ENDANGERED LANGUAGES

PROCEEDINGS OF THE BRITISH ACADEMY · 199

ENDANGERED LANGUAGES
Beliefs and Ideologies in Language Documentation and Revitalization

Edited by
PETER K. AUSTIN AND JULIA SALLABANK

Published for THE BRITISH ACADEMY
by OXFORD UNIVERSITY PRESS

Oxford University Press, Great Clarendon Street, Oxford OX2 6DP

First edition published in 2014

British Library Cataloguing in Publication Data
Data available

Library of Congress Cataloging in Publication Data
Data available

Typeset by Data Standards Ltd, Frome, Somerset
Printed in Great Britain by TJ International Ltd, Padstow, UK

ISBN 978-0-19-726576-5
ISSN 0068-1202

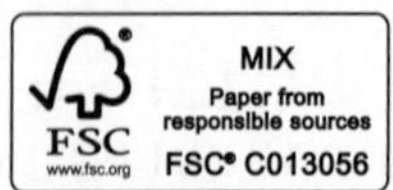

Contents

Figures

Tables

Notes on the Contributors

Peter K. Austin is Märit Rausing Chair in Field Linguistics and Director of the Endangered Languages Academic Programme, Department of Linguistics, School of Oriental and African Studies, University of London. His main research interests are the theory and practice of language documentation, syntax (with a focus on Lexical Functional Grammar), morpho-syntactic typology, computer-aided lexicography, and multimedia for endangered languages. He has extensive fieldwork experience in Australian Aboriginal languages and is currently involved in a language revitalization project in South Australia with the Dieri Aboriginal Corporation. He is also documenting Sasak and Samawa (Lombok and Sumbawa Islands, eastern Indonesia).

Michel Bert is a Lecturer (University Lumière Lyon 2) and Researcher (DDL Laboratory, Lyon). He has conducted extensive fieldwork in dialectology and sociolinguistics on both Francoprovençal and Occitan in the Rhône-Alpes region. He directed the FOR A sociolinguistic study on Francoprovençal and Occitan in Rhône-Alpes, and co-edited (with Colette Grinevald) *Linguistique de Terrain sur Langues en Danger: Locuteurs et Linguistes* (2010).

Jessica Boynton is a PhD candidate in Linguistic Anthropology at the University of Virginia. She received her BA in Linguistics at Eastern Michigan University, where she worked as a student editor at the LINGUIST List and on the E-MELD project. Her work on Australian language documentation was conducted through the University of Western Australia as a Fulbright Scholar. Her current research focuses on the sociolinguistics of language endangerment and the ethnography of language documentation.

James Costa is a postdoctoral fellow at the Centre for Multilingualism in Society across the Lifespan (MultiLing) at the University of Oslo. Educated at Aberystwyth (Wales), Rennes and Grenoble (France), James defended his doctoral thesis on language revitalization in Scotland and Provence in 2010. In his dissertation, drawing on ethnographic fieldwork, he argued for a critical understanding of revitalization processes as social issues and as recategorization. He subsequently developed an interest in competing movements of revitalization in Provence and on the social meanings of language revitalization in late-capitalist societies. More recently, he has been working in Oslo on social issues surrounding minority language standardization in Scotland, looking at both Scots and Gaelic.

Vicki Couzens is a Keerray Woorroong Gunditjmara woman, mother of five and grandmother of ten. She has been working in community language revival for nearly 20 years, continuing her father's work. Couzens completed her Master of Arts in 2009 and is currently a PhD candidate at Royal Melbourne Institute of Technology. Couzens contributes to language revival through her work as an artist and community cultural warrior. Creating works of art, recording stories, and regenerating cultural practices including dance, ceremony, and crafts, Vicki reclaims the language that belongs to these things: strengthening the people, healing the land.

Pierpaolo Di Carlo (University of Florence) is an anthropological linguist. He has been especially active in the domain of language documentation, with special attention to ethnography and verbal art performances. He has worked on Indo-Aryan (Kalashamon, north-west Pakistan) as well as Bantoid languages (Lower Fungom languages, Cameroon). His research interests include language ideologies, processes of cultural and linguistic reproduction, and linguistic prehistory.

Lise M. Dobrin is Associate Professor of Anthropology at the University of Virginia, where she also directs the Interdisciplinary Program in Linguistics. Her work focuses on the language, culture, and history of the Arapesh people of Papua New Guinea. She is the author of *Concreteness in Grammar: The Noun Class Systems of the Arapesh Languages*, as well as numerous studies in the areas of language documentation, the history of anthropology, and the changing status of linguistic research, especially vis-à-vis processes of language shift and language activism.

Christina Eira is the community linguist for the Victorian Aboriginal Corporation for Languages. This role is primarily targeted to Aboriginal communities reviving their languages, based on principles of the reclamation of authority in language. Christina's research has focused on the ramifications of this work for epistemological, methodological, and theoretical concerns, with particular interests in languages-in-process and the discourses of standardization. Initially working with immigrant communities on language maintenance, Christina has been working in Aboriginal language revival since 2001. She has co-produced dictionaries in five languages, and a contemporary grammar of Narungga, a revival language of South Australia.

Eloy Frank Gómez originates from the Panamahka community of Umbra, Río Coco, and is currently coordinator of URACCAN's Institute for Research and Promotion of Languages and Cultures (IPILC) in Rosita.

Jeff Good is Associate Professor in the Department of Linguistics at the University at Buffalo. His research interests include morphosyntactic typology, historical and comparative linguistics, and language documentation. His work in this last area focuses on description of the languages of the Lower Fungom region of Northwest Cameroon as well as the use of digital technologies in language documentation efforts.

Lenore A. Grenoble is the Carl Darling Buck Professor at the University of Chicago, holding appointments in the Department of Linguistics and the Department of Slavic Languages and Literatures. She studies language contact and shift, issues of language endangerment, and revitalization, with a focus on Arctic indigenous languages.

Colette Grinevald is Professor (Université Lumière Lyon 2), Researcher (DDL Laboratory, Lyon), and co-director with Michel Bert of the research programme LED TDR. She specializes in Latin American languages (Mayan languages of Guatemala, Rama of Nicaragua). She has coordinated the Rama Language Project, Nicaragua, one of her main sources of inspiration and maturation on issues of endangered languages (fieldwork issues, the role of linguists between academia and field). She recently co-edited (with Michel Bert) *Linguistique de Terrain sur Langues en Danger: Locuteurs et Linguistes* (2010).

Jeanette King is an Associate Professor in the Te Reo Māori programme in the School of Māori and Indigenous Studies at the University of Canterbury, New Zealand, where she also leads the bilingualism theme of the New Zealand Institute of Language, Brain and Behaviour. Her current research projects include corpus-based analysis of the use of non-verbal cues by Māori/English bilinguals, change over time in the phrasal lexicon of Māori, and children's use of written Māori in Māori immersion schools. As part of the Māori and New Zealand English (MAONZE) team she has also been investigating change over time in the sound system of Māori.

Yan Marquis is a freelance researcher, language teacher, and translator who has been documenting and teaching Guernesiais for 25 years. His research interests include language change, orthography, and teaching methods for endangered languages.

Anahit Minasyan is UNESCO Programme Specialist in the field of Culture and Focal Point for endangered languages. Before joining the United Nations Educational, Scientific and Cultural Organization in 2002, she worked in the non-profit sector (NGOs and academia) as an editor, researcher, and lecturer. She holds a graduate degree in Philology/Linguistics from Yerevan State University and another in Modern History from the Central European University (Budapest).

Tadhg Ó hIfearnáin works in the Irish-medium section of the School of Languages, Literature, Culture and Communication at the University of Limerick, Ireland. He is a sociolinguist researching and teaching from the social to the linguistic end of the discipline's spectrum with a particular interest in group, family, and individual language policy, ideology, and practice. His work focuses on the contemporary and historical sociolinguistics of the Gaelic languages (Irish, Manx, and Scottish Gaelic), but also on other minoritized languages and their speakers, especially in Europe and North America.

Anna-Kaisa Räisänen is actively involved in several language revitalization projects on the Kven language in Tromsø, Norway (online dictionary, film documentary project about the standardization process of Kven, teaching the language).

Olimpia Rasom is an educationalist serving at the Ladin School Board in Bolzano (South Tyrol, Italy). Born and brought up in Fascia Valley, she has, for years, been working on the protection of the Ladin language, her mother tongue, which she loves and passes on to her children. She is the author of a number of national and European projects in the fields of cooperation and promotion of minority languages (amongst others, she coordinated Euroscola 2001, Eurosnow 2006, the Comenius 2.1 INFO project, and Women in Art). Her PhD from the University of Bozen-Bolzano is about the way of thinking of Ladin women and their role in the process of transmission and promotion of the mother tongue. In 2007, she founded *Gana*, a women's magazine in Ladin. She writes Ladin TV and radio programmes for the Italian broadcasting company RAI and is active in educational research.

Julia Sallabank is Senior Lecturer in Language Support and Revitalization in the Endangered Languages Academic Programme, School of Oriental and African Studies, University of London. Her main research interests are sociolinguistics/sociology of language, endangered language documentation and revitalization, language policy and planning, and Channel Islands French.

Bernard Spolsky retired as Professor Emeritus at Bar-Ilan University in 2000, and since then has published three monographs, including *Language Policy, Language Management*, and, most recently, *The Languages of the Jews*. He has also edited a number of collections including *The Cambridge Handbook of Language Policy*, and has written a number of papers and chapters. He is at present carrying out research on the endangerment and current status of Jewish language varieties.

Tonya N. Stebbins is an Adjunct Associate Professor in the Linguistics Program at La Trobe University and a member of the Centre for Research on Language Diversity. She has worked in a range of communities on language description projects, including the Tsimshian Nation, Canada, the Mali (Baining) community in Papua New Guinea, and in partnership with the Victorian Aboriginal Corporation for Languages. She is currently an independent consultant working on a range of projects in education and human services.

Simone S. Whitecloud (Lac du Flambeau Band of Lake Superior Chippewa) is a PhD candidate at Dartmouth College studying ecology, with an interest in plant and animal communities. Her interest in ethnobotany stems from her uncle, a Cheyenne medicine man, and her desire to include humans in models of community ecology.

Preface

ACROSS THE world thousands of communities who speak a minority language are abandoning their heritage tongues (which are thereby becoming 'endangered languages') and switching to larger and more socially, politically, and economically dominant languages. Some community members have observed this happening and have been concerned to take steps to stem the tide of change and to revitalize their languages. The focus of this book is how these processes of language shift and revitalization of endangered languages are influenced by what speaker communities and others believe about languages, and the nature and use of human language in general.

This volume has its origins in a workshop on the topic of beliefs and ideologies about endangered languages held at SOAS, University of London on 27–28 February 2009 and partially funded by the British Academy.[1] The goal of the workshop was to highlight and discuss theoretical and practical issues in this area, and especially views that might have implications for language support and revitalization. We suggested that the study of language ideologies and beliefs may provide insights into the reasons why speakers shift languages and/or why they may be interested in language revival, and may help to determine the success or otherwise of language revitalization projects. Among the issues we asked speakers to consider were:

1. Are endangered languages fundamentally different from other languages when it comes to beliefs and ideology?
2. What, if any, are the consequences for language support and revitalization of the beliefs held by speakers of endangered languages?
3. To what extent can beliefs and ideologies be influenced by campaigning and language planning?
4. What beliefs and ideologies do linguists have about endangered languages? Are these in conflict with those of communities?

Following the workshop, we were invited by the British Academy to put together an edited volume of written versions of the presentations, the outline for which was then considered by its publications committee and Mark Turin, Yale University, as their external reviewer in 2010. The advice we received was to revise the volume by giving it more focus and invite other contributors to broaden the coverage of topics in the general area of beliefs and ideologies about

[1] See <http://www.hrelp.org/events/workshops/ideology/index.htm> (accessed 1 May 2014).

endangered languages. The resulting edited collection was reviewed by the publications committee and Mark Turin in 2012 and this volume is the outcome.

We are grateful to the original workshop presenters and participants for lively discussion and exchange which encouraged us to develop this book, and to the contributors whose work is presented here for writing up their research and bearing with us over an extended period as we requested revisions and developments to the text. We thank Mark Turin and the British Academy for their continued interest and support of our work over the last four years. We are also grateful to Samantha Goodchild for publications assistance in preparing the manuscript, to Elizabeth Stone for her editorial work on the final volume, and to Mary Chambers for efficient and thorough assistance with proof-reading and production of the index.

1

Introduction

PETER K. AUSTIN & JULIA SALLABANK

1.1 Language Endangerment

APPROXIMATELY 7,000 languages are spoken on earth today; however, the size and distribution of languages are far from uniform across the globe. Rather, there is a small number of very large languages with tens or hundreds of millions of speakers each, and a very large number of languages with just a small number of speakers, having sometimes only thousands or hundreds of people using them on a regular basis. Indeed, as Crystal (2000) and Austin (2008) point out, the top ten languages currently spoken account for over 40 per cent of the world's population; the population estimates in Table 1.1 are from Lewis et al. (2013).

Crystal (2000) also notes that 96 per cent of the world's population speaks just 4 per cent of its languages (around 300) while just 4 per cent of the population speaks 96 per cent of the languages (the remaining 6,700).

Over the past few centuries, and since the mid-twentieth century in particular, there has been a tremendous reduction in global linguistic diversity (or different ways of speaking) as people abandon minority language varieties and switch to larger and what they perceive to be more economically, socially, and politically powerful regional or national languages. In addition, governments have been promoting limited numbers of standardized official languages for use in schooling, media, and bureaucracy, often under a rubric of linguistic unity supporting, or even being a precondition of, national unity. A further factor that has been influential in more recent times is globalization, including the spread of computer and media technologies, which has given a further impetus to the widespread use and adoption of languages such as English and Mandarin Chinese.

This change in language choice is referred to as 'language shift' and it can take place quite rapidly, so that within one or two generations individuals and whole communities can move from speaking a given language to using another one in their daily lives. The result is that languages become 'endangered', in the sense that they are no longer being learnt by children and are only regularly used by an aging population in increasingly restricted domains. Over time, communities undergo 'language loss' and languages fall into disuse. Indeed, a widely accepted estimate is that at least 50 per cent of the currently spoken languages in

Proceedings of The British Academy, **199**, 1–26.

Table 1.1 Numbers of speakers of the world's top ten languages

Language		First-language speakers
1	Mandarin Chinese	1,200 million
2	Spanish	406 million
3	English	335 million
4	Hindi/Urdu	260 million
5	Arabic	223 million
6	Portuguese	202 million
7	Bengali	192 million
8	Russian	162 million
9	Japanese	122 million
10	Javanese	84 million

the world are endangered and likely to disappear during the twenty-first century. Language loss has been calculated to occur at a rate of roughly one language every three months (Campbell et al. 2013), a trend which is likely to accelerate in the future.

Since the 1990s there has been a significant increase in interest in minority languages and the phenomena of language shift, endangerment, and loss. As noted by Grenoble (2009): 'In this time, the issue of language endangerment has engaged increasing numbers of not only anthropologists and linguists, but also members of the general public.' Since the turn of the millennium there has been a steady trickle of books on the subject aimed at the (Western) general public, such as Crystal (2000), Nettle and Romaine (2000), Hagège (2000), Dalby (2002), Abley (2005), Harrison (2007), and Austin (2008), as well as workshops, papers, and volumes aimed at more academic audiences (Austin and McGill 2011; Austin and Sallabank 2011; Austin and Simpson 2007; Fishman 2001; Flores Farfán and Ramallo 2010; Gippert et al. 2006; Goodfellow 2009; Grenoble and Furbee 2010; Grenoble and Whaley 2006; Himmelmann 2006; Hobson et al. 2010; King 2001; King et al. 2008; Meek 2011; Mühlhäusler 2003; Romaine 2002, 2006; Tsunoda 2006). Two new academic journals have also been established (*Language Documentation and Description* in 2003 and *Language Documentation and Conservation* in 2007).

Some individuals and communities have become interested in 'language revitalization' as a response to the growing realization that many minority languages are under threat. This involves activities aimed at reversing language shift and redressing the loss of speakers and domains of use. Among indigenous communities, in the 1980s the Māori of New Zealand were among the first to make moves towards revitalization (see King, this volume), and they have been followed by other groups throughout the Pacific, Australia, the Americas, and Europe. There is a growing literature on language revitalization (Fishman 1991, 2001;

Grenoble and Whaley 2006; Hinton and Hale 2001; Hobson et al. 2010; Reyhner 1999; Reyhner and Lockard 2009). There have also been some attempts to encourage cross-disciplinary study in support of language revitalization efforts, for example by encouraging the involvement of applied linguists in the teaching of endangered languages (Cope 2012).

The reasons for language endangerment on the one hand, and for interest in language revitalization on the other, are complex and vary from one language community to the next; however, several characteristics do appear to be common across language groups and contexts. These include a shift away from negative attitudes and beliefs regarding minority languages towards positive ones. In language attitude research, negative attitudes are generally assumed to lead to language loss, and positive attitudes to support ethnolinguistic vitality or to assist revitalization (Bourhis and Sachdev 1984; Bradley and Bradley 2002; Currie and Hogg 1994). Schiffman (1996: 5) notes that:

> the beliefs (one might even use the term myths) that a speech community has about language (and this includes literacy) in general and its language in particular (from which it usually derives its attitudes towards other languages) are part of the social conditions that affect the maintenance and transmission of its language.[1]

In addition, judgements about the significance of minority languages as markers of individual and/or group identity are seen as key factors (high identity marking tending to support language maintenance and revitalization: see Kroskrity and Field 2009).

However, the processes of attitude change and how beliefs and ideologies are played out in the construction of linguistic identities and in supporting or undermining endangered languages have been largely unexplored by linguists and anthropologists. It is our contention—our belief, if you like—that the study of language ideologies and beliefs can provide insights into reasons for both language decline and revival, and may help us to assess the likely success (or otherwise) of language revitalization projects. We also contend that raising awareness of language ideologies can facilitate a more principled approach to language policies, from the family to the international level (cf. Spolsky 2004).

1.2 What Do We Mean by *Ideologies and Beliefs*?

Language ideologies have been described and (re)defined numerous times, so rather than propose a new definition we will explore some of those already

[1] Schiffman is here using the term 'speech community' differently from our interpretation: see section 1.4.

suggested in the literature. Language ideologies may be defined, very broadly, as:

> ideas about language and about how communication works as a social process; (Woolard 1998: 3)

or

> socioculturally motivated ideas, perceptions and expectations of language, manifested in all sorts of language use. (Blommaert 1999: 1)

Although these descriptions stress the social or sociocultural aspect of language, they do not adequately convey the systematic nature of ideologies, which is articulated more clearly by Steger (2003: 93):

> an ideology can be defined as a system of widely shared ideas, patterned beliefs, guiding norms and values, and ideals accepted as truth by a particular group of people.

This definition includes the word 'beliefs'—the joint focus of this book—and conveys the notion that ideologies are a social phenomenon shared by members of a group (see the discussion of 'speech community' in section 1.4); however, it does not make any mention of the unconscious acceptance of ideologies which  makes them all the more powerful as drivers of practices, since many people are unaware that their actions and reactions are based on socioculturally inculcated beliefs (Bourdieu 1977a, 1991). In this volume we aim to demonstrate that beliefs and ideologies do not simply arise without foundation: they are based on deep-seated predispositions and strongly held ways of thinking and perceptions concerning both language practices (what people do) and policies (what people *should* do). We therefore propose to follow McCarty's (2011) efficient summary:

> Ideologies about language are largely tacit, taken-for-granted assumptions about language statuses, forms, users, and uses that, by virtue of their 'common sense' naturalization, contribute to linguistic and social inequality. (McCarty 2011:10, who in turn acknowledges Tollefson 2006: 47)

Kroskrity (2000: 7) observes that:

> speakers' explicitly verbalised models are no longer scorned but valued as constructs that are by definition 'real' to the members of groups and can provide resources for members to deliberately change their linguistic and discourse forms.

This is akin to the increased attention being paid to 'folk linguistics' (Nieldzielski and Preston 2003) or non-specialists' perceptions of language (Long and Preston 2002; Preston 1989, 1999; Watts and Trudgill 2002). Such 'folk linguistic' beliefs are explored in many of the chapters in this book, especially by Ó hIfearnáin, Hadjidemetriou, Räisänen, Rasom, King, and Freeland and Gómez.

With regard to language shift, Kroskrity and Field (2009: 3–4) note that language practices such as:

> decisions about when to speak heritage and/or other languages, a community's linguistic repertoire and choices about whether to actively participate in language renewal efforts—or to assiduously avoid them—are prompted by *beliefs and feelings about language and discourse* that are possessed by speakers and their speech communities. These beliefs and feelings, which linguistic anthropologists term 'language ideologies', vary dramatically within and across native cultural groups. (Italics in original)

Such observations underline the importance of investigating ideologies and beliefs regarding language endangerment and revitalization.

It is clear from the literature that there is little consensus about terminology regarding language ideologies and beliefs. Baker (1992: 13) stresses that the notions of attitudes, ideologies, motives, traits, beliefs, concepts, constructs, and opinions are interrelated, observing that the lack of agreed definitions makes it difficult to compare theoretical propositions. Edwards (1999: 101, n. 1) suggests that many studies of 'language attitudes' are in fact studies of beliefs, which he does not define but clearly feels are less complex, or less advanced in the definitional hierarchy, than attitudes or ideologies. He remarks that it would take further probing (which is rarely done) to add the affective dimension needed for a fuller attitudinal evaluation: for example, one might believe French to be important while heartily disliking the language and its speakers. However, Spolsky (this volume), like McCarty (2011) and Kroskrity and Field (2009), equates ideologies and beliefs:

> I use the cover term language beliefs to include all the individual and group reactions to language, languages, language varieties, language variants, and language users, whether attitudes, motivations, or values, or gathered into recognizable ideologies.

Ideologies and beliefs can be seen as points on a continuum (though there seems to be no consensus as to where each comes, or what constitutes the continuum) or as manifestations of overall predispositions. In many of the chapters in this book, beliefs are treated as overt manifestations of implicit ideologies, or as the stated articulation of a (perhaps partial) recognition of an underlying ideology. Conversely, ideologies might be said to be social manifestations of implicit belief systems. Baker (1992: 14) cites Cooper and McGaugh (1966), who regard ideology as:

> an elaborate cognitive system rationalising forms of behaviour . . . Ideology tends to refer to codifications of group norms and values. At an individual level, ideology tends to refer to broad perspectives on society—a philosophy of life. In this sense, ideology may be a global attitude.

In the current orthodoxy in sociolinguistics and linguistic anthropology, ideologies are held to be more 'explanatory' than attitudes or beliefs; however, this too has become a disciplinary ideology that is rarely questioned.

Both Blommaert (1999) and Dorian (1994) stress that people are often faced with a lack of freedom in language choice, due, for example, to economic or political necessity; they then internalize ideologies of linguistic inferiority, which can lead to linguistic and cultural shift. This is analogous to the concept of *hegemony* elaborated by the Italian political theorist and linguist Antonio Gramsci (1891–1937) (Gramsci et al. 1971), who viewed ideology in terms of cultural beliefs presented by the bourgeoisie or capitalist state (or the group whose language practices are dominant) as a means of establishing and maintaining control. Hegemony propagates the notion that the status quo represents a 'common-sense' or 'normal' state of affairs and reflects 'natural' values.

Some of the arguments supporting the role of ideologies in the propagation, reproduction, and maintenance of beliefs about language can seem somewhat deterministic (Bourdieu 1977a; Kroskrity 2000; Schieffelin et al. 1998). However, one of the themes of this book is that the more aware speakers and members of speech communities are of ideologies, the more they can be challenged and contested. As Kroskrity (2000: 13) observes: 'even dominant ideologies are dynamically responsive to ever-changing forms of oppositions', for example the move from 'generic he' to 'he/she' (or even 'they') in English since the 1980s. Ideologies can thus be seen as similar to cultural patterning, which can be overcome through awareness-raising and human individuality or agency. Like Freeland and Patrick (2004: 12), we stress that Bourdieu's notion of *linguistic habitus*, like socialization, does not determine behaviour but predisposes social actors to respond in particular ways. This releases people from absolute associations of language and culture in a crude interpretation of linguistic determinism (one version of 'Whorfianism', see Deutscher 2011 for discussion), and explains why people can be both attached to and able to move beyond certain ways of behaving—and be motivated both to shift and to revitalize languages.

We are following current practice in linguistic anthropology in employing the term *ideology* in a wider sense than is usual in Italy, for example, where it can have negative connotations because of its use in political discourse (Olimpia Rasom, personal communication, 22 July 2011). There are, however, some overlaps between our use of the term and a Marxian understanding of 'ideology'. One of these is the notion of 'false consciousness', or the masses not being able to see their situation clearly. It is clear from many of the descriptions of 'naïve perceptions that directly energise stereotypical beliefs about ingroups and outgroups' (Cargile and Bradac, 2001: 355) that people are not necessarily aware of the ideologies that drive their language beliefs, policies, and practices.

Along with Gumperz and Cook-Gumperz (1982: 3), '[w]e do not intend to claim that ideology shapes language and that since language shapes social reality there is no way out'. We seek to challenge deterministic beliefs about ideologies themselves, so that language choice becomes liberating rather than constrained.

We propose that by researching and revealing unconscious language ideologies, and challenging consciously accepted ones, we can demonstrate that it is possible to overcome deeply ingrained beliefs about, for example, the inferiority of a particular way of speaking, the notion that acquiring a language of wider communication necessitates abandoning other languages and dialects, or the assumption that a small language needs to have all the attributes of a larger one. This leads us to the chapters in Part 2, which explore motivations behind and beliefs about language documentation and revitalization. The fruits of such investigations then enable suggestions to be made with regard to policies and practice(s).

As Jaffe (1999) comments, the dominant Western European language ideology is that linguistic or cultural homogeneity is 'normal'. Such beliefs are not only held by speakers of dominant or Western languages, but may also be 'naturalized', in Bourdieu's (1991) terms, by speakers of minority languages (see the discussion of hegemony above). This can lead to 'linguistic insecurity' and unwillingness to speak these languages. These kinds of beliefs are both a cause and an outcome of language shift and endangerment. The chapters in Part 1 of this volume explore these issues in communities around the world.

Resistance to dominant discourses does take place in communities who wish to see their languages and cultures continue in the face of pressure from dominant political and social groups. In addition, language planning (or *language management*, as Spolsky (2009) prefers to call it) is predicated on the notion that as discussed above, beliefs and ideologies can change. The chapters in this volume by Hadjidemetriou and Räisänen report on research into how beliefs and ideologies about endangered languages are changing, and how this may affect practices within communities.

Dauenhauer and Dauenhauer (1998: 63) distinguish between overt (stated, conscious, public) and private (unstated, unconscious, covert) beliefs, the latter being more likely to affect actual behaviour. Private beliefs may be seen as more closely reflecting underlying ideologies. In the Tlingit revitalization movement described by Dauenhauer and Dauenhauer, stated beliefs about the indigenous language were positive, and were reflected in involvement in revitalization efforts, yet unstated beliefs and ideologies prevented these efforts from affecting individuals' actual language practices. Such contradictions are explored in the chapters in this volume by Marquis and Sallabank, Boynton, Ó hIfearnáin, and Grenoble and Whitecloud. Endangered language communities and activists may, for example, find it easier to focus on a campaign to get their language introduced into the school curriculum than on changing their own intra-family behaviour by, for example, renewing the practice of speaking a particular language at home; this could be seen as an abdication of responsibility by effectively handing over custodianship of the language to schools (see also King 2001). As Costa's chapter reveals, it is by no means certain that children who learn a language only at school will speak it outside, or even that they will realize why they are learning it.

1.3 Studying Ideologies and Beliefs on Endangered Languages

Since the 1990s there has been a growing interest within the anthropological linguistics community in the study of both vernacular and disciplinary language ideologies (Bauman and Briggs 2003; Blommaert 1999; Errington 2003; Jaffe 1999; Kroskrity 2000; Mar-Molinero and Stevenson 2006; Schieffelin et al. 1998; Woolard and Schieffelin 1994). As discussed above, vernacular language ideologies can be defined as tacit or explicit ideas and beliefs that members of a speech community have with respect to their own linguistic repertoire (Woolard and Schieffelin 1994). Disciplinary language ideologies consist, instead, of more or less explicitly articulated theoretical principles and methodological practices that orient work undertaken by linguists and anthropologists engaged in language documentation and analysis (see, for example, Bauman and Briggs 2000; Errington 2001; Irvine and Gal 2000; Silverstein 2000). Several of the chapters in this volume examine the disjuncture, not to say conflict, between vernacular and disciplinary language ideologies, as well as between the beliefs of members of speech communities and the ideologies of institutions and governments with regard to language policies, and their implications.

This book would not have been written without the ideological shift since the 1990s towards broadly positive attitudes in favour of 'saving' endangered languages. As recounted in the chapters by Minasyan and Grinevald and Bert (this volume), this transformation led to the valorization of endangered languages in the 1990s, from the community to the international level. Indeed, it may be a sign that the study of language endangerment is becoming mature, or even mainstream, that there is debate and criticism of the rhetorics and methodologies of language documentation and revitalization, chiefly from the field of linguistic anthropology (Duchêne and Heller 2007; Hill 2002; Mufwene 2004) but also from within (Dobrin et al. 2009). There have been some important publications on this topic (such as Dobrin 2005, 2008; Duchêne and Heller 2007; Grenoble and Furbee 2010; Newman 2003) that have brought these issues to the consciousness of linguists concerned with the documentation, description, and revitalization of endangered languages. There has recently been an increase in the publication of edited collections of papers describing case studies of language revitalization efforts, but these rarely evaluate processes or outcomes or relate these to *ideological clarification* (Flores Farfán and Ramallo 2010; Goodfellow 2009; King et al. 2008). A number of publications do examine practices and ideologies in language revitalization, but most focus on 'fourth-world' indigenous communities in the Americas, Australia, or Europe, with little reference to other areas of the world (Jaffe 1999; King 2001; Kroskrity and Field 2009; Mar-Molinero and Stevenson 2006; Meek 2011; Reyhner and Lockard 2009; Urla 2012).

Although there have been individual calls for incorporating ethnographic methodologies and giving due attention to language ideologies in the endangered languages research agenda (see, for example, Newman 2003), the full potential of this line of research (theoretical and applied alike) has yet to be recognized. The chapters in Part 2 of this volume explore the reasons for this and suggest current and future directions for improved understanding.

More recently scholars have turned their attention towards analysing the ways in which language endangerment discourse is presented (Duchêne and Heller 2007), noting that the discourses involved valorize traditional people and practices in a way that pits them against 'modernity' while 'hypertraditionalizing' them, and, some say, dehumanizing participants in the population concerned. Furthermore, the ideologies that underpin such efforts reshape the way in which language is envisaged, sometimes through the discourse itself and at other times through the intersection of access to tangible (even if imagined) benefits and language-based processes of authentication. These ideologies can unintentionally effect ideological changes among the target population of language work and other political action (as Boynton discusses in her contribution here).

Relatively few book-length studies focus specifically on beliefs and ideologies with regard to endangered languages. The aim of this volume is to bring together chapters on theoretical and practical issues to do with ideologies and beliefs about language, especially with regard to the views of linguists and communities about the support and revitalization of endangered languages. The chapters in this collection go straight to the heart of ideological bases of reactions to language endangerment by community members and linguists. They draw their discussion from case studies on how language ideologies affect language practices (and vice versa). Theory emerges from the data rather than the other way round, and, as discussed below, each discussion sheds light on processes that both illustrate and extend the cutting edge of thinking in this field.

Part 1 of the book contains case studies that explore these issues in communities around the world. They demonstrate that situations are never as simple as acceptance of, or resistance to, subalternity by an oppressed minority. To a large extent, the beliefs that these chapters examine concern the definition (or construction) of a group, or language community, and its relationship with language as a marker of group identity (or not).

The chapters in Part 2 explore motivations behind, and beliefs about, language documentation and revitalization. They engage more critically with received ideas in language documentation and revitalization, and relate the common threads identified to insights into motivations, processes, and outcomes, in order to contribute to ideological clarification (Dauenhauer and Dauenhauer

1998; Fishman 1991, 2001; Kroskrity 2009). Several of these chapters deal with 'what is being revitalized?' (King) or 'what are we trying to preserve?' (Di Carlo and Good). The international, national, and local political contexts affecting ideologies and beliefs about language (as well as the rhetorics consequently taken up by linguists, communities, and indigenous support organizations such as Survival International) are also highlighted in several chapters (Austin, Boynton, Couzens and Eira—see also Minasyan in Part 3).

Part 3 takes up a theme that permeates several of the chapters in Parts 1 and 2: disjunctures in ideological perspectives between local and dominant language ideologies, or between what might be termed vernacular and institutional ideological positions (including within the discipline of linguistics). These chapters extend the book's perspectives to ideologies with regard to language endangerment at international and interdisciplinary levels.

1.4 Language and Speech Communities

Linguists going into the field to document endangered languages are generally concerned with one particular language and speak of the 'language community' as their primary target (sometimes adopting a puristic approach that aims to document the 'true' language, untainted by loans and language mixing). However, they may also need to think about the 'speech community' and the relationships that the language they want to document enters into with other codes, registers, and so on that speakers are choosing between and using in their daily lives, and, in some cases, shifting towards. Yet the concept of 'speech community' is deeply problematic: how can it be defined? What are its boundaries? What is its scale?

Documentary linguists often use the term 'community' in a rather vague manner (Grinevald and Bert 2011). Sometimes they mean a 'language community' as a group of people 'sharing a denotational code' (Silverstein 1996: 126) or 'a group of people who make use of a given lexicogrammatical code' (Jeff Good, personal communication, 18 September 2012).[2] In other words, they are people who consider that they speak the same language. Austin (this volume) also uses the term 'speaker community' for this notion. It is important to note that such a 'community' may not live in a traditional close-knit grouping (Gumperz and Cook-Gumperz 1982; Milroy 1987) or even in the same place. In the context described by Di Carlo and Good (this volume) they are dispersed within a region, but in other contexts they may have migrated to cities or to diaspora settings around the world—both of which are also key sites for both language shift and language maintenance and revitalization movements. Such

[2] The term 'denotational code' is discussed by Costa, this volume.

communities are increasingly linked through social media (Facebook, Twitter, blogs) or media technologies such as mobile phones and voice or video communication over the Internet.

Spolsky (1998: 24) explains that:

> for general linguistics, a speech community is all the people who speak a single language (like English or French or Amharic) and so share notions of what is same or different in phonology or grammar . . . Sociolinguists, however, find it generally more fruitful to focus on the language practices of a group of people who . . . share not just a single language but a repertoire of languages or varieties. For the sociolinguist, the speech community is a complex interlocking network of communication whose members share knowledge about and attitudes toward the language use patterns of others as well as themselves.

An important difference between documentary linguists working on endangered languages on the one hand, and linguistic anthropologists and sociolinguists on the other, has to do with the fact that the research object of the first tends to be 'a language', while the latter tend to focus on the 'speech community'.

However, decisions about what constitutes 'a language' or what is considered to be 'a dialect' are often ideologically or politically biased. In addition, authors influenced by postmodern thinking argue that boundaries between languages are largely constructed for the convenience of linguists and administrators (which can be argued to be true of any kind of boundary or label). The concept of language endangerment is, to a certain extent, predicated on the belief that languages can be delimited as discrete entities. In recent years it has become part of the disciplinary ideology of linguistic anthropology and sociolinguistics to call into question the notion of defining and enumerating languages (Dobrin et al. 2009; Hill 2002; Irvine and Gal 2000; Makoni and Pennycook 2006; Pennycook 2005; Ricento 2005). Mühlhäusler (1996) illustrates how beliefs about how languages should be defined and categorized were spread around the world by colonizers, missionaries, and linguists educated in the world view inherited from nineteenth-century European thinkers such as Herder and von Humboldt (who is considered by some to be the 'father of linguistics'). The consequences of such historically inherited beliefs and ideologies are explored in this volume by Stebbins, Costa, Freeland and Gómez, and Di Carlo and Good.

Postmodernist authors such as Pennycook (2007) also argue that the arbitrary chopping up of a chain of dialects (called a 'dialect continuum') is complicated further by 'transnational flows' of migration and worldwide social media, which have led to increased language contact, mixing, and hybridity. In this volume, Di Carlo and Good show that such 'hyperdiversity' is not necessarily a new or purely urban phenomenon. They also emphasize that languages never exist in isolation and are always embedded in relationships with other languages and varieties, and other codes, styles, registers, and so on, in what has been termed a *linguistic ecology* (Calvet 2006; Grenoble 2011; Haugen 1972; Mühlhäusler

1996, 2000). This is all the more so in the case of endangered languages, which, as noted by Schmidt (1985) and Nettle and Romaine (2000), never exist in isolation (indeed their status as being endangered comes from being in contact with other more dominant tongues) and are subject to extreme linguistic contact, rapid change, and fragmentation (Heinrich 2005), to the extent that members of the 'language community' may not agree on 'what is same or different phonology or grammar', what is 'correct' or desirable in terms of usage, or whether a particular way of speaking counts as a 'language'. The ideological tensions that such differences can bring about are explored in the chapters by Ó hIfearnáin, Marquis and Sallabank, Costa, King, Boynton, and Couzens and Eira.

Due to the fact that endangered languages researchers often work in plurilingual speech communities, it is essential to look at such languages in their linguistic ecologies (Grenoble 2011; Grenoble and Whitecloud, this volume). Placing languages in their broader context allows us to achieve a better perspective on speakers' ideas of their linguistic repertoire and on the place that a particular language has in the local linguistic market (Bourdieu 1977b; Harbert 2011). Both Di Carlo and Good's chapter and those by Costa, Stebbins, and Couzens and Eira challenge assumptions that linguists (and activists) may make about language(s). As Couzens and Eira note in their contribution to this volume:

> [T]he many points of lack of fit between learned practice and what is useful and needed in this context brings linguists into direct confrontation with the ideological underpinning of the discipline—that is, the systems refined over decades which define and constrain what constitutes a language, an analysis, a valid data source, language change, and so on.

This lack of fit with Western perceptions of language and identity is highlighted in Dobrin's chapter on linguistic and cultural shift in a community in Papua New Guinea, where 'repeatedly in this area of the world we find that high-level group boundaries fail to coincide with linguistic ones. In the Arapesh area there was never any basis for people to assume that they would share the most important features of their social identity with fellow speakers.'

Costa (this volume) cites Silverstein's (1998: 402) definition of language communities:

> groups of people by degree evidencing allegiance to norms of denotational … language usage, however much or little such allegiance also encompasses an indigenous cultural consciousness of variation and/or change, or is couched in terms of fixity and stasis.

He links these ideologies of 'what language is' to revitalization, commenting that: '[L]anguage communities are thus largely imagined communities based on a shared charter myth founding the group around language.'

In sociolinguistics, as Patrick (2002) notes, there is no unified definition of 'speech community', but the overall broad consensus seems to follow the definition proposed by Hymes (1967/72: 54–5): 'A community sharing rules for the conduct and interpretation of speech, and rules for the interpretation of at least one linguistic variety.' Spolsky (2004: 14) adds that:

> The members of a speech community share also a general set of beliefs about appropriate language practices, sometimes forming a consensual ideology, assigning values and prestige to various aspects of the language varieties used in it.

So a speech community can be multilingual, but importantly it is made up of people who share folk linguistic ideologies (Niedzielski and Preston 2003) of what language is and what it indexes: which varieties are most suitable for which domains, the social hierarchies associated with particular ways of speaking, and so on.

At other times the notion of *community* in documentary linguistics seems to extend to a *community of practice*, in the sense of Eckert (2000), as members who share practices (distinctive ways of speaking) and orientation to the world around them. Costa (this volume) too likens speech communities to 'communities of everyday shared practice, [which] can involve several "languages"'. It is important to note that the 'shared ideology' of a speech community does not imply that the 'general set of beliefs' is held consciously, or that the members of the community have somehow agreed on a particular viewpoint. Dobrin (this volume) points out the contrast between the way that modern Western group identities are ideological projections of the *possessive individual* (Handler 1988) and the construction of identity in traditional Melanesian culture, where 'a key concept is that of *relational personhood*: the way persons are idealized less as autonomous individuals than as the intersection of others to whom they are connected (Robbins 2004)'.

One of the problems with the use of the term 'community' in documentary linguistics is an often implicit assumption that 'the community' is in agreement about linguistic norms or community language policy—or that certain community members, notably 'elders', may be delegated (or take on themselves) the right to speak on behalf of the community in this respect. In contexts where some members of a community (however defined) have decided that it is desirable to reclaim, revitalize, or renew what they see as their heritage language (or at least some elements of it), not only may the language practices of younger generations differ from those of their parents' or grandparents' generation, but elders' preconceived notions of 'correctness' (or 'purity') may also clash with language activists' notions of 'progress'. The issues of who 'owns' language, and of legitimate authority on questions of language, are discussed in the chapters by Boynton, Costa, Dobrin, Marquis and Sallabank, Ó hIfearnáin, and Couzens and Eira. It thus appears that in contexts where language shift or loss is endemic, there may not necessarily be shared norms, knowledge about, or attitudes towards language use, or even 'a shared charter myth founding the group around language'.

We have spent some time on these definitions because the word 'community' is frequently used oversimplistically in the field of language documentation. As noted by Sallabank (2012), it is important to realize that communities are not monolithic: there are frequently conflicting beliefs and ideologies within speech (and language) communities regarding language, its status, domains, functions, and policy, and who has the authority or legitimacy to decide any of these. Such issues are often not discussed openly, as language movements have enough to contend with without criticism from people from whom they might reasonably expect support, such as linguists and anthropologists. But we have come to the conclusion that to hide issues relevant to ideological clarification 'under the carpet' does not help the cause of preserving linguistic diversity, or healthy language ecologies in viable speech communities (cf. also Dauenhauer and Dauenhauer 1998; Hoffman 2006; Whaley 2011).

In this discussion we are aware that we may be falling into a fallacy, first identified by Labov (1973), who raised the suspicion that linguists might be seriously different from the regular speakers of the languages and varieties they study. Linguists of all persuasions share what Spolsky (2011) calls 'lingui-centrism',[3] the assumption that language is at the centre of human culture and existence. The fact that so few people and governments, including so many of those most directly concerned in language shift, seem to care about the threat to the survival of the majority of existing varieties should warn us to think very carefully before we assume that the beliefs and ideologies of linguists, socio-linguists, and linguistic anthropologists are in harmony with those of the speech communities, and speakers of languages, and varieties that we study. This issue is addressed in this book in the chapters by Grinevald and Bert, King, Stebbins, Dobrin, Di Carlo and Good, and Couzens and Eira.

1.5 Language Ideologies and Revitalization

Language revitalization movements often unthinkingly follow what Dorian (1998) has called a 'western language ideology' of how languages ought to (be) develop(ed) and increase their domains, or an 'autonomous' model of standardization (Grenoble and Whaley 2006; Sebba 2007; Street 1984). One criticism of the approach of language planners for Welsh and Basque, for example, is that they focus on teaching a 'unified standard', which can be argued to contradict the stated aim of preserving linguistic diversity, as it entails loss of dialects (e.g. Sayers 2009). Woolard (1998: 17) observes that:

[3] Spolsky coined this word to distinguish it from 'linguacentrism', which, on analogy with ethnocentrism, would mean looking at things through the lens of a single language.

> movements to save minority languages are often structured, willy-nilly, around the same received notions of language that have led to their oppression ... language activists find themselves imposing standards, elevating literate forms and uses, and negatively sanctioning variability in order to demonstrate the reality, validity, and integrity of their languages.

While this might be adequate in Europe (as well as being a pragmatic policy that suits the funding model for regional and minority languages promoted by the European Union), situations vary greatly in other contexts. The processes of revitalization, including discourses, narratives, practices, ideologies, and myths, therefore need to be examined further.

At a community level, this dominant ideology of language revitalization influences expectations and assumptions which may stand in the way of achievable goals. For example, many communities embarking on revitalization projects state that their goal is to create fluent speakers or to reinstate intergenerational transmission, but omit to create domains of use for the language outside formal education, which may again be a feature of the 'western language ideology' of how languages ought to (be) develop(ed). Ideologies may thus contribute to a mismatch between desired results and methods, and, if these ideologies remain unconscious, the reasons why language planning measures are not working may remain undiscovered. In the Australian case study discussed by Boynton, a Western language ideology is assumed or imposed by (sometimes) well-meaning policy-makers who are unaware that 'language' might mean something quite different to indigenous people.

The chapters in this volume by Ó hIfearnáin, Freeland and Gómez, Marquis and Sallabank, Stebbins, Austin, and Costa illustrate both the pervasiveness of such ideologies, and also ways in which they are being challenged (implicitly or explicitly) by new generations who wish to add new uses for heritage languages to their linguistic repertoires. This volume thus responds to a call by Dorian (1993), who warned that research that only reports on the abandonment phase of a language, and which concentrates on negative attitudes and ideologies, can obscure a longer-term dynamic by overlooking revitalization efforts.

Languages learnt in school may not be native-like (the same as those learnt in childhood in the home), but in situations where all the native speakers are elderly, if language revitalization goes ahead, second-language speakers will soon be in the majority. A language restored for modern use is not necessarily the same as the one that was going out of use. Expansion of functions may lead to a reversal of traditional diglossic domains, so that the endangered language is used more in 'high' domains such as education, official documents, or ritual events than as a means of everyday communication. There may also be unrealistic notions of how much fluency can be retained or regained in daily use by second-language learners. This may accelerate language change, which is inevitable but not necessarily welcomed by 'elders' or by language enthusiasts.

As Bentahila and Davies (1993: 359) note, '[T]hose who feel moved to act in favour of reinstatement of the language are not always those for whom it is still an essential part of daily life.' Even the perception of the role of language in the everyday lives of traditional speakers may be coloured by the combined lens of nostalgia and ideology; as noted by Dorian (2009) and Grenoble (2010), people who are perceived by themselves and by 'the community' as 'good speakers' may rely on a restricted range of relatively simple formulaic language to give an impression of fluency, and may also have a very restricted range of interlocutors and domains of use (Sallabank 2010). This may also lead to tensions between linguists (who favour 'objective' corpus-based measures of fluency) and traditional speakers who may consider themselves 'language guardians'. In their chapter in this volume, Marquis and Sallabank highlight ideological differences between activists who want to see the language modernized, and purists whose attachment to their native language is also an attachment to a disappearing culture. Some purists may even prefer the language to die with them rather than survive in what they see as a garbled, or modernized, form (cf. King et al. 2009). Yet, as Thieberger (2002) argues, token maintenance (e.g. rituals, greetings) may be adequate for identity purposes (see also Austin's discussion in this volume). Also, as Boynton argues in her contribution, the *practice* of language may not be as relevant in questions of language rights or revival as the *idea* of language; and King observes how language itself may not be the prime motivator for activists.

Fishman's (1991) framework for language revitalization is prefaced by an important caveat, 'assuming prior ideological clarification' (that language activists have agreed basic foundations such as the relationship between language and culture) of what exactly it is they are trying to preserve or reclaim, and why it is desirable. In revisiting the framework ten years later, Fishman (2001: 541) admits that it is quite common for enthusiasts to embark on language planning and revitalization activities without such clarification, and without convincing arguments with which to counter critics. Similar points are made by Dauenhauer and Dauenhauer (1998) and Kroskrity (2009), who underline the significance of implicit beliefs in the success or otherwise of revitalization efforts. We thus hope that this volume will also contribute to the study of language revitalization, which itself is under-theorized, particularly with regard to *ideological clarification* (as Austin and McGill (2011) point out in their general introduction). Ideological clarification can itself be interpreted through ideological lenses. The chapters by Austin, King, Marquis and Sallabank, and Grinevald and Bert, for example, examine the relationship between practice(s) and ideology by comparing rhetoric regarding 'saving a language' with actions and results, providing a critical examination of the motivations, methods, and outcomes of language revitalization efforts. Dobrin draws attention to the 'Ethnic Revitalization Paradox', which is 'a term coined by Rindstedt and Aronsson (2002) to describe the disconnect these authors found between the way people speak *about* their languages on the one hand, and the way they actually *use* them on the other'. Simpson (2013) provides a detailed examination of this disconnect among Warramungu people in the Northern Territory of Australia.

This interpretation of ideological clarification overlaps with the focus of Stebbins, Couzens and Eira, Di Carlo and Good, Boynton, Freeland and Gómez, and Costa on the way in which language is envisaged, either from the point of view of the discipline of linguistics, or by community members, who may be more concerned with tangible (even if imagined) benefits from 'language rights' or language-based processes of authentication.

This leads to another intersecting theme of 'what is being revitalized?' (King) or 'what are we trying to preserve?' (Di Carlo and Good): language for its own sake or as a symbol of something else? Discrete languages and/or language ecologies, as discussed above? Cultural concepts or ideologies of language? Can these be separated?

1.6 Emergent Themes and Conclusion

The chapters in this collection explore the intersection of explicit and implicit beliefs and ideologies in contexts of language shift and revitalization. The apparent divergence between explicit and implicit, between practices and expressed beliefs, and even between what people believe they are doing, their observed practices, and the ideologies that these practices reveal, is explored, especially in the chapters by Austin, King, Boynton, Marquis and Sallabank, Grenoble and Whitecloud, and Grinevald and Bert.

In addition to continuing or (hopefully) advancing previous discussions in the field, this volume tackles new themes that are emerging from the research. The chapters by Rasom and Costa focus on sectors of the population who are often omitted from research into language revitalization: children and women. According to one of the key ideologies of both language documentation and revitalization, namely Fishman's (1991, 2001) insistence on the primacy of intergenerational transmission, they are crucial to its success (but see Romaine (2006) for an alternative view). Intergenerational transmission within the family is also treated as the key factor in language vitality by most measurement scales, such as UNESCO (2003) or Krauss (1997). It thus comes as somewhat of a shock to realize that Costa's chapter is one of the few studies of the beliefs and perceptions of children at the 'chalkface' of language revitalization, although so many language movements rely, through education, on children to carry languages forward. This chapter thus makes an important and thought-provoking contribution to ideological clarification in revitalization movements. Rasom's chapter moves on from the traditionally accepted view of women in language maintenance (as mothers or grandmothers whose main role is to transmit the language and reproduce speakers), by examining the beliefs of women who are proactive in a revitalization movement. Both Costa's and Rasom's chapters thus give voices to key players with agency in language maintenance and revitalization who are often treated simply as intermediaries.

Another recurrent theme in this book is disjuncture in language ideologies. The chapters by Ó hIfearnáin, Boynton, and King examine local language ideologies and the extent to which these resonate or conflict with the dominant ideology underpinning official language policy. Couzens and Eira, Di Carlo and Good, and Freeland and Gómez compare what might be termed 'institutional' or 'disciplinary' ideological positions within linguistics, with vernacular ideologies. Dobrin contrasts some assumptions of stereotypical Western language ideologies with the more culture-based focus of the field of anthropology. The chapters by Boynton and Grenoble and Whitecloud go beyond the tendency that can be discerned in the field to valorize (and 'exoticize') unquestioningly ways of knowing and learning privileged in Aboriginal and indigenous communities (also known as 'Traditional Knowledge') to examine the ideologies behind such valorizations. Grinevald and Bert examine conflicting ideologies in the various spheres, from individual to institutional, where policies about endangered languages develop. Hadjidemetriou, Räisänen and Marquis and Sallabank conduct detailed ethnographic examinations of ideologies at community level, where ideological disjunctures regarding change and continuity in language become apparent. All of these authors conduct collaborative community-based research and take a stance that we term *reflective engagement* to investigate (potential) clashes in ideological perspectives.

Finally, one word that might seem conspicuous by its absence in this book is *essentialism*. There has been some significant criticism of what might be termed the 'endangered languages movement' (Costa 2013; Duchêne and Heller 2007; Errington 2003; Freeland and Patrick 2004), especially with regard to what are perceived as its 'essentialist' underpinnings. This term is rarely defined, but has come to be perceived as a 'latter-day sin' (Schiffman 2002: 141). In this field it can be understood to include chiefly the demarcation and reification of languages as entities, and oversimplifying perceived links between languages thus defined with identity, culture, and ethnicity. As noted above, these and other issues are addressed in this book, but without the 'essentialist' label, which we feel has become an almost routine and meaningless denunciation that can obscure our preferred focus on ideologies at grass-roots level (see Sallabank 2009).

The editors of this volume openly and unashamedly position themselves as 'engaged' linguists supportive of efforts to maintain linguistic diversity (however it might be defined) and of efforts to overcome societal marginalization through linguistic empowerment. It is our belief that it is time to move on from both claims of essentialism and 'mud-slinging' to examine the ideological bases of reactions to language endangerment by those most closely involved (communities and linguists) as a basis for informed, reflective action in both language documentation and language policies, from family to international level.

References

Abley, Mark. 2005. *Spoken Here: Travels Among Threatened Languages*. London: Arrow.

Austin, Peter K. (ed.). 2008. *1,000 Languages*. London: Thames & Hudson.

Austin, Peter K. and Stuart McGill (eds.). 2011. *Critical Concepts in Linguistics: Endangered Languages*. London: Routledge.

Austin, Peter K. and Julia Sallabank (eds.). 2011. *Cambridge Handbook of Endangered Languages*. Cambridge: Cambridge University Press.

Austin, Peter K. and Andrew Simpson (eds.). 2007. *Endangered Languages*. Linguistische Berichte Sonderheft 14. Hamburg: Helmut Buske Verlag.

Baker, Colin. 1992. *Attitudes and Language*. Clevedon: Multilingual Matters.

Bauman, Richard and Charles L. Briggs. 2003. *Voices of Modernity: Language Ideologies and the Politics of Inequality: Studies in the Social and Cultural Foundations of Language*. Cambridge: Cambridge University Press.

Bentahila, A. and E. E. Davies. 1993. Language revival: restoration or transformation? *Journal of Multilingual and Multicultural Development* 14: 355–74.

Blommaert, Jan (ed.). 1999. *Language Ideological Debates*. Berlin: Mouton de Gruyter.

Bourdieu, Pierre. 1977a. *Outline of a Theory of Practice*. Cambridge: Cambridge University Press.

Bourdieu, Pierre. 1977b. The economics of linguistic exchanges. *Social Science Information* 16: 645–68.

Bourdieu, Pierre. 1991. *Language and Symbolic Power*. Cambridge: Polity Press.

Bourhis, Richard and Itesh Sachdev. 1984. Vitality perceptions and language attitudes: some Canadian data. *Journal of Language and Social Psychology* 3: 97–126.

Bradley, David and Maya Bradley (eds.). 2002. *Language Endangerment and Language Maintenance*. London: Routledge Curzon.

Calvet, Jean-Louis. 2006. *Towards an Ecology of World Languages*. Cambridge: Polity Press.

Campbell, Lyle, Nala Huiying Lee, Eve Okura, Sean Simpson, and Kaori Ueki. 2013. New knowledge: findings from the *Catalogue of Endangered Languages* ('ELCat'). 3rd International Conference on Language Documentation and Conservation.

Cargile, A. C. and J. J. Bradac. 2001. Attitudes toward language: a review of speaker-evaluation research and a general process model. In W. B. Gudykunst (ed.), *Communication Yearbook 25*. Mahwah, NJ: Lawrence Erlbaum Associates.

Cooper, J. B. and J. L. McGaugh. 1966. Attitude and related concepts. In M. Jahoda and M. Warren (eds.), *Attitudes—Selected Readings*. Harmondsworth: Penguin.

Cope, Lida (ed.). 2012. *Applied Linguists Needed: Cross-disciplinary Networking in Endangered Language Contexts*. Abingdon: Routledge.

Costa, James. 2013. Language endangerment and revitalisation as elements of regimes of truth: shifting terminology to shift perspective. *Journal of Multilingual and Multicultural Development* 34: 317–31.

Crystal, David. 2000. *Language Death*. Cambridge: Cambridge University Press.

Currie, M. and M. A. Hogg. 1994. Subjective ethnolinguistic vitality. *International Journal of the Sociology of Language* 108: 97–115.

Dalby, Andrew. 2002. *Language in Danger*. London: Penguin.

Dauenhauer, Nora Marks and Richard Dauenhauer. 1998. Technical, emotional, and ideological issues in reversing language shift: examples from Southeast Alaska. In Lenore A. Grenoble and Lindsay J. Whaley (eds.), *Endangered Languages*. Cambridge: Cambridge University Press.

Deutscher, Guy. 2011. *Through the Language Glass: Why the World Looks Different in Other Languages*. New York: Arrow Books

Dobrin, Lise. 2005. When our values conflict with theirs: linguistics and community empowerment in Melanesia. *Language Documentation and Description* 3: 42–52.

Dobrin, Lise. 2008. From linguistic elicitation to eliciting the linguist: lessons in community empowerment from Melanesia. *Language* 84: 300–24.

Dobrin, Lise M., Peter K. Austin, and David Nathan. 2009. Dying to be counted: the commodification of endangered languages in documentary linguistics. In Peter K. Austin (ed.), *Language Documentation and Description*, vol. 6. London: SOAS.

Dorian, Nancy C. 1993. A response to Ladefoged's other view of endangered languages. *Language* 69: 575–9.

Dorian, Nancy C. 1994. Choices and values in language shift and its study. *International Journal of the Sociology of Language* 110: 113–24.

Dorian, Nancy C. 1998. Western language ideologies and small-language prospects. In Lenore Grenoble and Lindsay J. Whaley (eds.), *Endangered Languages*. Cambridge: Cambridge University Press.

Dorian, Nancy C. 2009. Age and speaker skills in receding languages: how far do community evaluations and linguists' evaluations agree? *International Journal of the Sociology of Language* 200: 11–25.

Duchêne, Alexandre and Monica Heller (eds.). 2007. *Discourses of Endangerment: Ideology and Interest in the Defence of Languages*. London: Continuum.

Eckert, Penelope. 2000. *Linguistic Variation as Social Practice*. Oxford: Blackwell.

Edwards, John. 1999. Redefining our understanding of language attitudes. *Journal of Language and Social Psychology* 18: 101–10.

Errington, Joseph. 2001. Colonial linguistics. *Annual Review of Anthropology* 30: 19–39.

Errington, Joseph. 2003. Getting language rights: the rhetorics of language endangerment and loss. *American Anthropologist* 105: 723–32.

Fishman, Joshua A. 1991. *Reversing Language Shift: Theoretical and Empirical Foundations of Assistance to Threatened Languages*. Clevedon: Multilingual Matters.

Fishman, Joshua A. (ed.). 2001. *Can Threatened Languages be Saved? Reversing Language Shift, Revisited: A 21st Century Perspective*. Clevedon: Multilingual Matters.

Flores Farfán, Antonio José and Fernando F. Ramallo (eds.). 2010. *New Perspectives on Endangered Languages: Bridging Gaps Between Sociolinguistics, Documentation and Language Revitalisation*. Amsterdam: John Benjamins.

Freeland, Jane and Donna Patrick (eds.). 2004. *Language Rights and Language Survival Encounters*. Manchester: St Jerome Publishing.

Gippert, Jost, Nikolaus Himmelmann, and Ulrike Mosel (eds.). 2006. *Essentials of Language Documentation*. Berlin: Mouton de Gruyter.

Goodfellow, Anne Marie (ed.). 2009. *Speaking of Endangered Languages: Issues in Revitalisation*. Cambridge: Cambridge Scholars Publishing.

Gramsci, Antonio, Quintin Hoare, and Geoffrey Nowell-Smith. 1971. *Selections from the Prison Notebooks of Antonio Gramsci*. New York: International Publishers.

Grenoble, Lenore A. 2009. Review of K. David Harrison. 2007. When languages die: the extinction of the world's languages and the erosion of human knowledge. Oxford: Oxford University Press. *Anthropological Linguistics* 51: 179–82.

Grenoble, Lenore A. 2010. Switch or Shift: Code-Mixing, Contact-Induced Change and Attrition. Annual Public Lecture, Hans Rausing Endangered Languages Project, SOAS, University of London, 22 February 2010.

Grenoble, Lenore A. 2011. Language ecology and endangerment. In Peter K. Austin and Julia Sallabank (eds.), *The Cambridge Handbook of Endangered Languages*. Cambridge: Cambridge University Press.

Grenoble, Lenore A. and Louanna N. Furbee (eds.). 2010. *Language Documentation: Practice and Values*. Amsterdam: John Benjamins.

Grenoble, Lenore A. and Lindsay J. Whaley. 2006. *Saving Languages: An Introduction to Language Revitalisation*. Cambridge: Cambridge University Press.

Grinevald, Colette and Michel Bert. 2011. Speakers and communities. In Peter K. Austin and Julia Sallabank (eds.), *The Cambridge Handbook of Endangered Languages*. Cambridge: Cambridge University Press.

Gumperz, John J. and J. Cook-Gumperz. 1982. Introduction: language and the communication of social identity. In John J. Gumperz (ed.), *Language and Social Identity*. Cambridge: Cambridge University Press.

Hagège, Claude. 2000. *Halte à la mort des langues*. Paris: Odile Jacob.

Harbert, Wayne. 2011. Endangered languages and economic development. In Peter K. Austin and Julia Sallabank (eds.), *The Cambridge Handbook of Endangered Languages*. Cambridge: Cambridge University Press.

Harrison, K. David. 2007. *When Languages Die: The Extinction of the World's Languages and the Erosion of Human Knowledge*. New York: Oxford University Press.

Haugen, Einar. 1972. *The Ecology of Language: Language Science and National Development*. Stanford: Stanford University Press.

Heinrich, Patrick. 2005. What leaves a mark should no longer stain: progressive erasure and reversing language shift activities in the Ryukyu Islands. *Refereed Papers from the 1st International Small Island Cultures Conference, Kagoshima University Centre for the Pacific Islands (7–10 February 2005)*, 61–72. <http://sicri-network.org/ISIC1/j.%20ISIC1P%20Heinrich.pdf> (accessed 16 April 2013).

Hill, Jane. 2002. 'Expert rhetorics' in advocacy for endangered languages: who is listening, and what do they hear? *Journal of Linguistic Anthropology* 12: 119–33.

Himmelmann, Nikolaus P. 2006. Language documentation: what is it and what is it good for? In Jost Gippert, Nikolaus Himmelmann, and Ulrike Mosel (eds.), *Essentials of Language Documentation*. Berlin: Mouton de Gruyter.

Hinton, Leanne and Kenneth Hale (eds.). 2001. *The Green Book of Language Revitalization in Practice*. New York: Academic Press.

Hobson, John, Kevin Lowe, Susan Poetsch, and Michael Walsh (eds.). 2010. *Re-awakening Languages: Theory and Practice in the Revitalisation of Australia's Indigenous Languages*. Sydney: Sydney University Press.

Hoffman, Katherine E. 2006. Berber language ideologies, maintenance, and contraction: gendered variation in the indigenous margins of Morocco. *Language and Communication* 26: 144–67.

Hymes, Dell. 1972. Models of the interaction of language and social life (revised from 1967 paper). In John J. Gumperz and Dell Hymes (eds.), *Directions in Sociolinguistics: The Ethnography of Communication*. Oxford: Blackwell.

Irvine, Judith and Susan Gal. 2000. Language ideology and linguistic differentiation. In Paul V. Kroskrity (ed.), *Regimes of Language: Ideologies, Polities, and Identities*. Santa Fe, NM: School of American Research Press.

Jaffe, Alexandra. 1999. *Ideologies in Action: Language Politics on Corsica*. Berlin: Mouton de Gruyter.

King, Jeanette, Ray Harlow, Catherine Watson, Peter Keegan, and Margaret Maclagen. 2009. Changing pronunciation of the Māori language: implications for revitalisation. In Jon Reyhner and Louise Lockard (eds.), *Indigenous Language Revitalisation: Encouragement, Guidance and Lessons Learned*. Flagstaff: Northern Arizona University.

King, Kendall A. 2001. *Language Revitalisation Processes and Prospects: Quichua in the Ecuadorian Andes*. Clevedon: Multilingual Matters.

King, Kendall, Natalie Schilling-Estes, Lyn Wright Fogle, and Jia J. Lou (eds.). 2008. *Sustaining Linguistic Diversity: Endangered and Minority Languages and Language Varieties*. Washington, DC: Georgetown University Press.

Krauss, M. 1997. Indigenous languages of the north: a report on their present state. In H. Shoji and J. Janhunen (eds.), *Northern Minority Languages: Problems of Survival*. Senri Ethnological Studies 44. Osaka: National Museum of Ethnology.

Kroskrity, Paul V. (ed.). 2000. *Regimes of Language: Ideologies, Polities, and Identities*. Santa Fe, NM: School of American Research Press.

Kroskrity, Paul V. 2009. Language renewal as sites of language ideological struggle: the need for 'ideological clarification'. In J. Reyhner and L. Lockard (eds.), *Indigenous Language Revitalisation: Encouragement, Guidance and Lessons Learned*. Flagstaff: Northern Arizona University.

Kroskrity, Paul V. and Margaret Field (eds.). 2009. *Native American Language Ideologies: Beliefs, Practices, and Struggles in Indian Country*. Tucson: University of Arizona Press.

Labov, William. 1973. The linguistic consequence of being a lame. *Language in Society*, 2: 81–115.

Lewis, M. Paul, Gary F. Simons, and Charles D. Fennig (eds.). 2013. *Ethnologue: Languages of the World*. (17th edn.). Dallas: SOL International. See <http://www.ethnologue.com> for online version.

Long, Daniel and Dennis Preston (eds.). 2002. *Handbook of Perceptual Dialectology*, vol. 2. Amsterdam: John Benjamins.

McCarty, Teresa (ed.). 2011. *Ethnography and Language Policy*. New York/Abingdon: Routledge.

Makoni, Sinfree and Alastair Pennycook (eds.). 2006. *Disinventing and Reconstituting Languages*. Clevedon: Multilingual Matters.

Mar-Molinero, Clare and Patrick Stevenson (eds.). 2006. *Language Ideologies, Policies and Practices: Language and the Future of Europe*. Language and Globalisation. Basingstoke: Palgrave Macmillan.

Meek, Barbra A. 2011. *We Are Our Language: An Ethnography of Language Revitalisation in a Northern Athabaskan Community*. Tucson: University of Arizona Press.

Milroy, Lesley. 1987. *Language and Social Networks*. Oxford: Blackwell.

Mufwene, Salikoko. 2004. Language birth and death. *Annual Review of Anthropology* 33: 201–22.

Mühlhäusler, Peter. 1996. *Linguistic Ecology*. London: Routledge.

Mühlhäusler, Peter. 2003. Language endangerment and language revival. *Journal of Sociolinguistics* 7: 232–45.

Nettle, Daniel and Suzanne Romaine. 2000. *Vanishing Voices: The Extinction of the World's Languages*. New York: Oxford University Press.

Newman, Paul. 2003. The endangered languages issue as a hopeless cause. In Mark Janse and Sijmen Tol (eds.), *Language Death and Language Maintenance: Theoretical, Practical and Descriptive Approaches*. Amsterdam: John Benjamins.

Nieldzielski, Nancy A. and Dennis Richard Preston. 2003. *Folk Linguistics*. Berlin: Mouton de Gruyter.

Patrick, Peter L. 2002. The speech community. In J. K. Chambers, Peter Trudgill, and N. Schilling-Estes (eds.), *The Handbook of Language Variation and Change*. Oxford: Blackwell.

Pennycook, Alastair. 2005. Postmodernism in language policy. In Thomas Ricento (ed.), *An Introduction to Language Policy: Theory and Method*. Oxford: Blackwell.

Pennycook, Alastair. 2007. *Global Englishes and Transcultural Flows*. Abingdon: Routledge.

Preston, Dennis Richard. 1989. *Perceptual Dialectology*. Dordrecht: Foris.

Preston, Dennis Richard (ed.). 1999. *Handbook of Perceptual Dialectology*, vol. 1. Amsterdam: John Benjamins.

Reyhner, Jon and Louise Lockard (eds.). 2009. *Indigenous Language Revitalisation: Encouragement, Guidance and Lessons Learned*. Flagstaff: Northern Arizona University Press.

Ricento, Thomas (ed.). 2006. *An Introduction to Language Policy*. Oxford: Blackwell.

Rindstedt, Camilla and Karin Aronsson. 2002. Growing up monolingual in a bilingual community: the Quichua revitalization paradox. *Language in Society* 31: 721–42.

Romaine, Suzanne. 2002. The impact of language policy on endangered languages. *International Journal on Multicultural Societies* 4: 194–212.

Romaine, Suzanne. 2006. Planning for the survival of linguistic diversity. *Language Policy* 5: 441–73.

Sallabank, Julia. 2009. Review of Alexandre Duchêne and Monica Heller (eds.), Discourses of endangerment: ideology and interest in the defence of languages. *Journal of Sociolinguistics* 13: 106–12.

Sallabank, Julia. 2010. Endangered language maintenance and revitalisation: the role of social networks. *Anthropological Linguistics* 52: 184–205.

Sallabank, Julia. 2012. From language documentation to language planning: not necessarily a direct route. In Frank Seifart, Geoffrey Haig, Nikolaus P. Himmelmann, Dagmar Jung, Anna Margetts, and Paul Trilsbeek (eds.), *Potentials of Language Documentation: Methods, Analyses, and Utilisation*. Language Documentation and Conservation Special Publication No. 3. Manoa, HI: University of Hawai'i Press.

Sallabank, Julia. 2013. *Endangered Languages: Attitudes, Identities and Policies*. Cambridge: Cambridge University Press.

Sayers, David. 2009. Reversing Babel: declining linguistic diversity and the flawed attempts to protect it. Unpublished PhD dissertation, University of Essex.

Schieffelin, Bambi B., Kathryn A. Woolard, and Paul V. Kroskrity (eds.). 1998. *Language Ideologies: Practice and Theory*. Oxford: Oxford University Press.

Schiffman, H. F. 1996. *Linguistic Culture and Language Policy*. London: Routledge.

Schiffman, H. F. 2002. Comment. *International Journal of the Sociology of Language* special issue on Diglossia 157: 141–50.

Schmidt, Annette. 1985. *Young People's Dyirbal: An Example of Language Death from Australia*. Cambridge: Cambridge University Press.

Sebba, Mark, 2007. *Spelling and Society: The Culture and Politics of Orthography Around the World*. Cambridge: Cambridge University Press.

Silverstein, Michael. 1996. Monoglot 'standard' in America: standardisation and metaphors of linguistic hegemony. In Donald Brenneis and Ronald K. S. Macaulay (eds.), *The Matrix of Language: Contemporary Linguistic Anthropology*. Boulder, CO: Westview Press.

Silverstein, Michael. 1998. The uses and utility of ideology: a commentary. In Bambi B. Schieffelin, Kathryn A. Woolard, and Paul V. Kroskrity (eds.), *Language Ideologies: Practice and Theory*. Oxford: Oxford University Press.

Silverstein, Michael. 2000. Whorfianism and the linguistic imagination of nationality. In Paul V. Kroskrity (ed.), *Regimes of Language: Ideologies, Polities and Identities*. Santa Fe, NM: School of American Research Press.

Simpson, Jane. 2013. What's done and what's said: language attitudes, public language activities and everyday talk in the Northern Territory of Australia. *Journal of Multilingual and Multicultural Development* 34: 1–16.

Spolsky, Bernard. 1998. *Sociolinguistics*. Oxford: Oxford University Press.

Spolsky, Bernard. 2004. *Language Policy*. Cambridge: Cambridge University Press.

Spolsky, Bernard. 2009. *Language Management*. Cambridge: Cambridge University Press.

Spolsky, Bernard. 2011. Language and society. In Peter K. Austin and Julia Sallabank (eds.), *The Cambridge Handbook of Endangered Languages*. Cambridge: Cambridge University Press.

Steger, Manfred B. 2003. *Globalisation*. Oxford: Oxford University Press.

Street, Brian. 1984. *Literacy in Theory and Practice*. Cambridge: Cambridge University Press.

Thieberger, N. 2002. Extinction in whose terms? In David Bradley and Maya Bradley (eds.), *Language Endangerment and Language Maintenance: An Active Approach*. London: Curzon.

Tollefson, J. W. 2006. Critical theory in language policy. In T. Ricento (ed.), *An Introduction to Language Policy: Theory and Method*. Oxford: Blackwell.

Tsunoda, Tasaku. 2006. *Language Endangerment and Language Revitalisation*. Berlin: Mouton de Gruyter.

UNESCO (United Nations Educational, Scientific and Cultural Organization) (Ad Hoc Expert Group on Endangered Languages). 2003. Language vitality and endangerment: by way of introduction. Paris: UNESCO.

Urla, Jacqueline. 2012. *Reclaiming Basque: Language, Nation, and Cultural Activism*. Reno and Las Vegas, NV: University of Nevada Press.

Watts, Richard and Peter Trudgill (eds.). 2002. *Alternative Histories of English*. London: Routledge.

Whaley, Lindsay J. 2011. Some ways to endanger an endangered language project. *Language and Education* 25: 339–48.

Woolard, Kathryn A. 1998. Introduction: language ideology as a field of inquiry. In Bambi Schieffelin, Kathryn A. Woolard, and Paul V. Kroskrity (eds.), *Language Ideologies. Practice and Theory.* Oxford: Oxford University Press.

Woolard, Kathryn A. and Bambi B. Schieffelin. 1994. Language ideology. *Annual Review of Anthropology* 23: 55–82.

Part 1

Case Studies: Beliefs and Ideologies in Endangered Language Communities

2

Paradoxes of Engagement with Irish Language Community Management, Practice, and Ideology

TADHG Ó hIFEARNÁIN

2.1 Introduction: State Language Policy and Native Speaker Communities

IT HAS BEEN frequently observed that Irish has many parallels with other minority languages in Europe and around the world, where states or public authorities have tried to intervene in language contact situations to produce a societal outcome different from what the established dynamic would have ensured. In his study of the interaction of language policy and social reproduction of the language, Ó Riagáin (1997) observes that Ireland differs from most countries in two respects. Firstly, Irish language policy has been in operation for a much longer period, which makes the country's experiences more appropriate than many for testing the long-term effects of the community–state interface in language management, notably with regard to language-in-education policy. Secondly, he observes that, unlike other minority language situations, in Ireland the state attempted to deal with its minority language problem by seeking to re-establish it as a national language: 'No other minority language problem in Europe was tackled in this way, although the rather special (but relatively recent) cases of the regional languages in Spain have some similarities' (Ó Riagáin 1997: vii). It can be argued that the project to promote Nynorsk as a national language in Norway may represent another such case. However, this chapter proposes that it is not the actual action of the Irish state's promotion of the indigenous but minoritized language as the newly independent state's primary official and working language that is the appropriate basis for comparison, but the ideological grounding of that policy. In such a policy it is implicit that the minority of the population who used Irish as their home language, mainly Irish mother-tongue bilinguals living in rural Gaeltacht communities, could not be considered by decision-makers as a cultural group separate from the rest of the population. Instead, the ideology that marked and continues to be behind Irish

Proceedings of The British Academy, **199**, 29–52. © The British Academy 2014.

language policy is that the Anglophone majority are a post-language shift population and that there are no linguistic minorities; rather, there are varying degrees of linguistic ability and practice with regard to Irish.

In such a language ideology scenario, everybody has some kind of direct relationship to Irish. This is reflected by the fact that, over the twentieth century, Ireland's language policy contained a wealth of references to the 'revival', 'restitution', and 'recovery' of Irish (see, for example, Coimisiún na Gaeltachta 1926; Coimisiún um Athbheochan na Gaeilge 1963, 1964; Committee on Irish Language Attitudes Research 1975). Spolsky (2003) distinguishes between 'revitalisation' in home language acquisition and usage versus 'regeneration' in activities in wider society. It is this central focus on 'regeneration' that can be considered the ideological basis for language policy in Ireland. Even if an argument can be made that regeneration is an ideological construction and could be challenged by an alternative model that does not see the Irish language as a central component of Anglophone Ireland's identity, it is a position that a great part of the Irish national collective (meaning not just the state and educational apparatus but also the general public) take to be a reality and do not seek to subvert. As an example of this ideology in action, 14 per cent of Irish people claimed that Irish was their 'mother tongue' in the Eurobarometer survey on the knowledge of languages in the European Union (Eurobarometer 2003), despite the fact that less than 2 per cent of the population speak it on a daily basis. The idea that one can have a 'mother tongue' that would not meet the definitions used for census data in other jurisdictions—such as the first language learnt in youth and which one still speaks, as in Canada, or even simply a language in which one thinks or which one knows best, regardless of when it was acquired, such as in Switzerland or Finland (Arel 2002: 99)—is true for many people in Ireland. The Irish case shares this scenario with many other minority language situations in Europe and elsewhere. This fundamental stance of a large proportion of a post-language shift population to their ancestral tongue is increasingly present in populations that underwent language shift towards a dominant language during the nineteenth and twentieth centuries. This is a social reality that has led to responses from regional authorities and public organizations in many territories in contemporary times.

As such policies have been in place in Ireland for several generations, second-language speakers of Irish far outnumber those who speak it as a first language. 'Mother-tongue' data is not gathered by the Irish Central Statistics Office, as it would not be meaningful in this linguistic reality. Census returns based on self-reported language competence and frequency of usage reveal that those who claim to be able to speak Irish outnumber those who use it every day by 23 to 1 (see Table 2.1). In studies that offer respondents a more nuanced range of possible replies about their competence in Irish, even higher figures are revealed. In a national sample of 1,015 respondents, Mac Gréil and Rhatigan

Table 2.1 Population of Irish Republic over three years of age.

Ireland (Republic only)	**Gaeltacht (designated Irish-speaking areas)**
Population: 4,370,631	Population: 96,628
Irish speakers: 1,774,437 (40.6%)	Irish speakers: 62,238 (68.5%)
Speak daily outside education system: 77,185 (1.8%)	Speak daily outside education system: 23,175 (24%)

Source: Census of Population 2011 (Central Statistics Office 2012).

(2009) found that only 16 per cent of the Irish-born population claimed no ability in Irish, which should not come as a surprise as nearly all Irish-born residents would have experienced the Irish education system, where the language is a compulsory subject. Only 7 per cent in the same survey were not in favour of some measures to either preserve or develop the language.

First-language speakers of Irish and/or those who use Irish as their main home language are thus vastly outnumbered by those who habitually use English, but who have some knowledge of Irish, principally acquired through schooling. From a language policy perspective, the objective of the regeneration of Irish touches on the lives of the vast majority of the population, whereas revitalization, language maintenance, and development are matters directed at a very small part of the population indeed.

It is helpful to identify four stages in Irish language policy since the foundation of the state in 1922 (Ó hIfearnáin 2009). These four periods of language management by the state as chief agency were:

1. 1922–56: the foundations of Irish language management.
2. 1956–72: redefinitions of the role of the state.
3. 1973–92: consultation and reacting to pressure from the grass roots.
4. 1992 to the present: Linguistic minority rights and heritage.

Ó Riagáin (1997: 7–27), who at the time believed there was evidence for three post-independence stages, described state policy from the 1970s until the 1990s as one of 'benign neglect'. However, from the current perspective, that period can better be described as a repositioning of the way core language ideology was enacted, which in turn led to the emergence, since the early 1990s, of new explicit actions with regard to broadcasting, education, and the legal status of Irish in Ireland and the European Union. It has also engendered a new debate on the future definition of the Gaeltacht and whether it should continue to be defined as a geographic entity or as a linguistic community of practice of habitual Irish speakers living both inside and outside the core territory. All of these changes reveal how the state was starting to think of Irish in terms of being a minority language group issue (for maintenance and possible revitalization) on the one hand, and as a cultural heritage issue on the other. The four policy phases do not represent changes in essential policy priorities, but rather the emergence of the dominance of different strands and nuances that have always animated the state's conduct, reflecting the constant central ideology of the national role of Irish as the language of the Irish people, but expressing it in ways that were most acceptable to the majority of the people in each period. Language policy has thus never challenged the majority opinion, but has given substance to it. As such, the changes in tack that the policies represent have rarely proved to be controversial for the majority of the population, reflecting the deep-rooted consensus that such a core prevailing language ideology represents.

It is this chapter's contention that to properly understand the state's actions in the Irish language community, in the Gaeltacht in particular, one must understand that in some circumstances it is behaving covertly, as if the language community were a particular linguistic minority. But, at the same time, this stance is juxtaposed with a more overtly stated ideology that has been dominant since the foundation of the state (based on nineteenth-century romantic nationalist beliefs), which denies the existence of a separate Irish-speaking minority. This mismatch between action and beliefs, and the differing priorities for the role of Irish, nationally and in the Gaeltacht, has led to a series of misadventures in language policy. This chapter examines the manner in which policy practice, ostensibly in favour of Irish, inadvertently puts additional pressure on language retention in some marginal Gaeltacht areas by failing to identify two subgroups within that population—native and habitual Irish speakers on the one hand, and monolingual English speakers on the other—but instead tries to treat them as one homogeneous group who should have similar linguistic ambitions with regard to Irish.

2.2 Language Policy and Status Changes within the Speech Community

Language policies occur at many levels in society, including national and institutional language planning, but also in the complex matrices of language ideologies and the practices of families, communities, peer groups, and work environments. Spolsky (2009) explains what Baldauf (1994) and Eggington (2002) call 'unplanned language planning' as resulting from policies produced by central governments or other high sociopolitical levels, which do not take into account language policies that may already exist at other levels, albeit perhaps unconsciously. This hypothesis is a particularly useful approach when 'language policy' is to be understood according to Spolsky's (2004) tripartite model, consisting of (a) beliefs about language, (b) actual language practices, and (c) how these are managed or changed by agents within the community. This language policy paradigm is a way of describing the dynamics that exist within a speech community, where, for example, certain actors or inside groups that have different beliefs and/or language practices from the majority but who ultimately show themselves to have been trendsetters can be regarded as language planners or managers. The paradigm can also be used to describe how agencies such as the state itself, schools, or employers might also consciously set out to manipulate beliefs about languages and language practices (the way that people use their linguistic repertoires) in order to produce a result that fulfils their language planning goals, such as the acquisition of a new working language, a shift to the majority language in a peripheral community, or the enhancement of, or creation of, a new status for a language that had previously been undermined as a community asset. It is much more often the hidden rather than the overtly announced policy that is most effective. Communities that have undergone language shift from their traditional language to a dominant language often do not appreciate that their language is disappearing while the process is occurring, but instead only realize it when they notice that the younger generation can no longer communicate fluently in the ancestral language. Shohamy (2006) describes these undetected language dynamics as being driven by what she labelled 'covert ideologies', rather than the overtly expressed opinions about language and language planning goals. While Shohamy studied them in social terms, Kristiansen (2011), building on earlier work by Labov and Trudgill, has shown that linguistic change within a speech community's language is also subject to the overt/covert divide. Respondents might say that they prefer a local dialect or the 'high' or standard forms of their language, and that they dislike the variety of the capital or another major city. However, analysis of the same informants' speech reveals that in practice they have adopted many of the characteristics of the speech varieties that they said they did not like to use. It is the hidden aspects of beliefs about language, shown in actual preferences in language use, that are the real driving force of language shift or retention, and they represent the true challenge for language policy-makers. In order to make critical decisions about language policy initiatives in favour of the retention of Irish, or of other minoritized languages, the first task should be to understand what are the hidden ideologies at work in the community of speakers and how these may differ from those of the polity and the majority population.

Although language maintenance initiatives, and even long-standing policy positions created by national or regional governments or by local communities, often (if not always) share overt common aims, divergences between institutional revivalist policy and local retention strategies can actually be shown to reinforce older dominant/dominating diglossic language beliefs in the minority-speech community. These can be shown as most often resulting from differences in ideological stances between communities of speakers on the one hand, and 'authorities' and their language management or language planning strategies on the other. Work on the corpus of a language is necessary when it has been excluded from formal education but is then to be used in the education system either as a taught subject or as a medium of instruction. This involves changing the role of the traditional language within the community, and thus rearranging the speech community's collective practices and beliefs about the language(s) that they speak. Jaffe (2009) for instance, on Corsican evidence, argues that abstract changes in prestige accorded by authorities in language planning regimes may not actually change the underlying ideology of minority language speakers at all. What is seen as a key component of successful language management instead serves to embed deeply held linguistic ideologies, which purport that the local (minority) language has a functionality limited to family and local community, and lacks the legitimacy inherently needed for use in education, administration, broadcasting, print media, and other public domains. Endeavouring to modify attitudes so as to achieve regeneration and revitalization goals means encouraging the broadening of domains of usage whilst undercutting ideas that detract from the project by changing or manipulating them in such a way that they help to enhance the aims. However, it also requires a much broader change in ideology that can be difficult to achieve in an overt fashion over a short time. In the case of Breton, Le Dû and Le Berre (1996) have argued that the creation of a supra-regional normative version of the language (orignally developed by Breton nationalists in the early twentieth century as a 'national' version of the fragmented regional varieties for use in domains that the activists thought would eventually be necessary) has in fact undermined language maintenance of the traditional local varieties, which they labelled the *badumes* (from Breton *ba du-mañ*—'around our home'), a term now widely used in French-medium sociolinguistics. Unlike the regional proto-standards that had been used until the middle of the twentieth century in the Breton-language work of the Church, the normative version, designed for 'national usage', draws on linguistically purist terminology and on a synthetic amalgamation of regional dialectal usages, and has also been characterized as the language of second-language speakers who hold positions of power. This normative language variety has become the vehicle for the vast majority of language teaching in schools and language usage by the educational and regional administrative authorities since the 1990s. Yet it is so far removed from the local traditional dialects, with their limited social domains of usage, that it arguably does the opposite by undermining the legitimacy of the traditional varieties. However, there are indications that the situation may have moved into a new phase in the last ten years, to the extent that the linguistic and ideological gulf between traditional native speakers and language activists is not as great as that previously characterized in much of the sociolinguistic literature on Breton (Hornsby 2005; Ó hIfearnáin 2011). It may therefore be possible to say that, in the wider understanding of standardization and normativity in minoritized languages, the conflict between local versus (official) norm/standard varieties may represent a stage in development rather than a permanent situation, and that the coexistence of traditional varieties and an overtly planned variety may have various potential outcomes. The accommodation of traditional varieties and their speakers in 'national' language planning, without undermining either the goal of local maintenance nor of the language's role in national development, remains, however, a salient issue for all minoritized languages and regeneration/revival programmes within bilingual/multilingual contexts, and can be understood within the current language policy paradigm with its overt and hidden agendas.

2.3 The Irish State and the Gaeltacht Communities—the Changing Policy Environment

Ó Riagáin (1997) has argued that language management strategies for strengthening Irish in the Gaeltacht have never met their targets because they did not take adequate notice of the socio-economic reality. Further, I argue that covert ideological mismatches between national institutions and the Gaeltacht population, in relation to bilingual practices, have undermined the overt intentions of both groups to develop Irish (e.g. Ó hIfearnáin 2007, 2008, 2009). Ireland has now moved into a new policy-generating environment that includes fresh national language planning and local initiatives. It also includes a revision of how the core language ideologies, on which pro-Irish national language policy has been based since the foundation of the Irish state in the first quarter of the twentieth century, are expressed.

A number of documents illustrate the newly modelled stances of the state on the Irish language issue. These policy goals are embedded in ideologies that have much in common with more widely held European and Canadian concepts of aims and practices in relation to minority groups and their languages in the setting of globalization. The key documents for this discussion are the Gaeltacht Act 2012 (Tithe an Oireachtais 2012), the *20-Year Strategy for the Irish Language 2010–2030* (Government of Ireland 2010), which arose out of the government-commissioned studies: *Comprehensive Linguistic Study of the Use of Irish in the Gaeltacht* (Ó Giollagáin et al. 2007), two reports on Gaeltacht education (Mac Donnacha et al. 2005; Ó Flatharta 2007), the Official Languages Act 2003 (Tithe an Oireachtais 2003), and the *Report* of Coimisiún na Gaeltachta (2002).

Underlying this change in the language planning environment is a discourse that expresses a key concept: the desire for policy to be more 'democratic', in line with the neoliberal attitudes of states and the majority of the citizenry. Gaeltacht communities are being encouraged to make their own language plans and to take responsibility for their linguistic futures. Nevertheless, the framework for policy objectives remains centralized, emphasizing measurable success criteria. It relies, in particular, on (a) self-reported frequency of Irish language usage gathered by the national census and (b) community performance in Scéim Labhairt na Gaeilge, a scheme that existed from the 1930s until 2011, which gave a small financial reward to households whose children could be shown to be home-speakers of Irish and who regularly attended a Gaeltacht school. It should be noted that neither of these are reliable sociolinguistic tools for measuring language vitality in a community. However, as communities are now aware that some elements of their socio-economic well-being may, in future, depend on their answers to the language frequency question in the national census, it will be interesting to see if significant 'field contamination' of the local census data by the national language planning objectives may occur. The 2011 census data, for example, shows that there has been a net increase of 660 daily speakers of Irish since the 2006 census (CSO 2012), but the statistics released are only at the county level within the Gaeltacht regions and so do not yet show whether or not the increases are in any of the marginal Gaeltacht regions or whether they reflect rises in areas where Irish is more widely spoken. Since the Irish Government announced in April 2011 that Scéim Labhairt na Gaeilge would be discontinued, it seems that the two criteria used in measuring local and state language planning initiatives have actually been cast in doubt by the national authorities themselves.

Nevertheless, the principle that local communities should come up with local language plans in order to show their commitment to Irish is a core element of the newly emerging language policy regime. In this era of democratizing language policy, successful Irish language management has to accommodate shared overt objectives with the underlying beliefs and practices of communities of speakers who have been disempowered through centuries of marginalization and who have lived as 'targets' of national language planners. To expect such historically disenfranchised communities, who do not have any form of local municipal government, nor control over the language policies of their local schools, to develop meaningful language plans in a short space of time may not be realistic. Community empowerment, however superficial, also gives voice to opponents of pro-minority language policies. They had not previously had much media exposure or access to the state apparatus, due to the overt aims of local Gaeltacht language policy and national policy both being framed within the ideological context of the national language project to maintain and develop Gaeltacht Irish usage. Opponents of language promotion, or those who resist consolidating the special status of Irish in the Gaeltacht, reinforce the national minority/majority power differentials of an earlier era when Irish was being marginalized. These opponents must be a central concern of minority language management as they awaken hidden inferiority complexes in Irish speakers and fears about their English language skills.

A unifying element in the documents listed above is the notion that the territoriality of the traditional Gaeltacht regions is still paramount, although the

20-Year Strategy does declare that this may not be the only way to define an Irish-speaking community in the future, and the Gaeltacht Act (2012) holds out the possibility of recognition for 'Irish language networks' outside the designated Gaeltacht regions. Of particular interest is the idea that geographic regions within the Gaeltacht, where the number of daily Irish speakers is below a certain percentage, must come up with a strategy to increase the number of speakers. This would need to happen within a certain number of years in order for the area to continue to be recognized as a Gaeltacht community and so to benefit from special treatment in socio-economic development and in Irish-medium schooling. Under the heading 'Linguistic status of Gaeltacht communities: new legislation', the *Strategy* says in particular that new legislation should withdraw Gaeltacht status from weaker Irish-speaking communities if they do not increase the level of Irish usage:

> In the case of majority Irish-speaking communities, the emphasis will be on protecting and strengthening these strong language communities by ensuring the linguistic sustainability of Irish as the community language of these regions. In the case of other Gaeltacht regions where daily Irish speakers are a significant minority, the emphasis will be on strengthening the Irish language community networks that continue to exist there.
>
> Communities that cannot comply with the criteria in the new legislation will be afforded a period of two years to develop plans to ensure that they maintain their status as Gaeltacht communities.
>
> Communities who fail to develop acceptable sustainable plans within the two year period will no longer be included in the Gaeltacht.
>
> Plans will be reviewed every seven years and areas that do not achieve the linguistic criteria for the Gaeltacht set down in the new Act will cease to have Gaeltacht status. New areas may also be included in the Gaeltacht if they meet the linguistic criteria laid down in the new Act.
>
> (Government of Ireland 2010: 20)

This appears to be a threat directed at communities where Irish speakers are in a minority, but can be justified if one accepts the national ideology that these communities are culturally homogeneous, but simply that some of their members speak Irish and others do not. Removal from the Gaeltacht would simply make them part of the rest of Ireland where other language regeneration policies would apply. To avoid removal from the Gaeltacht, those who do not speak Irish in those areas should speak it more often. The ideological template set out in the *Strategy* did indeed inform the subsequent Gaeltacht Act, and in accordance with the Act the Minister of State defined 26 language planning areas within the Gaeltacht in September 2013, although many of these units are far from homogeneous in their sociolinguistic profile, containing both communities where Irish is widely spoken and where it is quite marginalized. The Act emphasizes the monitoring of the language planning process itself and retains exclusion from the Gaeltacht as an option for those areas which do not create a language plan with the help of Údarás na Gaeltachta (the Gaeltacht authority) or which fail to implement it adequately.

However, this approach may be fundamentally flawed as a way of considering these territorial communities if we instead consider that Irish speakers in many Gaeltacht areas form a distinct cultural minority that has a different attitude to language practice and a different set of beliefs from the monolingual English speakers who share their home areas. Indeed, it is the case that, in many areas in the official Gaeltacht, where Irish is now the first language of only a minority, this situation has arisen not only because of language shift, but also through widespread immigration of non-Irish-speaking people to the area. This has had an additional impact on language practices in that all Irish speakers are bilingual, and in a situation where non-Irish speakers are present they have a tendency to switch to English.

In the Gaeltacht, an Irish-only medium of instruction in education has been a pillar of language policy since the 1920s. Despite the fact that all Gaeltacht schools are meant to be Irish-medium units, Mac Donnacha et al. (2005), in their study of all Gaeltacht primary and post-primary schools, have documented how schools actually teach through Irish and English in a way that reflects the linguistic make-up of the community they serve. The linguistic 'compromises' identified may fit with the ideology of a homogeneous community with varying degrees of language ability, but could instead be interpreted as revealing the manner in which the distinct Irish-speaking community is denied access to Irish-medium education simply by the fact of their minority status. This was a view expressed in the qualitative feedback from the *Gaeilge 2010* survey discussed below. The situation is also at odds with the practice in many parts of Europe. For example, ever since the peace treaties after the First World War historical linguistic minorities have been provided with schooling in their own language once they have met a certain numerical threshold within the wider community. As an illustration Finland's Language Act (Ministry of Justice, Finland 2003) requires municipalities to be Swedish–Finnish bilingual, including educational provision, if 8 per cent or 3,000 or more of the population speak the minority language. This status changes if the linguistic minority drops below 6 per cent, although a municipality can choose to maintain its bilingual status in such circumstances. Arrangements for the provision of education to indigenous minority language groups in many other signatories to the European Charter for Regional or Minority Languages are discussed in their states' reports to the monitoring body and in its recommendations (Council of Europe 2012). Ireland has not signed the Charter.

2.4 Investigating the Minority/Majority Relationship of Irish Speakers and English Monolinguals in the Gaeltacht

The Gaeltacht regions (see Figure 2.1) have a local authority called Údarás na Gaeltachta, which has a socio-economic development agenda and has increasingly understood that role as being linked to Irish language maintenance and development (see Walsh 2011).

Údarás na Gaeltachta's main funding comes from the government department responsible for Gaeltacht affairs. For the period concerned in the studies

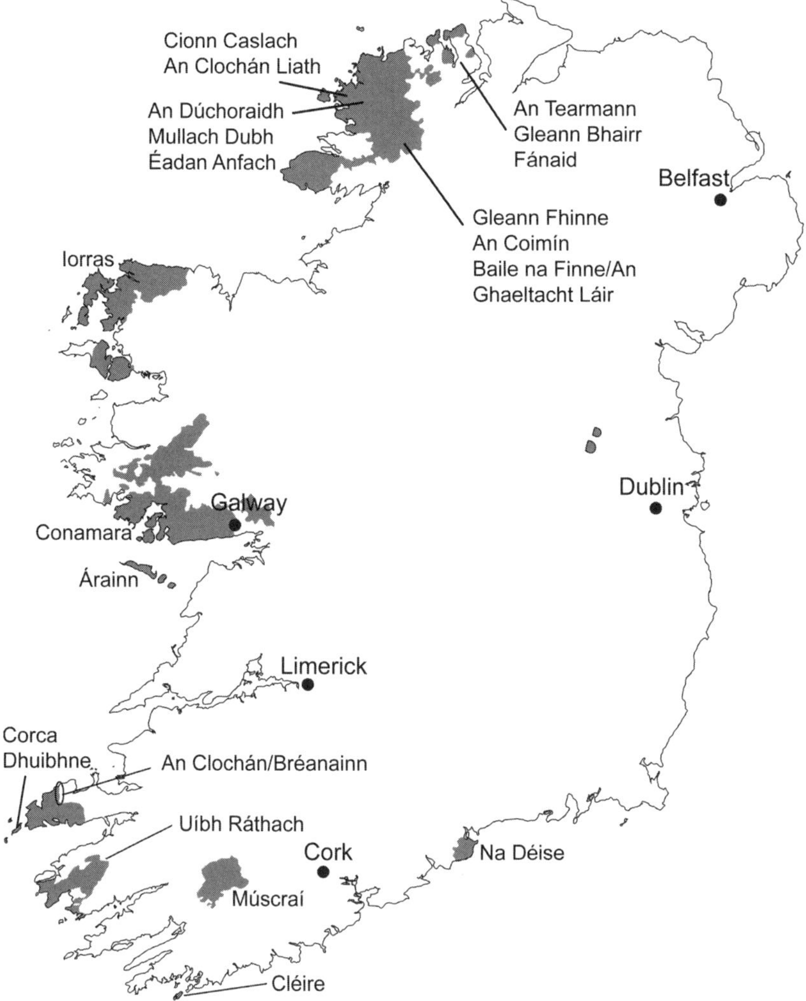

Figure 2.1 The Gaeltacht main regions (shaded) and those mentioned in the text. (T. Ó hIfearnáin)

described above, this was the Department of Community, Rural and Gaeltacht Affairs, becoming the Department of Arts, Heritage and the Gaeltacht in June 2011. In 2006 the Department invited Gaeltacht communities to submit projects to produce language plans under a limited budget initiative. Seven communities did this and were awarded some funding to proceed in developing a plan, mainly by employing a development officer to coordinate the project. A number of other communities also started to develop initiatives, but many regions remained largely inactive in this first wave of local language planning. In the absence of effective local/communal/municipal government, these projects were led by community groups, and there is, of course, some dispute as to the right or legitimacy of one group to lead a project rather than another. In the areas where no action had been reported, the Údarás and the Department came together to invite a local community organization to start to develop a language plan. To do this, a standardized questionnaire, entitled *Gaeilge 2010*, was developed as a tool to gather data in each community and to drive local initiative by asking the community what the aims of a language plan would be and what level of local support it would have. I was one of those consulted in the design of the questionnaire, but it was eventually put together by a committee of members of the two agencies and was put into practice before it had been reviewed. Unfortunately, some of the questions were formulated so that answers might be ambiguous. In addition, the English and Irish versions of the questionnaire asked slightly different questions or provided slightly different possible answers in some multiple choice and Likert-style questions, and so had to be analysed separately. Nevertheless, the results have provided a great deal of information, and constitute probably the biggest data-set available on attitudes to certain language planning issues currently available. It is not, however, a representative sample of the whole Gaeltacht population, but rather a sample of many of its constituent communities.

The data is from a household survey of 28 Gaeltacht regions carried out in 2007–8. There were 12,271 participants, and the information was gathered by community groups as part of an initiative to instigate local language initiatives (see Table 2.2). The areas concerned are mixed in the relative numerical strength of 'daily Irish speakers', ranging from some of the most strongly Irish-speaking communities in Conamara to some of the least Irish-speaking areas currently within the official Gaeltacht. More than half of the 28 communities concerned are affected by the two-year planning and seven-year probation period outlined in the *Strategy*.

It is very useful to compare some of the attitudes revealed with those of a much more far-reaching field survey conducted among fluent Irish speakers in the Múscraí Gaeltacht region in the south-west of the country during 2000–4. Múscraí is a small region with a population of approximately 3,600, where Irish is spoken regularly by the majority of people in only one of its four sub-areas.

Table 2.2 *Gaeilge 2010* overview of responses.

Number of households	4,454
Number of people in those households	12,721
Number of respondents (up to four from each household)	11,489

However, Múscraí was not one of the areas included in the survey of the 28 communities. Whereas the Údarás/Department survey was conducted among all households in the areas regardless of language, the Múscraí project was an Irish-medium study conducted only among Irish speakers in that particular mixed-language community.

The data, in both the survey of the 28 communities and the Múscraí project, highlight some persistent mismatches between community and institutional authority ideologies. There are also mismatches between the priorities for Irish with regard to its use in education in the home, in community, religious, and literacy practices, and with regard to English. Many of the new language policy initiatives being developed to maintain and regenerate Irish as a community language in the Gaeltacht continue to be based on language ideologies that are at variance with those of the language community, without strategies to modify those covertly held beliefs to achieve the policy goals. The data analysed also reveal new insights into some views of a monolingual English-speaking minority in the Gaeltacht and the extent to which they do not participate in, or actually oppose the revival/retention/regeneration policies of the community and state, a phenomenon that has manifested itself recently in conflicts over the medium of schooling and official place names in some areas (Warren 2012).

2.5 Monolingual English Speakers in the Gaeltacht

The challenge to language maintenance policies posed by non-Irish speakers in the Gaeltacht has not been the subject of sustained study, as it falls outside of the dominant belief system that does not see Irish speakers, or indeed monolingual English speakers in Ireland, as distinct groups. The extent to which monolingual English speakers see themselves as a distinct group within the Gaeltacht regions is particularly salient when we consider whether Irish speakers are indeed a separate group within the local community.

Table 2.3 and Figure 2.2 give an overview of the relative size of the communities in the *Gaeilge 2010* study, and of the linguistic make-up of each community. It should be noted that the questionnaire included a category of linguistic ability as 'native/fluent' (in both the Irish and English versions), but that no definition of how this was interpreted by the respondents is possible. While it may be assumed that fluent speakers have the language as their first or

Table 2.3 Linguistic profiles of respondents in the Gaeltacht communities as reported in the *Gaeilge 2010* data.

	Native/Fluent	Moderate	Weak	No Irish	Total
An Tearmann	27	62	49	41	179
Cionn Caslach	30	62	64	34	190
Gleann Bhairr	30	51	47	30	158
Cléire	38	15	13	9	75
Inis Meáin	43	1	1	1	46
An Clochán Liath	51	137	113	75	376
Inis Oírr	69	8	4	6	87
Gleann Fhinne	79	132	115	76	402
An Dúchoraidh	98	57	41	23	219
Mullach Dubh	98	149	73	34	354
Éadan Anfach	103	58	53	31	245
An Clochán/Bréanainn	113	163	100	26	402
An Coimín	125	48	27	35	235
Carna	126	23	11	5	165
Baile na Finne–An Ghaeltacht Láir	133	49	25	14	221
Rann na Feirste	141	26	4	5	176
Árainn	181	41	23	12	257
Fánaid	207	152	115	40	514
Uíbh Ráthach	210	376	217	92	895
Cill Chiaráin	275	12	13	6	306
An Fál Carrach	291	200	121	67	679
Camus	315	13	7	13	348
Anagaire	321	161	61	47	590
Ros Muc	367	16	6	7	396
Leitir Mealláin	555	31	34	19	639
Ceantar na nOileán	869	36	23	9	937
Gort an Choirce	952	150	89	53	1,244
An Cheathrú Rua	952	57	24	19	1,052

shared dominant language from early childhood, or that they have a very high level of competence in the language, it cannot be assumed in a bilingual community subject to language shift that somebody who is a 'native speaker' necessarily has a very broad and deep command of the language, although it seems that this is the most likely interpretation given the context of the study and the understanding between the people who administered the questionnaire and the respondents.

To investigate the areas in the Gaeltacht where Irish speakers are a minority, Figure 2.3 isolates those regions where those who described themselves as 'fluent/native' Irish speakers form half, or less than half, of the respondents. They are presented in four groups: the first one being in Munster and the other

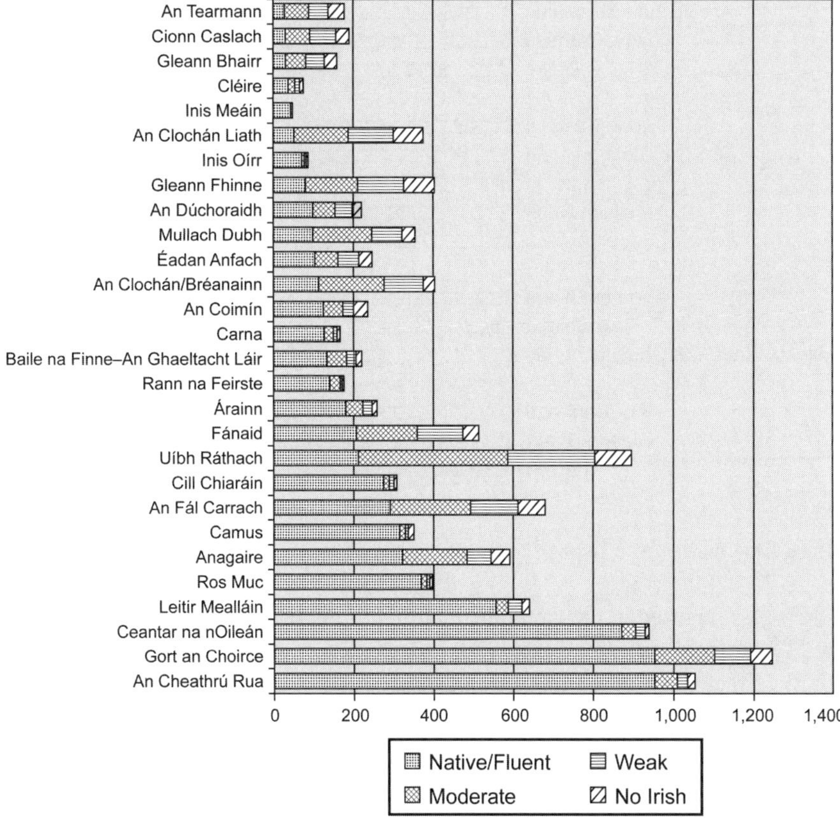

Figure 2.2 Graphic representation of the linguistic profiles of respondents in the *Gaeilge 2010* communities.

three being geographical groupings in three zones in the Ulster Gaeltacht regions of Donegal. One small community has been included, Baile na Finne (An Ghaeltacht Láir), where native/fluent speakers are a small majority. This is because the area forms a geographic unit with Gleann Fhinne and An Coimín and, when these areas are taken together, native/fluent Irish speakers form a minority.

Within these areas there is a correlation between the general support for Irish language promotion and different language abilities. Whereas over 95 per cent of native/fluent speakers support the promotion of Irish as policy, only 74 per cent of those who speak no Irish do so. The trend in all areas is the same, with support for Irish language promotion policies diminishing with linguistic ability. Although 74 per cent could be understood to represent relatively strong support for language promotion, it is actually similar or slightly lower than the support shown nationally by the general population for pro-Irish language

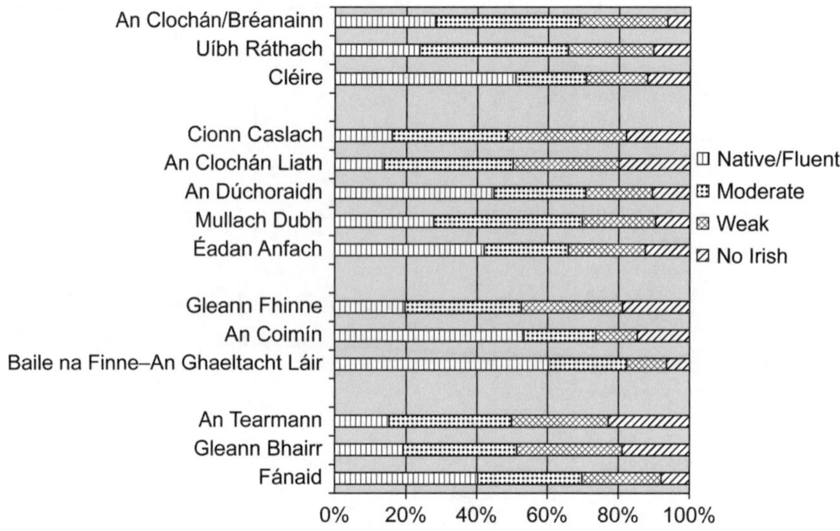

Figure 2.3 Communities in *Gaelige 2010* where Irish speakers are a minority.

policies, as reported in the Committee on Irish Language Attitudes Research and the ITÉ national surveys of the 1970s–90s (Ó Riagáin and Ó Gliasáin 1994). In the more recent national survey by Mac Gréil and Rhatigan (2009), over 90 per cent of the general population were reported as supportive, although the range of possible answers to the question and the possible proposed roles for Irish in society were more nuanced.

Gaeltacht society does, however, have many institutional supports that hark back to a national policy deeply rooted in the ideology of the 1920s and 1930s, which sought to make the Gaeltacht into a monolingual Irish-speaking region, or at least one in which all state services were conducted in Irish only and families were strongly encouraged not to speak English at home. Education is officially through the medium of Irish in these regions, and while it is true that Irish is not always the dominant language of schooling, it does have a very important role in schools and as a medium of instruction, even in areas where Irish is not spoken natively/fluently by the majority. In circumstances where a significant proportion of neighbouring people speak Irish as a home language and Irish occupies a very important role in local education, administration, and social life, it is perhaps surprising that monolingual English-speaking residents do not seem to have a strong compulsion to learn Irish in these Gaeltacht regions. Only 40 per cent had a desire to learn to speak the language, while very much smaller proportions wanted to read and write it (see Figure 2.4).

The trend is perhaps even more surprising when broken down by age group (see Figure 2.5). The analysis of the survey, in these marginal Gaeltacht areas, reveals that half of those aged five or under wished to learn Irish, and half did not

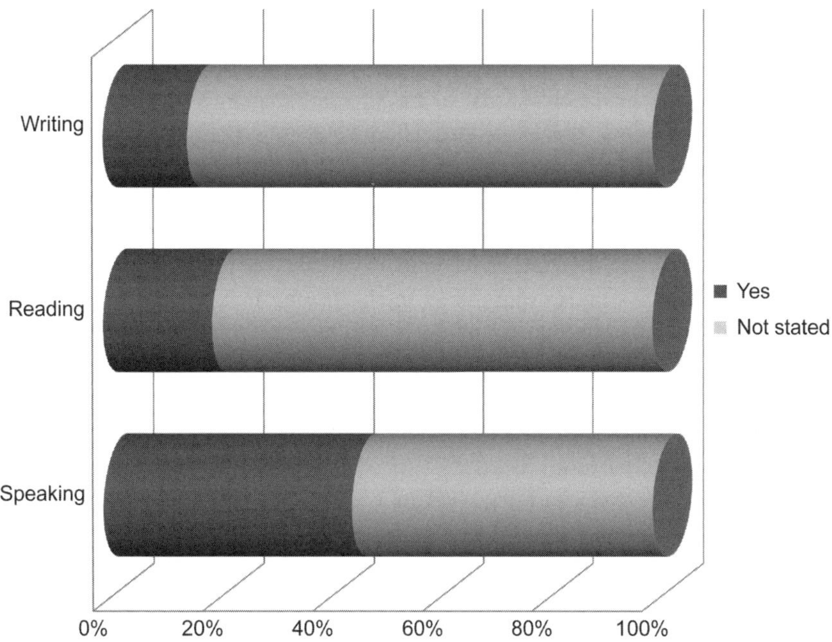

Figure 2.4 Target Irish-language skills of English monolinguals in Gaeltacht areas.

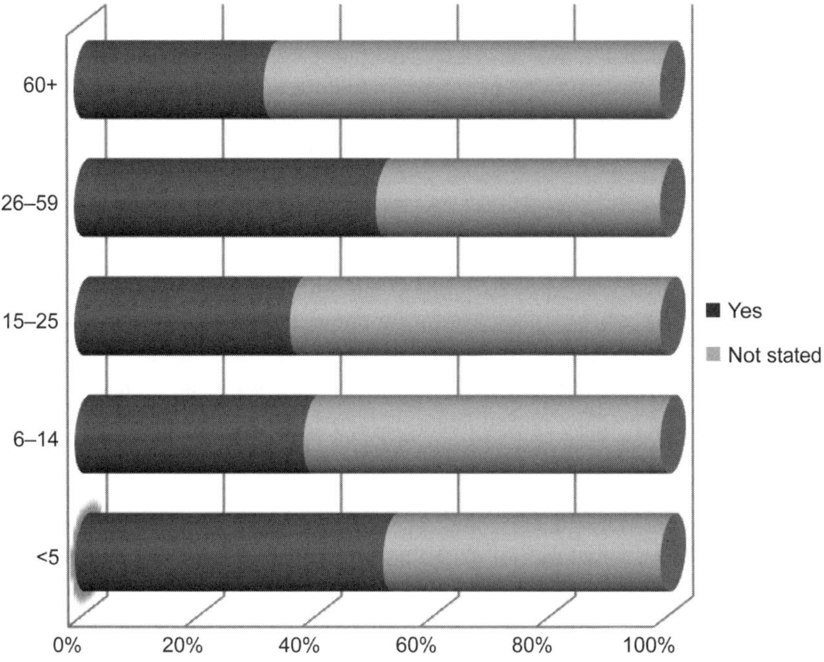

Figure 2.5 Gaeltacht-resident English-speaking monolinguals' desire to learn Irish by age group.

(this undoubtedly reflects the views of their parents rather than of the infants themselves). Antipathy to learning Irish among Anglophone children of school-going age in the Gaeltacht seems to be stronger than in other areas. This is despite the presence of Irish as a core school subject across the country and as a medium of education in the Gaeltacht, where it is also spoken socially in the community. There is little doubt that the special status given to the local language is a driving element of this resentment, as comments in the qualitative part of the survey highlighted. However, it is obvious from these results that few of the monolingual English speakers in the Gaeltacht feel the need to learn Irish in order to participate in their community, and thus must expect Irish speakers to use English with them, revealing a diglossic power relationship between native Irish speakers and monolingual English speakers in which Irish speakers must acquiesce.

The general trend in all the areas studied is that those with no Irish are the least likely to want to learn Irish, whereas a clear majority (ranging from 65 per cent to 87 per cent) of those who described themselves as having weak or moderate Irish language skills did wish to improve. It is therefore difficult not to arrive at the conclusion that a significant number of monolingual English speakers are living in designated Irish-speaking areas, be they recent arrivals or long-term residents, whose attitudes towards Irish show them to form a distinct group within the local population. This issue has come to the fore in the Gaeltacht since 2006 in a number of language policy disputes, in particular in relation to the language used in schools (disputes in Kerry, Mayo, and Donegal) and in disputes over the official usage of Irish-only signs for place names in official Gaeltacht areas.

2.6 Irish Speakers in the Gaeltacht as a Distinct Cultural Group

The results from the *Gaeilge 2010* project consistently show marked differences between the native/fluent Irish-speaking population and non-native speakers in the Gaeltacht regions in relation to their attitudes and ambitions for the language, and also in the way that they perceive the role of the state and its institutions in relation to the community and to themselves as Irish language speakers.

A central tenet of Irish language policy is that the state, which is the institutional incarnation of the majority opinion of the Irish population, regards Irish as the national language, and as a consequence all Irish people share ownership of the language. In the Múscraí study, there was some level of disagreement with this proposition. A total of 75.7 per cent of the informants believed that the people of the Gaeltacht formed a distinct cultural minority (101 people 'agreed', while 80 of the 239 interviewed 'strongly agreed' with the statement). This large majority opinion among Gaeltacht Irish speakers has serious consequences for language management, as the population clearly sees itself as different from the majority national population in matters of linguistic identity and consequently has different needs from a language management perspective. This language-centred identity in the Gaeltacht has gone unnoticed in discourse on language policy in Ireland because it runs against a fundamental element of national language ideology. Observers such as Hindley (1990: 208) have gone further, denying that there is any particular Gaeltacht identity. This is a misunderstanding of the nature of Gaeltacht identity among Irish speakers that arises from English-medium research in which the differing linguistic competences of Gaeltacht residents are not taken into consideration. It is certainly true that people identify with their wider region, their county, their province, and their nation, but there is little doubt among Irish-speaking Gaeltacht people about their linguistic minority status. Even in this small and relatively weak Irish-speaking district, there was little support for redrawing the Gaeltacht boundary (10 per cent) in order to concentrate work in areas where Irish was strongest. It was clear that informants understood themselves to be a linguistic minority within a wider Gaeltacht community, which has both linguistic members and more passive participants, to adapt Dorian's (1981, 1982) terms.

In 2000–4, Údarás na Gaeltachta (the Gaeltacht authority) was seen by nearly all informants in Múscraí as the legitimate institutional expression of their civic identity as Gaeltacht people. A total of 82.4 per cent agreed (92 respondents) or strongly agreed (105 people) that for Irish to survive it was essential that the Údarás be strong. Only 5 per cent of Irish speakers in the study thought that Irish speakers should not be privileged above non-Irish speakers in state-backed job creation in the Gaeltacht.

There was much more ambiguity in the Múscraí study as to the tangible benefits or failures of government policy towards the Gaeltacht and its people, as 38 per cent believed that recent governments had enacted the right policies while 39 per cent believed that they had not. Whilst 33.5 per cent of respondents believed that they did not have equal rights because they were Irish speakers, 47.3 per cent did not see it as an issue. Although the general opinion was that their rights were not infringed for linguistic reasons, it should nevertheless be a cause for concern at the national level, in the context of language maintenance and revitalization policy, that over a third of Irish-speaking Gaeltacht respondents in this study did feel this to be the case.

A particularly important outcome of this study was the feeling of solidarity that Gaeltacht Irish speakers felt with other Irish speakers throughout the country. Some 197 respondents (82.8 per cent) believed that all the institutional support mechanisms and schemes that have been developed for the Gaeltacht by national government and local initiatives should also be made available to Irish speakers and Irish-speaking families throughout the country. The Irish-speaking population, a national minority within a complex bilingual setting, identifies itself as being wider than the limits of the territorial Gaeltacht. This is a challenge to prevailing national language management policies which have, since the 1930s, tended to view the Gaeltacht population and speakers outside the Gaeltacht as different entities simply because of where they live, without any analysis of their interrelationships.

2.7 Conclusion

Although the Irish Government and language communities share the overt aims of stabilizing Irish in the Gaeltacht whilst favouring the national expansion of speaker numbers and functions of the language, the state-driven ideology of language management for millions of people, which targets the language use of a group of tens of thousands, has inevitably produced mismatches in ideologies that may, paradoxically, have further endangered the future of Irish as a community language. In December 2013 Seán Ó Cuirreáin, *An Coimisinéir Teanga* (the Irish language ombudsman), whose role included the monitoring of state bodies' compliance with the Official Languages Act (2003), resigned in protest at the government and state apparatus's failure to protect the language rights of Gaeltacht and other Irish speakers. In February 2014, a march in Dublin, called to bring attention to language-policy failures, drew 10,000 protestors, highlighting doubts among Irish speakers as to the veracity of the state's overt aims of supporting the language and its speakers. These events have illustrated the difficult context for the implementation of new language planning regimes in the Gaeltacht, where the state's commitment to Irish is increasingly called into question by both habitual Irish speakers and by those opposed to its special status. The Irish experience of mismatched national versus community language beliefs, practices, and management can serve as an example for the growing number of polities which seek to assign new expanded roles for their native languages, but which in doing so arguably run the risk of undermining the practices of the remaining speakers and the communities of language activists who, in some cases, have actually led the campaigns for these new roles.

The argument presented in this chapter is only a superficial investigation of the data revealed in the studies mentioned above, but gives ample evidence of how one particular aspect of the new language policy, for areas within the Gaeltacht where Irish is not spoken fluently, or daily, by the majority of the local population, might affect language shift in the area.

Significant numbers of the monolingual English-speaking community in the Gaeltacht do not share the goal of community language regeneration, nor do they want to participate in it. The majority of English-only speakers in the Gaeltacht agree with the discourse in favour of language retention and regeneration attested in national opinion polls and surveys, but only a minority appear to feel the necessity of engaging in language acquisition in order to participate in the community. The *Gaeilge 2010* study also revealed some native Irish speakers' ambiguous attitudes to retention and development strategies, in particular with regard to Irish-medium education. While over 80 per cent of Irish speakers in those regions believed that Irish-medium education was advantageous, less than three quarters thought that Irish-medium schooling was 'very important' to them. Although still a substantial majority, the lack of total consensus may well represent a more widespread underlying ambiguity on the issue, which may in turn lead to further conflicts about the medium of instruction in schools, and the use of Irish-only language in the public space and in service provisions.

Significant numbers of Irish speakers in the marginal Gaeltacht areas perceive themselves as being presented with bigger language management challenges than the larger, more strongly Irish-speaking areas. Irish activists in these areas feel they are being punished by the state for not being in the majority, for which they believe the state is largely responsible. It appears that an ideologically developed policy that does not see Irish speakers and monolingual English speakers as separate cultural groups is behind the proposal that areas within the Gaeltacht where Irish is not spoken daily by the majority of the population should lose that status unless speaking ability and frequency increases. However, current research shows that such a proposal places unreasonable demands on a marginalized Irish linguistic minority that is unlikely to be able to sustain its language. In fact it increases the power of the already dominant minority of monolingual English speakers. Successful language management in favour of Irish in these communities requires a multi-layered approach centred on Irish speakers and those wishing to participate in the Irish speech community. This approach should neither negate the rights of the non-Irish-speaking population who do not want to participate in language revitalization and regeneration projects, nor should it allow a monolingual minority to dominate all aspects of public activity and provisions in the local bilingual society.

References

Arel, Dominique. 2002. Language categories in censuses: backward- or forward-looking? In David I. Kertzer and Dominique Arel (eds.), *Census and Identity: The Politics of Race, Ethnicity and Language in National Censuses*. Cambridge: Cambridge University Press.

Baldauf, Richard B. 1994. 'Unplanned' language planning and policy. *Annual Review of Applied Linguistics* 14: 82–89.

Coimisiún na Gaeltachta [Gaeltacht Commission]. 1926. *Report*. Dublin: Stationery Office.

Coimisiún na Gaeltachta [Gaeltacht Commission]. 2002. *Tuarascáil/Report*. Dublin: Stationery Office.

Coimisiún um Athbheochan na Gaeilge [Commission on the Restoration of the Irish Language]. 1963. *Summary, in English, of Final Report*. Dublin: Stationery Office.

Coimisiún um Athbheochan na Gaeilge [Commission on the Restoration of the Irish Language]. 1964. *An Tuarascáil Deiridh* [The Final Report]. Baile Átha Cliath/ Dublin: Stationery Office.

Council of Europe. 2012. *Charter for Regional or Minority Languages: Reports and Recommendations*. <http://www.coe.int/t/dg4/education/minlang/Report/default_en.asp> (accessed 28 May 2012).

CSO (Central Statistics Office). 2012. *This is Ireland: Highlights from Census 2011, Part 1*. Dublin: Stationery Office.

Dorian, Nancy. 1981. *Language Death: The Life Cycle of a Scottish Gaelic Dialect*. Philadelphia: University of Pennsylvania Press.

Dorian, Nancy. 1982. Defining the speech community to include its working margins. In Suzanne Romaine (ed.), *Sociolinguistic Variation in Speech Communities*. London: Edward Arnold.

Eggington, William. 2002. Unplanned language planning. In Richard B. Baldauf (ed.), *The Oxford Handbook of Applied Linguistics*. Oxford: Oxford University Press.

Eurobarometer. 2003. *Europeans and Languages: Eurobarometer Special Survey 54*. Brussels: European Commission.

Government of Ireland. 2010. *20-Year Strategy for the Irish Language 2010–2030*. Dublin: Government of Ireland.

Hindley, Reg. 1990. *The Death of the Irish Language: A Qualified Obituary*. London and New York: Routledge.

Hornsby, Michael. 2005. Néo-breton and questions of authenticity. *Sociolinguistic Studies – Estudios de Sociolingüística* 6: 191–218.

Jaffe, Alexandra. 2009. The production and reproduction of language ideologies in practice. In Nikolas Coupland and Adam Jaworski (eds.), *The New Sociolinguistics Reader*. Basingstoke and New York: Palgrave Macmillan.

Kristiansen, Tore. 2011. Attitudes, ideology and awareness. In Ruth Wodak, Barbara Johnstone, and Paul Kerswill (eds.), *The SAGE Handbook of Sociolinguistics*. London: SAGE.

Le Dû, Jean and Yves Le Berre. (eds.). 1996. Badumes, standards, normes bretons. In *La Bretagne Linguistique*, vol. 10. Brest: CRBC.

Mac Donnacha, Seosamh, Fiona Ní Chualáin, Aoife Ní Shéaghdha, and Treasa Ní Mhainín. 2005. *Staid Reatha na Scoileanna Gaeltachta 2004*. Baile Átha Cliath: An Chomhairle um Oideachas Gaeltachta agus Gaelscolaíochta.

Mac Gréil, Micheál and Fergal Rhatigan. 2009. *The Irish Language and the Irish People: Report on the Attitudes towards, Competence in and Use of the Irish Language in the Republic of Ireland 2007–2008*. Maynooth: Department of Sociology, NUI Maynooth.

Ó Flatharta, Peadar. 2007. *Struchtúr Oideachais na Gaeltachta*. Baile Átha Cliath: An Chomhairle um Oideachas Gaeltachta agus Gaelscolaíochta.

Ó Giollagáin, Conchúr, Seosamh Mac Donnacha, Fiona Ní Chualáin, Aoife Ní Shéaghdha, and Mary O'Brien. 2007. *Comprehensive Linguistic Study of the Use of Irish in the Gaeltacht: Principal Findings and Recommendations*. Dublin: Stationery Office.

Ó hIfearnáin, Tadhg. 2007. Raising children to be bilingual in the Gaeltacht: language preference and practice. *International Journal of Bilingual Education and Bilingualism* 10: 510–28.

Ó hIfearnáin, Tadhg. 2008. Endangering language vitality through institutional development: ideology, authority, and official standard Irish in the Gaeltacht. In Kendal King, Natalie Schilling-Estes, Lyn Fogle, Jia Jackie Lou, and Barbara Soukup (eds.), *Sustaining Linguistic Diversity: Endangered and Minority Languages and Language Varieties*. Washington, DC: Georgetown University Press.

Ó hIfearnáin, Tadhg. 2009. Irish-speaking society and the state. In Martin Ball and Nicole Müller (eds.), *The Celtic Languages* (2nd edn.). London and New York: Routledge.

Ó hIfearnáin, Tadhg. 2011. Breton language maintenance and regeneration in regional education policy. In Catrin Norrby and John Hajek (eds.), *Uniformity and Diversity in Language Policy: Global Perspectives*. Bristol: Multilingual Matters.

Ó Riagáin, Pádraig. 1997. *Language Policy and Social Reproduction: Ireland 1893–1993*. Oxford: Clarendon Press.

Ó Riagáin, Pádraig and Mícheál Ó Gliasáin. 1994. *National Survey on Languages 1993: Preliminary Report.* Dublin: Institiúid Teangeolaíochta Éireann.

Shohamy, Elena. 2006. *Language Policy: Hidden Agendas and New Approaches*. Oxford and New York: Routledge.

Spolsky, Bernard. 2003. Reassessing Māori regeneration. *Language in Society* 32: 553–78.

Spolsky, Bernard. 2004. *Language Policy*. Cambridge: Cambridge University Press.

Spolsky, Bernard. 2009. *Language Management*. Cambridge: Cambridge University Press.

Tithe an Oireachtais. 2003. Acht na dTeangacha Oifigiúla/Official Languages Act 2003. 32/2003. Dublin: Irish Statute Book.

Tithe an Oireachtais. 2012. Acht na Gaeltachta 2012/Gaeltacht Act 2012. 34/2012. Dublin: Irish Statute Book.

Walsh, John. 2011. *Contests and Contexts: The Irish Language and Ireland's Socio-Economic Development*. Oxford: Peter Lang.

Warren, Simon. 2012. The making of Irish-speaking Ireland: the cultural politics of belonging, diversity and power. *Ethnicities* 12: 317–34.

3

Fluidity in Language Beliefs: The Beliefs of the Kormakiti Maronite Arabic Speakers of Cyprus towards their Language*

CHRYSO HADJIDEMETRIOU

3.1 Introduction

LINGUISTIC ISSUES IN SOCIETIES are charged with emotions, values, ideals, and loyalties, and so 'as with most "matters of the heart", they seem so compelling that to pause for clarification may seem, to many who favour reversing language shift ... to be not only unnecessary but unfeeling, uncaring and rigid' (Fishman 1991: 10). The endangerment of minority languages is mostly associated with extra-linguistic factors such as attitudes and beliefs, rather than linguistic ones. This chapter examines how the members of the Kormakiti Maronite Arabic (KMA)[1] community have expressed their beliefs towards their endangered language following the beginning of KMA revitalization efforts in Cyprus.

The study is based on empirical data obtained mainly from July 2002 to February 2003 (with some further audio and video recordings conducted from 2006 to 2008). In total, 48 speakers were interviewed, of whom 42 were KMA speakers and six were not. Six more speakers were interviewed in August 2008 with the purpose of obtaining more data on the speakers' views regarding their language and its significance for the Kormakiti Maronite community.

The cultural knowledge acquired during participant observation and while conducting sociolinguistic interviews enabled me to reach the following conclusions regarding the character of the two communities. The speakers' views on what constitutes their community identity and how they view their languages became evident during interviews, where quite often the respondents elaborated

* Special thanks to Julia Sallabank and Peter K. Austin, the editors of this volume, for their insightful comments during earlier drafts of this chapter. Any shortcomings are solely my own.

[1] There are different terms used to refer to this variety of Arabic, namely Cypriot Arabic, Cypriot Maronite Arabic, and Kormakiti Maronite Arabic. The use of 'Kormakiti Maronite Arabic' does not suggest that the speakers of this variety of Arabic are only located in Kormakitis. They can be found in different areas in Cyprus.

on this subject whether prompted or not. These issues were not the primary focus of the thesis and thus were not examined quantitatively.

3.2 Languages in Cyprus: An Overview

The two official languages in Cyprus, as stated in the 1960 constitution of the Republic of Cyprus, are Greek and Turkish. The recognition of only two official languages in the constitution raises the issue of the status of 'non-official' indigenous languages of the island, as discussed in the 2006 report from the European Charter for Regional or Minority Languages on Cyprus (ECRML 2006: 6):

> The Constitution divides the Cypriot population into two 'Communities', Greek and Turkish. The Communities are defined on the grounds of ethnic origin, language, culture and religion. The Constitution makes reference to 'religious groups'. As the denomination implies, religious groups are defined by their religious affiliation only. According to this classification, the only religious groups of Cyprus are the Armenians, the Maronites and the Latins.

The linguistic rights of these groups are not acknowledged, particularly those of the Armenians and Maronites, with the exception of the Latins as they are speakers of Cypriot Greek. According to the ECRML (2008a: 8), there are 3,000 Armenian speakers in Cyprus (of whom 400 are non-Cypriot Armenians who immigrated to Cyprus from Armenia). This number refers to the total number of Armenians in Cyprus and it is quite likely that some of these Armenians may not speak Armenian natively or at all. Hadjidemetriou (2009) refers to some Armenians who have not acquired Armenian and some who are semi-speakers of the language. Therefore, it is unclear how accurate the above number is. Regarding the number of Kormakiti Maronite speakers, the ECRML (2008a: 8) points out that there is no official data, but based on estimates, the number of speakers does not exceed 1,300. The total Maronite population in Cyprus, based on data from the ECRML (2006: 6), is 4,650. This number includes not only Kormakiti Maronites, but also Maronites from other Maronite villages, who have never spoken Maronite Arabic.

Since the Republic of Cyprus signed the European Charter for Regional or Minority Languages, it now has an obligation to abide by the recommendations of the Committee of Experts.[2] Regarding the Armenian language, the Republic of Cyprus declared that 'it undertakes to apply Part II of the Charter in accordance with Article 2, paragraph 1, to the Armenian language as a "non-territorial"

[2] 'The Republic of Cyprus has, by means of Law 39 (III)/1993, published in the Official Gazette of the Republic in December 1993, approved and, by an instrument of ratification deposited on 26 August 2002, ratified, the European Charter for Regional or Minority Languages' (ECRML 2005: 4).

language defined in Article 1c of the Charter' (ECRML 2008a: 7–8). The Republic of Cyprus made a similar declaration regarding KMA in 2008, recognizing that KMA 'meets the Charter's [European Charter for Regional or Minority Languages] definition of a regional or minority language' (ECRML 2009: 4). Whereas KMA has drawn the attention of linguists in the past (Borg 1985; Newton 1964; Roth 1975; Tsiapera 1969) and more recently (Hadjidemetriou 2009; Kossmann 2008, 2010), mainly for its uniqueness resulting from its contact with Cypriot Greek, it has yet to enjoy a similar status to that of Armenian.

3.3 Who are the Kormakiti Maronites?

The Kormakiti Maronites belong to the Cypriot Maronite community, which is a Catholic community.[3] The name 'Maronite' does not designate the ethnic or national origin of the community, but rather a religious sect (Dau 1984: 9). The arrival of the first Maronites dates back to the seventh century, according to Varnava (2002), to the eighth century (Cirilli 1898), or to between the eighth and ninth century (Grivaud 2000). Three further waves of Maronite migration had taken place by the thirteenth century (Hourani 1998: 1). First, the arrival of the Muslim Arabs led the Maronites to abandon Syria II and seek refuge in Lebanon due to violence inflicted by their religious enemies.[4] These were not limited to Muslims; inter-Christian conflicts between Jacobites and Byzantines also led to violence against the Maronites (Dib 1971: 51–2).[5] Nevertheless, religious conflict was not the only reason why the Maronites abandoned Syria II. Some of those who arrived in Cyprus had left for economic reasons (Dau 1984: 192). The second migration occurred in the tenth century, after the monastery of St Maron was destroyed by Arabs (Harb-Khoury 1995: 70; Hourani 1998: 2).

Thirdly, during the thirteenth century, with the acquisition of Cyprus by Guy de Lusignan, the island was thrown open to the defeated crusaders in Tripoli and

[3] Maronitism is a Christian movement that originated between the fifth and seventh centuries, after St Maron and his disciples converted the pagan population of Mount Lebanon to Christianity (Dau 1984: 9). The community's name is derived from this founding saint of the Maronite Church (Dib 1971: ix). After St Maron's death, the disciples who had united around him founded a monastery dedicated to him in an area near Apameus, in the valley of Orontes in Syria II (Dib 1971: 4). Salibi (1988) argues that the Maronites are possibly a community of Arabian origin and were the last Arabian Christians who arrived in Syria before Islam, settling in the valley of Orontes (1988: 89).

[4] Syria had been divided into two regions by Septimus Severus (AD 193–211) (Dib 1971: xv). These areas were Syria Magna and Phoenicia. Syria Magna was subdivided into three provinces: Syria I with Antioch as its capital, Syria II with Apameus as its capital, and Syria III with Hierapolis as its capital.

[5] The name of the Jacobite Church comes from the Bishop of Edessa, called Jacob Baradeus, who organized the Syrian Monophysitic hierarchy (Oxford English Dictionary Online 2012).

the Holy Land (Dib 1971: 65), and Maronites continued to follow the flow of migration to Cyprus in this period. The Maronites who arrived in Cyprus did not mix with the existing inhabitants. They settled in villages on the high plains of north Nicosia (Dib 1971: 65), where Guy de Lusignan offered them privileges (Cirilli 1898: 7). The Maronites flourished under the favour of the Franks, and during this era their colony became quite prosperous (Dib 1971: 65). The number of Maronite villages reached 72, and so the Maronite community became the second largest on the island after the Greeks (Dib 1971: 65). Historical sources show that at that time the Maronites numbered between 60,000 and 80,000 (Kypros 8,000 Chronia 1991: 491). After the Venetians took Cyprus from the Franks in 1489, the Maronites continued to emigrate to the island from all parts of Lebanon (Dib 1971: 65).

After the occupation of Cyprus by the Ottoman Turks (1571–1878), there were fewer Maronite villages (Cirilli 1898: 8). Cirilli claimed that the Turkish occupation of the island was detrimental to the Maronite colony: by the year 1596, there were only 19 Maronite villages left (1898: 8). Some Maronites returned to Lebanon during this period, while others dispersed elsewhere (Cirilli 1898: 10). Those who remained on the island were subject to assassinations, injustice, and violence. The Maronites who managed to escape did so, Cirilli argues, by either embracing Islam or Greek Orthodoxy. However, Varnava (2002) does not agree with this claim that the Maronites suffered during the Ottoman years; rather, he asserts that there is no evidence for this. Varnava further clarifies that the Maronites and the Greek Cypriots were equally 'burdened by the excessive taxes levelled at them by the Ottoman authorities' (Varnava 2002: 54).

The Maronites enjoyed more freedom after the Ottoman period, under British rule (Kypros 8,000 Chronia 1991: 491). With the more relaxed administration of the British, the Maronites became more active as a religious group (Kypros 8,000 Chronia 1991: 491). During British rule there were four Maronite villages (Kormakitis, Asomatos, Karpasia, and Ayia Marina Skyllouras), which survive to this day.

As of 2006, there were about 4,650 Maronites living in the government-controlled area (ECRML 2006: 7).[6] Before the 1974 Turkish invasion, all the Maronites were located in the aforementioned villages, but only in Kormakitis were the Maronites still bilingual in KMA as well as Cypriot Greek. Before 1974, there were 1,800 inhabitants of Kormakitis, but according to an estimate in the year 2000, there were by that time only about 135 Maronites, mainly elders (Fragkiskou 2000: 9). Inhabitants of the other three Maronite villages were monolingual Greek speakers, although there is no record of when the speakers shifted from Arabic to

[6] 'As a result of the Turkish invasion and continuing occupation of 37 per cent of the northern territory of the Republic of Cyprus the Greek Cypriots were forcibly expelled by the invading army from the area it occupied and are now living in the Government controlled area' (ECRML 2008b: 4).

Greek or even whether they ever spoke Arabic. After the Turkish invasion, the majority of Maronites from all four villages were scattered around the unoccupied part of the island, abandoning their villages in the occupied north.

3.4 Kormakiti Maronite Arabic

Kormakiti Maronite Arabic has been characterized as 'an Arabic dialect with a considerable admixture of Cypriot Greek' (Newton 1964: 43). Newton argued that KMA shows 'unmistakable signs of centuries-long Greek influence (e.g. loss of emphatic consonants and of distinctive vowel length, and Hellenization of idiomatic structure)' (Newton 1964: 43). Thomason and Kaufman claim that KMA is a mixed language and that 'the type of mixture it exhibits is an extreme version of ... borrowing of morphology (and phonology) along with lexicon' (Thomason and Kaufman 1988: 106). There is also an opposing view, which holds that KMA has never been a mixed language. Bakker (2003: 121) states:

> Other languages with heavy borrowing that have erroneously been called mixed, are Kormakiti Arabic of Cyprus, Chamorro, Maltese and some others in which also some of the basic vocabulary has been borrowed.

Thomason further stresses that the grammatical mixture arose from lexical mixture (2001: 200). Since the borrowed Cypriot Greek morphology is confined to Cypriot Greek loanwords, it seems unreasonable to consider KMA 'as a whole as a changed later form of Arabic' (Thomason and Kaufman 1988: 107). However, there are elements of morphology that are borrowed from Cypriot Greek and that are integrated into the KMA system, and these are not confined to Cypriot Greek loanwords only. In this case, KMA has changed because of contact with Cypriot Greek. Such prolonged interaction has given KMA a Cypriot Greek element, even though it has preserved much of its Arabic grammar (Thomason 1995: 18). Hadjidemetriou (2009) briefly discusses this issue and clarifies that the convergence is not mutual but unidirectional, with KMA exhibiting changes that approximate it to Cypriot Greek, but with the opposite not being true. However, based on available data, it is difficult to establish which mechanisms operated during the development of KMA.

Even though KMA has been in contact with Cypriot Greek for centuries, and its speakers have managed to resist language shift and avoid language death for a long time, it is now undergoing a very rapid process of shift and an interruption in intergenerational transmission is evident. The fact is that KMA has been classified as an endangered language in need of protection within the framework of the European Charter for Regional or Minority Languages. According to the categorization provided by Campbell and Muntzel, the type of language death facing KMA, unless revitalization efforts have an effect, is a gradual one (1989:

182–6). The shift from KMA was originally very slow, but accelerated after the Kormakiti Maronites were displaced from their home village. The shift had not reached completion in 2014, and there are still competent speakers who use the language and who consider KMA to be their first language.

However, there are increasing numbers of semi-speakers. Some interviewees pointed out that their own knowledge of KMA was not good. They claimed that they understood KMA better than they spoke it. Speakers with even scanter knowledge of KMA were also appearing in the community: some young adults and teenagers claimed that they had a rudimentary knowledge of KMA only, just simple phrases or words. Two teenagers reported knowledge of phrases such as 'I want some coffee' and 'our little dog is very nice' because their parents used them often.

Paulston (1994: 11) proposes a list of three factors that can 'help' language maintenance:

(i) a self-imposed boundary associated with non-linguistic factors, such as religion
(ii) externally imposed boundaries, either in the form of denied access to goods and services (e.g. jobs, as in the case of the African American community in the US) or in the form of geographical isolation, as in the case of Gaelic speakers in Scotland
(iii) a diglossic situation: the fact that two languages occupy different functions and are employed for different purposes and in different domains, as is the case with Spanish and Guarani in parts of Paraguay, can help maintain both varieties in a contact situation.

In terms of the social factors outlined by Paulston (1994), the situation of KMA can be viewed as follows. Originally, despite many years of isolation, the Kormakiti Maronite community had a certain degree of contact with Greek Cypriots. Moreover, Kormakiti Maronites received the same primary education as the Greek Cypriot children, with the exception of religious education, where textbooks on Maronite Christianity were used. In secondary education, some Kormakiti Maronites attended Greek high schools and some attended private Catholic schools where Greek was the language of instruction. Greek was also used in other institutions and public services. Life in Kormakitis entailed the use of both languages, with KMA being the dominant language; outside the village, it was the other way around. No problems were reported regarding any externally imposed boundaries, such as being denied access to services or jobs due to speakers' Maronite background. Quite a few of the respondents happened to work in various posts in the Cypriot Government in the government-controlled area of the island (e.g. the police force, public hospitals, various positions at different ministries). The Kormakiti Maronites who seemed to be struggling more than anyone else were those who still lived in their village enclave.

The sociolinguistic setting was suddenly changed with the displacement of the population from the village after 1974. My fieldwork observations revealed that the youngest fluent speakers of KMA were in their late thirties and early forties, meaning that these speakers were old enough to have lived in Kormakitis and to have been exposed to KMA there. They spent their childhood in the village, where KMA was still widely used among the majority of the speakers. When the community moved away from Kormakitis, speakers started to show immediate signs of language shift, and the younger generation that was born outside of Kormakitis did not acquire KMA. This conclusion is drawn from Kormakiti Maronites who did not acquire KMA, and from some KMA speakers who explained that their children born outside of Kormakitis had not acquired KMA. For the few who did acquire KMA, they had a 'semi-knowledge' of the language as described earlier. After centuries of language maintenance, it took merely one event to trigger the process of language shift. This shows how closely the language was related to life in Kormakitis and to what extent the Kormakiti Maronites associated KMA with the boundaries of their village.

3.5 The Kormakiti Maronite Arabic Community

The sociolinguistic profile of the KMA community focuses on: (i) the Kormakiti Maronites' subjective attitudes towards KMA and its speakers, and (ii) the ethnic identity value attached to KMA. The KMA community is clearly neither homogeneous nor one-dimensional. In particular, various opinions were observed regarding KMA revitalization efforts. The community may be seen as composed of subgroups with different views and opinions. The variation in these views refers to the different perspectives towards the revitalization processes and creates a rather 'fluid', non-uniform set of beliefs about what KMA represents, what should be the aims of its revitalization, and whether this should even be happening at all.

3.5.1 Attitudes

Gardner writes that attitudes are inferences that derive from behaviour and that 'the hypothesis is that once we know an individual's attitude toward some attitude object we have a better chance of understanding and predicting his/her behaviour toward that object' (1982: 132). In a similar fashion, Kristiansen defines language attitudes as 'complex psychological entities which involve knowledge and feeling as well as behaviour, and are sensitive to situational factors', such as the formality of a situation or the salience of language in a particular situation (Kristiansen 1997: 291).

Bradley (2002: 1), addressing the question of why one minority group assimilates while another maintains its linguistic and cultural identity, claims that what determines this difference is the attitudes of the speech community towards their own language. Bradley cites five minority and majority beliefs and preferences towards particular conditions that are important for minority language maintenance. It is important to establish (Bradley 2002: 1–2):

(i) whether bilingualism is accepted and valued, normal, and expected
(ii) how public use of a minority language is viewed in the majority monolingual environment
(iii) how the minority language speakers view the status of their language, as 'difficult' or 'hard to maintain'
(iv) what kind of attitudes the majority and minority communities have towards issues like the utility, importance, and beauty of the majority and minority languages, and
(v) how a society deals with the language maintenance of the minority language: whether it supports, tolerates, or represses this language.

Drawing on the work of Bradley, the following observations can be made with respect to the Kormakiti Maronites:

- When KMA was still being transmitted between generations, bilingualism was normal and expected. Now it is still accepted and valued, but no longer common.
- The Kormakiti Maronites view their language as being a unique linguistic system. Interviewees believe, for example, that their language shows features of Aramaic. This is a theory proposed by Borg (2004), which the Kormakiti Maronites have embraced proudly (possibly because to them it suggests a connection with Jesus). Of course, it is likely that KMA displays Aramaic influence in the same way that Levantine Arabic dialects do, given that Aramaic was very widely spoken in the region until the fourteenth century (Versteegh 2001: 105). Kormakiti Maronites also stress that this variety of Arabic is found nowhere else in the world, and that it has resisted language death for centuries.
- There is a discrepancy between the Kormakiti Maronites' positive attitudes to KMA and their failure to pass KMA on to their children. Some interviewees pointed to the importance of acquiring Cypriot Greek, since they live as part of the Cypriot Greek community. They believe it is unlikely that their language will be maintained, especially since the younger generation is not acquiring KMA.
- Nettle and Romaine (2000: 91) say that one type of language death is 'voluntary shift ... where a community of people come to perceive that they would be better off speaking a language other than their original

one'. This seems to apply to the Kormakiti Maronite speakers, as they stopped transmitting the language to their children because they believed that learning Cypriot Greek was more important for the children's future. Regarding the usefulness of Arabic, one speaker said (in Cypriot Greek) of why he did not speak to his children in Arabic: 'You couldn't move forward [progress] with Arabic.'

- Despite ongoing revitalization efforts, there are still speakers who feel that these efforts will not make a significant change to the vitality of the language.

3.5.2 The (Ethnic) Identity Value Attached to Kormakiti Maronite Arabic

Fishman (1977: 15) argued that 'the recent increase in societal attention to ethnicity has fostered a rebirth of interest in ethnicity among social scientists as well'. Years later, the same interest in the ethnicity of different groups still prevails. Fishman believed that the reason this link between ethnic identity and language exists is that 'language is so often taken as a biological inheritance that its association with ethnic paternity is both frequent and powerful' (Fishman 1977: 19).

Fought (2002: 444) stresses that 'ethnicity is not about what one is, but rather about what one does'. In Hadjidemetriou (2009) I point out that ethnicity is not simply about what one does, but also about what a community perceives the nature of its ethnicity to be, whether that is actualized in various social practices or not. For example, if a community believes that elements X, Y, and Z constitute their ethnic identity, then it is important to examine whether the X, Y, Z elements are practised or not. In case these elements are not practised, it is equally important to understand why a community identifies with these elements and why it is important for members of the community to do the same. Thus, the concept of (ethnic) identity as realized through interviews with individual speakers and from ethnographic observation during fieldwork led to observations on the nature of what indicates community identity according to the speakers themselves.

The link between language and ethnicity is constructed by social, contextual, and historical circumstances (Fishman 1977: 329). Eisenlohr maintains that 'language is involved in processes of group identification in that it provides a focus for explicit discourses of identity and constitutes a field of less overt practices for creating groupness' (2004: 59). Tabouret-Keller, on the other hand, provides a one-dimensional view of the relationship between language and identity, and claims that the language spoken by an individual and their identity as a speaker of a certain language are inseparable (1997: 315). While a particular language may be identified as an important cultural marker of a particular ethnic group, there is no direct correspondence between language and ethnicity (May 2001: 129). Moreover, as noted earlier, identifying language as an ethnic marker does not necessarily relate to linguistic practices. May (2001) states that linguistic differences do not always correspond to ethnic ones and that membership of a particular ethnic group does not necessarily entail an association with a particular language. One ethnic group can share a particular language with another, different, ethnic group. However, language is still regarded as a central and determining feature of ethnic and national identity: 'language seems straightforwardly a piece of culture' (Nash 1989, cited in May 2001: 130).

In examining the Kormakiti Maronite identity, the purpose is to locate those extra-linguistic characteristics that the speakers identify as markers of their community identity. It may be that what the speakers perceive as characteristic of their community is not what they actually 'do'. However, the focus remains on speakers' understanding of their community identity, and how this can relate to the fluidity of their beliefs towards their language before and during revitalization efforts, based on data collected and time spent with Kormakiti Maronites.

Language is still closely related to group identity for some Kormakiti Maronites. For instance, KMA was often referred to by interviewees who suggested that Kormakiti Maronites are more genuinely Maronites than those from other villages. This is what one speaker said in an interview:

> (1) *Íʃen éʃi tʃálla maronítika xorká éndʒe ksérumen praɣmatiká an íne maronítes allá ipoloɣi-[umen/ete] ipotíθete torá óti onomázunde maronítes ðióti emís ksérumen tin ɣlóssan pu kanénas ðéndin ikséri.*
>
> There were, there are other Maronite villages too. We don't really know if they are real Maronites but we esti-[mate] it is assumed now that they are called Maronites, because only we know the language, they don't.

The uniqueness of KMA as the language of Kormakitis is also pointed out in the following extract, where one of the younger and quite active members of the community proudly stresses the origins of KMA as deriving from Aramaic, the language of Jesus (see also section 3.1):

> (2) *I ɣlóssa aftí tu kormacíti pu arθrónnete akómi ce símmera pismatiká apó mia xúftan anθrópus éxi tis rízes tis stin aramaicín ðiálexton ti ɣlóssan tu xristú i opía ipárxi akóma ce símmera se kommátia tis θías lituryías pu ɣínete stin eklisían tu kormacíti. An lávi kanís ipópsin óti éxun apomíni móno ðekapénde xiliáðes átoma sólon ton kósmon na milún símmera tin aramaicín ɣlóssan apomonoména se tría xoriá tis sirías tóte i íparksi katalípon tis ɣlóssas aftís saftín tin mikrín ɣonián tis mesoɣíu íne apó móni tis spuðéo ce siginitikó sináma ɣeɣonós.*
>
> The language of Kormakitis, which is still spoken by some people, has its roots in the Aramaic dialect, the language of Jesus Christ, which is still preserved in some parts of the mass in the church in Kormakitis. If you take into consideration the fact that there are only about 15,000 people left who still speak the Aramaic language in three villages in Syria, then the existence of some elements of the Aramaic language in this small island in the Mediterranean is a magnificent and touching fact.

Heller argues that language use can promote group boundaries, within which shared experiences are realized through a common language (1987: 199). This can be seen in interactions between Kormakiti Maronites who are bilingual; these interactions are, of course, not open to those who are monolingual. But, as May says, membership of a particular ethnic group does not necessarily entail an association with a particular language (May 2001: 129); the children of Kormakiti Maronites who have not acquired KMA are still regarded as members. Moreover, even those Kormakiti Maronites who do not speak KMA offer it as evidence of their ancestry; they even proudly proclaim the presence of Aramaic elements in 'their' variety.

Another important element of Kormakiti Maronite identity is the strong sense of localism and pride in anything related to the village, whether this relates to the villagers themselves (and speakers of KMA) or to the customs and traditions of the village. The belief that things related to the past are better than the present (as is also the case with Arvanitika speakers in Greece; see Tsitsipis 1983) was also quite prominent during the interviews. One respondent expressed this briefly by stating, '*I zoí ómos ítan kalítteri pará torá*' ('But life was much better than it is now').

Their pride in the village was also highlighted when speakers stressed that it was so rich and the land so fertile that they did not need to buy any land in the capital. They were self-sufficient in their village. This is what one speaker said on this issue:

> (3) *Yíru tu xrónu en elípan i ðuliés. Étsi en eɣorázamen út- úte énan ikópeðon méstin xóran. En erkúmastin, úte pu ítan i xóra emís énekséramen ðióti i ðuliés mas en elípan … ímastin úlli t- tu tópu i ðuliés énelípan. ɣíru tu xrónu … ítan i protévusa ton perixóron ton perixóron ítan i protévusa … éne kséramen ee ii p- pu ítan i xóra. ðen ekséramen ðuléfkamen panda panda méston tópon mas … ɣiaftón éne ɣorázamen méstin lefkosían emís. Iðemí xoráfca étsi ta períxora tʃamé ta parapáno eɣɣorasména pu ton kormatʃítin ta parapáno xoráfca tus.*
>
> All year round, we had work. So, we didn't need to buy even a single piece of land in town [i.e. Nicosia]. We were not going, we didn't even know where the town was because we always had work to do … We were all in Kormakitis and work never ended. All year round … It [Kormakitis] was the capital of the surrounding villages, of the surrounding villages it was the capital … We didn't even know where the town was. We didn't know. We always worked in our village … That's why we didn't buy anything in Nicosia. Otherwise, the land of the surrounding villages, most of the land in the surrounding villages was bought by us, most of their land.

Older speakers still associate KMA with life in Kormakitis before 1974, and many of them claimed that KMA can only be revived if the Kormakiti Maronites are able to return to their village permanently:

(4) A: *Eán eminískamen ston kormacítin ðe θa exánnetun.*

If we had stayed in Kormakitis, it [i.e. KMA] wouldn't have been lost.

B: *Tʃambámen pale éθθa xaθí.*

And if we go again it's not going to be lost.

A: *E ambámen tʃe prolávumen.*

Eh, if we go and there's still time.

Comments such as those above are what Dauenhauer and Dauenhauer (1998: 73) call the community rhetoric of language survival. They refer to these attitudes as clichés (e.g. 'cultural values can only be transmitted in the language' or 'we can't save the culture without the language'). Such comments may also indicate a failure to see that language use and language transmission are connected (Dauenhauer and Dauenhauer 1998: 69). Language use does not need to be confined within the boundaries of Kormakitis village and language survival will certainly not be ensured if the speakers return to their home village. Dauenhauer and Dauenhauer (1998: 69) stress that even though parents fluent in the endangered language do not use it with their children, they 'still assume that somehow the children will magically learn the language through another channel'.

3.6 Prospects for Documentation and Revitalization

The ECRML (2006) report made the observation that the government of the Republic of Cyprus must recognize KMA as a regional or minority language. This was eventually declared in 2008. At the same time, it drew attention to the necessity of immediate protection and maintenance. The report also pointed out that:

> The codification of Cypriot Maronite Arabic is crucial for its maintenance since it facilitates its teaching at school, enhances its visibility in public life, for example in the press, and raises its cultural status. The committee of Experts encourages the Cypriot authorities to find means, in co-operation with the speakers, to codify Cypriot Maronite Arabic. (ECRML 2006: 13)

Within the framework of the above recommendation, on 9–10 November 2007, the Ministry of Education and Culture and the Ministry of the Interior of the Republic of Cyprus co-organized a symposium inviting members of the Kormakiti Maronite community, and linguists who have worked on KMA, including myself, to give their accounts of what they believe the future of KMA will or should be.

In Hadjidemetriou (2007), I stress the need to document KMA as a means of recording the language, since it is feared that the death of the language is imminent. However, there are also reservations as to whether documentation of

KMA will be adequate for the wishes of some Kormakiti Maronites, namely the wish for the survival of their language. The Kormakiti Maronites who are interested in maintaining their language rely heavily on the belief that teaching KMA at primary school level will work, although they also recognize the need to expand these lessons to make them available to adults, and to organize a range of events that promote the use of KMA. Of course, the proposed documentation of the language will facilitate their plans. However, any revitalization plan must surely focus not only on teaching KMA, but also on encouraging speakers to attempt other ways of restoring intergenerational transmission of the language.

3.7 Community Response

Since 2006 some Kormakiti Maronites have become involved in teaching KMA to children in the Maronite primary school, which was founded by the Republic of Cyprus following repeated requests by the Maronite refugees. In the past, Maronite children attended primary schools with the rest of the Greek-Cypriot children, as many of them still do, despite the fact that the community now has its own primary school in the capital, Lefkosia (Nicosia). As in Kormakitis before 1974, the school follows the same curriculum as other primary schools in Cyprus except for religious education. The new development, however, is the introduction of lessons in KMA. These are not part of the formal school curriculum (as this is defined by the Ministry of Education and Culture), but are an option for afternoon classes once a week only, in the same way that English is offered as an afternoon class option. Thus, the students are taught KMA as a foreign language. Additionally, an attempt to teach KMA to adult speakers was begun in 2007 when approximately 15 adult Kormakiti Maronites who do not speak KMA expressed an interest in learning the language and attended classes for a few months.

At the time of writing this chapter, the Maronites who were involved in teaching KMA lacked access to educational materials, as well as the training needed to teach their language. A writing system was created using the Greek script, but this was abandoned after the local community and the group of linguists chosen by the government decided to create a Latin-based writing system instead, following the example of Maltese. It may be that the Latin script was favoured and accepted by members of the community involved in the revitalization efforts in an attempt to 'reduce' any further Greek influence on KMA. It is possible to argue that this was an ideologically based decision to give KMA a script that would differentiate itself from Greek. The idea of using an Arabic script was rejected, mainly because it would possibly add an extra layer of difficulty for Maronites (particularly children) who wanted to learn KMA but who were unfamiliar with the Arabic script.

Furthermore, looking at how older KMA speakers view young people's efforts in learning the language, unreasonable expectations are also a problem. At an event organized by Kermia Ztite (a Maronite group focusing on the survival of KMA) in December 2006, some KMA speakers commented negatively on the accent of a group of children reciting a poem in KMA, which they had learned at primary school. The fact that revitalization might well produce a variety of KMA that the current native speakers are not familiar with is not an idea that had yet occurred to them. Marquis and Sallabank (this volume) highlight this issue and explain that there is an ideological conflict between members of a community involved in revitalization efforts who want to see the language modernized and members who have a 'purist' point of view and who do not want to see the language modernized. They stress that the purists are not only attached to their native language but are also attached to a disappearing culture.

As part of the effort to bring KMA into the classroom, a group of Maronites also founded a non-governmental organization with the name Hki Fi Sanna (Speak in Our Language), which had approximately 300 members in 2007 (some were not Maronites and not all were active members of the organization). Given that the total number of Kormakiti Maronites is approximately 1,950, this means that only about 15 per cent of the Maronites are members. Dauenhauer and Dauenhauer (1998: 69) see the creation of organizations to deal with language and cultural preservation as a 'bureaucratic fix'. They stress that such organizations are important but that 'they still require the efforts and cooperation of many individuals' (Dauenhauer and Dauenhauer 1998: 69).

At the December 2006 event organized by Kermia Ztite, the following aims were put forward (Kermia Ztite 2006):

(i) strengthening the Maronites' pride in their language and their culture
(ii) informing the wider Cypriot community and the world about issues concerning the Maronite community of Cyprus
(iii) dealing with racism in the Cypriot community
(iv) redevelopment of Kormakitis so that it can 'host' the revitalization efforts.

To accomplish the above, the following methods were suggested (Kermia Ztite 2006):

(i) providing lessons for people to learn the language of Kormakitis
(ii) giving lectures explaining the value of maintaining a language and the relationship of language to ethnic identity
(iii) running workshops on the use of the language
(iv) holding cultural events in Kormakitis for the promotion of learning the language, history, and traditions of the Maronites
(v) organizing excursions to take young people to the village and show them the most important places

(vi) creating material for teaching the language to primary-school children
(vii) making a TV documentary on the language of Kormakitis
(viii) publishing a newspaper in the language of Kormakitis with the title *Sanna*.

Since 2007 the Maronites have made many attempts to accomplish the above. They have organized summer camps for children in Kormakitis and various cultural events to present their efforts and their progress. They created and continue to make small video clips regarding their events. They also prepare short lessons, which they often make available on the community website or sometimes they publish them in community newspapers (the newspapers are in Greek, but they have short sections in KMA).

As mentioned in section 3.4, many interviewees argued that if the Kormakiti Maronites were ever to return to their village and start building their lives there again, the language could be revitalized and survive. This view was also expressed by a Kormakiti Maronite participant during the Symposium on KMA. He said:

> (5) *Nomízo to pco simandikó pu prépi na ɣíni ɣia na ðiasoθí i ɣlóssa íne na epistrépsun i maronítes píso sta xoriá tus.*
>
> I believe the most important thing that must happen in order for our language to survive is for the Maronites to return to their villages.

Moreover, in my fieldwork, it also became clear that many Kormakiti Maronites are unconcerned regarding the survival of their language. In one interview a speaker expressed the following idea:

> (6) *Pándos emás efánicen ítan pollá xrísimi ɣia llóumas. Torá ɣia tin néan ɣeɲán ɣia tin néan ɣeɲán enná xásun tʃíni éndʒenna xásumen emís.*
>
> KMA was very useful for us. *We* are not going to lose anything [if it disappears]; however, the younger generations will lose something [if the language is lost].

This speaker argues defensively that he (and possibly other speakers of his generation) benefited from learning the language and using it for inter-group communications, and the younger generations who do not speak the language will 'lose' that opportunity for inter-group communication in KMA.

This view that the break in intergenerational transmission will not be reversed was quite prominent. It seems clear to people that their language will be lost with its last native speakers. They have accepted that the language cannot be revitalized and they believe that it is highly unlikely that it will be spoken again by the younger generation. Some of these people, however, also hold the view that teaching materials for KMA are essential, not for the revitalization of the language as such, but for creating a legacy for future generations. They want to have a written record of the language so that it will never be 'lost'. This is, of course, very important and can be seen as a step towards permanently recording and thus safeguarding the language from total extinction in case the last native speakers of the language disappear. A lack of uniformity in how revitalization efforts should be organized is present within the KMA community and is a problem that is quite recurrent in language planning efforts (e.g. Freeland and Gómez this volume, Marquis and Sallabank this volume, Spolsky this volume, among others).

3.8 Fluidity in Language Beliefs

Since 2006, when revitalization efforts for the survival of KMA were initiated by the community, there has been an attempt to focus on creating a language identity for the Kormakiti Maronites. References to the language as signifying a part of the Maronite identity are stressed. For example, in August 2008, during the first summer camp conducted in KMA, which lasted five days, it became evident that the focus was to promote the idea that language is closely related to the Maronite identity, that is, in terms of how the Maronites perceive what their Maronite identity is composed of. This is what one of the participants said during the camp:[7]

> (7) *Erxómasten na epanaféromen káti to opíon íxamen xási sto parelθón. Káti to opíon pistévo sindíni istin epivíosin tis kinótitas mas. Íne mía istorikí stiɣmí ɣia tin kinótitan mas, epanaférumen káti to opíon íxamen xási sto parelθón, ce pistévo θa sinexísumen, ðen íne mónon aftí i prospáθia, θa ɣínun pollés prospáθies ɣia na epanaférumen tin ɣlóssan tis kinótitas mas.*
>
> We are here trying to bring back something that we have lost in the past. Something that I believe will contribute to the survival of our community. It is a historical moment for our community; we are bringing back something that we had lost in the past; and I believe that we will continue this. This is not just a one-time effort; more efforts will take place to bring back the language of our community.

This is how another member of the Kormakiti Maronite community expressed herself concerning the summer immersion camp:

> (8) *Prosopiká os maronitíssa nióθo perífani ce sigkiniména: i ɣlóssa íne I psixí enós éθnus íne foréas kultúras íne to erɣalíon tis sképsis tis epikinonías tis ékfrasis ce tis ðimiurɣías. Iðiká ɣia mas íne pára polí simandiki i epiviosi tis ɣlóssas ɣiatí θa simváli stin epivíosin tis kinótitas. Próta próta θa tonósi tin eθnicín tin θriskeftikín ce politistikín mas taftótitan ce éxumen xréos na tin metaðósumen stes epómenes ɣenjiés.*

[7] This opinion was expressed during the summer camp and was filmed by the Maronites themselves, who wanted to create a documentary about the summer camp.

> Personally, as a Maronite woman, I feel proud, and more specifically: the language is the soul of a nation, it is the carrier of culture, it is the tool of thought, communication, expression, and creativity. Especially for us, the survival of the language is extremely important because it will contribute to the survival of the community. First of all, it will stimulate our national, religious, and cultural identity; and we have a duty to transmit the language to the next generations.

How widespread the above view is within the Kormakiti Maronite community remains doubtful.

I mentioned earlier that the speakers themselves tend to express their pride in their language by pointing out the centuries it has managed to survive, its uniqueness, and that some lexical items might have Aramaic origins. However, these views are in contradiction with their views concerning which variety of Arabic they believe should be taught at school. In August 2008, while interviewing some KMA speakers, I posed the question: 'Which variety of Arabic should the children learn: KMA or Standard Arabic?' These are the answers provided by three different respondents:

> (9) *ta kalá aravikà* ('the good Arabic')
>
> (10) *ésto ta ɣnísia ta aravikà* ('at least the pure Arabic')
>
> (11) *makári na máθun ta ɣnísia ta aravikà* ('hopefully they will learn the pure Arabic').

After the speakers had stressed that it is Standard Arabic that young Kormakiti Maronites should learn, I asked them why they did not choose KMA. This is how one respondent replied to my question:

> (12) *Ma en ítan kaθarí ɣlóssa tʃíni pu emaθθénnamen olán índalos. Afú emaθθénnamen pu tus ɣonjús mas índa aravikà, éndʒe kséranda úlla. Pu tus ɣonjús mas éndʒitan kaθarí ɣlóssa.*
>
> But it is not a 'clean' language, the one we learned, come on! We learned it from our parents; what kind of Arabic [did they speak], they didn't know everything. It was from our parents, it wasn't a 'clean' language.

The idea that it is Standard Arabic that children should learn was also an important view in the November 2007 symposium on KMA, co-organized by the Ministry of Education and Culture and the Ministry of Interior in an attempt to gauge the community's reaction to the prospect of revitalization of KMA and to ascertain speakers' opinions regarding the fate of KMA.

There is also the idea of promoting KMA as the language of all the Maronites of Cyprus, thus referring to it as Cypriot Maronite Arabic. Whereas the language is referred to by its speakers as the language of the Kormakiti Maronites, it is now referred to by the Kormakiti Maronites involved in the revitalization efforts as the language of all the Maronites. In some interviews I conducted in August 2008, I asked respondents their opinion regarding the promotion of KMA for the

Maronites of the three other villages. This is what some Kormakiti Maronites said on this issue:

(13) *E én éxun lóɣon.*

They don't have a say in this.

(14) *Na su po xríso éni ksérumen allá pistéfko óti θa apantísun arnitiká. En tus enðiaféri tʃe pollá i ɣlóssa.*

Let me tell you Chryso, we don't know. But I believe that they will respond negatively. They don't care much about the language.

(15) *Ói ee éntus kófti. Róta tus allá enná su pun an θélun astín ðiatirísun an θélun as men tin ðiatirísun étsi enná su pun.*

No, eh, they don't care. Ask them but they will tell you if they [i.e. the Kormakiti Maronites] want [to save the language] or not. That's what they'll tell you.

In December 2006, Kermia Ztite organized the first event regarding KMA. During the event, KMA was referred to as 'the language of Kormakitis', which was also the name of the event: 'The Language of Kormakitis: Point Zero'.

Clearly, the effort to safeguard KMA has been 'accompanied' by the attempt to attach a language identity value to the community; that is, the attempt to promote the idea that KMA must be saved in order for the community to survive and to maintain its identity. Evidently, the Kormakiti Maronite identity and community have managed to survive without younger generations acquiring KMA. Despite their positive outlook on the language, and the idea that language and community identity are interrelated, some of the respondents expressed the opinion that the language chosen to be taught to children should be Standard Arabic. The argument is that if their children are going to learn another language, it should be a language that is going to be 'useful' to them in the future. Thus, some speakers do not see any use in the language anymore. The opinion that KMA is just a 'mixed dialect' (or '*machlut*' as they call it) and is not as 'complete' as Standard Arabic is what leads to the belief that Standard Arabic should be the focus of the revitalization efforts. This is despite the fact that Kormakiti Maronites have never been native speakers of another variety of Arabic. It seems that there is a contrast between the identity value attached to KMA, with proudly expressed opinions regarding the origins of KMA, and the belief that KMA is not 'sufficient' to offer younger generations any benefits in terms of progression in the job market. This belief that KMA, as used by the older generations, is not 'good' enough to be the variety to be revitalized is expressed by a Kormakiti Maronite in the following extract:

(16) *Ómos θélo na toníso óti ótan emiliótan i ɣlóssa mas i pappúðes mu tʃe i ɣonís mu emilúsan tin ɣlóssan sénan epípeðon morfotikón tis epoxies ecínis ikanopiúsen tes anáges tus … I ɣlóssa pu θa anazooɣonísumen pu θa ðiatirísumen pu θa metaðósumen prépi na andapokrínete stis anágkes tis ɣenjás pu θa tin máθun …*

> *Ce θa íθela tus akaðimaikús na mas pun apó pu θa kalípsumen ta cená pu ðanizómasten apó tin ellinikín?*
>
> But I would like to stress that when our language was spoken by my grandparents and my parents, they spoke the language in an educational level of those times that satisfied their needs ... The language that we are going to revitalize, that we are going to maintain and transmit, must satisfy the needs of the generations that are going to learn it ... And I would like the academics to tell us how we are going to cover all the voids we have and we borrow from Greek.

This extract highlights again the conflict between the Maronites who are actively involved in the revitalization efforts and understand the need for modernizing the language, and the Maronites who are native speakers of KMA who have been using it all their lives and do not understand the need for modernization.

3.9 Conclusion

This chapter has examined the Kormakiti Maronites' subjective attitudes towards KMA and their influence on revitalization efforts. It has shown how members of the community responded to the revitalization efforts. Furthermore, it has tried to understand the fluidity in the beliefs of Kormakiti Maronites towards KMA and its revitalization through opinions expressed in interviews with members of the Maronite community. It became clear that the lack of agreement over how the revitalization efforts should be organized, and the fluidity in beliefs that generate sometimes conflicting ideas about the direction of revitalization efforts, could prove to be problematic for the revitalization of KMA, although these competing ideas seem to be recurrent in language planning efforts in general.

Some members of the Kormakiti Maronite community are determined to implement any plans that would facilitate the survival of KMA. These members of the community are actively involved in planning and organizing events (e.g. summer immersion camps for children and the creation of online material on KMA) through the creation of non-governmental organizations, such as Hki Fi Sanna, or cultural groups, such as Kermia Ztite, that would possibly promote learning KMA. Dauenhauer and Dauenhauer (1998: 80) stress that trying to reverse language shift through cultural interaction in the endangered language, involving the older generation and encouraging mother-tongue transmission, is very demanding and requires 'a complete change of lifestyle followed by a lifetime commitment'. However, they also stress that efforts that focus on the acquisition of the endangered language as a second language for both young and old members of the community are relatively easy (Dauenhauer and Dauenhauer 1998: 80).

In August 2011, a two-year action plan for the revitalization of KMA was finalized through the cooperation of members of the Kormakiti Maronite community, linguists, and representatives from the Government of the Republic of Cyprus. The action plan included a detailed budget for the revitalization efforts, focusing on the documentation and codification of KMA, which would facilitate the production of material for educational purposes. Secondly, it stressed the importance of teaching KMA to speakers who have some knowledge of the language already (possibly referring to speakers with basic knowledge of KMA or semi-speakers of KMA). Finally, the action plan talked about the importance of informing Cypriot society and other experts (such as linguists) regarding the revitalization efforts in order to create a positive environment and help the revitalization efforts to succeed. The plan highlighted that these action points were the beginning of a lengthy effort to safeguard KMA, and it was believed that through these the survival of KMA would be promoted.

Currently, KMA is associated with the Maronite identity, whatever that may imply for the Kormakiti Maronite community and the Maronite community in general, in particular since the revitalization efforts commenced. There also seems to be an attempt to refer to Kormakiti Maronite as 'Cypriot Maronite Arabic' and to make reference to a pan-Cypriot Maronite Arabic language and identity. How widespread that belief is within the community is a different issue. How much success the people involved in these efforts are going to have in conveying this idea to the rest of the community (both the Kormakiti Maronite and Cypriot Maronite community in general) remains unclear. The real challenge is converting the fluidity in language beliefs into a uniform effort based on non-opposing ideas regarding the revitalization of KMA. No matter what the outcome, it is extremely important to note that these efforts were initiated by the community itself, and it is also encouraging that the survival of KMA might actually be possible and successful.

References

Bakker, Pieter. 2003. Mixed languages as autonomous systems. In Yaron Matras and Pieter Bakker (eds.), *The Mixed Language Debate: Theoretical and Empirical Advances*. Berlin: Mouton de Gruyter.

Borg, A. 1985. *Cypriot Arabic*. Stuttgart: Deutsche Morgenlandische Gesellschaft.

Borg, A. 2004. *A Comparative Glossary of Cypriot Maronite Arabic*. Leiden: Brill Academic Publishers.

Bradley, David. 2002. Language attitudes: the key factor in language maintenance. In David Bradley and Maya Bradley (eds.), *Language Endangerment and Language Maintenance*. London: Routledge Curzon.

Campbell, Lyle and M. C. Muntzel. 1989. The structural consequences of language death. In Nancy Dorian (ed.), *Investigating Obsolescence: Studies in Language Contraction and Death*. Cambridge: Cambridge University Press.

Cirilli, J. M. 1898. *Les Maronites de Chypre*. Lille: Imprimerie de l'Orphelinat de Don Bosco.

Dau, Butros. 1984. *Religious, Cultural and Political History of the Maronites*. Lebanon: B. Dau.

Dauenhauer, N. M. and R. Dauenhauer. 1998. Technical, emotional, and ideological issues in reversing language shift: examples from Southeast Alaska. In L. A. Grenoble and L. J. Whaley (eds.), *Endangered Languages: Language Loss and Community Response*. Cambridge: Cambridge University Press.

Dib, Pierre. 1971. *History of the Maronite Church*. Beirut: Maronite Apostolic Exarchate.

Eisenlohr, Patrick. 2004. Register levels of ethno-national purity: the ethnicisation of language and community in Mauritius. *Language in Society* 33: 59–80.

European Charter for Regional or Minority Languages. 2005. *Cyprus: Initial Periodic Report*. Strasbourg: ECRML.

European Charter for Regional or Minority Languages. 2006. *Application of the Charter in Cyprus: Initial Monitoring Cycle*. Strasbourg: ECRML.

European Charter for Regional or Minority Languages. 2008a. *Cyprus: Second Periodic Report*. Strasbourg: ECRML.

European Charter for Regional or Minority Languages. 2008b. *Core Document on Cyprus Drawn Up in Accordance with General Assembly Resolution 45/85 and the Consolidated Guidelines for the Initial Part of the Reports of States Parties (Document HRI/991/1)*. Strasbourg: ECRML.

European Charter for Regional or Minority Languages. 2009. *Application of the Charter in Cyprus: Second Monitoring Cycle*. Strasbourg: ECRML.

Fishman, Joshua 1977. Language and ethnicity. In Howard Giles (ed.), *Language Ethnicity and Intergroup Relations*. London: Academic Press.

Fishman, Joshua. 1991. *Reversing Language Shift: Theoretical and Empirical Foundations of Assistance to Threatened Languages*. Clevedon: Multilingual Matters.

Fought, C. 2002. Ethnicity. In J. K. Chambers, P. Trudgill, and N. Schilling-Estes (eds.), *The Handbook of Language Variation and Change*. Malden: Blackwell Publishers.

Fragkiskou, A. 2000. Το λεξικό της Αραβικής διαλέκτου του Κορμακίτη [*The Dictionary of the Arabic Dialect of Kormakitis*]. Nicosia.

Gardner, C. R. 1982. Social factors in language retention. In R. D. Lambert and B. F. Freed (eds.), *The Loss of Language Skills*. Rowley: Newbury House Publishers.

Grivaud, G. 2000. Les minorités orientales à Chypre (Époques médievale et moderne). *Chypre et la Mediterranée orientale* TMO 31: 43–70.

Hadjidemetriou, Chryso. 2007. Kormakiti Maronite Arabic: what comes after shift? Paper presented at the symposium *Cypriot Maronite Arabic in a New Era?* Ministry of Education and Culture, Republic of Cyprus.

Hadjidemetriou, Chryso. 2009. The consequences of language contact: Armenian and Maronite Arabic in contact with Cypriot Greek. Unpublished PhD thesis, University of Essex.

Harb-Khoury, A. 1995. *The Maronites: History and Constants*. Beirut: Al-Sindyana.

Heller, M. 1987. The role of language in the development of ethnic identity. In J. Phinney and M. Rotheram (eds.), *Children's Ethnic Socialisation: Identity, Attitudes and Interactions*. Newbury Park: Sage Publications.

Hourani, G. G. 1998. A reading in the history of the Maronites of Cyprus from the eighth century to the beginning of the British rule. <http://www.mari.org/JMS/july98/A_Reading_in_the_History.htm> (accessed 12 July 2005).

Kermia Ztite. 2006. *Programma Diasosis Tis Glossas Tou Kormakiti* [Programme for the Survival of the Language of Kormakitis]. Nicosia: Kermia Ztite.

Kossmann, M. 2008. On the nature of borrowing in Cypriot Arabic. *Zeitschrift für arabische Linguistik* 49: 5–24.

Kossmann, M. 2010. Parallel system borrowing: parallel morphological systems due to the borrowing of paradigms. *Diachronica* 27: 459–87.

Kristiansen, T. 1997. Language attitudes in a Danish cinema. In Nikolas Coupland and Adam Jaworski (eds.), *Sociolinguistics: A Reader and Coursebook*. London: Macmillan.

Kypros 8,000 Chronia: Istoria Kai Politismos. Tomos A [*Cyprus 8,000 Years: History and Civilisation. Volume A*]. Cyprus: Publications 2002.

May, S. 2001. *Language and Minority Rights: Ethnicity, Nationalism and the Politics of Language*. Harlow: Pearson Education.

Nettle, D. and S. Romaine. 2000. *Vanishing Voices: The Extinction of the World's Languages*. Oxford: Oxford University Press.

Newton, B. 1964. An Arabic-Greek dialect. *Word* 20: 43–52.

Paulston, C. B. 1994. *Linguistic Minorities in Multilingual Settings: Implications for Language Policies*. Amsterdam: John Benjamins.

Roth, A. 1975. *Le Verbe Dans le Parler Arabe de Kormakiti*. Leukosia: Kentron Epistemonikon Ereynon.

Salibi, K. 1988. *A House of Many Mansions: The History of Lebanon Reconsidered*. Berkeley: University of California Press.

Tabouret-Keller, A. 1997. Language and identity. In Florian Coulmas (ed.), *The Handbook of Sociolinguistics*. Oxford: Blackwell.

Thomason, Sarah. G. 1995. Language mixture: ordinary processes, extraordinary results. In Carmen Silva-Corvalán (ed.), *Spanish in Four Continents: Studies in Language Contact and Bilingualism*. Washington, DC: Georgetown University Press.

Thomason, Sarah G. 2001. *Language Contact: An Introduction*. Washington, DC: Georgetown University Press.

Thomason, Sarah G. and Terence Kaufman. 1988. *Language Contact, Creolisation, and Genetic Linguistics*. Berkeley: University of California Press.

Tsiapera, M. 1969. *A Descriptive Analysis of Cypriot Maronite Arabic*. The Hague: Mouton.

Tsitsipis, L. 1983. Language shift among the Albanian speakers of Greece. *Anthropological Linguistics* 25: 288–308.

Varnava, A. 2002. The Maronite community of Cyprus: past, present and future. *Al Mashriq: A Quarterly Journal of Middle East Studies* 1: 45–70.

Versteegh, K. 2001. *The Arabic Language*. Edinburgh: Edinburgh University Press.

4

Reflections on the Promotion of an Endangered Language: The Case of Ladin Women in the Dolomites (Italy)

OLIMPIA RASOM

4.1 Introduction

THIS CHAPTER AIMS to identify the beliefs and ideologies of Ladin women living in the Dolomites in Italy, an area where Ladin is spoken on a daily basis. The reasons that lead women to speak their heritage language in a progressively globalized European world were investigated, with the underlying aim of identifying the role that ideologies about language and culture play in shaping personal views. This study is based upon an ethnographic approach. Focus groups and life-history interviews were used to collect the data. In particular, focus groups—composed of small groups of women (no more than seven per group)—allowed the creation of a constructive setting where each woman could express her own ideas that progressively evolved as other women's opinions were heard. Life-history interviews were used to investigate the ideologies of women aged 70 and over. A total of 76 women between the ages of 17 and 84 were involved in the study (Ladin language professionals, mothers, students, and women over 70). Results support the view that women's ideologies contribute to shaping the cultural and linguistic female Ladin society. In particular, reflection among Ladin women may lead to a greater awareness of what it means to speak the 'mother tongue' and what the implications are for an endangered minority language. At the same time, reflecting together on certain issues makes women aware of their own skills and fosters a willingness to promote their own language and culture.

4.2 The Ladin Area in the Dolomites

The Dolomite valleys of Gherdëina, Badia, Fascia, Fodom, the town of Col, and the area of Anpezo form the Ladin area, which is located in the north-east of

Proceedings of The British Academy, **199**, 75–96. © The British Academy 2014.

Italy.[1] The administration of these areas is shared between two regions (Trentino/South Tyrol and Veneto), and three provinces (Bolzano/Bozen, Trento, and Belluno). The Ladin population of the Dolomites is approximately 30,000 people, who speak a total of five different varieties of the Ladin language. In Gherdëina and Badia, between 80 per cent and 100 per cent of the population are native Ladin speakers (there are some native Italian and German speakers in the villages where tourism is more prevalent). According to the 2001 census, around 80 per cent of the population in Fascia uses Ladin as their native language. In the province of Belluno, where Ladin is also traditionally spoken, data on the percentage of Ladin speakers is unavailable.

The Cultural Institutes of Badia (Bolzano/Bozen) and Fascia (Trento), and, more recently, the Institute of Col (Belluno), aim to safeguard and promote the Ladin language and culture. These institutions publish scientific reviews containing key essays about the history, language, and traditions of the Ladin people. They are also actively involved in research as well as in the dissemination of information about the Ladin language and culture through linguistic planning proposals, publications of various kinds, and cultural entertainment. They have also produced some important language material, such as Ladin dictionaries and a spellchecker. The Ladin Museum in San Martin de Tor is culturally very active, and attempts to stimulate the public's interest through exhibitions and publications. The institute in Fascia opened its Ladin Museum at the end of the 1990s. The museum offers workshops for schools and is an important means for the promotion of local history, knowledge, and culture. Over the past ten years, the cultural institutes have organized Ladin language courses for adults, open to both Ladins and non-Ladins alike. The courses aim to help students refine their accuracy in the spoken language and acquire a deeper knowledge of the written language. This assists students taking Ladin language examinations, which are compulsory for those seeking jobs in public administration or education.[2]

[1] Names in Italian: val Gardena, val Badia, val di Fassa, Livinallongo, Colle Santa Lucia, and Cortina d'Ampezzo; names in German: Gröden, Gadertal, Fassatal, Buchenstein, Colle Santa Lucia, and Cortina d'Ampezzo.

[2] The Second Statute of Autonomy, signed in 1972 between the Italian Government and the province of Bolzano/Bozen, consisted of a series of regulations, which, over the course of 20 years, brought about the recognition of the cultural and linguistic diversity of the two minorities, German and Ladin, in all social contexts. In the province of Trento different regulations have been implemented, with special reference to language policy and school management. Following this recognition, a new Ladin section was formed at RAI (the Italian state radio and television network, which broadcasts in Ladin), the diffusion of the Ladin newspaper *La Usc di Ladins* was increased in its weekly form, Ladin became compulsory in all schools, an office for language planning at the local administration of Fascia was built (Comun General de Fascia), and Ladin was introduced into public administration. All of these promotional activities permitted the creation of new jobs for teachers, translators, linguists, journalists, and others.

Schools in the Ladin valleys of Gherdëina and Badia have always used more than one language, due to their proximity to German- and Italian-speaking areas. Ladin is taught as a subject, and students use Ladin in the classroom whenever necessary for comprehension. In Fascia, parents can choose for their children a bilingual class in Ladin and Italian (at the moment this possibility is only available for primary schools). In secondary schools Ladin is taught for two hours a week. In Fodom, Col, and Anpezo, Ladin is taught sporadically. In cultural terms, there are various associations that promote the Ladin culture, the first and foremost being the Union Generèla di Ladins dla Dolomites. This deals with the preservation and revitalization of the Ladin culture and publishes the weekly newspaper *La Usc di Ladins* and the women's magazine *Gana–La Usc dles Ladines*.[3] Ladin-speaking media is limited, despite an increase since the early 2000s. Some programmes are broadcast in Bolzano by RAI, an Italian radio and television network, and some by a private television channel in Trento.[4]

As indicated above, Ladins live in three different provinces. They lack both administrative and political unity, as each province has its own policies towards Ladin minorities. In the province of Bolzano, the German-speaking majority holds the political power, although they themselves are a minority within Italy. Therefore, Ladins are in the peculiar situation of being a minority within a minority group, a situation that may have some advantages but which may also seriously hinder opportunities for free and autonomous development as a cultural and ethnic group.

The Ladin language is used consistently in the valleys, whereas in towns and villages, where tourism is more prevalent (bringing a greater percentage of immigrants as a consequence), it has less of a firm hold. There is a very clear difference between lifestyles in the globalized tourist areas and those in the more traditional countryside. In the more international resorts one may often observe cases of code-switching within a family away from the traditional Ladin language and in favour of Italian, or both Italian and German in South Tyrol (Verra 2000).[5] In this area, German seems to hold higher social prestige, as it is the language of business and politics. But language shifts are just one cause associated with the weakening of Ladin. Italian and German are regularly spoken

[3] The women's magazine appears every four months with an eye-catching layout. It is edited by a group of women who have a passion for promoting the Ladin language and who enjoy building relationships with other women. The articles in the magazine deal with the Ladin language as well as current affairs; topics are not limited to Ladin events (online edition: www.ganamagazine.com).

[4] The state network (RAI) transmits 15-minute daily television broadcasts and a 30-minute weekly cultural programme. The private network (TCA-TML) broadcasts programmes throughout the day in the minority languages spoken in the province of Trento. The broadcast in Ladin is about one hour a day.

[5] A recent survey by Dell'Aquila and Iannàccaro (2006: 77) observed different realities in the Ladin valleys. In some contexts, such as that of Fascia, the co-presence of Italian and Ladin does not diminish the importance of the Ladin language, even if a reverse in Ladin language shift cannot be expected.

in South Tyrol, and Ladin borrows numerous words from these languages, even when words for those concepts already exist in the Ladin vocabulary. Ladin also borrows syntactic and grammatical forms. According to Hagège (2002) and Crystal (2000), a language spoken by a limited number of speakers and surrounded by stronger languages risks disappearing due to repeated borrowings. In a bilingual (or trilingual) situation, the transformation of the original language at the phonological, grammatical, and lexical level is an almost invisible process, and code-switching becomes evident and more clearly observable.

4.3 The Research Study

This study explored women's attitudes towards language policy in the Dolomites. To identify the reasons that may lie behind women's views about passing on their native language, a total of 76 women were asked to join focus groups and participate in individual interviews. This chapter illustrates the introspective work carried out with these women and reports on some of the results. These concern the women's ideas about their heritage culture, language, territory, and history. The discussion also explores what it means to be a Ladin woman and the ties the participants share with other women, as well as their social and political status within the community in which they live.

4.3.1 Research Perspectives

The Ladin language (with the exception of the province of Belluno) enjoys a good level of protection. Ladin can be taught at school, and there is a Ladin weekly newspaper, radio and television programmes, various cultural associations, political parties, theatre companies, three publicly funded cultural institutes, and the opportunity to speak the language in administrative offices. In the Ladin area, a huge amount of work and human resources are devoted to translating laws and administrative acts. The same holds true for school activities and projects. However, it is mothers who most often speak the language with children, making them a significant part of Ladin society. Their role in transmitting the Ladin language and culture is undeniable. Some questions do arise therefore. Where do Ladin women position themselves in this world? What do they think? What is their policy towards their native language, if there is one? Ladin language policies were made almost exclusively by men. They are policies of laws, regulations, and rules. It is the law that defines the strategies within the social system. Is there anything else? What are women's views?

4.3.2 Methodology

Since the 1990s feminist literature has been very critical of the paradigms used for research, and several approaches have been developed that enrich research epistemology. A great deal of discussion has taken place concerning the methods that can be used to explore the world of women. Women in research institutes still need to devote substantial time to defining academic studies *about* women, *on* women, *with* women (Althoff et al. 2001; Behnke 1999; Jaggar 2008; Naples 2003; Roman 1992). Luigina Mortari states that a feminine epistemological voice 'is not one of the possible research philosophies, but a way of seeing the world, a different point of view, it is a glance that *cuts transversely* the way of conceiving research' (Mortari 2007: 131). This chapter follows this epistemological approach, which allows movement within a range of possible research methodologies, taking into account the *transversal cut* provided by being a woman, by studying women, and by being with and among women.

This ethnographic study was designed to uncover and explore the world of Ladin women, and the relationships they have not only with their own language and culture, but also with each other and with themselves, in different life contexts and in a particular historical moment. The data were collected from a total of 76 women in the valleys of Fascia, Gherdëina, and Badia. Four groups were created: (1) students, (2) mothers, (3) women active in language promotion, and (4) women over 70 years old. With groups 1, 2, and 3, focus group interviews were conducted (three times per group). The women in group 4 were interviewed individually. The data collected in the focus groups examined different issues. Discussions were encouraged, and pictures and ideas for short role plays were put forward. All answers became the basis for developing further reflections within the group. Women tried to imagine themselves in the future or attempted to find links with their past. The women who were interviewed individually were encouraged to talk about their lives, in particular in relation to their language and culture.

4.4 The Results

Throughout the study two dimensions began to take shape. On the one hand, the objectives originally set out were being met: the collection of data about women's worlds, their lives, their language, and their experiences in everyday life. On the other hand, a network of relationships between the women emerged and became more and more important, including for the author. The two dimensions intertwined and I became aware that the collection of important and interesting data occurred when the relationships with and among the women were particularly strong. Furthermore, the study developed beyond the mere collection of data. Another significant result of the study was that it gave the women the opportunity to reflect on the meaning of being Ladin, of speaking the Ladin language, and of transmitting and preserving the language and the culture. This joint reflection made it possible to open a window, making the language and cultural reality visible, and, in particular, allowing the women to become aware of their role in preserving the language.

If a mother decides not to speak Ladin to her child, and therefore not to pass on the language, intergenerational transmission is interrupted and a cultural void is created. The point of no return is reached, and the death of the language is not far off. Supporting reflection on these themes has to be considered one of the main goals of a researcher who studies minority languages. The researcher can help to bring to the surface needs, wishes, opinions, and points of view. Therefore, further decisions regarding whether to transmit the language and the culture are the result of reflection. They are not made by chance or—as often happens in these areas—as a consequence of an unconscious process of approval. Women who live with a minority language in a multilingual context have to be made aware of this. If they are, as they were during this research, then they gain an awareness that can transform them into main actors promoting the language, because they then consciously assign a value to their mother tongue, and also because the language of the mother has a very strong influence on the children.[6]

4.4.1 Experiencing Awareness

How does the awareness process start? For a large number of Ladin women the awareness process is born and developed at home, within the family, and with old friends. For others, it is a discovery through professional experiences, hobbies, or contact with a particular person. Chiara and Nicole, who were in the same focus group, told us how they tried to promote the Ladin language at

[6] The philosophers of the feminist philosophical community Diotima have written a great deal on the mother tongue (AA.VV. 1998); of particular interest and originality is the thinking of Luisa Muraro (1995, 2006), Chiara Zamboni (2006), and Jankowski (1998). Zamboni (2006: 10) describes the mother tongue in this way: 'The mother tongue is affective speaking, carnal speaking, learned in infancy, which accompanies us in the truest moments of our existence. Its truth is not immediately available. It is for that reason that we are searching: it is precisely in these times of ours that the truth is not manifest, and that the mother tongue is close to us and yet hidden. But this leads us to play a bigger, richer game, in which more bets are possible.' With regard to the experience of the mother tongue, Jankowski (1998: 31) writes: 'The experience of the mother tongue possesses a religious quality in that the first word—that absolute first word which the mother induces and receives like one word that contains everything, her entire self, her own name—will always remain beyond any dimension that is merely linguistic, it will never allow itself to be reduced purely to a word: it is promise, incantation, song and amazement, trust and nourishment, closeness and origin, it is tactile and sonorous, concrete and abstract, a symbol and yet not a symbol, it is where positive and negative are still kept together. Because of all of this, it opens up experience to the divine dimension.'

school throughout the 1970s, when interest in the Ladin language and culture was limited to an inner circle of activists.[7] Similarly, Nadia related how she was already involved with a cultural association that promotes Ladin culture in secondary school. When she had to decide the focus of her university thesis, she chose a topic in comparative linguistics, with the Ladin language as its main focus.

Maia developed her own awareness as a teenager outside of her family, in which Ladin was not spoken. Her father used to take her to the meetings of a cultural association where she played the role of 'the little secretary'. She had to write down addresses, put letters into envelopes, and send mail. After this, her voice was used on the radio, which at that time had begun to broadcast the first political shows in Ladin. When she was 20 she won a competition to secure a job at the local cultural institute. In the first few years she read many books about Ladin people, and her awareness became increasingly heightened.

Antonia told us how she was uninterested in the Ladin situation until she wrote her doctoral thesis. During this time she met other colleagues who were dealing with minority languages. In her own words, she became more aware of having 'something more than the colleagues who were studying other Italian dialects and I felt proud to give my culture and my language something by myself', something that other colleagues did not have. She was the only one who could work on a language that was also her mother tongue, and with which she had developed both an emotional tie and an academic interest.

The women involved in the study shared their pride in knowing the Ladin language. Some women—in particular, the younger ones—connected with Ladin culture and language because they were born in this area and because the language was part of their family history. Thus we find comments like: 'I like it very much when my grandfather tells me . . .' (Cleopatra). Many students said that they enjoy it when grandparents tell stories, convey local history, or relate community events. Some women expressed their desire to have a culture that connects one generation with another in order to avoid losing cultural and community experiences, and that only in this way can Ladin people understand the meaning of 'Ladin culture'.

The women noted a gap in cultural transmission. According to the participants, during the twentieth century, when the Ladin valleys transformed their economic system from agriculture to an economy based on tourism, most people tried to forget their origins and did not pass on the traditional ways of life or the Ladin language. The women observed that they needed to reconnect to their heritage and find reasons to maintain their Ladin culture. Sometimes, new traditions seemed to arise, as in the case of a young woman who was disappointed because, during the traditional celebration of her 18th birthday,

[7] All names are pseudonyms.

the girls in attendance did not wear the traditional flowered hat. However, it was traditionally only the men who used to wear it.

For the second meeting, participants were invited to bring an object that symbolically connected them with Ladin heritage, with the goal of investigating their connection with this culture. Without doubt, this was one of the best and most interesting parts of the research. The students primarily brought objects that connected them with the territory (one young woman brought her climbing shoe, another brought part of a bush, and another brought a picture of her valley). The mature women brought photos of their forefathers and told their histories to the group; others brought books written by people who worked to promote the Ladin language in the past. One woman brought her doctoral thesis, and another a dramatic work translated from English into Ladin in which she had played the main role. Other items shown were books of poetry, the Ladin flag, and the Ladin calendar.

All of the women enjoyed telling the group why they had decided to bring that particular object and how difficult or easy the decision had been, often saying: 'I also really thought a lot during this week.' The desire to share this experience with the other women was clearly visible. It was also gratifying to see how the women curiously awaited the turns of the others. During the meeting with a group in which the discussion had strayed away from the point, one participant (Federica), who needed to leave the session early, asked, 'Please, can we get back to the point, because I want to listen to all your voices!'

The awareness of being Ladin is expressed in terms of being able to understand Italian-speaking neighbours and German-speaking communities. In particular, in the Gherdëina and Badia valleys, Ladin women are aware of the added value of multilingualism. Language competence allows one to move across several worlds. Tania stated, 'I can stay here yet embrace both here and there.' Chiara reported that this does not mean that Ladin women are particularly tolerant, but that it allows them to enter into different intercultural dynamics. Sonia mentioned the multilingual dimension of the Ladin culture, and claimed that Ladin was the 'springboard' for knowledge of other languages and that it must be viewed as possessing a special and meaningful value. It is to be noted that women who were active in professional Ladin fields were more aware than mothers and students because they dealt with Ladin in a professional context on a daily basis. A better knowledge of the history, habits, customs, and traditions, and a good linguistic competence, brought with them a stronger commitment to and a more sophisticated awareness of Ladin.

4.4.2 Women and Territory

There was a strong relationship to the Ladin territory—the mountains, the natural environment, the forests, the lakes, and the rivers—for all of the women involved. This may indeed be the chief point that characterizes being Ladin. It seems to be the door that opens up the Ladin world: 'We couldn't be Ladin without our environment,' said Iris. This opinion was shared by all of the women in that particular group. 'The environment moulds our culture and our language,' added another, and Sofia stated that, 'When people arrived here from all over they were surely delighted by the marvellous mountains, and perhaps because of this they invented the stories of our origin that we know.'[8]

The Ladin territory influences the ideologies of the people who live in it. One woman in a focus group summarized the situation in the following words: 'The eyes don't stop on the rocks that tell us about the development of our society. The mountains are a fundamental good, to know the area and to keep alive the language, that has to be done.' She was able to express in just a few words what many women were trying to say in statements such as 'we are Ladin because we have these mountains' and 'without these mountains we lose our points of reference'.

The rocks are also particularly important points of reference in everyday life. In fact, a lot of the women had a favourite rock, often those they could they see from their home window. They admired the colours and the nuances; some women spoke with them, and others dreamt about them. One woman said, 'If I had to imagine paradise then I imagine it as this valley.'[9] There is an enthusiastic love for the rocks and even more for the forests. Walking in them, and taking time to think and reflect, is a cherished activity for many women.

Up until the beginning of the twentieth century, Ladin women had a good knowledge of local forests and pastures, and they took care of animals, were responsible for haymaking in the mountains, and knew all paths and tracks. Visiting the mountains as a source of delight is a recent innovation, and Ladin women joined this trend, transforming it into a cultural practice. It is not about a

[8] Ladin myths are very interesting and special, and are rich in female figures, particularly the *ganes*, mythical women with a great knowledge of the forces of nature who lived within female communities outside villages. The women could have relationships with human beings, but in the event of any cheating they would disappear. The *ganes* are known throughout the Alps under a variety of names. The *ganes* belong to the tales about roots, and are the common feature that connects all of the Ladin people of this area. The *contìes* (tales) tell us that the first men and women were made from stones or were animals, or else they came from the moon. All people look for their roots in the 'before time' (*illo tempore*) and usually make it conform to the world in which they live. The *croderes*, or stone people, were creatures without emotions, led by a woman named Tanna who had a human heart and who reigned over all the mountains, wearing a blue crown. Samblana was the queen of an ice realm. The queen reflected away the rays of sunshine with a blue mirror, thus maintaining her rule and keeping the soul of her twin in an ice-cold world. Similar to other female characters, women are, according to Ulrike Kindl, mistresses of time and space, of life and death, and as numinous figures are the equals of the mythical protagonists of other great cultures (Kindl 2007: 113).

[9] In an interview carried out for another study, a woman in her 80s described how, when she felt distressed, she prayed to the mountains and thanked them because they made her life less hard (interview with T. B.).

simple walk in the forest and mountains; it is also a walk into a world that Ladin women feel is their own property, a symbolic transposition of their own home, of their own origins, and perhaps a sort of 're-appropriation' of the Ladin territory. Some of the women in the study were more aware of this phenomenon than others, but several women saw it as an opportunity to reconnect with something that had been lost over time. With the shift from a farming culture to a tourist culture, Ladin women lost a direct link with nature and consequently the knowledge that came from that world, such as a familiarity with edible plants, medicinal herbs, place names connected with folktales, and so forth. Some women sometimes manifested this loss by criticizing those who were not aware of it, and sometimes through nostalgic behaviour.

It is easy to forget bad childhood experiences. In some focus groups women remembered how pleasant life was in the *viles*.[10] In another group they expressed how they missed the simple lifestyle of the past, giving their perception that it was a time when people were satisfied with very little, helped each other, and surrounded themselves with simple but pleasant things. These images, which are nearly idyllic, may have overridden memories of harsh living conditions, hunger, and low life-expectancy rates (Richebuono 1992: 111). Perhaps behind these desires there is a general discomfort with the hectic pace of living, which is common in modern Ladin society. In the Ladin valleys, time is measured by the tourist seasons, which entail a great commitment, in particular for women who are involved directly with hotels, restaurants, and apartment rentals. It is very difficult to escape this mechanism, as Gabriella claimed: 'It is a wheel; if you are on it you cannot get off,' but 'without the money coming from tourism we could not afford to be Ladin.' It is interesting that the women are aware that it is the well-established economic situation of the Ladin people that makes it possible for them to be a minority with great prestige.

4.4.3 Language Transmission

> Angela: 'How to get into the heart of the mother?'
>
> Tania: 'How to transmit desire and joy?'
>
> Angela: 'Everything begins from a personal passion that you live in your world.'
>
> Carla: 'For the love of your world, for the love of myself.'

The topic of language transmission emerged every time we met. How should one pass on the Ladin language and one's passion for it? Without passion, no language policy can be successful. This was the core argument when the women

[10] The *viles* were the typical homes of Ladin people. They were small groups of houses that included living quarters, a stable, and a barn. No more than eight to ten families could live in each *vila*.

spoke about the past, the present, and the future. A teacher (Deborah) said, 'I'm aware that now I transmit the Ladin world to my pupils with love and I see that they love it; they want to work harder and have more hours in Ladin.' A woman who is very active in a cultural association (Sofia) added, 'What else was it that distinguished women in the past if not passion and love for culture and language? They were successful in transmitting their heritage to us only because of this.'

When I asked the women to think of an era in the past in which they could imagine themselves living, answers were heterogeneous. Sometimes the respondents went back to prehistoric times, sometimes to the early twentieth century, and sometimes to the medieval period. But all of them saw themselves as having a unique mythological origin as Ladin people, even if many of the women were not especially versed in history. Considering the Ladin people to be unique was a common finding.

When thinking about the topic, the women seemed to be aware that if consciousness-raising activities did not involve all Ladins, within a short time this 'thread' of feeling would disappear. It should be noted that public cultural institutions work for their own local area, while public administrations vary throughout the Ladin area. Cultural associations, in particular the Union Generèla di Ladins dla Dolomites, try to promote activities together (such as festivals or meetings) but, due to the voluntary nature of this association, the task is incredibly challenging. There are also difficulties arising from other reasons. As one woman (Alice) said, 'Ladin people aren't used to collaborating, they have built walls because of difficulties experienced in the past [during Fascism]; if they don't work out the history and purge old resentments, they cannot imagine a common future.' Her view was shared by other participants in the group.

Other focus groups did not demonstrate such depth of analysis. Perhaps this was due to the fact that women's knowledge of other valleys is quite superficial in all groups (including students and mothers). A student in Gherdëina (Ottavia) asked me, 'There aren't people in Fascia who speak Ladin, are there?' Gherdëina and Fascia are physically very close to one another but the residents do not know each other well, with the exception of those with a particular interest in Ladin issues. The administrative division and in particular some of the political parties do not help in fostering the unity of Ladin people. Alice said, 'If we are able to construct a Ladin society we have a future, if not, we do not have other possibilities.'

4.4.3.1 Language Transmission at Home

Language transmission is a sensitive question and many of the women involved in the study argued that sensitivity is a female feature, in particular Maia. While it is true that many women decide to speak Ladin because they have no other option, it is also true that many other women change the language they speak for the same reasons. Chiara expressed the opinion that a better knowledge of the Ladin people is a good way to save the language. This mother decided to speak Ladin with her children while the father speaks a German dialect with them, a decision taken to promote both minority languages. When her first daughter began to attend primary school, the mother became aware that she herself did not know a lot about Ladin people: 'Often … you know nothing about yourself.' Because of this she let her daughter get involved in a project to become a museum guide, promoted by the local museum.

Transmitting a language means transmitting everything that the language may bring with it. Angela, for instance, gave us this example: 'Rather than telling the story of "Little Red Riding Hood" to my children, I tell them "La mort e la meseria".'[11] Both Angela and Nicole discussed how they try to pass on original tales to their children. Pia taught her child the games she herself knew when she was a little girl. Maia said she tried to teach language accuracy, finding the right word for the right thing every time it was needed.

For mothers who already had a good level of awareness it was a question of finding support; for other mothers it was a question of raising awareness with their partner. In fact, some women only needed a certain degree of practical support, as Anna said: 'Well, I reflected a lot during this week and I have to say that there is very little that can help us in this task.' How best to transmit the values associated with speaking the mother tongue was not an easy question for the women involved in the focus groups. Before discussing any kind of language policy it has to be understood why mothers change the language they speak. Is it because of an inevitable homogenization process, or because mothers are convinced by old stereotypes about minority language speakers?

4.4.3.2 Language Transmission in Society

Answering the question of how to awaken passion in other people, Angela said, 'We have to find new ways to let the inner self speak, such as music, theatre, poetry. We have to read the soul.' She added that activities that involve the individual had to be introduced, that every person was different, and a whole range of possibilities had to be considered. Maia told us about her experience as a teacher in adult Ladin courses: 'A lot of people come to the course for economic reasons. If they pass the examination they stand more of a chance of finding a job, but after a few weeks they tell me that I opened a window to the

[11] 'La mort e la meseria' ['Death and Misery'] is a tale in Ladin with Death and Misery as the main characters. It is a story that deals with some important existential questions. The tale is set in different environments and is known in other areas, such as Turkey and southern Italy, in a different form. Rather than focusing on the originality, it seems that the women interviewed tried to reconnect their culture with the cultural context of past generations.

Ladin world for them. I'm very happy when that happens because I feel that I have passed on something nice.' Iris added, 'The person who does the transmitting is very important', and Alice said, 'Just warming the heart is not enough.' Some of the women active in Ladin promotional activities developed other sorts of political awareness. Activist women know the language policy strategies used in minority language settings, and they considered it to be very important that language promotion activities were connected with personal and intimate factors. Alice said that she had been thinking about the social, linguistic, and political problems of the Ladin people for a long time. In her own words: 'I was thinking about this book, this is a path we have to follow, it is a book for the school, but we don't need a book in Badiot, one in Gherdëina, or in Fascia ... We need the same book for all pupils ... We have to work hard, we have to think rationally, we have to create an armour, we must have an armour and we have to create it for all Ladins.' Alice thought that division within the Ladin people was a problem, and that survival was possible only if Ladins actively worked together. Sofia focused on individuals with strategic roles in society who can make a difference in a promotional process: 'The right person in the right position.' Alice, Tania, and Nicole opened a discussion on the policies adopted in different valleys: 'We have to collaborate with other valleys.'

One fundamental issue for Alice, also shared by Nicole, was the fact that the Ladin people 'are poor when it comes to self-consciousness and they are disrespectful to themselves'. Without being respectful and assertive the creation of a common identity will not be possible, they said. This issue is also linked to language planning. A common (Standard Ladin) language has been in existence for several years but it remains relatively unused. This is an important issue from which a discussion about Ladin unity may start. It nevertheless seemed to be an unmentionable issue for a number of women. Many of them were not familiar with this political question—students and mothers in particular—while others were familiar with it but did not wish to share their views.

Ladin women also discussed the importance of finding 'smart' ideas for promoting the Ladin language and culture. Gabriella and Marcella said they did not want anything compulsory and excessively serious, but rather a language that spoke to their everyday world. Art was considered the primary tool for promotional activities: shows, plays, cabaret, music, and writing, in a mix of original and existing productions. Carla proposed an open singing session where she could transmit her 'enthusiasm'. Angela and Stella thought that better attention to Ladin theatre could convey a great deal of importance; other women, mostly students, said that dubbing movies, cartoons, and translating books for adults and children could make the Ladin language more modern. Maia proposed exploiting old Ladin anecdotes and stories that are usually appreciated by students learning the Ladin language in their courses. Sofia thought that it was necessary to start from the little things: greetings, the names of houses or objects close to them, and the use of the Ladin language in personal relationships (such as in greeting cards). She said it would also be important to speak about one's love for the language, rather than the economic interests associated with it.

4.4.4 Speaking Several Languages

The Ladin valleys form a unique language community, but each valley differs from the next with respect to the languages used. Every context is characterized by a particular multilingual setting and by individual plurilingualism. During the focus group conducted with women from Gherdëina, Caterina told us, 'Do you know why? When we went to school it happened that with one schoolmate you only spoke Italian; with another, only German; and with the third, only Gherdëina, while when we were all together such a mixture came out that those listening to us asked, "What kind of language is that?"' In fact, in Gherdëina the use of the three social languages (Ladin, German dialect, and Italian) is not a problem for the women involved in the study 'because that's how we grew up' (according to Amanda). This is also due to the educational system, where both German and Italian are used as the medium of instruction. A bilingual school programme is surely one of the factors (but not the only one) that allows people to achieve competence in more than one language. In Badia, even within the same school system, the use of the German dialect and Italian is associated with accuracy. Gherdëina women are able to speak to one another in different languages without loss of fluency, while in Badia (and also in Fascia), Ladin is the only language for communication. Pia said, 'It makes me laugh to speak Italian with a Ladin woman.'

Since the seventeenth century, the ability to speak languages such as German and Italian has allowed Ladin people to increase their trade, and to enjoy better job opportunities.[12] This multilingualism is as valuable today as it was in the earlier times. In the past, Ladin was not in danger until the valleys lost their seclusion, and other languages began to be spoken. The social prestige of Ladin began to diminish while that of other languages became stronger. Ladin remains the language of the heart but no longer the language of power, with some exceptions. In Fascia, Ladin is gaining new prestige. Nella said, 'Ladin is now in fashion … The people of Moena make an effort to speak Ladin and I find it ridiculous … In Moena we do not speak this way, you hear that it is not the same dialect.' In Fascia, Ladin has become something that is useful for gaining personal political prestige (administrative and/or political) and it has taken on a

[12] At the end of the seventeenth century the people of Gherdëina began to take their wooden goods outside the valley. The people of Fascia were known primarily as painters, but also as mediators at the markets in big towns outside of the valleys. The people of Anpezo did a great deal of business with Austria and Venice (in the timber and furniture trades).

new role in the social context. As Laura clearly stated, 'The Ladin language denotes power', at least in Fascia. This is not a unique reading of the reversal of language shift. People who are involved with the promotion of Ladin speak the standardized Ladin-Fascian in order to promote it. Furthermore, a young student said that she attended standardized Ladin courses in order to be able to speak the dialect spoken in the rest of the valley. She wished to be part of a larger community.

For Ladin women, multilingualism is an added value. Some women discussed intercultural reasons, such as Tina, who said, 'We are able to move across several worlds without losing anything, rather gaining some advantages.' Their opinion was that speaking a language allowed one to become familiar with other realities, giving one the skills needed to 'mix' with other people, and the opportunity to understand them. Other women saw multilingualism only as a useful skill for gaining interesting jobs.

In some focus groups we thought about adaptability. As is well known, minority language speakers adapt themselves to using other languages. Erica said, 'We change, we can do it, but it becomes increasingly more difficult for the Gherdëina language.' Nicole said, 'We don't feel our roots and one speaks the other languages without problems, but anything is better than our language, Ladin.' Sofia said, 'But is it right that we have to open ourselves to others in any situation and in all contexts?' For the women interviewed, Ladin was considered the most important language, a view shared by all speakers. If this does not happen, Maia said, 'One day the Ladin language will have disappeared.'

4.4.5 The Relationship of Women with Themselves

It seems to be quite difficult for Ladin women to communicate with each other. Perhaps they are not encouraged to do so because they do not need to interact with many other people; the economic situation in the Ladin area is very good, so there is no difficulty in finding a job with or without a university degree, and there is economic independence. Centuries of male dominance, along with attitudes that looked unfavourably upon social contact among women, is also likely to have contributed to this situation (Runggaldier Moroder 2006). After the focus group meetings I handed out a short evaluation questionnaire. It turned out that all of the women had enjoyed the meetings, where they could share their opinions, ideas, and beliefs, and where they 'could be together with other women' (an opinion expressed by Tania, Angela, Maia, Gabriella, and Carla). During the last meeting, Maia said, 'I would like to thank you for the idea of meeting without men. It was very interesting and unique. It is the first time I experienced that.'[13]

[13] The experience of being among women remains one of the core points of Italian feminism. Being with women permits the experience of feminine freedom, because freedom is not a set of

Relationships among Ladin women continue to be developed. When I asked women in Badia about relationships between women, Gabriella answered that because of her job she has no time to spend with other women. When she does have some time she prefers to spend it with her best friends. She also pointed out that when women have too much time, 'there is time only for gossip', something she does not like.

Another question that should be asked is whether there are personal relationships between women that are not characterized by friendship or professional links. This question was posed to the women participating in the study. Those from Badia talked about feminist associations that work within the territory, but they did not fully understand what the question meant. The question was reformulated as: 'Does it happen that women spend time together simply because it is pleasurable to do so? Could it be because you can talk about interesting things, or because you can exchange your opinions with a person who is not your friend?' Laura said that Ladin women were not taught to spend time with other women, and that they were not clear as to what they had to do. She did admit, though, that she would like to do so: 'It could be done ... nice ideas could come out of it ... but we have a lot of inhibitions, starting this kind of topic ... no, we are not ready to do it.' Other women indicated that the idea was intriguing. Carla brought up her idea of open singing events, discussed during the focus groups. During a meeting, one woman (Maia) stated that it was time to do something new for the promotion of Ladin.

Amanda said in an amusing way that in Gherdëina there is a 'female class division': 'On Monday the shopkeepers go skiing, two days after the hotel-keepers go skiing and on Sunday it is the teachers who go skiing.' Furthermore, women participate in meetings of political or religious associations (this also occurs in Badia).[14]

One student told us how she enjoyed Sundays, when she and her mother and sisters cooked *les tutres*, a typical Ladin dish. She said that she views this activity as a particularly female practice, where women can devote time to themselves. It seems to be a highly symbolic moment of sharing among women. As part of the value of cultural transmission, one can see a micro-setting where feminine ideologies are created. A similar experience was discussed by Antonia, who told us the history of her family and how it had been shaped by strong women.

Asia looked to share her points of view and customs with other women, not necessarily from within her family, so she turned to another woman for help.

constitutional, civil, and political rights but rather a space that makes it possible to feel the sense of being a woman (Cigarini 2004: 1). During the research women felt several moments of 'freedom'.

[14] The Ladin area has a long and strong tradition of Catholicism. The valleys are close to Trento, city of the Council of Trent during the years 1545 to 1563. The Ladin area is also close to the German area where the Protestant Reformation began. Several of the women interviewed considered faith to be an important feature of being Ladin in modern times.

Asia's mother comes from an Italian region, does not speak Ladin, and is not interested in the Ladin tradition. When Asia was in her teens she wanted to wear traditional dress, so the woman helped her to find the dress and the jewels.

During this study, several female figures turned out to be very important to the process of creating a Ladin identity. In Gherdëina one imparted values over several years in order to promote the minority language that emerged over the course of the time. Nicole said, 'She passed on to me the love for Ladin.' Cristina, from Fascia, said, 'When you listen to her you get the desire to know [Ladin issues] better.' Maria said, 'Her life, how she speaks Ladin, how she educates the children, I feel she is the real Ladin woman.' According to Anna Maria Piussi, relationships among women are important because they allow for female mediation. This mediation is a bridge between one woman and another, 'a transactional space between the mother-origin and a feminine "I" that emerged which permits at the same time to take the necessary distance and develop the identity without risk' (Piussi 1989: 89).

Women often identified with the female characters of Ladin tales and tried to find an image of themselves in the relationships with the characters. They enjoyed thinking that they were part of a life in which women had more power (in particular, freedom of speech and thought). They were convinced of their strength of character and will, because they inherited them from their grandmothers. This could also be read as a strategic promotion: conferring power to oneself and to other women means legitimizing all women, situating them in a symbolic order that forms a feminine world.

4.4.6 Women and Politics

There is not a strong tradition of Ladin women being involved in government politics. Only a few have political positions in local administration, and the number of women involved in political parties is small (in the municipal elections in 2010, Ladin women won 22.5 per cent of the total number of posts). The situation is quite similar in neighbouring areas and in Italy as a whole, where there is a significant lack of female involvement in politics.

Women in Ladin areas have always played the strongest role in managing the family, because men would emigrate for several months a year. They usually left the valley in spring and came back in autumn. During those months in the eighteenth, nineteenth, and early twentieth centuries, the women in a family had to look after the farm, tend the animals, and bring up the children.[15] After the Second World War, life in the Dolomites changed completely. A huge number of hotels, apartments, and restaurants opened, and this process engulfed the entire

[15] A very peculiar situation distinguished the women of the Gherdëina valley. During the eighteenth and nineteenth centuries many women used to carve and paint wooden objects, and houses became

population who lived in the valleys (in particular those in Anpezo, Fascia, and Gherdëina). People who did not own a business could nevertheless work for the tourist industry, and women understood that they had an opportunity to gain economic independence. A large number of tourist businesses are now run by Ladin women. With all of these interests and responsibilities, it is understandable that politics was not a priority. 'The only thing that belonged and still belongs to men is politics, all the rest is held by women in one hand,' said Sofia ironically.

The women who took part in the focus groups who did not take an active interest in politics thought that it was a field that was traditionally the province of men, and that entering it would mean adapting to a world that they do not like. Perhaps it would be best to say that they had an interest in politics, as was apparent when they spoke about their futures and pasts, of the different opportunities for Ladin people or villages. They did not like the politics of the various local and national parties, as they did not recognize themselves as playing a part in the way political issues are managed.[16]

But what do women think politics is? Politics is *tout court* the politics of parties, and the policies that administrate the public good (at the local, provincial, regional, and national levels). All of the activities that take place outside of political parties are not called 'politics' but rather 'volunteer activities', 'taking care of something', or 'devoting time to fulfilling a particular interest'. The women in this study worked for several associations and found it 'natural' and 'honest', while for most of them, being involved with a political party was viewed as an experience to be avoided. When they were invited to speak about politics most of them replied, 'No, please, politics no', 'I don't like politics', 'I don't understand politics', and so on. Since the 1980s, women and feminist movements have considered politics to be an arena for 'women's politics', in order to attempt to give additional meaning to policymaking in the world, including drawing attention to new points of view and promoting new roles for women (Cigarini 1995). Ladin women are generally not aware of these efforts.

Those women interviewed who were involved in politics considered their commitment to be problematic, and often felt alone. The only woman in the group who had experience as a local municipal representative admitted that 'politics is difficult and is connected with a lot of clichés'. She recognized the

cottage industries, leading to both advantages and disadvantages. The women gained powerful status, as a report from 1864 (Runggaldier Moroder 2006: 67) indicated: 'Recently women have begun to carve just like the men; some of them are better, and because of this they earn more. For this reason men of Gherdëina have to marry someone who is good at carving rather than someone who is rich but does not earn on her own.'

16 The students do not like the manner used by local politicians to gather votes. One student said, 'He came, asked me, "How old are you?" and when I answered, "Seventeen", he turned back without a glance.' Another student said, 'They come and buy you a pizza, they ask for your vote and then you'll never see them again.' Many of the mothers said, 'Politics is merely a compromise.'

difficulty in managing relationships in the political world, but she also admitted that women often do not support each other. She expressed the view that women were envious when other women wanted to leave the group, as a teacher (Deborah) said when speaking about relationships between teachers: 'That's alright if you remain in your role but if you try to fly high … stop! You can't.' It seems that Ladin women do not like it when other women attempt to do something different. They expect additional competence, skills, and knowledge. Isabella said, 'Because you don't trust a woman', and Gabriella said, 'If you are not well prepared, don't do it.'

Involvement with cultural associations is not considered to be 'real' politics, and is perceived as having less value. From the above discussions it emerged that it may be time to initiate a new way of getting Ladin women involved in society and politics, especially concerning language policies. All of the women in the study stated that they have extensive knowledge, abilities, and skills that could be used in a more targeted fashion. They were asked: where are all these strong women nowadays? Nicole replied, 'We are those women, we have great potential but we need to come out and take our place. We have to do it in cultural and educational fields.'

4.5 Conclusion

How can Nicole's proud stance above be interpreted? From the focus groups the following view has emerged with regard to safeguarding and promoting the Ladin language: the role of women is not yet visible, clear, or considered; their capabilities are yet to be revealed and expressed. Language policy does, however, have to consider women's needs and wishes. On the other hand, women have to reflect on and should give voice to their needs and wishes. During the research, one need emerged clearly: the need to reflect on senses and meanings. Many women wish to analyse and deepen the meanings that are assigned to important parts of their lives. If women do not find a link between the meaning assigned by themselves and the meaning assigned by language policy, then they become detached from the debate.

According to the results of this study, women do not like to actively take part in language policy. One of the reasons is the difference in meaning of various terms. Let us take as an example the meaning of 'mother tongue'. If language policy considers Ladin a 'minority language' or a 'lesser-used language', then the language consequently assumes these labels that are assigned to it. This is generally not how the women interviewed would describe the language themselves. The mother tongue is not *tout court* the minority language that has to be safeguarded. The minority language is politicized and sometimes also exploited for political reasons. In addition, the minority language is studied in its syntactical, grammatical, and lexical parts. For women, however, the mother tongue is indeed the language of their own mother, the language that permits them to interact with and experience the world. It is a living language that puts one at ease, and it is the language of confidence and trust.[17] Before designing a possible language policy—which should also include the feminine universe—it is necessary to reflect on the meanings that 'mother tongue' has for women. Reflecting on these issues, if possible among women, is the cornerstone upon which a language planning strategy that takes women into consideration should be constructed.

According to the results of this study, the participants were conscious of the richness of their heritage, and their awareness increased during our meetings, during which they tried to imagine themselves as the director of an advertising campaign promoting the language, or having to organize a 'Ladin Women's Day'. Being a part of a women's group that shares the same ideology (love for their history, love for their territory, and love for their traditions) gave strength to each of them, and set into motion ideas and the will to improve their language and culture. According to the results of the study, women do not need particularly expensive promotional activities; they are often satisfied with 'little things'. These should ideally have a personal meaning for everyone.

This important goal is actually not so easy to achieve. It means that language planners have to consider the individuality of each person living in a minority language context. In a few words, language planners have to face 'subjectivity', although it is seemingly easier to maintain a distance and work on 'objective' issues such as laws and scientific activities, rather than focusing on research that involves people, and which brings about a real change in the individual.

During the research the women interviewed demonstrated that they could create settings where the promotion of the language can embody both their own personality and the needs of women's communities. Even though they were having fun when proposing ideas for organizing an event, they genuinely showed the possibility of creating something effective that can encompass the whole person, body and soul, private and public, subjective and objective. These kinds of activities were usually closely connected with the arts. In fact, the women interviewed strongly believed in the power of the arts: theatre, music, poetry, cabaret, literature, fashion, and creativity in general. All of these could be used for promoting the value of the Ladin language and culture among women.

Those involved in the research consider Ladin culture as having passed its best. They are not used to thinking of Ladin as a culture created by each woman and man, day by day. Obviously, to be able to look to the past is important as a source for every culture; it is a place where women can find their roots, an oral

[17] With regard to the sense and value of a mother tongue that is simultaneously a minority language, see Rasom (2010).

history with a long tradition, and—in the case of the Ladin culture—an original mythology. But merely looking to the past in order to legitimize Ladin culture is a trap that risks transforming that culture into something without life. Keeping a culture alive means using the past to stimulate everyday life, thus allowing it to thrive in the future.

Language is the essential means for giving a voice to Ladin culture; at the same time the culture is in the content of the language. The results of this study demonstrate that Ladin women need to become more aware of their voice if they want to have opportunities in the future to be 'Ladin'. Women in minority language areas are often compelled to find meaning in speaking their language and living their culture, as opposed to women who speak national or widespread languages, who can take their culture and language for granted. For minority language speakers this is their strength and weakness at the same time. If Ladin women are able to construct meaning and to become aware of their reality, this could be a turning point that could enable the survival of the Ladin language and culture. Because what could be better and more satisfying than rescuing something that seems to be destined to disappear? What could be better than providing a future for a language that belongs to personal history? What could be better than creating a little bit of culture every day? Creating and recreating life is a question of sensitivity, and sensitivity is, according to the women who participated in this study, a female feature.

References

Althoff, M., M. Bereswill, and B. Riegraf. 2001. *Feministische Methodologien und Methoden: Traditionen, Kozepte, Erörterungen*. Opladen: Leske + Budrich.

Behnke C. and M. Meuser. 1999. *Geschlechterforschung und qualitative Methoden*. Opladen: Leske + Budrich.

Cigarini, L. 1995. *La politica del desiderio*. Parma: Nuova Pratiche Editrice.

Cigarini, L. 2004. Libertad relacional. *Duoda Revista d'Estudis Feministes* 26: 85–91.

Crystal, David. 2000. *Language Death*. Cambridge: Cambridge University Press.

Dell'Aquila V. and G. Iannàccaro. 2006. *Survey Ladins: Usi Linguistici nelle valli ladine*. Trento: Regione Autonoma Trentino-Alto Adige.

Hagège, Claude. 2002. *Morte e rinascita delle lingue: Diversità linguistica come patrimonio dell'umanità*. Milano: Feltrinelli. [Original edition: 2000. *Halte à la mort des langues*. Paris: Odile Jacob].

Kindl, U. 2006. Die ältere Geschichte: Numinose Frauengestalten in der ladinischen Erzähltradition. In *Eres tla Ladinia–Frauen in Ladinia–Donne nella Ladinia*. Ladin Ciastel de Tor: Museum San Martin de Tor.

Jaggar, Alison M. (ed.). 2008. *Just Methods: An Interdisciplinary Feminist Reader*. Boulder, CO and London: Paradigm.

Jankowski, E. 1998. Ascoltare la madre. In E. M. Thüne (ed.), *All'inizio di tutto la lingua materna*. Turin: Rosenberg and Sellier.

Mortari, L. 2007. *Cultura della ricerca e pedagogia: Prospettive epistemologiche*. Rome: Carocci.

Muraro, L. 1995. *Lingua materna, scienza divina. Scritti sulla filosofia mistica di Margherita Porete*. Naples: D'Auria.

Muraro, L. [1991] 2006. *L'ordine simbolico della madre*. Rome: Editori Riuniti. [French edition 2003: *L'ordre symbolique de la mère*. Turin: L'Harmattan. German edition 2005: *Die symbolische Ordnung der Mutter*. Rüsselsheim: Christel Götter Verlag].

Naples, A. N. 2003. *Feminism and Method: Ethnography, Discourse Analysis, and Activist Research*. London: Routledge.

Piussi, A. M. 1989. L'affiliazione magistrale. In A. M. Piussi (ed.), *Educare alla differenza*. Turin: Rosenberg and Sellier.

Rasom, Olimpia. 2010. Language policy strategy: does a focus on women lead to a change for the better? In Hywel Glyn Lewis and Nicholas Ostler (eds.), *Reversing Language Shift: How to Re-Awaken a Language Tradition*. Bath: Foundation for Endangered Languages.

Richebuono, G. 1992. *Breve storia dei ladini dolomitici*. San Martin de Tor: Istitut Micurà de Rü.

Roman, L. 1992. The political significance of other ways of narrating ethnography: a feminist materialist approach. In M. D. Le Compte, W. L. Milroy, and J. Preissle (eds.), *The Handbook of Qualitative Research in Education*. San Diego, CA: Academic Press.

Runggaldier Moroder, I. 2006. Stories d'ëiles tla valedes ladines. In *Eres tla Ladinia–Frauen in Ladinia–Donne nella Ladinia*. San Martin de Tor: Museum Ladin Ciastel de Tor.

Thüne, E. M. (ed.). 1998. *All'inizio di Tutto la Lingua Materna*. Turin: Rosenberg and Sellier.

Verra, R. 2000. *Plurilinguismo e Scuola Ladina*. Bolzano: Intendenza Scolastica Ladina.

Zamboni, C. 2006. *Il cuore sacro della lingua*. Padua: Il Poligrafo casa editrice.

5

Minority Language Use in Kven Communities: Language Shift or Revitalization?

ANNA-KAISA RÄISÄNEN

5.1 Introduction

THE LAST DECADES of the twentieth century saw a turn away from the ideal of the monolingual society towards active work on language pluralism in Scandinavian societies. According to Maria Wingstedt (1998), this turn meant a shift from nationalistic and monolingual language ideologies to plurilingual language ideologies. The nationalistic and monolingual views of language in Norway were indeed very strong when the state separated from Denmark in 1814, and later when the union with Sweden ended in 1907. During the period from the mid-nineteenth to the mid-twentieth century, minority languages posed a problem for the young nation-state, which resulted in a tendency to assimilate linguistic minorities into majority society (Eriksen and Niemi 1981).

The aim of this article is to shed light on language ideologies in a small bilingual Kven community in Northern Norway. Nowadays, the Kvens live in a Norwegian society, where the official political discourse resonates with pluralistic language ideology. However, there are, in addition, many other language ideologies affecting people's views of languages. Former Scandinavian research on language ideologies has revealed that discourses concerning minority and majority languages are infused with ecological, instrumental, monolingual, national, and ethnic ideologies (Wingstedt 1998). Some language ideologies support ongoing revitalization projects, while others actively support language shift among minority groups.

In this chapter, I examine the beliefs that speakers of Kven have about their language. I concentrate on the construction of their beliefs in discourses in which the interviewees discuss their own, and their family members', acquisition of the minority and majority languages. An essential part of my analysis describes the discourses associated with socialization (Schieffelin and Ochs 1986) into a minority language community, which describe the choices made in the respondents'

Proceedings of The British Academy, **199**, 97–108. © The British Academy 2014.

childhood family homes, and the choices that they themselves make with regard to their own children. I am interested in how individuals see the past from a present-day perspective. It is vital to understand the experiences that the speakers of a minority language have in a historical context, especially considering that former ideologies supporting monolingualism have undergone a major shift. This has resulted in ideologies that support the value of multilingualism and language revitalization. As Austin and Sallabank (this volume) point out, 'the study of language ideologies and beliefs can provide insights into reasons for both language decline and revival'.

5.2 The Kvens

The Kvens are a national minority in Norway. They once spoke a Finnic language, nowadays officially called Kven, before language shift started around the beginning of the twentieth century in Troms, and later in the mid-twentieth century in Finnmark (Aikio 1989; Eskeland et al. 2003; Lane 2010: 64). According to Eskeland et al. (2003), Kven was an important lingua franca in interethnic communication and was also a lingua sacra in the Laestadian religious movement in Northern Norway. However, in both local and peripheral Kven communities, it has lost ground while Norwegian has strengthened its hold.

Kven is generally used by the older generations, and it has an important role in the ethnic identity of the Kvens. The language is closely related to Finnish and has been considered a dialect of Finnish (termed *ruijanmurteet* or *kveenimurteet*) by both its speakers and linguists (Hyltenstam and Milani 2003). The Kven language received the status of an independent language in 2005, after a long political debate. The Kvens themselves have various interpretations of the origins of their own language. In the western part of Northern Norway, the Kvens regard their language as an independent language. It is called either *kveenin kieli* (the Kven language) or *kainun kieli* (the Kainu language); in Norwegian, the language is called *kvensk*. Despite the official status of the language, the Kvens in the eastern part of Northern Norway regard the Kven language as a dialect or a variety of Finnish called 'Old Finnish' or 'Norwegian Finnish'.

The main target of my study is the small Kven community in Eastern Finnmark, Bugøynes, which has 400 inhabitants, and where the onset of language shift was relatively late. As Lane (2010: 69) has pointed out, although since the 1970s parents have tended to speak only Norwegian to their children and grandchildren in Bugøynes, the minority language is still actively used among the community's oldest members, who learned Kven or Finnish as their first language. There have been some efforts to revitalize the language in Bugøynes, but until now the revitalization process has been restricted to the school environment as an optional subject.

5.3 Language Ideologies and Discourses

As many chapters in this book show, research on language ideology has been carried out from various viewpoints, in different language communities, and in many parts of the world. In this chapter, I shall use Blommaert's (1999) concept of language ideology to examine the discourses concerning language socialization among the Kvens. According to Blommaert's definition, language ideologies are 'socioculturally motivated ideas, perceptions and expectations of language, manifested in all sorts of language use' (Blommaert 1999: 1). These are not separated from any kind of language use but are present in language itself as well as in all its varied uses.

In the same way as language, language ideologies are also connected to other sociocultural, political and economic contexts, and to other ideologies and social practices affecting social life (Wingstedt 1998: 26). They have an influence on the way the language users perceive, interpret, and experience the language, but language and its uses also wield various influences on ideologies via discourse. As Woolard (1992: 235) points out, 'ideology stands in dialectal relation with, and thus significantly influences, social, discursive and linguistic practices'. As language speakers' ideologies are at work in their language(s) and in the linguistic choices they make, ideologies about languages should therefore be examined systemically in relation to language use, and especially to those semiotic processes that reveal these ideologies (e.g. Irvine and Gal 2000: 37).

In addition to linguistic ideology, discourse is the other important concept treated in this chapter. In conceptualizing discourse, I draw on Fairclough (2001), who considers discourse as a way of representing ideas and knowledge. By analysing discourses and their contexts, it is possible to reveal socially meaningful elements from different levels, originating from different historical, social, cultural, or ideological surroundings (Blommaert 2005: 174). Since language is an important semiotic system in which discourses are manifest, it is important to analyse language and its use.

5.4 The Data and Methods of Analysis

The data is taken from interviews with 12 native Kven speakers in Bugøynes. I collected the data (11 hours of recordings) in August 2007 when I worked as a field assistant in the project 'The Linguistic and Cultural Heritage Electronic Network', which was funded by the Research Council of Norway. The main focus of the project was Kven language documentation. Another aim was to gather and disseminate information about the situation of the Kven language (Lane and Räisänen 2008). The purpose of the interviews discussed in this chapter was to explore the attitudes and beliefs Kven speakers have with regard to their language. The interviews concentrated mainly on language, although some other particular themes about Kven culture were also discussed.

I analysed the data using Fairclough's (2003) discourse analysis method, paying attention to the content and linguistic structures of discourses in the data. Initially, I separated the excerpts in which the interviewees speak about language socialization into two generations: the first focused on the respondents' and their elders' use of language, and then about the respondents' own language use with their children. Secondly, I analysed how respondents linguistically conceptualize this kind of content concerning language choice within the family. In the analysis, attention was paid to the words and structures (especially to modal structures) that the participants used to express these themes and discourses. In the examination, there are two levels for analysing discourses: the micro-level linguistic choices, by which the respondents give meanings to language choices within families, and the macro-level choices that the interviewees make as members of a socio-cultural community. Finally, I examined what kind of language ideologies are constructed by these connected discourses regarding language and its intergenerational transmission. In addition to presenting the results of my study I shall discuss how different language ideologies relate to language shift and resistance to it.

5.5 Minority Language Transmission

A common feature in the interviews was that all participants who had learned Kven or Finnish as their first language described the use of the minority language as a normal and natural phenomenon at home during their childhood. The themes that arose in most interviews while talking about language use at home were connected to the interviewees' experiences of learning Norwegian and changes in the use of languages when starting school.

(1)

Haastattelija: *mitä kieltä teillä kotona puhuttiin.*

'What language did you use at home?'

Maria: *suomia joo se oli aivan suomia . joo ( ) joo. ei minun isä ja äiti ei puhuhneet ne ei ne osahneet oikiaa norjaa he. net oli puhuhneet aivan suomia . nii ( ) ko heän nehä esivanhemmat olthii Suomesta mm.*

—

nii joo ja se näi net puhuthii aivan suomia ja ja sillälailla se on (ollu sillon), samoten äitiki ni niin mii_en tiiä koska äiti on (–) mutta äitin äiti mie vain muistan, nii, kansa nii tä- se kuoli ko mie olin kuuev vuojev vanha, ( ) nii ( ) joo. niin mutta nehän oli su- suomesta se oli heillä aivan se suomi tuo nii ja kaikki met lapset jokka olemma ylöskasunheet kotona ni sehän oli suomia. ja nii nii niin kauan ko me aloimma kouhlun.

'Finnish, yeah, only Finnish. Yeah. ( ) Oh, my father and mother could not speak proper Norwegian. They spoke only Finnish. Yeah. ( ) Because their ancestors were from Finland mm.

—

So, yeah, and they spoke only Finnish and so it has been (has been then), and also mother, so yeah, I don't know, because mother is (–) but I remember my grandmother, yeah, too, she died when I was six, ( ) so ( ) yeah. But they were from Finland and had only Finnish and all of us children who were brought up at home, so it was Finnish. And so, it was so as long as we started school.'

(2)

Haastattelija: *joo no entä mikä on ollu sun ensimmäinen kieli, jonka sie oot oppinu.*

'Yeah, and what was the language you learned first?'

Reidun: *no sehän on tietenki suomi. hhh mutta mie olen siinä samassa norijaaki saanu jotaki, katto ko mulla on vanhempija, <syster> vanhin <syster> oli kaheksan vuotta vanhempi minua, sehän kulki jo koulua. se oli oppinu norijaa, ja ja:: minun vanhemmatki puhuthin norijaa aina joskus, ja ko kylä- joku ihminen tuli kylhän jol- joka osas aivan norijaa, niin niin opin vähän sillon norijaa jo. kotona puhu äiti oli oli <flink> hyvä puhumhan norijaa kotona, ja niin mie opin norijaa ennen ko mie menin koulhun. niin mie osasin jo norijaa.*

'Oh of course it was Finnish. But I did learn Norwegian as well, you see, because I had older ((siblings)), sister the oldest sister was eight years older than me, and she was already in school. She had learned Norwegian, and and my parents spoke Norwegian as well every now and then, and when someone visited us, someone spoke only Norwegian, so so I did learn a little Norwegian then already. My mother spoke at home, she was good at speaking Norwegian, and so I learned Norwegian before starting school. So I knew some Norwegian already.'

The discursive construction of speaking the Kven or Finnish language at home provides an immediate answer to the question about the language used at home in the interviewees' childhood. In line with other speakers in the study, Maria, in example (1), describes her home environment with her parents and grandparents as totally Finnish-speaking. This is a way of constructing a strong position for the minority language in private domains, which draws on discourses of monolingual environments where there are no other languages present—only the minority language. This is emphasized with the repetitive phrase '*aivan suomia*' (only Finnish). Like Maria, Reidun (2) too describes the home as a Kven-speaking domain: '*Sehän on tietenkin suomi*' (Of course, it's Finnish) contains a modal particle '*tietenkin*' (of course), which draws on discourses about Finnish as a natural first language in Bugøynes. These linguistic choices naturalize the linguistic socialization in the Kven language community and clearly echo the discourses of the Kven- or Finnish-speaking Bugøynes, where there is a strong tendency to compare their own minority community and its uniqueness to Norwegian-speaking majority communities.

The linguistic choices of the participants exploit discourses about bilingual Bugøynes, although the main explicit discourse refers to the minority language speaking community. In extract (2) Reidun emphasizes that her first language is Kven, but then she continues with the contrastive adversative conjunction *mutta* (but), followed by her description of learning Norwegian too. Reidun chooses contrastive linguistic elements to refer to her language socialization in the local community as a bilingual community member. Maria, also, recalls her bilingual childhood when she divides her family into two groups: those who could not speak proper Norwegian, and those (herself included) who spoke both Kven or Finnish, and Norwegian. These views of language use in childhood derive from discourses of bilingualism and the parallel use of languages, where participants are not able to keep the two languages separate when speaking about their linguistic environment during their childhood.

Both examples (1) and (2) demonstrate what an important effect school had in small bilingual villages, as the school was a monolingual Norwegian institution. School was the only domain where bilingualism was totally forbidden: only the use of Norwegian was permitted. In extracts (1) and (2) both Maria and Reidun construct discourses which create higher boundaries between private and public domains, thus these discourses connect the interviewees' beliefs about the different possibilities that the languages used in the community can provide; using Kven is opportune in the local village, but with Norwegian there are opportunities in society beyond the village.

The great majority of the participants learned Kven as their first language at home, yet the data includes two interviewees who say that they only learned Norwegian at home. However, these two respondents have been socialized in the minority community among other Kven speakers, and both of them have a strong identity as minority language speakers.

(3)

Haastattelija: *oo joo. ( ) no oliko teillä kotikielenä suomi vai, ( )*

'Yeah, yeah. ( ) Did you speak Finnish at home or,'

Irene: *äiti ja isä puhuthin suomia kyllä, mutta ei koskhan lasten aikana, ko lapset olthin siinä sillai, että mehän o- mehän olima norijalaisia, ja se oli se {p'edagogiik} sillon, että ei saa kahta kieltä. se_oli no se_oli väärin tietenki, mutta se oli se- sellainen {p'e-} niihän se_oli, että se oli {p'edagogiik} niin semmonen että yks kieli kerralhan. .hhh mutta ko me olima siinä kuuen kuuen vuen vanhana, niin kyllä sitä alko niin_ko ulkona*

> *kuuli, ( ) suomen kielen. .joo ja sitä alko sitten, mutta ehän sitähän kuuli suomen kielen ko vanhat ihimiset puhuthin niin se.*
>
> 'Mother and Father spoke Finnish but never when children were present, when children were there, because we were Norwegian, and it was the pedagogy then, that you are not allowed to speak two languages. It was, so, it was of course wrong, but it was kind of {p'e-} so it was, that it was {p'edagogiik} that one language at a time. But when I was six or so, then I started to learn, because I heard Finnish outside. Yeah, and I started to, because you heard older people speaking Finnish, yeah.'

In this extract (3), Irene describes how her parents decided to speak only Norwegian to the children, although they spoke Kven or Finnish to each other. After this, Irene focuses on the reasons why her parents did not pass on the language to their children. These reasons highlight the two beliefs that have been used to resist bilingualism and justify monolingualism in Norway: 'Norwegians speak Norwegian' and 'bilingualism is harmful'. From her present-day point of view, Irene explicitly expresses that a monolingual upbringing is 'väärin' (wrong), and impossible in a bilingual community; thus her statements reveal positive views of bilingualism. This example also shows how Irene constructs a strong contrast between discourses of defending or resisting multilingualism. The first is situated within the context of family and society, where her parents made the decision to shift languages, and the second within the context of a current plural postmodern society.

The previous analysis illustrates the contradictions between Kven and Norwegian, which are constructed through the discourses concerning the languages in the interviewees' childhood. The minority language represents home and the minority community, while the majority language represents wider society and its institutions. Although participants strongly emphasize the significance of learning Norwegian before they started school, they also highlight their primary socialization in the minority language community as a natural and normal process. Despite the discourse of bilingualism, participants draw on discourses where they construct contrastive views between languages as parallel linguistic resources existing in separate domains, where bilingualism refers to private domains and monolingualism to public domains.

The analysis also illustrates that discourses about language use in childhood draw on coexisting contradictory language ideologies. Although the dominant ideology in Norway during the respondents' childhood was a nationalistic and monolingual ideology, from the data it is obvious that this did not have a big impact on the Kvens in their local communities, and therefore did not radically affect the linguistic choices made in the home domain.

5.6 Language Transmission to the Next Generation

During the 1950s in Bugøynes, attitudes towards minority languages changed radically from positive to negative, as modern society and the education system did not support Kven language and its use (Lane 2010: 72). Although the interviewees perceived their own bilingualism as normal, they decided to shift from Finnish to Norwegian with their own children. As Lane (ibid.) states, 'mainly through the educational system, their mother tongue was devalued and this was one of the reasons that they did not pass it on to their children'.

However, according to the participants in the study, language practices varied greatly from family to family. Before the 1970s when most families shifted from Kven to Norwegian, some of the interviewees used only Norwegian with their children but still used Kven with their spouse, some used both languages with both their children and spouse, and some even shifted to Norwegian with their spouse after the birth of their first child.

(4)

Haastattelija: *mitä te yhessä ((Maria ja hänen miehensä)) puhhuitte.*

'What did you speak together ((with your husband)))'

Maria: *me me puhuimma suomia joo. hän praatasi suomen hänki. joo, ja sitte ko meilläki ko lapset tuota ni niinko se hääytti, me hääyimmä puhua norjaa sitte lapsille sitte ko lapset saathii kouhluu. ( ) niin ni että se ei ole niin ankara, niin nii ( ) mutta mehän tä- tavallisesti koti kotipuhe oli suomi. nii se oli suomi nii mutta, ( ) mutta niinko lasten vuoksi, ni lapsethan vai puhuthii, ni sitte sillähän opithii hekki sitte suomen ko ko met keskenhää puhuimma suomia ja ja puhuimma norjaa sitte lapsille.*

'We spoke Finnish, yeah. He spoke Finnish too. Yeah, and when we had children, then we had to, we had to speak Norwegian to children then when they started school. ( ) and so, so it is not so difficult, so so ( ) but we spoke Finnish at home usually. So it was Finnish so, but because of the children, so the children spoke only, so, and they learned also Finnish, because we spoke Finnish together and we spoke Norwegian to children.'

In extract (4) Maria divides up the description of her family's language shift from Kven to Norwegian with a temporal expression, '*sitten ko*', into two periods: the Kven-speaking era before the children started school, and the bilingual era that followed. Maria attaches 'we, the parents' to the Kven language. The parents are actors and direct the action, speaking to their children. These divisions of different periods and groups within the family construct the discourse, where Maria sees socialization in Norwegian society as more important than socialization in the Kven community (see also Lane 2010: 71–2). Furthermore, she does not see any possibilities of developing bilingual linguistic practices with the children. The deontic modal expression '*me hääyimmä puhua norjaa*' ('we had to speak Norwegian'), however, implies that the parents had to speak Norwegian to the children because of school and for later socio-economic success. Here, the modal verb '*häätyä*' expresses Maria's construction of obligation and duty, which is explicitly connected to school and implicitly to the larger society. Maria has experienced language shift as a force and necessity, which means that she did not shift of her own will. Example (4) could be summarized as 'You have to know Norwegian so that life will not be difficult'. Even though Maria partly refers to monolingual language ideologies, she also expresses resistance discourse, in which pluralistic ideological community wishes are expressed—the wish to continue their language and culture in present-day society—at least at the level of discourse.

As Dorian (1994) points out, people internalize ideologies of linguistic inferiority, which usually leads to linguistic and cultural shift, if they are faced with a lack of freedom in language choice. In this kind of situation, as the data show, people prefer to draw on discourses where the process of language shift is shown in a positive light. This discourse includes the presupposition 'It is good to know Norwegian so that life will be easier':

(5)

Idar: *((lapset puhuvat)) aivan norijaa ja [see nee nee*

'((Children spoke)) only Norwegian and [they they)'

Ida: *mutta ko mes] saama mek ko saima lapset sitten, niin sittem me vain, että elikkä se oli koko kylässä tässä että että kyllä se on parasta puhua lapsile norijaa. ko ne ko nes synnythin että ne se tullee niin_ko helpoks helpompi koulussa, kouhluun alkaa.*

'But when we had] children then, so then we only, so and the same was in the whole village, that that it is the best for the children that we speak Norwegian to them. When they were born that it will be easier at school, when starting school.'

Idar and Ida perceive the choice of Norwegian as a first language for their children as a decision that was made by the speech community, the '*koko kylän*' ('the whole village'), and where the responsible actor is the community and not single individuals. According to them, the decision was based on the belief that life in modern Norwegian society is '*helpompaa*' ('easier') if the children are monolingual in Norwegian. They refer to this with positive adjectives, '*parasta*' ('best') and '*ja helpompaa*' ('easier'), which describe their attitudes towards language shift as being much more positive than Maria's in example (4). These word choices connect example (5) to the discourse, which Lane (2010: 72) summarizes as the reasons for language choice made by Kven speakers in Bugøynes, 'We did what we thought was best for our children.' This discourse is linked to the ideology that the minority language belongs to the past and to the older generations, while Norwegian is the language of success in modern society (see Lane 2010).

As pointed out in Irene's example above, the attitude towards language shift is quite sceptical, even though the opposite attitude also exists. This is explicitly expressed in example (6), but it is also present in examples (4) and (5). The description of language shift as a forced process in example (6) presupposes that the natural and free choice for the interviewee would be speaking Kven to the children. The same discourses appear in the following example:

(6)

Lina: *nii se se sano ni että eihän ymmärrä ko te puhutta aivan, sehä on sehän koulutti {X:ssä} jo sillon ni sannoo että eihän ymmärrä ko oletta aivan puhuhneet norjaa heile, että {Nimi} se puhu aivan suomia lapsille ja sillä oltiin niin nopiat ne lapset. mutta mehäs sanomma että se oli se norja tietenni ko se on kirjotus ja sillai sitte se on ko me oomma Norjassa tieten. ( ) mutta: sehän otti sitten: mm: suomen: ( ) mitem mie sanon. {viideregooeende}*

'So he said that he does not understand why we spoke only, so he went to school in {X} then and he said that he does not understand why you have spoken only Norwegian to them, because he ((a man in a village)) spoke only Finnish and his children were so smart, those children. But we said that it was of course Norwegian, because of the written language and so and we live in Norway of course. ( ) But he chose Finnish at school, how do I say {viideregooeende}.'

This example points towards the changes of attitudes towards minority languages, strengthened by the references to the opinion held by Lina's son, who has criticized his parents' decision to bring up their children as monolinguals. This point of view reveals a critical attitude to monolingual discourses and represents a positive attitude to multilingualism. Although the children mainly use Norwegian with their parents and their own children, they have, however, studied their parents' language at school and achieved a level of skill such that they can now use the Kven language with Finnish-speaking people in Norway and Finland.

5.7 Conclusion

Whilst minority language use in the interviewees' childhood is seen as natural, language shift to Norwegian with their children is then seen as natural some decades later. The nationalistic ideology, which has produced a 'Norwegianization' process, has had an intense effect on language shift in the Kven communities in Northern Norway. The above analysis illustrates that it has not been only language ideology that affected language choices in the Bugøynes speech community. The process of language shift is still under way, but there are discourses evident that reveal a resistance to this process and a concomitant change of attitudes in a more positive direction. From this perspective interviewees regard past choices as unfavourable and wrong, and now refer to a progressive view of the minority language.

Language shift in the 1950s and 1960s was justified for educational and socio-economic reasons. The school as an institution had a remarkable role in strengthening national and economic language ideologies in the Kven communities. Once more, the school has a central role, but now in the present revitalization process: the arena that was formerly a place for assimilation is now promoting the reversal of language shift. Kven revitalization has begun in schools with the teaching of Kven as a second or foreign language, although revitalization efforts have yet to reach families and private domains. In addition to concrete revitalization projects, the change of beliefs and attitudes about Kven, from negative to positive, helps to shed some light on a possible avenue for the survival of minority languages.

References

Aikio, Marjut. 1989. The Kven and cultural linguistic pluralism. *Acta Borealia* 6: 86–97.

Blommaert, Jan. 1999. *Language Ideological Debates*. Berlin: Mouton de Gruyter.

Blommaert, Jan. 2005. *Discourse: A Critical Introduction*. Cambridge: Cambridge University Press.

Dorian, Nancy. 1994. Choices and values in language shift and its study. *International Journal of the Sociology of Language* 110: 113–24.

Eriksen, Knut Einar and Einar Niemi. 1981. *Den finske fare: sikkerhetsproblemer og minoritetspolitikk i nord 1860–1940*. Oslo: Universitetsforlag.

Eskeland, Tuula, Marjatta Norman, and Anna-Riitta Lindgren. 2003. Osima ja Baskabus: monet suomet Norjassa. In Helena Jönsson-Korhola and Anna-Riitta Lindgren (eds.), *Monena suomi maailmalla: suomalaisperäisiä vähemmistöjä*. Helsinki: Suomalaisen Kirjallisuuden Seura.

Fairclough, Norman. 2001. The discourse of New Labour: critical discourse analysis. In M. Wetherell, S. Taylor, and S. J. Yates (eds.), *Discourse as Data: A Guide for Analysis*. London: Sage.

Fairclough, Norman. 2003. *Analysing Discourse: Textual Analysis for Social Research*. London: Routledge.

Hyltenstam, Kenneth and Tommaso Milani. 2003. *Kvenskans status: Rapport for Kommunal- og regionaldepartementet og Kultur- og kirkedepartementet i Norge*. Stockholm: Stockholms Universitet, Centrum för tvåspråkighetsforskning.

Irvine, Judith and Susan Gal. 2000. Language ideology and linguistic differentiation. In Paul V. Kroskrity (ed.), *Regimes of Language: Ideologies, Polities, and Identities*. Santa Fe, NM: School of American Research Press.

Lane, Pia. 2010. 'We did what we thought was best for our children': a nexus analysis of language shift in a Kven community. *International Journal of the Sociology of Language* 202, 63–78.

Lane, Pia and Anna-Kaisa Räisänen. 2008. LICHEN-prosjektet: et humanioraprojektet I polarårsbuketten. *Ottar* 4: 12–19.

Schieffelin, Bambi and Elinor Ochs. 1986. Language socialization. *Annual Review of Anthropology* 15: 163–91.

Wingstedt, Maria. 1998. *Language Ideologies and Minority Language Policies in Sweden: Historical and Contemporary Perspectives*. Stockholm: University of Stockholm, Centre for Research on Bilingualism.

Woolard, Kathryn. 1992. Language ideology: issues and approaches. *Pragmatics* 2: 235–50.

6

Going, Going, Gone? The Ideologies and Politics of Gamilaraay-Yuwaalaraay Endangerment and Revitalization*

PETER K. AUSTIN

6.1 Background: The Linguistic Ecology of Eastern Australia

AT LEAST 35 LANGUAGES (including 120 dialects) were spoken in what is now New South Wales (NSW) in the eighteenth century when Europeans first settled in Sydney (Wafer and Lissarrague 2008: 4). A similar number of languages were to be found in what is now Victoria (Clark 2005). The nineteenth and twentieth centuries have seen massive language shift to English as Aboriginal groups were dispossessed of their lands and forced onto mission or government settlements, farms, or the fringes of country towns (and, in the twentieth century, increasingly into urban centres such as Sydney and Melbourne), and in some cases taken away from their families (what are known as the 'Stolen Generations'). The social and cultural disruption that affected the region resulted in Aboriginal languages being restricted to home and family domains, and rapidly becoming moribund (with only a handful of older speakers) or extinct. Cultural practices such as initiation and other ceremonies mostly ceased to be practised by the first quarter of the twentieth century, and children grew up speaking English and learning just a few words and expressions of the indigenous languages. The Gamilaraay and Yuwaalaraay languages of north-west New South Wales (see the map in Figure 6.1) present a well-documented case study that illustrates this (see section 6.2, for an outline of the history of research on these languages; see Austin (2008) and Wafer and Lissarrague (2008: 215–37) for more details on data sources).

* I am grateful to the many Gamilaraay and Yuwaalaraay people who assisted me with the study of their languages over the past 40 years, to R. M. W. Dixon and the late Stephen A. Wurm for access to their unpublished field materials, to David Nathan for collaborative work on web-based materials development, and to John Giacon for discussion of his work and recent events, especially the language and cultural revival currently taking place. Julia Sallabank provided detailed critical feedback on earlier drafts. I alone am responsible for any errors herein.

The last 25 years have seen a remarkable turnaround in the fortunes of these languages and the ideologies and politics that affect them (Walsh 2003). Until the mid-1980s, Aboriginal languages of south-eastern Australia were subject at best to benign neglect on the part of the non-Aboriginal population and of state and federal governments, and at worst to outright discouragement and suppression. This changed due to several political and social developments. Since the 1990s, language and culture revitalization programmes have been developed for a large number of languages from this area. Wafer and Lissarrague (2008: 4) identify at least 19 NSW languages that are currently being revived (see also Hobson et al. 2010; Lowe and Walsh 2004). In addition, the NSW state government introduced Aboriginal language programmes in 2002 and the NSW Department of Aboriginal Affairs established an Aboriginal Languages Research and Resource Centre.[1] The Aboriginal Education Board of Studies NSW has part of its website dedicated to Aboriginal languages.[2] The Federal Government Indigenous Languages Support scheme (and its predecessor the Maintenance of Indigenous Languages and Records (MILR) programme) has also funded a number of initiatives in NSW.[3] The Koori Centre and the Department of Linguistics at the University of Sydney have introduced the teaching of NSW Aboriginal languages at tertiary level and have supported several local efforts. Social media sites such as YouTube have also been used to promote NSW languages (see further discussion later in this chapter).

6.2 Gamilaraay and Yuwaalaraay

At the time of first settlement in the nineteenth century, Gamilaraay (also commonly known as Kamilaroi) was associated with a vast area of north-central NSW (covering some 75,000 square kilometres), from the Upper Hunter Valley around Jerry's Plains, north to Boggabilla on the Barwon River, and west to the area where Mungindi, Collarenebri, and Walgett are now located (see Figure 6.1).[4] To the north-west, Yuwaalaraay and Yuwaalayaay (also spelled Euhlayi) were spoken, covering a smaller area near present-day Goodooga, Lightning Ridge, and Walgett. The three languages are closely related (Austin, Williams,

[1] See <http://www.alrrc.nsw.gov.au/> (accessed 9 October 2012).

[2] See <http://ab-ed.boardofstudies.nsw.edu.au/go/aboriginal-languages> (accessed 9 October 2012). See also <http://www.curriculumsupport.education.nsw.gov.au/secondary/languages/languages/aboriginal/abl_qt/index.htm> (accessed 9 October 2012), for materials on the Quality Teaching Framework for Teachers of Aboriginal Languages established in 2010.

[3] <http://arts.gov.au/indigenous/ils> (accessed 9 October 2012).

[4] The name of the people and the language consists of *gamil* ('no') plus the affix *-araay* ('having'), that is, those who have *gamil* for 'no', a common naming practice in what is now New South Wales and Victoria. The misspelling 'Kamilaroi' derives from early written sources.

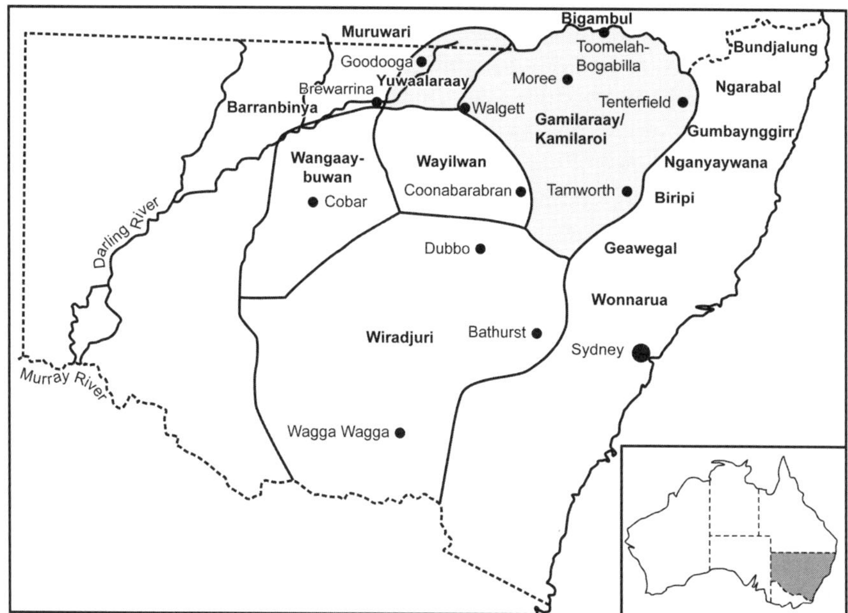

Figure 6.1 Location of Gamilaraay-Yuwaalaraay and neighbouring languages.

and Wurm (1980: 177) consider them to be 'dialects of a single language') and they share cognates and many grammatical features with central NSW languages to their south, namely Wangaaybuwan and Wayilwan (closely related and known collectively as Ngiyambaa) and Wiradjuri (Austin 1997; Austin, Williams, and Wurm 1980). Wafer and Lissarrague (2008) refer to the larger grouping as Central Inland NSW languages.

The Presbyterian missionary Reverend William Ridley came to the Gamilaraay area in 1852 and began to learn the language, later publishing a range of materials on it (see Austin 2008 for a list and assessment). It appears at that time to have been widely spoken, and the first language of many thousands of people (the exact population numbers will probably never be known, however O'Rourke (2009: 2) estimates '10,000 or more'). Around 50 years later (roughly two generations), when surveyor and amateur linguist and anthropologist R. H. Matthews collected vocabulary and sentences (see Austin 2008), it appears that extensive language shift had already taken place and that Gamilaraay was spoken only by middle-aged and older people. The causes of language shift probably included the mixing of populations in settlements and towns, intermarriage, and negative beliefs about Aboriginal people, cultures, and languages on the part of the non-Aboriginal population, which led to forbidding the use of indigenous languages in public. At this time Aboriginal people's lives were tightly controlled, especially those of people living on properties managed by the

Aborigines Welfare Board, and managers, staff, and schoolteachers were openly opposed to the expression of Aboriginal languages and cultures.

In 1938, anthropologist Norman Tindale collected vocabulary and a short traditional narrative text from two old speakers, noting that they no longer used the language regularly and had to work hard to produce the text, indicating that it was by now critically endangered.[5] By 1944, when Marie Reay did a sociological study of the Aboriginal community near Walgett (Reay 1945), it appears that some vocabulary items (she mentions kinship terminology, section names, and some plant names) and traditional songs were in wide use, but most people were speaking English only. In 1955 linguist Stephen Wurm was able to find and record just one fluent speaker of Gamilaraay, and five of Yuwaalaraay-Yuwaalayaay. In 1972–5 I found that there were no fluent speakers or semi-speakers of Gamilaraay, only those who could recall words and expressions (in what was often referred to as 'lingo') used by their parents and grandparents (as noted in Austin 2008, I recorded 212 cross-checked vocabulary items and half a dozen sentences). However, a limited number of lexical items were in wide use by people of all ages (terms for body parts, some animals and plants, food, and a handful of verbs) embedded within English sentences and often altered in pronunciation from their traditional form (Austin 1986). This vocabulary included taboo terms (for genitalia, bodily excretions, and sexual intercourse) as well as terms for police, and its continued use seems to have served as a kind of identity marker and 'secret code', expressing resistance to the dominance of non-Aboriginal authority.[6] Such resistance is reminiscent of Reay's discussion of Aboriginal expression of defiance in the 1940s to what they saw as unjust laws, that were in place until the 1960s, that made it unlawful for them to possess or drink alcohol. Reay (1945: 300–1) reports:

> If an aborigine having liquor in his possession knows that the police are near by, he drinks quickly and this hastens and exaggerates the intoxicating effects of the liquor. In any case, if an aborigine who is sober is caught with liquor in his possession, consciously and through years of habit he assumes drunkenness, for drunkenness is to him a symbol of defiance. It is the outward proof that he has been successful in flouting an unjust law. Imprisonment does not worry him, for there is no shame attached. Continual drunkenness increases his prestige among his fellows; it is a matter for boasting.

In 1976 Corinne Williams was able to elicit a range of grammatical materials and some brief texts from Fred Reece and Arthur Dodd, who were fluent, but rusty,

[5] Tindale NSW Notebook p. 39ff, and Kinship sheet 53; the text was published as Austin and Tindale (1986) with attempted phonemicization and analysis by Austin.

[6] Several of my consultants noted that a reason often given for prohibiting the speaking of Gamilaraay and other languages by the police and other authorities was that 'you might be saying bad things or swearing at us'. It is precisely the taboo vocabulary for doing so that continued to be passed on.

Table 6.1 Historical development of the vitality of Gamilaraay-Yuwaalaraay-Yuwaaliyaay.

Date	Probable vitality	Source
1852	Fluent speakers, all ages	Ridley
1902	Some middle-aged and older fluent speakers	Matthews
1938	Few fluent older speakers, no intergenerational transmission	Tindale
1955	Very few older speakers, no intergenerational transmission	Wurm
1972–6	Rememberers of Gamilaraay, two old rusty speakers of Yuwaalaraay	Austin, Williams
1994–	Rememberers of Yuwaalaraay-Yuwaaliyaay, handful of items recalled for Gamilaraay	Giacon

speakers of Yuwaalaraay-Yuwaalayaay (Williams 1980). Starting in 1994, John Giacon worked with rememberers in Walgett (especially Uncle Ted Fields) and collected 1,000 items of Yuwaalaraay vocabulary (Ash, Giacon, and Lissarrague 2003: 4; Giacon 2010: 409), but no grammatical information. Table 6.1 summarizes this historical development in the vitality of the three languages.

6.3 Language Revitalization

The seeds of language revitalization for Gamilaraay can be identified with the publication of two small dictionaries (Austin 1992, 1993), the second of which was adapted for Internet publication as the first fully hypertextual dictionary on the World Wide Web (Austin and Nathan 1996); and for Yuwaalaraay-Yuwaalayaay with Giacon's work in the Catholic Education service at Walgett, starting in 1994. There were also significant political developments in Australia around this time, which can be seen as having shifted the ground on relationships and perceptions and ideologies between Aboriginal and non-Aboriginal people, and opened up the possibility of Aboriginal people and languages being accorded the respect they had been denied for so long:

- the passing in September 1991 of the *Council for Aboriginal Reconciliation Act* by the Australian Federal parliament, that established a 'formal process of reconciliation between Aborigines and Torres Strait Islanders and other Australians' in order to 'address progressively Aboriginal disadvantage and aspirations in relation to land, housing, law and justice, cultural heritage, education, employment, health, infrastructure, economic development and any other relevant matters in the decade leading to the centenary of Federation, 2001'.[7]

[7] <http://www.austlii.edu.au/au/legis/cth/num_act/cfara1991338/> (accessed 9 October 2012).

- the 1992 Mabo decision of the High Court of Australia recognizing Aboriginal prior occupation and ownership of unalienated Crown land.[8]
- the Redfern Park speech on 10 December 1992 by Prime Minister Keating that included an admission of culpability on the part of non-Aboriginal settlers and boosted Reconciliation: 'We took the traditional lands and smashed the original way of life. We brought the diseases. The alcohol. We committed the murders. We took the children from their mothers. We practised discrimination and exclusion. It was our ignorance and our prejudice.'[9]

The hundreds of orders received from both Aboriginal and non-Aboriginal people for my small reference dictionary of Gamilaraay (Austin 1993), which had to be reprinted three times, surprised me at the time, but were perhaps symptomatic of the changed attitudes, changed level of interest, and a shift away from the ideology of the wider community that Aboriginal languages and cultures were 'doomed' (see McGregor (1993) for the origins and lack of empirical support for the 'Doomed Race' ideology) to an ideology of reconciliation.

Local developments took up support for the language in an educational context. As Giacon (2010: 403) describes:

> In 1996, after consultation with Aboriginal people at the school, a Yuwaalaraay language program began at St Joseph's Primary [in Walgett] … After further community meetings the NSW Department of Education and Training (DET) funded resource production and training as part of setting up a Year 7 GY program at Walgett High School. A language program also began in Goodooga around 1998. The model employed in the school programs included a linguist (myself) with Uncle Ted generally teaching the teachers.

Also in 1998, 'Marianne Betts (a teacher at Walgett High School) and I [John Giacon] prepared a 100-hour high school Gamilaraay-Yuwaalaraay (GY) course, with Marianne designing the programme and going through the time-consuming process of getting Board of Studies approval for the course' (Giacon 2010: 404). The official approval was to teach GY as a Language Other than English (LOTE) and hence as an alternative to the other foreign language courses required of school students in NSW. The status of the indigenous languages had now been changed to that of equivalent to Japanese, Indonesian, or French. The non-Aboriginal ideology that real languages are codified in books was no doubt a driving force that now led to the creation of GY reference materials, including the massive dictionary of Ash et al. (2003); (for a detailed account of its development see Giacon 2010: 405–15).

[8] See <http://en.wikipedia.org/wiki/Mabo_v_Queensland (No_2)> (accessed 9 October 2012).

[9] The full text is at <http://en.wikisource.org/wiki/Redfern_Speech> (accessed 9 October 2012). For a local example of the reconciliation process see Buckhorn (1997).

Giacon (2010: 403) suggests that there was at that time 'a hunger for language among many GY people. Most knew a few words but few knew many. And no-one knew how to put words into sentences and to string sentences together.' This desire to extend their knowledge led to a number of community-based meetings between 1999 and 2001 in Walgett, Moree, Boggabilla, Lightning Ridge, and other centres, and the production of a widely distributed community newsletter entitled *Yaama Maliyaa*, or 'Hello Friend' (also the title of the textbooks by Betts and Giacon (2002) and Giacon and Betts (1999), and the name of a youth group at Walgett Community College that won several national awards in the Young Achievers Australia competition in 2005).[10]

Aboriginal people began expressing their belief that, in the words of Aunty Rose Fernando, Walgett elder and Gamilaraay language rememberer, 'language is our soul'.[11] Lobbying at the state government level led in November 2001 to the NSW Minister for Aboriginal Affairs, Dr Andrew Refshauge, announcing that work had begun on developing a New South Wales Aboriginal languages policy, because 'Aboriginal communities have identified the maintenance of Aboriginal language as a priority for Aboriginal people'.[12] The reasons presented for this by the Minister are a mixture of practical and ideological:

> [A]necdotal evidence from schools currently teaching Aboriginal languages strongly suggests that Aboriginal children learning their language improves their general literacy significantly. Especially for young Aboriginal people, it helps them feel valued for their diversity, it maintains their cultural identity, and it improves their educational achievement.

Local institutionalization of the view that language (and culture) now has a significant role to play in Aboriginal people's lives is seen in documents such as Walgett Gamilaroi Community Working Party (2005: 5), which identifies 'our great culture and heritage, our history, our identity, our kinship and language' as components of 'What makes us happy and proud to be Aboriginal in Walgett'. This document also expresses a wish to have '[o]ur culture: taught in schools, respected and acknowledged, seen as an essential part of the whole community' through '[s]upport and maintenance of traditional languages, art and craft and culture (songs, stories, dances, radio and other media)' (ibid: 18).

Schools were seen as essential loci for language revitalization, and the focus of teaching at this stage was vocabulary (see Giacon 2001; Yuwaalaraay and Gamilaraay Language Program 2002, 2006), reflecting the widespread view of both Aboriginal and non-Aboriginal people that languages are collections of words.

[10] See <http://en.wikipedia.org/wiki/Walgett,_New_South_Wales> (accessed 9 October 2012).

[11] Quoted at <http://www.ourlanguages.net.au/languages/background-information/item/26-importance-of-indigenous-languages-quotes.html>, see also <http://www.alrrc.nsw.gov.au/> (accessed 9 October 2012).

[12] See <http://www.daa.nsw.gov.au/landandculture/statement.html> (accessed 9 October 2012).

Also important were songs, with a number of familiar nursery songs translated from English and professionally produced, recorded, and distributed (Yuwaalaraay and Gamilaraay Language Programme 2003).[13] Songs have been an important vehicle for revitalization elsewhere in Australia (Amery 2004: 83).

In 2004 the supporters of Gamilaraay and Yuwaalaraay received a further boost with the introduction of an Aboriginal Languages course for high school students by the NSW state government. This has given indigenous languages a new status in the eyes both of the Aboriginal and the non-Aboriginal community. The provision of government funds from the Aboriginal and Torres Strait Islander Commission and the federal Department of Communications, Information Technology and the Arts, as well as continuing support from the Catholic Schools Office, has also assisted with materials development. Yuwaalaraay and Gamilaraay Language Programme (2006) is a highly professional picture dictionary for children, and Chandler and Giacon (2006) is a resource book for language teachers and includes a CD-ROM. A website (http://www.yuwaalaraay.org/) was set up in 2008 and includes material on courses, lessons, resources and new words, a picture gallery, and a story collection. This latter collection, called *Guwaabal: Yuwaalaraay and Gamilaraay Stories*, contains 12 traditional narratives read by Giacon. These materials and more, together with a fully interactive version of Ash et al. (2003) and recordings of all the vocabulary and sentence examples in it, were published as Giacon and Nathan (2009). Since 2009, online courses have been available from New England Institute of TAFE Coonabarabran Campus.[14]

Wider political developments have accompanied and supported these local initiatives. The National Indigenous Languages Survey Report was published in 2005.[15] Following this, the Australian Federal Government announced its National Indigenous Languages Policy with a goal 'to coordinate action among the agencies involved in the maintenance and revival of Indigenous languages, including government, Indigenous languages organizations and educational and research institutions'.[16] The MILR (Maintenance of Indigenous Languages and Records) programme was established and provided funding for a range of activities in Gamilaraay and Yuwaalaraay, as shown in Table 6.2 (in 2011 MILR changed its name to ILS (Indigenous Languages Support) programme).

As Table 6.2 shows, activities have been concentrated in schools and sponsored by a limited number of organizations.

[13] Reay (1945) mentions women singing traditional songs during her fieldwork.

[14] See <http://www.youtube.com/watch?v=GIhH_aX3gKo> (accessed 9 October 2012).

[15] See <http://arts.gov.au/sites/default/files/pdfs/nils-report-2005.pdf> (accessed 9 October 2012).

[16] See <http://arts.gov.au/indigenous/languages> (accessed 9 October 2012).

Table 6.2 MILR/ILS funding.

Organization	Topic	2008–9	2009–10	2010–11	2011–12	2012–13
Armidale Roman Catholic Church	Deliver the Yuwaalaraay language programme to young people at St Joseph's Primary and community members in Walgett	$89,929				
	To support the revival of the Gamilaraay-Yuwaalaraay language in Dubbo		$90,000	$70,000		
	To develop online resources to provide access to the *Gayarragi Winangali* languages electronic collection.		$11,000			
Boggabilla Central School	Re-establish a Gamilaraay language programme	$40,600				
Barriekneal Housing and Community	Provide support for teaching Gamilaraay-Yuwaalaraay for all K-6 students at Lightning Ridge Central School	$39,000				
	To deliver a Gamilaraay-Yuwaalaraay language programme for youth		$40,200			
	To conduct community-based Aboriginal language programmes and provide language support services for indigenous communities in the Lightning Ridge region			$30,000	$30,000	$35,000
Dharriwaa Elders Group	Increase the use of the Yuwaalaraay-Gamilaraay languages in the Walgett community	$96,000				
	To develop a language programme to increase use of indigenous languages in Walgett		$90,000			
Murdi Paaki Regional Enterprise Corporation Limited	To develop a committee that will oversee future development and continuation of the Gamilaraay-Yuwaalaraay language			$13,200	$12,000	
	To develop web-based teaching resources and information for Gamilaraay-Yuwaalaraay learning, both for community and higher education study					$15,000
	To provide a series of language awareness and learning activities for the Walgett community					$20,000

6.4 Attitudes, Beliefs, and Ideologies about Revived Language Use

The focus of language teaching and learning in the school programmes has been on the iconic use of language for greetings and talking about family (a version of what Amery (2004) calls 'The Formulaic Method of Language Reclamation', and one that is commonly used in second language learning classes). Thus, one primary school student essay I have seen begins:

> Yaama. Gayrr ngay Barran. Ngay milan banay buligaa. Ngaya wilay-la-nha Walgett-ga. Gulibaa buwadhaa ngay.

We can analyse and translate this as follows:

Yaama.	*gayrrngay*	*Barran*	*Ngay*	*milan*	*banay*	*buligaa*	*Ngaya*
hello	namemy	boomerang	my	near	ten	four	I

wilay-la-nha	*Walgett-ga*	*Gulibaa*	*buwadhaa*	*ngay*
sit-continuous-present	Walgett-locative	three	older.sister	my

> 'Hello. My name is Barran [boomerang]. I am almost 14. I live in Walgett. I have three older sisters.'

Walgett teacher John Brown is quoted as follows on the NSW Aboriginal Board of Education website:[17]

> One of the most positive things for me is the language itself with the students and how they indulge in learning it. It's used in basic everyday activities at the school and outside the school. If I run into one of my students down the street they don't say 'Hello JB' or 'How you going JB'. I'm greeted in the traditional Aboriginal way of it, saying, 'Yaama JB'. And if I say 'Gabagaba nyinda?' they'll say, 'Gaba' back to me. So basically I think that's really great.

Also important are ritual speeches, such as 'Welcome to Country', that are performed at the beginning of significant public events within the region and are increasingly expected to be presented in the local indigenous language (see Couzens and Eira, this volume).[18] These are often memorized as a whole and repeated as set sequences, raising interesting issues of 'fluency' and the extent to which language learners fully comprehend such speeches and can analyse and modify them at will. According to local indigenous community ideology, the ability to perform iconic greetings and speeches does represent fluency, though this runs up against a rather different viewpoint that may be taken by non-Aboriginal language professionals, an issue explored in some detail in Hobson (2010).

[17] See <http://ab-ed.boardofstudies.nsw.edu.au/go/aboriginal-languages/learning/walgett/> (accessed 9 October 2012).

[18] For a Wiradjuri example, see <http://www.youtube.com/watch?v=veTusGR2IM4> (accessed 9 October 2010). See also Amery (2004: 87–9).

Another development, which appears to be relatively recent, is the use of Aboriginal languages in other official contexts, out of the indigenous home country, to display Aboriginal identity and authority to speak about matters relevant to Aboriginal people. Again, the use of a few words or sentences, with less-than-complex syntax, seems to suffice. An example of this occurs in a speech given by Anne Dennis, Councillor for the North West Region of the New South Wales Aboriginal Land Council, at the meeting of the Expert Mechanism on the Rights of Indigenous Peoples in Geneva, 9–13 July 2012.[19] The speech begins:[20]

> Thank you Mr Chair,
>
> Yaama Maliyaa. Anne Dennis ngaya. Gamilaraay ngaya. Australia-dhi ngaya. Nginda ngaya wingangay-lay-nha. Dhaymaarr ngaya wingangay-lay-nha. Guuguu ngaya wingangay-lay-nha.

We can analyse and translate the Gamilaraay material as follows:

Yaama	*maliyaa.*	*Anne Dennis*	*ngaya.*	*Gamilaraay*	*ngaya.*
hello	friend		I		I

Australia-dhi	*ngaya.*	*Nginda*	*ngaya*	*winangay-lay-nha.*
Australia-ablative	I	you	I	listen-continuous-present

Dhaymaarr	*ngaya*	*winangay-lay-nha*
land	I	listen-continuous-present

Guuguu	*ngaya*	*winangay-lay-nha.*
dead relative	I	listen-continuous-present

> 'Hello friend(s). I am Anne Dennis. I am Gamilaraay. I am from Australia. I am showing respect to you (singular) [or possibly you (singular) are showing respect to me?]. I am showing respect to the land. I am showing respect to the ancestors.'[21]

Note that there are some forms here that could be seen as errors in terms of traditional language forms and structures (as recorded in the work by Wurm and Williams, for example). The verb to 'hear, listen' is *winanga-*, not 'winganga' given in the text, and both *nginda* and *ngaya* in the fifth sentence are nominative case forms used for the subject of a sentence.[22] If the speaker intended 'I am showing respect to you' then the Gamilaraay would be *nginunha ngaya winangalanha* and if 'You are showing respect to me' then we would expect

[19] See <http://indigenouspeoplesissues.com/index.php?option=com_content&view=article&id=15675:new-south-wales-statement-on-the-role-of-languages-and-culture-in-the-promotion-and-protection-of-the-rights-and-identity-of-indigenous-peoples-5th-session-emrip&catid=24&Itemid=57> (accessed 10 October 2012).

[20] The translation was provided by John Giacon (personal communication).

[21] In Yuwaalaraay (and possibly Gamilaraay) *guuguu* is a noun used to substitute for the name of a deceased relative to observe a taboo on the mentioning of dead people's names. It appears to be being used here to refer to 'ancestors'.

[22] According to Giacon (personal communication) the verb *winanga-* is now used with the meaning 'show respect' (where it traditionally meant 'to hear, listen').

nginda nganha winangalanha. The parallel structure of the following two sentences suggests that *nginunha ngaya winangalanha* ('I am showing respect to you') was intended, but note that this is second person singular in Gamilaraay—if a plural addressee was intended then the form should be *ngindaaynya*. Interestingly, although the speaker identifies as a Gamilaraay person, she uses the Yuwaalayaay term for 'earth'—in Gamilaraay this is *dhawun*.

One issue that does not seem to have surfaced yet in discussions about the revival of NSW languages is the extent to which people adopt an ideology that the revived language use is meant to reflect 'traditional' language forms (phonology, morphology, syntax, as well as lexicon) or an ideology of 'modernization' and 'adaptation' to changed norms (cf. Couzens and Eira, this volume), especially given that there are no living first language speakers who can serve as models, and the recordings we have from the 1970s show various phonological mergers and grammatical changes (Austin 1986). Reid (2011: 18) notes that:

> contestations over authenticity have been discussed in the language revitalisation literature with respect to Hawai'ian (Wong 1999), Californian languages (Hinton [and Ahlers] 1999), and Maori (Crombie and Houia-Roberts 2001), but have received little discussion in Australia to date.

Recently, Zuckermann and Walsh (2011) have been promoting an adaptation approach modelled on Zuckerman's account of the development and revitalization of modern Israeli Hebrew. It remains to be seen to what extent this adaptationist ideology is accepted by Gamilaraay and Yuwaalaraay revitalization practitioners.

6.5 Insiders and Outsiders

The attitudes of Gamilaraay and Yuwaalaraay people towards 'outsiders' learning their languages are quite open and receptive. Thus, David Nathan found during local consultations in Moree and Boggabilla with Gamilaraay people in 1995, before the public launch of the online Gamilaraay dictionary (Austin and Nathan 1996), that they were keen to see their language represented on the Internet, and thus available for interested users from across the world to access. This is a rather different situation from that reported for some other indigenous groups in Australia. Thus, Amery (2004: 96) writes that for Kaurna of the Adelaide plains, South Australia:

> Kaurna people themselves have been reluctant to post much Kaurna language on the web and have generally disapproved of others doing so. Consequently, course material I have posted is password protected and, theoretically, only available to students of Kaurna and Kaurna people themselves.

The production and distribution of textbooks and CDs of Gamilaraay and Yuwaalaraay through bookstores and the IAD Press means that information on the languages is openly available to all who wish to purchase the materials.

NSW indigenous people and languages are becoming increasingly represented on the Internet and on social media, especially YouTube, with a few short videos in Gamilaraay-Yuwaalaraay, and many more in other NSW languages, such as Wiradjuri. Some of these videos explore the non-linguistic benefits of language study, including increased evaluation of self-worth and self-esteem, and reaffirmation of knowledge acquired within a family context, rather than school (see also King, this volume), expressing positive and affirming messages about language learning and the use of indigenous languages as a badge of group membership. Thus, Karen Flick, community language teacher from Walgett, says the following in a video on the Aboriginal Education Board of Studies website:[23]

> I think every Aboriginal person has got the ability to learn language. You've got it and soon as you just touch on a few words, 'oh yeah but Nan used to say that before' and then you just keep going with it and just try to build your vocab up. Everyone's got it within and it's not that hard to rattle it out and just say it. It's not. And it's only three years since I've had the job and now I'm doing Year 6 classes. Like three weeks with training and plus I had to do my own personal training and three weeks and I'm doing classes.

This has been taken up in the rhetoric of the Australian Federal Government. Thus, the National Indigenous Languages Policy website (http://arts.gov.au/indigenous/languages (accessed 9 October 2012)) refers to: 'the centrality of language to strong Indigenous culture, and the broader social benefits of functional and resilient families and communities'. Several of the chapters in Hobson et al. (2010) also point to perceived non-linguistic benefits of language revitalization, such as increasing children's self-esteem, reducing truancy from school, and improving employment opportunities (see King, this volume); however, Thieberger (2012: 129) is quite sceptical and notes that '[t]hese claims may be true, but no evidence is supplied to substantiate them'.

A recent development has been the extension of teaching GY into university-level courses, and the involvement of students who have no personal connection with the languages or the local area. In January 2007, John Giacon taught a Gamilaraay summer school at the University of Sydney that was attended by 15 students from throughout the metropolitan area. This has been followed by units like KOCR2605 Speaking Gamilaraay 1, offered through the University's Koori

[23] See <http://ab-ed.boardofstudies.nsw.edu.au/go/aboriginal-languages> (accessed 9 October 2012). Notice that Flick is here highlighting her belief about 'the ability to learn language'. Some indigenous groups take an ideological (and political) position that their languages are 'sleeping' rather than 'extinct', and can be 'woken up' by revitalization.

Studies Centre.[24] The language has thus moved well beyond its homeland to be embraced by interested Aboriginal and non-Aboriginal people more broadly.

6.6 Conclusions

The situation of Gamilaraay and Yuwaalaraay presents some interesting historical and contemporary data about beliefs and ideologies of language endangerment and revitalization in northern NSW, and eastern Australia more generally. Firstly, as for the case of Kaurna in South Australia (Amery 2004), we find an example of virtually extinct languages being revived as one expression of Aboriginal identity at both local and state government levels. This case also shows there is an essential role for good language documentation in order to provide resources and a framework for revitalization. It further demonstrates the need for clear goals and functions for the indigenous language, and clear politics and ideology: in this case the iconic use of language to express cultural identity and distinctiveness, within a politics of resistance and reconciliation. Actual use of language is for talk about family and domestic situations and for symbolic speeches. We have also seen the need for both local grass-roots community-based activity alongside government recognition and support (and consequently resources), and the leading role taken by schoolteachers, especially indigenous teachers. This case study also emphasizes the importance of collaboration between linguists, teachers, information-technology professionals, indigenous specialists, and local custodians of knowledge to lead to concrete outcomes, including outcomes that are non-linguistic and relate rather to perceived improvements in social well-being.

References

Amery, Rob. 2004. Kaurna language reclamation and the formulaic method. In Wesley Y. Leonard and Stelómethet Ethel B. Gardner (eds.), *Language is Life: Proceedings of the 11th Annual Stabilizing Indigenous Languages Conference*. Berkeley: University of California <http://linguistics.berkeley.edu/~survey/documents/survey-reports/survey-report-14.08-amery.pdf> (accessed 9 October 2012).

Ash, Anna, John Giacon, and Amanda Lissarrague. 2003. *Gamilaraay, Yuwaalaraay and Yuwaalayaay Dictionary.* Alice Springs: IAD Press.

Austin, Peter. 1986. Structural change in language obsolescence: some eastern Australian examples. *Australian Journal of Linguistics* 6: 201–30.

Austin, Peter. 1992. *A Dictionary of Gamilaraay, Northern New South Wales*. Melbourne: La Trobe University.

[24] See <http://sydney.edu.au/koori/studying/aborig_studies.shtml> (accessed 9 October 2012).

Austin, Peter. 1993. *A Reference Dictionary of Gamilaraay, Northern New South Wales*. Melbourne: La Trobe University.

Austin, Peter. 1997. Proto-central New South Wales. In Darrel Tryon and Michael Walsh (eds.), *Boundary Rider: Essays in Honour of Geoffrey O'Grady*. Canberra: Pacific Linguistics C-136.

Austin, Peter. 2008. The Gamilaraay (Kamilaroi) language, northern New South Wales: a brief history of research. In William McGregor (ed.), *Encountering Aboriginal Languages: Studies in the History of Australian Linguistics*. Canberra: Pacific Linguistics.

Austin, Peter and David Nathan. 1996. *Kamilaroi/Gamilaraay Web Dictionary*. <http://coombs.anu.edu/WWWVLPages/AborigPages/LANG/GAMDICT/GAMDICT.HTM> (accessed 8 October 2012).

Austin, Peter and Norman B. Tindale. 1986. Emu and brolga, a Kamilaroi myth. *Aboriginal History* 9: 8–21.

Austin, Peter, Corinne Williams, and Stephen A. Wurm. 1980. The linguistic situation in north-central New South Wales. In Bruce Rigsby and Peter Sutton (eds.), *Papers in Australian Linguistics No. 13*. Canberra: Pacific Linguistics.

Betts, Marianne and John Giacon. 2002. *Yaama Maliyaa*. Tamworth: Narnia Bookstore.

Buckhorn, Richard. 1997. *Boobera Lagoon: A Focus for Reconciliation*. Sydney: Australian Catholic Social Justice Council.

Chandler, Karan and John Giacon. 2006. *Dhiirrala Gamilaraay! Teach Gamilaraay! A Resource Book for Teachers of Gamilaraay*. Armidale: Catholic Schools Office.

Clark, Ian D. 2005. *Aboriginal Language Areas in Victoria: A Reconstruction*. Report to the Victorian Aboriginal Corporation for Languages, 25 August 2005.

Crombie, W. and N. Houia-Roberts. 2001. The rhetorical organisation of discourse: language revitalisation and the question of authenticity. *Journal of Maori and Pacific Development* 2: 57–73.

Giacon, Gianbattista (John). 2001. Creating new words in Gamilaraay and Yuwaalaraay. BA Honours thesis, School of Languages, Cultures and Linguistics, University of New England.

Giacon, John. 2010. The development of the Gamilaraay, Yuwaalaraay and Yuwaalayaay Dictionary. In John Hobson, Kevin Lowe, Susan Poetsch, and Michael Walsh (eds.), *Re-awakening Languages: Theory and Practice in the Revitalisation of Australia's Indigenous Languages*. Sydney: Sydney University Press.

Giacon, John and Marianne Betts. 1999. *Yaama Maliyaa, Yuwaalaraay–Gamilaraay: An Aboriginal Languages Textbook*. Walgett, NSW: Walgett High School, Yuwaalaraay Gamilaraay Program.

Giacon, John and David Nathan. 2009. *Gayarragi Winangali: Find and Hear*. CD-ROM. Armidale: Catholic Schools Office. <http://www.yuwaalaraay.org/> (accessed 1 October 2013).

Hinton, Leanne and Jocelyn Ahlers. 1999. The issue of 'authenticity' in California language restoration. *Anthropology and Education Quarterly* 30: 56–67.

Hobson, John. 2010. Questions of fluency in Australian languages revitalisation. In John Hobson, Kevin Lowe, Susan Poetsch, and Michael Walsh (eds.), *Re-awakening Languages: Theory and Practice in the Revitalisation of Australia's Indigenous Languages*. Sydney: Sydney University Press.

Hobson, John, Kevin Lowe, Susan Poetsch, and Michael Walsh (eds.). 2010. *Re-awakening Languages: Theory and Practice in the Revitalisation of Australia's Indigenous Languages*. Sydney: Sydney University Press.

Lowe, Kevin and Michael Walsh. 2004. California down under: indigenous language revitalisation in New South Wales, Australia. In Wesley Y. Leonard and Stelómethet Ethel B. Gardner (eds.), *Language is Life: Proceedings of the 11th Annual Stabilizing Indigenous Languages Conference, Survey Report 14*. Berkeley, CA: Survey of California and Other Indian Languages. <http://linguistics.berkeley.edu/~survey/resources/publications.php> (accessed 8 October 2012).

McGregor, Russell. 1993. The Doomed Race: a scientific axiom of the late nineteenth century. *The Australian Journal of Politics and History* 39: 14–22.

O'Rourke, Michael. 2009. The colonial discovery and occupation of east-central New South Wales, 1817–26—Oxley, Howe, Lawson and Cunningham—Mudgee, Merriwa, and Muswellbrook. Canberra. MS. <http://www.mudgeehistory.com.au/earlysettlement/passages_p1.html> (accessed 10 October 2012).

Reay, Marie. 1945. A half-caste Aboriginal community in north-western New South Wales. *Oceania* 15: 296–323.

Reid, Nick. 2011. The phonology of reawakened Aboriginal languages: issues in pronunciation and authenticity in language revival in Australia. Paper presented at CUNY phonology forum. <http://www.cunyphonologyforum.net/ENDANPAPERS/Reid.pdf> (accessed 10 October 2012).

Thieberger, Nick. 2012. Review of Hobson et al. 2010. *Australian Review of Applied Linguistics* 35: 128–31.

Wafer, Jim and Amanda Lissarrague. 2008. *A Handbook of Aboriginal Languages of New South Wales and the Australian Capital Territory*. Nambucca Heads: Muurrbay Aboriginal Language and Culture Co-operative.

Walgett Gamilaroi Community Working Party. 2005. *A Unified Community Working Together Creating a Great Future*. Walgett Gamilaroi Community Working Party Community Development and Strategic Plan 2004–2007. MS. <http://www.mpra.com.au/Action%20Plans/Walgett.pdf> (accessed 9 October 2012).

Walsh, Michael. 2003. Raising Babel: language revitalisation in NSW, Australia. In Joe Blythe and R. McKenna Brown (eds.), *Maintaining the Links: Language, Identity and the Land*. Proceedings of the Seventh Conference Presented by the Foundation for Endangered Languages. Bath: Foundation for Endangered Languages.

Williams, Corinne. 1980. *A Grammar of Yuwaalaraay*. Canberra: Pacific Linguistics.

Wong, Kerry L. 1999. Authenticity and the revitalisation of Hawaiian. *Anthropology and Education Quarterly* 30: 205–22.

Yuwaalaraay and Gamilaraay Language Programme. 2002. *Gamilaraay, Yuwaalaraay, Guwaaldanha Ngiyani: We Are Speaking Gamilaraay and Yuwaalaraay*. Tamworth, NSW: Coolabah Publishing.

Yuwaalaraay and Gamilaraay Language Programme. 2003. *Yugal: Gamilaraay and Yuwaalaraay Songs*. Tamworth, NSW: Coolabah Publishing.

Yuwaalaraay and Gamilaraay Language Programme. 2006. *Gaay Garay Dhadhin Gamilaraay and Yuwaalaraay Picture Dictionary*. Alice Springs: IAD Press.

Zuckermann, Ghil'ad and Michael Walsh. 2011. Stop, revive, survive! Lessons from the Hebrew revival applicable to the reclamation, maintenance and empowerment of Aboriginal languages and cultures. *Australian Journal of Linguistics* 31: 111–27.

7

Language Shift in an 'Importing Culture': The Cultural Logic of the Arapesh Roads*

LISE M. DOBRIN

> Papua New Guineans regarded their local languages as the main symbol of their local identities, which they held very dear.
>
> Stephen Wurm (2003: 26)

> There is ... a tacit acceptance of the 'one language = one culture' assumption, and a concentration on phenomena internal to the language or culture in question, with a consequent neglect, even underrating, of boundary problems of all sorts.
>
> Gillian Sankoff (1980a: 118)

7.1 Introduction: The Ethnic Revitalization Paradox

IN THIS CHAPTER I attempt to wrestle in an ethnographic way with a problem that is familiar to those concerned with endangered languages. One apt label for this problem in the literature is the 'Ethnic Revitalization Paradox', a term that was coined by Rindstedt and Aronsson (2002) to describe the disconnect these authors found between the way people speak *about* their languages on the one hand, and the way they actually *use* them on the other.[1] In the Quichua-Spanish bilingual community of the Ecuadorean Andes where Rindstedt and Aronsson worked, they found heightened ethnic consciousness, public advocacy for Quichua, and strongly positive mother-tongue ideology and rhetoric: 'I speak

* The arguments in this chapter were first presented at the *Sociolinguistics of Language Endangerment* workshop organized by David Bradley with funding from the Comité International Permanent de Linguistes in Boulder, Colorado, in July 2011. I am grateful to audiences there and at a University of Virginia Linguistic Anthropology Seminar presentation in Charlottesville, Virginia, in September 2012, for helpful questions and suggestions. I would also like to thank Peter K. Austin, Ira Bashkow, Ellen Contini-Morava, Eve Danziger, Jeff Good, Pierpaolo di Carlo, Don Kulick, Julia Sallabank, Saul Schwartz, Amanda Sweeny, Timothy Sonin, and my many friends on the Arapesh Facebook group for their feedback, assistance, and advice.

[1] A similar but somewhat more general concept used by Barbra Meek (2010: x) in her study of Kaska revitalization efforts is *disjuncture*, 'the everyday points of discontinuity and contradiction—between social or linguistic groups, within discourses, practices, or between them, even between indexical orders—that interrupt the flow of action, communication or thought'.

Quichua, I don't want to lose my Indian culture ... without [our maternal language] we are nothing' (Rindstedt and Aronsson 2002: 724–5). At the same time, however, the authors report that they would never have guessed this if all they had to consider were community linguistic practices, which included near universal bilingualism and thoroughgoing Hispanicization of Quichua, resulting in a classic pattern of three-generation language shift leading to language loss.

The Ecuadorean example is not the only one that could be given in which people seem to be voting with their feet against languages they nevertheless say they value (see, e.g., Dauenhauer and Dauenhauer 1998; Dobrin 2008; Kulick 1992; Perley 2011). Even when would-be speakers express regret about the language loss they notice taking place around them, this sentiment may coexist with a contradictory desire for development, a sense of shame or cultural inferiority, or a belief that language shift is inevitable and so not worth devoting limited energies to trying to overcome. In such cases, whatever value the traditional language might have as an anchor for ethnolinguistic identity is evidently not sufficient to override these attitudes and motivate people to maintain or reclaim it. We might interpret the paradox as indicative of the overwhelming power of a coercive world socio-economic system: it hardly matters what language people prefer to speak; what choice do they have but to adopt another language if they are to succeed in the wider society (Nettle and Romaine 2000)? Undoubtedly, to some extent this is true. But we might also seek insight into the *cultural models* people use to attribute significance to the languages in their local repertoires, and how exactly language use contributes to their sense of who they are. Here, following my conviction that we stand to learn more, including more that activists will find useful, about language shift from exploring matters of culture than we will from analyses of utility (Dobrin 2010), I aim to illustrate how *the ideological stances that bear on language may be grounded in implicit cultural assumptions that are not necessarily focused on language as such, but instead on more fundamental notions about how the social world works*. These include what makes a person or community good (Kulick 2002), what it means to exercise power (Dobrin 2008), beliefs about the lifespan such as how children learn (Paugh 2011) or appropriate comportment towards those in old age (Meek 2007), ideas about the nature of change, and so on. In other words, endangered language linguistics should concern itself not only with language ideologies, but with the full range of cultural ideas that may lead people who value their languages to nevertheless act in ways that diminish their use.[2] Because these ideas will vary dramatically from one local context to another, they cannot be addressed in the abstract; instead, they require detailed ethnographic exploration by observing what people actually say and do in the course

[2] See also Fishman (2002) and Spolsky (this volume) on linguists' overemphasis on language in addressing the problem of language shift.

of their daily lives. Clearly, there are larger patterns and commonalities to be found at the level of political economy, educational policy, colonial history, and so on. But as Sicoli (2011: 163–4) argues in trying to explain the different patterns of language shift from Zapotec to Spanish that he observed in Oaxaca, Mexico, a 'typology of language shift that we can apply across cultures does not exist ... [I]t is only through dedicated, long-term ethnographic work in and with particular speech communities that a maintenance effort can be designed to fit a specific situation.' The challenge is to understand what members of a given linguistic community think they are trying to do; what it feels like to be who they are, such that language shift follows.

7.2 Arapesh Language and Social Identity

In the rural Sepik region of New Guinea where the Papuan (Torricelli family) Arapesh languages are spoken, the revitalization paradox takes a somewhat muted, and locally distinctive, form. Language-related projects like vernacular schooling, Bible translation, and language documentation are generally welcomed by communities. I say 'welcomed' because these activities tend to be initiated or at least heavily facilitated by outsiders, such as educators, scholars, activists, and missionaries. A discourse promoting vernacular language vitality has little resonance as one moves out from urban middle class and educational policy circles and into rural areas, where local people are more concerned with the going price for their cash crops, rumours of sorcery, church politics, and pending development schemes than they are with planning for their cultural and linguistic continuity. It is difficult to interpret direct evaluative comments made by Melanesian villagers, who do not live in an 'interview society' like Westerners do (Atkinson and Silverman 1997; Briggs 2007), and who are culturally predisposed to seek common ground with their interlocutors while being culturally indisposed to place stock in verbal expressions of their inner states.[3] But when the question of how Arapesh people feel about their languages does arise, the answer is almost always positive. It is not unlike what Reiman (2010: 255) reports for the Kasanga people he worked with in West Africa: 'when told that their language and culture are valuable and worthwhile,' he says, they 'agree and appreciate it'. As Gray et al. (2008: 86) put it, in summarizing the results of their recent language survey in the Western Arapesh region, 'people stated positive attitudes towards the vernacular and asked for help in preserving their language, yet do not use the vernacular to speak to their children'.

[3] A 'doctrine of "the opacity of other minds"', a belief that one cannot know what other people are thinking, has been repeatedly noted in the literature on Pacific societies (Robbins and Rumsey 2008: 408).

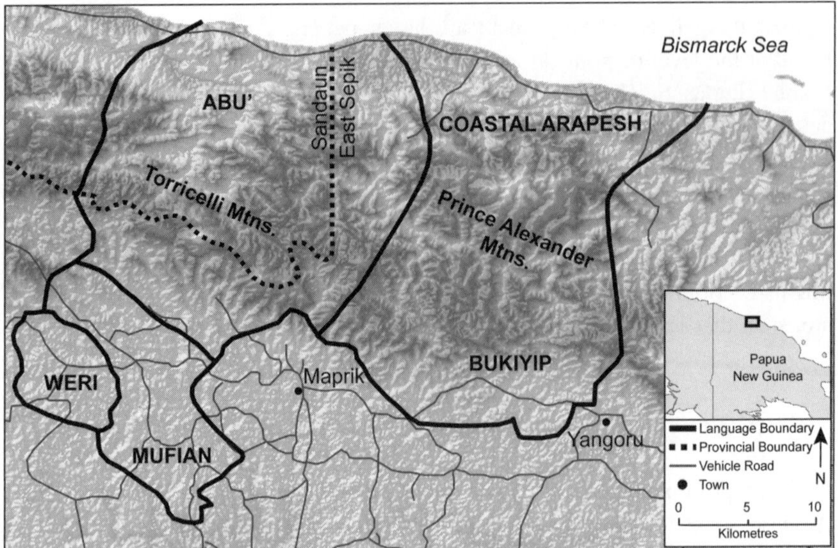

Figure 7.1 The Arapesh language area.

Like Papua New Guineans in other areas of the country, the Arapesh villagers I lived with on the Sepik 'West Coast' (see Figure 7.1) insisted that their traditional way of speaking was the correct or 'straight' way, in contrast to neighbouring villages where people are said to 'twist' their talk along the local dialect/language continuum, eventually to the point of incomprehensibility as one advances across the social landscape.

Although the Gapun villagers Kulick discusses in his seminal study of Sepik language shift view their language, Taiap, as difficult compared to neighbouring languages, they also describe it as 'sweet', deeply rooted, and richly expressive (Kulick 1992: 7). They like their vernacular speech, associate it with themselves and their lands, and wish their children would learn it. And yet, as in Gapun, in the coastal Arapesh villages the shift to Papua New Guinea's creole lingua franca, Tok Pisin, is well advanced, despite the fact that this has very little functional motivation and brings them little benefit.[4] There is nobody in any rural Arapesh community today who does not speak fluent Tok Pisin, and virtually all have learned it as a first language. In Apakibur village near the north-eastern boundary of the Arapesh language area, multiple attempts were made to establish a village-based vernacular (*tok ples*) preschool to revitalize the use of Arapesh, but as I have discussed elsewhere, because the school did not serve other important community needs, the efforts repeatedly failed (Dobrin 2008).[5]

[4] For an overview of the social history of Tok Pisin, see Romaine (1992).

[5] Apakibur children now attend a preschool adjoining the nearby community school. But because it integrates students from villages with different traditional languages, it operates exclusively in Tok

It has often been claimed that the spectacular linguistic diversity we find in New Guinea is a product of language difference being actively 'perpetuated as a badge of identification' and a 'form of deliberate boundary marking' (Laycock 1982: 34; Mühlhäusler 1996: 47). Indeed, the New Guinea area provides some of the clearest cases that have been made for esoterogeny, that is, languages in contact not converging but diverging because speakers actively exaggerate their differences (see, e.g., Salisbury 1962; Thurston 1987, 1989). But while this might be taken to suggest that people are mapping language onto cultural identity along similar lines to the Quichua case (i.e. viewing their traditional languages as markers of social group belonging), I believe it would be wrong to read it this way for the Arapesh situation, for at least three reasons.

First, repeatedly in this area of the world we find that high-level group boundaries fail to coincide with linguistic ones. In the Arapesh area there was never any basis for people to assume that they would share the most important features of their social identity with fellow speakers. Before pacification in the 1910s, Arapesh villagers in this region regularly joined forces with speakers of the genealogically distinct (Ndu family) Boikin language to their east, in defence against other Arapesh speakers, while fearing sorcery attacks by speakers of Bukiyip, a mutually intelligible Arapesh variety, farther inland. These historical patterns of alliance and conflict continue to influence people's feelings about local linguistic differences today. When the Arapesh New Testament was dedicated in 2004, Apakibur villagers were delighted to accept (indeed purchase) the books, to the extent that Western individuals and institutions were implicated in their production. That is, the value of these objects lay in their having been produced for them by caring outsiders concerned for the villagers' welfare. However, the villagers are disinclined to actually read them because lexical and orthographic elements they contain mark them as deriving from their former enemies, people they still see today as competitors.[6] Since the 1960s a wider Arapesh identity has emerged, in part as a byproduct of regional political events that transpired after the Second World War (discussed below). But this new Arapesh identity is still not so much linguistically or even socially motivated as it is *geographically* motivated, incorporating those communities on the northern side of the Torricelli watershed east of the province boundary, that share a common vehicle road. So traditionally, the identity indexed by 'one's own language' did not really extend beyond the sovereign political unit (the clan, hamlet, or village), always highly local, simultaneously kin- and residence-based groupings. Working with Yopno people in Morobe Province, Papua New Guinea,

Pisin and English. Its aim, to give village children a head start and improve their outcomes in formal schooling, therefore differs from that of the original Apakibur preschool, which villagers viewed as a space in which children would also return to speaking their vernacular language.

[6] The competing villages were affiliated with the two different 'roads' discussed below.

Slotta (2012: 5) describes this way of interpreting local linguistic diversity as 'socio-geographic provenance', a term that fits the Arapesh situation well.

Second, it is not at all clear that our analytic category of 'languages'—sets of linguistic features bundled up into distinct codes—is also the operative emic one for the communities in question. Consciousness of such units does not seem to be very well developed in Melanesia, where, as Mühlhäusler (1996: 35ff) points out:

> [t]he concept of a 'language', together with the metalinguistic labels for 'language', 'dialect' and similar entities are conspicuous by their absence. Language was not a self-contained object of inspection ... The difficulties of distinguishing between languages, dialects, communalects and such phenomena encountered by present-day linguists ... do not so much reflect their inability to find these 'objects' as their non-existence.

Linguistic differences are vigorously attended to, but distinct language varieties are more often identified simply by the name of the locality or kin group, a phrase that translates as 'our talk', or in other cases by contrasting sets of some emblematic form, such as the word for 'no' in the Torricelli area (*olo*, *one*, *au*, *weri*, etc.; see, e.g., Laycock 1975).[7] In fact, the label 'Arapesh' was coined by the anthropologists Fortune and Mead in the 1930s to fill just this gap:

> The Arapesh have no word in their language indicating their entire tribe or their entire country. The word *arapeʃ* means simply friends, and it is their word for their more distant personal connections. This word has been coined in the written form Arapesh in order to name their tribe, country, language, and culture. (Fortune 1939: 23)

Arapesh people apply the same term, *boraɲ*, equally to what a linguist would call 'the language' and to individual acts of speaking, raising questions about the cultural traction of whole languages construed as autonomous entities along the lines of Saussurean *langue*. In his forthcoming grammar of Taiap, now labelled 'Tayap Mer', Kulick argues that the idea of language as a shared system has little purchase in Gapun, where each speaker acts as if they own their own proprietary version of the language, dismissing all others as incorrect. He believes this has implications for language shift, since older speakers can each still have *their* Tayap irrespective of what the young people do. Here again, we find that a universe of discrete languages modelled according to the 'Herderian equation' that maps language and culture onto peoplehood (*Volk*) in Western language ideology, is not a structuring framework for traditional Melanesian social identities (Foley 2005; see also Silverstein 1996).

[7] This is, of course, not unique to Melanesia. The indigenous name for Welsh is *Cymru* 'comrades', in contrast to the English, who are called *saesnag* 'foreigners'. And languages in eastern Australia were named for the word for 'no', as Austin (this volume) notes.

Third, and most importantly, as Sankoff (1980b: 19) long ago noted:

> Over much of Papua New Guinea, though people had a great deal of pride in, and derived some of their identity from, their own local speech variety, often exaggerating its differences from the speech of their neighbors, this went hand-in-hand with an openness of attitude and an interest in the learning of other speech varieties.

This 'openness of attitude' is a more general cultural characteristic found all over New Guinea, and is what I want to consider in more detail in the remainder of this chapter, because I believe it is critical for understanding the role language plays in the construction of identity in this part of the world.[8] In brief, what I want to demonstrate is that the Arapesh appropriation of Tok Pisin follows an indigenous cultural logic that assigns value to, and works to attract, items and activities associated with cultural others. To that extent, although Arapesh language shift follows a familiar pattern in the sociolinguistic qualities it ultimately exhibits (disrupted intergenerational transmission, contraction of domains, frequent code switching, etc.), the phenomenon cannot be fully understood by viewing it as just one more case of 'politically dominant languages ... overwhelm[ing] indigenous and local languages and cultures' (Hale 1992: 1). It must also be understood as the result of culturally particular, ideologically motivated, agentive action on the part of the language's former speakers (see also Sicoli 2011).

7.3 Language in an Importing Culture

What Sankoff (1980b) is describing in her reference to Papua New Guineans' 'openness of attitude' is how mastery over other people's ways of speaking was never just a functional requirement for communication in the light of New Guinea's rightly renowned linguistic diversity, but a culturally elaborated method of enhancing an individual's social status: political power at the regional and village level has always been associated with multilingual skills. In order to facilitate trade relationships, the exchange of women, and war alliances, young men would be sent away to live in allied communities for a few years or be initiated into other groups' men's cults specifically to strengthen the relationship and gain fluency in the others' language (von Schlesier 1961). One manifestation of this assignment of value to foreign speech is the phenomenon of 'gratuitous translation', repeating oneself in another language, for a number of different

[8] For an argument that 'openness of attitude' has exerted an influence on linguistic structure, see Foley (2005). Evidence comes from the New Guinea Middle Sepik, where the ceremonial vocabulary is replete with foreign elements, and where the regional trade languages display morphosyntactic patterns that cannot be found in the local linguistic repertoire but instead seem to be modelled on languages spoken at a great social and geographic distance.

symbolic purposes, all of which mark the speaker as sophisticated and in control of both the situation at hand and the wider social scene, amounting to a claim that 'this speech is worth listening to' (Salisbury 1962). Historically, the second language used to serve this emphatic function would be that of a neighbouring community. Now it is often (or always) Tok Pisin (Kulick 1992: 75ff).

Similarly, in New Guinea and the surrounding islands it is common to find that a community's most highly prized oral texts, such as the powerful spells that make yams grow and traditional song/dance complexes (known in Tok Pisin as *singsing*s), are not in the local vernacular but in another language, not necessarily one that even the speakers understand. For example, although Kilivila speakers of the Trobriand Islands can generally recognize and label instances of their sung ritual register *biga baloma*, honouring the spirits of the dead, the forms used in this register are so unfamiliar (they are presumably archaic) that only those individuals highest in status know what they mean; the same goes for many Kilivila magical formulae, 'the meanings of which are completely unknown even to the magicians themselves' (Senft 2010: 81). As Malinowski (1978 [1935]: 221–2) explains, a 'coefficient of weirdness, strangeness and unusualness' is part of what gives such speech its power. The words of all but one or two of the traditional *singsing*s Apakibur villagers still know how to perform are indecipherable to anyone in the community, and as far as they know it has always been that way. Arapesh people account for this by saying matter-of-factly that the *singsing*s 'come from Madang', an area some 300 kilometres to the east, that can be compared to New York or Paris, in that they were the centres of the Arapesh fashion world. Arapesh villagers never went there themselves, but when they heard reports of the latest innovations taking place in the region they sought to activate their social networks to access and enjoy those innovations too (Mead 1935, 1937, 1938). The best-documented example we have of such an importation is a *singsing* that originated in the Murik Lakes region near the mouth of the Sepik River, and then made its way over a period of years during the early colonial period along the coast and up into the Torricelli foothills via local maritime trade circuits.[9] The incomprehensibility of all these highly valued speech forms is not (or not only) a consequence of specialized knowledge loss or top-down language shift. It is a stable cultural orientation that specifically draws value from the marking of some cultural element as distant, old, or foreign.

Summing up the argument to this point, a person's 'native language' traditionally contributed to the construction of Arapesh local identity in a place-based way, in that expectations about the way individuals should speak were tied to the kin-based group from which they hailed. Yet at the same time, the command of speech variation helped create a person's ethnolinguistic

[9] Photographic images documenting the transaction can be accessed at <http://www.arapesh.org/image_gallery.php?set=aa_01>.

identity, in that control of foreign varieties was an index of an individual's social reach, and hence influence and power.

7.4 Importation and Identity

In order to understand the cultural logic driving New Guinea people's openness to foreign features, linguistic and otherwise, it is necessary to appreciate how the Melanesian construction of group identity is derived from notions of property and personhood. And to do this, it will be helpful to make explicit the quite different logic by which these notions are implicated in the construction of identity familiar in the West. It is common to say that Western societies are 'individualistic' in their conception of the person, but linguists do not always appreciate the degree to which this conception underpins the Herderian language–culture–nation equation so central to Western language ideology. I should emphasize that the ideas presented here are not my own; they draw heavily from other anthropologists, especially Simon Harrison, whose thinking is shaped in part by fieldwork among Manambu speakers on the Middle Sepik, and whose writings on the relativity of cultural identity I find particularly insightful and extensible to issues of language (Harrison 2006).

In his influential anthropological study of identity and nationalism in Quebec, Handler (1988: 15–16) argues that modern group identities are ideological projections of the basic unit of the Western social universe, the *possessive individual*: 'The nation or ethnic group is taken to be bounded, continuous, and precisely distinguishable from other analogous entities. Moreover, from this perspective, what distinguishes each nation or ethnic group is its culture, which provides the "content" of group identity and individuality.' Thus, autonomous social groups are conceived of as bounded and unique person-like entities that seem to own or possess cultural 'things', their patrimony, that are primordially theirs. As Harrison (2006: 84) emphasizes: 'the most fundamental imperative of a nation or ethnic group is to define for itself a "culture", a body of "authentic" custom ... a patrimony capable of being encroached upon, appropriated, adulterated, defended, conserved', lost, and so on. This cultural logic, which defines group identity in terms of proprietary possessions originating within the group itself, leads naturally to an emphasis on groups as separate and independent from one another, while drawing attention away from the ways in which groups interrelate.

But traditional Melanesian culture assumes a very different mapping of persons on to cultural property, with very different implications for the way group identity is constructed. In the ethnographic literature on Melanesia, a key concept is that of *relational personhood*: the way persons are idealized less as autonomous individuals than as the intersection of others to whom they are connected (Robbins 2004). This idealization can perhaps be seen most clearly in the cultural practices set into motion at the end of life, when Papua New Guineans create their own analytic model of the person by decomposing the deceased back into their constituent relations as a way of marking the end of their productive social existence. Arapesh mortuary rituals illustrate this nicely. They consist of a series of food and money distributions that return something of value along each of the important lines of relationship out of which the deceased person was formed, most importantly the person's mother's brothers or mother's brothers' sons, hence repaying the debt of 'blood' inherited from the maternal line (Mead 1940: 430–2).

As a result of this understanding of what persons are, what is traditionally valued in both sociality and economy has less to do with one's possessions, an accumulation of enduring wealth, than on circulation and exchange, especially what one has demonstrably attracted away from others. This orientation has implications for Melanesian ideas about collectivities, which emphasize borrowings and importations because these index the relationships or social pathways through which they were acquired. Intangible cultural practices like magic and ritual, artistic styles, festival complexes, and other ways of speaking were traditionally valued as a form of cultural property not because they originated inside a community and were therefore the community's own, but because they were appropriated from others elsewhere. As Harrison puts it, groups would strive not to possess their 'own unique culture, but rather their own unique combination of elements from other cultures' (Harrison 2006: 70).

Kulick's (1992) ethnography of language shift in the Sepik village of Gapun analyses the assimilation of Tok Pisin into the villagers' linguistic repertoire as reflecting a radical reconceptualization of their sense of personhood, with Tok Pisin and Taiap mapped onto a series of new social oppositions that came about in the course of their colonial encompassment: modern versus jungle savages, Christian versus pagan, educated versus ignorant. But the root opposition Kulick posits is between the indigenous moral notions of *hed*, a selfish insistence on personal autonomy, and *save*, a desirable quality of social awareness and cooperation with others. Note the way this local distinction morally reverses the two types of identity construction just described above: the Western one in which value derives from what is produced and owned by the self, and the Melanesian one in which value derives from the effective pursuit of social relations. While I have never heard Arapesh villagers discursively elaborate a *hed–save* opposition in quite the way Gapuners do, there is no doubt about the overall appropriateness of Kulick's analysis for the Arapesh situation; indeed, I find reading his ethnography to be oddly eerie, almost like meeting a group of strangers who all speak another language in the voices of your friends. Contemporary Arapesh villagers, too, use Tok Pisin to symbolically incorporate qualities they associate with people of another kind.

But there is one way in which I believe Arapesh ethnography can shed additional light on the phenomenon of Sepik language shift, and that is by deepening our understanding of the traditional mechanisms that give the drive to embody *save* in its characteristic shape. In the chapter of his book that focuses on Christianity, entitled 'Preparing to change', Kulick (1992) makes repeated reference to the notion of a 'road' as the pathway for social improvement and transformation:

> Christianity is the 'road' (rot) that will lead to the metamorphosis they all anxiously await. (Kulick 1992: 163)
>
> Gapuners actively and creatively attempt to exploit the links they perceive between the written word, Christianity, and cargo in order to bypass the priests and find their own 'road' to the millennium. (Kulick 1992: 171)
>
> [A]mbitious young men ... spend much time trying to find the 'forms' and the addresses to mysterious places in America that they have heard will open a 'road' to the cargo. (Kulick 1992: 180)
>
> [S]chool is a 'road' preparing their children for another way of life. (Kulick 1992: 180)
>
> Each innovation seen as having its source in the outside world of school, church, or 'the countries' is viewed as a significant step further along the 'road' to the final transformation. (Kulick 1992: 186)

While we might interpret these repeated references to roads as metaphorical, they are not merely abstractions. Roads had, and continue to have, a real institutionalized existence all over New Guinea, and although they are organized somewhat differently from place to place, we can see what gives the metaphor meaning when we know how they operate in their more concrete form. The functioning of roads in Arapesh culture described below draws upon my own fieldwork with Ira Bashkow along the roads of today (Dobrin and Bashkow 2006 provides a detailed analysis), as well as on published and unpublished writings by Mead and Fortune, who did ethnographic and linguistic research among the Arapesh in the early 1930s when the traditional road network was just beginning to break down.

Before pacification in the early 1900s, Arapesh people did not travel around freely and thus come into contact with just anyone. Instead, wherever they went they followed particular roads. These were both real physical footpaths between localities, and more abstract conduits for social interaction and exchange (see Figure 7.2 and Figure 7.3).

In addition, individual Arapesh had 'road-friends' or 'road-men', inherited relationships with others in neighbouring localities. The names for these were essentially reciprocal gender-marked kin terms (road-friends were always male); so a man would have his *gəbɨkin*, while being the other's *kworiain*. These hereditary friendships were understood to be the product of risk and effort on the part of one's forefathers, and the roads they created had to be actively kept open or maintained. At the level of whole localities, roads represented stable alliances

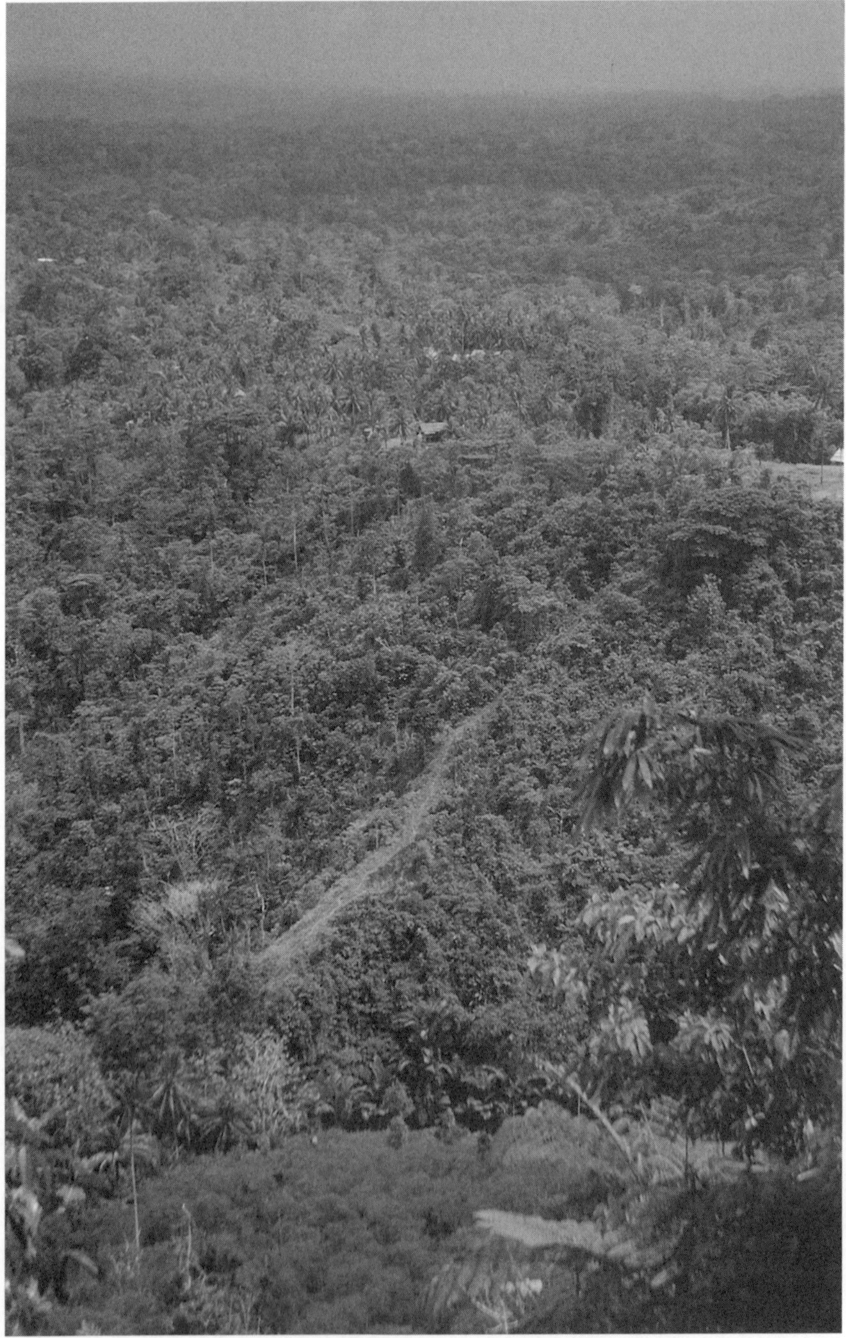

Figure 7.2 A ridgetop road in the Prince Alexander Mountains.

Figure 7.3 An Arapesh woman following a bush road to her garden.

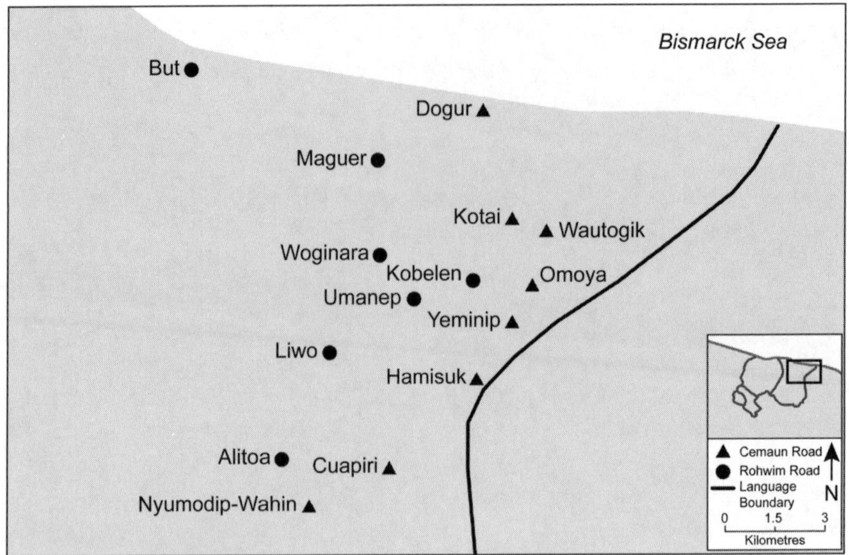

Figure 7.4 The Cemaun and Rohwim roads.

that allowed for safe passage, so that travellers would not have to fear ambush whenever they stepped off their own lands. The relationships they defined helped create confederacies that individuals called upon to support their efforts in feasting and warfare, and they set up very specific local channels for inter-community exchange.

In the eastern Arapesh region there were two major roads: the Rohwim and the Cemaun (see Figure 7.4 for a schematic diagram). These ran from the coast in the north up into the mountains separating the coastal Arapesh region from the Sepik plains in the south. These were not the only roads, just the ones that were most fully institutionalized in the region where Fortune and I both happened to work.

When looked at from an etic point of view, the roads were clearly a mechanism for diffusion. Following them one could trace bilingualism and borrowings, or trade items and artistic styles, as Mead (1938) was able to do. But when looked at emically, they must also be understood as a primary framework for defining Arapesh social identity. Each stage of advance along a road was justified by a principle of commutative relationship:

> A man has not scattered friends in various hamlets. He is one of a line of friends, inland to seacoast, who are friends of one another ... The natural friendships, following migration in former generation and the like, are usually between friends of friends, or friends two or three or four times removed. (Fortune n.d.: 67–9)

For both individuals and communities, when one acquired the things that came in along the roads (and this included not just tangible items like shell-ring valuables or carved wooden plates, but also intangible cultural forms such as hairstyles, linguistic skills, and ritual complexes like *singsings*), it publicly manifested the importer's political sophistication and demonstrated his influence in the region, because it presupposed his ability to mobilize relationships along the road that extended all the way to the source of those things. In his description of the purchase of a dance complex called *Shenei* at a major regional event that he attended in May 1932, Fortune describes the way the intermediate road relationships were all made visible in the gathering crowd of people, who all had a stake in the transaction. This would not be true every time one brought a friend a hand of bananas or picked up a new botanical term in the road-friend's language, but it illustrates the system's underlying logic: placement along a road implies a claim to recognition by association with those persons and items that pass through. Arapesh people could never simply walk somewhere new and acquire what they desired. Fortune says it was 'the gravest insult' to carry one's own pigs (analogous to currency) across another community's land; to do so was potentially dangerous and politically destabilizing because it represented a refusal to recognize one's road-men.[10] Mead and Fortune both speak of importations as happening in a piecemeal way, wrested up the roads from their begrudging owners through effort and expense, one step at a time. So the institution of the roads controlled and slowed the flow of diffusion, channelling the acquisition of imports of all kinds through a linear series of high-maintenance personal relationships.

By the time of Mead and Fortune's fieldwork, this system was beginning to disintegrate, and a good deal of the fierce competitive politics surrounding the dance transaction Fortune documented was devoted to managing the damage caused by two major disruptions to the roads as an institution for controlling the flow of social capital. The first of these was the white man's labour, especially plantations. These brought together individuals who would otherwise have had no grounds for direct interaction, and they were eager to avail themselves of their new, geographically unsanctioned friendships to access what had previously been beyond their social range. The other disruption was the white man's own road, what Mead and Fortune called 'the King's Highway'. This was the bridle path used by the colonial patrol officers, which presented a new model and metaphor for how roads, and hence interaction between localities, could operate. It assured safe passage, as its owners, the white men, demanded, eliminating the need for personal mediation and extending local people's reach into new areas. A decade later came the Second World War, parts of which were fought on and in the

[10] Still today people 'clear the road' to another locality by making gifts acknowledging their road-friends, before they attend or contribute to an event there, such as a funeral feast.

airspace above Arapesh lands. This devastated the people and completely upended their way of life. When those who survived returned from the bush where they had been scattered in hiding, they did not re-establish many of their former cultural institutions, including the system of roads.

But the desire to enhance one's identity through importation, which motivated Arapesh people to 'walk in search of shell rings', as the exploitation and enjoyment of road-friendships was euphemistically called, remains an aspect of Arapesh culture. And I believe we can see the effects of this cultural orientation in the shift to Tok Pisin that has taken place nearly to completion in the communities of the area.[11] Because those aspects of identity that are conceived of as being within one's own control are associated with importation, people are always looking for the roads they can follow to acquire distant valuable things. As in the past, these roads are simultaneously metaphorical and physical. In the 1950s, when the coastal Arapesh were regrouping their communities after the war, there arose an influential Arapesh leader named Pita Simogun who called for the Cemaun and Rohwim people to forget their past rivalries and build a new kind of road, a vehicle road that would connect their territory all the way to the town of Wewak to the east (Allen 2012). This they did. Using their *save* and working together, they felled 50 kilometres of huge trees by hand, creating what has now come to be known as the West Coast Highway. For Arapesh people on the northern side of the Torricelli watershed, that road is now the conduit to most modern forms of value (schools, towns, markets, health centres, and jobs), and the fact that they themselves built it provides a powerful anchor for what wider Arapesh group identity and pride exists in the region today.

The continuing prominence of roads in contemporary Arapesh discourse and social imagination is remarkable. Figure 7.5 presents a depiction of the mountaintop village of Apakibur as drawn by my village brother Timothy, at the time a ten-year-old boy. In it, his home, represented by the house at the top, is positioned in relation to other settlements on the way down to the coastal vehicle road, the row of trucks running at the bottom. As the drawing reveals, Timothy locates himself in social space in a way similar to that mapped out by the traditional road system (though note the aircraft that now flies overhead, obviating thousands of roads at once as it does so!).

With help from a village son who achieved significant stature in the national government, the Apakibur community was able to build a vehicle access road connecting their mountain home to the coast. It was washed out and rebuilt

[11] Suslak (2009: 205) describes a similar series of changes that took place in Mexico: 'In the 1970s... a campaign to obtain the road that would connect their village to the Valley of Oaxaca finally liberated the people of Totontepec from centuries of economic subordination to the Zapotec neighbors. Direct access to the urban markets of Oaxaca City and Mexico City opened up the flood gates to new flows of commercial goods, media, and people... Almost overnight, Spanish eclipsed Zapotec as the language of local commerce.'

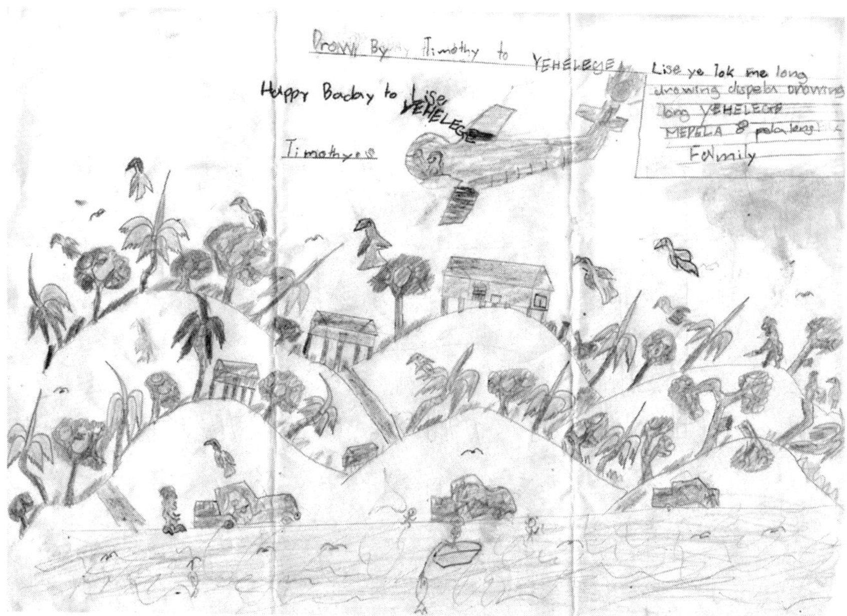

Figure 7.5 A ten-year-old child's drawing of Apakibur village.

several times, in a way reminiscent of the fate of their vernacular village preschool, and then settled into disrepair for about 15 years. The road was re-graded yet again a few years ago when the government leader died, so that the villagers could transport his body home for burial. In July 2013 I found it was again impassable (see Figure 7.6).

The roads have come to my attention in a new way over the past couple of years, since an Arapesh Facebook group has been formed in the hopes of creating 'avenues and institutions that will preserve our heritage and environment while empowering our people to develop economically sustainable activities that will benefit themselves and all Arapesh, from those in the village to those in towns and cities'. One important function of the Facebook group has been to provide a context for the use of the vernacular, although many of the contributors are primarily English and Tok Pisin speakers. Interestingly, when a query was posted about what challenges today's villagers faced, it generated passionate discussion, with most attention being given to the need for an effective system of modern roads. Several commenters expressed their belief that health care, education, and food security would follow naturally if the villagers only had roads. As one commenter put it, 'We cannot bring all services together, my people always tell me, we just need good roads, don't worry about others, with roads all other services will just complement together.' Of course, the difficulty of travel is a serious practical problem, with implications for rural people's daily lives. But this

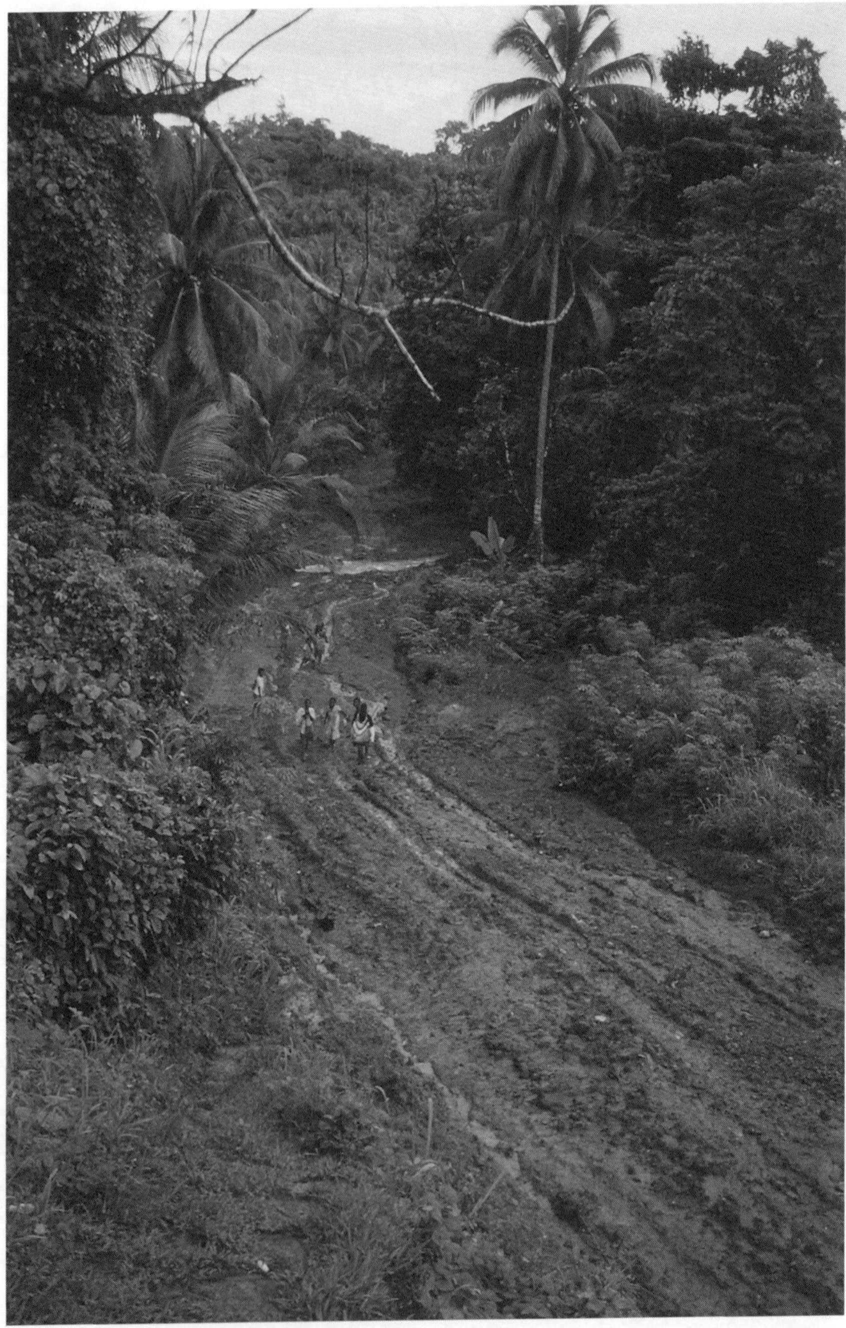

Figure 7.6 The Apakibur vehicle road, symbol of social efficacy, in disrepair.

should not preclude us from seeing that the problem is experienced by Arapesh people in a way that is distinctive because of how it is elaborated in their culture.

7.5 Conclusion: Arapesh Language Shift as a Modern Lifestyle Disease

Gillian Sankoff (1980a: 127) once described Tok Pisin as 'a neutral language', 'no one's vernacular', and as being in the public domain so that it 'can be learned with impunity'. That statement is, on the one hand, profoundly true, but on the other hand slightly misses the mark. Tok Pisin was never neutral. Its original socio-geographic provenance was a group of outsiders, the 'white men', who brought it with them from their home village across the seas, and its desirability derived not only from its utility for communication but also from the connection it indexed to them.[12] But in saying that Tok Pisin could be 'learned with impunity', Sankoff is absolutely correct. The reason it could be learned is not because language was otherwise a proprietary possession, but because *no mechanism existed to control its circulation*. The imposition of hierarchy that brought with it Tok Pisin, 'the King's Highway' that trumped all others, rendered obsolete not just place-based multilingualism, but the whole lateral system of inter-locality relations upon which Arapesh political life and identity had formerly been premised.

So have speakers of Sepik languages shifted to Tok Pisin because they weigh the language against their vernaculars along some scale of value and find the latter lacking? Not necessarily. Foreign cultural elements such as Tok Pisin skills were always learned and always associated with the better part of the self, but it was impossible for everyone to access them. In the view we get from the roads, the eager incorporation of Tok Pisin looks more than anything like a native cultural process gone haywire because the historical limits on importation have been rendered inoperative. In terms of its mechanism, then, we might see Arapesh language shift as like a modern lifestyle disease: we have heart attacks and get diabetes because we are surrounded by sugar, fat, and salt. Nothing against grains and vegetables, but our bodies are predisposed to hunger for sugar, fat, and salt, and since these are now all around and there is nothing to stop us, we consume them. In other words, as counterintuitive as it may sound, we must understand traditional Arapesh culture to be a factor driving linguistic change.

Over much of Papua New Guinea this system of values is now undergoing significant revision. With the rise of education, national consciousness, and a middle class in Papua New Guinea and throughout Melanesia, there is a

[12] For evidence that Arapesh speakers attributed Tok Pisin to a particular geographic location (that they saw it as having its own socio-geographic provenance) see Dobrin (2012: 18).

movement towards a Western nationalist model of identity like Handler (1988) describes, according to which language and culture take on meaning as the primordial possession of bounded social groups (Foster 1997, 2002). The reasons for this are clear: not only do people now participate in wider discourses about 'having a culture', but they are projected into the social role of the possessive individual as Christians with individual souls to be saved, as citizens who express their individual choices when they vote, and as advertising targets who are encouraged to make purchases that will satisfy their personal desires. Of course, these changes have implications for language renewal in an importing culture because they recast local languages as the valued possessions of speakers affiliated with modern ethnolinguistic communities. But for engaged linguists who would construe their linguistic preservation work as supporting indigenous cultures, there is an irony in this development: a genuine grass-roots movement for Arapesh language renewal can only begin in earnest once a profound kind of cultural assimilation is close to completion.

References

Allen, Bryant J. 2012. Simogun, Sir Pita (1900–1987). *Australian Dictionary of Biography*. Canberra: National Centre of Biography, Australian National University. <http://adb.anu.edu.au/biography/simogun-sir-pita-15747/text26935> (accessed 11 October 2013).

Atkinson, Paul and David Silverman. 1997. Kundera's immortality: the interview society and the invention of the self. *Qualitative Inquiry* 3: 304–25.

Briggs, Charles L. 2007. Anthropology, interviewing, and communicability in contemporary society. *Current Anthropology* 48: 551–80.

Dauenhauer, Nora Marks and Richard Dauenhauer. 1998. Technical, emotional, and ideological issues in reversing language shift: examples from Southeast Alaska. In Lenore A. Grenoble and Lindsay J. Whaley (eds.), *Endangered Languages*. Cambridge: Cambridge University Press.

Dobrin, Lise M. 2008. From linguistic elicitation to eliciting the linguist: lessons in community empowerment from Melanesia. *Language* 84: 300–24.

Dobrin, Lise M. 2010. Review of *Language and Poverty*, by Wayne Harbert, Sally McConnell-Ginet, Amanda Miller, and John Whitman. *Language Documentation and Conservation* 4: 159–68.

Dobrin, Lise M. 2012. Ethnopoetic analysis as a resource for endangered language linguistics: the social production of an Arapesh text. *Anthropological Linguistics* 54: 1–32.

Dobrin, Lise M. and Ira Bashkow. 2006. 'Pigs for dance songs': Reo Fortune's empathetic ethnography of the Arapesh roads. In Regna Darnell and Frederic W. Gleach (eds.), *Histories of Anthropology Annual*, vol. 2. Lincoln: University of Nebraska Press.

Fishman, Joshua A. 2002. Commentary: what a difference 40 years make! *Journal of Linguistic Anthropology* 12: 144–9.

Foley, William A. 2005. Personhood and linguistic identity, purism and variation. In Peter K. Austin (ed.), *Language Documentation and Description*, vol. 3. London: SOAS.

Fortune, Reo F. 1939. Arapesh warfare. *American Anthropologist* 41: 22–41.

Fortune, Reo F. n.d. Pigs for dance songs. Manuscript reconstructed from fragments in R. F. Fortune papers at the Alexander Turnbull Library, Wellington, New Zealand.

Foster, Robert J. (ed.). 1997. *Nation Making: Emergent Identities in Postcolonial Melanesia*. Ann Arbor: University of Michigan Press.

Foster, Robert J. 2002. *Materializing the Nation: Commodities, Consumption, and Media in Papua New Guinea*. Bloomington: Indiana University Press.

Gray, Rachel, Thom Retsema, and Rachel Hiley. 2008. *A Sociolinguistic Survey of the Abu' Arapesh [aah], Ulau-Suain [svb] and Kap [ykm] Languages*. Ukarumpa: SIL PNG.

Hale, Kenneth. 1992. On endangered languages and the safeguarding of diversity. *Language* 68: 1–3.

Handler, Richard. 1988. *Nationalism and the Politics of Culture in Quebec*. Madison: University of Wisconsin Press.

Harrison, Simon. 2006. *Fracturing Resemblances: Identity and Mimetic Conflict in Melanesia and the West*. New York: Berghahn.

Kulick, Don. 1992. *Language Shift and Cultural Reproduction: Socialization, Self, and Syncretism in a Papua New Guinean Village*. Cambridge: Cambridge University Press.

Laycock, Donald C. 1975. The Torricelli Phylum. In Stephen A. Wurm (ed.), *New Guinea Area Languages and Language Study*, vol. 1: *Papuan Languages and the New Guinea Linguistic Scene*. Pacific Linguistics C-38. Canberra: Australian National University.

Laycock, Donald C. 1982. Melanesian linguistic diversity: a Melanesian choice? In R. J. May and Hank Nelson (eds.), *Melanesia: Beyond Diversity*, vol. 1. Canberra: Research School of Pacific Studies.

Laycock, Donald C. and C. L. Voorhoeve. 1971. History of research in Papuan languages. In Thomas A. Sebeok (ed.), *Current Trends in Linguistics*, vol. 8: *Linguistics in Oceania*. The Hague: Mouton.

Malinowski, Bronislaw. 1978 [1935]. *Coral Gardens and their Magic*, vol. 2: *The Language of Magic and Gardening*. New York: Dover.

Mead, Margaret. 1935. *Sex and Temperament in Three Primitive Societies*. New York: William Morrow.

Mead, Margaret. 1937. The Arapesh of New Guinea. In Margaret Mead (ed.), *Cooperation and Competition among Primitive Peoples*. Boston, MA: Beacon Press.

Mead, Margaret. 1938. *The Mountain Arapesh: I, An Importing Culture*, vol. 36, part 3. New York: Anthropological Papers of the American Museum of Natural History.

Mead, Margaret. 1940. *The Mountain Arapesh: II, Supernaturalism*, vol. 37, part 3. New York: Anthropological Papers of the American Museum of Natural History.

Meek, Barbra A. 2007. Respecting the language of elders: ideological shift and linguistic discontinuity in a northern Athapascan community. *Journal of Linguistic Anthropology* 17: 23–43.

Meek, Barbra A. 2010. *We Are Our Language: An Ethnography of Language Revitalization in a Northern Athabaskan Community*. Tucson: University of Arizona Press.

Mühlhäusler, Peter. 1996. *Linguistic Ecology: Language Change and Linguistic Imperialism in the Pacific Region*. London: Routledge.

Nettle, Daniel and Suzanne Romaine. 2000. *Vanishing Voices: The Extinction of the World's Languages*. Oxford: Oxford University Press.

Paugh, Amy. 2011. Local theories of child rearing. In Alessandro Duranti, Elinor Ochs, and Bambi B. Schieffelin (eds.), *The Handbook of Language Socialization*. West Sussex: Blackwell.

Perley, Bernard C. 2011. *Defying Maliseet Language Death: Emergent Vitalities of Language, Culture, and Identity in Eastern Canada*. Lincoln: University of Nebraska Press.

Reiman, D. Will. 2010. Basic oral language documentation. *Language Documentation and Conservation* 4: 254–68.

Rindstedt, Camilla and Karin Aronsson. 2002. Growing up monolingual in a bilingual community: the Quichua revitalization paradox. *Language in Society* 31: 721–42.

Robbins, Joel. 2004. *Becoming Sinners: Christianity and Moral Torment in a Papua New Guinea Society*. Berkeley: University of California Press.

Robbins, Joel and Alan Rumsey. 2008. Introduction: cultural and linguistic anthropology and the opacity of other minds. *Anthropological Quarterly* 81: 407–20.

Romaine, Suzanne. 1992. *Language, Education, and Development: Urban and Rural Tok Pisin in Papua New Guinea*. Oxford: Oxford University Press.

Salisbury, R. F. 1962. Notes on bilingualism and linguistic change in New Guinea. *Anthropological Linguistics* 4: 1–13.

Sankoff, Gillian. 1980a. Multilingualism in Papua New Guinea. In Gillian Sankoff (ed.), *The Social Life of Language*. Philadelphia: University of Pennsylvania Press.

Sankoff, Gillian. 1980b. Political power and linguistic inequality in Papua New Guinea. In Gillian Sankoff (ed.), *The Social Life of Language*. Philadelphia: University of Pennsylvania Press.

Schlesier, Erhard von. 1961. Über die Zweisprachigkeit und die Stellung der Zweisprachigen in Melanesien, besonders auf Neuguinea. In *Beiträge zur Völkerforschung: Hans Damm zum 65 Geburtstag*. Leipzig: Museum für Völkerkunde.

Senft, Gunter. 2010. Culture change—language change: missionaries and moribund varieties of Kilivila. In Gunter Senft (ed.), *Endangered Austronesian, Papuan, and Australian Aboriginal Languages: Essays on Language Documentation, Archiving, and Revitalization*. Pacific Linguistics 618. Canberra: Australian National University.

Sicoli, Mark A. 2011. Agency and ideology in language shift and language maintenance. In Tania Granadillo and Heidi A. Orcutt-Gachiri (eds.), *Ethnographic Contributions to the Study of Endangered Languages*. Tucson: University of Arizona Press.

Silverstein, Michael. 1996. Monoglot 'standard' in America: standardization and metaphors of linguistic hegemony. In Donald Brenneis and Ronald K. S. Macaulay (eds.), *The Matrix of Language: Contemporary Linguistic Anthropology*. Boulder: Westview Press.

Slotta, James. 2012. Dialect, trope, and enregisterment in a Melanesian speech community. *Language and Communication* 32: 1–13.

Suslak, Daniel F. 2009. The sociolinguistic problem of generations. *Language and Communication* 29:3: 199–209.

Thurston, William R. 1987. *Processes of Change in the Languages of North-Western New Britain*. Pacific Linguistics B-99. Canberra: Australian National University.

Thurston, William R. 1989. How exoteric languages build a lexicon: esoterogeny in West New Britain. In Ray Harlow and Robin Hooper (eds.), *VICAL 1, Oceanic Languages: Papers from the Fifth International Conference on Austronesian Linguistics*. Auckland: Linguistic Society of New Zealand.

Wurm, Stephen A. 2003. The language situation and language endangerment in the greater Pacific area. In Mark Janse and Sijmen Tol (eds.), *Language Death and Language Maintenance: Theoretical, Practical, and Descriptive Approaches*. Current Issues in Linguistic Theory, vol. 240. Amsterdam: John Benjamins.

Part 2

Language Documentation and Revitalization: What and Why?

8

Ideologies, Beliefs, and Revitalization of Guernesiais (Guernsey)

YAN MARQUIS & JULIA SALLABANK

8.1 Introduction

In this chapter we examine language ideologies in a small community (Guernsey, Channel Islands) which reflect wider issues concerning the aims and effectiveness of language-related activities. By 'ideology' we are referring to deep-seated and strongly held beliefs and perceptions concerning both language practices (what people do) and policies (what people *should* do). These ideologies are largely unstated yet profoundly influence language planning and policy at both personal and public levels. Although there has been a shift since the 1980s towards broadly positive overt attitudes in favour of maintenance of Guernsey's indigenous language in the community as a whole (among both speakers and non-speakers), it seems from our research that ingrained covert negative attitudes linger in some sections of the community. 'Traditionalist' ideologies regarding the status of 'High' and 'Low' languages, 'correctness', and the 'ownership' of a language are largely impervious to shifts in public opinion, which has led to debates regarding control over the direction of language maintenance and revitalization. From these observations we identify two main divergent trends in beliefs and ideologies, concerning who has authority to speak on behalf of 'the community' and to make decisions regarding the future of an endangered language (if indeed a future is envisaged). We also relate our observations to the concept of 'prior ideological clarification' (Fishman 1991, 2001; Kroskrity 2009), and compare rhetoric regarding the desirability of language maintenance and revitalization with actions and outcomes (cf. Dauenhauer and Dauenhauer 1998).

8.2 Sociolinguistic Background

The case study described focuses on the indigenous language of Guernsey, Channel Islands. Some form of Romance language has been spoken in the

Proceedings of The British Academy, **199**, 151–166.

archipelago for around 2,000 years, and over time each island evolved its own distinctive variety of Norman, one of the regional languages of northern France. The Channel Islands belonged to the Duchy of Normandy at the time of the Norman conquest of England in 1066, after which a version of the Norman language was used by the English court and nobility for some 300 years. Following the incorporation of mainland Normandy into France in 1204, 'English' gradually became established as the language of England, but not without borrowing many Norman words (Bailey and Maroldt 1977; Milroy 1984; Thomason and Kaufman 1988). Guernsey, along with the other Channel Islands, retained allegiance to the English Crown but continued speaking Norman, although the use of Guernesiais (the speakers' preferred name for the indigenous variety of Guernsey) declined considerably in the twentieth century.

The Channel Islands thus have a long-standing connection with the British Crown. Their political allegiance is to Britain, although they are not part of the UK, have their own parliaments, and are self-governing in domestic policy. Guernsey, the second largest island, is the administrative centre of the Bailiwick of Guernsey, which encompasses several smaller islands; this chapter discusses only the language of the island of Guernsey itself. The main industries are finance and tourism, but before the Second World War the economy was based on agriculture and horticulture. The islands are not members of the European Community and are not party to European agreements such as the Charter for Regional and Minority Languages.

8.2.1 Language Vitality and Status

The UNESCO Atlas of Endangered Languages (Moseley 2009) categorized Guernesiais as 'severely endangered', that is, intergenerational transmission has ceased. However, we have found that Guernesiais is rapidly approaching the UNESCO classification of 'critically endangered': 'the youngest speakers are grandparents and older, and they speak the language partially and infrequently' (ibid.). Most speakers (of any level of proficiency) are over the age of 60, and we know of no children who are able to speak the language fluently.

In the 2001 census 1,327 people reported speaking Guernesiais fluently.[1] This represented 2.22 per cent of the population, which at the time was just under 60,000.[2] In the census, 3.13 per cent of the population (1,871 people) reported understanding Guernesiais 'fully'. The degree of endangerment is indicated by

[1] The 2001 census (States of Guernsey 2002) was the first and only one to ask a language question. Before 2001 censuses were held every five years in Guernsey. The 2006 census was cancelled for financial reasons, and in 2010 proposals were made to replace the 2011 census with a 'rolling electronic census' (Billet d'Etat XVII, July 2010). This has not yet been implemented, and officials are unwilling to state whether a language question will be included in future censuses.

[2] The population is now thought to be just over 62,000 (States of Guernsey 2009).

the statistic that 70.4 per cent of speakers (934 people) who reported being fluent were over the age of 64 in 2001. Since then the number of fluent speakers appears to have declined dramatically. In our documentation project we have interviewed over 100 'native speakers', of whom at least a third proved to be significantly less fluent than expected. Clearly there has been age-related attrition (see Sallabank 2010), but this does not account fully for the discrepancy. We conjecture that, in the absence of any objective measure of fluency, over-optimistic perceptions of proficiency may have translated into over-reporting of fluency in the 2001 census; we therefore estimate that there may now be fewer than 300 fully fluent speakers, mainly over the age of 80.

These perceptions of proficiency are based on beliefs about what constitutes a 'native speaker', which is interpreted by many as having been brought up in a home where Guernesiais was (one of) the language(s) of socialization. However, many of these 'native speakers' use Guernesiais infrequently and find it difficult to speak it without preparation. In many cases they might more accurately be described as 'semi-speakers', as defined by Grinevald and Bert (2011), in that they do not speak Guernesiais regularly in their everyday lives, their receptive skills are higher than their productive skills, and the language they produce is largely formulaic (see Marquis and Sallabank 2013).

Beliefs and ideologies about language thus play a role in self-perception and self-reports, which in turn may potentially affect public policy and language-related research and documentation, which may not be seen as so pressing if there is thought to be a larger number of fluent speakers than is actually the case.

Although the States of Guernsey (the island government) appointed a Language Support Officer (Yan Marquis, one of the authors of this chapter) in 2008, Guernsey's indigenous language remains unofficial and unrecognized, and is not used in the education system. This reflects the historical situation, where Guernesiais was in a diglossic relationship with French from *c.*1650 to the early twentieth century. French was used in all High domains, such as education, government, and religion, and was the official written form. Although a number of local writers published poetry in Guernesiais (e.g. Georges Métivier, Denys Corbet, and Thomas Lenfestey), for most people Guernesiais remained an unstandardized vernacular. Contemporary writers praised Métivier for having 'placé le guernesiais au nombre des idiomes reconnus et vivants' [placed Guernesiais among the ranks of recognized and living tongues] (Boland 1885: 68), but this in effect meant attempting to 'civilize' Guernesiais by importing French elements. This reflects an ideology that can still be discerned today in attitudes towards Guernesiais: that it is inferior to French, and even an inferior *form* of French (patois). This affects both language policy, as French is seen as a more legitimate variety to promote and teach, and perceptions of what is 'correct' in Guernesiais usage. We were frequently asked whether Guernesiais is a language or a dialect, and are informed that it 'can't be written' (see 8.3.2).

Trudgill (1992) observes that whether a variety is designated a language or not is related not only to linguistic characteristics (such as degree of relatedness to or difference from the majority language), but also to social and economic factors, and, of course, to ideologies of 'correctness'. Although Hudson (2002) claims that Low status in diglossia does not necessarily imply inferior social status, it almost inevitably leads to the Low variety being seen as inferior, reflecting a lack of social mobility (Ager 2005; Eckert 1980; Williams 1992). Nevertheless, Guernesiais maintained its ethnolinguistic vitality in a relatively stable diglossic relationship with French for several hundred years. French was learnt through education but was rarely spoken in day-to-day life; the majority of the population probably only had a passive knowledge (e.g. enough to understand newspapers and Bible readings). This might help to explain the relative ease with which it was replaced by English as the High variety. English has been used in Guernsey since the late Middle Ages, but only started to become widespread in the nineteenth and twentieth centuries; this was due initially to the Napoleonic wars between Britain and France in the early nineteenth century, during which increased numbers of British troops were stationed in Guernsey, and then to increased immigration (Crossan 2007). English is now the default language in all domains, and all Guernesiais speakers are bilingual or even dominant in English.

Until relatively recently, English was used for utilitarian events such as commercial and official transactions, while Guernesiais fulfilled a more affective and domestic role. However, this domain is disappearing as speakers' family members and friends pass away (see Sallabank 2010). Symbolic language use in language-related events and performances is therefore becoming an increasingly important forum for using Guernesiais, but it does not ensure language maintenance or further Fishman's (1991) key criterion of intergenerational transmission.

8.2.2 Language Attitudes and Beliefs

The language attitudes and beliefs of older community members (both speakers and non-speakers of Guernesiais) were shaped by the predominant ideologies of the period when they grew up. Their linguistic human rights were ignored by the Guernsey establishment: one interviewee reported that when his brother started school in the 1950s, he was told to 'go home and come back when you can speak English'. There was strong societal pressure to shift to the dominant language:

> When I was little it [Guernesiais] was the first language that I learnt and my mother took a lot of stick for allowing me … 'oh gosh you know you're letting her speak patois and when she goes to school she won't be able to learn—she'll be a dunce.' (GF39)

The views referred to in this interview excerpt are predicated on a monolingual ideology which was prevalent in the mid-twentieth century, and which saw a minority language as 'holding people back', rather than promoting additive bilingualism or self-confidence in speakers' own ethnic and linguistic identity as a firm base from which to acquire other language varieties.

Given such experiences, combined with the di/triglossic relationship where Guernesiais was always the Low partner first to French then to English, it is not surprising that attitudes towards Guernesiais among these generations reflect a classic social–psychological split of 'status versus solidarity' (Giles and Johnson 1987; Giles and Ryan 1982).

Many older speakers thus express emotional attachment to Guernesiais and regret its demise, especially as part of the 'golden era' of their childhood. But this regret does not necessarily entail any remedial action, such as passing the heritage language on to a new generation. This discourse of Guernesiais as 'a language of the past' (see section 8.4) is compatible with a continued ingrained belief in the inferiority or lack of utility of Guernesiais ('French is more useful').[3] More implications of such beliefs will be discussed in section 8.3.

8.2.3 Public Opinion and Support for Guernesiais

Since the 1980s, grass-roots campaigning has contributed to a political climate in which government support for the indigenous language became seen as desirable by both the general public and politicians. Positive attitudes and awareness-raising cannot in themselves 'save' a language without more concrete measures; however, they can lead to public support for such measures.

Although Guernesiais has traditionally held Low status, a survey conducted by Sallabank in 2004 indicated overwhelmingly positive attitudes among the majority (Anglophone) population (Sallabank 2013). According to these findings, the indigenous language is seen as a marker of island distinctiveness in the face of perceived Anglicization and the homogenizing effects of globalization, as suggested by Trudgill (2004). Some comments from interviews and questionnaires included:

> Guernsey is a unique island and needs to be kept that way. Our language is important in identifying Guernsey people. (AQ113)
>
> Guernsey French identifies the island even though I don't speak it . . . necessary to keep it going to keep island identity. (AQ88)

[3] This does not necessarily entail action either: although the excuse that 'major European/Asian languages are more useful' is common, it does not mean that those expressing it actually learn those languages. In practice there is a 'monolingual mentality': everyone speaks English so that is the only language needed.

> The language adds something different to the culture. I'm sorry I never learnt it—I was evacuated and came back aged 5.[4] (AQ65)

> [Guernesiais is] still part of what being Guernsey's about and being slightly different—in the modern world should we be all homogenized and become all the same kind of people, the same views, the same language, the same standard—I don't want to be part of that. (AQ112)

This view of language as a 'marker of distinctiveness' is reflected in government policy as a strategic element in positioning the island on the world stage. The foreword to the cultural strategy of the government's Culture and Leisure Department for 2010–14 states:

> Our difference from everywhere else in the world is what makes Guernsey unique and if we wish to remain unique and independent we must use every opportunity and every difference that we have from the rest of the world to make that case. Why is it important to promote and preserve our differences? I offer a simple answer, and one that has been used widely by others—extinction is forever. Our Guernsey French language is an example of what we could lose unless we take the appropriate steps to preserve it. (States of Guernsey 2010: 3)

The same document goes on to stress that preserving distinctiveness does not necessarily imply a purely preservationist, backward-looking perspective:

> However, the cultural identity of Guernsey is forever moving on; change is a fact of life, and should be embraced as an opportunity for expansion and development. The challenge is to ensure that change is balanced with the continued care and respect for cultural identity and historic environment. (States of Guernsey 2010: 7)

As will be seen later in this chapter, this acceptance of cultural identity as dynamic is not fully shared by all of those involved in language-related activities.

Another factor influencing government policy has been the British–Irish Council, which was created as part of the Northern Ireland peace process under the agreement reached in the Multi-Party Negotiations in Belfast in 1998 'to promote positive, practical relationships among its Members, which are the British and Irish Governments, the devolved administrations of Northern Ireland, Scotland and Wales, and Jersey, Guernsey and the Isle of Man' (States of Jersey 2011). As the only member not to have recognized or promoted its indigenous language, the need for Guernsey to initiate a language policy to support Guernesiais became apparent; this may have been in part due to the wish/need to 'project the desired external image' (Ager 1996: 26). The political consensus in Guernsey at the time of writing seems to be in favour of the maintenance of a

[4] The majority of Guernsey children were evacuated to the UK just prior to the German invasion in 1940, and did not return until 1945; this is blamed by many islanders for the break in intergenerational transmission of Guernesiais.

distinct language, although what that means in policy and practice remains a matter for debate (see sections 8.3 and 8.4).[5]

Politicians wish to be seen to respect public opinion, if only to improve their own standing. However, even those who are sincere in their support for the language know little about either the language itself, or about language policy. They are therefore susceptible to lobbying from influential community members who claim to represent 'the speaker community' and also to be authorities on the language (and who dismiss expertise from outside of the island as a 'waste of money'). By and large, those seeking to influence policy hold particular ideologies about what language represents and what it can/should do—and who has the authority to decide.

8.3 Ideological Debates and Language Revitalization

Beliefs about who is a legitimate speaker, and thus who has the authority to decide how Guernesiais should develop, bedevil language planning in Guernsey.

8.3.1 Who is Qualified to Teach Guernesiais?

The main focus of current language maintenance efforts in Guernsey is extra-curricular lessons in primary schools (students aged six to eleven). These sessions are taught by volunteers and receive little (if any) official support. As discussed further in Marquis and Sallabank (2013), the volunteer teachers are mainly in their 60s and 70s and are generally considered to be 'native speakers' because Guernesiais was one of their primary languages of socialization, which is deemed to endow them with authority and expertise. However, as noted in section 8.2, many could more accurately be described as 'semi-speakers': they do not use Guernesiais on a day-to-day basis and are insecure about their own grammatical judgements, which can lead to influence from French due to ideologies of 'correctness' in a diglossic relationship and a formal teaching situation.

Becoming a teacher of Guernesiais, even only on a voluntary basis for half an hour a week, valorizes the knowledge and status of 'native speakers', who for most of their lives have suffered from the negative attitudes described earlier in this chapter. Most of the volunteers did not transmit Guernesiais to their own children due to these widespread societal attitudes. Being involved in teaching Guernesiais provides a powerful boost to their own self-image on two grounds: firstly by affirming their language expertise, and secondly by enabling them to assuage any guilt they might feel at not having taught Guernesiais to their own

[5] Guernsey's political system operates on a consensus-based model and does not have political parties.

children and grandchildren. Furthermore, the sessions provide an opportunity for social interaction between teachers, and between teachers and pupils. For some volunteers it also provides opportunities they had not previously thought possible: one recounted how she had always wanted to be a teacher, but her education had been disrupted due to the German occupation of Guernsey in the Second World War and she did not have the qualifications required. Volunteering to help in after-school Guernesiais classes thus enables her to fulfil a long-held dream. For such volunteers there is thus a blurred line between language revitalization and personal revitalization (see also Chapter 11 in this volume).

In this valorization of the 'native speaker', the effectiveness of the lessons themselves, and of the overall programme, holds minimal importance. There is little or no coordination between the volunteer teachers, little or no teacher training (apart from helping a more experienced volunteer for a few months), no syllabus, few materials, and no linguistic progression in the lessons. Neither is there any planning for the future provision of teachers of Guernesiais, although the majority of the volunteer teachers are in their 60s and 70s.

Being perceived as a 'native speaker' is thus important in claiming legitimacy as a teacher. As in many language teaching contexts, being a 'native speaker' is viewed as a more legitimate qualification for passing the language on than teaching qualifications or experience. This is despite Medgyes' (1992) suggestion that having been through the process of learning a language can potentially lead to a teacher being in a better position to explain it.

The fact that most of the volunteer teachers are already of retirement age might be expected to encourage moves to develop replacements. There are no opportunities for formal training to teach Guernesiais; however, there is interest among some learners in becoming teachers. In 2009–10 a group of students aged 16–18 requested lessons in Guernesiais as one of their college options. One of the students proved to be very keen, and with another group of students she produced a children's book and CD in Guernesiais. Several students who were considering mainstream teaching careers participated in an initiative to pass on their knowledge of Guernesiais to primary school pupils. Reactions to these attempts from older volunteer teachers ranged from scepticism ('they'll never be good enough to teach the language') to outright disapproval.[6]

8.3.2 Orthography and 'Modernization'

Despite the body of nineteenth- and early twentieth-century literature discussed in section 8.2, Guernesiais is generally considered to be an unwritten vernacular. Most speakers do not write Guernesiais, and a significant proportion of islanders

[6] An additional cause for disapproval was that the children's book used a 'learner orthography' that has been contested by 'traditionalists'; see section 8.3.2.

(both speakers and non-speakers) maintain that it cannot be written at all. There is no official standard spelling, although a dictionary published by a language society (De Garis 1967, revised in 1982 and 2012) enjoys considerable prestige. In general it follows French spelling conventions, but it contains numerous inconsistencies. Many speakers and learners find this dictionary difficult to use due to its inconsistencies and lack of pronunciation guidance. The majority of interviewees who write in Guernesiais claim to follow the dictionary; but in practice it is rarely adhered to, leading to a wide variety of spellings being in use (Sallabank 2002). This is just one area in which practices are less powerful than perceptions and ideologies. Orthography development is dealt with in more detail elsewhere (Marquis and Sallabank, 2009 and forthcoming); in this chapter we focus on ideological debates in which orthography seems to be a trigger for deep-seated ideologies and fear of 'language change'.

Younger generations in Guernsey (i.e. anyone under the age of 60), as well as many older islanders, are mainly monolingual and literate in English. They have little knowledge of French and its spelling conventions. Problems arising from using a French-based system with such learners are evident in the neighbouring island of Jersey (Sallabank 2011), as learners of Jèrsiais have little exposure to the spoken language, yet its pronunciation is opaque from the spelling in the written materials that lessons rely on. Some learners (or potential learners) of Guernesiais have requested a spelling system that is more systematic and more transparent for Anglophones in order to facilitate learning, while influential 'elders' insist on the primacy of the De Garis (1967/1982) dictionary despite not always following its principles themselves.

In August 2010 the authors of this chapter conducted a small-scale experiment, asking both native speakers and learners of Guernesiais to listen to recorded words and phrases and write them however they felt looked right. While the resulting spellings were so diverse as to be difficult to analyse for the purposes of orthography development, the process was very revealing of attitudes and ideologies. Learners were more willing to 'have a go' than native speakers, some of whom expressed concern that they might not spell 'correctly' and even seemed too intimidated to try. The experiment itself was strongly criticized by a prominent speaker with considerable influence in the community, who raised concerns about what was perceived as an attempt to 'change the language' by challenging 'traditional' prestige spelling. Discussion of orthography and revitalization (as opposed to maintenance: see Marquis and Sallabank 2013) is perceived by self-identified 'traditionalists' as driving, rather than reflecting, language change, and is therefore rejected as pernicious.

The development of effective learning and teaching materials is thus hampered by the lack of a practical or universally agreed orthography. As well as rejection (and lack of awareness) of any need to discuss issues surrounding orthography, there is an unpreparedness to innovate in language use, for example vocabulary terms for items commonly used in schools and by the middle and younger generations, such as computers and mobile phones. The lack of vocabulary dealing with modern items is common to many endangered languages (e.g. 'televisions' and 'refrigerators' are usually referred to by their English names). Some teachers in Guernsey are developing terms as required for objects such as mobile phones and computers; these terms tend to be criticized by 'traditionalists' unless they have the cachet of having been invented by someone perceived as a 'native speaker'. However, even some of those who claim language 'ownership' express a lack of confidence in their authority to create neologisms. There seems to be no room in the 'traditionalist' interpretation for Guernesiais to develop its own identity (known as 'differentiation' in some of the revitalization literature, 'individuation' (Thiers 1986), or *Ausbau* in the terms of Kloss 1967); the only options seem to be convergence towards English or French.

Nevertheless, it should be possible through language documentation to identify established, traditional methods of word creation that could be harnessed for future language development. For example, the verb *taextotai*, 'to (small) text', has been created from *taext* (text) with the suffix *-otai*, a much-used infinitive form which indicates that an action takes place in a reduced/diminished manner. One might even hope that, for traditionalists and purists, such an approach would be more acceptable than the practice of inserting an English term such as 'refrigerator', which is seen as evidence of deficit by some non-speakers. The perceived lack of modern vocabulary in Guernesiais is frequently cited by opponents of language maintenance/revitalization as evidence of its inferiority and lack of adaptability to the modern world. Such borrowing has also been observed to lead to more sustained code-switching and abandonment of attempts to communicate in Guernesiais. The focus on 'traditional' (French-based) spelling can also be seen in this light: opponents have cited its 'corrupt' look (e.g. it often contains apostrophes to indicate where 'full' French forms have been 'elided') as further evidence of inferiority, although these 'full' forms are not a feature of Guernesiais.

The belief that schools should play a major role in language maintenance is at odds with purist or so-called 'traditionalist' attitudes towards language, although both are often voiced by the same individuals. Because of their age and relative lack of familiarity with information technology, 'elders' dismiss the inclusion of technology in language teaching and revitalization (e.g. texting, tweeting, blogs, social networking sites) as irrelevant, although the majority of language revitalization movements embrace technology as key to motivating younger learners and to the digital preservation of language records (Holton 2011; Moriarty 2011). Ideologies may thus contribute to a mismatch between desired results and methods in teaching Guernesiais.

8.3.3 Language 'Ownership', Documentation, and Language Policy

In a section on 'potential problems and how to avoid them' in their book *Saving Languages*, Grenoble and Whaley (2006: 177) recommend that 'effort should be made to avoid potential flash points which involve who "knows" the language, who is "qualified" to teach it, who has the "ownership" rights to the language'. This is, however, more easily said than done. Yan Marquis resigned from the post of Guernsey Language Officer in July 2011 due to the intractability of the entrenched views and associated problems. In September 2011 the Ministry of Culture and Leisure announced the setting up of a 'Language Commission' to advise on language policy, but at the time of writing little or no progress had been made.

Grenoble and Whaley (2006: 177) go on to suggest that:

> Where there are differences of opinion as to what form is 'correct' or as to who speaks 'better', an early resolution, one often involving compromise, is called for. This is one area where a professional linguist can provide much-needed help.

Unfortunately, even documenting or discussing such issues as orthography and language change has led to the researchers in this instance not being seen as neutral but as 'changing the language'. In addition, as noted by Hoffman (2006: 114), drawing attention to intra-group conflicts may not be welcome for some community members. Nevertheless, 'ideological clarification' is essential for effective language planning. Mason (2002: 56) sees 'people, and their interpretations, perceptions, meanings and understandings, as the primary data sources' for qualitative research. People's perceptions, as gleaned from statements, observed practices, and reactions, form a central source of information for researchers into language endangerment and revitalization. Although Spolsky (2009) maintains that language practices are the basis of language management, it is our observation that beliefs and perceptions about practices, especially quasi-purist views on what people *should* do, are more potent drivers of unstated/accidental language policy, which can make or break stated and planned policies.

Dorian (1993) warns that research which only reports on the abandonment phase of a language, and which concentrates on negative attitudes, can obscure a longer-term dynamic by overlooking 'reactivation' efforts by later generations. Crystal (2000: 106) adds that 'this kind of reaction [regret at not knowing the heritage language] is common among the members of a community two generations after the one which failed to pass its language on'. In Guernsey we are finding a clear interest among young people and adults in learning and promoting Guernesiais. This means that at some point attention needs to turn to the needs and opinions of those who actively seek access to a heritage language.

One Guernsey teenager reported:

> I began [t]o think very early on, 'I've been robbed' (which surprised me, because I've never been overly interested in my own heritage—it must have been taught in a very dry way at school, because it certainly never inspired me; and I was never taken to any of the local traditional things when I was little—bit of a pity, really, but never mind.) ... Still, now that I feel I've missed out, I reckon young kids should definitely have access to it.

The following post appeared on a language-interest Internet blog in November 2005, following a link to a post about Guernsey on another blog:[7]

> Hi, I am so keen to learn Guernsey French and always listen to Radio Guernsey on a Saturday morning so i can hear the news in Guernsey French. An old work colleague of mine was teaching me when our shop was closed and I think it is so so important to keep this language alive. It is part of our heritage and we should not be allowed to lose it. This is coming from a 19 year old and seeing as we are the future of our Island, i think the young people should have a say ... Hear our cry!![8]

However, at the time of writing the views and needs of learners and potential learners seem to be conspicuously absent from discussion of language policy (if and when there is any open discussion). The continued focus on 'native speakers' can mean that potential supporters of revitalization (including non-speakers with useful skills to offer) may be deterred, feeling unsure whether they are 'allowed' to get involved:

> If anyone wants any advice in computer-mediated education then I'm willing to pitch in of course but I have not pushed this since I think our priorities today are with speakers. (GE13)

However, it could be argued that due to the rapid decline in the number of fluent speakers, a more urgent priority is to train a cohort of adults with the skills to document and teach Guernesiais. This is actually being taken up at the time of writing.

8.3.4 Divergent Ideologies

From consideration of the issues described above we have identified two main diverging trends in language ideologies in Guernsey, which for ease of description we call the 'Static' and 'Dynamic' viewpoints. It must, of course, be borne in mind that the definitions below are extreme points on a continuum. We should also stress that for the most part these ideologies are implicit and have been deduced from observations, and that the 'debates' we refer to are largely unspoken too.

This chapter has focused largely on the 'Static' view, in which the indigenous language has a mainly nostalgic value which is expressed through performance

[7] See <http://www.nakedtranslations.com/en/2005/09/000504.php> (accessed 2 April 2006).

[8] Source: <http://www.languagehat.com/archives/002118.php> (accessed 12 August 2006).

rather than by day-to-day use. The focus of efforts is on maintenance of the current language community, and its authority and legitimacy, rather than on the development of new users or uses. In this view, French is still seen as the High or 'roof' language (in the terms of Kloss 1967) and as the only valid source of linguistic prestige.

Parallel to this we have identified a 'Dynamic' view of language, in which the local language is promoted as a source of shared identity for all. Supporters of this position aim to increase the number of speakers through second language teaching and 'reactivating' 'semi-speakers' and 'rememberers' (in the terms of Grinevald and Bert 2011). They also aim to expand the domains of use of Guernesiais and increase its prestige as a language in its own right. This may entail language development in terms of vocabulary, orthography, and distanciation from French. Its proponents no doubt see this as a pragmatic viewpoint in that to retain some of the language is better than none, but it is no less ideologically based than linguistic purism. It assumes that it is desirable 'to have local languages and cultures continue in whatever form they may take' (Goodfellow 2009: 21), whereas some 'traditionalists', whose attachment to 'the language of our youth' is linked to nostalgia for a bygone age, would rather Guernesiais did not survive than change from the language they remember and love.[9, 10]

While some proponents of the 'Static' view are vocal and influential in the speaker community, our research suggests that the 'silent majority' probably sits somewhere between these two standpoints. In some cases, as in the orthography experiment reported in section 8.3, people feel intimidated when questioning 'traditionalist' views in public, although some will express less constrained opinions or concerns in private.

8.4 Conclusions

While these broad-brush trends are of necessity an oversimplification of a complex situation, they are presented in an effort to establish 'ideological clarification'. Raising awareness of unstated perceptions and ideologies may help to address expectations and assumptions that may stand in the way of achievable goals for language maintenance or revitalization (see also Dauenhauer and Dauenhauer 1998; Dorian 1994, 1998; Hinton and Ahlers 1999; Kroskrity 2000, 2009).

[9] As noted, many of these older people are 'rememberers' whose mastery of Guernesiais is incomplete or imperfect, but since they are seen as 'native speakers' they are unaware of any need to refresh their knowledge.

[10] There is a parallel contrast between 'static' and 'dynamic' views of language documentation and archiving too: 'preservation' could be seen as a 'static' view of archives, with 'revitalization' as the 'dynamic' end of the continuum. The analogy could even be extended to 'bounded system' vs. 'ecological' views of languages (see Introduction and Chapters 9 and 12, this volume).

Language ideologies in Guernsey reinforce the assumption that the indigenous language belongs to 'native' and 'traditional' speakers, who see themselves as its 'guardians' but who are using it less and less. Until relatively recently there was little consultation about the future of the language with younger people, the learner community, and the general public, who might be seen as the future custodians of linguistic heritage.

Issues of nostalgia and ownership were stated publicly for the first time at a meeting in February 2013 to announce the formation of a new Language Commission. This is made up of disinterested people, that is, they have no stake in the language or associated groups, but instead have expertise in fundraising, marketing, museum services, education, and public relations. The Commission's approach seems to be reactive rather than to put forward a strategic framework, and so it is arguable that by the time this book goes to press, language policy development will have progressed little, either at macro (ideological/strategic) level or at micro level (detailed measures and practices).

We conclude that it is likely that, as in the Isle of Man, language revitalization may not be possible until covert negative attitudes have disappeared—unfortunately along with the last 'native' speakers. We therefore feel that it is necessary to prioritize language documentation in order to build a record of Guernesiais in use which can be accessed by anyone interested as a resource for reference and revitalization, thus implying a 'dynamic' rather than a 'static' view of language archiving too.

References

Ager, Dennis E. 1996. *Language Policy in Britain and France: The Processes of Policy.* London: Continuum.

Ager, Dennis E. 2005. Prestige and image planning. *Current Issues in Language Planning* 6: 1–43.

Bailey, C.-J. N. and K. Maroldt. 1977. The French lineage of English. In J. M. Meisel (ed.), *Langues en Contact*. Tübingen: TBL-Verlag Narr.

Boland, Henri. 1885. Les institutions de langue française à Guernesey. *Revue Internationale* 8: 66–85 and 190–212.

Crossan, Rose-Marie. 2007. *Guernsey, 1814–1914: Migration and Modernisation.* Woodbridge: The Boydell Press.

Crystal, David. 2000. *Language Death.* Cambridge: Cambridge University Press.

Dauenhauer, Nora Marks and Richard Dauenhauer. 1998. Technical, emotional, and ideological issues in reversing language shift: examples from Southeast Alaska. In Lenore A. Grenoble and Lindsay J. Whaley (eds.), *Endangered Languages: Language Loss and Community Response*. Cambridge: Cambridge University Press.

De Garis, Marie (ed.). 1967. *Dictiounnaire Angllais–Guernésiais*. Guernsey: La Société Guernesiaise.

De Garis, Marie (ed.). 1982. *Dictiounnaire Angllais–Guernésiais* (3rd edn.). Chichester: Phillimore.

Dorian, Nancy. 1993. A response to Ladefoged's other view of endangered languages. *Language* 69: 575–9.

Dorian, Nancy. 1994. Purism vs. compromise in language revitalization and language revival. *Language in Society* 23: 479–94.

Dorian, Nancy. 1998. Western language ideologies and small-language prospects. In Lenore A. Grenoble and Lindsay J. Whaley (eds.), *Endangered Languages: Language Loss and Community Response*. Cambridge: Cambridge University Press.

Eckert, Penelope. 1980. Diglossia: separate and unequal. *Linguistics* 18: 1053–64.

Fishman, Joshua A. 1991. *Reversing Language Shift: Theoretical and Empirical Foundations of Assistance to Threatened Languages*. Clevedon: Multilingual Matters.

Fishman, Joshua A. (ed.). 2001. *Can Threatened Languages be Saved? Reversing Language Shift, Revisited: A 21st Century Perspective*. Clevedon: Multilingual Matters.

Giles, Howard and Patricia Johnson. 1987. Ethnolinguistic identity theory: a social psychological approach to language maintenance. *International Journal of the Sociology of Language* 68: 66–99.

Giles, Howard and Ellen Bouchard Ryan (eds.). 1982. *Attitudes Towards Language Variation: Social and Applied Contexts*. London: Edward Arnold.

Goodfellow, Anne Marie (ed.). 2009. *Speaking of Endangered Languages: Issues in Revitalization*. Cambridge: Cambridge Scholars Publishing.

Grenoble, Lenore A. and Lindsay J. Whaley. 2006. *Saving Languages: An Introduction to Language Revitalization*. Cambridge: Cambridge University Press.

Grinevald, Colette and Michel Bert. 2011. Speakers and communities. In Peter K. Austin and Julia Sallabank (eds.), *Cambridge Handbook of Endangered Languages*. Cambridge: Cambridge University Press.

Hinton, Leanne and Jocelyn Ahlers. 1999. The issue of 'authenticity' in Californian language restoration. *Anthropology and Education Quarterly* 30: 56–67.

Hoffman, Katherine E. 2006. Berber language ideologies, maintenance, and contraction: gendered variation in the indigenous margins of Morocco. *Language and Communication* 26: 144–67.

Holton, Gary. 2011. The role of information technology in supporting minority and endangered languages. In Peter K. Austin and Julia Sallabank (eds.), *Cambridge Handbook of Endangered Languages*. Cambridge: Cambridge University Press.

Hudson, Alan. 2002. Outline of a theory of diglossia. *International Journal of the Sociology of Language* 157: 1–48.

Kloss, H. 1967. 'Abstand languages' and 'Ausbau languages'. *Anthropological Linguistics* 9: 29–71.

Kroskrity, Paul V. 2000. Regimenting languages. In Paul V. Kroskrity (ed.), *Regimes of Language: Ideologies, Polities, and Identities*. Santa Fe, NM: School of American Research Press.

Kroskrity, Paul V. 2009. Language renewal as sites of language ideological struggle: the need for 'ideological clarification'. In John Reyhner and Louise Lockard (eds.), *Indigenous Language Revitalization: Encouragement, Guidance and Lessons Learned*. Flagstaff: Northern Arizona University.

Marquis, Yan and Julia Sallabank. 2013. Speakers and language revitalisation: a case study of Guernesiais (Guernsey). In Mari Jones and Sarah Ogilvie (eds.), *Language*

Endangerment: Documentation, Pedagogy, and Revitalization. Cambridge: Cambridge University Press.

Marquis, Yan and Julia Sallabank. Forthcoming. Issues in orthography development: examples from Dgernesiais/Guernésiais/Giernesiei/Djernezié. Paper presented at workshop on *Writing Systems: Analysis, Acquisition and Use 2*, Institute of Education, London, 28 November 2009. Full version in preparation.

Mason, Jennifer. 2002. *Qualitative Researching* (2nd edn.). London and Thousand Oaks, CA: Sage.

Medgyes, Péter. 1992. Native or non-native: who's worth more? *ELT Journal* 46: 340–9.

Milroy, James. 1984. The history of English in the British Isles. In Peter Trudgill (ed.), *Language in the British Isles*. Cambridge: Cambridge University Press.

Moriarty, Máiréad. 2011. New roles for endangered languages. In Peter K. Austin and Julia Sallabank (eds.), *Cambridge Handbook of Endangered Languages*. Cambridge: Cambridge University Press.

Moseley, Christopher (ed.). 2009. *UNESCO Atlas of the World's Languages in Danger of Disappearing*. UNESCO. <http://www.unesco.org/culture/ich/index.php?pg=00206> (accessed 23 June 2011).

Sallabank, Julia. 2002. Writing in an unwritten language: the case of Guernsey French. *Reading Working Papers in Linguistics* 6: 217–44.

Sallabank, Julia. 2010. Endangered language maintenance and revitalisation: the role of social networks. *Anthropological Linguistics* 52: 184–205.

Sallabank, Julia. 2011. Norman languages of the Channel Islands: current situation, language maintenance and revitalisation. *Shima: The International Journal of Research into Island Cultures* 5: 18–41.

Sallabank, Julia. 2013. Can majority support save an endangered language? A case study of language attitudes in Guernsey. *Journal of Multilingual and Multicultural Development* 34: 332–47.

Spolsky, Bernard. 2009. *Language Management*. Cambridge: Cambridge University Press.

States of Guernsey. 2002. *2001 Guernsey Census: Report on the Census of Population and Households*. Guernsey: States of Guernsey Advisory and Finance Committee.

States of Guernsey. 2010. *Our Way of Life: A Cultural Strategy for Guernsey 2010–14*. <http://www.gov.gg/ccm/cms-service/download/asset/?asset_id=13534853> (accessed 23 June 2011).

States of Guernsey Policy and Research Unit. 2009. *Annual Population Bulletin*. St Peter Port: States of Guernsey Policy and Research Unit.

States of Jersey. 2011. About the British–Irish Council. <http://www.gov.je/britishirishcouncil/Pages/index.aspx> (accessed 12 September 2011).

Thiers, Ghjacumu. 1986. Epilinguisme, élaboration linguistique et volonté populaire, trois supports de l'individuation sociolinguistique corse. *Langages* 21: 65–74.

Thomason, Sarah G. and Terence Kaufman. 1988. *Language Contact, Creolization, and Genetic Linguistics*. Berkeley, CA: University of California Press.

Trudgill, Peter. 1992. Ausbau sociolinguistics and the perception of language status in contemporary Europe. *International Journal of Applied Linguistics* 2: 167–77.

Trudgill, Peter. 2004. Glocalisation and the Ausbau sociolinguistics of modern Europe. In Anna Duszak and Urszula Okulska (eds.), *Speaking from the Margin: Global English from a European Perspective*. Frankfurt: Peter Lang.

Williams, Glyn. 1992. *Sociolinguistics: A Sociological Critique*. London: Routledge.

9

Local Language Ideologies and Language Revitalization among the Sumu-Mayangna Indians of Nicaragua's Caribbean Coast Region

JANE FREELAND & ELOY FRANK GÓMEZ
WITH GLORIA FENLY & STRINGHAM MONTERO CISNEROS*

9.1 Introduction

THIS CHAPTER AIMS to contribute to the growing literature on language ideologies and language revitalization (e.g. Blommaert 1999; Duchêne and Heller 2007; Kroskrity and Field 2009; Schieffelin et al. 1998) with a case study that explores how local language ideologies vary not only between but within ethnic groups. It also adds to the relatively scarce literature that focuses not only on language loss but on successful language maintenance (Dorian 1998).

We compare two Sumu-Mayangna communities. In both communities another, more powerful indigenous language, Miskitu, forms part of the community repertoire. One community, however, shows a marked and growing tendency to shift towards Miskitu, whilst in the other the local language is secure and gaining new ground. Yet in both communities the language enjoys the same institutional support under Nicaragua's progressive language policies: official status, intercultural–bilingual education programmes, and strong backing from the local university, URACCAN.

In seeking to explain these differences, we focus on the local language ideologies that have developed historically in the two communities, and explore the extent to which these resonate or conflict with the dominant ideology underpinning Nicaragua's language policy. We argue that such resonance, or the lack of it, profoundly affects the success of language maintenance and

* Gloria Fenly and Stringham Montero Cisneros are Tuahka-speaking members of the community of Wasakin; at the time of writing they were both primary school teachers in the Sumu bilingual programme.

Proceedings of The British Academy, **199**, 167–194. © The British Academy 2014.

revitalization measures, and that where it is lacking new approaches to revitalization need to be sought.

The chapter is based on our work since 2005 with the Sumu-Mayangna Indians of Nicaragua's Caribbean Coast region. It includes ethnographic work in several communities, and extensive classroom discussions with Sumu-Mayangna students on two courses co-taught by Freeland and Frank Gómez at the University of the Autonomous Regions of Nicaragua's Caribbean Coast (URACCAN). This is in addition to a sociolinguistics unit for the URACCAN *Licenciatura* (BA) in Intercultural Bilingual Education, in 2005, and the first two sessions of a Community Diploma in Sociolinguistics and Language Revitalization for community leaders, initiated in 2009 with finance from the Norwegian educational NGO, SAHI, which ended in August 2011.

A fuller discussion of the diploma course appears in the conclusions to this chapter, since it was developed as a direct response to the problems examined here. The course brought together village elders and younger members from different communities and enabled them to carry out basic research in their own communities on the particular situation of Sumu-Mayangna and how it developed. The aim was to empower them to develop revitalization strategies appropriate to their community language ideologies. We cite some survey data from students on this course. However, since data are still being processed, and their eventual use consulted with the communities, we can only refer to it here in broad general terms.[1]

The chapter comprises six sections. In section 9.2, we set out our conceptual framework. In section 9.3 we contextualize the Sumu-Mayangna demographically, territorially, and in the changing power structures of Nicaragua's Caribbean Coast region. Sections 9.4 and 9.5 trace the historical development of two very different social ecologies of language and their related language ideologies, and explores their degree of resonance with the 'official' ideology. We conclude by discussing the implications of our findings for the maintenance and revitalization of their language that all Sumu-Mayangna ostensibly desire, and for language revitalization in general.

9.2 Language Ideologies and Language Ecologies

We take a community's 'local language ideology' to be its beliefs and commonsense notions about language in general and about its own and other people's

[1] The ethnographic work was carried out in 2005–6 by Frank Gómez for his URACCAN Master's thesis in social anthropology, supervised by Freeland, and through a research project on Sumu-Mayangna language ideologies, financed by a British Academy Small Grant and managed by Freeland. Frank Gómez was the Nicaraguan coordinator and co-researcher and Fenly and Montero were research assistants. The Community Diploma in Sociolinguistics and Language Revitalization (2010–11) is financed by the Norwegian NGO, SAHI.

languages in particular (Kroskrity 1998; Kroskrity and Field 2009; Schieffelin et al. 1998; Silverstein 1998a, 1998b). The degree to which such beliefs are consciously held is variable: they may be explicit and culturally highly salient, or part of a community's practical knowledge as evident in its everyday practice (Field and Kroskrity 2009: 6–7).

We focus particularly on the aspect of language ideologies that concerns the relationship between language and ethnic identity, taking 'identity' to be 'a relational and socio-cultural phenomenon that emerges and circulates in local discourse contexts of interaction rather than as a stable structure located primarily in the individual psyche or in fixed social categories ... *identity is the social positioning of self and other*' (Bucholz and Hall 2010: 19, authors' emphasis, see also Bucholz and Hall 2004). Such a 'broad and open-ended definition' (Bucholz and Hall 2010: 19) is particularly important when comparing local language ideologies, as they concern language and *ethnic* identity. Much of the discourse on ethnic identities, especially in the pursuit of identity politics, tends to represent them in 'primordialist/essentialist' terms, as fixed, pre-existing categories marked by a set of inherited cultural traits whose change or loss is interpreted as identity loss. Language tends to be seen as one of the most important of these traits; latterly it has assumed an increasingly prominent place in the discourse on indigenous and minority rights. However, according to this broader view of identity, ethnic identity is not the only, or even the most salient, identity available to indigenous or ethnic minorities. Correspondingly, although language is one of the principal means for socially positioning oneself, the language associated with an individual's ethnic identity is not necessarily the most important one for a member of an ethnic group.

We approach Sumu-Mayangna local language ideologies through the analysis of their 'popular discourse on language' as it occurs in formal or informal talk about language, through their daily communicative practice, and particularly through the relationship between the two. The 'official' ideology of language is expressed primarily in Nicaragua's legislation on diversity and on minority languages in particular (though a rather wider corpus of texts is analysed in Freeland 1999 and 2011).[2] Of course, Sumu-Mayangna popular discourse on language also incorporates interpretations of the 'official' discourse, as well as the discourses of linguists and anthropologists with whom they have interacted. These interpretations are sometimes dismissed as mere 'folk linguistics' that distort or misunderstand those discourses; in our view they should be considered part of local language ideology (Cameron 1995; Niedzielski and Preston 2003), much as long-borrowed lexicon is considered part of a language.

[2] Legal texts can be 'seen as ... reified ideology, if we take it that ideologies are ... networks of given ideas ... that reflect the interests of the dominant groups that formulate laws' (Martel 1999: 52–3).

Finally, we assume a relationship between 'local ideologies of language' and 'social ecologies of language'. Generally speaking, the 'ecological discourse' on language revitalization has not explicitly included ideologies of language. In Haugen's original definition, a language ecology is constituted by the 'interactions between any given language and its environment', so that the 'true environment of a language is the society that uses it as one of its codes . . . [and] the language only functions in relating these users to their . . . social and natural environment' (Haugen 2001 [1972]: 57). Consequently, he emphasized, this relationship is 'sociological: its interaction with the society in which it functions as a medium of communication'. The ecology of a language 'is determined primarily by the people who learn it, use it, and transmit it to others' (Haugen 2001 [1972]: 57), and is rooted in their historical experience. Had Haugen been writing today, he might well have drawn out the implication of this definition: that community perceptions of these relationships—their local ideologies of language—are part of any language ecology and its development.

9.3 The Sumu-Mayangna in Context

Demographically, the Sumu-Mayangna are one of the smallest of the Coast region's five ethnic and indigenous minorities, whilst the Miskitu are the largest.[3]

Table 9.1 Demography of Nicaragua's Caribbean Coast region. (PNUD 2005)

Ethnic group	Mestizos	Miskitu	Creoles	Sumu-Mayangna-Sumu	Ulwa	Rama	Garífuna (Black Caribs)
First language	Spanish	Miskitu	English Creole	Northern Sumu *c.*13,000	Miskitu (Ulwa)	English Creole (Rama)	English Creole (Garífuna)
% of Coast population	72	40.88	11.83	5.23	0.41	0.55	0.43

[3] Namings are sensitive in this region. The phrase 'indigenous and ethnic groups' was adopted nationally to include non-indigenous, Afro-Caribbean minorities and so avoid the issue of aboriginality, which became contentious in early rights negotiations with the Sandinista revolutionary government. Until the mid-1990s, the Sumu-Mayangna were referred to in literature about the Coast, and self-referred, as 'Sumu'. This name included the groups labelled 'Sumu-Mayangna' and 'Ulwa' in Table 9.1. Since then, reacting to pejorative connotations given to the name Sumu by the Miskitu, the name 'Mayangna' has gained currency. However, not all Sumu accept this, notably the Ulwa, who consider themselves part of the Sumu 'family' but not Mayangna. Even some 'Mayangna' prefer the denomination 'Sumu'. We adopt here the usage 'Sumu-Mayangna' stipulated by the newly formed Sumu-Mayangna 'national' government for both the ethnicity and the language, and use Panamahka, Tuahka, and Ulwa to refer to the subgroups so named and to the variants of Sumu-Mayangna that they speak.

A rough United Nations Development Programme (UNDP) census in 2005 estimated Sumu-Mayangna numbers at about 13,000 in Nicaragua, but no full census has yet been conducted. Together with the Ulwa, the Sumu-Mayangna constitute just 5.7 per cent of the Coast's population and a minuscule proportion of the national population of approximately 3 million.

Linguists refer to the Sumu-Mayangna's language as 'Northern Sumu', a member of the small Central American Misumalpan family that also includes Miskitu.[4] Two variants—Panamahka and Tuahka—are spoken in Nicaragua, whilst a third—Tawahka—is spoken in Honduras. Southern Sumu, or Ulwa, a different but related language (Benedicto and Hale 2000), is spoken in the south of the region. Benedicto and Hale (2000) estimate between 10,000 and 12,000 Panamahka speakers and about 2,000 Tuahka speakers in Nicaragua, and between 850 and 1,000 Tawahka speakers in Honduras.[5]

The traditional Sumu-Mayangna territories span the much-disputed Nicaragua–Honduras frontier, but are more extensive in Nicaragua. As the map in Figure 9.1 shows, these territories are not clearly separated.[6] Some are closely contiguous with those of ethnically different groups, whilst other territories and even villages are shared by different ethnic groups—more so in some parts of the region than others. Consequently, linguistic and territorial boundaries are not neatly isomorphic. Social interaction in the region takes place through four languages: Spanish, Miskitu, Sumu-Mayangna, and English/Creole, and complex multilingual practices are the norm (Freeland 2003).

About 70 per cent of the Nicaraguan Sumu-Mayangna live in the BOSAWAS Reserve, a UNESCO Biosphere Reserve designated in 1991, which also incorporates the traditional territories of about 14,000 Miskitu Indians (Stocks 1994). The remaining 30 per cent of the Mayangna live in an area known as the Mining Triangle. Our comparison is between communities in these two areas.

9.3.1 A History of Heterogeneity

Heterogeneity and interethnic relations predate European contact with the region, when Central America was home to numerous, loosely knit indigenous groups

[4] The name Misumalpan combines syllables of the names of three of its member languages: Miskitu, Sumu, and Matagalpan. 'The unity of the family was established by ... Lehmann (1920), who also assembled in his work most of the Misumalpan linguistic data available in his time ... [T]he first serious comparative work seeking to reconstruct aspects of the putative proto-language is that of Constenla Umaña (1987)' (Benedicto and Hale 2000: 95).

[5] Their estimate is based on the work of several linguists up to 1997, since when speaker numbers are likely to have changed. Nevertheless, these figures are probably more reliable than those currently given on the *Ethnologue* site. The discrepancy between population and speaker numbers is a rough indicator of language displacement.

[6] Given that this map was drawn up in the early stages of indigenous territorial demarcation, it may even slightly exaggerate territorial discreteness.

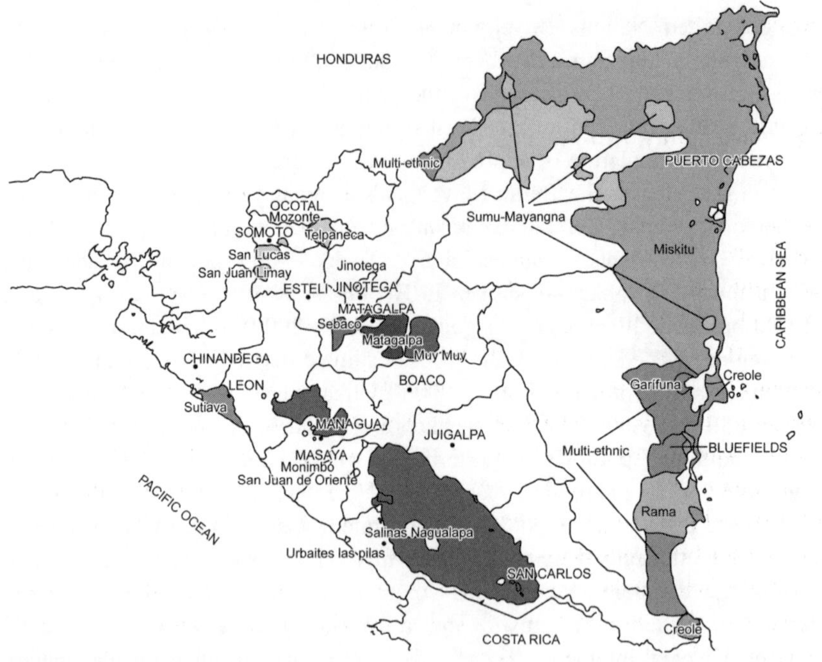

Figure 9.1 Indigenous peoples and ethnic communities of Nicaragua. (Buss 2004: 10)

who merged or split in response to pressures and opportunities offered by trade, war, or internal differences (Offen 1999; Romero Vargas 1995; von Houwald 2003). Many of these groups have now 'disappeared'. Early English and Spanish chroniclers mention many more groups than the three (Panamahka, Tuahka, and Ulwa) identified nowadays as 'Sumu' or Mayangna. The received wisdom was that these groups died out in wars with the Miskitu during the eighteenth century. However, there is now evidence they were not killed off, but 'transculturated' towards other ethnic communities, adopting their language and at least some elements of their culture.[7] Jamieson (2001: 10–11) has studied a community in the south of the region that may have belonged to one such group, the Tungla. Today they speak Spanish and are classified by outsiders as Mestizo, but older community members still identify themselves as 'Sumu', the community retains

[7] Whitehead points out, in discussing ethnogenesis in Suriname, a comparably heterogeneous and multiply colonized region (1499–1681), that when groups ostensibly 'disappear', it is more often the case that 'new group identities were formed and old ones fell into disuse … than that persons themselves were destroyed'. The issue is 'how self-representation and the definition of others work as synergetic processes for the formation of group identity' (Whitehead 1996: 21). The volume in which this study appears (Hill 1996) carries several studies of such merging and splitting among American Indians, and their implications for contemporary indigenous rights claims.

many Sumu-Mayangna cultural practices, and the main Ulwa-Sumu community now accepts them as 'Spanish-Sumu'. More recently, Gurdián (2001) has traced the 'transculturation' of a formerly Sumu-Mayangna community that now self-identifies as Miskitu, apparently motivated by the pressures of counter-revolutionary war in the 1980s.[8]

Perhaps unsurprisingly, this region is regarded by linguists as part of a long-established and well-defined 'linguistic area': both Miskitu and Sumu-Mayangna have borrowed lexicon from each other, and 'the syntactic structures of the present-day Misumalpan languages exhibit the characteristics of grammatical "merger" not uncommon in such areas, though it is difficult to trace the history of these mergers at all precisely' (Benedicto and Hale 2000: 97).

Europeans first arrived in the mid-seventeenth century. Spain and England, vying for control of this geopolitically strategic part of the Caribbean Basin, occupied respectively the western and the eastern halves of the Central American isthmus, each seeking possession of the other half. In the nineteenth century, as Britain gradually withdrew, the region became an economic enclave of the United States, within a Mestizo-dominated Nicaraguan state. The mid- to late nineteenth century saw increasing efforts towards state unification and strong resistance from *Costeños* (Coast peoples) determined to defend what they perceived as their autonomy from Hispanic dominance. The region was forcibly incorporated into the Nicaraguan state in 1894, though resistance continued whenever opportunity presented itself. The latest episode was a Miskitu-led uprising against the Sandinista revolution, which became co-opted into the US-backed counter-revolutionary war of the 1980s.[9] In 1987, peace negotiations led to a new constitution proclaiming Nicaragua 'a multi-ethnic nation', and to an autonomy law granting extensive political, cultural, and economic rights to the peoples of the Coast. Initially, only the linguistic rights were consistently developed, largely through the institution in 1985 of primary school level intercultural–bilingual education programmes (PEBI) in Sumu-Mayangna, Miskitu, and English/Creole, which became the principal sites for minority language maintenance and revitalization. Since 1994, however, there has been important progress on the demarcation and titling of historic territories.

As Coast peoples responded to these changes of external and internal power, there emerged a shifting hierarchy of political and socio-economic power, reflected

[8] Indeed, such fluidity is still so important to Coast peoples that it had to be recognized in the Autonomy Law of 1987, discussed below: its Article 13 gives individuals and groups 'the right to define and determine their own ethnic identity'. (All quotations of the Autonomy Law are from the official English translation, ODACAN 1994.)

[9] For accounts of the Coast's dual colonization and its effects, written within different ideological and methodological frameworks, see Dunbar Ortiz (1984), González Pérez (1997), Hale (1994), Offen (1999), and Vilas (1989).

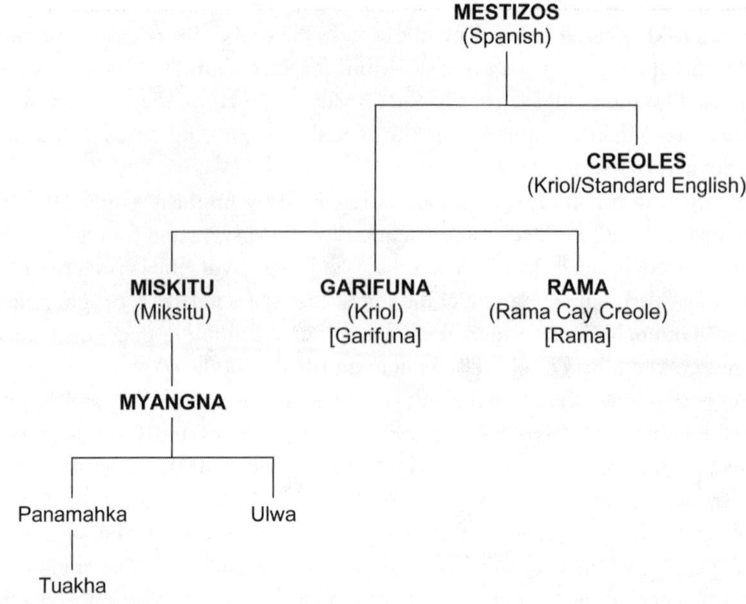

Figure 9.2 Ethnolinguistic hierarchy of the Caribbean Coast region of Nicaragua.

Key: **Name of group**; (language in daily use); [original language almost in disuse]

and maintained by a corresponding hierarchy of symbolic power, of which the current form is represented in Figure 9.2.

Figure 9.2 shows the whole hierarchy, but we shall focus here only on the relationship between Sumu-Mayangna and Miskitu. The balance of power between these two groups was tipped towards the Miskitu when they became special allies of the British, exercising a form of indirect rule on their behalf over the other indigenous groups. During this period, Miskitu became a regional lingua franca. Moravian missionaries further cemented Miskitu dominance in the nineteenth and early twentieth centuries by adopting their language to evangelize among both the Miskitu and the Sumu-Mayangna. They translated the Bible into Miskitu and, when they 'indigenized' the church in the north of the region in the twentieth century, they trained Miskitu pastors to lead it. This association of the Miskitu language with Christianity, 'civilization', and writing gave it a prestige that it still retains, and correspondingly limited the power and scope of Sumu-Mayangna, which remained unwritten until the mid-twentieth century. From the 1894 incorporation of the Coast into the Mestizo-dominated Nicaraguan state until the Sandinista revolution of 1979, successive governments imposed strict Hispanization policies in the interests of national unity, prohibiting all other languages in state education (Freeland 1999, 2003, 2011). As a result of these processes, Sumu-Mayangna became doubly subordinated to Miskitu and Spanish.

9.3.2 Language Rights Under the Sandinistas

Under the Sandinista Autonomy Law of 1987, all the communities of the Caribbean Coast region were accorded 'absolute equality of rights and duties, regardless of the size of their population and level of development' (Art. 11.1). As with ethnic groups (or 'communities', as the legislation calls them), so with languages: there was to be no discrimination on grounds of the number of speakers or of the languages' state of development/decline. Whether still in use or not, all the Coast's languages acquired 'official status within the Region' (Art. 5). All groups gained the right to 'promote and develop their languages, religions and cultures' (Art. 11.2), and 'to be educated in their mother tongues (*en su lengua materna*), through programmes that take into account their historical heritage, their traditions and the characteristics of their environment, all within the framework of the national education system' (Art. 11.5). In 1993 these provisions on language were further elaborated through a Law of Official Use of the Community Languages of the Atlantic Coast of Nicaragua (Law No. 162), which came into effect in 1996. It defines 'official use' more precisely and provides for the Coast languages to be taught as a subject at secondary level and in teacher training (ODACAN n.d.).

Like much egalitarian legislation, however, this overlooks the need for asymmetric policies to achieve the equalities it proposes, and takes little account of the complex social ecology outlined above. Moreover, it rests on essentialist assumptions of the kind that underlie the Euro-American model of nation-building adopted in Latin America, assuming that cultural unity is created through a shared language that expresses the essential spirit of the group. It therefore treats Nicaragua's indigenous and ethnic groups as though they were discrete, homogeneous nation-like entities, identified by and identifying with equally discrete, homogeneous languages.[10] It is true that all *Costeño* groups, in claiming their indigenous rights from those who use this discourse, present themselves with 'strategic essentialism' (Jaffe 1999: 121) as single, unified *ethnias*. However, communities vary considerably in their interpretation of this discourse. The Sumu-Mayangna are a particular case in point: they have only relatively recently begun to conceive of themselves as a single people/nation (Frank Gómez, personal communication); most refer more readily to the 'Sumu family' and to themselves by their subgroup names—*Tuahka*, *Panamahka*, *Tawahka*.

It is this variation that we shall now examine in more detail, focusing on differences in the local ideologies of language that have developed in the Reserve and the Mining Triangle communities, and their relationship to the dominant ideology of language.

[10] For fuller critical analyses of this ideology, see Freeland and Patrick (2004a), Jaffe (1999), and Cameron (2007).

9.4 Local Language Ideology in the Reserve

In the villages of the Reserve, local and 'official' discourses on language chime well with each other. These villages are located in the ancestral environment of rivers and rainforest where Sumu-Mayangna culture originated. Since the mid-1990s, they have developed important alliances with international conservation NGOs in support of their claims to have their traditional territories recognized and demarcated under the provisions of the Autonomy Law, and to make the case for indigenous state co-management of the Reserve, with indigenous villagers as forest wardens (e.g. Stocks 1994; Stocks et al. 1998). Since the Sandinistas returned to power in 2006 such co-management is realized through 'ecological battalions' of the army, consisting entirely of Sumu-Mayangna whose role is to protect the Reserve. Such developments have legitimated and greatly enhanced the status of traditional Sumu-Mayangna culture and its value in the national economy.[11]

The Reserve holds the largest concentrations of Sumu-Mayangna villages, so that interactions between communities, such as trading and social events, take place predominantly in Sumu-Mayangna. Importantly, these communities also maintain the Sumu-Mayangna tradition of endogamy, but have adapted it to modern realities. Mixed marriages are now permitted if the aspiring non-Sumu-Mayangna partner can demonstrate prior links with the community and commits to learning Sumu-Mayangna and speaking it in the home. Surveys carried out in 2010 by students on the URACCAN Sumu-Mayangna Community Diploma course in two Reserve communities show relatively few Sumu-Mayangna/Miskitu mixed marriages, and provide evidence that non-Sumu-Mayangna partners, both male or female, become completely integrated into Sumu-Mayangna mores. Importantly, too, in these communities the Moravian Church is no longer dominated by Miskitu; services are now conducted entirely in Sumu-Mayangna by Sumu-Mayangna pastors using Sumu-Mayangna Bibles.

However, these are not monolingual communities isolated from interethnic contact; they need to engage with Miskitu communities whose traditional territories also lie in the Reserve, with communities of later-constituted Mestizo peasant settlers, with the Nicaraguan State, and with conservation NGOs, interactions that all require multilingual skills. Table 9.2 shows the results of a 1996 survey of community multilingualism in two Reserve territories, Mayangna Sauni As (MSA), comprising 16 communities, and Sikilta, the only territory

[11] Stocks (2005) and Stocks (1998) provide excellent accounts of Sumu-Mayangna historical and contemporary land tenure issues, the processes of territorial demarcation, the development of co-management plans, and the case for co-management. They also cogently analyse the differences between indigenous and government conceptions of 'land' and 'territory' that have created conflict and stand in the way of co-management plans.

Table 9.2 Multilingualism in two Sumu-Mayangna territories of the BOSAWAS Reserve.

Bi/multilingualism	**Territory**			
Total <16 years old	**Mayangna Sauni As***		**Sikilta****	
	Men n=1,610	Women n=1,577	Men n=71	Women n=70
Monolingual Sum	777 ***24.4%***	907 ***28.5%***	0 ***0%***	4 ***2.8%***
Bilingual Sum-Myn/Msk	191 ***5.99%***	362 ***11.3%***	2 ***1.41%***	32 ***22.69%***
Bilingual Sum/Span	137 ***4.29%***	74 ***2.32%***	6 ***4.25%***	5 ***3.54%***
Bilingual Sum-Myn/Span	0 **0%**	0 **0%**	0 ***0%***	1 ***0.71%***
Trilingual Sum-Myn/Msk/Span	505 ***15.8%***	234 ***7.34%***	63 ***43.75%***	28 ***19.86%***
Total Sumu-Mayangna speakers	1,610 ***100%***	1,577 ***100%***	71 ***100%***	70 ***100%***

* Source: 'Libro territorial Mayangna Sauni As' (1997) Appendix 1: Table 10

** Source: 'Libro territorial Sikilta' (1997) Appendix 1: Table 9

comprising a single community. Some MSA communities are contiguous with Miskitu communities, whereas Sikilta is surrounded by both Miskitu and Mestizo communities.

In both territories, 100 per cent of the population over 16 years of age speaks Sumu-Mayangna, but in MSA more of them are monolingual in Sumu-Mayangna than in Sikilta. In MSA there is a higher incidence of monolingualism than in Sikilta, in both men and women (though it is more prevalent among women); in Sikilta monolingualism is exclusive to women. Sikilta shows a higher overall incidence of bi- and trilingualism than MSA, and in both territories men are more multilingual than women (in Sikilta 100 per cent of the men and 61 per cent of the women, against 51 per cent of the men and 42 per cent of the women in MSA), though skills are differently distributed between languages. Overall, many more men than women speak Spanish, but there are fewer Spanish speakers in MSA than in Sikilta (in MSA 40 per cent of men and only 19.5 per cent of women, in Sikilta 97.1 per cent of men and 48.5 per cent of women). Miskitu skills are more evenly distributed, though again more pronounced in men (in MSA 43 per cent of men and 37 per cent of women; in Sikilta 91 per cent of men and 87 per cent of women). Since these figures are not disaggregated by age, they give no information on the spread of multilingualism; nor is there any clear definition of what respondents understood by 'speaking a language'. Preliminary analysis of Community Diploma student surveys of two other Reserve villages in 2010 suggests that this pattern has not significantly changed.

In all these communities, the local language ideology establishes and maintains clearly defined functions for Sumu-Mayangna, Miskitu, and Spanish, such that they take their place within a balanced social ecology of language, of the kind that Mühlhäusler (1996) considers critical to the maintenance of even very small languages in multilingual and multi-ethnic conditions like these (see also Kroskrity 1998). Firstly, there is a clear division between 'our' language, Sumu-Mayangna, and 'theirs', Miskitu or Spanish: it is deemed inappropriate to use anything but Sumu-Mayangna for within-community talk, and this is supported by the rules governing marriage and language. Correspondingly, it is considered 'natural' to speak to others in 'their' language when receiving them as visitors or visiting them in their communities. When we suggested to Sumu-Mayangna sociolinguistics students that this was a sign of Sumu-Mayangna's subordination to Miskitu, they denied it vehemently, saying that it was simply 'natural', and a matter of courtesy.[12]

In the villages of MSA, the main contact is with Miskitu. The relationship with Spanish is more classically diglossic, largely because the use of Sumu-Mayangna in public contexts is not yet fully normalized: Spanish is still the language of secondary and most higher education, of negotiations with state officials and with the NGOs that figure largely in Sumu-Mayangna life (though Sumu-Mayangna speakers are now more frequent among local officials). In Sikilta, where contiguous Mestizo peasant communities bring Spanish closer and, as we saw, there is a higher incidence of Sumu-Mayangna-Spanish bilingualism, the 'ours' and 'theirs' separation becomes equally important between Sumu-Mayangna and Spanish. Indeed, there is even evidence that, when Reserve Sumu-Mayangna migrate to the Spanish-speaking municipal capitals, they take their local language ideology with them. A survey carried out by Community Diploma students in Sumu-Mayangna *barrios* of Rosita suggests that, despite the close proximity of Spanish and the lack of PEBI provision in the schools, Sumu-Mayangna from the Reserve tend to maintain Sumu-Mayangna in the home more consistently than those originating elsewhere.

The sense of indigenous identity in the Reserve communities and of Sumu-Mayangna as its icon has considerably intensified over the last 30 years. These territories became strategic during the war of the 1980s.[13] As a peace negotiation concession, the Sumu-Mayangna were allowed to do their national service defending their own communities. However, some elders on the Community

[12] Additionally, many Sumu-Mayangna, from both Reserve and Mining Triangle villages, are loath to contemplate the idea that the Miskitu might learn and speak to them in Sumu. An often-cited reason rests on the notion of Sumu as a secret, private language.

[13] See Flores Farfán (2001) on similar intensifying experiences among the Nahua of Mexico's Alto Basas region.

Diploma course tell of how young men hunting with arms were regarded with suspicion and sometimes captured by either Sandinista and/or resistance forces. To prove they were indeed Sumu-Mayangna, they were required to speak Sumu-Mayangna before trusted witnesses, which made the link between language and identity a matter of life and death.

A threat of a different kind arose when the UN Biosphere Reserve was first mooted. Originally, it was to be based on a very strict model that excluded humans from the most ecologically delicate areas, and would entail relocating communities from their traditional territories. Sustained and well-organized protest by the Reserve communities, on the grounds that these areas had survived thanks to, not despite, their presence, eventually persuaded the UN to revise the model (Howard 1993, 1996; Stocks 2005). This struggle further motivated the Reserve Sumu-Mayangna to demand full recognition, demarcation, and titling of their territories according to the Autonomy Law.

In sum, circumstance and ideology have kept the Sumu-Mayangna language (Panamahka) vital and secure in the Reserve villages and contributed to its steady 'iconization' (Gal and Irvine 1995). The traditional Sumu-Mayangna culture in which it is embedded has acquired new economic potential as both Nicaragua and the world revalue rainforest environments. Although, in an increasingly interethnic context, they need multilingual skills, and have become more vulnerable to the potential dangers of intermarriage, the people's adaptation of traditional Sumu-Mayangna endogamous marriage has so far permitted them to control the influx of outsiders and to integrate them into their communities. Consequently, Sumu-Mayangna fulfils clearly differentiated functions within a relatively balanced sociolinguistic ecology.

This local language ideology resonates strongly with two powerful legitimating discourses: that underpinning Nicaragua's language policies and the PEBI, with its essentialized concept of discrete indigenous identities, unified though an identifying 'mother tongue'; and that of the international conservation agencies that have supported these communities in claiming and demarcating their territories. Indeed, the two discourses have recently come together in the concept of *biolinguistic diversity*, on which much of the language endangerment literature draws, which emphasizes the importance of indigenous languages as repositories of environmental knowledge (see e.g. Crystal 2000; Hale 1992; Nettle and Romaine 2000, and critiques of the use of this metaphor in Cameron 2007; Freeland and Patrick 2004b; Muehlmann 2007). To what extent these resonances are 'natural' and to what extent they are the result of astute strategic alliances on the Sumu-Mayangna's part, is difficult to determine (but see Stocks 2003 on the complex interactions of conservationist and indigenous agendas). The point is that, at least for now, they operate in favour of these communities' survival and development.

9.5 Local Language Ideology in the Mining Triangle

The situation of the Mining Triangle Sumu-Mayangna could not be more different; here, Sumu-Mayangna seems insecure and the institutional support that works well in the Reserve is not helping. This bodes particularly ill for the Tuahka variety of Sumu-Mayangna, which is spoken only in these villages. However, differences between Reserve and Mining Triangle ideologies cannot simply be attributed to dialectal differences, though as we shall see, these are a complicating factor. Sumu-Mayangna is also fading in the Panamahka-speaking villages of this area.

As we saw, these villages gradually became interspersed with Miskitu and Mestizo communities since the 1940s, when North American companies began mining gold, silver, and copper there. This activity brought a rapid influx of Miskitu migrant workers, some of whom settled. In the heyday of the mines, the Sumu-Mayangna became the main suppliers of fruit and vegetables to these workers (Frank Gómez 2006). Over time, Sumu-Mayangna villages became interspersed with new Miskitu settlements. Since the 1960s, national governments have also encouraged land-hungry Spanish-speaking Mestizo peasants to colonize so-called 'virgin lands' that in fact form part of Sumu-Mayangna traditional territories. Ethnically mixed Miskitu/Sumu-Mayangna villages have become increasingly common; indeed, one village we studied was founded by a mixed Miskitu/Sumu-Mayangna couple. Consequently, interaction between villages, and increasingly within them, is now interethnic and inevitably multilingual.

Mining, and the new trading relationships it generated, brought these villages into much closer association with the money economy than those of the Reserve. Although their forest and riverine environment is still important to their economies, and people still pursue traditional agricultural and hunting practices, Mining Triangle Sumu-Mayangna cannot easily claim to be natural conservators, so this role cannot hold the economic promise it does for the Reserve. Indeed, as Freeland's interviews with women reveals, they tend to associate traditional skills with poverty.

So there is much less continuity, and even some conflict, between traditional conservationist culture and modernity than in the Reserve villages. In fact, Wasakin, the Sumu-Mayangna 'capital' village of the area, acquired titles to its territory in 1905, through an older process; now it both allows and participates in relatively uncontrolled logging by foreign companies (Offen 1997).[14] Nor have these communities had the identity-heightening experiences we noted in the Reserve. During the 1980s, both Sumu-Mayangna and Miskitu refugees were relocated to the Mining Triangle area, especially from the strategic River Coco

[14] The titles were granted under the 1905 Harrison–Altamirano Treaty, signed as part of the incorporation of the Coast into the Nicaraguan State (Howard 1993).

zone, which further contributed to their ethnic mix. In current processes of territorial demarcation, language is not a criterion.

This history, then, has created a very different social ecology of language from that of the Reserve, and a concomitantly different local language ideology. These Mining Triangle Sumu-Mayangna share with the Reserve villagers the 'natural' tendency to speak to outsiders in their own language, but with different consequences. Mining Triangle villagers recall how their parents cautioned them to keep silent once they left their community, unless they could speak Miskitu. To what extent this parental injunction was motivated by the need to protect trading relations is unclear. The upshot was that as villages became more ethnically mixed this deference to Miskitu simply moved within community boundaries, and has facilitated a gradual capitulation.

Nor do the Mining Triangle villages regulate intermarriage, as do those of the Reserve. Indeed, many Sumu-Mayangna women consider a Miskitu partner to be a good catch; Miskitu men are seen as industrious and better earners than Sumu-Mayangna. Miskitu men, for their part, find Sumu-Mayangna women more docile and compliant than Miskitu women who, they think, are becoming 'too flighty'. When we mapped regular travel in three of these villages in 2006, to see how it related to multilingualism, we found that men and women travelled regularly to quite distant Miskitu villages, not only for trade, work, and social activities, but also, they said, to seek spouses. In all but a very few mixed households, Miskitu predominates.

Indeed, this is not unique to mixed families. In seven Mining Triangle communities surveyed by the Community Diploma students in mid-2010, a common pattern emerged: although with few exceptions people identified unhesitatingly as Tuahka or Panamahka, the habitual language of most homes was Miskitu. In class discussions of these findings, the younger Mining Triangle students in particular felt there was no necessary link between being Sumu-Mayangna and speaking Sumu-Mayangna, and spoke of 'feeling good' when speaking Miskitu.[15] Moreover, according to the Community Diploma students' survey of the Sumu-Mayangna *barrios* of Rosita, families whose members originated from Mining Triangle communities tended not to maintain Sumu-Mayangna in the home as consistently as those originating from the Reserve, though they, too, brought their community ideology with them.

Today, in the Mining Triangle villages, Miskitu is the first language of most school-age children, even when their parents speak Sumu-Mayangna; children feel it is easier to speak Miskitu, and many refuse to speak Sumu-Mayangna

[15] In one village, people in one sector of the village identified themselves as 'mix' (by which they meant Sumu-Mayangna/Miskitu). The surprise this provoked among the other students suggests it is a relatively new phenomenon; it triggered a heated discussion in the classroom, in which those who either lived in or originated from Reserve villages insisted that one had to be either Sumu-Mayangna or Miskitu, otherwise how would people know who to trust in a crisis?

even when they can. In discussions of intergenerational transmission during a village assembly in Dibahil, 2006, led in Sumu-Mayangna and Miskitu by Eloy Frank Gómez, we heard frequent interventions along these lines:

> Woman 1: I speak to them in Sumu—but they answer in Miskitu and they don't want to speak [Sumu].
>
> Woman 2: I never abandon my language with adults—but with my children I never use Mayangna because they don't want to speak it.

Miskitu also dominates key public spaces; in Wasakin, in late 2009, the Sumu-Mayangna headman (*síndico*) said he felt obliged to hold community meetings in Miskitu. The Sumu-Mayangna Moravian pastor interviewed there by Frank Gómez in 2006 said he favoured using Sumu-Mayangna as they do in the Reserve, but that his parishioners insisted he preach and read in Miskitu. In an exercise during the first term of the Community Diploma, when students plotted contexts of language use in their communities, it emerged that in all but one of the Mining Triangle villages represented, the Moravian pastor would not even let them sing hymns in Sumu-Mayangna; in discussions during the second term, the failure of the Moravian Church to legitimate Sumu-Mayangna became a recurrent theme.

This was brought powerfully home to us in August 2010, when Freeland, Frank Gómez, and two Diploma students from Reserve communities attended a Moravian Sunday service in Wasakin, conducted by a different Sumu-Mayangna pastor from the one quoted earlier. We had gone, with the pastor's consent, to talk about the course during the news exchange that traditionally follows Sunday service. The service was conducted entirely in Miskitu, apart from one Bible reading in Spanish. The Reserve students were dismayed when the pastor introduced us in Miskitu and then commented on our contribution also in Miskitu; in his view, Sumu-Mayangna was not in real danger, and responsibility for maintaining it lay entirely with parents.

In these communities, then, there is little sense that Sumu-Mayangna is 'our' language and Miskitu 'theirs'. Indeed, Miskitu has become so intrinsic to community interaction as to be indispensable, as the following quotation illustrates. During the lunch break at Dibahil village assembly, Frank Gómez informally sounded out attitudes to Miskitu:

> I asked them which of these languages do you think is best? Then some were like: 'well they're all important, so [the children] can learn Miskitu—or some other language—but they shouldn't miss out on Miskitu'. So the thing is not to stop speaking Miskitu, it's important that the child should speak Miskitu.[16]

[16] Since a major theme of the assembly was language revitalization, more strongly pro-Sumu declarations might have been expected.

Indeed, not only do Mining Triangle villagers find it easy to separate ethnic identity and language, but many seem uncomfortable with making too close an association between them. As one elder complained of the predominance of Miskitu in Dibahil, his words echoed the 'official' essentializing discourse, but they also tell of unsuccessful exhortations towards an ideal that people seem unwilling to embrace:

> I'm always telling the children that ... our language *must* always remain alive among us—*we're people too, but if we speak in the language of others we don't know who we are* ... you're not Miskitu but you only speak in Miskitu—you can't feel like a Miskitu if you're Mayangna—*you have to be Mayangna*, identify yourself as Mayangna—so there are days when we scold them like this. (Frank Gómez 2006, interview with Don Zacarías, village elder of Dibahil, emphasis added.)

Don Zacarías, whose wife is Miskitu, speaks Miskitu at home himself; in fact, he turned away from this conversation to address his grandchildren in Miskitu, though in the Diploma classes he revelled in speaking Tuahka and Panamahka with his colleagues.

In discussing indigenous identity, many emphasize bloodlines as the key marker. So, in the same village assembly, a young Sumu-Mayangna man—echoing the spirit of Don Zacarías's words above—complained that he was beginning to doubt whether he was really Tuahka, since he didn't speak the language. Don Zacarías then proceeded to prove his Tuahka authenticity by tracing the young man's genealogy, and that of most of the Tuahka present, through the traditional maternal line.

Consider, too, this account of his genealogy from a Wasakin man, using phenotypical features to index blood links (though to outsiders phenotype is not a reliable guide to ethnic identity):

> My grandfather was a Miskitu from the Río Coco, he came to Rosita as a rubber cutter. In Wasakin he encountered my grandmother ... and they married. He stayed in Wasakin, *now he too is a Sumu because he speaks Sumu*. My grandmother, though, *is an authentic Sumu*. My mother *looks Miskitu, but she's Sumu*. My father is a Miskitu from the Río Coco, he worked for a company that transported cargo to the mines. He met his wife in Wasakin, *now he is also Sumu*. My father has curly hair, but *his kids have straight hair, therefore we are more Sumu*. (Offen 1997, emphasis added.)[17]

This suggests that a Miskitu can 'become' Sumu-Mayangna by learning the language, but if your mother is Sumu-Mayangna you are authentically Sumu-Mayangna even if you don't speak the language. In principle, then, children of mixed parentage can settle the issue by their choice of language. At present, since most children prefer to speak Miskitu, if forced to link language and

[17] Straight hair is seen as a typically Sumu-Mayangna trait, whereas curly hair is a Miskitu/Creole trait, associated with their historic tradition of intermarriage with Creoles.

identity they might just choose the Miskitu identity to go with the language. As it is, some prefer to keep their options open, like one child whom Frank Gómez found playing in Miskitu with a group of Sumu-Mayangna children but speaking Miskitu. To the question of why he spoke only Miskitu when his father is Sumu-Mayangna, he replied: 'Look, my hair's curly and the colour of my skin's different, maybe I'm not Sumu, maybe I'm Miskitu' (conversation quoted by Frank Gómez 2006: 38). Identities in these villages, then, are more cross-cultural, and less clearly bounded than in the Reserve. In daily social interaction and language choice, the demands of local community relations seem more salient than a wider, more abstract 'ethnic identity', and Miskitu is crucial in negotiating them.

All this has serious implications for the PEBI, which is designed, projected, and implemented as a 'mother-tongue' programme. Its underlying ideology assumes, as we saw, that indigenous groups, like nations, are unified by loyalty to a common language. So a group's *mother tongue* is assumed to be both its language of identification and its first language (Skutnabb-Kangas 1981). Since this is not the case here, for most children the PEBI resembles the kind of submersion programme in an unfamiliar language that it was meant to replace. In many homes, there is little or no support for the variety of Sumu-Mayangna the children do learn; in some, students report, parents laugh at children trying out their school Sumu-Mayangna at home. The upshot is that the PEBI in these communities not only fails children educationally, but also fails in its purpose of legitimating or supporting their 'mother tongue'.

As Freeland (2003 and 2011) shows in detail, the problem is further complicated by Sumu-Mayangna dialect variation. Sumu-Mayangna is not standardized; indeed, the Sumu-Mayangna actively resist standardization because they value the Panamahka and Tuahka variants as markers of these identities, though they have been happy to work on a unified orthography for both variants (Benedicto 1999). In the oral culture of these communities, people could choose to converge around common understandings or emphasize differences, according to circumstances. Problems arise, however, with the advent of writing (which is relatively recent in Sumu-Mayangna). Assuming mutual intelligibility, the PEBI textbooks were originally only developed in Panamahka, the demographically dominant variant. Since this compounded the difficulties outlined above, some early reading texts in Tuahka have been introduced, thanks to pressure from Tuahka teachers.

In the Ulwa, Rama, and Garífuna communities in the south of the region, the mother tongue (language of identification) has long fallen out of use, but there is a strong desire to 'rescue' it (*rescatar*), at least symbolically. A successful solution adopted here is to deliver the PEBI in the children's L1 (Miskitu for the Ulwa, Creole for the other two), and to introduce the mother tongue using second- or other-language teaching methods. In theory, this could also be a useful interim measure for the Mining Triangle communities, to build on children's Sumu-Mayangna comprehension skills. However, when we suggested it in one or two Tuahka communities, the idea was roundly rejected as the ultimate surrender to Miskitu, and a betrayal of their identity. At the same time, teachers reportedly resort frequently to Miskitu in class. On the face of it, this rejection appears to contradict our observation that these communities are unwilling to associate language too closely with identity. Indeed, as our analysis shows, this is only one among many 'contradictions' in Mining Triangle attitudes towards their language: they both proclaim and reject the idea of language as a mark of identity, and whilst they publicly assert a concern to revitalize Sumu-Mayangna, their daily communicative practice seems to undermine that assertion. It would be easy to conclude that this public rhetoric is produced merely for the 'experts', and that they are not really interested in maintaining Sumu-Mayangna.

However, it may be worth viewing these contradictions not as evidence of dishonesty or even confusion, but as instances of 'heterogeneous discourse' (Fairclough 1992), where two or more ideologies are opposed.[18] On the one hand, in the social ecology of language that has developed in this area, and in the face of institutional and local persecution of their language and identity, these Sumu-Mayangna communities have evolved cross-cultural, multifaceted identities, and a utilitarian ideology of language that links it only weakly with ethnic identity.[19] On the other hand, the essentializing and iconizing discourse on language that has become hegemonic in Nicaragua is also ubiquitous: it was used strategically in early claims for indigenous rights made to the Sandinista government, and it permeates the Autonomy Law that responds to those claims and the discourse on language rights upon which current language revitalization strategies and the PEBI are founded. This is the discourse of the Reserve communities, a major and much-admired section of the Sumu family. Indeed, they sometimes use it to impugn the Mining Triangle villagers' authenticity as Sumu-Mayangna. In the early stages of the Community Diploma, we heard

[18] Closer ethnographic studies in particular communities, such as those of Hill (1984) and Warren (1998), would clarify how these different ideological strands are represented in different individuals or strata of the community, according to personal experience and social category (e.g. age, gender, and social role).

[19] In light of our earlier discussion of the Coast's long history of heterogeneity and interethnic contact, it is arguable that this utilitarian attitude is a continuation of pre-contact traditions according to which indigenous groups fused with other groups by adopting their language. If so, then the more 'iconized' relationship that has emerged in the Reserve communities would be a continuation of pre-contact adaptive responses of fission and differentiation. Kroskrity (2009), Reynolds (2009), and Bunte (2009) point out that not all indigenous communities traditionally link language and identity. Their work studies 'utilitarian' attitudes to language among, respectively, the Western Mono of Central California, Guatemalan Kaqchiquel communities, and the San Juan Paiute, and the gradual emergence of a more iconized relationship in response to specific pressures or opportunities.

Reserve village students accusing Mining Triangle students of betraying the Sumu-Mayangna identity by 'losing' their Sumu-Mayangna; as a participant observer of Sumu-Mayangna sporting events and religious assemblies, Frank Gómez (2006) heard Mining Triangle villagers being taunted as 'not real Sumu-Mayangna' because they did not speak Sumu-Mayangna. Hence, perhaps, the urgent tone of Don Zacarías's plea, quoted earlier, which seems both to echo and deny these taunts: 'We are people too, but if we speak in the language of others we don't know who we are—we're not Miskitu but we speak their language.'

Like other hegemonic discourses, this one effectively silences voices that go against its assumptions. Whilst it empowers their brothers in the Reserve, to the extent that it excludes cross-cultural identities and their corresponding linguistic ideology, it silences the voice of the Mining Triangle communities, effectively preventing them from conceptualizing clearly and articulating with confidence their own language ideology.

9.6 Conclusions

These findings, then, raise a number of questions. In the circumstances of the Mining Triangle communities, what are the most appropriate strategies for revitalizing Sumu-Mayangna? Or does this question raise too many others? Given their heterogeneous discourse on the matter, how do we know this is what these communities really want? As academic researchers, and in Frank Gómez's case as a Sumu-Mayangna, what role should we now play in the light of our findings? Should we conclude, with Ladefoged (1992) and Newman (2003), that it is none of our business, and leave these communities to their own devices, even if that leads to the demise of Tuahka? After all, Tuahka is now well recorded, and Panamahka, a closely related dialect, is thriving elsewhere. Might these communities' worries over revitalization simply be an artefact of the dominant ideology, which we academics have reinforced by spotlighting language endangerment and 'loss'? If so, are we not responsible now for responding to it? If so, how?

Such questions are increasingly being raised in the sociolinguistic, linguistic, and anthropological literature on language 'endangerment' and 'loss'. Certainly academics 'need to understand their own language ideologies and ensure that these accord well with community perspectives with regard to setting and achieving realistic goals for language revitalisation' (Collins 1998, cited in Field and Kroskrity 2009: 25–6). Our own research has been motivated by Frank Gómez's strong personal commitment to the survival and maintenance of Sumu-Mayangna, and by our joint sense that, in trying to answer some of the above questions, we needed a better understanding of Sumu-Mayangna 'community perspectives'. Conceivably, we could use our findings to 'manipulate' the Mining

Triangle ideology towards the 'iconizing' ideology of the Reserve, a strategy Loether (2009) controversially suggests.[20] Yet, despite plenty of official and internal Sumu-Mayangna pressure to move in that direction, this ideology has not yet 'taken' in the Mining Triangle communities. We have also observed its counter-productive, guilt-inducing effects. In any case, is the survival of Sumu-Mayangna sufficient reason for these communities to abandon the intercultural identities and language practices they have evolved as survival strategies?

Instead, we have been exploring ways of developing revitalization strategies more in tune with the Mining Triangle communities' existing ideology, through the Community Diploma in Sociolinguistics and Revitalization to which we have been referring. It ran from 2010 to 2011 at the URACCAN, and it brought together village elders and younger leaders from selected Reserve and Mining Triangle communities, with a view to putting into their hands some basic research tools to discover the situation of Sumu-Mayangna in their communities, including people's attitudes towards its revitalization.[21] These tools were adapted from sociolinguistic research methodology through discussion and practice, to make them culturally appropriate and communicable to the students' communities.

The goal was to involve the communities' younger and older generations in constructing their own 'prior ideological clarification' (Dauenhauer and Dauenhauer 1998) of whether and why they might want to revitalize Sumu-Mayangna, and how to develop revitalization strategies based on local circumstances and attitudes. Rather than insisting on radical change, the idea was to replace the abstract and hardly conceivable goal of 'we must speak our language' with modest, feasible goals that people can fit into their daily lives. The emphasis of the course was primarily on the process rather than the product; nevertheless, though the data produced are arguably weakened by having been gathered by beginner researchers, they are starting to refine our understanding of the sociolinguistic situation of Sumu-Mayangna language ecologies and ideologies.

The course consisted of three *encuentros* (intensive four-week sessions held at approximately six-month intervals) at URACCAN's Mining Triangle campus, between which the students applied their research training in their own communities, with periodic visits from two members of the URACCAN team to discuss problems, achievements, suggest possible modifications, and so on. The first

[20] Loether, and other contributors to Kroskrity and Field's 2009 volume (Bunte, Gómez and García, Axelrod, and Lochler) find an iconic sense of the relationship between language and identity to be most conducive to successful revitalization.

[21] Our ideas have, of course, been influenced by the work of Hinton and Hale (2001). We are also grateful for the interest and support of Jose Antonio Flores Farfán, who has been involved in developing and teaching the 2009–10 Diploma in Language Revitalization, for indigenous students from throughout Latin America, jointly with the Universidad Nacional Mayor de San Marcos, Guatemala, the Institución de Investigación de Lingüística Aplicada—CILA—of Peru, and the Centro de Investigaciones y Estudios Superiores en Antropología Social—CIESAS—in Mexico, under the auspices of the International Indigenous University.

encuentro focused on collecting household data on the relationship between ethnic allegiance, the languages used at home, and on the relationship between competence in Sumu-Mayangna, gender, and age. These surveys were shared and discussed extensively at the beginning of the second *encuentro*, and will be analysed in more detail. The second *encuentro* developed skills in interviewing and taking life histories, to fill out this data and give insights into the significance of Sumu-Mayangna in people's lives. Both *encuentros* also explored ways in which students could engage their communities in recovering or collecting songs, stories, and histories in Sumu-Mayangna, rather than focusing on revitalizing language per se. In the third and final *encuentro*, the results of this work were shared, and the issue addressed of how best to use the collected stories, songs, and histories to stimulate further interest in the communities. It was agreed to create CDs of stories and songs, with accompanying illustrated booklets, regular radio broadcasts based on them, and a web page, now that solar-powered computer resources are coming to some communities.

Overall, the survey data suggests that Sumu-Mayangna is less 'lost' in the Mining Triangle communities than the blanket statement 'we/you are losing our language' implies. Children may not speak Sumu-Mayangna, but many understand it well. The interview data suggest that, in households that declared Miskitu as their family language, older and younger adult family members both could and did continue, easily and willingly, conversations initiated in Sumu-Mayangna. One explanation to be explored further is that it has become habitual to initiate conversations in Miskitu and that initiating in Sumu-Mayangna is 'marked'. As one student suggested, Sumu-Mayangna 'is there, but it's silent'. Some students now feel encouraged to try opening conversations in Sumu-Mayangna as a way to start reactivating it. It will be interesting to see whether this stimulates readier use, or provokes reactions that reveal more negative attitudes.

Discussion of the surveys enabled comparison between communities, which has begun to alter perceptions among the Reserve students. They now feel that the situation of Sumu-Mayangna in the Reserve is not as dire as they supposed, and are willing to acknowledge that maintaining it there is more difficult than in their own communities. Interestingly too, it has alerted them to the possibility that Sumu-Mayangna in the Mining Triangle may be more vulnerable than they had supposed. Closing sessions of the course explored how the Reserve communities might help encourage revitalization strategies elsewhere.

One recurring theme was the role of the Moravian Church in supporting Sumu-Mayangna, and how to persuade church leaders to assume greater responsibility. Whilst this might appear merely to delegate responsibility to someone else, the church's considerable political and moral power in the communities makes its support or otherwise for Sumu-Mayangna highly charged. In the third and final *encuentro*, a meeting with local pastors took place, and a dialogue was initiated that the Moravians themselves welcomed.

Students reported more Sumu-Mayangna usage the following Sunday, and a weekly religious broadcast was arranged by Radio URACCAN, conducted in Sumu-Mayangna by two local pastors.

It may be that, following this course, some Mining Triangle communities will nevertheless opt not to pursue revitalization. At least they will make that decision from a clearer sense of their interests and values. At best, we hope communities may gradually define clear functions for Sumu-Mayangna that will revive its status and value in the community, and enable it to take its place within a balanced multilingual ecology. Either way, the experiment should contribute to a general understanding of the conditions under which language revitalization succeeds or fails.

References

Benedicto, Elena. 1999. Normalización de la Lengua Mayangna. MS, IPILC-URACCAN. Rosita, RAAN (Nicaragua).

Benedicto, Elena and Kenneth L. Hale. 2000. Mayangna, a Sumu language: its variants and its status within Misumalpan. In Elena Benedicto (ed.), *The UMOP Volume on Indigenous Languages*. University of Massachusetts Occasional Papers. Amherst: GLSA, University of Massachusetts.

Blommaert, Jan (ed.). 1999. *Language Ideological Debates*. Berlin and New York: Mouton de Gruyter.

Bucholz, Mary and Kira Hall. 2004. Theorizing identity in language and sexuality. *Language and Society*, 33: 501–47.

Bucholz, Mary and Kira Hall. 2010. Locating identity in language. In Carmen Llamas and Dominic Wyatt (eds.), *Language and Identities*. Edinburgh: Edinburgh University Press.

Bunte, Pamela A. 2009. 'You keep not listening with your ears!' Language ideologies, language socialization, and Paiute identity. In Paul V. Kroskrity and Margaret Field (eds.), *Native American Ideologies: Beliefs, Practices and Struggles in Indian Country*. Tucson: University of Arizona Press.

Cameron, Deborah. 1995. *Verbal Hygiene*. London: Routledge.

Cameron, Deborah. 2007. Language endangerment and verbal hygiene: history, morality and politics. In Alexandre Duchêne and Monica Heller (eds.), *Discourses of Endangerment: Ideology and Interest in the Defence of Languages*. London: Continuum.

Collins, James. 1998. Our ideologies and theirs. In Bambi B. Schieffelin, Kathryn Woolard, and Paul V. Kroskrity (eds.), *Language Ideologies, Practice and Theory*. New York and Oxford: Oxford University Press.

Crystal, David. 2000. *Language Death*. Cambridge: Cambridge University Press.

Dauenhauer, Nora Marks and Richard Dauenhauer. 1998. Technical, emotional and ideological issues in reversing language shift: examples from Southeast Alaska. In Lenore Grenoble and Lindsay J. Whaley (eds.), *Endangered Languages: Language Loss and Community Response*. Cambridge: Cambridge University Press.

Dorian, Nancy. 1998. Western ideologies and small-language prospects. In Lenore A. Grenoble and Lindsay J. Whaley (eds.), *Endangered Languages: Language Loss and Community Response*. Cambridge: Cambridge University Press.

Duchêne, Alexandre and Monica Heller (eds.). 2007. *Discourses of Endangerment.* London: Continuum.

Dunbar Ortiz, Roxanne. 1984. *Indians of the Americas: Human Rights and Self.* London: Zed Books.

Fairclough, Norman. 1992. *Discourse and Social Change*. Cambridge: Polity Press.

Field, Margaret C. and Paul V. Kroskrity. 2009. Introduction: revealing Native American language ideologies. In Paul V. Kroskrity and Margaret C. Field (eds.), *Native American Ideologies: Beliefs, Practices and Struggles in Indian Country.* Tucson: University of Arizona Press.

Flores Farfán, José Antonio. 2001. Culture and language revitalization, maintenance and development in Mexico: the Nahua Alto Balsas communities. *International Journal of the Sociology of Language* 152: 85–97.

Frank Gómez, Eloy. 2006. El Cambio Lingüístico y la Identidad: Un Estudio Etnográfico de la Comunidad de Wasakin. Unpublished Masters dissertation, University of the Autonomous Regions of the Caribbean Coast of Nicaragua.

Freeland, Jane. 1999. Can the grassroots speak? The literacy campaign in English on Nicaragua's Atlantic Coast. *International Journal of Bilingual Education and Bilingualism* 2:3: 214–32.

Freeland, Jane. 2003. Intercultural–bilingual education for an interethnic–plurilingual society? The case of Nicaragua's Caribbean Coast. *Comparative Education* 9: 239–60.

Freeland, Jane. 2011. Gaining and using language rights in a multilingual region. In Luciano Barraco (ed.), *National Integration and Contested Autonomy: The Caribbean Coast of Nicaragua*. 243–82. New York: Algora Publishing.

Freeland, Jane and Donna Patrick (eds.). 2004a. *Language Rights and Language Survival: Sociolinguistic and Sociocultural Perspectives*. Manchester: St Jerome Publishing.

Freeland, Jane and Donna Patrick. 2004b. Language rights and language survival: sociolinguistic and sociological perspectives. In Jane Freeland and Donna Patrick (eds.), *Language Rights and Language Survival: Sociolinguistic and Sociocultural Perspectives*. Manchester: St Jerome Publishing.

Gal, Susan and Judith T. Irvine. 1995. The boundaries of languages and disciplines: how ideologies construct difference. *Social Research* 62: 967–1001.

González Pérez, M. 1997. *Gobiernos Pluriétnicos: La Constitución de Regiones Autónomas en Nicaragua.* Mexico: URACCAN/Plaza y Valdés S.A.

Gurdián, Galio. 2001. Mito y memoria en la construcción de la fisonomía de la comunidad de Alamikangban. Unpublished PhD dissertation, Austin, University of Texas.

Hale, C. R. 1994. *Resistance and Contradiction: Miskitu Indians and the Nicaraguan State, 1894–1987*. Stanford, CA: Stanford University Press.

Hale, Ken. 1992. On endangered languages and the safeguarding of diversity. *Language* 68: 1–10.

Haugen, Einar. 2001 [1972]. The ecology of language. In Alwin Fill and Peter Mühlhäusler (eds.), *The Ecolinguistics Reader.* London: Continuum.

Hill, Jane. 1984. *Speaking Mexicano: Dynamics of Syncretic Language in Central Mexico*. Tucson: University of Arizona Press.

Hinton, Leanne and Ken Hale (eds.). 2001. *The Green Book of Language Revitalization in Practice*. New York: Academic Press.

Howard, Sara. 1993. Autonomía y derechos territoriales indígenas: el caso de la RAAN. *Wani: Revista del Caribe Nicaragüense* 14: 1–17.

Howard, Sara. 1996. Autonomía y derechos territoriales de los sumus de BOSAWAS: el caso de Sikilta [Autonomy and territorial rights of the Sumu of BOSAWAS: the case of Sikilta]. *Wani: Revista del Caribe Nicaragüense* 18: 3–18.

Jaffe, Alexandra. 1999. *Ideologies in Language: Language Politics on Corsica*. Berlin: Mouton de Gruyter.

Jamieson, Mark. 2001. Miskito, Sumo y Tungla: variación lingüística e identidad étnica. *Wani: Revista del Caribe Nicaragüense* 27: 6–12.

Kroskrity, Paul V. 1998. Arizona Tewa Kiva speech as a manifestation of a dominant language ideology. In Bambi B. Schieffelin, Kathryn Woolard, and Paul V. Kroskrity, *Language Ideologies*. New York and Oxford: Oxford University Press.

Kroskrity, Paul V. 2009. Embodying the reversal of language shift: agency, incorporation and language ideological change in the Western Mono community of Central California. In Paul V. Kroskrity and Margaret Field (eds.), *Native American Ideologies: Beliefs, Practices and Struggles in Indian Country*. Tucson: University of Arizona Press.

Kroskrity, Paul V. and Margaret Field (eds.). 2009. *Native American Ideologies: Beliefs, Practices and Struggles in Indian Country*. Tucson: University of Arizona Press.

Ladefoged, Peter. 1992. Another view of endangered languages. *Language* 69: 809–11.

Loether, Christopher. 2009. Language revitalization and the manipulation of language ideologies: a Shoshoni case study. In Paul V. Kroskrity and Margaret Field (eds.), *Native American Ideologies: Beliefs, Practices and Struggles in Indian Country*. Tucson: University of Arizona Press.

Martel, Angéline. 1999. Heroes, rebels, communities and states in language rights activism and litigation. In Miklos Kontra, Robert Phillipson, Tove Skutnabb-Kangas, and Tinor Váradu (eds.), *Language, A Right and a Resource: Approaching Linguistic Human Rights*. Budapest and New York: Central European University Press.

Muehlmann, Shaylih. 2007. Defending diversity: staking out a common global interest? In Alexandre Duchêne and Monica Heller (eds.), *Discourses of Endangerment*. London: Continuum.

Mühlhäusler, Peter. 1996. *Linguistic Ecology: Language Change and Linguistic Imperialism in the Pacific Region*. London: Routledge.

Nettle, Daniel and Suzanne Romaine. 2000. *Vanishing Voices: The Extinction of the World's Languages*. Oxford: Oxford University Press.

Newman, Paul. 2003. The endangered languages issue as a hopeless cause. In Mark Janse and Sijmen Tol (eds.), *Language Death and Language Maintenance*. Amsterdam and Philadelphia, PA: John Benjamins Publishing Company.

Niedzielski, Nancy A. and Dennis R. Preston. 2003. *Folk Linguistics*. Berlin: Mouton de Gruyter.

ODACAN (Oficina de Desarollo de la Autonomía de la Costa Atlántica de Nicaragua). 1994. *Autonomy Statute for the Regions of the Atlantic Coast of Nicaragua*. Managua: ODACAN.

ODACAN (Oficina de Desarollo de la Autonomía de la Costa Atlántica de Nicaragua). n. d. *Ley de Lenguas: Ley No 162 en Español, Miskitu, Sumu, Inglés*. Managua: ODACAN.

Offen, Karl. 1997. Interpreting the Mayangna past: the view from Wasakin, northeastern Nicaragua. *Human Organization* 62/4: 382–92.

Offen, Karl. 1999. The Miskitu kingdom: landscape and the emergence of a Miskitu ethnic identity, northeastern Nicaragua and Honduras, 1600–1800. PhD dissertation, Department of Geography, University of Texas.

Reynolds, Jennifer H. 2009. Shaming the shift generations: intersecting ideologies of family and linguistic revitalization in Guatemala. In Paul V. Kroskrity and Margaret Field (eds.), *Native American Ideologies: Beliefs, Practices and Struggles in Indian Country.* Tucson: University of Arizona Press.

Romero Vargas, Germán. 1995. *Las Sociedades del Atlántico de Nicaragua en los Siglos XVII y IX.* Managua: Fondo de Promoción Cultural, BANIC.

Schieffelin, Bambi, Kathryn Woolard, and Paul V. Kroskrity (eds.). 1998. *Language Ideologies, Practice and Theory.* New York and Oxford: Oxford University Press.

Silverstein, Michael. 1998a. The uses and utility of ideology. In Bambi Schieffelin, Kay Woolard, and Paul V. Kroskrity, *Language Ideologies, Practice and Theory.* New York and Oxford: Oxford University Press.

Silverstein, Michael. 1998b. Contemporary transformations in local linguistic communities. *Annual Review of Anthropology* 27: 401–26.

Skutnabb-Kangas, T. 1981. *Bilingualism or Not: The Education of Minorities*. Clevedon: Multilingual Matters.

Stocks, Anthony. 1994. Case study: the Bosawas Natural Reserve and the Mayangna (Sumu) ethnic group of Nicaragua. <http://www.alistar.org.ni/documentos/default.htm> (accessed 1 June 2013).

Stocks, Anthony. 1998. Indigenous ecological activism in Nicaragua: the case of Bosawas. In J. F. Schwaller (ed.), Proceedings of the Annual General Meeting of the Rocky Mountains Chapter of the Latin Studies Association. Las Cruces, NM.

Stocks, Anthony. 2003. Mapping dreams in Nicaragua's BOSAWAS Reserve. *Human Organization* 2: 344–56

Stocks, Anthony. 2005. Too much for too few: problems of indigenous land rights in Latin America. *Annual Review of Anthropology* 34: 85–105.

Vilas, C. M. 1989. *State, Class and Ethnicity in Nicaragua: Capitalist Modernization and Revolutionary Change on the Atlantic Coast*. Boulder, CO and London: Lynne Rienner.

Von Houwald, Götz Freiherr. 2003. *Mayangna: Apuntes Sobre la Historia de los Indígenas Sumu en Centroamérica.* Serie Etnología, No 1. Managua: Fundación Vida/Colección Cultural de Centroamérica.

Warren, Kay B. 1998. *Indigenous Movements and Their Critics: Pan-Mayan Activism in Guatemala*. Princeton, NJ: Princeton University Press.

Whitehead, Neil Lancelot. 1996. Ethnogenesis and ethnocide in the European occupation of native Suriname, 1499–1681. In Jonathan D. Hill (ed.), *History, Power, and Identity: Ethnogenesis in the Americas, 1492–1992*. Iowa City: University of Iowa Press.

'Libros territoriales'

Lino, Baudilio Miguel, Mollins Erans, and Fidencio Davis (1994) *Mayangna Sauni As. Tradición Oral de la Historia Mayangna* [Mayangna Sauni As. Oral Tradition of Mayangna History]. Arlington, VA: The Nature Conservancy.

Sikilta, Comunidad (1996) *Sikilta, Censo y Estudio Socioeconómico* [Sikilta, Census and Socioeconomic Study]. Managua: The Nature Conservancy.

Interviews conducted by Eloy Frank Gómez for Frank Gómez (2006), and by Jane Freeland, Gloria Fenly Montiero, and Stringham Montiero Cisneros, British Academy project, 2006.

Unpublished community censuses (2010) conducted by students on the Diplomado Comunitario en Sociolingüística Aplicada a la Revitalización de la Lengua Sumu-Mayangna [Community Diploma in Sociolinguistics Applied to the Revitalization of Sumu-Mayangna], University of the Caribbean Coast Region of Nicaragua (URACCAN).

10

Must We Save the Language? Children's Discourse on Language and Community in Provençal and Scottish Language Revitalization Movements*

JAMES COSTA WILSON

10.1 Children and Language Revitalization

WHEN CONCERNED WITH CHILDREN, sociolinguistic work on language revitalization has concentrated on patterns of language acquisition or on bilingualism, and very rarely, if ever, on the discourse that the children involved in such programmes articulate. This mirrors a tendency in anthropology to avoid considering the points of view expressed by children, so much so that the anthropologist Lawrence Hirschfeld (2002) asked, in a famous paper: 'Why don't anthropologists like children?'.[1] Yet, according to the author, 'anthropology is premised on a process that children do better than almost all others, namely, acquire cultural knowledge' (Hirschfeld 2002: 624).

While qualitative and critical ethnographic sociolinguistics—the perspective I adopt in this chapter—have possibly paid more attention to what children have to say, studies on issues of language revitalization remain remarkably silent on that matter. In this respect, tribute ought to be paid to the pioneering work of Fabre back in the 1980s in the Nîmes area near Montpellier in southern France (Fabre 1985). In her 1985 article, Fabre seeks to assess the ways in which local children consider their own speech and the opinion they have of Occitan, the local language. Her focus remains, however, the *language*, and not the *children* themselves.

In contrast, this chapter focuses on the very discourses of children, asking a set of crucial questions: what do they have to say about the minority languages they are made to study? How does this shape their understanding of their human

* I am grateful to Alexandre Duchêne and Julia Sallabank for their insightful comments on an earlier draft of this chapter. Any remaining weaknesses are obviously my own.

[1] A similar opinion about children in linguistic anthropology is expressed in Ochs (2002: 99–100).

environment? And, last but not least, in what way is this relevant to the academic study of language revitalization?

I will concentrate on data collected during interviews with groups of three to five children, aged 9 to 11, while doing ethnographic fieldwork between 2007 and 2009 in and around two primary schools: the first was an Occitan immersion school situated in northern Provence, and the second was an ordinary state-funded primary school located in central Scotland. A comparative approach was particularly useful for identifying community belonging and for shaping it as a sensitive issue that the children had to deal with in everyday life.

While geographically unrelated, language issues in Provence and Scotland bear many resemblances. In particular, language advocates there make strong references to the prestigious literary past of Occitan and Scots respectively. The relationship of both languages to the now-dominant languages, English and French, is also very similar. Typological similarities between minority and majority languages enable the development of specific discourses caused by this proximity. This results in the use of such terms as 'patois' or 'semi-language', and Scots and Occitan are often referred to as corrupt varieties of the dominant languages. Yet both speech varieties evolved in different ideological contexts, making comparisons relevant in highlighting how pupils in both contexts react and relate in different ways to dominant ideologies of language.

As I have argued elsewhere (Costa 2010), language revitalization movements are not merely about 'restoring language', whatever that may mean locally. They are primarily about semiotizing and reinvesting linguistic forms made relevant by groups of activists to the invention of a new social project, in which groups are redefined and group belonging is reshaped according to linguistic criteria. Language revitalization movements are part of contact processes where (minority) groups are shaped according to criteria set to enable them to renegotiate terms of contact with another 'dominant' or 'majority', group. As such, they are social movements where language is one primary focus of thought and action.

In their sociology textbook on social movements, Della Porta and Diani (2006: 20) identify three main features characterizing such movements:

- they are 'involved in conflictual relations with clearly identified opponents';
- they are 'linked by dense informal networks';
- they 'share a distinct collective identity'.

While the first two features apply to language revitalization movements, the third feature is particularly problematic. In the case of revitalization movements, that 'distinct collective identity' is often still a project, central to the shaping of collective action, and a central issue to the enterprise.

Children are pivotal in this process. As such, an analysis of their discourse on language and other speakers of the minority language is of particular interest for at least two reasons:

- it sheds light on the types of discourse circulating among adults, and on the elements that adults deem relevant to pass on;
- it gives us insights as to how new categories of belonging connected to language are integrated into the everyday lives of children, and how those categories shape their socialization as members of those linguistic groups in the making.

Such work is essential, particularly among older children in a given school, as their discourse reflects the types of discourse that might be passed on to younger pupils outside the classroom and outside the reach of teachers. Children may move on, grow up, and forget the minority language, yet discourses on language remain and endure in schools among younger generations, so that beyond idiosyncrasies, more stable elements might be discernable.

As such, narratives of revitalization, particularly among the young, afford us an opportunity to analyse the types of language ideologies circulating in language-based social movements in a condensed form, a form deemed suitable to be transmitted to the next generations. In this chapter, language ideologies are to be understood as a shared body of ideas mediating forms of speech (and in this case, language choices) and social structure (Kroskrity 2004), in other words a set of naturalized ideas underpinning, as well as shaping, discourse.

In order to analyse ideologies of group belonging and conceptualizing with respect to language practice, I will first explore the discourse of children on language itself, and will then proceed to examine how this discourse shapes their views of the groups and communities around them.

10.2 Using a Minority Language at School

The next two sections will provide background information on the types of schools I studied, and will show instances of children's discourse on the languages they teach.

10.2.1 Teaching (through) Minority Languages in Provence and Scotland

The data I analyse in the following sections were collected in semi-structured interviews conducted between 2007 and 2009. The schools where I completed my study were distinct from neighbouring schools in their own ways:

- the children in Provence attended a Calandreta primary school,[2] an immersive bilingual school founded by an association of parents and running mostly through the medium of Occitan (locally known as Provençal, a term generally used by the children themselves);[3]
- the children in Scotland attended a school where teachers had initially introduced Scots in some classes, then gradually in all aspects of education and everyday life, in order to sustain literacy skills among pupils (in the view of teachers, pupils suffered from the distance between their own speech and the Standard English of school, hindering their general progress).[4]

In this respect, the two contexts are fairly different. While the Calandreta school teaches most subjects through Occitan, and although pupils in Scotland are entitled to use Scots at all times, there are only a few dedicated Scots-language moments per week. In terms of initial language proficiency, both contexts are also very distinct. It can safely be said that no child, save rare exceptions, comes to the Calandreta with any working knowledge of Occitan, although for some the language might be present in their environment through family or neighbours. In the Scottish school, on the other hand, teachers and other educators broadly consider that most children speak a variety of Scots at home. In fact, they tend to categorize any production containing elements of non-standard language as Scots.

These differences highlight another fundamental difference, residing in the approach to language. The approach to Occitan is heavily normative, while the attitude to the norm in Scots is more relaxed. The dominant attitude towards Scots since the early 2000s has been to accept any form that children might know, and to let them write in whichever way they find meaningful. These forms may then be discussed in class. Normative ideologies are on the surface less present among pupils in Scotland.

[2] 'Calandreta' is an association running dozens of immersion schools throughout the South of France. This system concerns over 2,000 pupils across a vast area encompassing the regions of Provence, Languedoc, Gascony, Limousin, and Auvergne. As little literature exists on these schools, readers interested in the subject are directed to the schools' website at <http://c-oc.org/calandreta/> as well as to Dompmartin-Normand (2002), Boyer (2005), and Sumien (2009). The first two articles are concerned with the discourse of former Calandreta pupils, the third one with Calandreta teacher training.

[3] A strong controversy emerged at the turn of the millennium in some circles in Provence as to whether Provençal should be considered a language in its own right or as a dialect of a wider language, Occitan (see Blanchet 2004; Costa 2010 for differing analyses). In this chapter I use both terms interchangeably and consider Provençal as the Occitan variety spoken in Provence, as does the Calandreta federation.

[4] Scots regroups the Germanic vernacular varieties spoken in Scotland. There is an ongoing linguistic and sociolinguistic debate as to whether it constitutes an autonomous language or a set of eccentric varieties of English (see Millar 2010; McClure 2009).

This has considerable implications as to who counts as a speaker of Occitan or Scots: while speaking Occitan is submitted to considerable evaluative activity, speaking Scots tends to be much more broadly conceived. In other words, language proficiency is not the only criterion for identifying someone as a speaker of Scots. Whereas Occitan is regularly reported as being spoken by some three million people (Sibille 2002), and Scots by well over a million people (McClure 2009), the structure of these populations of speakers, their motivations, and their patterns of language use differ radically, as will become obvious through analysing the discourse of children. Although Occitan might be well established as a 'language', it is seldom heard in public. The status of Scots is far more insecure, yet varieties included under that label can be heard throughout Scotland on a daily basis. Consequently, comparing the discourse of children in both contexts provides very diverse examples of how school pupils problematize 'community' in language revitalization processes.

Schools are heavily constrained places where ideologies of language are inculcated, reproduced, and rarely challenged.[5] Discourse elicited from such places is therefore itself dependent on such constraints, and it is likely that children speak more or less freely than otherwise. Yet, as will be seen, children retain a degree of agency in the shaping of their own narratives, in which elements are borrowed from both discourse on minority and dominant languages, and in which others are formed locally.

10.2.2 Narrating Revitalization

The children I interviewed had been mustered by their teachers into groups of three to six, and the questions primarily concerned their own experience with the 'new' language and the programme they were involved in. In this chapter, I focus on one group in each context.

In Provence, the children chose to use Occitan as the language of interview, whereas in Scotland using Scots was not an option, for an array of reasons—in particular, being an outsider to their normal group of socialization, I might not have been perceived as a legitimate speaker. Also, the interviews took place inside the school, a place where Standard English is still perceived to be the legitimate variety in Scotland. Using Scots would have also meant raising many questions as to what the children spoke, and as to how they might have reacted to my using a brand of Scots learnt from a book.

The children in Scotland had been following Scots language workshops for several months, concentrating on reading and writing. Interviews in Scotland were conducted with the assistance of M. F., a prominent Scots language writer

[5] 'Places' are to be understood in this context as 'spaces made social, hence becoming a space in which humans make social, cultural, political and historical investments' (Blommaert 2008: 211).

who had been teaching the Scots classes in the school during the previous term. The pupils in Provence had been in the Calandreta school for four to seven years, depending on whether they had been to the Calandreta pre-primary school or not.

Talking about the language itself proved a source of great satisfaction for children in both locations, and all were enthusiastic about recounting their feelings and ideas on that topic. In Provence for example, one pupil, Léa, explicitly referred to 'saving' Provençal. This is part of a conversation with another pupil, Carla, as they argue over the place Provençal should have in public life. The following extract is part of an hour-long interview with three girls, Carla, Léa, and Sarah. Only Carla and Léa interact here.

Extract 1:[6]

1	**Léa**	**perdequé en mai es una coma ditz carla es una bela lenga** *because also it is as carla says a beautiful language*
2		**/ fau la sauvar tròbe perdequé** *it should be saved i think because*
3	**Int.**	**fau la sauvar? de que vòu dire fau la sauvar?** *it should be saved ? what does it mean it should be saved ?*
4	**Léa**	**ben / coma dire la sauvar / fau pas la laissar tombar fau /** *well / how can i say to save it / we shouldn't let it down we should*
5		**au contrari fau pas laissar per exemple l'anglés [envaír tot** *on the contrary we shouldn't let for example english [invade everything*
6	**Carla**	**[òc / nos a** [yes daniel
7		**dich aquò danieu** *told us that*
8	**Léa**	**o: lo francés envaïr tota la França** *or french invade all of France*
9	**Carla**	**es lo provençau que fau que envaís tota la França** *it is provençal which should invade all of France*
10	**Léa**	**ben justament sariá pas tròp ben tanben aquí faudriá que *y*** *well precisely that wouldn't so good also there it would be*
11		***ait que y ait* un pichòt de tot de'n partot** *better if there were a bit of everything everywhere*
12	**Carla**	**ben tota la provença / provençau** *well in all of provence / provençal*

Two distinct parts can be identified in this extract, enacting two different types of voices. One voice represents widely circulating language activists' discourse (lines 2 to 7), as exemplified in Carla and Léa's proclaiming of Provençal as beautiful. This standard piece of discourse echoes other studies on language

[6] Note that my own use of the term 'Scots *language*' was dictated by the context, where the 'Scots language' syntagm was the norm set to become dominant by teachers and the school administration.

revitalization where children are socialized into ideologies of minority languages as beautiful (Friedman 2011: 641). The other voice exemplifies the children's own voice (line 1, and lines 8 to 12).

From line 2 to line 6, the children are re-entextualizing discourse, lifting texts out of their original interaction contexts and making them relevant to new texts and contexts (Bauman and Briggs: 1990). They are transforming discourse that is widely circulating in minority language activist circles and which is made available to them to reframe in a meaningful way. In this particular case, they are framing language contact in terms of conflict and competition. This, the children accomplish through summoning the voice of their teacher, Daniel, who represents an authoritative view on language—the only such view most children are ever exposed to. This view situates Provençal with respect to both French and English, in such a way that constructs children as defenders of that language—a role Léa and Carla are apparently willing to endorse. The defence of Provençal occurs in a military setting, where other languages are ascribed agentivity and can 'invade' the territory of weaker languages. The minority language is thus framed as a special and rare item entrusted to children, who in turn live in a world where they are surrounded by monolingual others, known only through the language they speak.

The world where the children evolve is thus one where languages are items deserving preservation, in a world where dominant others prey on smaller languages. Yet the reasons for this remain unclear—hence the development of a number of empirical (and essentially idiosyncratic) arguments for 'saving Provençal'.

As mentioned above, at the beginning of the extract Léa (referring to what Carla said before) presents us with an aesthetic judgement on language: Provençal is 'a beautiful language' (line 1). While participating in a very common set of discourse, Léa thus chose to convoke very subjective (and to her more meaningful) reasons rather than the universalistic claims circulating among activists (such as the benefits of worldwide linguistic diversity).

Meaning is also constructed through debate on the status of languages in conflict. From lines 8 to 12, Carla and Léa develop their own argument over responses to the dominance of French, with two different types of arguments. While Carla extends the 'invasion' metaphor and argues in favour of increased linguistic homogeneity through the imposition of Provençal throughout France, Léa apparently insists on a more generous point of view, 'a little bit of everything everywhere'. However, while both pupils are able to express themselves in both French and Provençal, they do not present bilingualism as an option. Instead, they display a view on languages in contact as juxtaposed entities, and frame languages as autonomous entities without consideration for the individuals or groups who speak them. Carla finally links language and territory (line 12) in a way common among proponents of minority language groups in Europe, while still ignoring actual speakers.

Interestingly also, Carla refers to Provence, a term attached to lived everyday experience, rather than to 'Occitania', a historical, linguistic, and geographical construct promoted by the Occitan language movement and encompassing all Occitan-speaking regions. In doing this, she relates to her own experience outside school rather than to the types of discourse she is exposed to in class.

The discourse developed by Carla and Léa is both embedded in the one they hear at school, and yet it expands in an autonomous way and is subject to debate among the children. This allows both girls to develop their own position as regards subjects such as linguistic diversity and global linguistic conflict. This is, however, set within a wider frame of conflict, as promoted within the Occitan language movement, and Carla and Léa's discourse remains largely disincarnated, with speakers conspicuously absent from their debate.

The next extract, from Scotland, provides the first replies to my questions on the nature of Scots.[7] I had initially expected very similar responses to those collected in Provence. Yet it soon became apparent that language was conceptualized in a significantly different way. Teachers in the school also advocated 'saving Scots', as a sign proclaimed in one classroom, yet for the children this did not appear to be a pressing issue. To them, this was the language they all spoke on a daily basis, and Scots was understood to be simply a new label reframing their speech from 'slang' to 'language'. Scots just was, and if it had to be anything, then it was 'rude', 'broad', 'coarse', 'posh', or, as in the next extract, 'popular'. Language is therefore not characterized for itself, but is correlated to social and moral evaluations.

Extract 2

Int.	so er ok can you tell me a wee bit what the scots
	language IS / then
Teresa	er / it's like / it's awfie // popular noo at school / a
	lo(t) bigger / like xxx with other things that's happening
Connor	schools are allowed to speak in scots
Teresa	it's like if you'd speak to like someone / scottish or
	whatever she would be like / stop talking slang and noo
	i can say / we get taught that at school

Scots is presented as evolving in a lived-in social space, with both Connor and Teresa talking about it not in abstract terms but in relation to speakers, and to a social reality they can refer to. This compares strikingly with the abstract language conjured by Carla and Léa above.

[7] See Williamson (1982, 1983) for a historical account of the ban on vernacular forms in education in Scotland.

In their opposition between a present that allows public use of Scots ('noo' [now], line 3) and a past that did not, Connor and Teresa too replicate the discourse of language activists. Yet the past they refer to corresponds to a reality they had themselves experienced or one that had been narrated to them by parents or older siblings. Until very recently, using dialectal forms was strictly forbidden in schools and in all formal settings in Scotland, and this situation still endures across many parts of the country, as I witnessed myself in several other schools.[8]

The discourse on language serves to express a discourse on shifting authority between a 'before' where Scots was banned and associated with uncouth speech, and a today where it is 'authorized', and where previous structures are replaced by potential agentivity. In Teresa's words, she now has arguments to legitimize her own speech when told off by adults. This possibility is afforded by the presence of an even greater authority—school—and Scots language classes taught by a famous writer.

The shifting of authority takes place against the backdrop of a densely populated social landscape, expressed through the 'popularity' of Scots at school, through the presence of an authority allowing or disallowing the use of Scots in schools, and through the existence of individuals criticizing the linguistic choices of children. This short piece of narrative on Teresa and Connor's view of vernacular forms of speech relates to a thriving community outside the school walls for whom the vernacular is either an interest or a concern.

Carla and Léa conceptualized language as an object, a threatened entity adults had entrusted them with, yet a strangely disembodied object. Conversely, Teresa and Connor focus on language practice, group categorization, and social evaluation on behalf of all-too-real 'others', and construe their participation in the Scots language movement as empowering and relevant to their daily lives. Such opposing views on language (as object vs as practice) unsurprisingly bear on how the children construct the groups they belong to or evolve in, as I will show in the next section.

10.3 Conjuring Groups through Language

Social movements based on language project an idea (and an ideal) of the group they claim to represent. At the same time, their discourse is performative: it seeks to bring into existence the very groups it designates or describes (see Bourdieu 1991: 221 and 223–4). The analysis of how groups are invented through language

[8] This survey should, however, be taken cautiously, as the very notion of language is not defined. The statement to which the population sample was to react was thus phrased: 'I don't really think of Scots as a language, it's more just a way of speaking' (TNS-BMRB 2010: 15).

is therefore central to an understanding of language revitalization movements, since such discursive moments reveal who is part of them and who is not. Discourse on groups is therefore central to the analysis of ideologies associated with language social movements.

To understand how children in Provence and Scotland involved in language revitalization programmes construct the linguistic worlds in which they evolve, it is important to bring in a distinction between language communities and speech communities (section 10.3.1). This will allow us to analyse why pupils in both settings talk about their linguistic environments in the way they do (sections 10.3.2 and 10.3.3).

10.3.1 Language and Speech Communities

Silverstein (1998) distinguishes between two types of groups based on language: 'language communities' and 'speech communities'. According to him, language communities are 'groups of people by degree evidencing allegiance to norms of denotational ... language usage, however much or little such allegiance also encompasses an indigenous cultural consciousness of variation and/or change, or is couched in terms of fixity and stasis' (Silverstein 1998: 402). 'Denotational language usage' here stands for 'language' in the most common sense of the term in the Western world: allegiance to a set of more or less fixed grammatical forms, forms of speech usually 'influenced by explicitly codified registers deemed ... correct or standard' (Silverstein 1996: 129). In short, those are the standard languages as we know them, set as an ideal for minority languages by generations of sociolinguists working along the lines of a Fishmanian paradigm—a current particularly strong in Catalan and Occitan sociolinguistics (see Sumien (2006) on the creation of seven distinct yet interrelated regional norms for Occitan). Language communities are thus largely imagined communities based on a shared charter myth founding the group around language.

Speech communities, in contrast, '[indicate] that there are perduring, presupposable regularities of discursive interaction in a group or population' (Silverstein 1998: 407). They are communities of everyday shared practice, and can involve several 'languages'.

In an ideal situation (as defined by most European language revitalization movements), both types of communities should coincide with one other within a well-defined territory, and preferably under one political (and linguistic) authority. Schools are central places where this ideal model is presented as an actual reality, and through the construction of a closed educational community revitalization movements can perform such imagined schemes (e.g. through textbooks, advertising material, or school language policy), hoping to make them eventually happen throughout their target society.

In most cases this remains a political ideal and project rather than a social reality. Minority language communities remain for the most part theoretical, and speech communities are dwindling everywhere in Europe. In this respect, a contrastive analysis of the Occitan and Scottish (Scots) cases is of particular interest to study the internal dynamics of language revitalization movements and minority group formation. In the Occitan case, over 150 years of activism have succeeded in shaping a 'language' as a set of norms of denotational usage, with well-established (yet often competing) standards, dictionaries, and grammars, but with less and less regular discursive interaction taking place outside limited settings such as language activists' meetings. Scots, on the other hand, barely exists as a denotational standardized code (see for instance the TNS-BMRB (2010: 15) Scottish Government survey, indicating that 'the majority of adults in the sample (64 per cent) agree that they do not think of Scots as a language').[9] Non-standard forms of speech (i.e. Scots, according to Scots language movements) are, however, the everyday medium of communication across many parts of Scotland, and certainly so in the small Central Belt town where I conducted my fieldwork.

In the next section, I set out to explore the ways in which the children I interviewed used language to construct groups as categories relevant to their understanding of the world. More specifically, I show that for a number of reasons, the pupils cannot identify with the construct of the activists to superpose language and speech communities.

10.3.2 Looking for a Speech Community

Here I wish to show that the idea of a language community remains obscure (but constantly invoked by those in authority) for the pupils of the Provençal school, while their construction of a speech community is only tentative, and generally restricted not even to the school, but to the classroom.

The following extract follows Extract 1 (Carla and Léa) chronologically, and provides an example of how both pupils debate on issues of language conflict and the social presence of Provençal outwith the classroom.

Extract 3

1	**Léa**	**imagina / aquí lo *français* seriá lo provençau a la plaça** *imagine / here french would be provençal instead*
2		**dau *français* e que lo *français* eh ben sariá lo provençau** *of french and french well would be the provençal*

[9] 'Int.' stands for 'Interviewer'; 'Daniel' is the name of the class teacher. /, //, and /// indicate breaks, and capitalization indicates an emphasis by the pupils on a particular term or sentence. Italics indicate use of French.

3		**qu'eriam en trin de l'aprendre / eh ben diriam parier diriam** *that we would be learning / well we'd say the same we'd say*
4		**qu'es una polida lenga que faudriá la la sauvar** *that it is a pretty language that should be saved*
5	**Carla**	**mai dau provençau fau que [se sòrt** *but about provençal it must [get out*
6	**Léa**	**[ieu tròbe** *[I think*
7	**Carla**	***parce que* es que dins lei classas calandretas senon i a jamai** *because it is only in the calandreta classes otherwise there*
8		**de de de entendem jamai parlar de gens defòra / provençau** *is never we never here people talk outside / provençal*
9		**donca:s fau que parlon encara provençau de gens / fau cridar** *so they should speak provençal people / we should shout*
10		**PARLATZ PROVENÇAU ((laughter))** *SPEAK PROVENÇAL*

As we saw above (section 10.2.2), both girls agree on the necessity to 'save Provençal', which, like saving the whales, is presented as a natural and obvious thing to do. How to proceed is, however, cause for debate, or at least reveals conflicting ideas on the nature of the group that is supposed to use the minority languages, and on its relationships with the dominant language.

Léa presents languages as interchangeable: if French were the minority language, she would learn it all the same, framing the question in terms of equity in language diversity and relativizing the beauty argument. Carla, on the other hand, presents herself as a language advocate, and argues in favour of concrete measures of language planning, namely getting people to speak the language outside the classroom.

In doing so, Léa and Carla present two outlooks on the linguistic situation of France, and on the Provençal speech community, understood in this case as the total number of people in their environment capable of holding a conversation in Provençal. While Léa displays a certain awareness that they, as schoolchildren *learning* Provençal, act as little other than a piece of equipment used to convey and support language (lines 1–4), Carla views their role as a potentially active one. What she advocates is for people to be told to use the language in everyday life; yet, and rather ambiguously, her use of impersonal forms ('fau', *one should* or *must*, lines 5 and 9) contrasts with both the active language of Léa (e.g. 'diriam', *we would say*, line 3) and her own ('entendem jamai', *we never hear*, line 8). The pupils' experienced reality thus highlights the distance from an ideal world, the coming of which is left to the actions of hypothetical 'others'. In fact, those 'others' can only be conjectural, since, as Carla states, they never hear Provençal outside the school; it is therefore quite likely that both girls would find it practically difficult to identify those who ought to save the language.

A further ambiguity lies in Carla's use of the imperative 'parlatz provençau', *speak Provençal* (line 10), to encourage people to use the language, indicating that she assumes people are capable of speaking it. This suggests either that she has never tried to use Provençal outside school time, or that she is unaware of the processes that led to language minorization and to her own subsequent learning of it.

This extract points to a linguistic inside, the (effectively) bilingual school, and to a linguistic outside, where the use of French is not only the norm but also possibly, with some level of uncertainty, the only available medium for general communication. In effect, Léa and Carla's understanding of the Provençal speech community is reduced to the school, and possibly, given the quasi-absence of use of Provençal during recess, to the classroom. This leaves pupils with an idea of an imagined and rather mythical language community based on a 'language' they have little first-hand experience of outside school time, Occitan or Provençal (a distinction that remains unclear for most), and a speech community limited to a small group of peers. This inevitably raises some questions as to the role of immersion in education in cases where intergenerational linguistic links no longer favour using the minority language as a primary medium of communication. Indeed, revitalization processes are presented in Provence as a way to restore a broken link between the language of the people, and the children, who are said to have lost the language.

In fact, both pupils mention some contact with Provençal outside the school, but it remains sporadic, and often raises questions about their own speech, as it is often met with incomprehension. Léa exchanges a few formulaic phrases with an older gentleman at her music club, and Carla occasionally speaks some Provençal with an uncle living further south, but says she does not really understand him. I suggest this latter issue strengthens the pupils' sense of community around the classroom.

The speech community issue resurfaced later during the interview, as we discussed the case of a local woman, Mrs R., a native speaker of Occitan whom I had met for another interview a year before, when she was 87. I presented the children with an audio extract of the interview, in which Mrs R. recounted in Provençal a dream she had had a few nights before. When I explained that she had only learnt French at school at the age of ten, the pupils expressed bewilderment:

Extract 4

1	**Carla**	**DETZ ANS / avans parli provençau** *TEN YEARS / before I speak provençal*[10]
2	**Int.**	**parlava QUE provençau** *she spoke ONLY provençal*

[10] While this last segment literally means: 'before, I speak Provençal', I interpreted it as meaning 'she only spoke Provençal' and reformulated it thus (line 2). The pupils aligned with my reformulation apparently without any problem.

3	**Carla**	***la cha::nce*** *how lucky*
4	**Carla, Léa, and Sarah**	***la chance*** *how lucky*
5	**Carla**	***elle est née quand?*** *when was she born?*
6	**Int.**	***elle a* vuechanta vuech ans doncas *elle est née en 1921 euh*** *she is eighty eight so she was born in 1921 er*
7		***qu'est-ce que je vous dit 1921 22 quelque chose comme ça*** *what am I talking about 1921 22 something like that*
8	**Carla**	***ouh la la*** *oooh*
9	**Léa**	***en 1921*** *in 1921*
10	**Carla**	***21*** *21*

This extract apparently depicts the pupils' encounter with a reality they had not been aware of, namely the existence of people who had only learnt French at school. The 'monoglot speaker of Provençal' type is seemingly absent from the pupils' own conceptualization of the Occitan or Provençal language community. This is not surprising given the Calandreta schools' emphasis on the value of bilingualism; yet it also displays a lack of awareness of the process of language change that took place throughout the twentieth century, a central element in the charter myth of the Occitan language movement (see Merle (1977) for a collection of accounts on those processes, exemplifying how common these narratives are among native speakers).

The pupils' *how lucky!* (lines 3 and 4) is difficult to interpret in this context, and should probably not be understood as a praise for a time when people could be monoglot speakers of Occitan. Yet the revelation that there was a time when the use of the language they are learning as pupils was widespread enough for monolingual speakers to exist certainly opened up a new dimension in their representation of Occitan as a language, and as their language. In fact, they switch to French upon hearing about the elderly woman's linguistic history, illustrating the contrast between their participation in a plurilingual speech community rather than in a monolingual one. Later during the interview, Carla expressed her wish to have been born at the same time as Mrs R., displaying perhaps less empathy towards Mrs R. and her own personal sociolinguistic story as a regret at not being able to participate in similar socialization networks.

On a more general level, these excerpts show how children involved in a programme of minority language revitalization react both to the aim of activists to bring into existence a language community and its corresponding speech community or communities, and to the awareness of their solitude as speakers of

Provençal. In short, the categories adults promote remain abstract to them, and the give and take of everyday life implies the construction of a speech community where both French and Provençal are used not according to rules set by the institution, but according to emerging interactional patterns depending on factors such as interlocutors, moments, place, and so on, as I was able to observe during my time in the school.

10.3.3 Articulating Existing Speech Communities with a Newfound Language Community

The Scottish situation provides an interesting contrast to the Provençal one. According to the children themselves, there is no shortage of people who understand or speak what they now call Scots, whether at school, at home, or more generally throughout Scotland. There is therefore an easily identifiable 'Scots' speech community in the immediate environment. However, the introduction by language advocates of the term 'Scots' to replace what the children formerly identified as 'Scottish', 'slang', or referred to as 'just the way we speak' implies the merging of the local speech community into a wider language community, distinct from the English language community. This provides pupils with a new array of categorizing terms they can use to shape community membership around them, and leaves them with the task of articulating both types of community. In the following extract, the children express their lack of confidence as to who is concerned or not by the 'Scots language' label.

Extract 5

Int.	and would you say / it's more old people than young people
	who speak scots today / or
Robert	i think it's more young people
All pupils	((approve))
Int.	yeah? why / how would ye explain that
Robert	we:ll because er maybe cause old people didn't do that much
	scots in school / so they probably didn't know that much /
	and we know more cause we're doing it in school

In questionnaires I had asked them to complete, most pupils wrote 'Scots' as their home language. Yet it remained unclear throughout both the interviews and my observations what reality this term addressed. In the extract above, as I raise a generational issue, Robert links knowledge of Scots with formal education, without, however, specifying what he means by 'knowing Scots'. What this reveals, however, is a certain unawareness of the full extent of language registers used by other generations, a fact confirmed through further observations. In fact, Scots, whatever it might refer to, is widely used among peers, whereas vernacular forms tend to be shunned in the family for intergenerational use, with children being told to 'speak properly'.

This, however, leads to a strong paradox: while language advocates present Scots as the language the children use every day, it is connected to formal education and to acquisition at school. While the children previously experienced a dichotomy between the high variety of the school and the everyday vernacular they used among peers, that latter variety is suddenly given high status and presented to them in written form. In other words Scots comes to designate both the everyday vernacular of the children and the prestige variety found in books, a duality that needs accommodating to by the children.

When Robert depicts Scots as spoken mainly by young people (lines 6–8), he is therefore playing it safe, and referring to a speech community consisting mainly of his peers without voicing too much of an opinion regarding the membership (or not) of adults. I suggest the children are developing a view on what their Scots speech community is from their own experience at school and with peers, leaving their linguistic contact with other vernacular speakers aside because of the ambiguous nature of Scots, standing between its status as a written medium and as an everyday language. This in turn underlines the insecure (and recent) nature of their representation of the Scots language community they are presented with at school. This is a representation that further destabilizes their perception of the speech communities they take part in. Throughout interviews and observations, the children used the term 'Scottish' rather than 'Scots', possibly illustrating further their insecurity with regard to the latter term.

10.4 Conclusion

Speech and language communities are places of socialization for children, and the importance of how they are presented and represented should not be underestimated. Language revitalization movements typically aim at destabilizing existing views on such communities to replace them with others. Those other representations, being in essence mainly discursive and not (fully) effective in practice, potentially leave much space for insecurity as they replace existing frameworks of thought. The new categories proposed by adults are not fully functional, so that children must adapt them or create new ones, perhaps temporarily, to get on with the give and take of everyday life.

Overall, the children I interviewed seemed happy to participate in such programmes—and never questioned their participation. However, taking part in these programmes demands a strong capacity for adaptation and interpretation, as the often unclear views of adults, be it on language, community, or any other matter, are projected onto the children without any further consideration. The issue of the target groups where children are to be socialized is never raised, and it is assumed that they will integrate into a local community without any particular reflection about its nature.

The first conclusion I draw from my work in Provence and Scotland concerns the importance of paying attention to the discourse of children. Not only does it reflect the discourse of adults and the ideologies this is premised upon—in this case the necessity of making language and speech communities coincide—but it also reveals how children adapt the categories of adults to their own everyday reality. That reality is not one of language advocacy, or of language revitalization, hence possibly the lack of discussion about language among children. Those languages have become their own, and they need not justify this, unlike adults perhaps. What they need to deal with is how to categorize their environment, and how language fits into that categorizing process.

A second conclusion concerns the importance of comparative work. Contrasting such different contexts as the Provençal and Scottish ones highlights different processes taking place under a similar ideological matrix, namely the necessity of making speech and language communities coincide. In this, social movements based on language seek to imitate processes of nation-state construction, which points to the fundamentally modern nature of language revitalization movements (in the historical sense of the term). Other areas still need investigating, in particular the role of the written word in both programmes.

Finally, in terms of analysing language revitalization, and language revitalization movements, this chapter raises several questions, in particular about the socialization of children into groups that are still mostly imaginary (i.e. they are in the process of being created) and into wider (e.g. regional or national) language or speech communities. This dimension is rarely taken into account in the conception and implementation of language immersion programmes, especially in contexts where the target language is no longer a language of everyday use. This is especially true, I suggest, in cases where pupils are likely to cease being exposed to language revitalization programmes (and to a more or less normative, or academic, version of the language) after primary school (this is especially the case in Provençal).

References

Bauman, Richard and Charles L. Briggs. 1990. Poetics and performance as critical perspectives on language and social life. *Annual Review of Anthropology* 19: 59–88.

Blanchet, Philippe. 2004. Provençal as a distinct language? Sociolinguistic patterns revealed by a recent public and political debate. *International Journal of the Sociology of Language* 164: 125–50.

Blommaert, Jan. 2008. Writing locality in globalized Swahili: semiotizing space in a Tanzanian novel. In Cécile B. Vigouroux and Salikoko S. Mufwene (eds.), *Globalization and Language Vitality*. London and New York: Continuum.

Bourdieu, Pierre. 1991. *Language and Symbolic Power*. Cambridge: Polity Press.

Boyer, Henri (ed.). 2005. *De l'école occitane à l'enseignement public: vécu et représentations sociolinguistiques. Une enquête auprès d'une groupe d'ex-calandrons*. Paris: L'Harmattan.

Costa, James. 2010. Revitalisation linguistique: Discours, mythe et idéologie. Approche critique de mouvements de revitalisation en Provence et en Ecosse. PhD thesis, Université de Grenoble. <http://tel.archives-ouvertes.fr/AOM/tel-00625691/fr/> (accessed 15 October 2011).

Della Porta, Donatella and Mario Diani. 2006. *Social Movements: An Introduction*. Oxford: Blackwell.

Dompmartin-Normand, Chantal. 2002. Collégiens issus de *Calandreta*: quelles représentations de l'occitan? *Etudes de Linguistique Appliquée* 101: 35–54.

Fabre, Sylvette. 1985. Approche de la représentation que les enfants se font de la langue régionale. *Repères* 67: 59–70.

Friedman, Debra. 2011. Language socialisation and language revitalisation. In Alessandro Duranti, Elinor Ochs, and Bambi B. Schieffelin (eds.), *The Handbook of Language Socialization*. Oxford: Blackwell.

Hirschfeld, L. A. 2002. Why don't anthropologists like children? *American Anthropologist* 104: 611–27.

Kroskrity, Paul V. 2004. Language ideologies. In Alessandro Duranti (ed.), *A Companion to Linguistic Anthropology*. Oxford: Blackwell.

McClure, John Derrick. 2009. *Why Scots Matters* (3rd edn.). Edinburgh: Saltire Society.

Merle, René. 1977. *Culture occitane per avançar*. Paris: Editions Sociales.

Millar, Robert McColl. 2010. An historical national identity? The case of Scots. In Carmen Llamas and Dominic Watt (eds.), *Language and Identities*. Edinburgh: Edinburgh University Press.

Ochs, Elinor. 2002. Becoming a speaker of a culture. In Claire Kramsch (ed.), *Language Acquisition and Language Socialization*. London and New York: Continuum.

Sibille, Jean. 2002. *Les Langues Régionales*. Paris: Flammarion.

Silverstein, Michael. 1996. Encountering language and languages of encounter in North American ethnohistory. *Journal of Linguistic Anthropology* 6: 126–44.

Silverstein, Michael. 1998. Contemporary transformations of local linguistic communities. *Annual Review of Anthropology* 27: 401–26.

Sumien, Domergue. 2006. *La standardisation pluricentrique de l'occitan: nouvel enjeu sociolinguistique, développement du lexique et de la morphologie*. Turnhout: Brepols.

Sumien, Domergue. 2009. Comment rendre l'occitan disponible? Pédagogie et diglossie dans les écoles *Calandretas*. In Patrick Sauzet and François Pic (eds.), *Politique linguistique et enseignement des langues de France*. Paris: L'Harmattan.

TNS-BMRB. 2010. *Public Attitudes towards the Scots Language*. Edinburgh: Scottish Government Social Research. <http://www.scotland.gov.uk/Resource/Doc/298037/0092859.pdf> (accessed 15 October 2011).

Williamson, Keith. 1982. Lowland Scots in education: an historical survey (1). *Scottish Language* 2: 54–77.

Williamson, Keith. 1983. Lowland Scots in education: an historical survey (2). *Scottish Language* 3: 52–87.

11

Revitalizing the Māori Language?

JEANETTE KING

11.1 Introduction

THE THEME of this chapter is the range of responses to the question 'what is being revitalized?' In New Zealand, the rhetoric at vernacular and language planning levels indicates that it is the Māori language that is being revitalized. For example, linguists, language planners, politicians, and the general population alike readily describe developments such as the preschool 'language nests' (*kōhanga reo*) and concomitant education initiatives as 'language revitalization initiatives'. This description is not inaccurate, but it obscures a much deeper and more nuanced situation: that the language revitalization movement in New Zealand was founded on and developed from the idea of revitalizing people as much as revitalizing an endangered and indigenous language (King 2003: 116).

Accordingly, this chapter describes not so much differences in beliefs about language but beliefs about the nature of revitalization, and so concerns itself with what might be termed 'revitalization ideologies' and how these differ at institutional and vernacular levels.

We begin by examining the beginnings and development of *kōhanga reo*, the initiative at the vanguard of language revitalization in New Zealand, and the participatory motivations of the first and second generation of adults involved in these initiatives. The motivations of these adults differ somewhat from the revitalization ideologies espoused by language planners in New Zealand, both at tribal and national levels. These institutional ideologies have shaped perceptions of what is necessary to secure motivation for revitalization amongst the populace.

11.2 The Kaupapa of *Kōhanga Reo*

Fishman reminds us that revitalization movements typically involve larger ethnocultural goals (1991: 18). This is undoubtedly true of the experience with the Māori language in New Zealand. The Māori language revitalization movement is generally agreed to have gained widespread momentum with the development of the preschool Māori immersion initiative, *kōhanga reo*, in the

Proceedings of The British Academy, **199**, 213–228.

early 1980s. Although described and understood as a language revitalization initiative, the *kōhanga reo* movement has always had a much wider *kaupapa* (philosophy).

Kōhanga reo were formed as a result of a radical new direction in the Department of Māori Affairs, which was initiated when Kara Puketapu took over the leadership of the department in 1977. At that time, the department's role was to promote 'the social, cultural and economic well-being of the Māori people' (Puketapu 1982: 2). But, facing the reality of urban situations where Māori unemployment and crime were becoming major issues, Puketapu decided that instead of 'promoting Māori well-being' the department needed to take a more active role to empower Māori development. Puketapu gathered senior members of the department around him and charged them with coming up with a new way of addressing the challenges facing Māori. These senior officials were all native speakers of Māori who had been raised in rural areas. One of them was Iritana Tāwhiwhirangi, who was to become the leader of the *kōhanga reo* movement:

> We said, from now on don't anybody talk about Māori problems in front of us, we're going to talk about how wonderful it is to be Māori. [John] Rangihau said, '*e kōrero nei tātou mō te tū tangata o te tangata*' ['we're talking about people standing tall'], and wrote '*tū tangata*' on the board. Then, we agreed that, if we could touch the lives of our people in a positive way to say, 'you're okay', we could harness their talents. (Tāwhiwhirangi, quoted in Diamond 2003: 97)

The phrase '*Tū Tangata*' became the name of the programme and soon three '*Kōkiri*' units were established in the Wellington area. The word *kōkiri* means 'to rush, to charge', and was undoubtedly chosen as being the Māori word closest in meaning to 'development' and to promote the idea of 'advanc[ing] into the twenty-first century' (Walker 1990: 237). Each unit worked with the local community to devise cultural, social, and economic programmes in response to the community needs. The basic idea of the *Kōkiri* units was to reverse the usual operating procedure of government departments, which was to implement policy from the top down. That is, whereas departments usually took government policies and translated them into actions and programmes for the community, in Puketapu's plan *Kōkiri* units would work alongside the community to develop programmes to address community needs: a bottom-up approach.

> So in launching its *Tū Tangata* programme the Department of Māori Affairs has attempted to hold a mirror up to the people, to encourage them to see themselves as they really are and as they could be, and not through the distorting mirrors of other people's stereotypes and assumptions. (Department of Maori Affairs 1979)

Unlike earlier policies, *Tū Tangata* advocated the retention of Māori cultural values as crucial to Māori advancement and self-definition. The validity of Māori language and culture was promoted on the assumption that uncertainty over cultural identity contributed to the poor attainment of Māori at schools and in the marketplace. Thus the cultural basis of Māori society was depicted not as a problem for the New Zealand Government to solve but as a source of untapped energy which, if handled correctly, would enhance the well-being of society in its entirety (Sissons 1993). Puketapu (1982: 4) states: 'What we are saying is that the process should be one of letting "culture be the catalyst".'

Part of the *Tū Tangata* initiative at the nationwide level was to consult with tribal elders to find out what strategies and emphases were needed. As a consequence the department ran a number of annual strategic conferences (*hui*) in Wellington. At the national conference held in the Legislative Council Chamber at Parliament in October 1981, one of the main focal points was the Māori language. Concern about the state of the language, which had been heightened by activist groups such as Ngā Tamatoa, was confirmed by the comprehensive sociolinguistic research carried out by Richard Benton during the mid-1970s (Benton 1991). Benton's study showed that there were only a few pockets left in the country where Māori could still be described as a community language. The importance of this research as the catalyst for the revitalization of Māori has been noted elsewhere (Pawley 1989: 16) and cannot be overstated.

> The research we did helped drive home the point that the language wasn't endangered just in Mōtatau or Hiruhārama, but everywhere, and those who cared about it would have to act quickly if they were to be able to change things. It was also very obvious that schools weren't going to be able to change things by themselves. (Richard Benton, personal communication, 24 April 1996)

In particular, participants at the conference were informed that few, if any, Māori children were being raised as speakers of Māori. Not only did the conference make language revitalization an 'urgent target', the elders also came up with a strategy to make it happen: they wanted 'Māori-speaking supervisors to run day-care centres' (Hayes 1982: 3). As a result of these discussions and decisions the Department of Māori Affairs set up the first *kōhanga reo* in a building already housing a *Kōkiri* unit in Wainuiomata (a Wellington suburb with a high Māori population; see Figure 11.1). The facility also housed a gym and was the centre for other Māori training programmes set up under the *Tū Tangata* programme.

The Pukeatua *kōhanga reo* was opened in the back half of the top level of the building on 13 April 1982. The idea of *kōhanga reo* spread like wildfire around New Zealand, with *kōhanga* opening up on *marae* (traditional community meeting places), in community halls, and even in private homes. By the end of 1982 there were 107 *kōhanga reo*, and three years later there were 337.

Kōhanga reo were initially funded through the Department of Māori Affairs. The umbrella organization Te Kōhanga Reo National Trust was set up to organize and administer the initiative at a national level. Iritana Tāwhiwhirangi, a native speaker from the Ngāti Porou tribe, became the Trust's general manager. She took the *Tū Tangata* development policy into her management of

Figure 11.1 Pukeatua Kōkiri Centre, 2002. Entrance to Pukeatua Kōhanga Reo at top right. (Author's photograph)

kōhanga reo and was staunch in maintaining that *kōhanga reo* was a Māori development initiative rather than a childcare initiative or solely a language revitalization initiative.

> When it started, *kōhanga* was very much a Māori development issue, in the hands of Māori, the *kaupapa* was driven by the trustees and the people. (Iritana Tāwhiwhirangi, quoted in Diamond 2003: 102)

Kōhanga reo were particularly based around the idea of development of the whole *whānau* (extended family). *Kōhanga* weren't just about the children becoming fluent in Māori; they were about all age groups in the Māori community working together and improving their skills and abilities, not only in the Māori language and culture, but in a range of areas. In defining this philosophy, *kōhanga reo* became the forerunner for other initiatives based on a 'by Māori, for Māori, in Māori and about Māori' approach (Black et al. 2003).

Iritana Tāwhiwhirangi steered *kōhanga reo* on a course that included as one of its precepts the idea that all *kōhanga reo* were to be autonomous. Being autonomous meant that each *kōhanga reo* was run by the *whānau*, that is, the group of parents, elders, and teachers associated with each centre. This was to ensure accountability and the training of parents who, by taking on administrative roles, would learn new and transferable skills.

Kōhanga reo took the *Tū Tangata* philosophy that Māori culture and language were the key to survival, and extended it. If Māori culture and language were the key, where was that key? It was inside every Māori. This philosophy is exemplified in the *kōhanga reo* teacher training package that received New Zealand Qualification Authority accreditation in 1991 (Irwin 1992: 90). Students in the *Whakapakari Tino Rangatiratanga* training programme learn through conducting their own research into the ten areas of the curriculum (King 2001: 124–5). Their study is supported by the whole *kōhanga* in which the student is based. Thus, the pedagogy is based on the idea that answers are to be found within Māori people and their families. The practical outcome is a group that consistently looks to itself rather than outside for direction.

11.3 Generation 1

The main stalwarts of the first 20 years of the Māori language revitalization movement have been adult second language speakers of Māori. These adults were typically young urban parents involved in Māori immersion schooling initiatives as parents and teachers of the new generation of Māori-speaking children (King 2007). However, the original model of *kōhanga reo*, shown in Figure 11.2, describes it as a vehicle for transmitting the language from older native speakers to the youngest members of the community.

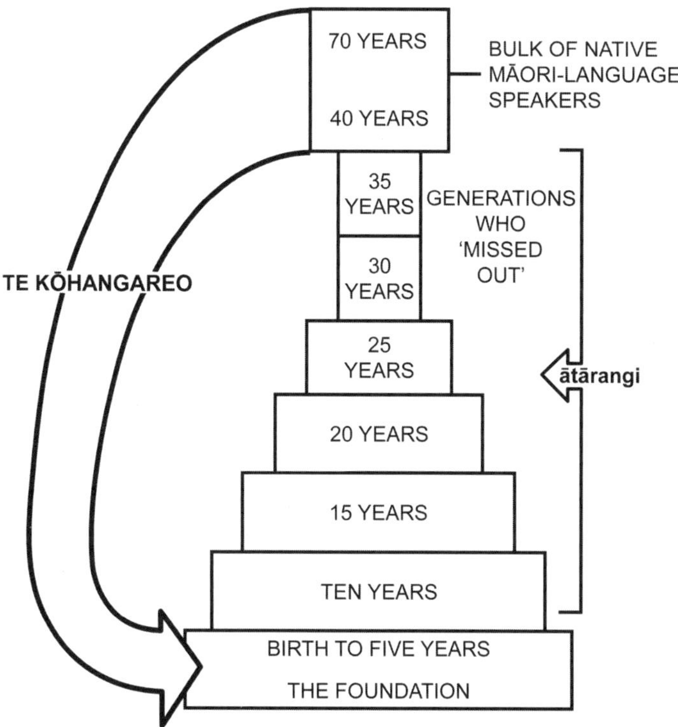

Figure 11.2 Diagram from Te Kōhanga Reo National Trust. (Te Kōhanga Reo National Trust 1985: 2)

In stressing the importance of native speakers in *kōhanga reo*, Iritana Tāwhiwhirangi noted:

> As I explained to the people, when I went around the country, 'all of you fluent speakers are the goldmine to launch this and we need you!' (Iritana Tāwhiwhirangi, quoted in Diamond 2003: 101)

Despite this lauded aim, a large number of *kōhanga reo* throughout the country have had second language speakers rather than native speakers as the majority of the teachers and adults in daily contact with the children. Although it is hard to find definitive statistics, a recent publication found that in only two out of six *kōhanga* studied were elders involved (Mitchell et al. 2006: 73). Second language adult speakers have therefore played a large role in the *kōhanga reo* movement as both parents and teachers (Benton and Benton 2001: 430). These adults, described in Figure 11.2 as the generations who 'missed out', and here termed Generation 1, are the first generation of Māori parents since the development of language revitalization initiatives to be involved in raising their children as speakers of Māori.

Generation 1 adults have made a personal and conscious decision to engage with the Māori language. Their internally focused relationship with the Māori language is illustrated in the words of a song composed by Te Rita Papesch in 1995. Entitled 'He Mauri Te Reo', a line in the song poses the question 'from whence comes my language?' (*nō whea te reo?*). The reply is given, 'from within yourself' (*tēnei anō au*).

The relationship that Generation 1 has with the Māori language is also revealed in the range of metaphors that these second language adult speakers employ to describe the Māori language (King 2003). Interviews conducted with 32 Generation 1 adults from a range of urban and rural backgrounds and tribal areas highlight their use of metaphors of transformation and growth. The four main metaphors they employ are 'language is a path' (cf. Dobrin, this volume), 'language is a canoe', 'language is food', and 'a language learner is a plant'. These metaphors allow Generation 1 adults to describe an initial state of being without the heritage language, a subsequent engagement with the language, and a continuing relationship with it.

The 'language is a path' metaphor is a version of the conceptual metaphor 'language is a journey' (Lakoff and Johnson 1980). Before being involved in learning Māori, these adults spoke of searching for a path (cf. Dobrin, this volume, on 'road' as a metaphor for linguistic connections).

> *Ka kimikimi haere i tētahi huarahi mōku. Kātahi ka tīmata au ki te ako i te reo.*
>
> 'I was searching around for a path I could take. Then I began to learn Māori.'

The high level of commitment evident in Generation 1 speakers is expressed using the path metaphor.

> *Ko te huarahi kotahi hei whāinga māku ko te reo.*
>
> 'The sole path for me to follow is the language.'

One aspect about the choice of becoming a fluent speaker is the realization that it is a long-term project.

> *E kore rawa au e tū ki te whai i te reo, e rawa au e kapi i tērā huarahi. He whāinga tērā mai i tō whānautanga, tae noa atu ki tō matenga ki a au.*
>
> 'I'll never stop following the language; I'll never get to the end of that path. To me, it's something you follow right from your birth, up until you die.'

The second version of the 'language is a journey' metaphor used by these adults is 'language is a canoe'. Canoes have had an important role in Māori society; they were the means by which Māori came to New Zealand many centuries ago and they also played an important role in transportation and fishing into the first half of the nineteenth century. With the importance of water transport in an island country such as New Zealand it is not surprising that Generation 1 adults use canoe imagery. With the 'language is a canoe' metaphor, the Māori language is referred to as a canoe, *waka*. Informants speak of being lost, *ngaro*, getting onto the canoe, *eke ki runga i te waka*, and paddling, *hoe*. The canoe can be under the direction of a leader, *kaihautū*, and moving in a forward direction, *ahu whakamua*.

> *Nā tēnei, ka haere katoa mātou ki te kōhanga reo, ko taku tama me taku pēpi me ahau. Kātahi au i tino peke ki runga i te waka rā.*
>
> 'Because of this we all went to *kōhanga reo*, my son, my baby and me. It was then that I really jumped on that canoe.'

The 'language is food' metaphor allows Generation 1 adults to talk about how, before learning the Māori language, they were hungry (*hiakai*, *matekai*) or not being fed the language, *kāore i te whāngai atu*. In learning the language they are being fed, *whāngaihia*. Informants see the possibility of feeding others, particularly children, with the language. In this schema the adult learner's original diet (without the language) is lacking; Māori language is seen as a special food necessary for surviving in the world.

> *I taku tīmatanga atu kāore kau he reo, nō reira nā aku kaiako i whāngaihia mai tērā reo me ō rātou āhuatanga, ngā tikanga, ngā mea katoa.*
>
> 'When I started I didn't have any language, so it was my teachers who fed me the language and its aspects, the customs, everything.'

This food enables Generation 1 adults to grow, with this idea being expressed through the 'a language learner is a plant' metaphor. Speakers refer to the Māori language as a seed, *kākano*, which is planted, *whakatō*, inside the learner, enabling them to grow and flower, *puāwai*.

> *Ka whai huarahi ahau kia puāwai tērā kākano i whakatōngia e tōku pāpā.*
>
> 'I followed a path so that that seed planted by my father would flower.'

In summary, these metaphors enable Generation 1 adults to stress the ongoing, transformative nature of learning and speaking Māori.

The metaphors also emphasize a strong theme of the inner life of the individual, echoing the philosophy encapsulated in the title of Puketapu's publication *Reform from Within* (1982). This personalized relationship with the Māori language is also reflected in the motivations Generation 1 adults cite when asked why they are involved in speaking the Māori language. Generation 1 adults are not primarily motivated by a sense of responsibility towards the Māori language (King and Gully 2009). Instead, these individuals typically cite very personal reasons for their commitment, reasons that centre on their own identity and well-being needs, as well as those of their children.

> *I te whakaaro, he Māori wā mātou tamariki, me whāngaihia te reo ki a rātou. Kāore au i titiro mō tērā atu, mō te whakaora i tō tātou reo rangatira.*
>
> 'I thought, our children are Māori, better feed the language to them. I didn't look at that, about revitalizing our chiefly language.'

Although Generation 1 adults mention concern for the future of the Māori language as an important motivation, it is not as salient as the other two areas of focus (King and Gully 2009).

Although at the wider level Generation 1 adults are engaged in language revitalization, at the personal level they see themselves as being revitalized, and feelings of responsibility towards the revitalization of the language are not their primary concern. That is, they are motivated by personal imperatives and the belief that the Māori language is important for them, not that they are important for the Māori language.

11.4 Generation 2

Since the turn of the century and the passing of the 20th anniversary of the founding of *kōhanga reo*, the focus of attention has shifted to the second generation of adults to be involved in revitalization of the Māori language: the offspring of Generation 1 adults. These are 'the foundation' generation of young children shown in Figure 11.2 as the focus of *kōhanga reo*. Even if these young adults, referred to here as Generation 2, have not personally participated in *kōhanga reo* and Māori-language immersion schools and programmes, they have grown up in an environment where these initiatives have existed. That is, their experience is quite removed from the idealism and protest stages of language revitalization that were the cornerstone of the experience of Generation 1 adults (as per Colin Williams, cited in Baker and Prys Jones 1998: 193). With the consequent legitimization and institutionalization of Māori immersion education initiatives, there has been some concern about whether there might be complacency amongst Generation 2 adults who have not had to fight for their language (Henare 2010).

However, Papesch contends that new community-centred arenas are arising amongst Generation 2 adults as sites for communication in the Māori language (Papesch 2010). These sites parallel the importance that the *marae* had for earlier generations.

The *marae* has always been a strong setting for ritual use of the Māori language, and is a 'symbolic focus of Māori social and culture life' (Walker 1989: 159). Traditionally, a *marae* consisted of a group of buildings comprising a meeting house, dining room, and kitchen facilities (Barlow 1991: 73), though the word also refers to the open place in front of the meeting house, which is the site of ritual encounters.

With the post-Second World War urbanization of the majority of the Māori population, a number of *marae* were built in the main cities (Sissons 1993: 102–3). Many of these urban *marae* had a pan-Māori rather than tribal focus. Another development has been that the traditional ceremonies conducted on *marae*, in particular welcome ceremonies, are now routinely conducted in non-*marae* settings such as at schools and other institutions. That is, both the structures and the performances associated with the *marae* have been adapted to the urbanized setting.

In an examination of the role of *kapa haka* (Māori performing arts) in today's society, Papesch contends that for many Generation 2 adults *kapa haka* groups and performances are discharging the social function that the *marae* had for previous generations.

> A modern Māori identity may be wrapped around 'performance' relationships super[c]eding the 'being' relationship that is *marae* and *tūrangawaewae* [a place of belonging]. For the 'modern' Māori who is divorced from his *marae* and *tūrangawaewae* maybe we are supplanting *tūrangawaewae* of land with one of practice. (Papesch 2010, emphasis added)

New venues that create a sense of belonging have also appeared on the internet, with Māori creating 'virtual *marae*' (Greenwood et al. 2011). It seems that sites are developing where Māori language will increasingly be required for full participation in Māori events. Anecdotally, it appears that the use of Māori language is increasing at events such as regional and national *kapa haka* and speech competitions. Previously the use of Māori at these occasions was often limited to the actual performances, but now it is becoming common, and even expected, that most public, and many private, interactions at the venues will take place in Māori. These events also involve people from all age groups of the

Māori community, precisely the sort of events encouraged by Fishman as opportunities for intergenerational interaction (Fishman 1991: 395). It is interesting that the increasing use of the Māori language has developed naturally at these events, no doubt as a result of the normalization of the use of the language amongst Māori in Māori-focused arenas.

It also appears that Generation 2 adults cite different motivations with regard to speaking, and supporting, the Māori language. In a small pilot study, nine speakers of Māori, in their early twenties, were asked what motivates them to be speakers of the Māori language. Their responses indicated a strong sense of awareness of their role in revitalizing the Māori language and passing the language on to future generations. This is in contrast to Generation 1 speakers who were most strongly motivated by identity needs. With their upbringing strongly rooted in Māori-immersion education it seems that Generation 2 adults have a solid sense of who they are as Māori, and are therefore more aware of their role in language regeneration.

11.5 Language Planners

It is the purview of language planners involved with minority and endangered languages to care passionately about the language they have some responsibility for. Because it is their job to support and facilitate the use of minority languages they are, by necessity, motivated by a belief that they are facilitating the revitalization of a language. To discharge this obligation effectively, language planners endeavour to stimulate the motivations of individuals within their target population. Until recently, language planners at both tribal and national levels in New Zealand appeared to assume that because they themselves are highly motivated by the idea that they are revitalizing a language, any promotional encouragement should remind their intended audience of the individual's role in revitalizing the Māori language. That is, language planners often seem to believe that the most effective ideology with respect to the Māori language is based on encouraging an individual's sense of responsibility towards the language.

At a national level in New Zealand, this assumption is revealed in statements that note that many adult speakers of Māori lack 'critical awareness' of their role in language revitalization, and this is noted as a problem to be rectified. Individuals need to be aware of their role 'in not only maintaining the Māori language but also in revitalising it' (Chrisp 2005: 177). This sort of statement implies that the most effective motivator is to encourage the target population to believe that the individual is personally responsible for the revitalization of the Māori language.

In 2007 the South Island tribe Ngāi Tahu ran a series of advertisements in their tribal magazine aimed to encourage language engagement and use. The tribe's 25-year language strategy (*Kotahi Mano Kāika* or '1,000 homes') aims to

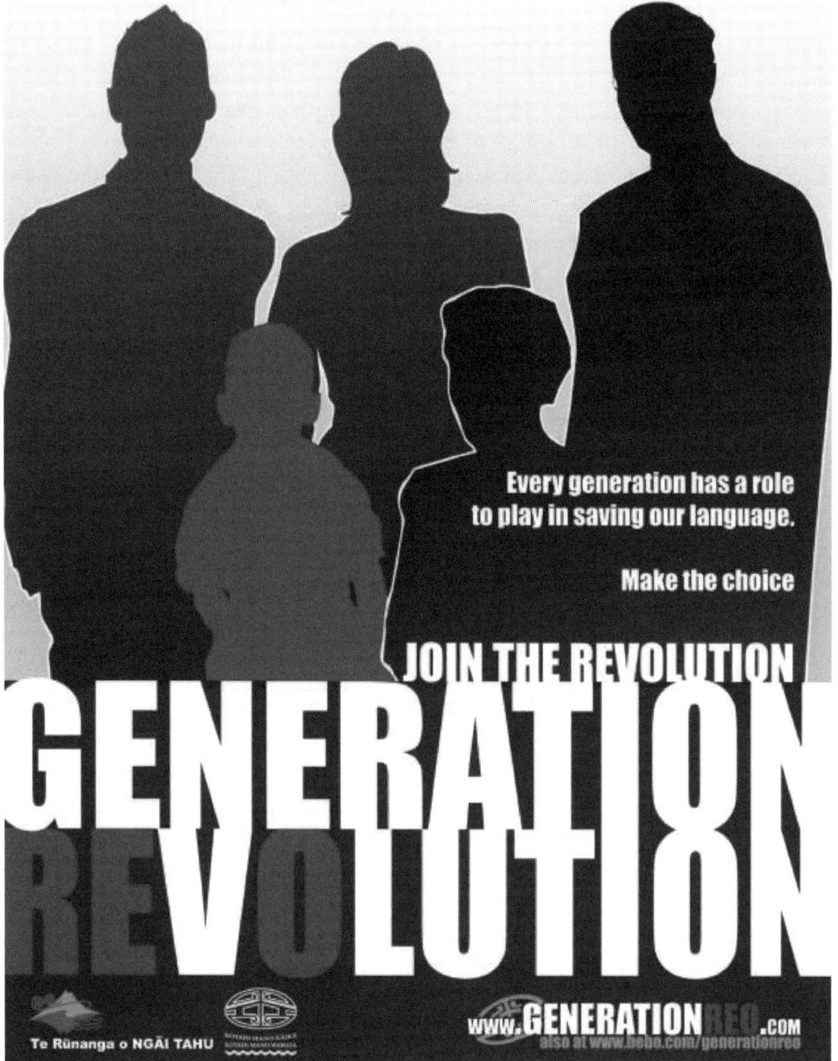

Figure 11.3 Tribal language advertisement ('Every generation has a role'). (2007: 6; copyright Te Rūnanga o Ngāi Tahu and Kotahi Mano Kāika language revitalization strategy.)

have 1,000 homes speaking Māori by the year 2025, and particularly focuses on young families (O'Regan 2009). Figure 11.3 shows one of the tribal language advertisements.

The idea expressed in the advertisement that everyone 'has a role to play in saving our language' is based on the appeal that saving the language, or revitalizing the language, is what potential speakers of the language see themselves as doing. Furthermore, the implication is that such appeals will exert an effective moral pressure on readers to commit themselves to speaking the language. In addition, the advertisements and other material on the website <www.generationreo.com> evoke a battle metaphor encapsulated in the word 'revolution' shown at the bottom of the advertisement, where the word is printed in two colours to reveal the word *reo* (language). The use of the word 'revolution', and the targeting of new generations of parents, is designed to reignite the passion and commitment evident amongst the Generation 1 adults (Te Rūnanga o Ngāi Tahu 2003). Tribal members are encouraged to make 'the cause of our generation be saving the language' (quoted in Greenwood et al. 2011: 69–70).

As these examples show, it appears that language planners often believe that the only effective ideology with respect to the Māori language is based on an individual's sense of responsibility towards the language. But, as discussed earlier, a closer examination of the beginnings of the language revitalization movement in New Zealand, and the motivations of the first generations of adults involved in the revitalization initiatives, reveals different motivating forces. Nevertheless, it seems that the second generation of adults may be more receptive to this type of message, and indeed, the success of ongoing revitalization efforts are now in their hands.

When it comes to encouraging people to use Māori, language planners in New Zealand are in a difficult position. They are aware that it is hard to appeal to notions of identity in promoting language learning and use, for the definition of 'who is a Māori' is strong, and is based entirely on genealogical descent, with some commentators also including a requirement for tribal affiliation (see Kukutai 2004: 91–4). It is certainly true that an ability to speak Māori was previously an important component of ethnic identity, until about the 1970s. The statesman Sir Apirana Ngata is reported as saying that 'the Māori language was an essential means of communication between Māoris' (Belshaw 1939: 26) and this sentiment has been repeated by other commentators (for example, Biggs 1968: 82; Williams 1987: 101; and Reedy, as quoted in Waitangi Tribunal 1986: 52). However, suggestions that there is a linguistic component to Māori identity are not generally supported. For example, in a 1995 survey the majority of Māori respondents (83 per cent) did not agree with the statement that 'you have to be able to speak Māori to be a real Māori' (Te Puni Kōkiri 1998: 57). More recent attempts by the Māori Language Commissioner, Haami Piripi, to assert that Māori leaders needed to be speakers of Māori, received an immediate and strong backlash (Gifford 2006). Accordingly, it is difficult to 'market' the Māori language on the basis of it having an important role in Māori identity, since Māori identity is based largely on genealogical heritage rather than linguistic practice.

In response, language planners involved with the Māori language have become more nuanced and aware in recent years in their promotion of the language. The main emphasis since the early twenty-first century, both nationally and tribally, has been to encourage the use of Māori in the home, as per level 6 of Fishman's Graded Intergenerational Disruption Scale (GIDS) (Fishman 1991: 395). There has also been a recent recognition of the importance of community language use, and an effort to encourage intergenerational language interaction before the current generation of elders dies (Te Paepae Motuhake 2011).

One example of this at the national level is the promotion of the annual Māori Language Week held in late July. Celebrated since 1975, it is only since 2008 that a theme has been associated with the event. In 2008 the theme was 'language in the home' and in 2009 'language in the community'. The focus on home and community language use is also relevant in the face of concern that the populace may be placing too much dependence on schools as sites of language revitalization. In 2010 the theme for Māori Language Week was '*Te Mahi Kai*' (the language of food). There was widespread coverage of the food theme, with a national supermarket chain using prominent Māori slogans in their newspaper advertisements and with Māori translations of recipes, measurements, and shopping lists available in the supermarkets themselves.[1] Of course, a focus on the language of food encourages the use of Māori in the home, so this theme was a much less overt, but arguably more effective, way to encourage the use of Māori in the home.

11.6 Discussion

There are differing revitalization beliefs among various sections of the Māori population. The ideology of national and tribal language planners revolves around the idea that what is being revitalized is a language. However, this is tempered by an examination of the agenda of the *kōhanga reo* movement and the motivations and beliefs of the first generation of adults involved in Māori-immersion education. Speakers of the first generation were motivated by the fact that they could see the Māori language reviving them, rather than vice versa. However, their children, the second generation, take their relationship with the language for granted, as the Māori language has always been in their wider environment. Instead, it appears that they may be internalizing a message that the Māori language is increasingly required for full participation in key Māori cultural events, and there are some signs that they are more receptive than their parents to their responsibilities in revitalizing the Māori language. However,

[1] See <http://www.korero.maori.nz/resources/shop.html> for a list of food-focused resources produced to promote the Māori Language Week theme.

further investigation of the motivations and attitudes of this group of speakers is required to be able to make more definitive statements.

The analysis of the differing institutional and vernacular revitalization ideologies in New Zealand leads us to a number of conclusions of relevance to language planners.

1. The role of language planners is to aid and support language revitalization. As a result they believe that they are primarily engaged in revitalizing a language.
2. The major aim of language planners is to stimulate use of the target language by individuals and communities. However, the target audiences for language revitalization will commonly have different language and revitalization ideologies from those of language planners.
3. These vernacular ideologies will vary amongst different groups within the population and over time, especially between generations.
4. In that ideology shapes action (Spolsky 2004), the most effective ways to promote language use will involve appealing to the strongest motivators for the relevant target group.

The Māori language has a special place in the wider indigenous language revitalization movement because of the development of *kōhanga reo* and other Māori immersion schooling initiatives. Accordingly, this analysis of the differing revitalization ideologies has relevance to other jurisdictions that have modelled their initiatives on the New Zealand experience.

References

Baker, Colin and Sylvia Prys Jones (eds.). 1998. *Encyclopedia of Bilingualism and Bilingual Education*. Clevedon: Multilingual Matters.

Barlow, Cleve. 1991. *Tikanga Whakaaro: Key Concepts in Māori Culture*. Oxford: Oxford University Press.

Belshaw, Horace. 1939. *Report on Young Māori Conference held at Auckland University College, May 22nd–May 26th, 1939*. Auckland: Auckland University College.

Benton, Richard. 1991. *The Māori Language: Dying or Reviving*? Hawaii: East-West Center.

Benton, Richard and Nena Benton. 2001. RLS in Aotearoa/New Zealand 1989–1999. In Joshua Fishman (ed.), *Can Threatened Languages Be Saved?*. Clevedon: Multilingual Matters.

Biggs, Bruce. 1968. The Māori language past and present. In Eric Schwimmer (ed.), *The Māori People in the Nineteen-Sixties*. Auckland: Blackwood and Janet Paul.

Black, Titoki, Phillip Marshall, and Kathie Irwin. 2003. Māori Language Nests in NZ: Te Kōhanga Reo, 1982–2003. Paper presented at the United Nations Permanent Forum on Indigenous Issues, New York.

Chrisp, Steven. 2005. Māori intergenerational language transmission. *International Journal of the Sociology of Language* 172: 149–81.

Department of Maori Affairs. 1979. What is Tū Tangata? *Te Kāea* 1: 7–8.

Diamond, Paul. 2003. *A Fire in Your Belly: Māori Leaders Speak*. Wellington: Huia.

Fishman, Joshua. A. 1991. *Reversing Language Shift*. Clevedon: Multilingual Matters.

Gifford, Adam. 2006. *Watea News Update*. <http://waatea.blogspot.com/2006_07_23_archive.html> (accessed 10 October 2010).

Greenwood, Janinka, Lynne Te Aika, and Niki Davis. 2011. Creating virtual marae: an examination of how digital technologies have been adopted by Māori in Aotearoa New Zealand. In Patricia R. Leigh (ed.), *International Explorations of Technology Equity and the Digital Divide: Critical, Historical and Social Perspectives*. Charlotte, NC: Information Age Press.

Hayes, L. 1982. Whakatauira 1981: Māori leaders proposals. *Tū Tangata* 4: 3–6.

Henare, Erima. 2010. Language holds the promise of change. *New Zealand Herald*, 3 August. <http://www.nzherald.co.nz/nz/news/article.cfm?c_id=1&objectid=10663107> (accessed 14 April 2014).

Irwin, Kathie. 1992. Māori education in 1991: a review and discussion. *New Zealand Annual Review of Education* 1: 7–112.

King, Jeanette. 2001. Te kōhanga reo: Māori language revitalization. In Leanne Hinton and Ken Hale (eds.), *The Green Book of Language Revitalization in Practice*. San Diego: Academic Press.

King, Jeanette. 2003. 'Whāia te reo: pursuing the language': how metaphors describe our relationships with indigenous languages. In Jon Reyhner, Octaviana V. Trujillo, Roberto L. Carrasco, and Louise Lockard (eds.), *Nurturing Native Languages*. Flagstaff: Northern Arizona University.

King, Jeanette. 2007. Eke ki runga i te waka: the use of dominant metaphors by newly-fluent Māori speakers in historical perspective. PhD dissertation, University of Canterbury.

King, Jeanette and Nichole Gully. 2009. Towards a theory of motivation: describing commitment to the Māori language. 1st International Conference on Language Documentation and Conservation (ICLDC), Mānoa, Hawaii. <http://hdl.handle.net/10125/4991>.

Kukutai, Tahu. 2004. The problem of defining an ethnic group for public policy: who is Māori and why does it matter? *Social Policy Journal of New Zealand* 23: 86–108.

Lakoff, George and Mark Johnson. 1980. *Metaphors We Live By*. Chicago: University of Chicago Press.

Mitchell, Linda, Arapera Royal Tangaere, Diane Mara, and Cathy Wylie. 2006. *Quality in Parent/Whānau-led Services*. Wellington: New Zealand Council for Educational Research and Te Kōhanga Reo National Trust.

O'Regan, H. 2009. A language to call my own. In Anne Marie Goodfellow (ed.), *Speaking of Endangered Languages: Issues in Revitalization*. Newcastle: Cambridge Scholars Publishing.

Papesch, Te Rita. 2010. Composing Māori, composing tradition in Kapa Haka. Paper presented at the *Symposium of the Māori Performing Arts*. AUT University, Auckland.

Pawley, Andrew. 1989. Can the Māori language survive? *Hurupā* 10: 12–23.

Puketapu, Kara. 1982. *Reform from Within*. Wellington: Department of Māori Affairs.

Sissons, Jeffrey. 1993. The systemisation of tradition: Māori culture as a strategic resource. *Oceania* 64: 97–116.

Spolsky, Bernard. 2004. *Language Policy*. Cambridge: Cambridge University Press.

Te Kōhanga Reo National Trust. 1985. *Resource Manual: Te Kōhanga Reo National Wānanga, 1985, Tūrangawaewae Marae, Ngāruawāhia*. Wellington: Author.

Te Paepae Motuhake. 2011. *Te Reo Mauriora*. <http://www.tpk.govt.nz/_documents/te-reo-mauriora.pdf> (accessed 20 August 2011).

Te Puni Kōkiri. 1998. *The National Māori Language Survey*. Wellington, NZ: Author.

Te Rūnanga o Ngāi Tahu. 2003. *Tēnei Te Ruru*. Christchurch: Author.

Waitangi Tribunal. 1986. *Finding of the Waitangi Tribunal Relating to Te Reo Māori and a Claim Lodged by Huirangi Waikerepuru and Ngā Kaiwhakapūmau i te Reo Incorporated Society (The Wellington Board of Māori Language)*. Wellington: Author.

Walker, Ranginui. 1989. Colonisation and the development of the Māori people. In Michael C. Howard (ed.), *Ethnicity and Nation-Building in the Pacific*. Tokyo: United Nations University Press.

Walker, Ranginui. 1990. *Ka Whawhai Tonu Mātou: Struggle Without End*. Auckland: Penguin.

Williams, Haare. 1987. Broadcasting and the Māori language. In Walter Hirsh (ed.), *Living Languages: Bilingualism and Community Languages in New Zealand*. Auckland: Heinemann in association with the Office of the Race Relations Conciliator.

12

What Are We Trying to Preserve? Diversity, Change, and Ideology at the Edge of the Cameroonian Grassfields*

PIERPAOLO DI CARLO & JEFF GOOD

12.1 Preserving Languages or Language Dynamics?

A CONSPICUOUS FEATURE of the endangered languages discourse is the focus on the consequences (whether scientific or social) of the loss of *languages*. This is perhaps most strikingly seen in statements like, 'the coming century will see either the death or the doom of 90% of mankind's languages' (Krauss 1992: 7), which choose to characterize the 'crisis' of endangerment in numerical terms that suggest languages are easily conceptualized as discrete objects. It is also an essential part of characterizations of the significance of endangered languages to stress their role as 'repositories for cultural knowledge' (Harrison 2007: 7), clearly implying that the loss of the language implies the loss of 'treasures' contained within them (see also Crystal 2000: 32–6, and Nettle and Romaine 2000: 14, among others). Hill (2002) has critiqued motifs like these under the headings of *enumeration* and *hyperbolic valorization*, and the forces that have caused linguists to adopt them are clear enough: they are effective at 'selling' the need for significant efforts to be devoted to the world's less-resourced languages (Dobrin et al. 2009: 38–40; Hill 2002: 119. See also Duchêne and Heller 2007 for a broader contextualization).

The ideologies in which this approach to endangered languages are embedded are clearly open to criticism on general academic, and perhaps even more

* The research on which this chapter is based has been supported by generous funding from the Max Planck Institute for Evolutionary Anthropology Department of Linguistics, the US National Endowment for the Humanities (under NEH fellowship #500006 and NEH grant RZ-50817-07), the US National Science Foundation (under NSF Grant BCS-0853981), the Endangered Languages Documentation Programme, and the University at Buffalo College of Arts and Sciences and Humanities Institute. We would like to thank our many linguistic consultants who made this work possible, in particular Ngong George Bwei Kum, whose support of this work since 2004 has been invaluable, as well as Scott Farrar, Roland Kießling, Jesse Lovegren, Alice Mitchell, Rebecca Voll, and audiences in London and Berlin for helpful comments on the work leading to this chapter.

Proceedings of The British Academy, **199**, 229–262.

broadly sociopolitical grounds (see, e.g., Edwards 2010: 51–6). However, the observation that guides this chapter is more narrowly linguistic in nature. In conducting work on the languages of a small but exceptionally diverse region of Cameroon, what appears to make them 'special' is not their value as self-contained storehouses of a culture but, rather, their utility as tools for the flexible construction of multiple identities. In an African context, this is not a fundamentally novel idea, as the 'complicated' (Childs 2003: 175) nature of multilingualism in Africa has been discussed in detail elsewhere (see, e.g., Blommaert 2007; Irvine and Gal 2000: 47–59; Lüpke 2010). Our new contribution here is first to offer an account of the development of linguistic diversity in such a multilingual context in a region which has, heretofore, seen relatively little study, thereby introducing an additional case to the unfortunately small catalogue of available studies that have been conducted along these lines (Storch 2011: 213) (section 12.3). We then look at our analysis of the history of the region's linguistic diversity in the light of contemporary ideas of language documentation (in the sense of Himmelmann (1998) and Woodbury (2011)) and suggest that it calls for a more nuanced approach to the relationship between documentary methodology and ecological contexts than has generally been found to this point (sections 12.4 and 12.5).

On the whole, we hope that this chapter will make clear the need for work on endangered languages to become more sensitive to the cultural contexts in which these languages are embedded, rather than assuming that ideas about language that make sense in Western contexts straightforwardly apply to other parts of the world. We acknowledge, at the outset, that this point may be obvious to many readers, but our impression is that it has yet to significantly inform most work on language documentation, making it worthwhile to emphasize it in the context of a volume like this one. We begin by giving a general overview of the linguistic situation of our area of focus in section 12.2.

12.2 Lower Fungom: Ethnolinguistic Background

12.2.1 Languages and Villages

Our area of focus, the Lower Fungom region of Northwest Cameroon, is one of the most linguistically diverse parts of the Cameroonian Grassfields, itself an area whose linguistic diversity has been noted for some time (Stallcup 1980: 44). Located in the Grassfields' north-west periphery (see Figure 12.1), the core inhabited area stretches roughly 10 kilometres both north to south and east to west, making it about the size of Guernsey. Including less densely settled outlying areas, the entire region is around 240 square kilometres, comparable in area to the Pacific island of Niue.

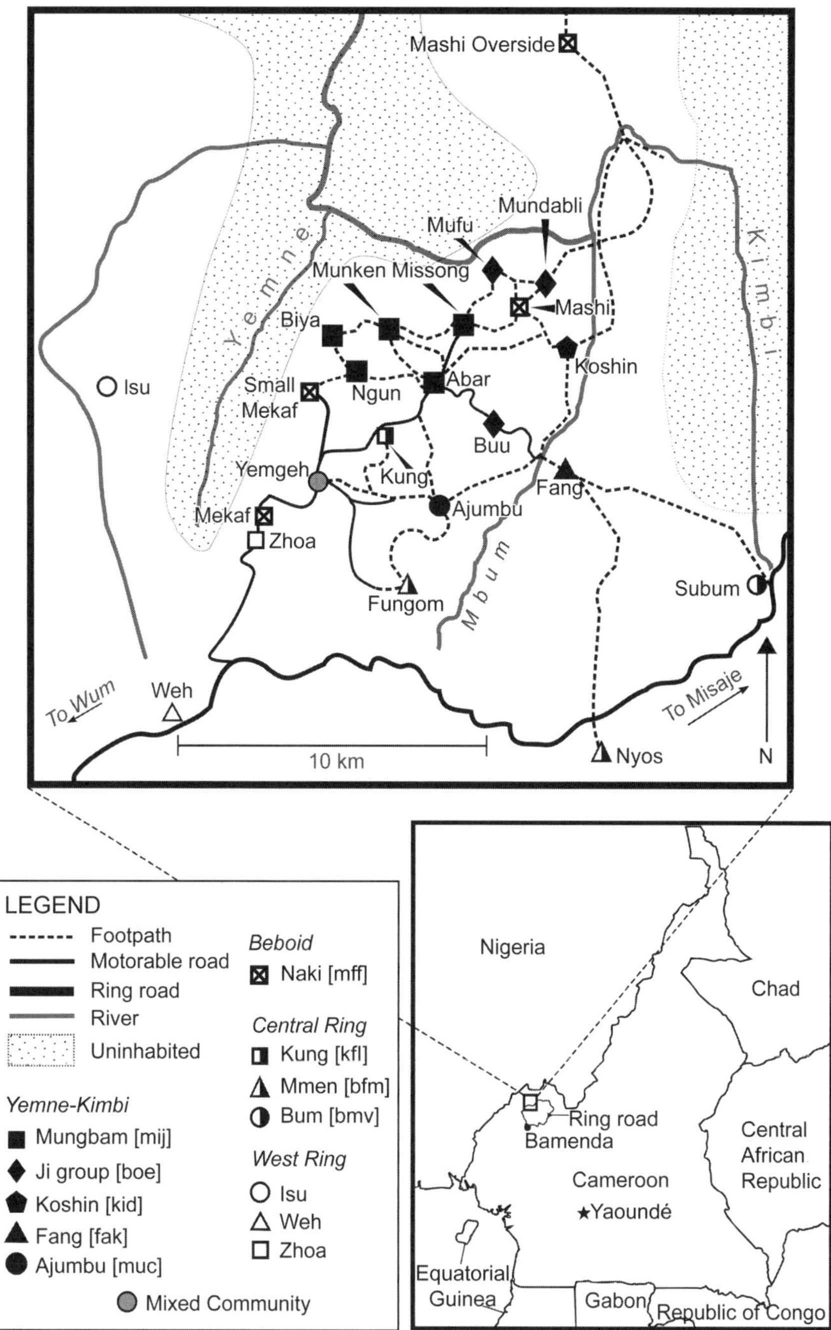

Figure 12.1 Lower Fungom and surrounding area.

Table 12.1 Lower Fungom villages.

Subgroup	Language	Village	Population
Yemne-Kimbi	Mungbam [mij]	Abar	650–850
		Munken	around 600
		Ngun	150–200
		Biya	50–100
		Missong	around 400
	Ji [boe]	Mundabli	350–450
		Mufu	80–150
		Buu	100–200
	Fang [fak]	Fang	4,000–6,000
	Koshin [kid]	Koshin	3,000–3,500
	Ajumbu [muc]	Ajumbu	200–300
Beboid	Naki [mff]	Mashi	300–400
Central Ring	Kung [kfl]	Kung	600–800

Seven languages, or small language clusters, are spoken in Lower Fungom's 13 recognized villages, meaning there is about one language per 34 square kilometres. By way of comparison, the famously linguistically diverse country of Vanuatu (see Evans 2010: 214) has about one language for every hundred square kilometres.[1] Four of Lower Fungom's languages are restricted to a single village. While its languages can all be reasonably classified as Bantoid (see section 12.2.2), five of them do not have any established close relatives outside of the region, nor can they be straightforwardly shown to be closely related to each other (see section 12.2.3). The linguistic picture is paralleled by an ethnographic one which shows considerable diversity in social organization across the region's villages as well. The discussion in this section provides an overview of the pertinent features of the region. More detailed analysis is provided in Good (2013), Good et al. (2011), and Di Carlo (2011).

Table 12.1 lists the linguistic affiliations of each of the Lower Fungom villages, along with rough population estimates. Two varieties in the table, Missong and Buu, are sufficiently distinctive from closely related varieties that they are probably best associated with their own 'language' if only linguistic criteria (such as unacquired mutual intelligibility) are considered. Mungbam, the Ji group, Fang, Koshin, and Ajumbu are only known to be spoken within Lower Fungom and have no established close relatives outside of the

[1] See François (2012) for a discussion of the language dynamics of a region of north Vanuatu which, superficially at least, appears to show comparable patterns to those found in Lower Fungom.

area.[2] Unlike these, Naki is spoken in Mashi as well as in villages outside of Lower Fungom, three of which (Mekaf, Small Mekaf, and Mashi Overside) appear in Figure 12.1. Kung is spoken only within the village of Kung, but has been classified with the Central Ring languages found to the south, which include Mmen (bfm). A dialect of Mmen is spoken in Fungom, a village to the south of Ajumbu, which, for largely accidental historical reasons, lent its name to the wider region. The label 'Lower Fungom' was then applied to refer to the lower-elevation territories found within this area.

In terms of social identification, with the partial exception of Mashi, which in some respects acts as part of a larger Naki unit, even villages speaking closely related varieties in Lower Fungom view themselves as autonomous, each having their own chief, and identify their language as being spoken only within the village itself, though they often recognize that other villages speak languages that 'rhyme' with theirs (i.e. that are perceived as lexically and grammatically similar). On the whole, then, the region can be characterized as dominated by a localist attitude with respect to language, rather than a distributed one (see Hill 1996).

The languages of Lower Fungom appear to be relatively vital, despite their small size. Children born and raised in its villages generally still speak the language associated with their home village. Anecdotal observations suggest that the increasing use of the local lingua franca, Cameroonian Pidgin, may be leading to the decline of knowledge of local languages as second or third languages insofar as bilingualism in one's native language and Cameroonian Pidgin may be replacing older patterns of multilingualism. However, this issue has yet to be examined systematically (see also Hamm et al. 2002: 20).[3] It does seem clear, however, that the *idea* of a lingua franca in the region is of relatively recent provenance, arising due to European contact. Menang (2004: 903–4) gives a date around the mid-nineteenth century for the first major influx of a pidgin English variety along the Cameroonian coast, which was the precursor to contemporary Cameroonian Pidgin. Before this, communication between different linguistic groups was apparently achieved via multilingualism rather than a dedicated trade language (Warnier 1980: 832).

[2] Throughout the chapter, we follow a convention of referring to Mungbam as though it were a language, while referring to the Ji group rather than the Ji 'language', for two reasons. First, the divergence between Buu and the other members of the Ji group appears to be greater than that between Missong and the rest of Mungbam, giving strong evidence for distinct languages within the group. Second, the name Mungbam has been specifically crafted to refer to the speech varieties of this language in what we believe is a reasonable way (Good et al. 2011: 114–24), while the label Ji references a local isogloss involving the word for 'dog', rendering it inappropriate as a language name.

[3] François (2012: 105–6) describes a similar pattern in northern Vanuatu, on the basis of more detailed data than are available to us.

12.2.2 Linguistic Context

The languages of Lower Fungom have all been classified in the Bantoid group (see Watters 1989). This puts them among the closest relatives of the well-known (Narrow) Bantu group of languages, which dominate southern sub-Saharan Africa. The primary basis for this classification is their Bantu-like systems of noun classes (see Good et al. 2011), which are nevertheless divergent enough from the noun class systems associated with Bantu languages (Katamba 2003; Maho 1999) to suggest that they should be treated as part of a higher-level grouping within Benue-Congo, the subgroup of Niger-Congo in which the Bantu languages have been classified.[4]

Nevertheless, we believe a general note of caution is required when discussing issues of classification in this part of the world. It has often been assumed that tree-based models of language classification can be usefully associated with the Bantoid languages. This is, perhaps, best evidenced by the tree diagrams seen in handbook chapters such as Williamson and Blench (2000) that are propagated as much by 'scholarly inertia' (Childs 2003: 47) as empirical evidence (Dalby 1971: 17; Heine 1980: 295). It is also seen in various attempts at lexicostatistical classifications (Bastin et al. 1999; Piron 1997; see also Nurse 1994–5). However, as pointed out in the recent overview by Schadeberg (2003: 154–60), despite success in reconstruction, establishing clear-cut subgroups for Bantu and its Bantoid relatives has proved difficult. This is not a new concern. Möhlig (1979, 1981), for example, develops an approach to diversification in Bantu that emphasizes the role of wavelike change in shaping the family, while markedly de-emphasizing the role of traditional genetic descent.

Beyond providing general context for the discussion of diversity in Lower Fungom to be presented below, the issue of how to model language change and language classification within Bantoid has direct significance regarding how we should understand the region's diversity. The earliest survey work on the region, described in Hombert (1980), privileged the 'unilinear monogenetic model of language history' (Möhlig 1981: 251) and interpreted its diversity as being primarily the result of divergence of varieties of the various villages from a common proto-language, a model which was sustained in the later survey by Hamm et al. (2002). The analysis to be presented here in section 12.3, by contrast, will highlight the role of social changes in triggering the region's diversity, most prominently changes involving increased sociopolitical risk in the area (a complement to Nettle's (1996) notion of 'ecological risk'). This, in turn, will have consequences regarding how the situation of Lower Fungom should

[4] See Dimmendaal (2011: 318–24) for an up-to-date overview of the composition of the Niger-Congo family.

potentially prompt us to refine documentary methodology, as will be discussed in section 12.4.

12.2.3 Sociocultural Context

As already indicated, Lower Fungom's linguistic diversity is not an isolated pattern but, rather, represents an extreme within the already diverse Cameroonian Grassfields. This area has been culturally distinctive potentially since the Iron Age in this part of Africa, which dates to, perhaps, two or more millennia ago (Rowlands and Warnier 1993: 514), and has been characterized by Stallcup (1980: 44) as the most linguistically 'fragmented' part of the so-called sub-Saharan Fragmentation Belt (Dalby 1970: 163), a region of sub-Saharan Africa characterized by high language density.[5] The Grassfields region is also characterized by relatively high population density (Warnier 1980: 831), local economic specialization (Warnier 1979: 410), frequent internal migration (Warnier 1979: 412–13), and pervasive multilingualism (Warnier 1980: 832) (see also Voorhoeve 1980: 66 for brief remarks on this last point).

Despite being at the geographic periphery of the Grassfields and not speaking languages of the Grassfields group, Lower Fungom's societies are clearly part of the Grassfields cultural area, if not 'core' members of it. The most widely accepted reconstruction for the history of the Grassfields (exemplified in Warnier 1985: 15–20) connects patterns of economic specialization with patterns of socio-political consolidation and stratification, conditioned, in part, by local ecologies. In particular, groups in lower-elevation and moister peripheral areas of the Grassfields (which include Lower Fungom) have tended to specialize in the production of palm oil and have been associated with less centralized socio-political institutions. By contrast, as one moves south from Lower Fungom towards the centre of the Grassfields, progressively more centralized and internally hierarchical societies are encountered and the production of more specialized products (e.g. iron tools and wood carvings) begins to dominate the local economies. Lower Fungom's position in an area not characterized by much political consolidation—where villages do not join into larger units such as kingdoms—has clearly been an important factor in fostering its linguistic diversity.

In the next section, we will offer a reconstruction of Lower Fungom's recent linguistic history on the basis of linguistic, ethnographic, and historical evidence.

[5] We use the term 'Fragmentation Belt' here, following earlier work. However, one must be cautious in applying the fragmentation metaphor too literally, insofar as it has a possible implication of a former 'unity' which has since broken apart. A more appropriate label, at least for the Grassfields, might be to consider the region to be marked by 'singularity' rather than fragmentation, in the sense of Fowler and Zeitlyn (1996: 1), where language differences are emphasized as part of the justification of a multiplicity of distinct political communities rather than as resulting from the dismantling of a once-coherent unit.

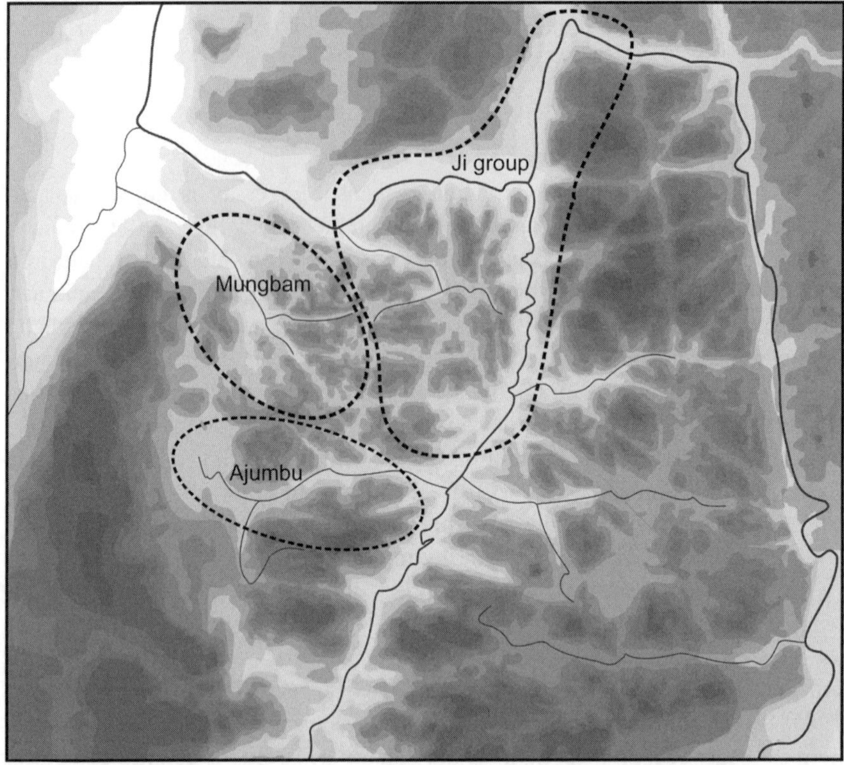

Figure 12.2 Reconstructed historical language distribution in Lower Fungom (*c.*1800).

12.3 Lower Fungom: Historical Reconstruction

12.3.1 Two Historical Phases

The key elements of our reconstruction of Lower Fungom's recent linguistic history are depicted in Figures 12.2 and 12.3. Figure 12.2 proposes a language distribution for the region of about two centuries ago, where predecessors of three of the region's languages or language groups were dominant. Rather than populations being concentrated in compact settlements, as is the case today, they would have been more dispersed, perhaps even in the form of relatively isolated compounds associated with individuals claiming common descent in the form of a kin group, or, perhaps, as a series of federated hamlets. While we can only reconstruct this pattern for Lower Fungom, it is attested for nearby groups to the south-west of the region, which bear a similar geographic and economic relation to the rest of the Grassfields (see, e.g., Masquelier 1978; Warnier 1985: 200–6).

Figure 12.3 depicts the settlement patterns of the present day, in a less schematic fashion than that given in Figure 12.1. The locations of the recognized

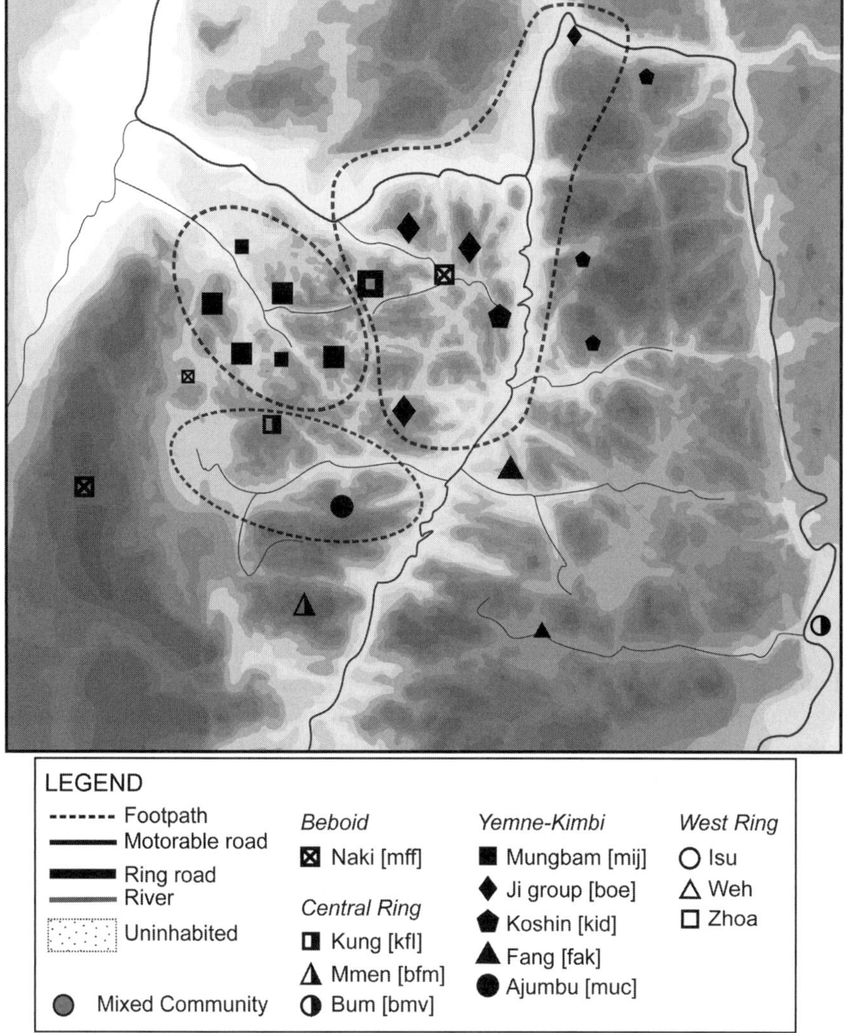

Figure 12.3 Present-day distribution of settlements and languages, shown according to the latter's genealogical affiliation.

villages are given with larger symbols (following the same conventions as those in Figure 12.1), with outlying settlements, always associated with one of the villages, indicated with smaller symbols of matching shapes. The symbols for Naki-speaking villages and for Kung are also somewhat smaller than those of groups with no known close relatives outside of Lower Fungom. The village of Missong, speaking a distinctive variety of Mungbam, is associated with a special symbol for reasons to be made clear in section 12.3.4. The reconstructed areas associated with the earlier language group distributions in Figure 12.2 are included in Figure 12.3 for ease of comparison.

In section 12.3.2, the historical phase depicted in Figure 12.2 will be discussed in more detail, and in section 12.3.3, the historical phase depicted in Figure 12.3 will be discussed. Our evidence for these two phases involves a combination of linguistic, ethnographic, archaeological, and ethnohistorical information, in some cases supplemented by archival records. We will discuss some aspects of the evidence where relevant. Fuller documentation can be found in Good et al. (2011) for the linguistic points and Di Carlo (2011) for discussion of other domains.[6]

12.3.2 The First Phase: Three Dispersed Language Groups

Based on linguistic evidence alone, two of the Lower Fungom language groups—the Mungbam dialect cluster and the Ji group—would already be good candidates for having occupied the region for some time, due to their association with multiple distinctive varieties.[7] Whatever the precise conditions under which the different varieties arose, a topic we will explore in sections 12.3.3 and 12.3.4, their presence suggests these language groups have been located in Lower Fungom longer than languages like Fang, Koshin, Kung, and Naki, which are all restricted to a single village (for a fuller analysis of Lower Fungom linguistic geography see Di Carlo and Pizziolo 2012).

Ajumbu is a special case in this context. It, too, is a one-village language at present. However, this appears to be a relatively recent development. As late as the early twentieth century, another language, most generally referred to as Lung, now only remembered by a handful of speakers, was also found in Lower Fungom (see Troyer et al. 1995: 9–10 and Di Carlo 2011: 83). The vocabulary data we have collected strongly indicates that Lung was a close relative of

[6] Of course, as is often the case with the sort of historical reconstruction attempted here, the data we have collected from different sources do not seamlessly integrate to create a simple historical narrative. Moreover, the two historical phases we reconstruct are deliberately idealized, and the facts on the ground would have deviated in the past (and continue to do so in the present) from these idealizations in some ways, most notably seen in cases where contemporary villages are associated with various outlying hamlets, as found, for instance, for Fang, Koshin, Abar, Munken, and Mundabli. Indeed, as will be discussed in section 12.3.4, Lower Fungom habitation patterns are well understood as responses to different degrees of risk in the region's ecology (understood broadly to encompass both natural and human factors), which have not resulted in changes between discrete 'states' of settlement but, rather, initiated processes favouring a more dispersed pattern of settlement over a more concentrated one. As such, the attestation of cases intermediate between idealized models of dispersion and concentration should be considered unsurprising from a historical perspective.

[7] Of course, alternative interpretations for such diversity are available. For instance, related groups could have migrated into the area, thereby 'importing' their diversity. However, in this case, evidence from other sources, to be discussed immediately below, uniformly point towards a scenario where the presence of the three groups discussed here predates the presence of the languages limited to a single village, as will be discussed in section 12.3.3.

contemporary Ajumbu. This relationship appears to be confirmed by ethnohistorical accounts. As two of our consultants (one from Ajumbu, the other a Lung rememberer) have described, 'Ajumbu had no boundaries with Lung [and vice versa]; we were like brothers'.[8] Thus, Ajumbu's status as a one-village language within Lower Fungom is almost certainly innovative historically. There is no evidence for anything comparable for the other one-village languages.

These linguistic facts are largely complemented by evidence from a number of other domains. Oral histories collected throughout Lower Fungom, for instance, consistently treat Fang, Koshin, Naki, and Kung as more recent entrants to the region (though, as will be discussed in section 12.3.4 and section 12.3.5, oral histories also treat some Mungbam and Ji villages as being more recent entrants.) Similarly, excepting superficial resemblances in economic and symbolic terms, the cultures of the villages of Fang, Koshin, and Kung (and, to a lesser extent, Naki-speaking Mashi) differ from those of Mungbam- and Ji-speaking villages, as well as from each other, suggesting they have been subject to distinct influences (see section 12.3.5 for relevant discussion of Ajumbu on this point.)

While we have collected less archaeological data, what we have uncovered is also consistent with the scenario depicted in Figures 12.2 and 12.3. For instance, there are remains of previous areas of habitation that are suggestive of a shift from more dispersed to more concentrated settlement that can be associated with contemporary Ajumbu-speaking and Ji-speaking groups.[9]

There is also indirect evidence for reconstructing this change in settlement patterns. Before the early nineteenth century we are not aware of any need for inhabitants of the region to have settled in the dense settlements that characterize the area today, particularly in cases like Mufu, Mundabli, and Ajumbu, where the villages are located on relatively steep hilltops, which are good locations for defensive purposes but otherwise quite inconvenient. Other villages associated with apparent 'newcomer' groups, such as Fang and Koshin, are also found on hilltops. In these cases, we believe that groups entering Lower Fungom from the outside would have immediately chosen hilltops for village locations—also for defensive purposes—rather than coalescing in such locations from other parts of Lower Fungom. This interpretation is corroborated in an oral history collected from a Koshin speaker, as seen in the text fragment in (1).[10]

[8] This description is drawn from Di Carlo's fieldnotes and was provided by Sah Nicholas and Pa Joe.

[9] At least one of these 'Ajumbu' settlements appears to have been occupied by Lung groups, who, as discussed, would have spoken a variety closely related to Ajumbu rather than Ajumbu specifically.

[10] The text fragments in (1) and (2) are drawn from an oral history recited by Nji Ndinkwa Manessah Tah and transcribed by Good with the assistance of the speaker as well as Tah Christopher. Transcription conventions largely follow Tadadjeu and Sadembouo (1984) (see Good et al. 2011: 13 for further details). While the most crucial aspects of the meaning of the fragment for present purposes are believed to be secure, the glosses may not fully reflect all grammatical distinctions,

(1) a. *Mwìn kə́ bī WHY bə̀ nə̀ nì gə̀ dɔ́m ŋgàŋ wə̄.*
1.person FUT ask why 3p leave walk go settle 5.hill 5.DET
'Someone might wonder why they went and settled on that hill.'

b. *Bə̀ nə́ gə̀ dɔ́m ŋgàŋ wə̄ njəkə̄ TIME wə̄ dzʉ̀m*
3p leave go settle hill 5.DET because time that warfare
nə̀ nyā TOO-MUCH.
PST be too.much
'They settled on the hill because there was too much warfare at that time.'

It seems certain that the need to locate villages in easily defensible positions arose in conjunction with the so-called 'Chamba raids', a number of violent waves led by bands of mounted raiders coming from the north and north-east of the Grassfields, which swept through these and surrounding regions during the first half of the nineteenth century (Chilver and Kaberry 1968: 15–19, 132–4; Fardon 1988: 85ff; Geary 1976: 89–93; Nkwi and Warnier 1982: 81–8, 190). By virtue of being located away from the main trade routes and characterized by a remarkably hilly environment, it seems likely that Lower Fungom was raided only on isolated occasions and, therefore, became a refuge for groups displaced by Chamba raids (Di Carlo 2011: 91–2).[11]

In speaking of refugee movements here, we must be careful to distinguish organized migrations of multiple kin groups, or even whole villages, which we believe to have significantly altered the level of ecological and sociopolitical risk in Lower Fungom, to small-scale movements of individual kin groups, which we do not refer to using the label 'refugee' here. Movements of the latter type appear to have been long characteristic of the Grassfields region (and presumably beyond) (Warnier 1984: 399; 1985: 5, 213–14), and there is no reason to suspect they were particularly disruptive to local systems of social organization when they took place. Quite the contrary: societies in the region appear to have had standard means of incorporating relatively small incoming groups (see Kopytoff 1987). The need to make a distinction between these two kinds of population movements will become clearer in section 12.3.3 and subsequent sections.

---

especially those coded primarily via tone, and the tone transcriptions themselves reflect the surfacing tone patterns rather than a tonemic representation. Elements of Cameroonian Pidgin origin in the text are capitalized since their level of integration into Koshin is not known. Glossing abbreviations for the data in (1) and (2) are as follows: 1, 2, 5: noun class; 3p: third-person plural pronoun; CONT: continuous; DET: determiner; FUT: future; LOC: locative; PRT: tense-aspect particle; PST: past. Further grammatical information on Koshin can be found in Good et al. (2011: 140–6).

[11] For an instance of synoecism caused by the emergence of external violent threats in the Grassfields, see Warnier (1975: 86ff) for Mankon. On the same process accompanied by fortification, see also Warnier (1984: 405). For an instance of how strong an impact Chamba raids had on easily reachable areas, see Geary (1976: 74, 88; 1979: 54) on Weh.

12.3.3 The Second Phase: Village Crystallization and In-migration

As discussed in section 12.2.1, Lower Fungom societies can, in 2014, be described as occupying what we have termed 'villages'. We employ this term in a rather specific sense (which we believe is fully consistent with its use in the wider literature on Grassfields' societies). It refers not merely to a 'clustered' settlement, but rather a settlement with a specific social, political, and physical character. The two most prominent features of what we term 'canonical' Lower Fungom villages (see Di Carlo 2011: 65–77) for present purposes are: (i) that they do not have a fully unified social structure but, rather, are composed of exogamous quarters which typically occupy a distinct physical space from each other and serve as the primary units of economic and political organization (see section 12.3.4 below) and (ii) that their inhabitants recognize the ritual authority of a single chief who, though relatively weak in political terms, is traditionally credited to own special powers capable of ensuring the villagers' well-being. As consultants describe it, the chief must give *bush*, *chop*, and *pikin*. Translated from Cameroonian Pidgin, this means the chief should provide an abundance of 'harvest', 'game', and 'children', respectively.

We focus on these two features since they establish villages as representing only a weak unification (via the ritual chief) of otherwise competing interest groups (quarters). They are therefore characterized by a constant tendency towards 'fission' (Kopytoff 1987: 26) rather than serving as the 'primordial embryo' (Kopytoff 1987: 7) of a language-culture complex of the sort that is presently valorized in much of the endangered languages discourse. This model of village structure also puts our second phase of Lower Fungom history into an appropriate perspective. The Mungbam and Ji villages and the village of Ajumbu appear to represent innovative political formations from previously 'acephalous' patterns of social organization, which underwent a process that we informally refer to here as 'crystallization' (see also Kopytoff 1981: 373). This process did not create a new, indivisible community. Rather, it resulted in a politically expedient 'federation' of kin groups which retained significant autonomy.

This process of crystallization must be contrasted with the quite distinct pattern of in-migration of refugee groups, as introduced in section 12.3.2, which effectively brought whole villages, as units, into Lower Fungom. That such in-migration explains the presence of two villages in Lower Fungom, Kung, and Mashi is essentially incontestable. The historical analysis prompted by the linguistic facts (see section 12.2.1) converges with analyses indicated by non-linguistic evidence. For example, oral histories regarding the Kung and the Mashi place their origins outside of Lower Fungom, and each has distinctive cultural traditions from other Lower Fungom villages.

The villages of Koshin and Fang also appear to have entered Lower Fungom via in-migration of refugee groups, though the lack of known close linguistic relatives of the Koshin and Fang languages means that this can only be established by virtue of non-linguistic evidence. As with Kung and Mashi, oral histories treat both groups as having outside origins. Furthermore, each is culturally distinctive within the Lower Fungom context and both notably show indications of having had close relations with communities with more stratified social structures than what appears to have been the historical norm in palm oil producing areas like Lower Fungom (see section 12.2.3).

Most likely due to their relatively high populations, social cohesion, and the nature of their movements being triggered by mounted raids (see section 12.3.2), the migrations of the Kung, Mashi, Koshin, and Fang into Lower Fungom were not associated with incorporation into existing societies but, rather, merely shifted their physical location, leaving their social structure relatively intact. Oral histories are consistent with this view. For example, the sentences in (2) depict the last stage of a migration that would bring Koshin speakers to Lower Fungom. It portrays them moving as a unit and settling in one location. Moreover, as seen in (1), which is drawn from the same oral history and almost immediately follows the fragment given in (2), Koshin history treats the group as forming a dense settlement on a hilltop upon their arrival in Lower Fungom.[12]

(2) a.

SO	*bə̀*	*ká*	*gwá*	*fə̂*	*bə̀*	*ká*	*tīká*	*bānyɛ́*	*bə̄bɔ̀*	*Sáwì.*
so	3p	CONT	separate	exit	3p	CONT	leave	2.brother	2.their	Sawi

'They then separated and left their brothers from Sawi.'

b.

Bə̀	*ká*	*nê*	*ká*	*nî*	*kə̀*	*bà*	*wə́*	*mə̀*	*SOTEE*
3p	CONT	leave	CONT	walk	PRT	5.bank	5.DET	LOC	so.long
ká	*dí*	*jīɛ̄*	*fə́*	*bā*	*mɔ̀*	*fɔ́*	*wɛ̄n.*		
CONT	come	reach	place	3p	be	there	now		

'They then went along the banks until they came and reached where they are today.'

We believe it is likely that these in-migrations were the main trigger of the crystallization processes affecting the older inhabitants of Lower Fungom just described above. As antagonistic newcomers entered the region, those already present underwent processes of synoecism.[13] This involved shifting from previously autonomous kin groups into federated villages in order to increase their potential for controlling increasingly scarce natural resources.[14]

[12] See the discussion surrounding (1) for details on the source of the data in (2) and on the glossing conventions.

[13] See Fleisher (2010) for discussion of synoecism in a sub-Saharan African context.

[14] For the most part, the oral histories of Lower Fungom's villages that we have collected neither corroborate nor contradict this claim, except for those of the Missong (see section 12.3.4), which do support it. However, we do not believe this is particularly surprising since explicitly referencing a process of synoecism in an official oral history would partly contradict the historical justification for the existence of the village as a 'natural' entity.

Therefore, at the time of contact with colonial administrators and surveying linguists, the situation in Lower Fungom was not the result of 'natural' differentiation of languages into dialects, which, in turn, developed into new languages, as implied by the earliest serious linguistic treatment of the area (Hombert 1980). Rather, what was (and still can be) witnessed is a moment of exceptional 'hyperdiversity' triggered by the chance confluence of social, ecological, and historical factors. This underscores the observation of Kopytoff (1987: 7) that, rather than adopting the stereotype of Africa as a 'continent mired in timeless immobility', we should instead view it as characterized by a 'ceaseless flux among populations' (see also Zeitlyn and Connell 2003).

While we believe that the overall picture presented above is more or less valid as a general framework for understanding recent Lower Fungom history, not surprisingly the details of some of the villages complicate the story somewhat. We discuss aspects of the problems they raise in the next two sections, paying special attention to the case of the Mungbam-speaking village of Missong, whose history offers a clear counterbalance to the prevailing notion of languages as the storehouse of unique cultural 'treasures' (see section 12.1).

12.3.4 The Exemplary Case of Missong and the Rest of Mungbam

The historical reconstruction we have given here implies, in some sense, that villages in Lower Fungom speaking varieties of Mungbam represent a continuation of speech varieties of an 'indigenous' population of the region. However, three of the Mungbam-speaking villages, Biya, Munken, and Missong, are actually associated with oral traditions treating them as newcomers to the area. When this is set against the fact that the two other Mungbam villages, Abar and Ngun, are not associated with such traditions, the linguistic facts are unambiguously at odds with the historical representations. There is, however, a straightforward way to account for this: villages like Biya, Munken, and Missong may very well have been founded (at least partly) by immigrants to the area who eventually shifted to a Mungbam variety. We will explore this possibility via an examination of the village of Missong, which is the most exceptional of the Mungbam villages (see Lovegren 2013 for a polylectal grammar of the five Mungbam villages).

In Figure 12.3, Missong was given a special symbol intended to suggest an 'imperfect' connection between it and the other Mungbam varieties, as it is distinctive in both linguistic and cultural terms. As discussed in Good et al. (2011: 115), Missong is linguistically differentiated from the other Mungbam varieties lexically, phonologically, and morphologically, to the point where it may in fact be most reasonable to treat it as a distinct language. Di Carlo (2011: 84–5) further delineates Missong's cultural distinctiveness. For example, the structure and distribution of its secret associations reveal that in Missong, unlike most of the other villages of the region, the balance of control over ritual and political power is skewed towards quarters, at the expense of the village as a united whole.[15] Indeed, Missong quarters could almost be seen as miniature villages insofar as they are not even exogamous units, as in the overwhelming majority of Lower Fungom societies, but each of them is in fact composed by two exogamous moieties.

Oral traditions reinforce the observed lack of political cohesion among quarters. All the kin groups we have contacted, for instance, claim distinctive provenances, to the point where there seems to be virtually no lineage that could be held as 'indigenous' to the village site. For example, when asked to specify the provenance of their forefathers, one of our Missong consultants mentioned 'Fang side', the village chief offered 'Adjumə, not far from Dumbu', while another man recalled 'Tsha' (location unknown) and 'Ufayu' (probably today's Mashi Overside).[16] If such statements are treated as instances of direct historical data, the composite structure of Missong would be obvious. Alternatively, one could treat them as political statements intended to legitimize some form of ownership or power—that is, as a kind of Malinowskian charter, as in the famously debated case of the historical role of the Tikar in the Grassfields (see Chilver and Kaberry 1971; Jeffreys 1964; and, more recently, Fowler and Zeitlyn 1996: 6–15). If this were the case, however, they would represent elements of an unusual kind of charter where historical 'differentness' is used to justify present-day political consolidation. This leads us to believe that the historical interpretation is the more likely one, at least in its broad outlines.

Moreover, the list of remembered chiefs in Missong is comparatively short in the Lower Fungom context, consisting of just four names rather than a more typical six to eight, suggesting that the village is understood by its inhabitants to be a relatively recent amalgamation, regardless of its actual history.[17] This is

[15] Secret associations, at least in the Grassfields, are 'secret' primarily by virtue of the fact that their members have access to and know secret objects, practices, words, songs, and so on which are believed to have magical powers and are kept secret from the non-initiated. There are secret associations for men as well as women in the Lower Fungom villages (and in much of West Africa as well), and they play a highly significant role in the maintenance of social cohesion in the area. See Di Carlo (2011: 67–70) for further discussion of Lower Fungom's secret associations and Horton (1972: 101–3) for discussion of the key role of secret associations in processes of confederation of diverse kin groups into villages in the history of West Africa.

[16] See the map in Figure 12.1 for the locations of Fang and Mashi Overside. Dumbu (also known as Dumbo) is roughly to the east of the Lower Fungom, but not particularly distant from it, and is associated with the Beboid language Kemezung (see Brye and Brye 2002: section 3.5)

[17] Length of genealogies cannot be taken as an immediate historical index (see Irvine 1978 and Vansina 1985: 182–5). However, among the social distortions of genealogical knowledge there is the so-called 'structural time depth' (Vansina 1985: 118)—that is, the possibility that in a given tradition genealogical steps are fixed in number. At the very least, then, genealogies of appreciably different length from that encountered most commonly in a given area can be taken as indices of a given village's distance from local norms. (See Goody and Watt 1963: 308–11, for discussion of how colonial ideologies of 'history' and the interpretation of genealogies clashed with those of the Tiv, a group primarily based in Nigeria in an area roughly to the north of Lower Fungom.)

exemplified in the words of Buo Makpa Amos, a senior member of the Bambiam moiety of the Bikwom quarter of Missong, during his reconstruction of village history (all the following names refer to exogamous units found within the village): 'Bikwom was the first, the early people, then the Bidjumbi came, then the Biandzəm, then we, the Bambiam, and the Bakpaŋ and finally the Myam.' Although they would not necessarily agree on all details, we believe the claim that Missong was progressively populated by unrelated kin groups would be shared by many, if not most, Missong elders.

Significantly in the present context, the local perception of the linguistic variety associated with Missong follows a similar pattern. Far from being understood as the 'ancestral code' (see Woodbury 2005, 2011) of its people, it is instead taken to be of recent provenance. Furthermore, this perception is not limited to Missong but is also found in other Mungbam-speaking villages, some inhabitants of which have characterized Missong people as having 'stolen' their language. Moreover, the Missong do not question this history, and some Missong consultants have even suggested that the group is particularly adept at learning the languages of others—a positive reorientation of outside perceptions.

What appears to be the most straightforward historical account for what we see in Missong is that the village represents an amalgamation of immigrant groups of diverse origin. Before proceeding further with our historical reconstruction, it is probably best to reproduce here an excerpt, drawn from Di Carlo's fieldnotes, again from Buo Makpa Amos, that elucidates both this process and its underlying ideology. Parts of the excerpt of particular interest to the present discussion have been italicized:

> As my father told me, we were from Fang side, even in Bum side there were many of us. *When you people are cooperating you speak one language. If you speak one language, you cooperate.* As a group of relatives moves, the brothers may decide to split, each choosing a different place to stay. This is what happened to us. We left the early place in Fang side as a whole and arrived in Abar. From here we scattered. Now, we Bambiam from Missong have relatives in Abar, in Buu, in Ngun. Each family attached itself to a village and therefore had to speak the general language used there. For example, *we Bambiam attached ourselves to Bikwom and hence had to adopt their language; Bikwom people are attached to Bidjumbi and Biandzəm to form the village of Missong, and this is why they all had to use the same language, that is, Missong.* This is why all the descendants of the family that moved from Fang side now speak different languages.

We believe, therefore, that the development of Missong can best be understood as resulting from a twofold process. On the one hand, immigrant groups underwent a process of mimesis with surrounding Mungbam-speaking groups, probably facilitated by high intermarriage rates.[18] On the other hand, the

[18] In Missong, as in most of Lower Fungom societies, residence is virilocal, meaning that women, once married, are expected to move to the husband's father's compound. Therefore, high numbers of

emerging group was motivated to develop a locally distinctive idiom for political reasons and did so by incorporating influences of the original languages of the new immigrant groups (see also Zeitlyn and Connell 2003: 119), which, over time, added to Missong's population. If we situate this process with respect to the two idealized phases of Lower Fungom history discussed above, we can speculate that some of the earliest kin groups that would come to form Missong—of presumably diverse linguistic origin—had settled among Mungbam-speaking groups during the first phase, but had not been fully incorporated into these societies when the second phase, that of crystallization, took place. They then amalgamated with members of other incoming immigrant groups into a partly crystallized village for purposes of defence, with the adoption of a common language being one of the most overt signs of this new political entity.

Under such a scenario, the Missong variety of Mungbam could be considered to be a partly mixed language, along the lines of the celebrated case of Ma'á (Mous 1994, 2003a, 2003b; Thomason 1983, 1997). The mixture would have been between closely related, and grammatically broadly similar, languages. Thus, it would be less striking than the Ma'á case, but, nevertheless, sufficient to make Missong's distinctiveness in the local context both readily detectable by the linguist and quite salient to speakers of other Mungbam varieties.

12.3.5 Ajumbu

As indicated in Figure 12.2, we also believe the Ji group of languages and Ajumbu to represent a continuation of societies that have been present in Lower Fungom for some time, as opposed to the other groups that appear to be the result of relatively recent refugee movements. The multi-village Ji group shows comparable patterns to Mungbam insofar as there is evidence to suggest that some of its villages may represent historical amalgams of groups of distinct ultimate provenance. Ajumbu raises additional issues insofar as we have no reason to suggest that it has incorporated outside groups, but it nevertheless shows cultural divergences in comparison with the other 'older' groups in the region, which calls for some explanation. We briefly discuss the latter case in this section, focusing on points of relevance to the relationship between a community, a culture, and a language.

Unlike Mungbam and the Ji group, there is only one extant village speaking Ajumbu (though see section 12.3.2 for evidence that there were once at least two villages speaking this language, or very closely related languages). Therefore, we do not have the problem of explaining divergences among villages. However, as

---

Mungbam-speaking women in a village of otherwise composite nature may have fostered the adoption of a Mungbam variety as the village-wide lingua franca.

mentioned above, Ajumbu cultural traits are distinctive enough from those of the other groups that we believe to have been present in Lower Fungom in our reconstructed first phase (see Figure 12.2) as to require some discussion. For example, its oral traditions represent it as indigenous to the area. At the same time, other Lower Fungom groups do not show evidence of close connections to Ajumbu, and its strongest relations appear to be outside of Lower Fungom, with the village of Fungom (see Di Carlo 2011: 83–4).

Our conclusion from this is that the predecessors of today's Ajumbu speakers were probably somewhat culturally distinct from those of Mungbam or the Ji group even during our reconstructed first phase in Figure 12.2, though we cannot say more beyond this with any certainty. It is important to bear in mind that the time depth of the caesura between our first and second phase is relatively shallow, at about two centuries, while the Grassfields cultural area is, perhaps, two millennia old (see section 12.2.3). This leaves plenty of room for historical developments to have affected the region, which are, at least at present, beyond the reach of our ability to reconstruct; it is not impossible to imagine, for instance, that the Ajumbu may represent an older layer of habitation than the Mungbam or the Ji (or vice versa), which could help explain these divergences.

There is one additional aspect of Ajumbu oral history, not directly relevant to its position within Lower Fungom, but nevertheless of significance for the broader topic of this chapter, which is worth mentioning here. While Ajumbu's oral traditions give no suggestion of culturally diverse origins—unlike, for instance, those of Missong, Munken, or Mundabli—they do explicitly claim that groups historically associated with Ajumbu have contributed to the formation of amalgamated groups in locations to the south and the east of Lower Fungom. For example, the Ajumbu claim to be the point of origin for groups to the south-west in Obang, whose inhabitants are classified as speaking the Befang language of the Menchum subgroup of the Grassfields group (see Boum 1980). They also claim to have contributed to the population of the village of Mbuk in the Bum area, which is reported to speak its own language (Lamberty 2002: 3). According to one of our consultants, this can be characterized as a 'mix' of Ajumbu and Bum elements.[19] A text fragment from an oral history describing this is given below in (3).[20]

[19] The available data on the language of this village are quite limited (comprising a wordlist of less than 50 terms (Chilver and Kaberry 1974: 40)). Therefore we cannot verify this description.

[20] The text fragment in (3) is drawn from an oral history recited by Che Martin and transcribed by Good with the assistance of Zang Martina. Transcription conventions largely follow Tadadjeu and Sadembouo (1984) (see Good et al. (2011: 13) for further details). While the most crucial aspects of the meaning of the fragment for present purposes are believed to be secure, the glosses may not fully reflect all grammatical distinctions, especially those coded primarily via tone, and the tone transcriptions themselves reflect the surfacing tone patterns rather than a tonemic representation. Glossing abbreviations are as follows: 2, 5, 8: noun class; 3p: third person plural pronoun; DET:

(3) a. *Ādzú āgyə́ gyàŋ nyɛ̀ny fɛ̂ bā nyɛ̀ny yì Bûm Mbūkə́.*
2.Ajumbu 2.some separate leave here 3p leave go Bum Mbuk
'Some Ajumbu split and left here for Mbuk in Bum.'

b. *Bā bâ dû kə̀ dú ādzú yə̀ bā dú kwɛ̄ny kə̀*
3p now speak PRT 5.language 2.Ajumbu 5.DET 3p speak meet PRT
bā dú ádzú zó bə̀sə̀ yɔ̀ dú yɔ̀
with 5.language 2.Ajumbu call mix go.IPFV language go.IPFV
bə̀sə̀ yɔ̀ nyū bāgyə́ ā dú Bûm yɛ̄ mā.
mix go.IPFV 8.thing 8.some LOC 5.language Bum 5.DET LOC
'They now speak a language close to Ajumbu that sounds as if it was mixing with things from the Bum language.'

The conceptualization of Ajumbu as a village associated with diaspora communities, who no longer necessarily speak the Ajumbu language, is clearly significant for understanding the nature of Ajumbu 'identity'. It also attests to the fact that, in local terms, incorporation is not viewed as a strictly one-way process of one group 'absorbing' another group. The fission of a group into multiple new groups is also explicitly recognized as a possibility, as already pointed out by Kopytoff (1987).

12.4 Lower Fungom Ideologies and Documentary Ideologies

12.4.1 Multilingualism, Solidarity, and Identity

We have provided above a partial reconstruction of the linguistic history of Lower Fungom, emphasizing the relationship between certain sociopolitical entities (i.e. villages) and 'languages' in the region, which we believe have bearing on our understanding of the connection between languages and cultures, a topic we will explore in the present section.

Lower Fungom's linguistic history may appear to be somewhat distinctive when set against, say, that of better-known European languages, though we should be quick to point out that we do not believe it to be particularly unusual in the context of the Grassfields, where comparable situations have often been reported, if not as well explored. Indeed, the earliest comprehensive ethnographic study of the Grassfields has already provided an outline for the historical scenarios discussed above:

---

determiner; IPFV: imperfective; LOC: locative; PRT: tense-aspect particle. Further grammatical information on Ajumbu can be found in Good et al. (2011: 133–40).

> The major problem of historical reconstruction in this area is the incompatibility of language distribution with alleged ethnic origin and institutions ... The present politico-social units of the [Cameroon] Grassfields are for the most part composite units, sometimes grouped round intrusive dynasties or built by conquest, or by the slow adhesion of smaller groups in favoured areas, or, more recently, by the temporary agglomeration of small groups seeking protection from attack. The history of the [Cameroon] Grassfields, therefore, must do without simple schematic maps showing broad directions of migration, though some of the effects of invasion in the early 19th century or the expansion of particular states can be demonstrated. (Chilver and Kaberry 1968: 6–7)

Chilver and Kaberry's (1968) ethnohistorical insights have largely gone unheeded in the linguistic literature on the Grassfields, which has, instead, tended to uncritically assume the classic *Stammbaum* or family tree model of language differentiation.[21] However, our own examination of Lower Fungom aligns quite well with their depiction, and our impression is that, at least in cases like that of Missong (see section 12.3.4), it offers a more insightful characterization of the linguistic situation than applying models of historical reasoning devised from examinations of European languages onto the Grassfields landscape (see, e.g., Greenberg 1972: 196).

The repercussions of even partly accepting such a model of language development have significance across a number of domains. Here, we would like to highlight its impact on the conceptual understanding of the nature of a 'language' in a given society. To do so, we must attempt to characterize key aspects of the language ideologies we are uncovering in Lower Fungom. Our present understanding of them must be considered somewhat tentative. Nevertheless, we feel confident enough that they lend sufficient insight to the overall picture to provide a sketch of it at this point, and we begin by contextualizing multilingualism in the area, since that will help elucidate the relationship between *individual* identity and language, and thus add to the discussion above on the relationship between *village* identity and language.

Throughout Lower Fungom, at birth every child (traditionally) receives two names: one is given by their (social) father, the other by their mother's father.[22] While the former is more likely to become the most used, and ultimately the only name recognized by Cameroon's administration, the latter—not a nickname but a real personal name usually taken from the repertoire of names peculiar to the

[21] The adoption of this assumption was hardly a foregone conclusion in African linguistics where, before the widespread acceptance of Greenberg's (1966) classification of African languages, analyses involving language 'mixture' were not uncommon (see, e.g., Welmers 1974: 2–3 for a critical discussion).

[22] Comparable patterns of assigning multiple names to a child are found elsewhere in the Grassfields (and beyond), though not necessarily with precisely the configuration we have found in Lower Fungom. The collected articles in Mbunwe-Samba et al. (1993) give an overview of naming practices for a number of Grassfields groups.

maternal kin group—is kept somewhat hidden and used only by the child's maternal kin. This twofold identity can also have a linguistic side. If the child's parents come from two different villages and, hence, are speakers of two different languages (at least in local perception), then the child is expected to learn both languages and use them in the appropriate circumstances. Simplifying somewhat, the father's language is the exclusive code to be used for communication with their paternal kin, whereas the mother's language must be used with their maternal kin. In essence, the child acquires distinct identities with respect to each kin group. This is the clearest (though not the only) instance of the significance of multilingualism for the region's traditions.[23] It indicates that the local culture acknowledges (and prizes) the possibility for an individual to develop multiple social identities, stressing language as a major means to symbolize them.[24]

Indeed, this is merely one prominent, linguistically oriented example of a more general tendency of maintaining (often latent) networks of solidarity groups apparently common to much of sub-Saharan Africa:

> [E]ach person was attached to several groups of solidarity. Depending on the context, one expected support from each and offered it to each of them. In times of conflict, one tried to mobilize the maximum contextually relevant group. Since traditional African societies were structured in terms of corporate groups, individual survival was possible only by being under the protective umbrella of one or another such group, and the larger and more powerful it was, the safer one was. The most immediate and most secure groups of support were those based on ties of kinship. (Kopytoff 1987: 24)

We have already seen the extremely localist sociolinguistic attitudes that dominate Lower Fungom resulting in a coincidence between villages and languages (see section 12.3.4).[25] At the same time, one must also recognize the

[23] For example, it is not uncommon for the same pattern to apply with respect to grandparents, so that by learning the languages associated with their villages a child can gain additional affiliations (though they do not receive additional names in such cases). Of course, individuals may also learn to speak multiple languages for more familiar reasons, such as by going to school in an area with a local language distinct from theirs or to gain access to economic opportunities where knowledge of another language is useful.

[24] Wolff (1967) gives another example of how names have been linked to social solidarity (or lack thereof) in a nearby area of Nigeria where subordinate groups adopted names from historically dominant groups, with the pattern shifting away from this with a change in political attitudes towards the relevant subordinate–superordinate relationship.

[25] We have adopted Hill's (1996) sense of 'localist' here. However, we should point out an interesting difference between the cases she considers and ours. In her interpretation of Tohono O'odham dialect differentiation, speakers associated with a geographic area that had less access to crucial resources (especially water) were analysed as more likely to adopt a distributed stance over a localist one, as manifested by their greater propensity towards employing linguistic traits of other dialects as part of a strategy to help gain access to resources of other groups. In Lower Fungom, comparable goals appear to be achieved via multilingualism. A key difference here is that Hill was concerned with change in

possibility for *individuals* to use different idioms in order to maintain multiple affiliations, and hence social identities, regardless of their 'official' village of residence.

12.4.2 Essentialism and Indexicality

In order to make sense of these patterns, we believe it is useful to consider two heuristic 'orientations' that can be associated with language ideologies, 'essentialist' and 'indexical', each of which references a kind of social meaning that can be applied to a given lexicogrammatical code. The essentialist orientation can be understood in terms of the matrix of cultural assumptions through which:

> '[l]anguages are loaded with particular ontological commitments, including ... notions of "purity", the notion that languages can isomorphically (iconically) reflect the essences of their speakers ... and the notion that particular languages embody qualities ranging from rationality to recidivism' (McIntosh 2005: 1920).

The essentialist orientation is a key component of the so-called 'Herderian equation' of language, culture, and nation (see, e.g., Foley 2005 and Hymes 1968, 1972) that intimately informs dominant language ideologies in the West and elsewhere.[26]

In considering the indexical orientation of language, we are interested in the ways in which the use of language in a given context associates a speaker with 'particular ways of being and acting' (Johnstone and Kiesling 2008: 7).[27] McIntosh (2005) relates essentialism to indexicality as follows:

> Not only is language essentialism important to the way people conceptualize language; it also has implications for the way we think about language-in-use. It is common for sociolinguistics and linguistic anthropologists to suggest that particular linguistic practices, including code choice, constitute an 'index' of identity, context, social relations, or interpretive frames ... *Yet the notion of 'index' risks treating language as nothing more than a semiotic pointer to something else, and obscures the fact that sometimes language is treated as if it were the bearer of special ontological properties in and of itself.* (McIntosh 2005: 1921; emphasis added)

McIntosh's (2005) warning about the potential problems with overemphasizing language's role as an 'empty' semiotic pointer is an important one. At the same time, our own understanding of the linguistic situation of Lower Fungom

---

dialects within a single language community, rather than a set of communities speaking distinct languages (whether in linguistic or local terms).

[26] Nichols (1993) presents a study of the Slavic expansion of clear interest in the present context that suggests that it was, at least partly, driven by the dynamics that developed when Slavic speakers with a strongly essentialist linguistic orientation came into contact with speakers of other languages whose relationship to their primary speech varieties emphasized the indexical orientation.

[27] For more on our use of indexical, see, for example, Silverstein (2003) and Johnstone and Kiesling (2008).

suggests that the language ideologies of the region do indeed stress the indexical orientation of languages without necessarily loading them with particular ontological commitments associated with the essentialist orientation.

Lower Fungom is an area where discrete social groups live close to each other and, on the whole, perceive themselves as being of nearly equivalent socio-economic status. The absence of a recognized hierarchical relationship between villages, and hence of an agreed-upon preference for a given target identity, is embedded in a context where key cultural features are shared at a regional level. This situation is probably to be seen as a fertile ground for 'pure' indexicality to become central to local language ideologies, which assign languages only a marginal role as expressions of some cultural essence exclusively connected with a given 'ethnic' group. This pattern is seen both when examining the historical development of a village like Missong and when looking at the social significance of multilingualism in the region. We explore these points in more detail in the next section.

12.4.3 Indexicality in Lower Fungom (and Possibly Beyond)

If it is the case that languages in Lower Fungom are associated with ideologies that treat them as strongly indexical but only weakly essential, then this has clear implications for our understanding of what is 'lost' when a language ceases to be spoken. For instance, if a language is conceptualized as one of the outward manifestations of something more fundamental, such as an ethnicity or a nation, the loss of that language will be taken to imply the loss of that deeper thing, including the 'culture' shared by its speakers. By contrast, if language is conceptualized first and foremost as an index of group identity and, hence, primarily as a symbolic resource allowing a group to claim political independence (see section 12.3.4) and, through multilingualism, for an individual to maintain multiple affiliations with different groups, then it is legitimate to wonder just what would be 'lost' when such a language disappears. We can examine this issue in both synchronic and diachronic terms.

On the diachronic side, we have argued that, once aggregated, newly emerged village communities, such as Missong, voluntarily crafted what were to become their common and unique languages and cultures as a means to establish cohesion and autonomy in a fluid regional context. It would, therefore, seem clear that the language and culture that we observe today in a place like Missong represent historically quite shallow innovations obtained through variations on linguistic and cultural 'themes' that the newly emerged group could absorb from surrounding groups or retrieve from the pre-confederation past of its forming segments. If Missong, and similar villages in Lower Fungom, were to disappear, it appears to be undeniably true that some kind of 'culture' would be lost. However, the nature of this culture, arising as the result of a temporally recent response to changing ecological and social conditions, is not of the type that is so frequently valorized in the rhetoric surrounding endangered languages, which emphasizes the significance of language as a link to some sort of ancient 'indigenousness' (see Errington 2003: 724–6).

On the synchronic side, due to traditional predominance of multilingualism, if we wanted to establish the number of total speakers of a given language of Lower Fungom, we would be obliged to consider the whole area and not confine ourselves to the village that gives the name to the language. This means that, at any given moment, the 'speech community' associated with a particular language consists both of those resident in its associated village and of significant numbers of non-residents. A given individual, therefore, has the potential to participate in the 'cultures' of more than one village-language complex. Since patterns of multilingualism are linked to the specific life (and especially family) history of an individual, the implication is that residents of Lower Fungom are bearers of diverse assortments of not only multilingual, but also multicultural, competences, rendering the relationship between individuals and local cultures intrinsically variegated. The loss of a village-language complex in such a context cannot reasonably be associated with the loss of a 'people' or an 'ethnicity', at least as commonly understood, since inhabitants of Lower Fungom do not segregate into the neatly defined groups that such notions presuppose. Rather, the loss of one of these 'hyper-local' cultures would merely represent a shift among the kaleidoscopic array of allegiances that characterize the Lower Fungom social space.

Both of these considerations emphasize the independence of the indexical and essentialist orientation in language ideologies and make visible the lack of generality of commonplace assumptions often found in the endangered languages literature, such as the uniformity and continuity of the relationship between language and culture in the history of a community and the idea of a unified (and prototypically geography-bound) speech community that is the bearer of a consistent 'culture' (see also Errington (2003) for a relevant discussion).[28]

To return to our exemplary case, what this means is that, under our interpretation, people who speak Missong do so when they wish to index their affiliation with the current village of Missong, without the specific intention to express some deeper sense of 'Missonghood' associated with differential ethnic markers. Furthermore, the ability to speak Missong merely gives one the power to index such affiliation, rather than implying an immutable feature of identity.[29]

[28] The relative lack of clearly bounded speech communities in the Grassfields adds to the number of examples calling for the dismissal of such a concept and its substitution with the broader notion of 'community of practice' (see, e.g., Bucholtz 1999 and Eckert 2000).

[29] Of course, one may find individuals in the community who outwardly attribute deeper significance to the language, though we suspect these would most likely be those with the greatest stake in the ongoing cohesion of the village, who, as a result, would have a strong interest in ensuring key indices

Seen from this perspective, we believe it would be a mistake to equate the loss of Missong (or presumably any of the languages of Lower Fungom) with something as extreme as 'dropping a bomb on the Louvre', to quote one popularized instance of Hill's (2002) thematic category of hyperbolic valorization.[30] To stretch the analogy a bit, the language of Missong is perhaps better understood as an individual work of art in the Louvre of the wider Grassfields 'ecumene' (Kopytoff 1981), rather than as an entire museum in and of itself.[31]

There is a potentially negative conclusion one can reach on the basis of this last point: that the indexical orientation of Lower Fungom language ideologies makes its languages, in some sense, less 'valuable' than languages associated with a strong essentialist orientation that are, thereby, conceptually intertwined with their associated cultures. In fact, this conclusion would appear to be inescapable if we choose to emphasize the role of endangered languages as repositories of cultural knowledge that constitute 'priceless treasures' (see Hill 2002: 123–35). Cultural knowledge is, of course, encoded within the speech variety of Missong, but most of this knowledge can also be found in other languages of the Grassfields. The 'treasures'—if we choose to adopt such a word—are better understood to be found at the level of the 'palm oil belt' of the Grassfields (and perhaps beyond), rather than in any one language. We will explore this issue, and its consequences for language documentation, in the next section.

12.4.4 Lower Fungom and Documentary Agendas

At present, as implied by programmatic work such as Himmelmann (1998, 2006), and made more explicit in work such as Woodbury (2005, 2011), typical documentation projects are oriented towards documenting a speech variety that is idealized as being uniquely associated with a community and conceptualized as an 'ancestral code'. Such projects not only align well with *nostalgic* (see Woodbury 2011: 178) impulses to document codes, or features of codes, whose near-term loss is anticipated, but they also cohere with the default stance of linguists that a documentation project's most natural descriptive outputs are characterizations of a language in the form of a grammar, a dictionary, and a set

of village identity would be maintained as a way of demonstrating village strength—that is, the original indexical significance of the Missong language would acquire an additional indexical significance of a higher order, in the sense of Silverstein (2003).

[30] The original source for this appears to be Ken Hale as quoted in an article in the August 1999 issue of *National Geographic*.

[31] At the same time, we are aware that there are cases of African languages that show other, apparently more 'essential', patterns. Rottland and Okoth Okombo (1986), for example, describe a case in sub-Saharan Africa where language attitudes appear to align more closely with something like the Western notion of ethnicity than what we see in Lower Fungom. Lüpke (2010: 160–1) describes something similar. In both cases, however, these are relatively recent developments.

of annotated texts, that is, a language is treated as a stable synchronic object rather than as a dynamic entity whose character is bound to a sociohistorical context (see also Silverstein 1998 for a relevant discussion).

Such a documentary ideology partners naturally with language ideologies dominated by essentialist claims, which is not surprising to the extent that language documentation has arisen in contexts where languages are normally conceptualized in these terms. It matches up less comfortably, however, with ideologies emphasizing primarily the indexical quality of languages. This is because the social significance of languages associated with such ideologies does not derive from their perceived intrinsic relation to some ancestral inheritance but, rather, from the way they are opposed to, and therefore derive their social meaning from, the other languages of their milieu. In other words, the 'meaning' of Missong is only recoverable when one realizes that the variety is *not* the same as Abar, Munken, or Buu, and so on, and that its differences are locally construed as sufficient to classify it as a distinct language (regardless of the linguist's judgement). Of course, languages understood in essentialist terms also derive some of their significance by means of oppositions to other languages, but there is a critical difference in conception: for such languages, the differences among them will ultimately be understood as deriving from ethnic 'essence' rather than from an individual's overt signalling that, at a given moment, they are expressing solidarity with one group over another.

This suggests at least three lessons with respect to the documentation of languages like those of Lower Fungom, where indexical ideologies of language predominate. First, any documentation of them that does not take their socio-historical context into account is likely to be inadequate if one of the ultimate uses of documentation is not merely to make a record of the language but also to explore connections between the structure of the language and the culture of its speakers. Moreover, it seems especially important for such languages to document their relationships to the other languages that play a significant role in their local ecology. Cobbinah (2010) and Lüpke (2010) make similar points with respect to the documentation of the Baïnounk group of languages spoken in Senegal, which appear to be found in an environment with important similarities to what is found in Lower Fungom. It may be reasonable to suggest, therefore, that a key lesson that sub-Saharan African languages may hold for work in language documentation is that we must be wary of the usually implicit assumption that the 'normal' way to document is to delineate a single lexicogrammatical code as the object of investigation, and that we should view this, instead, as a response only appropriate to certain contexts.

A second lesson, related to the first, is that we must be careful not to get caught up in our own rhetoric and allow it to define our approach to language documentation in a time of extensive endangerment. If it is the case that languages of Lower Fungom, and perhaps of a good deal of sub-Saharan Africa, are more typically characterized by indexical rather than essentialist orientations, this is clearly an important and interesting dimension of linguistic variation, on top of variation within lexicogrammatical codes themselves, which needs to be documented if we are (perhaps nostalgically) to capture the range of known linguistic variation.

Finally, we must bear in mind that issues like those discussed here are difficult to discern when researchers are embedded in an ideological context that assigns primary value to languages in their role as 'repositories' as opposed to other possible roles they have, such as their use in constructing a larger social space. Put differently, in the context of the Lower Fungom, if we focus on only documenting 'languages', we will be failing to gather information on what lessons the region has to offer us in the area of language dynamics. This is a striking gap when we consider that the extreme linguistic diversity of this region may provide important lessons for the maintenance of small languages in other parts of the world.

12.5 A Methodological Conclusion

We have argued above that 'canonical' notions of documentation at present derive from ideologies that may align quite poorly with local language ecologies, and we would like to conclude with a brief methodological point. Each of the villages of Lower Fungom comprises an entity that is relatively clearly circumscribed in local terms and also maps well on to Western notions of settlement. Moreover, the local context assigns a particular lexicogrammatical code to each village, signifying its 'talk'. It would, therefore, be quite simple for a linguist to arrive in, say, Missong and to document its language in the canonical way and apparently improve the state of our understanding of an endangered language.

However, what we have seen here is that, if they were to adopt such an approach, they would fail to see the lesson Missong offers for understanding the local significance of 'language' in Lower Fungom, prompting us to wonder what other important linguistic facts might be masked by approaches that emphasize the documentation of individual ancestral codes as the primary academic response to endangerment. What has been required to overcome this problem, in our case, has been an approach to language documentation that integrates comparative grammatical data with the results of ethnographic and historical investigation. Such work is inevitably more difficult than more grammatically focused documentation, and we are well aware it is beyond the reach of many projects. Nevertheless, if the documentary endeavour is to result in a record not merely of endangered codes but also of endangered ways of deploying codes in social interaction, it would seem to be essential.

References

Bastin, Yvonne, André Coupez, and Michael Mann. 1999. *Continuity and Divergence in the Bantu Languages: Perspectives from a Lexicostatistical Study*. Tervuren: Musée Royal de l'Afrique Centrale.

Blommaert, Jan. 2007. Linguistic diversity: Africa. In Marlis Hellinger and Anne Pauwels (eds.), *Handbook of Language and Communication: Diversity and Change*. Berlin: Mouton de Gruyter.

Boum, Marie Anne. 1980. Le groupe menchum: morphologie nominale. In Larry M. Hyman (ed.), *Noun Classes in the Grassfields Bantu Borderland*. Southern California Occasional Papers in Linguistics 8. Los Angeles, CA: University of Southern California Department of Linguistics.

Brye, Edward and Elizabeth Brye. 2002. *Rapid Appraisal and Intelligibility Testing Surveys of the Eastern Beboid Group of Languages (Northwest Province)*. SIL Electronic Survey Reports: SILESR 2002-019. <http://www.sil.org/silesr/2002/019/SILESR2002-019.htm> (accessed 1 October 2013).

Bucholtz, Mary. 1999. 'Why be normal?' Language and identity practices in a community of nerd girls. *Language in Society* 28: 203–23.

Childs, G. Tucker. 2003. *An Introduction to African Languages*. Amsterdam: Benjamins.

Chilver, Elizabeth M. and Phyllis M. Kaberry. 1968. *Traditional Bamenda: The Precolonial History and Ethnography of the Bamenda Grassfields*. Buea: Ministry of Primary Education and Social Welfare.

Chilver, Elizabeth M. and Phyllis M. Kaberry. 1971. The Tikar problem: a non-problem. *Journal of African Languages* 10: 13–14.

Chilver, Elizabeth M. and Phyllis M. Kaberry. 1974. *Western Grassfields (Cameroun Republic) Linguistic Notes*. Occasional Publication No. 29. Ibadan: Institute of African Studies, University of Ibadan.

Cobbinah, Alexander. 2010. The Casamance as an area of intense language contact: the case of Baïnounk Gubaher. *Journal of Language Contact*, THEMA 3: 175–201.

Crystal, David. 2000. *Language Death*. Oxford: Oxford University.

Dalby, David. 1970. Reflections on the classification of African languages: with special reference to the work of Sigismund Wilhelm Koelle and Malcolm Guthrie. *African Language Studies* 11: 147–71.

Dalby, David. 1971. A referential approach to the classification of African languages. In Chin-Wu Kim and Herbert Stahlke (eds.), *Papers in African Linguistics*. Carbondale, IL, and Edmonton, AB: Linguistic Research Inc.

Di Carlo, Pierpaolo. 2011. Lower Fungom linguistic diversity and its historical development: proposals from a multidisciplinary perspective. *Africana Linguistica* 17: 53–100.

Di Carlo, Pierpaolo and Giovanna Pizziolo. 2012. Spatial reasoning and GIS in linguistic prehistory: two case studies from Lower Fungom (Northwest Cameroon). *Language Dynamics and Change* 2: 150–83.

Dimmendaal, Gerrit J. 2011. *Historical Linguistics and the Comparative Study of African Languages*. Amsterdam: Benjamins.

Dobrin, Lise M., Peter K. Austin, and David Nathan. 2009. Dying to be counted: the commodification of endangered languages in documentary linguistics. In Peter K. Austin (ed.), *Language Documentation and Description*, vol. 6. London: SOAS.

Duchêne, Alexandre and Monica Heller. 2007. Discourses of endangerment: sociolinguistics, globalization, and social order. In Alexandre Duchêne and Monica Heller (eds.), *Discourses of Endangerment: Ideology and Interest in the Defence of Endangered Languages*. London: Continuum.

Eckert, Penelope. 2000. *Linguistic Variation as Social Practice: The Linguistic Construction of Identity in Belten High*. Oxford: Blackwell.

Edwards, John. 2010. *Minority Languages and Group Identity: Cases and Categories*. Amsterdam: Benjamins.

Errington, Joseph. 2003. Getting language rights: the rhetorics of language endangerment and loss. *American Anthropologist* 105: 723–32.

Evans, Nicholas. 2010. *Dying Words: Endangered Languages and What They Have to Tell Us*. Chichester: Wiley-Blackwell.

Fardon, Richard. 1988. *Raiders and Refugees: Trends in Chamba Political Development 1750 to 1950*. Washington, DC: Smithsonian Institution.

Fleisher, Jeffrey B. 2010. Swahili synoecism: rural settlements and town formation on the central East African coast, AD 750–1500. *Journal of Field Archaeology* 35: 265–82.

Foley, William A. 2005. Personhood and linguistic identity, purism and variation. In Peter K. Austin (ed.), *Language Documentation and Description*, vol. 3. London: SOAS.

Fowler, Ian and David Zeitlyn. 1996. Introduction: the Grassfields and the Tikar. In Ian Fowler and David Zeitlyn (eds.), *African Crossroads: Intersections Between History and Anthropology in Cameroon*. Providence, RI: Berghahn Books.

François, Alexandre. 2012. The dynamics of linguistic diversity: egalitarian multilingualism and power imbalance among northern Vanuatu languages. *International Journal of the Sociology of Language* 214: 85–110.

Geary, Christraud. 1976. *We: Die Genese eines Häuptlingtums im Grasland von Kamerun*. Wiesbaden: F. Steiner.

Geary, Christraud. 1979. Traditional societies and associations in We (North West Province, Cameroon). *Paideuma* 25: 53–72.

Good, Jeff. 2013. A (micro-)accretion zone in a remnant zone? Lower Fungom in areal-historical perspective. In Balthasar Bickel, Lenore A. Grenoble, David A. Peterson, and Alan Timberlake (eds.), *What's Where Why? Language Typology and Historical Contingency: A Festschrift to Honor Johanna Nichols*, 265–82. Amsterdam: Benjamins.

Good, Jeff, Jesse Lovegren, Jean Patrick Mve, Nganguep Carine Tchiemouo, Rebecca Voll, and Pierpaolo Di Carlo. 2011. The languages of the Lower Fungom region of Cameroon: grammatical overview. *Africana Linguistica* 17: 101–64.

Goody, Jack and Ian Watt. 1963. The consequences of literacy. *Comparative Studies in Society and History* 5: 304–45.

Greenberg, Joseph H. 1966. *The Languages of Africa*. The Hague: Mouton.

Greenberg, Joseph H. 1972. Linguistic evidence regarding Bantu origins. *Journal of African History* 13, 189–216.

Hamm, Cameron, Jason Diller, Kari Jordan-Diller, and Ferdinand Assako a Tiati. 2002. *A Rapid Appraisal Survey of Western Beboid Languages (Menchum Division, Northwest Province)*. SIL Electronic Survey Reports: SILESR 2002-014.

Harrison, K. David. 2007. *When Languages Die: The Extinction of the World's Languages and the Erosion of Human Knowledge*. Oxford: Oxford University Press.

Heine, Bernd. 1980. Methods in comparative Bantu linguistics (the problem of Bantu linguistic classification). In Luc Bouquiaux (ed.), *L'expansion Bantoue: Actes du Colloque International du CNRS, Viviers (France) 4–16 avril 1977*, vol. 2 Paris: SELAF.

Hill, Jane H. 1996. *Languages on the Land: Towards an Anthropological Dialectology.* David Skomp Distinguished Lectures in Anthropology. Bloomington: Indiana University, Department of Anthropology.

Hill, Jane H. 2002. 'Expert rhetorics' in advocacy for endangered languages: who is listening, and what do they hear? *Journal of Linguistic Anthropology* 12: 119–33.

Himmelmann, Nikolaus P. 1998. Documentary and descriptive linguistics. *Linguistics* 36: 161–95.

Himmelmann, Nikolaus P. 2006. Language documentation: what is it and what is it good for? In Jost Gippert, Nikolaus Himmelmann, and Ulrike Mosel (eds.), *Essentials of Language Documentation*. Berlin: Mouton de Gruyter.

Hombert, Jean-Marie. 1980. Noun classes of the Beboid languages. In Larry M. Hyman (ed.), *Noun Classes in the Grassfields Bantu Borderland*. Southern California Occasional Papers in Linguistics 8. Los Angeles: University of Southern California Department of Linguistics.

Horton, Robin. 1972. Stateless societies in the history of West Africa. In J. F. A. Ajayi and Michael Crowder (eds.), *History of West Africa*, vol. 1. New York: Columbia University.

Hymes, Dell H. 1968. Linguistic problems in defining the concept of 'tribe'. In June Helm (ed.), *Essays on the Problem of Tribe: Proceedings of the 1967 Annual Spring Meeting of the American Ethnological Society.* Seattle, WA: University of Washington.

Hymes, Dell H. 1972. Linguistic aspects of comparative political research. In Robert T. Holt and John E. Turner (eds.), *The Methodology of Comparative Research*. New York: Free Press.

Irvine, Judith T. 1978. When is genealogy history? Wolof genealogies in comparative perspective. *American Ethnologist* 5: 651–74.

Irvine, Judith T. and Susan Gal. 2000. Language ideology and linguistic differentiation. In Paul V. Kroskrity (ed.), *Regimes of Language: Ideologies, Polities, and Identities*. Santa Fe, NM: School of American Research.

Jeffreys, M. D. W. 1964. Who are the Tikar? *African Studies* 23: 141–53.

Johnstone, Barbara and Scott F. Kiesling. 2008. Indexicality and experience: exploring the meanings of /aw/-monophthongization in Pittsburgh. *Journal of Sociolinguistics* 12: 5–33.

Katamba, Francis. 2003. Bantu nominal morphology. In Derek Nurse and Gérard Philippson (eds.), *The Bantu Languages*. London: Routledge.

Kopytoff, Igor. 1981. Aghem ethnogenesis and the Grassfields ecumene. In Claude Tardits (ed.), *Contribution de la Recherche Ethnologique à l'histoire des Civilisations du Cameroun*. Paris: CNRS.

Kopytoff, Igor. 1987. The internal African frontier: the making of African political culture. In Igor Kopytoff (ed.), *The African Frontier: The Reproduction of Traditional African Societies*. Bloomington: Indiana University Press.

Krauss, Michael. 1992. The world's languages in crisis. *Language* 68: 4–10.

Lamberty, Melinda. 2002. *A Sociolinguistic Survey of Bum*. SIL Electronic Survey Reports: SILESR 2002-071.

Lovegren, Jesse. 2013. Mungbam grammar. PhD dissertation, University of Buffalo.

Lüpke, Friederike. 2010. Language and identity in flux: in search of Baïnounk. *Journal of Language Contact* THEMA 3: 155–74.

McIntosh, Janet. 2005. Language essentialism and social hierarchies among Giriama and Swahili. *Journal of Pragmatics* 37: 1919–44.

Maho, Jouni. 1999. *A Comparative Study of Bantu Noun Classes*. Göteburg: Acta Universitatis Gothoburgensis.

Masquelier, Bertrand M. 1978. Structure and process of political identity: Ide, a polity of the Metchum Valley (Cameroon). PhD dissertation, University of Pennsylvania.

Mbunwe-Samba, Patrick, Paul N. Mzeka, Mathias L. Niba, and Claire Wirmum (eds.). 1993. *Rites of Passage and Incorporation in the Western Grassfields of Cameroon: Birth, Naming, Childhood, Adolescence, the Incorporation of Royal Wives, and Some Palace Rituals*. Bamenda, Cameroon: Kaberry Research Centre.

Menang, Thaddeus. 2004. Cameroon Pidgin English (Kamtok): phonology. In Edgar W. Schneider, Kate Burridge, Bernd Kortmann, Rajend Mesthrie, and Clive Upton (eds.), *Handbook of Varieties of English*, vol. 1: *Phonology*. Berlin and New York: Mouton.

Möhlig, Wilhelm J. G. 1979. The Bantu nucleus: its conditional nature and its prehistorical significance. *Sprache und Geschichte in Afrika* 1: 109–41.

Möhlig, Wilhelm J. G. 1981. Stratification in the history of the Bantu languages. *Sprache und Geschichte in Afrika* 3: 251–316.

Mous, Maarten. 1994. Ma'a or Mbugu. In Peter Bakker and Maarten Mous (eds.), *Mixed Languages: 15 Case Studies in Language Intertwining*. Amsterdam: IFOTT.

Mous, Maarten. 2003a. The linguistic properties of lexical manipulation and its relevance for Ma'á. In Yaron Matras and Peter Bakker (eds.), *The Mixed Language Debate: Theoretical and Empirical Advances*. Berlin: Mouton.

Mous, Maarten. 2003b. *The Making of a Mixed Language: The Case of Ma'a/Mbugu*. Amsterdam: Benjamins.

Nettle, Daniel. 1996. Language diversity in West Africa: an ecological approach. *Journal of Anthropological Archaeology* 15: 403–38.

Nettle, Daniel and Suzanne Romaine. 2000. *Vanishing Voices: The Extinction of the World's Languages*. Oxford: Oxford University Press.

Nichols, Johanna. 1993. The linguistic geography of the Slavic expansion. In Robert A. Maguire and Alan Timberlake (eds.), *American Contributions to the Eleventh International Congress of Slavists*. Columbus, OH: Slavica.

Nkwi, Paul Nchoji and Jean-Pierre Warnier. 1982. *Elements for a History of the Western Grassfields*. Yaoundé: Department of Sociology, University of Yaoundé.

Nurse, Derek. 1994–5. 'Historical' classifications of the Bantu languages. *Azania* 29/30: 65–81.

Piron, Pascale. 1997. *Classification Interne du Groupe Bantoïde*, vol. 2. Munich: Lincom.

Rottland, Franz and Duncan Okoth Okombo. 1986. The Suba of Kenya: a case of growing ethnicity with receding language competence. *Afrikanistische Arbeitspapiere* 7: 115–26.

Rowlands, Michael and Jean-Pierre Warnier. 1993. The magical production of iron in the Cameroon Grassfields. In Thurstan Shaw (ed.), *The Archaeology of Africa: Food, Metals, and Towns*. London and New York: Routledge.

Schadeberg, Thilo C. 2003. Historical linguistics. In Derek Nurse and Gérard Philippson (eds.), *The Bantu Languages*. London: Routledge.

Silverstein, Michael. 1998. Contemporary transformations of local linguistic communities. *Annual Review of Anthropology* 27: 401–26.

Silverstein, Michael. 2003. Indexical order and the dialectics of sociolinguistic life. *Language and Communication* 23: 193–229.

Stallcup, Kenneth. 1980. La géographie linguistique des Grassfields. In Larry M. Hyman and Jan Voorhoeve (eds.), *L'expansion Bantoue: Actes du Colloque International du CNRS, Viviers (France) 4–16 Avril 1977*, vol. 1: *Les Classes Nominaux dans le Bantou des Grassfields*. Paris: SELAF.

Storch, Anne. 2011. Ritual pathways: contact in a framework of difference, imitation and alterity. In Osamu Hieda, Christa König, and Hirosi Nakagawa (eds.), *Geographical Typology and Linguistic Areas: With Special Reference to Africa*. Amsterdam: Benjamins.

Tadadjeu, Maurice and Etienne Sadembouo (eds.). 1984. *General Alphabet of Cameroon Languages (Bilingual Edition)*. Yaoundé: University of Yaoundé.

Thomason, Sarah G. 1983. Genetic relationship and the case of Ma'a (Mbugu). *Studies in African Linguistics* 14: 195–231.

Thomason, Sarah G. 1997. Ma'a (Mbugu). In Sarah G. Thomason (ed.), *Contact Languages: A Wider Perspective*. Amsterdam: Benjamins.

Troyer, Duane, Paul Huey, and Joseph Mbongue. 1995. *A Rapid-Appraisal Survey of Mmen (ALCAM 821) and Aghem Dialects (ALCAM 810), Menchum Division, Northwest Province*. Yaoundé: SIL Cameroon.

Vansina, Jan. 1985. *Oral Tradition as History*. Madison: University of Wisconsin.

Voorhoeve, Jan. 1980. Bantu and Bane. In Larry M. Hyman and Jan Voorhoeve (eds.), *L'expansion Bantoue: Actes du Colloque International du CNRS, Viviers (France) 4–16 Avril 1977*, vol. 1: *Les Classes Nominaux dans le Bantou des Grassfields*. Paris: SELAF.

Warnier, Jean-Pierre. 1975. Pre-colonial Mankon: the development of a Cameroon chiefdom in its regional setting PhD dissertation, University of Pennsylvania.

Warnier, Jean-Pierre. 1979. Noun-classes, lexical stocks, multilingualism, and the history of the Cameroon Grassfields. *Language in Society* 8: 409–23.

Warnier, Jean-Pierre. 1980. Des précurseurs de l'école Berlitz: le multilingualisme dans les Grassfields du Cameroun au 19ème siècle. In Luc Bouquiaux (ed.), *L'expansion Bantoue: Actes du Colloque International du CNRS, Viviers (France) 4–16 Avril 1977*, vol. 3. Paris: SELAF.

Warnier, Jean-Pierre. 1984. Histoire du peuplement et genèse des paysages dans l'ouest camerounais. *Journal of African History* 25: 395–410.

Warnier, Jean-Pierre. 1985. *Echanges, Développement et Hiérarchies dans le Bamenda Pré-colonial (Cameroun)*. Wiesbaden: F. Steiner.

Watters, John R. 1989. Bantoid overview. In John Bendor-Samuel (ed.), *The Niger-Congo Languages: A Classification and Description of Africa's Largest Language Family*. Lanham, MD: University Press of America.

Welmers, William E. 1974. *African Language Structures*. Berkeley: University of California.

Williamson, Kay and Roger M. Blench. 2000. Niger-Congo. In Bernd Heine and Derek Nurse (eds.), *African Languages: An Introduction*. Cambridge: Cambridge University Press.

Wolff, Hans. 1967. Language, ethnic identity and social change in southern Nigeria. *Anthropological Linguistics* 9: 18–25.

Woodbury, Anthony C. 2005. Ancestral languages and (imagined) creolisation. In Peter K. Austin (ed.), *Language Documentation and Description*, vol. 3. London: SOAS.

Woodbury, Anthony C. 2011. Language documentation. In Peter K. Austin and Julia Sallabank (eds.), *The Cambridge Handbook of Endangered Languages*. Cambridge: Cambridge University Press.

Zeitlyn, David and Bruce Connell. 2003. Ethnogenesis and fractal history on an African frontier: Mambila-Njerep-Mandulu. *Journal of African History* 44: 117–38.

13

The Cost of Language Mobilization: Wangkatha Language Ideologies and Native Title*

JESSICA BOYNTON

13.1 Introduction

AS A RESPONSE to the threat of global language loss, many linguistic anthropologists have turned their attention to documenting, describing, diagnosing, and revitalizing endangered languages (Dorian 1989; Fishman 1991; Hale et al. 1992; McKay 1996, 2008; Newman and Ratliff 2001; Schmidt 1990). Likewise, traditional language has been championed as part of indigenous rights movements the world over (Dalby 2003; Wurm and Heyward 2001: 127). More recently, scholars have turned their attention towards analysing the ways in which language endangerment discourse is presented (Duchêne and Heller 2007), noting that the discourses involved valorize traditional people and practices in a way that pits them against modernity and, some say, dehumanizes participants in the population concerned. Furthermore, the ideologies that underpin such efforts reshape the way in which language is envisaged, sometimes through the discourse itself and other times through the intersection of access to tangible (even if imagined) benefits and language-based processes of authentication. These ideologies can unintentionally effect ideological changes among the target population of language work and other political action.

Language ideologies are subject to influence not only when language is the focus of political action, but also when language is mobilized, that is, invoked as a necessary or logical component of action, as a political tool for an indirectly related political struggle, as often occurs in indigenous rights movements. These ideological shifts present a paradox: they are created, formalized, or at the very least highlighted as a result of attempts to valorize traditional values and

* This chapter is based on a presentation made at the *Workshop on the Sociolinguistics of Language Endangerment* in Boulder, Colorado, 2011. I would like to thank the Australian American Fulbright Commission and the University of Western Australia for funding the research undertaken here, and David Bradley, Julia Sallabank, John Henderson, Lise Dobrin, Saul Schwartz, and Daniel Hieber for feedback on initial drafts. Any flaws that remain are entirely my own.

practices. This chapter investigates the nature of ideological transformation among Wangkatha language consultants in Australia, as has been highlighted in the wake of Native Title legislation designed to determine the veracity of Aboriginal claims to land rights. After providing some basic background about research methods and locations, it discusses Native Title in general, presenting the legislation and its rationale, identifying a schism between the actual and perceived benefits of success, and finally focusing on the role of language in Native Title cases as discussed by anthropologists and linguists who have served as expert witnesses. Next, the use of language to establish continuity is discussed, focusing on the kinds of change and continuity that may be presented. Critically, the actual expectations of the judge do not directly affect language ideologies or practices; nor do the observations and theoretical background of experts in language and language change; it is, rather, on-the-ground perceptions about how linguistic practices may be interpreted by a Native Title judge that influence practice and, potentially, ideology. Finally, the ideological refocusings that these sorts of perceptions highlight are identified, namely the transition from a dialect mesh to an ideologically bounded mosaic, from the prestige of language ownership to the power of language proficiency, and from extreme individual multilingualism to language guardianship. In all cases, the transformations are attributable to more than Native Title, but the current political climate highlights and sharpens them because it demands that claims to identity and group membership are presented according to criteria that are likely to be accepted by a non-Aboriginal judge. When it comes to language, this often means that proficiency in an unchanged, well-bounded traditional language is simultaneously venerated and guarded, while traditional ideologies about linguistic identity are overshadowed, at least in the political and legal context.

13.2 Methods and Background

The data for this study were collected via semi-formal interviews with 16 Aboriginal language consultants in and around Kalgoorlie, Western Australia. Most consultants were referred by the Karlkurla Language and Culture Aboriginal Corporation, although some were referred by other consultants or Aboriginal businesses surveyed around the area. The selection criteria were rather open, mandating only that consultants initially self-identify as Wangkatha, at least in part. However, preconceptions among community members regarding the appropriate type of person for a female to consult regarding language and culture meant that most consultants were women who were either of advanced age (typically 60 years or older) or who had held some sort of position in Aboriginal Affairs, education, or language or social work. Five consultants, however, were male, and two of those were in their 20s.

Additional insight was gleaned through informal observations made during seven months' combined fieldwork conducted somewhat sporadically over the course of two and half years. During these field visits, I initially undertook language elicitation work and happened upon concerns about sharing language and teaching it, as well as desire to clarify the confusion about language/group boundaries. Later, during a language ideological enquiry, I consulted with Aboriginal people by day while cohabiting with non-Aboriginal people in a youth hostel. This split experience tended to bring questions of Native Title to the fore because both populations voiced concerns about its legislation and its implications.

Two locations are central to this research: Kalgoorlie, where most fieldwork was conducted, and Mt Margaret Mission, often seen as the melting pot from which modern Wangkatha identity has emerged. The map in Figure 13.1 shows these locations, among others that are important in the Western Goldfields.

Kalgoorlie, located on the fringes of the Western Desert and 700 kilometres east of Perth, is considered the urban hub of the Australian Goldfields. It is by far the largest town of the area, so people travel there to make use of the services it offers. These, crucially, include a well-equipped dialysis centre. Additionally, many Aboriginal people have settled there at least semi-permanently from more rural Goldfields locations because of the availability of jobs, especially mining jobs, during the resources boom that began shortly before this research. Most Aboriginal Kalgoorlians were either raised in Mt Margaret Mission or are related to someone who was, so that particular setting can be considered a major shaping force in the perceptions, ideologies, and even realities of Aboriginal Kalgoorlie.

While many modern incentives can contribute to ideological transformation, Native Title is the focus here because it was a heated topic among consultants. The Wangkatha group's sizable Native Title claim had just been dismissed in February of 2007, and many component groups were gathering resources to follow Judge Lindgren's advice of submitting more individualized claims (see Harrington-Smith on Behalf of the Wongatha People vs. Western Australia).

13.3 Native Title

Native Title law was introduced as part of the reconciliation process, in the same vein as the measures proposed in the 'Bringing Them Home' report (1997), which was requested by the Australian Attorney General as a record of the acts committed in Australia's strongly assimilatory past. The report was intended to identify the effects of the policies of Australia's Stolen Generation era, spanning from the late 1800s to the mid-1900s, during which Aboriginal children were taken from their families and placed in missions and boarding schools in an effort to 'protect' them from their Aboriginal heritage and prepare them for their

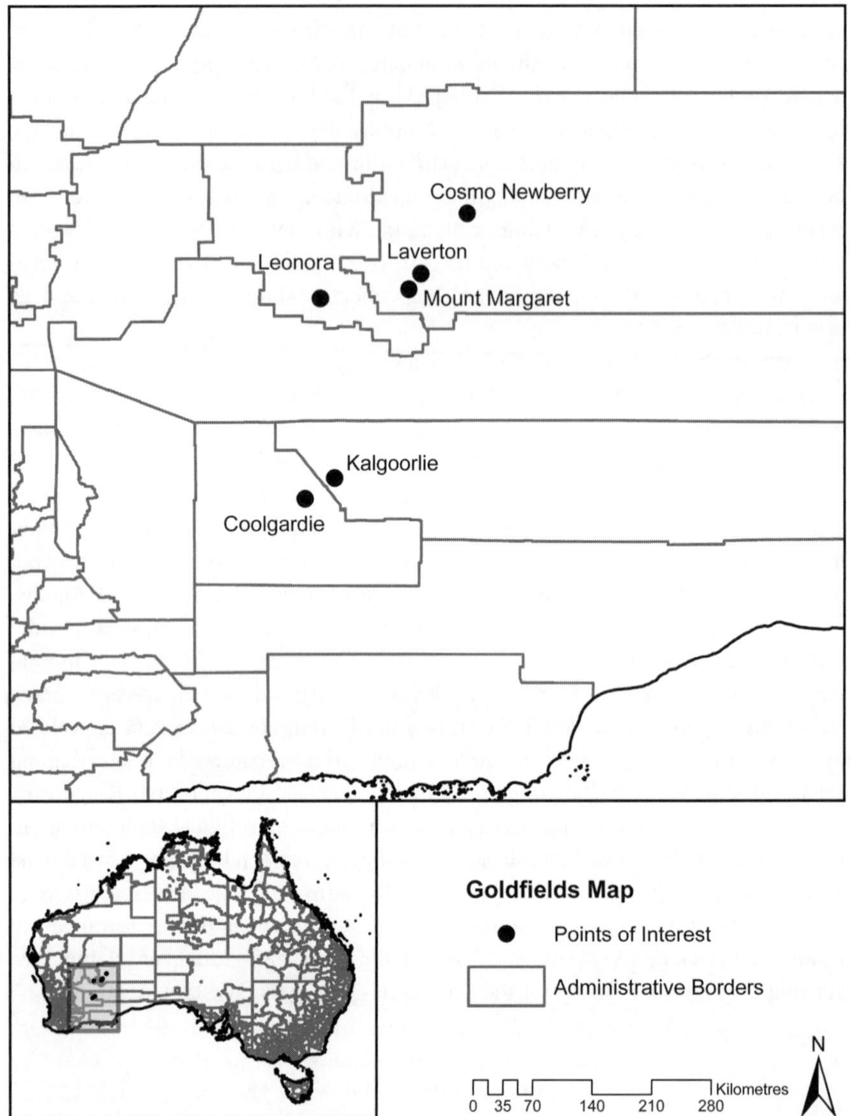

Figure 13.1 The Goldfields region of Western Australia.

'appropriate' roles in wider society. The report also examines current legislation to propose any changes necessary to best realize self-determination among Aboriginal Australians, and to recommend any necessary compensation in the light of these past actions, primarily through facilitating reconnections between families that were separated from each other and groups that were separated from their cultural property. The law regarding Native Title predates this report, finding its roots in the civil rights movement of the 1960s and '70s, but its significance is couched in similar terms. The law is intended to grant property rights to groups that were unlawfully separated from their land during colonization, although, unlike most elements of reconciliation, it is actually necessary to prove that ties to cultural practices have not been lost in order to win these rights. Like an overwhelming percentage of indigenous rights policies the world over, the actual legislation was written by non-indigenous people and is enacted through non-indigenous practices (e.g. courtrooms), thereby maintaining the authority of the non-indigenous in determining indigenous fates.

Basically, successful Native Title claimant groups are recognized by Australian law as the native title holders of their claimed land, and—to a certain degree—their rights to their land are officially seen as never having been legally extinguished. Claimants must meet certain requirements to demonstrate that they qualify as Native Title recipients—a caveat that meets with sharp criticism from many Aboriginal people because those requirements do not necessarily align with Aboriginal values and tradition. The benefits that result from successful Native Title claims vary greatly depending upon the diplomatic prowess of group representatives and the value of the land to outsiders such as the mining industry, but many Australians perceive significant automatic benefits that incentivize specific behaviours, such as speaking a certain language. Language can be used in Native Title to help identify the relevant group, and many (especially Aboriginal) people believe that language is instrumental in validating that group's authenticity and validating an individual's membership to that group.

13.3.1 Requirements

Native Title law has seen the development of requirements that must be met by Native Title claimants in order to ensure that rights are not given fraudulently. This process of authentication is often criticized because the standards were set by non-Aboriginal legislators and therefore do not necessarily reflect Aboriginal ideologies about authentication. Additionally, the evidence presented by expert witnesses is interpreted by non-expert judges.

13.3.2 Meeting Requirements

Essentially, interpretations of Native Title law expect claimants to establish their identity with a land-owning group at the time that the British Crown declared sovereignty and to demonstrate a continuous link between that historical group and the modern group of claimants—basically, there must be a continuing system by which rights in land are held. Case law has seen that proof for these requirements can be demonstrated through the continuing practice of Aboriginal Law, languages, or other cultural habits that can be traced back to sovereignty or as near to it that records were kept. Current cultural attributes do not have to be identical to more traditional practices, but continuity (with change) must be demonstrable.

13.3.3 Criticism of Requirements

The proof required in Native Title hearings is often criticized because it forces Aboriginal claimants to prove their Aboriginality to the very institutions that once legislated to obliterate it, and pass a test of authentication that is judged by people who are not themselves authentically Aboriginal. One consultant (S05) remarks:

> You can't blame people for being invaded, and you can't punish them for following assimilationist policy and losing their language and culture. Native Title is unfair in saying that you need proof; you've got a really high bar for proof. People end up in the scuttle for language and culture, and sometimes it isn't theirs.

Such a perspective is not uncommon to measures that ostensibly support indigenous empowerment but require authentication by non-indigenous processes. Historically, indigenous people have rarely been involved in formulating the measures that are allegedly adopted in support of their human rights (Niezen 2000: 127); this is the very process, in fact, that resulted in the assimilationist legislation of the Stolen Generation era. The law does not necessarily intend to redefine indigenous concepts; it simply adheres to Western concepts of rights and makes determinations accordingly.

Often, foreign authentication processes require a demonstration of traditional culture for legitimization—a requirement that often eliminates the groups that have been most sharply dispossessed (Muehlmann 2008: 33). Ginsburg and Myers (2006: 36) observe that this practice makes 'a cruel joke of legislation initially anticipated to acknowledge indigenous autonomy'. For the Native Title Act in Australia, this results in the perception (and oftentimes reality) that the legislation justifies a further denial of rights, as opposed to an assertion of them (Bell 2002: 52). The valorization of traditional culture also exacerbates distinctions between more traditional populations (often more remote or settled on reserves) and urban ones, creating a schism between indigenous populations that might not otherwise be so decisively juxtaposed (Ginsburg and Myers 2006: 36).

Muehlmann (2008) presents the paradox of external authentication in discussing the response of the Cucapá to similar practices. When asked to demonstrate linguistic ability in order to prove their authenticity as Cucapá, Cucapá people respond with Cucapá profanity that will not be understood by the person judging their authenticity and will therefore be accepted as proof. The language is not spoken fluently by many people, but the judges of authenticity are typically outsiders who have no command of the language whatsoever, so fluent use of profanity suffices to impress (and simultaneously expose the ignorance of) the outsider judge. This technique is apparently somewhat unusual, but the Cucapá's disdain for foreign authentication processes can be generalized to other populations. This disdain is not obviously demonstrated among the Wangkatha in a regularized social practice, but rather in discourse about Native Title.

Globally, the emphasis on foreign processes of authentication also ignores, and possibly even overshadows, traditional authentication processes that do not align with legislative criteria (Muehlmann 2008: 39). The schism between insiders and outsiders, then, is not necessarily formulated in ways that hold traditional value; traditional values did not immunize people against social divisions, but the divisions were defined according to internal, not external, criteria. With Native Title law, the divisions are made according to criteria that have been set by non-Aboriginal legislators and practitioners of law who, while responding to Aboriginal protests, did not necessarily understand or capture the essence of Aboriginal goals. Even if they did, those goals were curtailed by the assumption that Western law and society must continue unhindered and that Aboriginal rights could be granted only so far as they fit into the Western system.

13.3.4 Judged by Non-experts

In addition to the problematic nature of its formulation, Native Title methods mean that expert evidence is judged by non-experts in the various relevant fields. Expert linguistic witnesses often present extraordinarily complex historical linguistic evidence, as well as findings about land and language associations, dialect groups, proficiency, and naming. Walsh (2002: 238) points out that judicial reactions to these kinds of expert testimony varies, and that some published reasons for judgements demonstrate misunderstandings about the linguistic evidence on the part of the judge (Walsh 2002: 240). For their part, lawyers sometimes demonstrate impressive knowledge of linguistic matters in cross-examination (Evans 2002: 77), but this depends upon the quality of their briefings. Therefore, even if the external criteria for authentication were accepted by the claimant group, the evidence presented in regards to these criteria is not necessarily evaluated consistently.

13.3.5 Benefits

The actual benefits awarded to successful Native Title claimants are often quite modest compared to expectations: groups gain enough authority to give them greater power to bargain for compensation for profits made off their land. In some cases, groups have bargained for quite gainful compensation, but others have not. The newly recognized landowners exercise some authority over that land's use; Native Title can only be won over land where other overriding rights have not been granted by the Crown. People in general, whether Aboriginal or non-Aboriginal, typically perceive much greater tangible benefits than are associated with successful claims to identity. This perception makes cultural behaviour, such as language, much more politically loaded than it would otherwise be because, in additional to the social benefits that typically go with group identification, these behaviours now may provide access to legal benefits as well. The familiar concept of social capital is of even greater import because tangible benefits quite objectively decrease in value as they are dispersed across a larger population. Behaviour that could be used to assert authenticity, then, potentially becomes an automatic authenticator or de-authenticator to a claim.

13.3.6 Perceived Benefits

The perception of valuable benefits that come from successful claims makes the possibility of succeeding in a claim salient. While no consultant made a laundry list of expectations during interviews, a few of them criticized others for changing their behaviour for the sake of Native Title, and some shared their hopes that they would come into money soon because of unspecified court proceedings and that their lives would improve after that. Overall, consultants painted a somewhat vague picture about how they or others perceive Native Title benefits—a picture that, despite its vagaries, underscores hopes, at the very least.

Many Aboriginal people seem to perceive a successful claim as an ascendance to power and a financial windfall. They seem to envision finally having definitive control of their traditional lands and being able to share in the profits that have come from dispossessing them of it in the first place. Non-Aboriginal parties, who were often keen to share their opinions if given any opportunity, also frequently perceive a successful claim as an automatic contract with any mining companies that will send a significant percentage of profits to Aboriginal people; they worry that Aboriginal people will gain the power to kick non-Aboriginal people back out of Aboriginal land. Native Title does not automatically ensure either circumstance, and the legislation is written to protect many interests of non-Aboriginal parties, but these perceptions hold. With these perceptions, then, come strong attitudes about cultural behaviour and the potential motives and outcomes to practising it. The perceptions do not mean that all Aboriginal people adjust their behaviour to better position themselves for Native Title, or even that most do; instead, they mean that evaluations of others' behaviour take into account the possibility that those others are making such adjustments because of greed, selfishness, and, as it is ultimately perceived, disrespect for authentic Aboriginality.

13.3.7 Sociocultural Capital and Benefits

Theories about social capital see the spread of any ethnic indicator as potentially eroding the unique value of the ethnic identity it indicates; when a successful claim to that identity is connected to access to tangible benefits as well, the risk is far greater. If a Native Title claim is successful, the benefits derived from it are typically spread among all claimants, even those who are seen as inauthentic by other claimants. This means that every inauthentic member of the claimant group depletes the benefits to authentic members.

Furthermore, if a Native Title claim is unsuccessful, its failure may be blamed on the inclusion of inauthentic claimants. This seems to be the exact perception regarding the 2007 Wangkatha Native Title case: the claim, which by the end included a myriad of groups and last-minute claimants, was not successful. In the eyes of consultants who see their claim as having been unfairly dismissed, the inclusion of groups that fail to demonstrate authenticity potentially lost the case for everybody. In fact, Judge Lindgren listed the composition of groups in the claim as the primary reason for his judgement.

13.3.8 Cultural Behaviour

If linguistic behaviour in particular is an authenticator of identity, then language use becomes essentialized with authentic identity and a claim to it. Amongst the widespread pursuit of identity and benefits, any practice that may be used in court to determine Native Title becomes politically charged. Under the requirement of continuity (discussed later), any action that may establish continuity could potentially be used in court to support authentic and inauthentic claims alike. Conversely, any action that may establish a lack of continuity could potentially be used in court to argue against authentic and inauthentic claims alike. Both possibilities are threatening, and both colour perspectives on language. For example, language guardianship, by which some individuals seek to control others' access to language learning, demonstrates a reluctance to enable outsiders to demonstrate authentic claims.

13.4 Language in Native Title

Henderson (2002: 3) presents the following uses of language in a Native Title claim:

> Language is relevant to the extent that (i) it is involved in identifying the relevant group of people, (ii) evidence for the continuity of a language contributes to a claim for the continuity of tradition and (iii) terms in the language are used in describing the cultural system.

The two that are most central here are the ability to identify the relevant group, discussed briefly below, and the role of language in establishing continuity, to which section 3 is devoted later.

Central to this study is the extent to which Aboriginal people view language as a determining factor in Native Title cases. Some consultants identify language as a major factor in Native Title, and even more report that this perception holds in the community. Language is generally seen as important because it can help validate a group and individual's memberships to a given group.

13.4.1 Identify Relevant Group

Language can be used in court to identify the group that is relevant to a Native Title claim (Henderson 2002: 3). The process involves analysing language naming (McConvell 2002: 279), establishing time depths (Alpher 2002: 245; McConvell 2002: 259), and, most importantly here, identifying the continuing ideological nature of the dialect group. If a dialect group can be demonstrated to have diverged from related codes, the ideological distinctiveness of the speech community can be convincingly argued to have been salient at the time of divergence (Bowe 2002: 126). The enduring salience of the group distinction can then be demonstrated by continued divergence.

Henderson (2002: 4) notes that there is clearly no legal requirement that a language and group be demonstrated as coextensive: a single group can speak more than one language, and a single language can be spoken by more than one group. However, the use of language to identify group boundaries drives many people, including the consultants for this study, to envision sharp divides, often on the model of distinctive dialect groups.

13.4.2 Validate Group

Linguistic identity can be used to authenticate a group as a whole. This type of authentication affects language practice because different authenticating bodies (Aboriginal or non-Aboriginal) interpret the relationship between linguistic identity and language use differently. Aboriginal linguistic identity has been argued time and again to be a matter of language ownership, not proficiency (Sutton 2002: 24), meaning that a person's linguistic identity is not determined by the language(s) he or she speaks (as a first language, in specific domains, or necessarily at all), but rather by complex connections to tracts of land and the language(s) associated with them. However, the potential that outsiders will see proficiency as the true marker of linguistic identity makes language practice a crucial factor. This concept, and its correlation to traditional practice, will be discussed in greater detail in section 13.4.1.1. Here, it suffices to note that insecurities about Native Title drive some to claim the existence of a distinctive dialect spoken only by members of their group.

13.4.3 Validate Individual

Language can also be taken to validate individuals' claims and, by extension, their inclusion in Native Title claimant groups. At least one consultant shared his experience in a Native Title court, in which he felt that he demonstrated the superior validity of his claim by speaking traditional language more fluently than other claimants. In his story, he did not focus on any statements made on the stand, but rather on language use in casual conversation during breaks—a distinction that suggests the importance of validity in the face of one's competitors, because the demonstration was made in a way that would not directly impact the official court proceedings. A couple of consultants also discussed the use of inappropriate place or group names by claimants: to them, using the wrong name to denote a group or name a modern location demonstrated a lack of familiarity with Wangkatha language and, by extension, a lack of authentic Wangkatha identity. In particular, one consultant identified the ethnonym for a claimant group in an unsuccessful case that determined Native Title for many Goldfields groups—this consultant claimed that their ethnonym was actually the word for 'vagina'. This group's adoption of the ethnonym, then, was taken by the consultant to demonstrate their ignorance about language and culture.

13.5 Continuity

Even without the influence of Native Title, the use of language as an authenticator of indigenous identity often requires continuity of form. Authenticating discourse typically dictates that, in order for a language, or the use of a language, to assert one's authentic place within a traditional culture, that language must closely resemble the language that was spoken during traditional times. The use of language in Native Title hearings calls these assumptions into question more so than any other context because continuity is a specific requirement that can potentially be demonstrated through language. However, some language change is inevitable, and language loss demands a different perspective on the link between language and culture.

13.5.1 Language as Proof

Continuity can be established through arguments about language, among other factors that are less relevant to this chapter. Henderson (2002: 5) identifies three facets to continuity of language: the current state of knowledge about the language and ability to speak it, a demonstrable relationship between the language and the land under question, and unbroken descent of the language from sovereignty to current times.

13.5.2 Current State of Knowledge and Proficiency

The current state of knowledge of and proficiency in the relevant language can demonstrate a continuous cultural trait. Henderson (2002: 3) notes that court precedent shows that the ability to speak a language is not necessary for making a Native Title claim, and speaking ability alone is not sufficient. However, he poses the remaining question of whether at least some members of a claimant group must have command of the language, as court cases have left the answer to that question undetermined.

Furthermore, while broad linguistic identity has often survived better than traditional estates as the focus for traditional grouping (Sutton 2002: 24), the interpretation of expert linguistic evidence is left to a judge, and anticipations of these interpretations weigh on the minds of actual and potential claimants in ways that are discussed in the remainder of this section. Walsh (2002: 240) argues that the judgement in at least one Native Title hearing demonstrates a misunderstanding about the distinction between ownership and use.

13.5.3 Land/Language Relationship

In order for language to be invoked in a Native Title case, its relationship to the claimed land must be established. This kind of relationship can be established in the court through a history of documented association between the language and the location, etymologies of place names (Evans 2002: 55), analyses of dreamtime stories (McIntyre and Doohan 2002: 187), and, most important here, analyses of ideological connections. The last paints a complicated picture, belying the dogma of a 'static model of the relationship between language and land' (McConvell 2002: 283).

Silverstein (1998: 404) notes that a language group can only exist if there are perceived contrastive markers of membership and if there is some consensus about methods by which someone can demonstrate participation in a language community. Woolard (1998: 18) explains that any marker of identity and group membership is necessarily ideological—language use, for example, is not itself an indicator of any particular identity; interpretations of language use are. In her words:

> Simply using language in particular ways is not what forms social groups, identities, or relations . . . rather, ideological interpretations of such uses of language always mediate these effects. (Woolard 1998: 18)

Connections between language and land are similarly ideological. In Aboriginal Australia, land, people, and language are connected, at least with regard to ownership—people who are connected to the same land are also often connected to the same language, because the ownerships are acquired according to the same criteria (discussed in greater detail in section 13.5.4). Therefore, language as it is ideologically conceived connects to groups as they are ideologically conceived, and both connect to territories as they are ideologically conceived. Simplistic arguments that connect a reified language to uncontested territory in a direct manner almost always overlook the complex ideological underpinnings. Explaining the underlying complexities in a courtroom, however, is problematic.

13.5.4 Unbroken Descent

Especially in cases where language attrition has taken place, the notion of unbroken descent can be problematic (Henderson 2002: 5). It is not clear in law exactly how much language heritage must be demonstrated, as the degree of maintenance required is interpreted on a case-by-case basis. Complicating factors include: the fairness of requiring a marginalized or banished population to demonstrate unbroken descent (Bowe 2002: 127), the status of revived languages (Henderson 2002: 6), and, most central to this chapter, the relative importance of linguistic form and sociolinguistic link (Bell 2002: 47; Bowe 2002). This problematic topic could provide the material for volumes of analysis; for this chapter, it merits extended discussion for the remainder of this section.

13.6 Language Change

The requirement of continuity is often perceived by consultants and officials alike to demand that some claimants or their recent forebears, at least, have some degree of fluency in a traditional language. Additionally, many consultants suggest that others believe they must demonstrate that the language has not changed at all since contact. Linguists (and anthropologists who focus on linguistics) testifying as expert witnesses have established ‘normal language change’ as a mitigating factor for continuity. However, judges who are unfamiliar with language change may not interpret this convention accurately. Furthermore, (potential) claimant groups are not necessarily aware of this mitigation, so any change in language, however small and however natural, can be seen as a saboteur to an otherwise authentic claim to those on the ground.

13.6.1 Change as Threat

With regard to Native Title, the threat of language change lies precisely in the possibility that these changes will be taken to demonstrate a lack of continuity, and that lack of continuity will result in a denial of Native Title claims. This focus helps explain the sharp perceptual line exhibited by many consultants, which distinguishes between traditional causes of language change (such as borrowing due to tabooing) and modern causes of language change (such as borrowing due to introduced technologies). Any change to language is seen as threatening, but at least a traditional kind of change can be argued to be a sign of continuity: borrowing due to tabooing, while it requires a slight change in language, demonstrates continuity with an important and widely recognized Aboriginal tradition. Borrowing in order to name newly introduced technologies not only presents a change to language, but also exposes the adoption of a modern lifestyle and that lifestyle's integration into the very parlance of the most traditional community language speakers.

13.6.2 Lexical Change

Concerns about the integrity of language are manifested in criticism about a Wangkatha dictionary that was compiled by community linguists—it is accused of reflecting or even causing lexical confusion. This lexical confusion becomes especially worrisome because traditional group boundaries were articulated largely according to lexical distinctions.

Focus on lexical integrity is common among speaker populations, and this general trend is made even more pronounced by the very lexical nature of group distinctions in traditional Aboriginal society. The names of many Western Desert dialect groups, past and present, are derived from words that distinguish one group from another—shibboleths (McConvell 2002: 271). Often, the suffix *-tjara* ('having') was added to the end of a word that was seen as distinctive in the speech of the referents. For example, the Yankunytjatjarra have the root *yank'* for 'go', whereas the Pitantjatjara have *pitja* for 'go'. Even in cases where that lexical distinction fades, the name that was based upon such distinctions may remain, especially since the more Western-style crystallization of Aboriginal ethnonyms.

When an incentive to prove the validity of boundaries emerges, the lexical distinctions that are evoked by the very names of the groups in question regain importance. Lexical borrowing, then, might be perceived as a threat because it could potentially jeopardize the authenticating power of words and their social boundaries, as the process of borrowing introduces the possibility that the word used to denote the group will change.

13.6.3 Phonetic Change

Concerns also manifest in criticism about the orthography: that it may cause mispronunciation, especially as shift to English phonology occurs among language learners. Once again, such criticisms are hardly rare, especially in minority language communities with a limited set of fluent speakers and where the producers of language materials are viewed as outsiders. Salience is highlighted in this case partially because, in some cases, phonetic differences between cognates can serve as shibboleths and partly because of ideologies about literacy.

Correct pronunciation is perceived as important because of language's role in maintaining boundaries in a dialect mesh where lexical and slight phonological variation is boundary-defining. One consultant in particular (S03) worried that teaching pronunciation incorrectly would result in a mixed-up language. After some real equivocation about whether it would be better to lose language altogether or to keep language but with bad pronunciation, she concluded:

> Speaking at all is good, but you gotta learn it proper. Learning with any sounds is better than not at all, but it's really not good. It'd be all mixed up.

Additionally, there is an expectation among the Wangkatha that English literacy will, or should, guarantee Wangkatha literacy. Few consultants entertain the notion that one might learn Wangkatha literacy independently of learning English literacy. Materials written in the current orthography, which follows the model for other Western Desert dialects, will absolutely be mispronounced if read aloud following the rules of English literacy. Some consultants fear that these materials, potentially being primary sources for future language transmission, will eternalize 'bad' language and spell the doom of authentic Wangkatha. Some consultants have developed their own orthographies, and one woman even created a new dictionary using an orthography that she developed. In nearly all cases, consultants are certain that the faults with the writing system are due to the inability of non-Aboriginal language workers to fully understand Aboriginal language and the wants and needs of Aboriginal people. Most are certain that the Aboriginal-created orthographies that they support do not pose the same risks that the current one does because they were created by the 'correct' people.

Overall, fears about language change can be attributed, at least in part, to fears about the effect of those changes on Native Title determinations. Such fears are also common to any standardization efforts, and can be attributed to the unique situation posed by standardization of endangered languages: if a standardized language perishes, then the standard that was recorded becomes the sole means of transmission. Native Title highlights many concerns that would have existed anyway because it brings them into the courtroom during arguments about group composition and continuity.

13.7 Language Shift

Many Native Title claimant groups are undergoing some degree of language shift—a fact that is hardly surprising given the morbidity of Aboriginal languages across the continent. Establishing continuity with a shifting language becomes problematic in the community, first because the traditional language and culture becomes valorized in a way that frowns upon the kind of modern innovations that vitalize languages and cultures, and second because continuity of form is frequently valued above continuity of the ideological link between language and culture. It is vital to note that continuity is not so problematic from a legal perspective—one person with a reasonably extensive knowledge of language would probably make a reasonable basis for continuity, and innovations that reflect cultural changes can attest to the vitality of a language (Henderson, personal communication). Valorization often accompanies language shift, especially in cases where language is in any way mobilized. This section, therefore, describes processes that would probably be underway even without Native Title law, and that do not actually align with legal requirements. However, it seems that Native Title does bring the processes into sharper focus.

13.7.1 Shift and Valorization

Continuity comes into question in cases of language shift because the Native Title legislation, like many tools of indigenous mobilization, valorizes the traditional in juxtaposition against the modern. This juxtaposition has been characterized in many ways: the noble savage versus the obscene substance abuser (Muehlmann 2008: 42), frozen traditionalism versus total assimilation (Ginsburg and Myers 2006: 28), traditional past versus dystopic present (Ginsburg and Myers 2006: 31). In all cases, valorization means that claimants must present their connection to tradition in an atmosphere that often sees that tradition as mutually exclusive with modernism. While current culture is crucial to Native Title law, the cultural expressions that most benefit a Native Title case are those that show continuity with traditional culture. The resulting cultural expression has been characterized as museumification (Errington 2003: 729) or immobilism (McConvell 2002: 262–3)—an ironic term considering that, in this case, the immobilism is caused by mobilization. Simply put, this juxtaposition denies claimant groups the right to adapt to their changing social landscape and punishes those who did so in the past. These effects mirror exactly the criticism often levied against the requirements for Native Title claims.

Valorization of tradition also presents a pair of paradoxes: first, the future of a cultural representation obtains its value solely from its association with the past (Dobrin and Berson 2011: 189); and second, the very traits that were attacked during assimilationist eras (such as the Stolen Generation era) become necessary for recognition of special indigenous status (Muehlmann 2008: 35).

The role of language in this ideological stance pivots on its essentialization with culture. It has been recognized for some time that this essentialization is in many ways problematic. Walsh (2002: 236) discusses the phenomenon with regard to Native Title in particular:

> Something is being lost as fluency declines, but much of the culture is being retained and much of it is being transformed. Whether land ownership relies so heavily on the parts of culture being lost (or transformed) that the land ownership will be negated must be determined on a case by case basis.

Because Native Title specifically requires cultural continuity, not linguistic continuity, language can be used to demonstrate continuity only as far as it can be linked to culture. Essentialist perspectives demand that the linguistic form be maintained, whereas more sociolinguistic perspectives focus the maintenance of ideological links between language and culture.

13.7.2 Continuity of Form

One approach to linguistic continuity argues that a language's form must be similar to the form recorded in early history, although the natural change that occurs with any living language must be tolerated. This approach with regard to Native Title is probably best discussed by Bowe (2002: 105) in reporting Sommer's contributions to the Yorta Yorta (also spelled Yoda yoda) Native Title hearing. According to Bowe (2002: 105), Sommer presented the current morbidity of the language as evidence that continuity had not been maintained. The findings most central to this conclusion, as provided by Bowe (2002: 106), were that:

- In the social domain, the speakers of Yorta Yorta lack the language resources to engage in meaningful conversation even on culturally relevant topics.
- Yorta Yorta language revival programmes may serve a valid purpose in supporting Yorta Yorta identity and cohesion, but the resulting use of Yorta Yorta can only be regarded as symbolic.
- If Yorta Yorta is not actually dead, it is at best permanently frozen at a point of imminent morbidity by the language revival programme.

Bowe concedes that the language could be considered moribund or dead if one focuses on transmission of language structure (Bowe 2002: 127), but maintains that this exclusive focus on linguistic form misses important aspects of continuity—such as ideological continuity. Similar arguments about the flawed, structural focus that linguists tend to bring with them to the field abound. Dobrin and Berson (2011: 195), for example, note that such a focus 'runs the risk of undertheorizing the important role of mobility, diffusion and mixing in shaping endangered vernaculars, and in some cases sustaining their speakers', adding later that a form-focused approach to preservation may even violate indigenous ideologies about continuity and community (Dobrin and Berson 2011: 200).

More specifically regarding Native Title, McConvell (2002: 287) argues against the assumption that language change equates to 'a break in continuity of tradition', thereby refuting notions that language loss should be taken to automatically nullify Native Title claims. Despite the fruitful scholarly debate on the subject, however, consensus has yet to be reached and scholarship is not always reflected in courtroom judgements. Focus often falls on the continuity of linguistic form, resulting in understandable tendencies towards purism among potential claimants.

13.7.3 Continuity of Link

A more sociolinguistic approach to linguistic continuity argues that the use of salient linguistic elements, particularly lexemes, that can be identified as part of the traditional language, demonstrates continuity of the relationship between a language and a culture. In fact, even discourse that bemoans the loss of language typically demonstrates an ideological link between language and culture.

Bowe (2002) argues the importance of this link in refuting the arguments she presented from Sommer. She observes that the Yorta Yorta people may have lost fluency in their language, but that they have clearly demonstrated a continued link between the language and culture by using remnants of the language to mark their identity—even just a few words known by a handful of people could suffice in some cases. Likewise, Sutton (2003) argues that a loss of traditional language cannot be taken as evidence against the authenticity of claims to linguistic identity, noting that linguistic identity is about owning or belonging to a language rather than speaking it. Bell (2002: 44) makes a similar argument:

> Goori people believe strongly that our languages are still very much a part of who we are and language continues to be one of our main spiritual connections to country. The form and use of our language has changed dramatically over the past 50 to 100 years due to numerous factors, but the continuity of connection has remained.

It must be recognized that the relationship between a language and a culture is an ideological construct that is the property of individuals within a society and is subject to change. Endurance of these ideological constructs, which can only be demonstrated by practices that can be traced to the ideologies, is therefore a form of continuity.

13.8 Ideological Changes

The mobilization of language, in this case through Native Title claims, inspires and highlights ideological changes. The speaker region, typically considered a dialect mesh by researchers, becomes an ideologically bounded mosaic in part because Native Title law creates a situation that requires groups with clearly defined boundaries. The traditional prestige of language ownership is overshadowed by the power of language proficiency in part because Native Title proceedings blur the salient distinction between the two concepts. Finally, an area known for extreme individual multilingualism becomes home to language guardianship attitudes in part because the Native Title process provides tangible incentives to limit the population of speakers.

13.8.1 Mesh to Boundaries

Where traditional practice saw remarkably individual-based affiliations between people, land, and language, as well as extraordinarily ephemeral naming and composition for large groups, modern practice attempts to approximate miniature nation states with clear-cut boundaries. Therefore, a linguistic area that is typically studied as an extreme example of borrowing and cross-linguistic synonymity is ideologically broken up. Group boundaries did exist in some sense before Native Title, and corporate groups have been emerging since contact; now, Native Title law inspires the creation of clear boundaries. The many associations that are currently posited in court, however authentic they may be regarding traditional grouping, must now be argued in terms that convince a judge rather than in terms that have meaning in a traditional context.

13.8.2 Traditional Dialect Groups

Scholarship generally agrees that, in most of Australia, groups of people were strongly affiliated with particular tracts of land and with the language belonging to that land, despite highly nomadic movements around more loosely bounded territories (Rumsey 1993: 193; Schmidt 1990; Sutton 2003). Social and linguistic identity in Aboriginal Australia was, and still is, strongly correlated to a connection with the land and, consequently, the named speech variety attributed to that land. That named variety does not necessarily have a simple correlation to actual linguistic forms used by people who identify with it (Evans 2001: 253; Rumsey 1993: 201; Walsh 2002).

In the Western Desert, the connection to land is less clearly associated with recognized groups because ownership of territory was defined on a far more individual basis. Each individual within a group was tied to specific areas, determined by place of conception, birth, raising, responsibility, and ancestry (McIntyre and Doohan 2002; Sutton 2003). Larger groups could share land and language rights primarily because their individual-based affiliations overlapped. In many cases, these larger groups were referred to according to salient dialectal differences—a practice that continues, in a more corporate form, today.

If dialect groups are taken to be synonymous with named entities, then the nature of traditional naming practices helps illustrate the problem with any concept of well-bounded dialect groups. Traditional naming was descriptive and ephemeral, and it was not group-instantiating. Simply put, there was no single-layered, consistent system of groupings underlying group names—a simple collection of group names in an area does little to inform about the number of groups associated with that area, the number of dialects (whatever that might be taken to mean) spoken in that area, or the social system of that area. Groupings beyond small family groups that travelled together were largely ephemeral, even if groupings posited by long-standing vendettas and ceremonial connections endured for those specific purposes.

13.8.3 Shift since Contact

The tendency towards Western naming practices and the normalization of groups that were reified by Westerners who adhered to these practices contributed to the increasing corporatization of language groups, in ideology and practice alike, because it created groupings that were expected to endure. In early contact, missionaries, law enforcement agents, and government authorities typically played the strongest roles in group naming and attribution of memberships outside of Aboriginal practice, although a handful of researchers also had their impact.

For the Wangkatha, group composition was based primarily on Mt Margaret Mission residence. Many Goldfields children who were institutionalized during the Stolen Generation were residents of Mt Margaret and, as in most institutions associated with the Stolen Generation, were lumped together with little or no regard for their traditional affiliations or speech variety. Initial understanding that the local Aboriginal population was 'Wangkatja' resulted in the application of this name to all future residents of the mission. Due to this crystallization of ephemeral groupings into proper names, and their eventual adoption by the Aboriginal population themselves, these names endure to the present day—in some cases along with associations to their early contact constituencies and locations.

The children of Mt Margaret lived together in dormitories, forming close relationships with fellow 'inmates' who became, more than classificatory kin, lifelong friends and the closest thing many of them experienced to family. Older children helped care for younger ones, forming parent–child-like bonds—a fairly traditional practice at any rate. Mission staff, although non-Aboriginal, also formed family-like bonds with their charges. Thus the 'group' in mission settlements became more corporate in character, in that there were longer-term broad associations and coextension between the relatively discernible group and their stable territory. Australia-wide, sharp, corporate-like delineations such as this probably did not exist until after contact (Sutton 2003), so such corporatization can be seen as contact-induced ideological change.

13.8.4 Role of Native Title

The introduction of benefits that are tied to Aboriginal group membership has contributed to the corporatization of groups because corporate groups are the most easily defined on the ground. There is no legitimacy to any claim that

Aboriginal society saw no link between people, land, and language, and the link that was traditionally posited is of continuing importance (Sutton 2002: 23). Group boundaries of some type have always existed; however, before Native Title those groups could more easily be defined and redefined in reaction to social purposes, day in and day out, as any social groupings are. The Native Title era creates an incentive to prove that group boundaries exist, not just to operate according to them in daily life, and to prove that they existed before contact with unbroken descent to modern-day groups.

Sometimes, this incentive may cause people to create new distinctions, or try to manifest distinctions through language in cases where language was never the basis of differentiation. This repurposing of social distinctions is a common social trait; however, with Native Title in the background, the new distinctions may be made according to criteria that will best suit Native Title purposes and crystallize that way. Even if Native Title does not constrain an individual's creation of group delineations, it conditions the way that others perceive that individual's posited groups. One consultant (S02) notes that:

> Because of Native Title, some people reckon they speak different languages when they really don't.

Therefore, Native Title comes into play when people evaluate others' claims to linguistic and social distinctions, colouring the political underpinnings of social habit.

The shift is that many associations that are currently posited, however authentic, must now be argued in terms that have limited meaning in a traditional context, or are interpreted to have this underlying caveat. The complex relationships that were forged before contact are often conceptually traded for much simpler bounded entities that can be more easily adopted by individuals on the ground, thus crystallizing through Native Title claim the results of a process that began during early contact. The maps presented by expert witnesses demonstrate the dialect mesh scenario, but people who take part in the claims often believe that this mesh must be 'sorted out' in court for language to play a clear part in a Native Title claim.

13.8.5 From Ownership to Proficiency

The use of language proficiency as an authenticator of a group as a whole and of individual members in that group ignores the traditional value placed on language ownership, which does not require language proficiency. The line between ownership and proficiency, which always delineated a complex relationship, was salient in traditional practice but is blurred in modern proceedings.

13.8.6 Traditional Ownership

Language 'ownership' in Aboriginal Australia is a person's birth right to a particular language that does not depend upon usage of that language. Critically, language ownership does not require proficiency in the owned language—proficiency was not traditionally required in order to prove ownership and was not a responsibility included with it. For example, Chanda and Hume (2003) address the issue for Mirning people:

> Mirning people are to be considered as language owners but not necessarily language speakers. The language is their heritage, and they still use some of it, although they may not be fluent speakers.

That being said, proficiency has traditionally played a role in the level of authority a language owner might have—if some people who 'own' a language are fluent speakers, while other owners are not, those who are fluent would probably be afforded a more authoritative role in language-related decisions.

The precise relationship between language ownership and land ownership is interpreted widely. Some consultants claim that there are direct relationships between land and language, and that an individual's ownership of language is mediated through their ownership of land. S12 shares:

> Language is not owned by people; it belongs to the land. People are the custodians of both. I would like to know more about that connection.

However, S08 disagrees, attributing the concept of ownership to anthropologists rather than practice:

> The land language connection is part of academic speak—it's not part of my experience. But certain words in certain places release energies, and some spirits don't understand English as well as their own language.

Sutton (2002: 23) observes that language is indeed associated with particular areas of country 'in a way that is normally of substantial local cultural significance' and, even taking apparent discrepancies into account, consultants agree.

Even consultants who did not reflect directly on the nature of language ownership demonstrate related opinions when discussing the nature of language work. With ownership of a language come the rights associated with that language. Perhaps the most salient rights are the right to be consulted about language-related decisions and the right to refuse to give approval. This is why consultants universally agree that language materials must be made in consultation with appropriate owners, and some disapprove of anybody but language owners having authority positions in language work. These reservations are partially due to fears about language proficiency but are more concerned with showing proper respect—an evaluation that demonstrates a continued distinction between ownership and proficiency.

13.8.7 Proficiency as an Authenticator

Whether or not they continue to make a distinction between ownership and proficiency, some individuals view proficiency in a language as an automatic strengthener to any claim to identity or land. Some governments indeed require language proficiency for proving indigeneity (Muehlmann 2008: 40). In the Australian situation, Walsh (2002) identifies proficiency as potentially relevant information that can be used to strengthen a Native Title claim in New South Wales. These requirements and expectations do not value the language in itself, but rather the use of language to distinguish coherent communities (Errington 2003: 728). However, the requirement that individuals or groups have proficiency in a purified traditional language ignores the fact that such proficiency may have faded as a result of the exact policies that current legislation aims to correct. Furthermore, it assumes that such proficiency was ever common (Dobrin and Berson 2011: 191)—an assumption that is not necessarily any more accurate for traditional languages than it is for textbook English or any other reified linguistic code.

In some cases, like with the previously discussed Cucapá, these sorts of requirements result in a mocking display of proficiency (Muehlmann 2008). In others, such as among the Wangkatha, the requirements create insecurity about language use. It is unclear whether Wangkatha people have adopted an ideology that prizes proficiency over ownership or whether they simply recognize that determiners of Native Title cases may have that ideology. Regardless of the locus of the ideology, its influence catalyses a change in, or at least a reinterpretation of, practice.

It is worth noting that the distinction between ownership and proficiency only comes into play when there is disjunction between the speakers and owners: speakers who are not owners or owners who are not speakers (Henderson, personal communication). While language speakers who are not owners would have abounded during traditional times, their existence wanes as languages fall out of use. Conversely, very few language owners would have lacked at least some proficiency in traditional times, while post-contact language attrition adds significantly to this number. The relationship between ownership and proficiency, always complex, has changed since contact. The need to distinguish clearly between the two groups has been highlighted with the introduction of language maintenance efforts, and insecurities about judges who may fail to make the distinction emerge from Native Title.

13.8.8 Modern Caveats

Consultants are hesitant to require proficiency in any traits that are perceived to have been eradicated through assimilationist policies. Valorization juxtaposes the traditional against the modern, but most people on the ground do not fault individuals for turning to modern conventions when traditional ones were lost due to forced removal from families or similar practices of the Stolen Generation. However, the same people generally fear that external judgements of memberships might not take such caveats into consideration, and even they are less willing to apply them to individuals who they think should be excluded from the group for other reasons.

Valorizing ideologies suggest that authenticating practices are superior to the modern lifestyle and cannot coexist with it. Accordingly, use of inauthentic Aboriginal language would negate any claim to authentic Aboriginal identity. Furthermore, social habits, evaluated through anything from job title to management of resources, that are associated with Western culture would disauthenticate any traditional practices that would otherwise substantiate a claim to Aboriginal identity. For example, Aboriginal people who 'go bush' regularly are often considered more authentically Aboriginal, but if they hold down Western-style jobs and keep their earnings to themselves rather than sharing them around, they are seen by some as 'wannabes'. Additionally, use of English, while necessary to the point of nearly being exempt from this ideology, is taken to result in subtractive bilingualism; in turn, this subtractive bilingualism is taken as another indicator that Aboriginal populations in the cities are less traditional than those living 'in the lands' who have not developed English proficiency.

Consultants exhibit variation in their degree of adherence to this ideology in particular. Some are reluctant to put any strong restrictions against the adoption of modern ways where doing so is often necessary for wider success, and most are unwilling to blame people for losing traditions that they were coerced into abandoning—perhaps because they themselves may be open to such criticism, or because they wish to protect family members who would be. However, the value judgements about traditional versus modern living hold whether or not individuals' practices are criticized: valorization argues that, in the best of worlds, Aboriginal people would still be practising traditional lifestyles and speaking the language of their people as it was before contact. Native Title means that, caveats or not, people are afraid that any lack of linguistic ability may nullify a claim, regardless of the reasons for loss.

13.9 Multilingualism to Guardianship

When language is used to instantiate and authenticate group membership, language proficiency becomes a potentially necessary and exclusivizing practice in an area that traditionally boasted extreme multilingualism. Language guardianship, an ideology through which individuals seek to control who is permitted to learn and speak a language, nevertheless has reflexes in pre-contact secret languages and initiation patterns.

13.9.1 Traditional Multilingualism

Traditionally, Aboriginal people were expected to learn the language of whatever group they encountered; through traditional roaming practices, this expectation would easily amount to a dozen languages. Significant movement of people occurred at the group and individual level. Individual roamers were typically men who left their small family group and travelled afar, eventually returning to their own country. These ‘walkabout’ trips were common practice, with some travelling literally hundreds of kilometres in their journeys—Hansen reports one consultant’s 700-kilometre trip (1984: 7). Each individual would typically learn the languages of those groups that they visited (Rumsey 1993: 195; Sutton 2002: 24). These individuals, however, would not claim multiple linguistic identities; their proficiency in more than one language did not secure them membership to more than one group or claim to multiple linguistic identities (Sutton 2002). Some consultants (S05, S10) likewise remark that they or their family members could speak multiple languages but were still only part of the group they were from.

Some language learning was protected—for example, the teaching of sacred words or languages was reserved for people who demonstrated appreciation for and understanding of certain elements of culture and met other criteria, such as initiation as ‘Law Men’ (Evans 2001). Conversely, some cultural knowledge was available exclusively to people who had learned their language. However, the bulk of language was available to all learners, and language learning was expected through adulthood.

13.9.2 Native Title Insecurities

In the Native Title era, the practice of language proficiency becomes potentially dangerous in the eyes of consultants who then seek to protect it, first because a failure to demonstrate command of the language may jeopardize an otherwise well-founded claim to identity and, second, because an ability to demonstrate command of the language may strengthen an otherwise ill-founded claim.

Individuals who feel that they have an authentic claim to identity but who are linguistically insecure may refuse to speak the language among people who might expose their linguistic knowledge to those who would deny their claim. Individuals may also be wary of language instruction because it would give more people language proficiency, which could in turn strengthen an inauthentic claim to identity. This is reportedly the case in one community near Kalgoorlie: a family that is fabled to speak the language fluently both refuses to work with linguists and protests the teaching of their particular dialect in local schools.

While this family refused to talk to me (a linguist), others in the area explained that their sentiments were probably due to fears about Native Title. Henderson (2002: 17) likewise notes that:

> Claimants may be concerned that having researchers document their knowledge of language and other things may amount to surrendering it to other groups. This is probably more likely in areas where few if any claimants have substantial knowledge of the local traditional languages.

Language consultants share similar perspectives in more general terms:

> Some people don't let others learn the language ... They're depriving their kids that way. They see knowledge as a threat, and with Native Title they're worried about down the track, thinking their family will miss out. (S11)

> It's important for kids to speak language if they can. It's part of their identity. But who teaches it? It could be in schools, but which language should be taught? Until Native Title is settled, they won't let any be taught. (S05)

Whether or not Native Title is actually the motivator for the actions of language guardians, the perceptions shared by Aboriginal consultants demonstrate that such fears are anticipated, and Henderson's concurring observation suggests these trends extend beyond the Wangkatha group.

13.9.3 Sanctification

Language guardianship can be partially explained independently of Native Title. Language attrition often causes formerly mundane domains of language to become sanctified. Florey (1993) describes how, as the registers that were once sacred fall completely out of use, elements of the language that were not traditionally viewed as sacred are sanctified, and Dobrin and Berson (2011: 197) report Moore's (1988) finding that the Wasco sanctify their linguistic property in response to language loss in a way that makes linguistic elicitation sessions hazardous. It is likely that sacred words, contexts, and languages have likewise faded in the community studied for this chapter, and therefore foreseeable that languages that were formerly available to any and all learners may now achieve sacred status. The Native Title adds additional rationale for a process that may have taken place anyway.

13.10 Conclusion

The ideological shifts that result, at least in part, from language mobilization present a paradox: they are created, formalized, or at the very least highlighted as a result of attempts to valorize traditional values and practices. Likewise, Native

Title law, which ostensibly aims to empower Aboriginal groups and respect their traditions, requires that claimants make their case in non-Aboriginal settings according to non-Aboriginal processes and for non-Aboriginal judges. The irony of such a system is not lost on language consultants, nor is it unique to Aboriginal Australia.

That being said, many of the ideological shifts that seem to be taking place can also be attributed to other factors and have reflexes in pre-contact tradition. Worries about language purity abound worldwide; even 'safe' languages such as English and French are subject to concerns about encroaching modernisms such as 'textisms'. Among the Wangkatha, insecurities about language change and shift have to do with more than Native Title; they can also be attributed to the normal workings of social capital, valorization of tradition, and are a common result of language standardization. Native Title law, however, puts the situation into a harsher light and exacerbates fears because extensive language shift really can have an impact on court proceedings. Furthermore, some people fear that even minor shifts can have an effect, which impacts behaviours and attitudes as well.

As for the crystallization of group boundaries, early contact saw the introduction of more corporate groups, in practice and ideology alike. Furthermore, more recent anthropological scholarship (McConvell 2002; Sutton 2003) has criticized views of historical Aboriginal group composition for over-emphasizing its lack of boundaries, calling for a focus on the implications of the ownerships and naming practices that did exist traditionally. At any rate, it can safely be said that Native Title law creates a situation that requires groups with clearly defined boundaries, if only to help determine the allocation of claimed resources among claimants. For the Wangkatha, the shift is that many associations that are currently posited, however authentic, must now be argued for in terms that have limited meaning in traditional context.

The recent value placed on language proficiency, as opposed to language ownership, was also not completely introduced by Native Title. Language proficiency was always expected of Aboriginal people: they were expected to learn the language of whichever groups they might encounter. Furthermore, proper custodianship of owned land often required proficiency in the language associated with that land because that language was the only one understood by the spiritual beings residing there. The traditional value of proficiency cannot be denied and should not be overshadowed. However, it is through Native Title proceedings that the salient distinction between language proficiency and ownership becomes blurred, and it is through language mobilization that simply using a language potentially becomes a claim to identity or political position.

The shift to language guardianship seems to pose the most drastic ideological change—Aboriginal Australians are well known for multilingualism and lexical borrowing across group boundaries, such as they may be. The traditional existence of secret languages, which could typically only be learned by initiated men, provides an analogue for the modern tendency, and Florey's (1993) discussion of similar patterns among the Alune provides an explanation for the modern shift that is independent of Native Title. Essentially, when sacred linguistic registers vanish, elements of the mainstream language that were never before considered sacred become sanctified. This analysis, extended to the Wangkatha situation, helps explain the adoption of guardianship attitudes. The Native Title era reshapes the process in three ways: it provides a very tangible rationale for guardianship; it provides critics of guardianship attitudes with a perceived selfish motive to attack, as they can claim that guardianship is due solely to Native Title greed; and it potentially provides a legal framework through which exclusive language rights could actually be claimed in court.

Perhaps the most important learning point from this research with regard to Native Title itself is the importance of ideology in relationship to continuity. First, because the link between language and group is ideological and therefore subject to change, the endurance of that ideological link serves as evidence of continuity in its own right, regardless of language proficiency. Second, political efforts like the Native Title Act are increasingly criticized for actually requiring ideological change among the championed population in order to work. Finally, and directly related to the second, the ideological 'changes' revealed in this research have reflexes in pre-contact populations and, therefore, can be taken as modern adjustments that nevertheless demonstrate an unbroken descent from pre-contact practice.

References

Alpher, Barry. 2002. Can lexicostatistics contribute an absolute time-scale to discussions of continuity of occupation in Native Title determinations? In David Nash and John Henderson (eds.), *Language in Native Title*. Canberra: Aboriginal Studies Press.

Bell, Jeanie. 2002. Linguistic continuity in colonized country. In David Nash and John Henderson (eds.), *Language in Native Title*. Canberra: Aboriginal Studies Press.

Bowe, Heather J. 2002. Linguistics and the Yorta Yorta Native Title claim. In David Nash and John Henderson (eds.), *Language in Native Title*. Canberra: Aboriginal Studies Press.

Bringing Them Home. 1997. *Report of the National Inquiry into the Separation of Aboriginal and Torres Strait Islander Children from their Families*. Sydney: Human Rights and Equal Opportunities Commission.

Chanda, Mary and Sharon Hume. 2003. Reviving an endangered language: the case of the Mirning language. Paper presented at *Maintaining the Links: Language, Identity and the Land*. Broome, Western Australia.

Dalby, Andrew. 2003. *Language in Danger: The Loss of Linguistic Diversity and the Threat to Our Future*. New York: Columbia University Press.

Dobrin, Lise M. and Joshua Berson. 2011. Speakers and language documentation. In Peter K. Austin and Julia Sallabank (eds.), *The Cambridge Handbook of Endangered Languages*. Cambridge: Cambridge University Press.

Dorian, Nancy C. 1989. *Investigating Obsolescence: Studies in Language Contraction and Death*. Cambridge: Cambridge University Press.

Duchêne, Alexandre and Monica Heller. 2007. *Discourses of Endangerment: Ideology and Interest in the Defence of Languages*. London: Continuum.

Errington, Joseph. 2003. Getting language rights: the rhetorics of language endangerment and loss. *American Anthropologist* 105: 723–32.

Evans, Nick. 2001. The last speaker is dead: long live the last speaker! In Martha Ratliff and Paul Newman (eds.), *Linguistic Fieldwork*. Cambridge: Cambridge University Press.

Evans, Nick. 2002. Country and the word: linguistic evidence in the Croker Sea claim. In David Nash and John Henderson (eds.), *Language in Native Title*. Canberra: Aboriginal Studies Press.

Fishman, Joshua A. 1991. *Reversing Language Shift: Theoretical and Empirical Foundations of Assistance to Threatened Languages*. Philadelphia, PA: Multilingual Matters.

Florey, Margaret J. 1993. The reinterpretation of knowledge and its role in the process of language obsolescence. *Oceanic Linguistics* 32: 295–309.

Ginsburg, Faye and Fred Myers. 2006. A history of Aboriginal futures. *Critique of Anthropology* 26, 27–45.

Hale, K., M. Krauss, L. J. Watahomigie, A. Y. Yamamoto, C. Craig, L. V. M. Jeanne, and N. C. England. 1992. Endangered languages. *Language* 68: 1–42.

Hansen, K. C. 1984. Communicability of some Western Desert communilects. *Working Papers of SIL-AAB Series B* 11: 1–112.

Harrington-Smith on Behalf of the Wongatha People vs. State of Western Australia. 2007. No. 9, SCA 31.

Henderson, John. 2002. Language and Native Title. In J. Henderson and D. Nash (eds.), *Language in Native Title*. Canberra: Aboriginal Studies Press.

McConvell, Patrick. 2002. Linguistic stratigraphy and Native Title: the case of ethnonyms. In David Nash and John Henderson (eds.), *Language in Native Title*. Canberra: Aboriginal Studies Press.

McIntyre, Greg and Kim Doohan. 2002. Labels, language and Native Title groups: the Miriwung-Gajerrong case. In David Nash and John Henderson (eds.), *Language in Native Title*. Canberra: Aboriginal Studies Press.

McKay, Graham. 1996. *The Land Still Speaks: Review of Aboriginal and Torres Strait Islander Language Maintenance and Development Needs and Activities*. Canberra: Australian Government Publishing Service.

McKay, Graham. 2008. *WA Aboriginal Language Policy: Discussion Paper*. Perth, WA: Edith Cowan University.

Moore, Robert. 1988. Lexicalization vs. lexical loss in Wasco-Wishram language obsolescence. *International Journal of American Linguistics* 54: 453–68.

Muehlmann, Shaylih. 2008. 'Spread your ass cheeks': and other things that should not be said in indigenous languages. *American Ethnologist* 35: 34–48.

Newman, Paul and Martha Ratliff. 2001. *Linguistic Fieldwork*. Cambridge: Cambridge University Press.

Niezen, Ronald. 2000. Recognizing indigenism: Canadian unity and the international movement of indigenous peoples. *Society for Comparative Study of Society and History* 42: 119–48.

Rumsey, Alan. 1993. Language and territoriality in Aboriginal Australia. In Michael Walsh and Colin Yallop (eds.), *Language and Culture in Aboriginal Australia*. Canberra: Aboriginal Studies Press.

Schmidt, Annette. 1990. *The Loss of Australia's Aboriginal Language Heritage*. Canberra: Aboriginal Studies Press.

Silverstein, Michael. 1998. Contemporary transformations of local linguistics communities. *Annual Review of Anthropology* 27: 401–26.

Stanton, J. 1984. Conflict, change and stability at Mt Margaret: a community in transition. PhD thesis, University of Western Australia.

Sutton, Peter. 2002. Linguistic evidence and Native Title cases in Australia. In David Nash and John Henderson (eds.), *Language in Native Title*. Canberra: Aboriginal Studies Press.

Sutton, Peter. 2003. *Native Title in Australia: An Ethnographic Perspective*. Cambridge: Cambridge University Press.

Walsh, Michael. 2002. Language ownership: a key issue for Native Title. In David Nash and John Henderson (eds.), *Language in Native Title*. Canberra: Aboriginal Studies Press.

Woolard, Kathryn A. 1998. Introduction: language ideology as a field of inquiry. In Bambi B. Schieffelin, Kathryn A. Woolard, and Paul V. Kroskrity (eds.), *Language Ideologies: Practice and Theory*. Oxford: Oxford University Press.

Wurm, Stephen A. and Ian Heyward. 2001. *Atlas of the World's Languages in Danger of Disappearing*. Paris: UNESCO.

14

Finding the Languages We Go Looking For*

TONYA N. STEBBINS

14.1 Introduction

SPEAKER COMMUNITIES at different times and for a range of reasons (generally having to do with the need for 'official' rccognition of their status as a language community with a 'real' language) struggle to gain recognition for their language, its structure, and their relationship to it by (a representative of) the discipline of linguistics. Such recognition is important as a means for achieving entitlements over a range of domains, from vernacular education to land rights, and gives linguists, as representatives of the discipline, an extraordinary amount of power as mediators between communities and various statutory bodies.

In order to achieve official recognition, languages, and the materials that have been produced in relation to them, are assessed according to linguistic criteria. As shown in Eira and Stebbins (2008), these criteria are in fact ideologically founded and frequently have distinctive, often competing, counterparts within each speech community. Ideological differences pose a problem when they become barriers to official recognition.

Ideological struggles affect not only the identities of languages but also the ways in which they are analysed and the support that is made available to them. Among the types of languages that have struggled for acceptance as bona fide objects of study within our discipline are creoles and sign languages (see Branson and Miller 2007). These types of language, for different reasons, challenge our assumptions about what language is like, the former by virtue of their mixed provenance and the latter by virtue of their non-linear use of space, in addition to their linear practice of making signs in time. The history of linguistic typology shows that language structures that are not evident in Indo-

* I thank Catherine Easton, Mark Planigale, Christina Eira, and Vicki Couzens for their contributions to this paper. Stephen Morey and Julia Sallabank also provided comments on an earlier draft. Although this material is presented here as a single-authored paper, it is important for me to acknowledge that the thinking behind it has developed over many years through work with Christina Eira (Eira and Stebbins 2008) and from my newly developing involvement with a Victorian Corporation for Aboriginal Languages project with Christina and with Vicki Couzens called *Meeting Point: Parameters for a Typology of Revival Language* (see Couzens and Eira, this volume).

European languages can take a long time to become recognized, let alone well understood. Ergative case marking is an obvious example. Seely (1977) tracks the development of the concept of ergativity and associated terminology.

Both linguists and the speech communities with whom they work vary greatly in their ability to articulate their own ideologies about language or to assert them through interactions with others. Where linguists and communities have conflicting ideologies, and each group becomes committed to their views about what language is like and how language should be managed, progress on language retrieval and development projects can be greatly impeded. The linguistics literature reveals a relatively recent and lively strand of discussion about how linguists should negotiate these ideological differences given the importance of cohesive relationships with communities if a true partnership is to be possible in working against the pressures associated with language endangerment (Dobrin 2008; Dwyer 2010; Franchetto 2010; Guérin and Lacrampe 2010; Hinton 2010; Rice 2009, 2010; Speas 2009; and Whaley 2011, among others).

To engage with alternative ideologies of language is critical if we are to address the underlying power structures that have created the conditions for language endangerment (see also Eira 2007; Eira and Stebbins 2008; Musgrave and Thieberger 2007; Rice 2006). As a contribution towards this project, this chapter presents a framework for understanding the impact of ideological differences in relation to language and explores some of the effects of ideological differences in relation to work with endangered languages.

This chapter begins by developing a framework for understanding the effects of contrasting ideologies in interactions between linguists and community groups (section 14.2). A description of the ways in which ideologies contribute to the construction of languages and dialects is given in section 14.3, taking Mali Baining as a case study. In section 14.4, I present a range of effects of linguistic ideologies on our understandings of what language is like and how it should be managed. Section 14.5 is concerned with the tensions around ideas of authentic speakerhood and diachronic continuity in relation to language change. Finally, in section 14.6, I summarize the potential consequences of an ideologically dominant position for linguistics in relation to the languages we study.

14.2 Framework: Viewing Language through Filters and Lenses

What is language? In introductory linguistics textbooks it takes about a chapter to answer this question, and answers are typically framed in terms of signs and rules, with some discussion of what does and does not 'count'. For example, animal languages do not count. To speakers, there is much more to language than this. For speakers, language is essentially an experiential phenomenon—something we do and respond to when others do it around us. For speakers, the elements of language, however speakers may identify them, are also intimately bound up with collective and individual memory. Meaning arises because of the memory of what experiences have been associated with particular words or utterances in the past.

Of course, it is not possible for us to be conscious of everything relating to our own language experiences, let alone the experiences of others. In order to render the study of language manageable, we narrow down its meaning and identify particular areas of study. One way to think about this is to say that we filter out certain aspects of language. The things we can see, we view through the lenses provided by our training as linguists. The effect of this filter is that some things are lost from view. The effect of the lens is to predispose the viewer to particular interpretations of what is available to view. This model is set out in Figure 14.1.

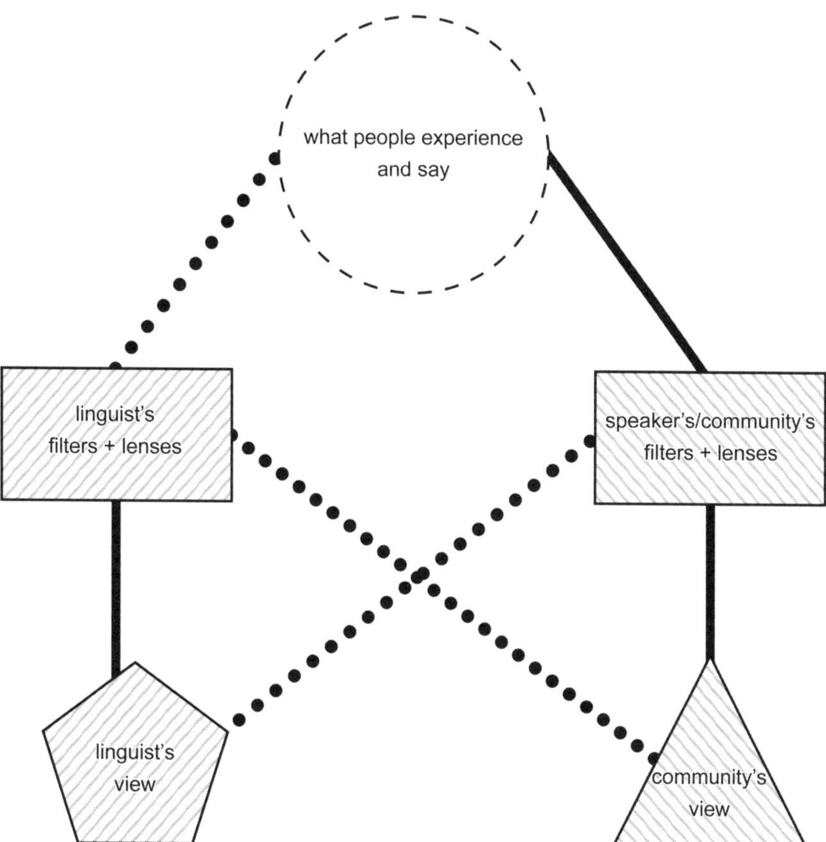

Figure 14.1 Relationship between experiences and representations of language: how lenses colour our views and filters reshape them. The dotted lines represent weaker lines of experience and influence; double lines represent stronger lines of experience and influence.

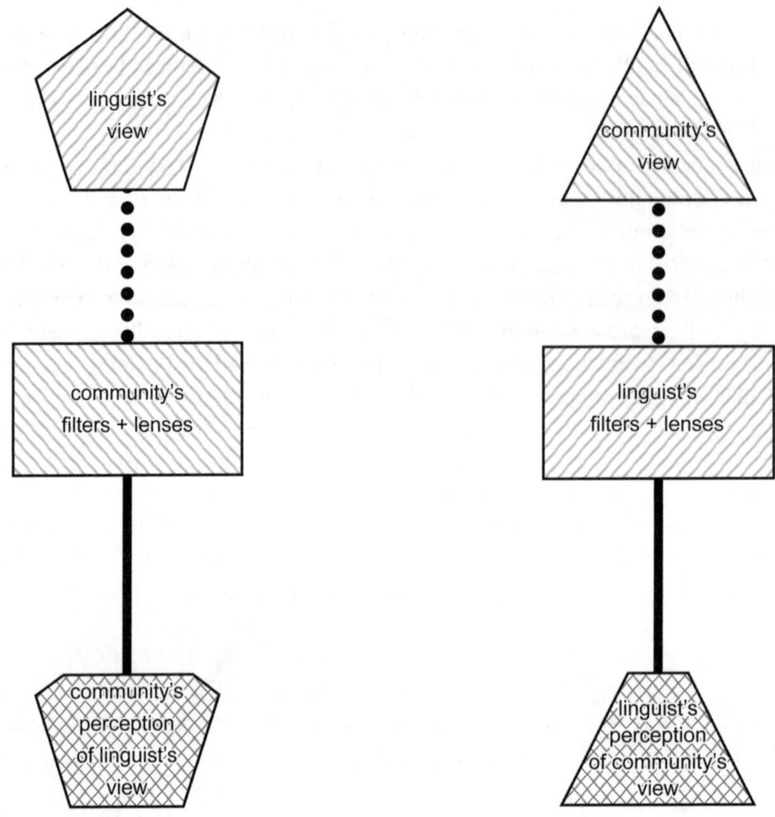

Figure 14.2 Views of 'other' representations of language.

This model can be used to explain the effects of ideological conflicts between linguists and communities, that is, why misunderstandings and disappointments for speakers arise over what a linguist attends to in their research and produces as a result. Figure 14.2 shows how partial and discoloured each group's view seems to the other when viewed through their own lenses. I will return to this point in section 14.6.

The image in Figure 14.2 is intended to show how our views of language are doubly distorted when we view them through each other's lenses in addition to our own. In each case, the final product does not match with what is viewed from a single perspective, and importantly, nor is it anything like the original view of the other group. This figure helps us to see the reasons why it can be so difficult for all interested parties in language documentation and development work to find common ground.

14.3 On Becoming an Object of Study (i): Language versus Dialect

In this section I want to show how the filters we apply to language can influence our ability to identify a particular variety as a language or a dialect. I particularly want to highlight the fact that this is less a matter of the filters we acquire through linguistic training than the filters that arise in the sociopolitical contexts in which we work.

The difference between 'being a dialect' and 'being a language' can have quite significant consequences for speech communities. In the context of language endangerment these consequences are often very readily apparent. A language can attract researchers, documentation funds, teacher training, publications, Bible translators, and so on in a way that a dialect cannot. Often, as will be illustrated below in an example from Papua New Guinea, this is justified in terms of economies of scale.

The process of filtering information and experience in order to establish languages as distinct entities has been described by Gal and Irvine (1995) and subsequently by Irvine and Gal (2000). They identify three semiotic processes that operate to establish languages as distinct entities in association with specific communities:

- *Iconization*: 'The attribution of cause and immediate necessity to a connection ... that may be only historical, contingent, or conventional' (Irvine and Gal 2000: 37).
- *Erasure*: 'Facts that are inconsistent with the ideological scheme either go unnoticed or get explained away' (Irvine and Gal 2000: 38).
- *Fractal recursion*: 'The projection of an opposition, salient at some level of relationship, onto some other level' (Irvine and Gal 2000: 38).

Communities are co-constructed by association with their languages (see Makoni and Pennycook (2007) for discussion of this theoretical point). Gal and Irvine are concerned with the way:

> observers' ideologies defined the object of study of linguistics and ethnology—the material claimed to be the particular area of expertise of each—by producing the appearance that language is separate from questions of social process ... They [practitioners of these disciplines] have therefore obviated questions that would link the two kinds of inquiry, questions about the varying ways in which the boundaries of languages may be constructed, or the diverse ways in which named languages and unnamed varieties are linked to social groups. (Gal and Irvine 1995: 985)

This is certainly true in connection with Papua New Guinea, where Romaine (1994: 12) notes that 'any attempt to count distinct languages will be an artefact of classificatory procedures [involving both filters and lenses] rather than a reflection of communicative practice'. Lexicostatistics were widely used within

Papua New Guinea as a preliminary means of determining language boundaries (Wurm 1975, 1976). The examples below indicate that other perspectives on the relative status of language communities played an important role in determining which languages were counted and compared in the first place. As the following examples show, the delineation of ostensible speech communities within Papua New Guinea is established primarily through the processes of iconization, fractal recursion, and erasure. This is consistent with Irvine and Gal's (2000: 74) observation that 'linguistic differentiation crucially involves ideologically embedded and socially constructed processes. Moreover, the scholarly enterprise of describing linguistic differentiation is itself ideologically and socially engaged.'

For much of the twentieth century, the main preoccupation of those concerned with identifying languages in Papua New Guinea was to find ways of grouping speech varieties together in order to 'reduce' the number of languages so that each language would be spoken by more people. Wurm and Laycock (1961–2: 143) sought to defend the use of local languages by arguing that:

> There is no need to stress the importance of this [grouping of varieties into languages] at a time when arguments against the use of any native language in New Guinea for administrative and elementary educational purposes are largely based on the assumption of the enormous multiplicity of the New Guinea languages, and the smallness of the number of the speakers of individual languages.

The tide of this practice has begun to turn now that language endangerment provides more favourable outcomes (in terms of funding opportunities at least) to small and dwindling language groups in preference to large and robust ones. Education departments across Papua New Guinea have realized that there is value in beginning children's education in their mother tongue. Both the pull towards local varieties and questions of scale continue to be weighed against each other. For example, within the Papua New Guinea branch of the Summer Institute of Linguistics (SIL) many communities hope to attract a Bible translation team, but within SIL the practicalities of the translation process still push for economies of scale.

Local sociopolitical factors have contributed to the filtering out of much of the complexity within the Baining language family, whose speakers live on the Gazelle Peninsula in East New Britain, Papua New Guinea. The Baining language family consists of a group of at least five non-Austronesian languages: Kaket, Kairak, Ura, Mali, Simbali, and possibly Makolkol, which is reportedly extinct and is said by speakers of Simbali to be a mixture of Simbali and Nakanai (the Austronesian language immediately to the west). Speakers of the Baining languages identify themselves as members of a single ethnic group. This self-identification is strongly reinforced by the opposition between Bainings and the locally dominant cultural group, the Austronesian-speaking Tolais (who live in

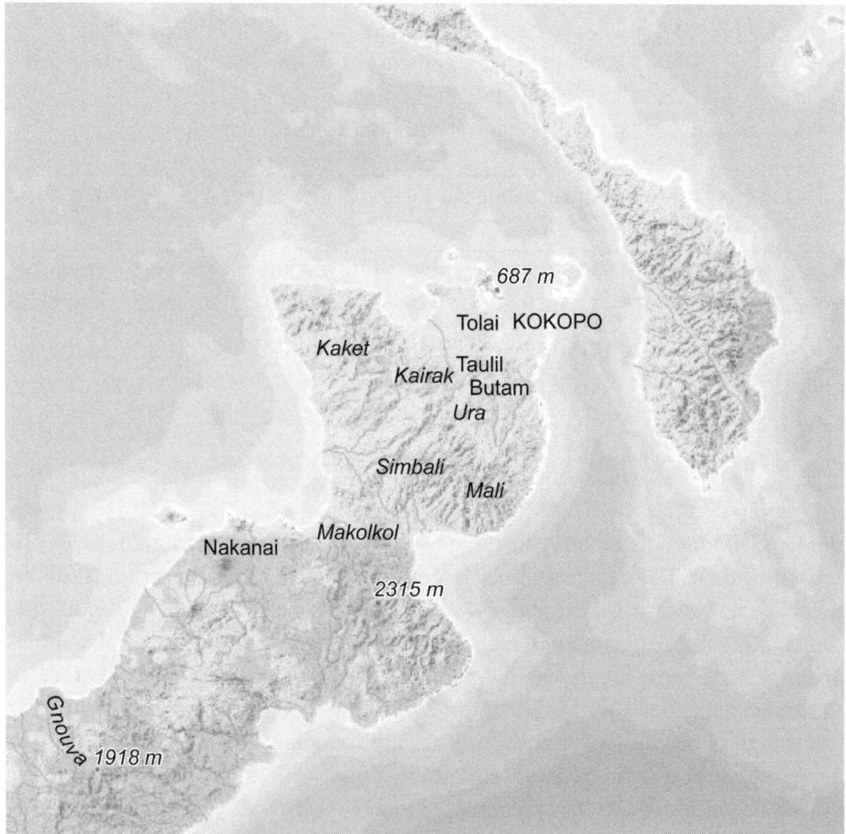

Figure 14.3 Languages of the Bismarck region.

the Austronesian-speaking region to the north of the Gazelle Peninsula (just above Taulil and Butam on Figure 14.3).

Rohatynskyj (2000) argues that the socially subordinate position of the Bainings was significantly reinforced by the fact that the capital of the German colony of the Bismarck Archipelago was on Tolai land at Kokopo, formerly known as Herbertshöhe. The imbalance in the representation of the two groups is nicely shown by the following quote from a *Lonely Planet* guide (McKinnon et al. 2008: 213):

> Most of the 184,000 people in ENB are Tolai who share many cultural similarities with southern New Irelanders. Traditional enemies of the Tolai … the semi-nomadic Baining people of the mountains.

The Bainings are frequently characterized as an undifferentiated, backward group with limited capacity for cultural expression (see also Stebbins and Planigale 2009). This contempt has made its way into the national culture in the use of

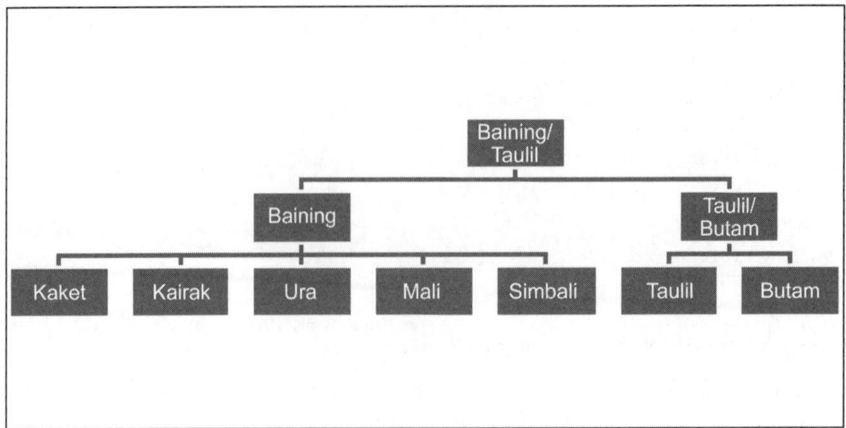

Figure 14.4 Presumed links between Baining languages and Taulil/Butam.

the word *Baining* as a derogatory term, referring to a backward individual. The prosody of the Baining languages is quite distinctive from the prosody of the neighbouring Austronesian languages, and Austronesian speakers report that the Baining languages sound like meaningless babble to them. Iconization is apparent here since the distinctive prosody of their language becomes iconic of the characterization of the Baining—as exemplified by expressions such as 'meaningless babble', as opposed to 'strange sounding' or 'difficult to learn'.

I began fieldwork in New Britain in 2001 with a view to producing a grammar (Stebbins 2011), dictionary (Stebbins with Tayul 2012), and text collection (Stebbins 2009, Tayul and Stebbins 2004) for the language. The initial phase of the fieldwork involved a series of discussions about how the community regarded themselves and their language and what aspirations they had relating to each. One of the key areas identified by Malis in which they aspired to improve their lives was overcoming invisibility on the world stage (see Stebbins 2004). This may seem like a rather strange concern to have. It makes sense in the context of understanding how the distinctive identity of the Mali community has been erased. Research on the languages of the Gazelle Peninsula occurs in a context in which the Tolai community dominates outsider perceptions of others in the region. This situation and its resonances are summarized in Rohatynskyj (2005).

Although there is a group of people who self-identify as Baining, the term has also been used more generally to refer to 'non-Tolai' people.[1] This may have

[1] See, for example, the dictionary of the Tolai language published by Bley (1900), whose entry for 'Butam' (cited in Laufer 1959: 186) reads 'Name für die in der Mitte der Gazelle südlich vom Varzin wohnenden Baininger' ('Name for the Bainings living in the middle of the Gazelle in the south of Varzin').

had a strong influence on the decision to group the Taulil and Butam languages with the Baining in previous studies of the non-Austronesian languages of the region (for a summary see Stebbins 2009). Substantial linguistic evidence for this connection has yet to be established. The move to group together non-Tolai people under the umbrella of 'Baining' is an example of fractal recursion, which, in this case, involves 'supercategories that include both sides but oppose them to something else' (Irvine and Gal 2000: 38).

One of the effects of this move is to erase distinctions within the Baining ethnic group through a process that 'renders some persons or activities (or sociolinguistic phenomena) invisible' (Irvine and Gal 2000: 38). Not only do the Malis identify themselves as speakers of a distinct language within the Baining language family, but they also identify two major dialects and several other minor varieties. If the Baining language family is treated as including Taulil and Butam alongside the Baining languages then the conceptual space for dialects of these languages, and even the languages themselves, may be erased (see Figure 14.4).

The main result of this erasure has been the ongoing use of 'Baining' to refer particularly to Kaket, one of the demarcations possible within the Baining community in terms of either language or social groupings (see, for example, Fajans 1997; Rascher 1904; Parker and Parker 1977). The result is that other speech varieties represented within the Baining community are relegated to the status of dialects and neither they nor their communities are then visible enough to warrant specific attention.

The strength of feeling associated with this concern about the invisibility of the Mali language and the Mali community was evidenced in the first encounter I ever had with a member of the Mali community. This person was a man working for the East New Britain Provincial Department of Education in a senior position. I introduced myself and explained that I was hoping to be able to study his language, and was quite surprised when he burst into tears on hearing this news. This was because he considered that much has hinged on the Mali community being able to get people to take the existence of their language seriously. For example, until an orthography for the language was recognized by the East New Britain Provincial Department of Education, it was not possible for the community to operate a Tok Ples primary school (local language schooling up to grade two).

The ideological perspectives of a range of viewers have impacted on the accessibility of the sister languages within the Baining language family. At different times, and for a host of reasons, these languages have been characterized as more or less distinct. Outside perspectives have also had a significant impact on outsiders' abilities to engage with members of the wider Baining community on their own terms, and this has had a direct effect on language attitudes within the community.

14.4 On Becoming an Object of Study (ii): Ticking the Linguists' Boxes

The situation outlined in section 14.3 refers to an example in which languages are obscured by the filters and lenses through which they are viewed. Having acknowledged that languages are socially constructed and are identified in part by virtue of their association with particular constellations of political power, we find ourselves in the troubling field of questioning what languages are and how they could be identified.

In this section I consider how the disciplinary filters and lenses of linguistics influence our representations of the languages we choose to study. In this context, external sociopolitical pressures, as experienced by the community, are often treated as irrelevant since they do not directly inform any part of the analysis. In order to identify places where the filters and lenses of the discipline may be at work, I consider two areas of frequent dissent between communities and linguists. These seem to me to signal areas in which there are mismatches between the representations of each group that have led to power struggles between disciplinary and community understandings about language. The power struggles that are apparent here relate to the intertwined questions of authenticity and rights to decision-making in relation to languages. Specifically, whose representation is to be taken to be the truth? Needless to say, power struggles in these areas, while they may represent work towards decolonizing the languages in question, also involve the use of a great deal of energy that could better be deployed in other activities relating to language support.

One of the challenges of fieldwork is working effectively with people whose models of language differ from our own. In Eira and Stebbins (2008), we argued that, like linguists, individuals within communities and sometimes communities in a more collective sense have theories (filters and lenses) of language and frameworks (filters and lenses) for assessing the authenticity of language. Until a language becomes an object of academic study, these issues are not within the scope of the discipline, and the community is free to deal with them as they see fit; often this may involve divergent practices in various segments of a community. Most tellingly of all perhaps, we noted that within our discipline, linguists from different traditions also have different filters and lenses or ways of thinking about what languages are (and should be) like. As La Polla (2001: 236) has noted:

> In India, linguists are trained in Sanskrit grammar, and so are familiar with paradigms and participles. They generally look for them in the Tibeto-Burman languages they describe, and often find them. They are not very familiar with tones, and do not consider them that important, and so even if the language has tones, they often will not be included in the description. On the other hand, the Chinese

> linguists are trained in Chinese linguistics, and so are often not familiar with paradigms and participles, but are very familiar with tones. They then generally do not describe the languages as having tight paradigms, etc., but very often find and describe Chinese-like tonal systems, even in languages (e.g. Burmese, rGyalrong) that could be argued to have register or pitch-accent systems.

A significant result of becoming an object of study in linguistics, particularly at the stage of being assigned to a particular language family, is that the speech variety concerned will then be represented as having certain features that linguists 'know' to assign to the languages they study because of the filters and lenses they bring to the task. To a certain extent the features concerned may relate specifically to the tradition in which the linguist is trained, but they can also relate to language in much more general terms.

Collins (1992: 407) identifies the ideological significance of the relationship between our roles as experts on language and the types of things we are able to recognize in connection to it:

> We academics are people who make authoritative pronouncements about language. Our categories of analysis are part of linguistic practices that characterize social realities, and we inhabit positions as specialists in state-certified institutions that make our statements and our silences unavoidably ideological.

In this quote Collins identifies two issues of concern here: the existence of filters and lenses that provide us with particular views of language, and the relatively powerful positions linguists hold as experts that make our representations of language ideological even as we consider them to be scientific. Collins provides an example of a three-way conflict between community members, academic linguists, and certifying officials in his discussion of his experiences working with the Tolowa community in north-western California (Collins 1992: 414):

> In the local/nonlocal encounter over 'authentic' Tolowa we have a multiparty conflict: academic linguists undermine local efforts in the name of an always-earlier, more systematic system; certifying officials seek expert opinion, to validate an image of ethnic cultural-linguistic tradition-as-test; and local people question the presumption of a general representation, while recognizing that without efforts at such representation, the language tradition is indeed 'lost'.

Among the specific issues under contention from the perspective of linguists were the treatment of the verb system, which in Athabaskan languages centres on aspect rather than tense, and the use of the Unifon alphabet, which failed to represent the language phonemically. The conflict was heightened by the fact that each group had ideological investments in its position and because the language programme and more generally the protection of the language in a systematized way were at stake.

Collins observes that the key teaching text used in the Tolowa language programme 'is based on a simplified English plan' (1992: 411). The influence of the model of European grammar (via the locally dominant language, in this case English) on speakers working towards descriptions of their own languages without (much) prior training in linguistics has also been noted elsewhere (for example, Eira and Stebbins 2008: 22). In the context of this chapter it should hardly be surprising that, like linguists, community members working on their languages seek to apply categories with which they are already familiar, even when these categories may not be the most suitable from other perspectives. Knowledge about language that is available to them acts as a filter and a lens, just as it does for us. The important difference, which causes some of the conflict, is the source and status of the knowledge.

Decisions around orthography are also a widely recognized area of contention between linguists and communities, so it is hardly surprising to find unhappiness among linguists with the use of the Unifon alphabet. Easton (2007: 7–19) identifies a significant gap between the theory of language planning (including orthography development) and its practice. In other words, the ways in which linguists sometimes believe orthographies should be developed and used are not how things really happen. Easton considers (2007: 18) that although a more sophisticated model of language ideology, one that identifies linguists' as well as communities' ideologies (filters and lenses), helps us to understand the causes of these conflicts (for example, the importance that linguists but not always communities typically attribute to the representation of phonemes), it does not help us to solve them.

She argues (2007: 270–2) that these tensions are more likely to be resolved productively (resulting in orthographies that communities (variously self-defined) can 'own' and so are more likely to use) when appropriate representatives from the community hold the authority to design their own orthography—one consistent with a representation of the language based on their particular filters and lenses. In describing the orthography development workshops she facilitated in Papua New Guinea, Easton (2007: 271) notes that linguistics:

> provided some tools that participants could choose to access … these were not presented as answers, but as contextual information for discussions of orthography options … As part of the decision making process, the workshop participants and linguistic facilitators created a list of advantages and disadvantages of the various orthographic options … Then community models of decision-making took over. This often involved lengthy discussions … The process was … a deep renegotiation of self and community.

This section has highlighted a range of ways in which the ideologically driven approaches of linguists to language impact on both our analyses and our advice to communities. Unless community representatives have extensive linguistics training and have consequently been acculturated into the discipline, it is unrealistic to expect that they will readily accept all of these ideas. Moreover, as Easton argues, it is possible for us to provide analytical methods and tools for use within communities without at the same time expecting that, in using these tools for their own ends, they will produce the outcomes we would expect of ourselves. Community representatives can make meaningful knowledge for themselves using a combination of linguistics techniques and their own ideological positions. The challenge for us is to recognize these new perspectives on language for what they are and to find ways to make our own meanings in relation to them.

14.5 On Becoming an Object of Study (iii): Sorting out Pedigrees

There is currently tension expressed in relation to documentary linguists, who often find that anthropologists' concerns for the risk of reifying dynamic ethno-linguistic realities can easily end up ignoring the urgency of documenting languages that are on the verge of extinction. As Eira and Stebbins (2008) noted, lineages are an extremely important concept both in linguistics and in speech communities.

Our philological heritage predisposes us to believe more deeply in languages whose genetic lineages we can establish. In the context of language endangerment, and most especially in the context of language revitalization/revival, where languages are radically transformed through processes of contact with majority languages and there is no longer any possibility of imagining a slow progression through orderly stages of development, it can be difficult for us to know how to view new varieties and their speakers.

A useful first step in addressing these issues is to take care in distinguishing between the histories and present characteristics of languages and the histories and speech varieties of particular speakers. We need to know where a speaker fits in to the picture of language continuity, change, and contact and, knowing this, we can then treat whatever language variety they speak as a valid and potentially interesting object of study.

The overarching issue here crops up not only between descriptive and sociologically oriented (sub)disciplines of linguistics/anthropology but also within the descriptive (documentary, typological) tradition in the form of debate about the status of the speakers consulted in the research (see also Evans 2001; Warner et al. 2007 on speakerhood). Do they have 'full command' of the language or not? This is a question that points to the ideologically founded assumptions about what is meant by 'full command' of a language and the identity of the 'language' itself in some sort of historically 'correct' or 'pure' or somehow more 'real' form. In the context of intensive language contact, we are perhaps being called to a more sophisticated understanding of what language is, and a great deal of care will be required to ensure that our conceptual struggles in relation to language change are not projected onto speakers in the form of blaming them for failing to speak historical versions/visions of the language to which we very often no longer have direct access in any case.

This issue comes to a head in the context of language endangerment, and especially language revitalization or revival, since in these contexts there can be a large disjunction between versions of a language spoken in the past and current forms and practices. Linguists sometimes struggle to understand the relationship between historical and present-day varieties of these languages, especially in settings where very little information about the language as it was spoken before contact remains. We tend to think that the historical form of the language is the target of revitalization or revival and offer our services in explicating this target to communities using our skills at interpreting archival sources (see also Couzens and Eira, this volume). Communities, however, while they too may want to be as faithful as possible to historical forms, may view archival records as resources rather than targets; this is a very practical approach where records are limited.

In fact, this period represents an enormous opportunity for us to enrich our understandings of what language is and how it works by engaging more fully with the dynamics and effects of intensive language contact—a long-established field but one that has not perhaps been recognized as being as central to the formation of languages as it might be, given the traditional predominance of multilingualism across much of the world. Ironically, the focus on language contact as central to our understanding of language is emerging just as multilingualism is threatened by the ever-expanding dominance of a few major languages.

Insofar as philologically biased perspectives are a reflection of historical and ideological forces within our discipline (in this case the development of linguistics out of the tradition of philology), these are likely to be quite opaque to community representatives. In effect, these issues are problems for us, generated by unexamined ideological positions that we bring to the data and the context in which we work. However, because of our greater power in real terms, because we are experts and are able to say what is real and correct, we have the capacity to shift the conflict away from ourselves. Projecting the conflict onto speakers whom we consider to have less than full command of a threatened language is an easy but ultimately destructive act, one that undermines our best intentions to provide support to the communities concerned.

14.6 Costs and Benefits in Becoming an Object of Study

Branson and Miller (2007: 128), in their discussion of the relationship between linguistics and sign languages, provide a useful summary of the risks to languages in becoming objects of study:

- we find what in Western and academic terms makes sense;
- we state that this is the case, representing the language to others in these terms;
- we are in a dominant power situation—bestowing legitimacy;
- our model of the language is assumed correct because of the apparently scientific nature of the recording process;
- the model is taken on board by those studied as theirs, the authority of the linguist becoming the basis for the evaluation of linguistic correctness;
- rules therefore become established;
- the language becomes formalized;
- the language is fundamentally transformed.

One of the attractive aspects for me of working in the tradition of language description and typology (as opposed to working in a more formalist tradition) is the fact that there is an expectation that we do not know everything there is to know about languages—that there are grammatical categories in language that we have not yet identified and cannot yet explain. In writing a descriptive grammar there is some room for not knowing. Indeed, the empirical method, properly applied, requires that we clearly acknowledge where our data and our analytical tools are inadequate to solve the puzzles we find in describing the language. We are not supposed to be making things up. So too, in working with communities on language retrieval and development projects, it is critical in negotiating ideological positions that we are able to distinguish shared understandings from the views of only one group, the things that are real to everyone from the things that are not. Working relationships are not supported by the imposition of one group's ideological certainties on the others'.

For example, there are clearly systematized ways of marking contrasts in information status in Mali that I can see but that I do not understand. These same patterns of contrast, marked in a variety of ways, also appear in grammars of other languages of the region, described in only minimal terms presumably because the writers of the grammars, like me, do not have the means to express what the languages are able to express.

A less complex example is the contrast in Mali and in some other languages of the region between pragmatically unmarked and pragmatically marked possession by way of additional morphology. This is not an established contrast in linguistic typology, but I was able to identify it in Mali, I can recognize it in other grammars from the region, and, with enough evidence, I could write a paper on the topic and establish the distinction for other grammar writers in the future. The challenge in this case is that the contrast is pragmatically determined; it draws the listener's attention to possessions that are particularly precious or under threat of being stolen and as such it is harder to demonstrate than a paradigmatic contrast across established grammatical categories.

The difficulty that Branson and Miller identify is that if the contrast is not identified—if the filters and lenses of linguistics happen to block it from view—and some other explanation is made, the language may be transformed insofar as speakers of the language (are required to) take the description to heart. In contexts where a grammar and dictionary are prerequisite to language teaching in schools, it is hard to see how such a situation could be avoided. I have no doubt that all of us conflate contrasts we fail to recognize, misread contrasts that we cannot ignore, and generally cast the language to some extent in the image of our own interests and abilities and prejudices. It is no small wonder in the context of these inevitable failings that the speech communities concerned might worry about what we are doing to their languages—we make them into our own (see also Makoni and Pennycook 2007: 7).

There are many outsiders' representations of language, including the views of anthropologists, missionaries, government officials, and workers in NGOs in addition to linguists, and they influence each other as well as potentially influencing the representations available to the language community. Where outsider representations of language are imposed on communities it is clear that power has been exercised over communities by outsiders. All of these views have something to offer, and many of them can contribute constructively to the project of responding to language endangerment. The analytical methods of linguistics are an obvious case in point. They give us meaningful access to archival sources and a heuristic for organizing what we can know about the structure of a language, as well as common ways for talking about these with each other. However, they are not likely to represent the ultimate goal in language development work for the community and hence are likely to be most effective when they are viewed as part of the means to other ends.

Eira (2007) notes that there are serious institutional barriers to transforming our ways of knowing and our uses of the knowledge we co-produce with the communities in which we work. Dealing with these issues is beyond the scope of this chapter (but see Czaykowska-Higgins 2009; Gerdts 2010; Rice 2009 for discussion). I raise them here simply to signal that the project of transforming the way we work means much more than developing effective models of project work. We have to learn new ways of knowing about language so that we can see (most of) what speakers see and can adapt our conceptual tools for their purposes. As Rice (2006) proposes in her description of ethical fieldwork, and as Branson and Miller (2007) also signal, our relationship to this learning (in terms of how we represent it and gain from it) must also be transformed if we are to make any headway in transforming our relationships to the communities we say we serve.

14.7 Conclusion

In this chapter I have proposed a model of language that explicitly identifies the effects of ideologies on our definitions of language and our ability to engage with the concepts we consider to be relevant. We apply filters that remove from view certain aspects of language and disciplinary lenses that predispose us to particular interpretations of what remains. These effects can be seen across the full spectrum of linguistics-related concerns. They influence:

- how languages are organized in relation to each other and in relation to associated dialects;
- how languages are characterized in terms of their typological categories;
- what kinds of descriptions and representations of language we are likely to produce, to consider valid, and the means of developing these;
- who will be considered to be a reliable consultant for a research project; and
- what forms of the language varieties currently spoken are understood to be worthy of study.

We are required to make judgements and decisions about all these issues and we can only make them based on our understandings of language from where we currently stand. In order to make more effective decisions in relation to all these issues, and many others, it is useful to be aware of their ideological correlates and the potential for conflict, and the possibility of negotiation with all parties potentially involved in the area: speech communities, linguists, anthropologists, missionaries, government officials, workers in NGOs, and so on.

Engagement with speakers of endangered languages challenges us on many levels. This chapter has identified ways in which our existing ideologies can act as barriers to deeper, more sophisticated understandings of the language around us and to constructive engagement with communities whose heritage includes an endangered language.

The challenge for us in moving into new ways of encountering language and making sense of what we learn as we work alongside speech communities is to renegotiate these ideological stumbling blocks at various points; in doing this effectively, our current ideologies will be tested repeatedly.

References

Bley, B. 1900. *Woerterbuch der Neu-Pommerschen Sprache (kanakisch-Deutsch)*. Munster: Tumbrink.

Branson, Jan and Don Miller. 2007. Beyond 'language': linguistic imperialism, sign language and linguistic anthropology. In Sinfree Makoni and Alistair Pennycook (eds.), *Disinventing and Reconstituting Languages*. Clevedon: Multilingual Matters.

Collins, James. 1992. Our ideologies and theirs. *Pragmatics* 2: 405–15.

Czaykowska-Higgins, Ewa. 2009. Research models, community engagement, and linguistic fieldwork: reflections on working within Canadian indigenous communities. *Language Documentation and Conservation* 3: 15–50.

Dobrin, Lise. 2008. From linguistic elicitation to eliciting the linguist: lessons in community empowerment from Melanesia. *Language* 842: 300–24.

Dwyer, Arienne M. 2010. Models of successful collaboration. In Lenore A. Grenoble and N. Louanna Furbee (eds.), *Language Documentation: Practice and Values*. Amsterdam: John Benjamins.

Easton, Catherine. 2007. Orthography developments in Papua New Guinea: the interaction of linguistic structures and language attitudes. PhD dissertation, La Trobe University.

Eira, Christina. 2007. Addressing the ground of language endangerment (Victoria, Australia). In Maya Khemlani David, Nicholas Ostler, and Caesar Dealwis (eds.), *Proceedings of the XIth Conference of the Foundation for Endangered Languages, with SKET, University of Malaya, Working Together for Endangered Languages: Research Challenges and Social Impacts. Kuala Lumpur, Malaysia, 26–28 October 2007*. Bath: Foundation for Endangered Languages.

Eira, Christina and Tonya N. Stebbins. 2008. Authenticities and lineages: revisiting concepts of continuity and change in language. *International Journal of the Sociology of Language* 189: 1–30.

Evans, Nicholas. 2001. The last speaker is dead: long live the last speaker! In Paul Newman and Martha Ratliff (eds.), *Linguistic Field Work*. Cambridge: Cambridge University Press.

Fajans, Jane. 1997. *They Make Themselves: Work and Play Among the Baining of Papua New Guinea*. Chicago: University of Chicago Press.

Franchetto, Bruna. 2010. Bridging linguistic research and linguistic documentation: the Kuikuro experience. In José Antonio Flores Farfán and Fernando F. Ramallo (eds.), *New Perspectives on Endangered Languages: Bridging Gaps between Sociolinguistics, Documentation and Language Revitalization*. Amsterdam: John Benjamins.

Gal, Susan and Judith T. Irvine. 1995. The boundaries of languages and disciplines: how ideologies construct difference. *Social Research* 62: 967–1001.

Gerdts, Donna B. 2010. Beyond expertise: the role of the linguist in language revitalization programs. In Lenore A. Grenoble and N. Louanna Furbee (eds.), *Language Documentation: Practice and Values*. Amsterdam: John Benjamins.

Guérin, Valerie and Sébastien Lacrampe. 2010. Trust me, I am a linguist! Building partnership in the field. *Language Documentation and Conservation* 4: 22–33.

Hinton, Leanne. 2010. Language revitalization in North America and the new direction of linguistics. *Transforming Anthropology* 18: 35–41.

Irvine, Judith T. and Susan Gal. 2000. Language ideology and linguistic differentiation. In Paul Kroskrity (ed.), *Regimes of Language: Ideologies, Polities, and Identities*. Santa Fe, NM: School of American Research Press.

La Polla, Randy J. 2001. The role of migration and language contact in the development of the Sino-Tibetan language family. In Alexandra Y. Aikhenvald and R. M. W. Dixon (eds.), *Areal Diffusion and Genetic Inheritance*. Oxford: Oxford University Press.

Laufer, Carl. 1959. P. Futschers Aufzeichnungen über die Butam Sprache (Neubritannien). *Anthropos* 54: 183–212.

McKinnon, Rowan, Jean-Bernard Carillet, and Dean Starnes. 2008. *Papua New Guinea and Solomon Islands* (8th edn.). Footscray: Lonely Planet.

Makoni, Sinfree and Alistair Pennycook. 2007. Disinventing and reconstituting languages. In Sinfree Makoni and Alistair Pennycook (eds.), *Disinventing and Reconstituting Languages*. Clevedon: Multilingual Matters.

Musgrave, Simon and Nicholas Thieberger. 2007. Who pays the piper? In Maya Khemlani David, Nicholas Ostler, and Caesar Dealwis (eds.), *Proceedings of the XIth Conference of the Foundation for Endangered Languages, with SKET, University of Malaya, Working Together for Endangered Languages: Research Challenges and Social Impacts. Kuala Lumpur, Malaysia, 26–28 October 2007*. Bath: Foundation for Endangered Languages.

Parker, Jim and Diane Parker. 1977. Baining grammar essentials. MS. Summer Institute of Linguistics, Ukarumpa.

Rascher, M. 1904. Grundregeln der Bainingsprache. *Mitteilung des Seminars für Orientalishce Sprachen zu Berlin* 7: 31–85.

Rice, Keren. 2006. Ethical issues in linguistic fieldwork: an overview. *Journal of Academic Ethics* 4: 123–55.

Rice, Keren. 2009. Must there be two solitudes? Language activists and linguists working together. In Jon Reyhner and Louise Lockard (eds.), *Indigenous Language Revitalization: Encouragement: Guidance and Lessons Learned*. Flagstaff: Northern Arizona University.

Rice, Keren. 2010. The linguist's responsibilities to the community of speakers: community-based research. In Lenore A. Grenoble and N. Louanna Furbee (eds.), *Language Documentation: Practice and Values*. Amsterdam: John Benjamins.

Rohatynskyj, Marta A. 2000. The enigmatic Baining: the breaking of an ethnographer's heart. In S. R. Jaarsma and M. A. Rohatynskyj (eds.), *Ethnographic Artifacts: Challenges to a Reflexive Anthropology*. Honolulu: University of Hawai'i Press.

Rohatynskyj, Marta A. 2005. On knowing the Baining and other minor ethnic groups of East New Britain. In P. J. Stewart and Andrew Strathern (eds.), *Anthropology and Consultancy: Issues and Debates*. Studies in Applied Anthropology Series). New York and Oxford: Berghahn Books.

Romaine, Suzanne. 1994. *Language in Society: An Introduction to Sociolinguistics*. Oxford: Oxford University Press.

Seely, Jonathan. 1977. An ergative historiography. *Historiographia Linguistica* 4: 191–206.

Speas, Margaret 2009. Someone else's language: on the role of linguists in language revitalization. In Jon Reyhner and Louise Lockard (eds.), *Indigenous Language Revitalization: Guidance and Lessons Learned*. Flagstaff: Northern Arizona University.

Stebbins, Tonya N. 2004. Mali Baining perspectives on language and culture stress. *International Journal of the Sociology of Language (Small Languages and Small Language Communities)* 169: 161–75.

Stebbins, Tonya N. 2009. The Papuan languages of the Eastern Bismarcks: migration, origins and connections. In Bethwyn Evans (ed.), *Discovering History through Language: Papers in Honour of Malcolm Ross*. Canberra: Pacific Linguistics.

Stebbins, Tonya N. 2011. *Mali (Baining) Grammar*. Canberra: Pacific Linguistics.

Stebbins, Tonya N. with the assistance of Julius Tayul. 2009. *Mali (Baining) Texts*. Canberra: Pacific Linguistics.

Stebbins, Tonya N. with the assistance of Julius Tayul. 2012. *Mali (Baining) Dictionary.* Canberra: Pacific Linguistics.

Stebbins, Tonya N. and Mark Planigale. 2009. Explaining the unknowable: accessibility of meaning and the exegesis of Mali Baining songs. *Australian Journal of Linguistics* (special issue on 'The Language of Song') 30: 141–54.

Tayul, Julius and Tonya N. Stebbins (eds.). 2004. *Asek Dechama Mambu Neva Bang: Stories and Songs from the Village*. Melbourne: Planigale Publications.

Warner, Natasha, Quirina Luna, and Lynnika Butler. 2007. Ethics and revitalization of dormant languages: the Mutsun language. *Language Documentation and Conservation* 1: 58–76.

Whaley, Lindsay J. 2011. Some ways to endanger an endangered language project. *Language and Education* 25: 339–48.

Wurm, Stephen A. (ed.). 1975. *New Guinea Area Languages and Language Study*, vol. 1: *Papuan Languages and the New Guinea Linguistic Scene*. Canberra: Pacific Linguistics.

Wurm, Stephen A. (ed.). 1976. *New Guinea Area Languages and Language Study*, vol. 2: *Austronesian Languages*. Canberra: Pacific Linguistics.

Wurm, Stephen A. and Donald C. Laycock. 1961–2. The question of language and dialect in New Guinea. *Oceania* 32: 128–43.

15

Meeting Point: Parameters for the Study of Revival Languages*

VICKI COUZENS & CHRISTINA EIRA

15.1 Introduction

IN ABORIGINAL AUSTRALIA, community-based language and linguistics work is increasingly targeted to language revitalization and revival (see also Austin, this volume). The relative recency of this shift, however, leaves both communities and linguists working without an established foundation from which to understand the goals, processes, and outcomes of this work. The most commonly assumed initial goals or ideals of language revival have been the restoration of the language as at the time of colonization. This is taken by most participants to imply the lexicon and phonology, and by others also the grammatical and semantic structure and/or the cultural meaning and knowledge embedded in the language. It is becoming clear, however, that at many levels, revived languages in present-day use are not going to be the same as their historical counterparts. This is due to a variety of reasons, starting with loss of language from community memory, limitations of historical records, and unprecedented levels of language mixing during the mission period. The languages in the present reflect the means and priorities by which they are reclaimed, and changes—both planned (in particular, lexical elaboration) and unavoidable—in the genres, modes, domains, and conceptual systems of language use in the twenty-first century.

The manner, means, and timeline of the changes involved pose problems for linguistic theory in the recognition and characterization of revival languages. Yet an adequately functioning theoretical basis is necessary for linguists to be able to work with such languages effectively. The many points of lack of fit between learned practice and what is useful and needed in this context brings linguists

* This chapter emerges from research made possible through AIATSIS Grant no. 2008/7366. We would like to express our appreciation to Uncle Sandy Atkinson, Alice Rigney, Jeanie Bell, Paul Paton, and David Tournier for project direction, and to the many people involved in language revival on the ground who contributed their views and experiences to the research through interviews. Sincere thanks are also due to Tonya Stebbins for her patient and thoughtful responses to a series of drafts. Tonya is now working with us in the next phase of this project.

into direct confrontation with the ideological underpinning of the discipline—that is, the systems refined over decades that define and constrain what constitutes a language, an analysis, a valid data source, language change, and so on. On the other hand, language revival communities—like any communities in the process of intensive or extensive language planning—are working on a daily basis with ideologies developed in the context of the work to maintain or reclaim cultural cohesion and continuity, individual and group identity, and authority in their own business.

In this light we can see ideologies per se as not only natural to social and intellectual life, but potentially important and necessary, as they provide frameworks for contextualizing, and thereby guiding, ourselves and our purposes in various key arenas. What is important to understand from this, however, is that it reveals community linguistics work as deeply cross-cultural, requiring as it does a productive understanding and connection between sets of ideologies formed for very different purposes, from within very different social and intellectual heritages. While in the present day we are beginning to achieve far more balance in terms of people working with their own languages, these recent changes have as yet had very little impact on the ideological frameworks that guide the discipline more broadly.

The vision of our current project is, firstly, to develop a framework to describe current revival language practice in a way that is meaningful given the above cross-cultural conditions, and, particularly, is meaningful to people on the ground working with language revival. A model in which only the historical language is valid misses that which a literally descriptive approach could tell us about what is actually happening in these languages. The latter is a vitally important study, as 'the languages now emerging from the historical languages as well as from the culturo-linguistic pathways of the past 150 years or so encode much that is crucially important to understanding both the source and the pathways' (Eira 2010). The understanding of revival languages to be gained by this can then be put to work to assist both communities and linguists to work more effectively—with each other, with what is most needed at a given stage, with expressed and less overt goals, and with what is feasible. Finally, we are hopeful that this endeavour will have significant contributions to make to community linguistics work in other contexts, as the methodology we employed to respect and respond to the views, experiences, and analyses of the communities of use has ripple effects into the heart of linguistics theory and practice.

15.2 Meeting Point

Language revival presents a unique situation for language analysis, in that language is researched, learned, and developed in one single, overarching process. While there are many world situations in which language learning is accompanied by intensive language planning, it is highly unusual for those researching and learning the language to also be developing it and making the language planning decisions at the same time. This means that it is simply not possible to study the languages in any meaningful way without incorporating 'vernacular' approaches as well as 'disciplinary'. The languages are just not available for 'objective' academic study outside of community-internal motivations, processes, and analyses.

For this reason, amongst others, we saw it as crucial to first prioritize the perspectives of Aboriginal people involved in language revival. The degree to which our research was oriented to linguistics questions of description and classification, a rebalancing of the field of *what is possible to know*, in this way was quite simply a requirement for the integrity and ultimate relevance of the research itself.

Our model envisions an expanded epistemology in which 'what there is to know' is *a priori* and paradigm-free. Approaches to science, or knowledge, necessarily develop in contexts of people, culture, and environment in the broadest sense. What we have rather simplistically called 'Western science' is one such epistemology, out of which core linguistics emerges, with a focus on analytical units, systematic patterns, the observable and repeatable, the forms of language and structures in which they appear, and so on. We have labelled another epistemology 'Aboriginal ways of knowing/being/learning/doing', out of which emerge approaches to language as revealed in our interviews, which we discuss further below. Our goals were to more adequately represent Aboriginal community perspectives within academic research, and in this way to make linguistics research more relevant to and useable by Aboriginal people reviving their languages. Our aim is to build a 'meeting-point' epistemology that can do justice to both streams (Figure 15.1).

This emphasis reflects an important principle that Vicki Couzens brings to this project, which she refers to as *wangan ngootyoong* ('respect' in her language, Keerraywoorroong) or *dadirri*, a Ngangikurungkurr concept recently brought into the public arena by Miriam Rose Ungunmerr's essay on deep listening (Ungunmerr n.d.). In Vicki's words:

> My father told me as a young woman in my twenties ... 'sometimes you have to wait, listen to people and let them feel that they own it, you sometimes have to wait' ... Gradually over the years this awareness grew, I learned to listen, to hear people's stories and I learned to wait. The awareness is a living and growing process through which we attain learning and knowledge. This brings responsibility. (Couzens 2009)

The principles encapsulated in Ungunmerr's essay are attracting attention amongst Aboriginal researchers in particular, for their potential in underpinning

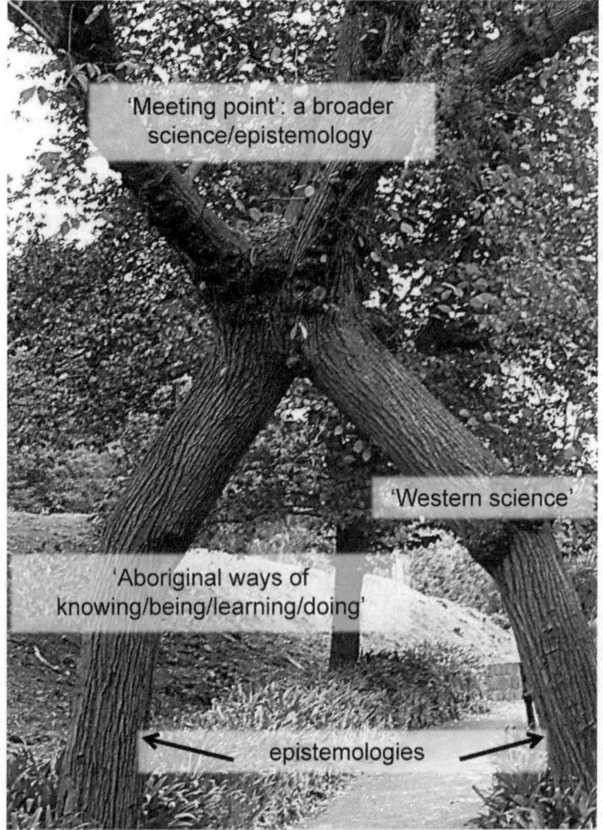

Figure 15.1 Meeting-point epistemology tree. (Photograph courtesy of Tonya Stebbins)

a research methodology seen as more appropriate for working with Aboriginal people and issues. Atkinson (2002) is an early example of an academic reworking of Ungunmerr's ideas. For her, in a context of working with family violence, a *dadirri*-inspired approach assumes:

- the diversity as well as the interconnectedness of Aboriginal communities,
- the principle of reciprocity in research,
- an attempt on the part of researchers to maintain awareness of their own assumptions or biases,
- that learning comes from listening, without judgement or prejudice, and
- that the activity of learning introduces a responsibility to act with integrity and fidelity to what has been learnt.

These principles are highly relevant to our research: we intended that what people told us would inform what, how, and why we were to carry out our analysis of revival languages. Our roles in communities and relationships with the people we interviewed require that what we produce is oriented to their needs at least as much as to those of academic linguistics. In particular, this mandated a model that was both concrete enough to be useable, and flexible enough to accommodate the variation in views and processes that we encountered. In setting up the theoretical foundation for our project, our first priority was to listen to what was meaningful to our interviewees, and respond to what we learned in our research.

15.3 Foundational Themes

To begin building our model, we first obtained over 30 hours of interviews with Aboriginal people involved in language revival, across 13 different language groups and three states. Those interviewed range from young adults through to the most senior elders, who are involved as language workers, teachers, students of language and/or linguistics, participants in language committees, or simply interested community members. We thematized the interviews, drawing out recurring themes to establish initial parameters for our analytical model. Using these themes, we have now developed a model for revival language data analysis, through intensive sampling of selected languages in the throes of language revival. This was an ongoing reflexive process in which initial results feed back into the model itself. This phase also incorporated further insights from relevant subfields of linguistics, including language contact, 'new' and 'mixed' languages, sociolinguistic typologies, and critical applied linguistics.

The 'meeting-point' concept of our project highlights interactions not only between community ideologies and those of linguistics, but also between preservative/restorative goals and modernizing/progressive goals, between oral and written modes, between locating authority for decision-making with elders, linguists, or particular historical sources, and so on.

The question of meeting points arises in relation to specific issues within the themes, with variation in how smoothly the different positions can currently meet. One goal of the larger project, then, is to consider further how to increase a productive mutual understanding at the more troublesome meeting points. For example, we identified 'developing new words' as a relatively smooth meeting point:

Community ways of thinking	*MEETING POINT*	*Linguistics ways of thinking*
Getting inside the 'head space' of how elders or ancestors think.	New words following old patterns.	Identifying principles of word formation in old records (metonymy, shape metaphor, etc.).

There is more difficulty around the smooth meeting of the 'bottom line' of authority in some cases:

Community ways of thinking	*MEETING POINT*	*Linguistics ways of thinking*
Accurate language will fit with what is dreamed/ culturally authorized/ intuitively understood.	Different possible interpretations of sources, and so on, can be authorized/rejected/further modified according to community principles for determining what is correct.	Accurate language is largely determinable through records and comparing language characteristics.

For the purposes of this chapter, we will explore just a few of the themes that emerged prominently from the community interviews. Our task was, firstly, to engage deeply with what people were saying, and secondly, to turn around to linguistics with the new understandings gained and consider what each theme implies for a meaningful linguistic study of revival languages.

15.3.1 Language = Culture

> Cause language is culture, culture is language, language is land, land is language, family: language, family—if you can understand what I am saying, it's that spiral stuff again, one can't live without the other . . . as I keep saying, language is our culture, language is everything, it's a part of one another. (David Tournier)

The understanding that language is inseparable from culture is at some levels familiar in linguistics. However, what emerged from our interviews is that Aboriginal people can assume this at a level that linguistics has not come close to accommodating. Regardless of what might be assumed to be their English language-culture environment and education, many of our interviewees took for granted a broader definition of 'language', responding to our linguistically oriented questions in terms of family, education, understanding of the land, song, and so on. Some articulated this clearly as a deep layering of meaning implied or evoked by each word:

> Their name is not just reflective of what the animal does, it's reflective because the animal is also part of the spirit world. Sometimes the name, you can't really get a handle on the name until you realise that it's a spirit name for the animal. (Bruce Pascoe, in Couzens et al. 2014: 37)

A language word references inward-spiralling layers of meaning. Starting with the form of the word, at the outermost layer, then its semantic meaning, the spirals move through the associated meanings of various senses of the word. For example, in Keerraywoorroong (Vicki's language), the network of words for 'wind' includes *lalarr koorn parrakee* 'north wind, hot wind' and *koorreen* 'south wind, south, mist'. So far we are still within the range of linguistic meaning. Next, we move to daily life knowledge, such as methods for preparing food or medicine, and maintaining the growth of plants for such purposes. Keerraywoorroong *porran porran koola moothang* is a storm which destroys wattle blossoms (*moothang* 'blackwood', *koolang moothang* 'blackwood blossom'), thus indicating when a certain wattle is blooming, with associated seasonal events including the nesting season for swans and a plentiful availability of bream. This level raises all manner of cultural practice questions—who has what roles in gathering eggs or fishing for bream? What tools and techniques are used? Some of this might conventionally be included in an encyclopaedic dictionary, but clearly the scope for cultural learning is broad.

Then there are Dreaming trails and stories linked with specific words. These take us still further, into deeper knowledges including values for relationships, and social and geological history buried in the Dreamings. In Gunnai/Kŭrnai, the Gippsland language, there is a major Dreaming concerning the ancestors Borun and Tuk. *Borun* means 'pelican' and *tuk* means 'musk duck'. In the present, however, use of the word *borun* or *tuk* necessarily evokes this Dreaming, which is often told, appears in art, and features on public signage in the country. This Dreaming holds buried knowledge about history, possibly encoding an ancient journey of one or more groups of people, and the evolving relations between different groups of people and their lands. The still-buried knowledge is part of what people are reclaiming when they reclaim the words *borun* and *tuk*. In the current situation, where loss and reclamation are so strongly in focus, it is possible that these layers of meaning are even more salient in the perception of the words than in the past.

Although in linguistics we are aware that these connections exist, we have not yet come to terms with their centrality to the very processes and goals of reclamation. To reclaim, say, 100 words in an Aboriginal language, is to undertake the work of reclaiming these inward-spiralling layers of meaning for each one. In this light, a crucial function of the form of the word is to signal all that is underneath. This has at least two important ramifications. One is that to reclaim 100 words is a substantial undertaking—countering the linguistics assumption that where only very scanty records of a language have survived, there is little point in attempting language reclamation. A second is that it is possible to carry out a very significant amount of language reclamation without even necessarily knowing the form of the words. Perhaps incomprehensible within linguistics at first, this view becomes recognizable in the context of Saussurean semiology, in which the system of signs is understood primarily as a conceptual system—the signifier being in some ways irrelevant.[1] We will not

[1] Thanks to Nick Nicholas for this observation.

pursue this analogy too far, however, as the *signified* in this epistemology is considerably broader than de Saussure would have recognized—nor do Aboriginal people necessarily agree that the *signifier* is arbitrary.

Both in Standard English and in linguistics terminology, the word 'language' implies linguistic language. However, this does not map onto the meaning of 'translation equivalents' in all language cultures. Heryanto (2007), for example, describes the semantic history of *bahasa*, showing that the contemporary meaning 'language' developed after the introduction of that concept through European colonization. The former meaning in Malay communities was a singular concept incorporating 'religion, culture, manners, norms, speech' (Errington 1974, in Heryanto 2007), and intrinsically bound up with levels of status, integrity, and stature. Similarly, it is clear in our interviews that the concept of 'language' and its reclamation extends deeply into cultural understanding and practice, in a way that goes beyond elements traditionally recognized as 'linguistic':

> When I'm at a conference and here's 70-year-old Unc sitting there and hasn't got no lunch, I just go over and say 'Would you like me to go over and get you some lunch Unc?' He goes 'yes I would daught'. I go get him some lunch and then I go get my lunch. That's what language is. (Lynette Solomon-Dent, in Couzens et al. 2014: 182)

To view and treat these aspects of language as integral to its description will require a shift of methodology, supported by a shift in theoretical frameworks, which entails a shift in ideology within the discipline. It seems to us that such a shift could alleviate the risk of reductionism which a linguistic approach to language revival appears to pose, and thereby open the gates to greater inclusion of linguistics tools and knowledge in community language revival work. It suggests that a parameter of *reclamation of cultural knowledge* as well as linguistic knowledge is required for adequate study of a revival language. If language is really inseparable from culture, then what is being reclaimed is *all* the layers of meaning. Reclamation in this multi-layered sense can mean that the linguistic layers proceed very slowly, and not necessarily as the highest priority. It is conventional in linguistics to assign studies of culture in language to sociolinguistics or other 'satellite' areas of the discipline. What we are arguing is that the stages and types of cultural reclamation must be accounted for within a linguistic description—in order to get a fuller picture of what and how much is actually happening, and to be able to support the process adequately and appropriately.

Lines of investigation that enable us to start incorporating this broader notion of language reclamation into the analysis of language data might include:

- the balance, or points of meeting and tension, between cultural and linguistic priorities and decision-making criteria in the language;

- non-verbal language components evident in or significant to language and cultural expression in the language community;
- ways in which the land of the language and people is reflected in language development and use;
- ways in which the link between language and identity affects decisions and processes as evidenced in language use; and
- ways in which the forms and instantiations of language function as identifiable expressions of identity at the levels of individual, family, community, or other groupings.

15.3.2 Authority and Protocols

> It's not my decision to make, that's the other thing a lot of people don't understand too, is that all aspects of Aboriginal ways of doing things—not only language: education, health, employment, housing—there's all those protocols, the cultural protocols that still exist today. People try to tell us that our culture's gone . . . people don't understand that our culture's been ingrained in us, and always will be and there are certain rules that are there, that have never been spoken to you about, but you know they're there. (David Tournier, in Couzens et al. 2014: 67–8)

It is crucial in both practice and analysis of language revival to account for the effects that protocols and authority have. The primary recognized line of authority may refer to a particular elder or group of elders, one or more ancestors or lines of descent, a trained language worker, teacher, or linguist from the community, a reference group, an internalized sense of 'rightness' or a set of guiding principles. Elders may hold roles of decision-making or at least approval of directions chosen as part of their cultural authority role, independently of their linguistic level of language reclamation.

> I think the most important thing is for us to be true to ourselves and teach our way with our Elders. And whether that's our Elders want us to do a dictionary, or they want us . . . to do these resources, or they want us to just go out there and speak language, then it is for us and our Elders to decide that. (Lynnette Solomon-Dent, in Couzens et al. 2014 182–3)

A small subset of historical sources may be accepted as authoritative—because of familial links with the speakers represented, because of the circumstances and relationships contextualizing the original collection, or as a strategy to make manageable the sea of records and their apparent contradictions. For some, authority is vested in a collaborative process whereby a linguist's interpretation of the archives, together with their knowledge of Aboriginal languages more generally, forms the basis for community-based language planning targeted to present-day purposes.

Any of these choices has immediate ramifications for what forms of language are and are not utilized. They largely determine the acceptable geographical limits of lexical sources, the degree of attention paid to reclaiming grammar, the acceptability of an orthography, and more. Aunty Dot discusses the role of authority in regard to sharing words across what linguistics would conventionally class as dialects:

> I have to get permission ... to use another person's language as part of your language as well. (Aunty Dot Moffat, in Eira and Couzens 2010)

What for linguistics is simply words in a single language is highlighted here, and by many of our interviewees, as an issue for careful negotiation of protocols among different community-defined language groups. This is a clear example of the points at which an exclusively linguistic perspective can miss important explanatory factors defining a language and its use. A linguistic perspective alone does not allow us to make sense of all that happens in language revival. It can also risk characterizing communities as making decisions out of ignorance, rather than seeing and understanding the bases on which those decisions are consciously made.

The location of authority emerges directly from the productive ideologies of the group, as the selection of particular individuals, processes, or sources embodies deep-lying principles of what is important, what is valid, and the accepted lineage of knowledge. This holds for both community and academic perspectives. In Tsimshian (British Columbia) language revitalization for example, an approved genealogy of speakerhood is essential for a given person to be seen as holding language knowledge. Compare this to standard practice within the academy, where it is a requirement to validate research findings in the context of previous research accepted as credible (Eira and Stebbins 2008).

Some sources of authority may even appear quite impractical from the perspective of an academic discourse:

> I might go out bush and yell it out in Dhudhuroa ... listen Ancestors you can hear that? Can you hear that? Am I on the right track? (Tom Kinchela, in Couzens et al. 2014: 206)

It is important to recognize the overlaps and disjunctions between operative lines of authority in one ideological framework (such as that of linguistics) and another as just that—rather than, for example, disregarding factors that nonetheless continue to be highly significant to decisions and language outcomes. It is not essential that a non-Aboriginal linguist personally take on the same lines of authority implied by the quote from Tom Kinchela above. But it is vital to understand in very practical ways their importance in any language development decisions that are made. This could mean, for example, accepting that a feature of grammar evidenced in historical sources but dispreferred by living elders may simply no longer be part of the language. This acceptance will include supporting the alternative new or emergent grammar at all levels.

A final point worth noting is the continuing practice of transmission of authority and responsibility in language to selected, known persons. This has implications for the identity of key people in a language programme, and partly explains the tendency for family groups within a language community to interact with language in ways specific to themselves. Sometimes it may encourage the diversification of varieties within the language, despite the expressed unhappiness of many with this situation. Principles governing the transmission of knowledge at times come into direct conflict with the academic ideology that knowledge is an independent asset, to be preserved for, and made available to, an undefined posterity. This view of knowledge cannot be assumed to be universal, which has direct effects for access to language knowledge.

> The language that you have that you were given, the language that you know, it has to be kept within your families or within your mob. All right. Your words are easy to identify, and different things that meant this and that. But that's only as a common thing spoken. When you go into the deepest language, nope it's not for sale at any price. Cause I've had, um, the linguist come down, and you get, um, botanists and they all want to know what this plant is and what it was used for, and I say Not for sale, sorry, sorry. Not for sale. (Uncle Albert Mullet, in Eira and Couzens 2010)

15.3.3 Authenticity

> And then she said, oh, but the words should be dead. I said, yeah, I know, we got a sliding scale on that. (Uncle Lewis O'Brien, in Eira and Couzens 2010)

Authenticity is a topic currently brought into focus by the accelerating occurrence and heightened awareness of language contact, shift, rapid change, and revitalization, as highlighted in Amery (2001), Austin (this volume), Goodfellow (2003), and Thieberger (2002). It has clear and direct connections with the lines of authority operative in the community, as outlined above. Our interest here lies not so much in engaging with the debates on what constitutes authenticity, as in recognizing that the assessment of authenticity can have different ideological foundations.

Appropriate cultural process is for many a condition of authenticity, so that work done on a linguistically sound basis that is seen as overlooking protocols, key people, or thorough community consultation may be considered suspect, if not ignored, for language reclamation purposes:

> And that may be the correct pronunciation, but my Elders, they've always taught me it's Dhurga so that's what I call it ... And I don't know but my Elders are important to me, what they have taught me is important, and okay I know that the audio and the other sources are important but I certainly don't want to disrespect my living Elders and say you don't know what it is, it is this. (Ursula Brown, in Eira and Couzens 2010)

Definitions of authenticity are closely entwined with attitudes to language change. Very broadly speaking, three general ideological positions can be identified: 'purist', 'middle-of-the-road', and 'focus on now'. It should be understood that these are by no means mutually exclusive in practice.

15.3.4 Purist

Many Aboriginal people entertain a strong desire for an authentic language, defined according to a view of pre-colonization language practices as internally homogeneous and clearly bounded. Some may be hesitant to approve learning and teaching until a comprehensive certainty about grammar, meanings, sounds, and so on can be attained. Loanwords from related languages or English are strongly dispreferred, and clean boundaries around what is and is not a given language are desired. A purist position commonly characterizes the start of the language revival journey, which may then be reviewed and relaxed as part of the process of coming to terms with linguistic realities on the ground, and the status of language records and memories. Linguists may take up a purist position in the sense of viewing what can be reconstructed as the language at the point of colonization as the only, or at least the ideal, goal of language reclamation.

15.3.5 Middle-of-the-Road

Many communities take a compromise view in which the cultural and linguistic basis of the language should be solidly in place as far as possible, but balanced with the priority of using the language, which necessarily entails some compromise to a historically oriented ideal. This view may license, for example, the use of wordlists from a more extensive area than does a purist approach, or may accept that people will at least initially pronounce the language on an English model or on the basis of 'spelling pronunciation'. Many linguists working in this field also take a position in the middle, working towards a more historically evidenced version of the language while also supporting the acceptance and practice of recent and contemporary knowledge.

> I was saying: we need to have people pronounce our language right. And we need to have fluency as a measure to tell us that we're doing okay. And we stuck pretty hard to them, that, you know, these are important features of our language. Well, the experience taught us several different things about these complexities. Firstly, fluency. That people are actually shying away because they weren't fluent. And the insistence on fluency was a hindrance as well as a positive. But what we did find was that we had to give up some of these ideals, but we were very rigorous on, all introductions should be done properly. (Dr Lester-Irabinna Rigney)[2]

[2] Quote sourced from project interview, by permission.

15.3.6 Focus on Now

Other Aboriginal language programmes have a future-oriented approach to language change, which places use of the language and its function for people in daily life at the higher end of the priority scale. This approach promotes the use of what is available at a given stage, encouraging people to speak whatever they can as best they can, assuming that linguistic understandings such as grammatical structures will develop more slowly and cumulatively, and accepting the cross-fertilization of languages that has occurred both for historical contact reasons and as a result of more recent forced relocations, mixing, and separations of peoples. An emerging shift within linguistics is also beginning to allow for better accommodation of this end of the scale, recognizing and validating a difference between more analytical goals of historical reconstruction and more functional goals of reclaimed or recreated languages (Walsh 2005).

> I don't see a problem with today's Wathaurong people saying, no, we haven't got a word for swimming, and we're going to use the one that this mob uses, because we would have heard it anyway. And ... the fact that we don't have that word is a tragedy, but we've got to live, now we have to overcome tragedy as we've always done, we are survivors ... So the way to do it is to say we are going to have a word for swimming, we insist on the right to have a word for swimming, and we're gonna choose this. And that's part of your cultural survival. (Bruce Pascoe, in Couzens et al. 2014: 39)

These three positions, which are intended as broad characterizations only and not as cleanly defined categories, imply different priorities, yardsticks, and criteria for the success of a language reclamation endeavour. They are, in other words, functional, productive ideologies, which provide people with a working foundation for how to proceed in a given phase of reviving their language.

Lines of investigation targeted to authenticity and related issues of authority could include: attitudes to the loss and mixing of the languages resulting from colonization in relation to the language in the present; aspects of language which are the focus of *correctness* for cultural appropriacy purposes; the primary location of authority for the language programme as a whole, for key individuals within it; and the pattern of other sources of authority (for example, a hierarchy of authority, or reference to one authority source for particular questions and a different source for other questions); and, of course, how these patterns of authority can be traced in language outcomes.

15.4 A Model for Analysis

Considering the themes that emerged from our interviews in this way, we are now beginning to work with the following as broad starting parameters for the study of revival languages (Figure 15.2):

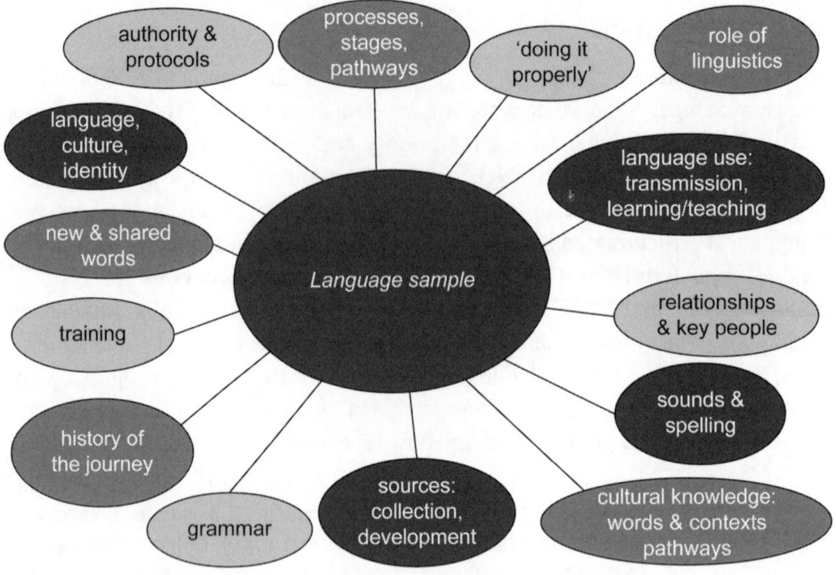

Figure 15.2 Parameters for the study of revival languages.

In order to demonstrate how this model might work, we have selected as a sample for analysis the opening speech Vicki Couzens gave at an initial presentation of the 'meeting-point' model at the Australian Linguistics Society conference in 2009. Our challenge is to incorporate the perspectives and priorities highlighted for us by our interviewees in a study that is also directly linguistic, thereby contributing both to the theoretical understanding of revival languages (and thereby the capacity of human language in general), and to the practical needs of language revival processes.

In considering Vicki's speech, our overarching question is: *What does this sample show about the language for each of the parameters we are considering?* We have selected a number of the parameters proposed in Figure 15.2 for our discussion. (See Eira and Couzens (2010), for a comprehensive description and discussion of all the parameters, including extensive extracts from interviews and possible questions for a descriptive investigation.)

Example 1. Vicki Couzens, Acknowledgment of Country speech

Ngatanwarr	*wooka*	*ngootoowan*	*ngathoongan.*
greet	give	2PL.POSS	1PL.INC

Ngathook	*mayapa*	*wangan*	*ngootyoong*	*wanyoo*
1SG	make	hear/understand	good/healthy	PREP

kulin	*alam meen,*	*koorrookee,*	*ngapoon*	*ba*	*ngarrakeetoong.*
person	ancestor	MM	MF	and	many/family/crowd

Mayapa	*wangan*	*ngootyoong*	*wanyoo*
make	hear/understand	good/healthy	PREP

kulin	*meerreeng*	*makatepa.*
person	country	today

'We greet you all.
I pay respect to the Kulin ancestors
the grandmothers, grandfathers and families.
Pay respect to the Kulin people and Country today.'

15.4.1 New and Shared Words

A range of strategies for lexical development are evident in this speech, including the creation of words, collocations, and phrasal lexemes, and semantic and/or functional extension of existing words.

Ngatanwarr is now commonly used as a greeting. The word is listed in the community dictionary (Krishna-Pillay and Gunditjmara Aboriginal Cooperative 1996) as *ngatanwarr* 'greeting salutation', from Dawson (1881) <gna tanwarr>, and is analysable as *ngata-n-warr* greeting-?HORT-2DU.[3] The word form, then, is not a product of recent language reclamation efforts, but its conventionalization as a greeting probably is, and allows its use generally, obviating the need for alternation of pronominal suffixes.

The collocation *mayapa wangan ngootyoong* is an intentional new construction, comprising [make [hear/understand good/healthy]] 'pay respects'. Vicki particularly liked the word *ngootyoong* when she found the stem *ngooyt* glossed in the dictionary as 'cure', adding layers of meaning to her new phrase.[4] The suffix *-n* is included on *wangan* largely because of the word's attestation in this form in Dawson (1881). Dawson (1881) is Vicki's preferred primary source, due to the confidence inspired by James Dawson and his daughter Sarah (both contributors) having taken time to learn the language themselves, through their extended relationship with key people such as Kaawirn Kuunawarn and Yarruun Parpur Tarneen. The phrase appears in this speech in both declarative and imperative moods, differentiated by the presence or absence of the 1SG pronoun.

In regard to *ngootoowan* 2PL.POSS: no personal pronoun is listed in the dictionary for 2PL, although in Blake (2003) it is *ngutuwar*. As the community dictionary is a primary reference in this community, the use of *ngootoowan* effectively constitutes an instance of meaning extension in the face of limited lexico-grammatical resources.

[3] The morphemic breakdown and verb gloss are from Blake (2003); the glosses for the suffixes are our suggestions.

[4] Word-final palatals are spelt with the 'y' of the digraph first in this orthography.

15.4.2 Cultural Knowledge: Pathways

The first thing to note is that acknowledging country is in itself a reclamation of cultural practice. Samples of the exact words and phrases were used in the past, or the specific components required for such an acknowledgment in this region, is not to our knowledge recorded, so what is reclaimed here appears to be primarily the *genre* of a speech event. Today, the components of an acknowledgment or welcome to country have become fairly standard across community groups, suggesting that either the general principles of what they involve may in fact have been retained despite the loss of passed-down conventional speeches, or that implicit rapid agreement has developed across a broad area as people have heard the speeches of others in recent cultural revival history.

Secondly, the content of the speech clearly invokes a relationship between people, language, and land, bringing this back to the foreground as a crucial consideration for any formal event. Acknowledging ancestors and elders also invokes a particular orientation of respect that differs from the respect conventions of 'mainstream' Australia. The convention now in speeches of this genre is to acknowledge 'Elders, past, present and future'. In Vicki's expression of this general meaning, she specifically highlighted *koorookee* (MM) and *ngapoon* (MF), which additionally reflects the matrilineal outlook of her people.

15.4.3 Authority

It is not uncommon in language revival processes for the main responsibility for the work to fall on the shoulders of a very few. Creators of texts may be working more or less alone, basing their decision-making authority on their right as traditional owners of the language, or in some cases as authorized language workers who refer to an elder or reference group in the broad sense, but not necessarily for a specific text project. Similarly, Vicki will consult with key community members, in particular her father, Uncle Ivan Couzens, but this is a procedure more of protocol than of detailed language construction. For that, she relies primarily on herself in her authority as traditional owner, and on her experience in language work over some years. The importance of Uncle Ivan is both as an icon of the family status in the language community and as the initiator of very significant milestones in the language reclamation process—particularly the development of the community dictionary.

Authority systems are especially crucial when a desired meaning is not simply available to look up in a dictionary. In these cases, Vicki's conceptualization of the process is *dreaming* the words and phrases. By this, she means the interweaving of a wide range of principles, including the construction of words according to semantic and morphological principles—but requiring that their choice and development resonate with her intuitive or spirit sense of what is appropriate at the time. This is *wangan ngootyoong* or *respect* in operation—recognizing that language is not only linguistic but also cultural, actively recognizing the authority of language custodianship. While keenly aware that in a linguistic sense the language is still undergoing development, such as in the use of primarily English grammatical systems in this version of the speech, Vicki is proactive in using the language as it is at a given stage, so long as this level of community and/or intuitive authority is respected.

Secondary to this authority system, the selection of words is constrained by what is available in the dictionary. Then, choices are made from within that, according to criteria such as the specific language identified by a given source (in this case, preferring Keerraywoorroong over related languages also included in the community dictionary), and simple practicalities such as ease of pronunciation.

15.4.4 Sounds

The sounds of words are a particular focus for many people reclaiming their language, as there is a general awareness that the sounds originally differed from those of English, yet the new generations of speaker/learners are L1 English speakers. (It should be noted, however, that some of the phonology and phonotactics of heritage languages are retained in Koorie English.) In addition, elders who are the cultural authority on language have often themselves learned the words of their language from written records, although some have childhood memories of hearing their own elders speak in their language. For these and other reasons, current practice can vary considerably from the linguistic reconstruction of the words from historical sources. Where individuals elect to re-learn the historical phonology, a hierarchy of priority begins to emerge, based on criteria such as salience, ease of pronunciation (from an English base), iconic differentiation from English, and disambiguation (see Reid 2010 for an extended discussion of related issues).

In Vicki's speech on this occasion, she focused on the reclamation of initial /ŋ/ and the dental stop. These are highly salient in terms of position in the word and type of articulation respectively, and draw attention as a learning focus for new speakers. The stop is quite distinct not only from the English alveolar, but also, importantly, from the English dental fricative otherwise implied by the digraph <th> used in this orthography. In contrast, the historical palatal stop was pronounced throughout as English <j>. This shift is common in reclaimed languages of the south-east, although speaker/learners may be aware of its earlier articulation. Vicki suggests here that economy of effort is an important, though not always conscious, principle of language reclamation. As the easier (for L1 English speakers) articulation triggers no disambiguation issues and no ripple effects in the phonological system, there is no practical need to focus on the earlier articulation in this case.

Rhotics in south-eastern Australia are typically problematic for reconstruction, so they tend to all be pronounced as either an Australian English approximant or a trill. In this speech, Vicki selected the latter, which then became an indication of 'a non-English sound'. She left the final /r/ of *ngatanwarr* unarticulated, probably by analogy with vowel-final Australian English pronunciation of orthographically <r>-final words.

A commonly held community view is that it is not possible to really know how the words were once pronounced. In regard to vowels, at phonetic level in fluent discourse, a realistic linguistic evaluation would probably have to concur with this. Vowels today can be highly variable, responding partly to word- and sentence-level stress and English models. In Vicki's speech, the short vowels generally approximated the historical [a, u, i], with a tendency to raise and lengthen the long vowels (orthographic <ee> and <oo>) at the ends of words.

In line with the principle noted above of *redreaming* language, Vicki also talks about the need to listen to the land for the sounds to use in the language. As an illustration or example, she points out how the wind is the same everywhere, but sounds different in a particular landscape because of the trees, or hills, or water there. This correlates well with the approach of some to *sing* their hearing of the land, whether or not they also have language to sing with. It also engenders significant interest in onomatopoeic words, such as the names of some birds.

15.4.5 Stages and Pathways

On a linguistic level, Vicki intends that there will be changes to the speech and its variants as the language develops. She is particularly interested in researching word order, and more intensive implementation of suffixes. Although a sketch grammar is available in Blake (2003), only at language programme or authorized speaker/learner level is it feasible to review and implement this and other possible inputs, at word level, for each required context. There is also the question of grammatical 'gaps' in the records, and Vicki is looking at ways to fill these, at the same time developing principles of validation for such *redreamed* grammar.

There are elements in the current speech that Vicki is uncertain of at this stage, such as the use and meaning of *wanyoo*. This highlights an important principle of language reclamation—to use the best available at a given time, always keeping in mind that it may be advanced to a new stage later. Without this principle, language reclamation would rapidly come to a standstill in many places, as the status of historical records and current understanding entails that both community and linguistics knowledge are a work in progress.

> I just teach 'em and it might be based along English way ... because that's how they're trying to fit it in, into their English structure. If you don't do it along that line that they're comfortable with, if I try to do it in the proper Aboriginal grammatical way then they're just all mixed up. So we just wanna get 'em talkin'.
>
> And all of that will come eventually. Like this is the proper way that you actually put those things, and this is the marker that you add to it ... But we never go there until they're really comfortable. (Lynette Solomon-Dent, in Couzens et al. 2014: 171)

The window provided into present-day Keerraywoorroong by this one sample reveals characteristics that are strongly conditioned by the particular pathway of language revival taken by the Gunditjmara language programme so far. In the first place, certain pathways were motivated by the very low levels of language knowledge active in the community when the programme started. Archival rather than contemporary sources were prioritized, triggering in turn the centrality of writing and orthography, and a dictionary as the main linguistic source for building language. Secondly, linguistic analysis of the sources was outsourced to a linguist, which is a common but not inevitable choice. This is then reflected in orthographic choices and the component elements assumed for the dictionary. The community target audience and consultation is apparent primarily in the plain language of the dictionary, the choice of illustrations, and a Foreword by Uncle Ivan Couzens.

Emerging standards for speeches and other relatively fixed texts undoubtedly reflect the very small number of people actively involved in language development to date, as well as the prevalence of one family in that number. This may shift in future as more people and organizations take on a more active role. One possibility on the table is differentiated language development, for some aspects of language, for different culturo-linguistic groups within the region.

15.5 Conclusions: Ideology and Linguistic Analysis

Through this examination of one text for one language, it becomes apparent that a wide comparison of language samples and languages could readily allow identification of basic pathways, stages, patterns of lexical development, priorities for cultural reclamation, relationships between oral and written language, and so on. We see it as intrinsic to each point of the analysis to account for the many aspects of language traditionally put aside as 'extra-linguistic'. These are predominantly the aspects of language that people talked about in our 30+ hours of interviews, and they are integral to the language forms appearing in current language data. Many of these factors are tied firmly to prevailing ideologies, whether intentionally and fluidly designed for the purpose, or inherited as part of the legacy of being a colonized people reclaiming culture, identity, and language.

Perhaps one of the most important overall points to emerge from the study of Vicki's speech is that every aspect of her speech is motivated. A view from a conventional linguistics perspective might assume that the historical grammar and phonology are the goal, leaving anything outside of this as understandable only in terms of lack of knowledge or experience in the language. This view is specific to one ideology, with an authority system that privileges analysis of recorded language forms, on the basis of previous analysis of language data in the same broad language family. We have shown, however, that there are many factors consciously involved in the design of this particular speech, which are based in quite different ideologies—including different lines of authority, the importance of relationships both past and present, and of certain cultural meanings. To make sense of this piece of language data within linguistics, then, requires a much broader view of what is involved in linguistic analysis. It requires a deep listening at discipline level, to hear what other ideologies are important and relevant to our understanding.

It is our hope that this research will ultimately have multiple benefits in several directions. A thorough description of 'what revival languages are like' will allow both linguists and communities to work with such languages more effectively. If we know what kinds of elements are more readily 're-learnable', or more readily combined, for example, we can promote these elements or combinations as early language revival targets. If we know the likely linguistic corollaries of particular language revival pathways, then we know how to vary recommendations for priorities for different language revival situations. An analysis of contemporary use of revival languages will also have the effect of validating the languages as they are and as they are being developed. But in our view these sorts of goals are only really possible by recognizing the ideologies that inform a linguistic approach as well as those underlying community views and practices, and finding ways to open out linguistic ideologies to accommodate those of community language revival at the core of our methodologies. It is this that will enable greater understanding of less visible or less directly linguistic parameters, such as cultural reclamation or stages of language revival, and how they function to shape the actual language forms produced. In our view, it is this *wangan ngootyoong*-informed methodology—the practice of engaging respectfully with diverse ideologies—that gives us the tools to develop broader epistemologies, intertwining the best of Western scientific traditions with current and reclaimed Aboriginal approaches to knowledge and research.

References

Amery, Rob. 2001. The right to modernize. Paper presented at the Indigenous Languages Panel, Australian Federation of Modern Languages Teachers Associations, Canberra.

Atkinson, Judy. 2002. *Trauma Trails—Recreating Song Lines: The Transgenerational Effects of Trauma in Indigenous Australia*. North Melbourne: Spinifex Press.

Blake, Barry. 2003. *The Warrnambool Language*. Research School of Pacific and Asian Studies, ANU. Canberra: Pacific Linguistics.

Couzens, Vicki. 2009. *Meerta Peeneeyt, Yana Peeneeyt, Tanam Peeneeyt*. (Stand strong, walk strong, proud flesh strong). Unpublished Masters thesis, Royal Melbourne Institute of Technology.

Couzens, Vicki, Christina Eira, and Tonya Stebbins. 2014. *Tyama-teeyt Yookapa: Interviews from the Meeting Point Project*. Melbourne: VACL.

Dawson, James. 1881. *Australian Aborigines: The Language and Customs of Several Tribes of Aborigines in the Western District of Victoria, Australia*. Melbourne, Sydney, and Adelaide: George Robertson.

Eira, Christina. 2010. Languages of revival: understanding a new type of Aboriginal language. *Ngoonjook* 35: 74–83.

Eira, Christina and Vicki Couzens. 2010. Meeting point: setting up a typology of revival languages in Australia. Unpublished report. <http://www.vaclang.org.au/projects/meeting-point-language-revival-typology-project.html> (accessed 11 April 2014).

Eira, Christina and Tonya N. Stebbins. 2008. Authenticities and lineages: revisiting concepts of continuity and change in language. *International Journal for the Sociology of Language* 189: 1–30.

Goodfellow, Anne. 2003. The development of 'new' languages in Native American communities. *American Indian Culture and Research Journal* 27: 41–59.

Heryanto, Ariel. 2007. Then there were languages: Bahasa Indonesia was one among many. In Sinfree Makoni and Alastair Pennycook (eds.), *Disinventing and Reconstituting Languages*. Clevedon: Multilingual Matters

Krishna-Pillay, Sharnthi and Gunditjmara Aboriginal Cooperative (eds.). 1996. *A Dictionary of Keerraywoorroong and Related Dialects*. Warrnambool, Australia: Gunditjmara Aboriginal Cooperative.

Reid, Nicholas. 2010. English influence on the pronunciation of re-awakened Aboriginal languages. In John Hobson, Kevin Lowe, Susan Poetsch, and Michael Walsh (eds.), *Re-awakening Languages: Theory and Practice in the Revitalisation of Australia's Indigenous Languages*. Sydney: Sydney University Press.

Thieberger, Nicholas. 2002. Extinction in whose terms? Which parts of a language constitute a target for language maintenance programmes? In David Bradley and Maya Bradley (eds.), *Language Endangerment and Language Maintenance*. London: RoutledgeCurzon.

Ungunmerr-Baumann, Miriam-Rose. n.d. *Dadirri: A Reflection*. <http://www.liturgy planning.com.au/documents/main.php?g2_view=core.DownloadItemandg2_itemId=4696> (accessed 11 April 2014).

Walsh, Michael. 2005. Will indigenous languages survive? *Annual Review of Anthropology* 34: 293–315.

Part 3

From Local to International: Interdisciplinary and International Views

16

Conflicting Goals, Ideologies, and Beliefs in the Field*

LENORE A. GRENOBLE & SIMONE S. WHITECLOUD

16.1 Introduction: Conflicting Goals, Ideologies, and Beliefs

FOR LINGUISTS WORKING with endangered language communities, language documentation is of the utmost priority. Where speakers of a language consist of only a very small number of elderly speakers, documentation is viewed as urgent; it is seen as the activity that warrants the bulk of our time and energy. Linguistic analysis is critical, or one runs the danger of not understanding the documented language and may miss crucial parts of the language: there is no way to evaluate if a documentation is 'complete' or 'thorough' unless one has a good grasp of the linguistic system as a whole. Our work as linguists rests on our training as Western scientists, which requires us to be objective and detached from our object of study. The current model of linguistic analysis assumes that languages can be studied in isolation from a host of environmental, social, and political issues, and that it is the linguist's job to conduct such an analysis. At the same time, our commitment to ethical research requires that we work collaboratively with the communities where the endangered language is (or was) spoken. Many linguists find it nearly impossible to live within a community long enough to build the ties required for a deep documentation while maintaining detachment. In many cases it is difficult, if not impossible, to gain the trust of community members without first becoming personal friends. Investment in the community is required to succeed but it is not just a ticket to success, it is what most field linguists want. Our speakers are our friends and often adopt us into their families.

However, the basic priority of documentation for linguists is often fundamentally at odds with those of many speaker communities, who place a premium on language revitalization, language instruction, and the development of pedagogical materials and methods. There is an increasing desire among

* Research on this project was funded by the National Science Foundation, IGERT 0801490 and BCS-105649, the Institute of Arctic Studies at Dartmouth College, and the Humanities Division of the University of Chicago. We are grateful for their support. We would like to thank the many people in Greenland who worked with us on this project. The views expressed here are our own.

communities to have linguists work on community-driven projects in lieu of documentation and analysis. When speakers are few, it is argued that their time should be spent teaching others the language rather than in documentation efforts. Moreover, community leaders are often activists and see the need for external linguists to join them in this activism, which is fundamentally at odds with the neutrality required of Western scientists. At times the expectations of community members are unrealistic: few linguists are positioned or trained to be effective language teachers or activists, for example. In many communities language documentation is not even a goal, much less the primary objective of language projects. Instead, many communities find that the revitalization process is an important part of community building and healing; that the collaborative effort of building language programmes unites people where other projects have failed. This may be due to the fact that revitalization tends to be a community-driven project, but also surely because a language requires speakers and a community in order to thrive.

One of the most discussed aspects of ethical research in recent years is the notion of collaborative research models that include community members. This represents a radical shift from previous linguistic and ethnographic work, in which an external researcher visited the community for some period of time, and then left. This model has become so outdated as to be nearly abandoned, although it may be persistent in more instances than we would feel comfortable admitting.[1]

In this chapter we consider just one aspect of this complicated issue, the differing perspectives between Western scientists and community members on what counts as science, what counts as data, and what kind of analyses should be done. Our thinking on this topic is shaped and influenced by our experiences working in the Arctic and circumpolar regions, in areas referred to as the 'Far North' in Russia. Our thoughts here reflect conversations with Northern and Arctic peoples, in the field, in conferences and workshops, and around the dinner table. We bring to this discussion our own different backgrounds and training: Grenoble is a linguist, and has been working with indigenous communities in Siberia and the Arctic since the mid-1990s. Whitecloud is an ecological and evolutionary biologist, a member of the Lac du Flambeau Anishinaabeg tribe, and is trained in the use of medicinal plants by her uncle. We have been working collaboratively since 2010 to study the uses of Arctic plants in the Circumpolar Arctic, primarily in Greenland. Our collective approach to research has been

[1] This issue is noted by Nadasdy (1999: 3) in his discussion of the politics of traditional ecological knowledge (TEK): 'On one occasion a biologist told me outright that the only value she sees in consulting with native elders is that she must do so in order to secure community support for her projects, which in the current political climate is now required.' Although this quote, and this attitude, are now outdated, we wonder how often it still holds.

shaped by the differences and commonalities in our backgrounds, and by multiple conversations with one another and with Arctic peoples.

Just as research in the natural and social sciences in the Arctic today strives to incorporate TEK (traditional ecological knowledge) into its findings, the topic of differing goals and priorities for linguists and language activists has received considerable attention in the last few years. We centre our discussion on differences in ideologies between Western science on the one hand, and TEK on the other, focusing on the perspective of linguistic research. Ongoing work has expanded the notion of TEK to encompass what is alternatively called traditional, indigenous, or local knowledge: knowledge of local community members (see section 16.2.2). This knowledge is acquired through experience and collective practices, usually stemming from traditional practices and lifestyles. It is often valorized to the point of being romanticized as more basic, truer to indigenous experience and roots, and as being anchored in indigenous systems of beliefs. We argue that Western science, and thus Western linguistics, brings with it a host of challenges, and we illustrate some of these with a discussion of how these differences have shaped our collaborations in Greenland (see section 16.3).

Our own research in Greenland into so-called traditional uses of plants has challenged this conceptualization of local knowledge at its very core, questioning the extent to which it is anchored in traditional beliefs and practices, and questioning the assumptions of external researchers like ourselves that such traditions are held at a premium by local practitioners.

16.2 Differences in Approaches

The differences in ideologies go even deeper than the differences in goals outlined in section 16.1. Rather, they extend to the very heart of the enterprise of research and knowledge. There is increasing pressure, from Arctic communities and from funding agencies, for researchers to take local knowledge and values into account. For external linguists, this often translates into collaborative research, with pedagogical projects as side projects, in addition to documentation. The hard sciences (biology, geology, engineering, and so on) have recently begun to value and incorporate indigenous knowledge into their research. In Arctic research as a whole, there is an ever-increasing pressure to consider local knowledge systems. These knowledge systems are sometimes referred to as TEK, but this label erroneously implies both that they are traditional (in the sense of antiquated as opposed to modern) and that they involve only biological ecologies. Other groups use the term *indigenous knowledge* but, as we argue in sections 16.2.2 and 16.3, the knowledge under consideration is not always, strictly speaking, 'indigenous'. For that reason, many reject all these labels, and refer to this knowledge as local knowledge (which encompasses TEK, traditional, and indigenous knowledge), a practice we follow here. The question of how local knowledge should be integrated into Western science is of central concern in the Arctic today, where climate change threatens subsistence lifestyles and the knowledge therein.

16.2.1 Western Science

Scientific enquiry is central to Western conceptions of all kinds of knowledge, and is fundamental to Western society. Froude (1890: 595–6) argues that 'neither history, nor any other knowledge, could be obtained except by scientific methods'.

In its broadest sense, the English word 'science' can be used to refer to any systematic knowledge, but it is currently associated not only with knowledge, but also with method. The scientific method rests on the core principle that scientific hypotheses that are invoked to explain phenomena are supported (or disproved) by data collected through studies that can be replicated by others. Western science is empirical, data-driven, and its conclusions are both testable and replicable. This ideology is so fundamental to Western culture that basic dictionary definitions include hypothesis testing rather than solely systematic knowledge: 'Principles and procedures for the systematic pursuit of knowledge involving the recognition and formulation of a problem, the collection of data through observation and experiment, and the formulation and testing of hypotheses' (*Merriam Webster*); or 'a method or procedure that has characterized natural science since the seventeenth century, consisting in systematic observation, measurement, and experiment, and the formulation, testing, and modification of hypotheses' (*Oxford English Dictionary*). One of the key differences between Western scientific knowledge and local knowledge is the principle of measurements and testing that that science entails. This is in direct contrast to many indigenous knowledge systems, which include experience and culture as a means of defining what is known.

16.2.2 Local Knowledge

Local knowledge or its subset, TEK, are driving forces in discourse of the North and the so-called 'human dimensions' of the Arctic and the Arctic response to climate change. Such knowledge, as defined by the Convention on Biological Diversity, Article 8 (j), is developed over centuries through experience and is part and parcel of local culture and environment.

As defined by the Convention on Biological Diversity, Article 8 (j):[2]

> Traditional knowledge refers to the knowledge, innovations and practices of indigenous and local communities around the world. Developed from experience gained over the centuries and adapted to the local culture and environment, traditional knowledge is transmitted orally from generation to generation. It tends to be collectively owned and takes the form of stories, songs, folklore, proverbs, cultural values, beliefs, rituals, community laws, local language, and agricultural practices, including the development of plant species and animal breeds. Traditional knowledge is mainly of a practical nature, particularly in such fields as agriculture, fisheries, health, horticulture, and forestry.

Local knowledge thus differs radically from scientific knowledge. The former is collectively owned and includes not only the names of plants and animals but also cultural values, rituals and belief systems, community laws, local language, and agricultural practices. Such knowledge is transmitted orally from generation to generation and thus it is viewed as community, not individual, intellectual property. Western scientific knowledge can be copyrighted, whereas the notion of intellectual property is unknown in many communities outside of the Americas and Europe. Since traditional knowledge includes beliefs, values, and practices, traditional knowledge is not recognized as knowledge per se by all who study it; it falls outside of the purview of the basic tenets of (Western) scientific methodologies, which require that results be testable and replicable. (See in particular Nadasdy (1999) for the politics and difficulties of integrating Western science and indigenous approaches to knowledge.) Beliefs, cultural practices, and the like have no place in Western views of science; if anything, they are considered to be an impediment to scientific enquiry, which is supposed to be detached from belief systems and values.

Bringing Western science and local knowledge together has become a critical issue for many Arctic Indigenous leaders. The IPY (International Polar Year) 2012 Conference in Montreal, the last in a series of conferences to consider the research and impact of the IPY (2007–8), hosted daily sessions on Indigenous Knowledge Exchange.[3] One example is Inuit Qaujisarvingat: The Inuit Knowledge Centre, established in Ottawa, Canada, at the Inuit Tapiriit Kanatami headquarters. Inuit Qaujisarvingat was established 'to bridge the gap between Inuit knowledge and western science and build capacity among Inuit to respond to global interests in Arctic issues' (http://www.inuitknowledge.ca/), a goal that has become increasingly urgent due to rapid climate change in Arctic regions.

[2] See <http://www.ser.org/iprn/tek.asp>.

[3] In fact, there was a designated programme committee chair to focus on indigenous knowledge (Nancy Karetak-Lindell, Director of the Jane Glassco Arctic Fellowship Program, Walter and Duncan Gordon Foundation). An indication of how important this topic is for Polar Science is at <http://www.ipy2012montreal.ca> (accessed 1 October 2013).

The Inuit perspective is articulated by Martin Lougheed in an interview reported in *National Geographic News* (Braun 2011):

> Inuit perspective and knowledge are key to understanding things like the changes in sea ice, where modern-day researchers use tools to measure what the Inuit see and know already. It's the understanding of the changes—the weather, the water, the sun—that are key players in the inter-workings of these different systems that are not as well understood in the outside world. That form of knowledge needs to be incorporated alongside measurements, alongside probing with tools, so that the full extent of knowledge is available to people who want to know it.

Lougheed speaks here with specific reference to climate change, but his statement can be expanded to a fuller understanding of the environment. In this view, local knowledge does not replace Western science but the two supplement each other, providing outlooks and data that are not available to the one without the other. Not only do they enrich one another, but neither alone can provide a complete picture of the physical environment.

16.2.3 Linguistics, Science, and Knowledge

For linguists, linguistics is the scientific study of language, and thus is founded on the core principles of (Western) scientific enquiry: language is seen as an object of study, language data are extracted from context of usage, and linguistic experiments are replicable. In contrast, speaker communities often view language as an integral part of human society that cannot be separated from the speakers themselves. They may interpret the tendency of linguists to objectify language as objectifying the people, or at least to be uncaring about the people themselves. As Berardo and Yamamoto (2007: 112) note, the tradition of linguistic description has its own culture and values, which do not necessarily intersect with those of local communities: 'the linguist does impose a linguistic approach to language description, which has been developed outside the values, attitudes, beliefs, assumptions, and traditions of the local culture'.

One commonly held belief is that knowledge and language are inseparable: that there is a need to protect and document local languages centres in the belief that knowledge will be lost if the languages are lost. In part these assumptions stem from a belief that such knowledge is not translatable, and in part from recognition that the knowledge encoded in local languages is often not retained as communities transition to a dominant culture, because the dominant language does not encode the said knowledge, According to the Biodiversity Indicators Partnership:[4]

[4] See <http://www.bipindicators.net/indicators/traditionalknowledgepractices/linguisticdiversity.2010> (accessed 1 October 2013).

> There is a fundamental linkage between language and traditional knowledge related to biodiversity. As languages go extinct, there is an irrecoverable loss of unique cultural, historical and ecological knowledge. Local and indigenous communities have elaborated complex classification systems for the natural world, reflecting a deep understanding of local flora, fauna, ecological relations and ecosystem dynamics. This traditional ecological knowledge is both expressed and transmitted through the local or indigenous language. When young people no longer learn the language of their ancestors, special knowledge is often lost, as it is not transferred into the dominant language that replaces it . . . Information on status and trends of numbers of speakers of indigenous languages may therefore be used as a proxy for measuring trends in the status of traditional knowledge, innovations and practices.

This suggests that the transfer of local knowledge and language are intimately connected. The Convention on Biological Diversity includes the local language as a component of traditional (local) knowledge. It explicitly recognizes the value of TEK and makes a serious attempt to integrate it into any models for protecting biodiversity. Moreover, the Convention recognizes the intimate connections for people between biological environment, sociocultural environment, and language. For indigenous peoples, these are all deeply intertwined. This points to two major discrepancies between Western linguists and indigenous groups.

First is the disjuncture between knowledge attained by scientific method and that gained by local knowledge. This gap is most frequently discussed with regard to biological and ecological knowledge. Western science relies on measurements and recorded, quantifiable data; findings should be replicable and are viewed as presenting 'facts'. Traditional knowledge is experientially based and relies on direct observation, meaning that it is not quantifiable and is not replicable. Davis and Wagner (2003) provide a useful critique of the challenges in identifying local experts. In linguistics, this tension is exemplified in the difference between etymologies attained through the methods of historical reconstruction and through folk etymologies. Historical linguistics relies on careful reconstruction through the comparative method; folk etymologies tend to be based on synchronic surface forms without an understanding of the history of these forms. For example, speakers assume that the word 'housewife' derives historically from the compound 'house' + 'wife', but this etymology is incorrect: Old English *hūs-wīf* (literally 'house wife') would not have resulted in the Modern English 'housewife' but rather 'hussy'. An oft-repeated false etymology is that the English phrase 'rule of thumb' comes from an English law which permitted men to beat their wives with sticks no thicker than their thumbs. In fact, no such law existed (although wife beating was sanctioned by common law).[5] Concrete examples such as these make linguists sceptical about the value of relying on local knowledge of the origins of words.

[5] For a discussion of the possible origin of this widespread false etymology, see Freyd and Johnson (1998). The *Oxford English Dictionary* cites the first attestation of the phrase 'rule of thumb' as 1685

Second, and even more fundamental, is the methodology of Western linguists, which extracts language from its context of usage, abstracting from spoken forms to create idealized forms and rules. Many of these idealized forms are in fact theoretical constructs (such as abstract phonemes or underlying morphemes) that are never realized on the surface in these abstract forms. In other cases, such extraction from the context can mean that we do not record or know how to use certain structures, words, or phrases felicitously in conversation. For example, work by linguists on Arctic languages, such as reference grammars of Kalaallisut (Bjørnum 2003; Fortescue 1984; Sadock 2003) or of Evenki (Bulatova and Grenoble 1999; Konstantinova 1964) provide theoretical discussions of polysynthesis or agglutination, descriptions of cases and tense-aspect systems, and grammatical paradigms, but do not provide any information about how to conduct a conversation in the language. The idea behind such approaches to linguistic description is that, in the ideal, a reference grammar provides all sufficient and necessary information to understand the structure of the language, to generate and to analyse sentences in the language. Yet they have little to say about the necessary components of communicative competence. They describe what is grammatical without describing what is necessarily felicitous in any particular context.

In stark contrast, at least in many of the Arctic communities where we work, language cannot be abstracted from its context of usage. Brower (2008) and Simon (2008), Inuit leaders from Alaska and Canada respectively, make compelling statements about the centrality of language to knowledge. This is part of the overarching claim that language and identity are inherently linked. Although most, if not all, linguists would agree with this, they are hard put to define exactly how they are linked because they are constrained by the requirements of the (Western) scientific method. The ties between language and identity are neither measurable nor testable in the way that syntactic structures are, or the way that the links between syntax and lexicon are. But in the Inuit view, such things cannot be separated from one another in this way. Taken at face value, this represents a fundamental difference between many approaches by Western-trained scientists to local knowledge systems. They try to use local knowledge to inform science. For example, Si (2011) makes the argument for studying ethnobiology and indigenous knowledge of local ecosystems by pointing to the kinds of information that local communities have about different species, including breeding, migration, and feeding habits. Inuit hunters and fishermen can help track changes in fish and sea mammals, not only in terms of changes in migration but also changes in body fat and fur that add to our understanding of climate change. Still, this additive approach to knowledge, with one informing

in James Durham's *Heaven upon Earth*, but provides no etymology for the phrase, just for the individual words. For a related discussion of Greenlandic etymology, see section 16.3.

the other, differs from the Inuit view in which different kinds of knowledge are inseparable and can only be taken together as a whole. And critically, language is an integral component in that system.

Greenland is unique in the Circumpolar Arctic in terms of language vitality. The number of native speakers of Kalaallisut is growing, and children learn the language as their first language. The Greenlandic people have long recognized language as integral to identity, and made language policy a key issue during Home Rule (1979–2009). Subsequently, beginning with the institution of self-government in June 2009, language policies have been reinforced. As a result, 88 per cent of the population today speaks Kalaallisut. The language enjoys high prestige, and there is pressure from both the government and the people to strengthen its position in society. But, we argue, it provides a counterexample to common beliefs that knowledge will be preserved if language is preserved. In Greenland, there is a practical approach to knowledge: people want to know what they need to know. This is not to suggest a lack of curiosity but rather the opposite, an expanded sense of inquisitiveness that prioritizes knowledge for its own sake and for utilitarian purposes, regardless of the source.

16.4 Case Study: Reconstructing Plant Knowledge in Greenland

Beginning in the summer of 2010 we began preliminary research on the uses of plants in Greenland, and then conducted fieldwork in two locations in southern Greenland (Qassiarsuk and Nanortalik) in August 2011. Kalaallisut, or West Greenlandic, is the official language of Greenland and is robustly spoken. Children learn the language as a first language and the number of native speakers has shown a steady increase over the last few decades. Although the overall total number of speakers is not large by some standards (an estimated 88 per cent of Greenland's population of 56,749; Statistics Greenland 2011), it is large in comparison to other Arctic indigenous languages. As the official language of Greenland, it enjoys higher legal authority than any other Arctic indigenous language, and is the prestige language in Greenland.

We are interested in all aspects of plant usage (medicinal, food, decorative, and utilitarian purposes), preparation, and collection, as well as indigenous taxonomy, and linguistic documentation of all these aspects (including a linguistic analysis of the plant names and their etymologies, and a linguistic documentation of their uses, histories, legends, and so on). Thus we began by researching what is currently known about plant usage in Greenland. Publications, and especially guidebooks, for plant use in Greenland are sparse to non-existent. At most, plants are associated with food and uses can be found in cookbooks. Greenlanders tend to assume that all knowledge of medicinal uses has been lost. Elsewhere in the Arctic there are texts available that describe plant uses. *Walking with Aalasi* (Ziegler et al. 2009) records plant uses according to elder Aalasi Joamie in English and Inuktitut. *Nauriat Niginaqtuat* ('Plants That We Eat') (Jones 1983) is a book in English with Iñupiaq plant names documenting Inupiat uses. One scientific guide to the plants of Alaska by Hultén (1968) contains plant uses and references the peoples to whom they originate. Viereck (1987) is an extensive guide to Alaskan plants, their medicinal uses, and constituents. The fact that it was already in its tenth printing speaks to the demand for such guides. Notably, it is entirely in English, except for the Latin names of the plants, and draws on a wide range of sources, including those of native Alaskans and early settlers (understood to be non-native). Even ancient uses of Sami plants have been documented (Bergman et al. 2004), drawing on a large body of literature on their uses.

Our own research began with published (Western) scientific accounts, such as Porsild (1953) and anthropological and ethnographic accounts (e.g. Petersen 2010). Unlike many other indigenous communities, Greenlanders have a field guide to plants, *Nunatta Naasui* ('Greenland's plants', Danish title *Grønlands flora i farver*), by Foersom et al. (1997). This is a bilingual guide, in Kalaallisut and Danish. Each plant entry is complete with an illustration, the common name in Danish and Kalaallisut, the Latin scientific name, the location of the plant on a map of Greenland, and a brief entry in Kalaallisut and Danish describing the plants. These entries are in keeping with a Western field guide to flora or fauna, such as an Audubon guide, with purely descriptive information about the plants, and no information about uses. A typical entry is given here in English translation, the entry for a well-known plant, the crowberry:

> **Paarnaqutit** 5–25 cm
> **Fjeld revling** *Empetrum nigrum ssp. hermaphroditum*
>
> The plant is most common in the southern coastal heaths, often in wind-exposed areas with little snow cover. It is also found in most other plant communities except the wettest, in the north and inland, most generally in moist soil. Wintergreen dwarf shrub with very small flowers, seen in early spring. These favourite 'crowberries' are stone fruits.
>
> (Foersom et al. 1997: 68)

This kind of 'scientific' information is readily available to Greenlanders, but published information (in Kalaallisut or Danish) about how to use plants is found in cookbooks, such as Olsen (2001), which provides recipes and some discussion of historical uses, or Larsen and Oldenburg (2000), a trilingual volume (in Kalaallisut, Danish, and English) that also includes ethnographic and cultural information about food in southern Greenland for the last 1,000 years. These documents lack the scientific information described above.

In Greenland, who are the experts and what are the sources of their knowledge? The inhabitants believe that the knowledge of plants has largely been lost, and they are in the process of reconstructing it from a variety of sources. They are less concerned with the overall source of the knowledge than with the knowledge itself, evident through the resources we were shown during our research. Jespersen (1985) is an unpublished collection of all kinds of information about plants, using newspaper clips, notes, recipes, drawings, photographs, illustrations and descriptions from *Nunatta Naasui*, information about vitamin and mineral content, and some handwritten notes. It is written in Danish, although the Kalaallisut name is also provided for some plants. Photocopies of this book-length manuscript of approximately 130 pages are circulating in Greenland among people interested in plants. It is one of the key sources. One person recommended to us Anderson et al. (1977), a scholarly book (in the tradition of Western science and ethnography) about Inuit–Yupik plant use in Alaska, and written in English. Another loaned us a copy of Ziegler et al. (2009), *Walking with Aalasi*, a book about Inuktitut plants aimed at plant users. It is written in English and Inuktitut, using the syllabary, which would not be comprehensible to most Greenlanders because Kalaallisut is written in the Roman alphabet. In other words, people we talked to discussed an overwhelming desire to learn about plants. They were not especially concerned whether the information came from 'traditional' Inuit sources or from Western science. For that reason, they are very supportive of our work and are eager for us to distribute our findings, preferably in the form of a guidebook to plant uses.

For ethnobotanists and linguists alike, people are generally the primary source of information. Our queries about local expertise were often met with the response that Greenlanders do not know about plants but are trying to learn about them. One exception in this regard is Anne Sofie Hardenberg, a self-taught plant expert and author of an award-winning cookbook on Greenlandic fusion cuisine, published in 2008. Hardenberg, who has been identified as Greenland's food ambassador, is a public figure who has done much to promote the use of native plants in Greenland, and is the single most visible advocate for the use of natural native foods in Greenland. Hardenberg describes herself as self-educated in the use of plants, and has gathered information from wherever she can find it.

Beyond Hardenberg, it is difficult to identify local experts. Most people claimed not to know anything about plants, although a few people admitted to knowing a little. We were constantly directed to southern Greenland, on the assumption that more plants grow in the south and so more people would know about them. Without having conducted extensive interviews in other parts of Greenland, it is difficult to know if this is the case. But what is true is that people know considerably more about plants than they profess. This became apparent in interviews and through casual conversation. For example, one woman who said she knew nothing about plants, then brewed a tea of *qajaasat* (*Rhododendron groenlandicum*, 'Labrador tea') to help soothe a cold. The interest in plant uses is genuine and profound, and many professed a deep love of plants. People were particularly interested in learning of Whitecloud's expertise and were happy to consult with her about plants. (On one occasion she was asked to identify an invasive grass species that had presumably been accidentally introduced with the sheep feed.)

One point that became eminently clear in our interviews and informal conversations with Greenlanders was that they were very interested in learning about plants. The idea of publishing a multilingual guide to plant uses emerged from these talks; locals were interested in having the resource in Kalaallisut, we were interested in including an English version, and everyone generally agreed that it might be useful to include Danish. To make it maximally accessible, people hoped for both a paper copy and a digital copy to be made available. Many people were eager to contribute to such an endeavour, and even more were enthusiastic about having such a guide. We entered this project focused more on the ethnobotanical and linguistic information for the advancement of science, with an eye towards integrating what we were construing as local knowledge with Western biology. Initially, we foresaw logistical challenges in identifying local experts who could tell us about plants, and intellectual challenges in integrating Western biology, local knowledge, and linguistics. But our views of the project have been reshaped by the Inuit specialists, who in many cases served more as collaborators than consultants. They want a guidebook, and are most happy to contribute to its making. This underscores the point that true collaboration is not only ethical, it can radically change the outcome of research (Mithun 2001). The implications of our work can extend far beyond our intent. In many (or even most) indigenous societies, language use is a form of cultural capital, and can serve to mark a user both as a member of a certain community as well as someone actively involved with traditional culture (Ahlers 2006). In Greenland, it is knowledge that is the cultural capital. Language use is an issue for only a small segment of the population: those who have been raised and educated in Denmark.

Thus it is important to keep in mind that these are not speakers whose language is undergoing shift. They are fluent, and they live in a community of fluent speakers who use Kalaallisut in all aspects of life. Many speakers knew the common (Kalaallisut) names of plants that are frequently found and used, although some speakers referred to plants that they were more accustomed to seeing in a Danish context with their Danish name. Rosemary—Kalaallisut *tupaarnaq*, Danish *timian*—is such an example. It is sold in grocery stores in packages with the Danish name, but a wild species grows in part of Greenland. Moreover, Kalaallisut is a highly polysynthetic language and, in our experience, speakers are readily able to parse the names of plants and explain what they mean. For example, there are a number of plants whose name is based on some variety of a colour word, referring to the colour of the flower. These meanings are transparent, as is the meaning for the name for Labrador tea (*Rhododendron groenlandicum*), or *qajaasaq*. The word *qajak* + *-usaq* combines 'kayak' with 'something like', 'imitation/false', or 'sort of'. Thus *qajaasaq* means 'model kayak', here in reference to the shape of the plant's leaf.

But what of so-called traditional knowledge? Of the people we interviewed, only three, including a married couple, spoke of the way their parents used plants and what they learned as children. One woman recalled travelling to a place where the peat was deep, and of cutting blocks that were used to heat their home. She also recalled that her ancestors used a certain plant, but did not know how. Within her community she was seen as the expert because she had attended a class taught by Hardenberg, not because she recalled these traditional uses. This was despite the fact that her community included the granddaughter of Jespersen, who had Jespersen's personal field guide (*Nunatta Naasui*) with his handwritten notes in the margin, and a copy of her grandmother's unpublished manuscript. The couple were the only people to give any spiritual uses for plants (such as burning *Juniperis communis* to chase away bad spirits) or what might be classically considered traditional uses of plants, such as puffball mushrooms (*Lycoperdon perlatum*, Agaricaceae) as a wound dressing, or the use of *Eriophorum sp.* (Cyperaceae) as an abortive. However, they produced several books in Danish on plant uses, and referred to these when presented with a plant with which they were not familiar. There are few accounts of older, traditional uses of plants. Kristine Raahauge of Nanortallip Katersugaasivia (the Nanortalik Museum) interviewed elders about plant usage and has graciously shared transcripts of those interviews with us.[6] Some of these interviews included both plants and usages we did not find elsewhere, such as the use of *Euphrasia frigida* or 'eye bright'. Most of the speakers we interviewed neither recognized the plant nor knew of any of its uses. However, one of the elders who was interviewed gave instructions for how to boil it with water, strain it, and use it to soothe inflamed eyes. As in English, the Kalaallisut name is suggestive of its use: *isiginnaq* (*isi* means 'eye').

What is more striking is that all speakers interviewed were fluent Kalaallisut speakers. This is their preferred, everyday language. Where many cultures lose the language but keep the subsistence knowledge, Greenlanders appear to have done the opposite. Or at least so they claim. Some of the most striking differences between our own beliefs and theirs have not to do with their levels of knowledge but rather what counts as knowledge. For many, knowledge was seen as legitimate if formally learned (as in a class such as Hardenberg's), or from published sources, especially books. This strikes us as a very Western

[6] We first received copies of some interviews from Natuk Lund Olsen of Nunatta Katersugaasivia Allagaateqarfialu (the Greenland National Museum and Archives) in Nuuk; Natuk also introduced us to Kristine Raahauge. We are very grateful to both for their generosity in sharing materials with us and their collaborations in our efforts to document plant knowledge.

ideology of knowledge, both of what constitutes knowledge and of how it is acquired. In oral cultures, knowledge is transmitted orally and experientially, in contrast to written cultures, where knowledge is conveyed in formal settings and where primacy is placed on published (and refereed) authorities. Our goal to publish a guidebook to plant uses emerged as a result of multiple conversations with Greenlanders who encouraged us to do this, and who were eager to contribute their knowledge. (Not only did they want the information to be available, but at least some consultants saw the need to have their own knowledge validated by such a publication.) We see this as an evolving collaborative database with multiple users; this vision has been collaboratively shaped, and we hope its contents and format are as well.

16.5 Conclusion

The differences in ideologies go even deeper than the differences in goals outlined in section 16.1. Rather, they extend to the very heart of the enterprise of research and knowledge. As we, the external, Western-trained scientists, struggle to learn and understand local knowledge systems, beliefs, and ideologies, we need to be careful not to impose our own conceptions of scientific enquiry on communities. That includes not imposing our own conceptions of local knowledge and beliefs. Our work in Greenland has constantly required us to assess and reassess the ways in which we frame our inquiries and the results that we expect. Our collaborators and consultants want more than a recapitulation of their collective knowledge; they want access to all different kinds of knowledge about plants, regardless of its source. In part because we have been trained in a different context, in native North America, we expected local knowledge to include aspects of plants, such as sacred and spiritual uses, but we found it difficult to find this. Surprisingly, what we might consider to be 'traditional' knowledge is not necessarily highly valued, in part because such traditional knowledge is associated with an antiquated lifestyle of the past, when Greenlanders used seal oil lamps and travelled in kayaks. The fact that sphagnum moss (*issuatsiaat*) can be used for lamp wicks (information that we gathered from Raahauge's interviews) is of historical interest, but not useful in the modern world. Their views challenged our own preconceived notions of what would 'count' as local knowledge. By and large our consultants were less interested in traditional (i.e. historical) uses of plants than they were in modern uses. They were more interested in the ways that plants could be put to use in a modern Greenland by modern Inuit. For some this means moving away from imported foodstuffs and medicines, which can certainly be construed as a return to traditional lifestyles, but is more part of a larger move towards self-determination and independence. Not only did this force a reconsideration of our own beliefs on entering the project, but their interest in all aspects of plant usage made our own knowledge valuable to them as well. Unlike previous instances of conflicting goals between documenting versus teaching language, our work in Greenland provided a win-win situation where the community desired access to the documented information as a means of preserving it. We can aid in this preservation not only by documenting, but by sharing recorded knowledge with other consultants and ultimately with the people of the Arctic once our guide is made available. This shows that the differences in ideologies and beliefs are not insurmountable, but rather can provide valuable points of entry into new ways of thinking and seeing the world, and new ways of packaging knowledge.

References

Ahlers, Jocelyn C. 2006. Framing discourse: creating community through native language use. *Journal of Linguistic Anthropology* 16: 58–75.

Anderson, Douglas B., Wanni W. Anderson, Ray Bane, Richard K. Nelson, and Nita Sheldon Towarak. 1977. *Kuuvaŋmiut Subsistence: Traditional Eskimo Life in the Latter Twentieth Century.* Washington, DC: Department of the Interior, National Park Service.

Berardo, Marcellino and Akira Yamamoto. 2007. Indigenous voices and the linguistics of language revitalization. In Osahito Miyaoka, Osamu Sakiyama, and Michael E. Krauss (eds.), *The Vanishing Languages of the Pacific Rim*. Oxford: Oxford University Press.

Bergman, Ingela, Lars Östland, and Olle Zackrisson. 2004. The use of plants as regular food in ancient subarctic economies: a case study based on Sami use of Scots Pine. *Arctic Anthropology* 41: 1–13.

Bjørnum, Stig. 2003. *Grønlandsk grammatik.* Nuuk: Atuagkat.

Braun, David. 2011. Inuit knowledge critical to Arctic science. *National Geographic News*. <http://newswatch.nationalgeographic.com/2011/08/18/inuit-knowledge-critical-to-arctic-science/> (accessed 12 May 2012).

Brower, Ronald. 2008. Protecting culture and transferring traditional knowledge. Paper presented at the *Arctic Indigenous Languages Symposium*, Tromsø, Norway, 19–21 October 2008. <www.arcticlanguages.com/presentations/session2/ronald_brower.pdf>.

Bulatova, Nadezhda and Lenore Grenoble. 1999. *Evenki.* Munich: Lincom.

Convention on Biological Diversity. See <http://www.cbd.int/traditional/intro.shtml> (accessed 29 December 2011).

Davis, Anthony and John R. Wagner. 2003. Who knows? On the importance of identifying 'experts' when researching local ecological knowledge. *Human Ecology* 31: 463–89.

Foersom, Th., F. O. Kapel, and O. Ole Svarre. 1997. *Nunatta Naasui. Grønlands Flora i Farver.* Nuuk: Atuakkiorfik Ilinniusiorfik.

Fortescue, Michael D. 1984. *West Greenlandic.* London: Croom Helm.

Freyd, Jennifer J. and J. Q. Johnson. 1998. Commentary: domestic violence, folk etymologies, and 'rule of thumb'. <http://dynamic.uoregon.edu/~jjf/essays/ruleofthumb.html> (accessed 29 April 2012).

Froude, James Anthony. 1890. Scientific method applied to history: an address to the Devonshire Association for the Encouragement of Science and Literature. In *Short Studies on Great Subjects*, vol. 2. London: Longmans, Green, and Co.

Hardenberg, Anne Sofie. 2008. *Igassat. Opskrifter*. Nuuk: Atuakkiorfik.

Hultén, Eric. 1968. *Flora of Alaska and Neighboring Territories*. Stanford, CA: Stanford University Press.

Jespersen, Kirsten. 1985. *Vilde Grønlandske Planter Til Mad Drikke og Helse*. Unpublished manuscript, Narssaq.

Jones, Anore. 1983. *Nauriat Niginaqtuat* (Plants That We Eat). Kotzebue, Alaska: Maniilaq Association Traditional Nutrition Program.

Konstantinova, O. A. 1964. *Èvenkijskij Jazyk: Fonetika, Morfologija*. Moscow: Nauka.

Larsen, Finn and Rie Oldenburg. 2000. *Neri ... Kujataamiut Nerisaat Ukiuni 1000-ni. Mad i Sydgrønland i 1000 år. Food in Southern Greenland for 1000 years*. Højbjerg: Forlaget Hovedland.

Merriam Webster. See <http://www.merriam-webster.com/dictionary/scientific%20 method> (accessed 29 December 2011).

Mithun, Marianne. 2001. Who shapes the record: the speaker and the linguist. In Paul Newman and Martha Ratliff (eds.), *Linguistic Fieldwork*. Cambridge: Cambridge University Press.

Nadasdy, Paul. 1999. The politics of TEK: power and the 'integration' of knowledge. *Arctic Anthropology* 36: 1–18.

New Nordic Food 2008. New Nordic cuisine. Nordic Council of Ministers, Copenhagen. <http://nynordiskmad.org/fileadmin/webmasterfiles/PDF/Ny_Nordisk_Mad_Low.pdf>.

Olsen, Tupaarnaq Rosing. 2001. *Takanna: Nunatta Pissarititaanik Igaat*. Nuuk: Atuakkiorfik.

Oxford English Dictionary. See <http://www.oed.com/view/Entry/172685?redirectedFrom=scientific%20method#eid23962743> (accessed 29 December 2011).

Petersen, H. C. 2010. *Kalaallit Ilisimaat: Pisuussutsit Uumassusillit Nunattalu Pissarititai Nalillit. Local Knowledge: Living Resources and Natural Assets in Greenland*. Montreal: International Polar Institute Press.

Porsild, A. E. 1953. Edible plants of the Arctic. *Arctic* 6: 15–34.

Rice, Keren. 2009. Must there be two solitudes? Language activists and linguists working together. In Jon Reyhner and Louise Lockard (eds.), *Stabilizing Indigenous Languages: Encouragement, Guidance, and Lessons Learned*. Flagstaff: Northern Arizona University.

Rice, Keren. 2010. The linguist's responsibilities to the community of speakers: community-based research. In Lenore A. Grenoble and N. Louanna Furbee (eds.), *Language Documentation: Practice and Values*. Amsterdam: John Benjamins.

Sadock, Jerrold. 2003. *A Grammar of Kalaallisut (West Greenlandic Inuttut)*. Munich: Lincom Europa.

Si, Aung. 2011. Biology in language documentation. *Language Documentation and Conservation*: 169–86.

Simon, Mary. 2008. Good intentions are not enough. Keynote address presented at the *2008 Arctic Indigenous Languages Symposium*, Tromsø, Norway. <www.arcticlanguages.com/presentations/keynote/mary_simon.pdf> (accessed 29 December 2011).

Statistics Greenland. 2011. <http://www.stat.gl/> (accessed 29 December 2013).

Viereck, Eleanor. 1987. *Alaska's Wilderness Medicines: Healthful Plants of the Far North*. Edmonds, WA: Alaska Northwest Publishing.

Ziegler, A., A. Joamie, and R. Hainnu. 2009. *Walking with Aalasi: An Introduction to Edible and Medicinal Arctic Plants*. Toronto and Iqaluit: Inhabit Media.

17

Whose Ideology, Where, and When? Rama (Nicaragua) and Francoprovençal (France) Experiences*

COLETTE GRINEVALD & MICHEL BERT

17.1 Introduction

AS FIELD LINGUISTS we have been involved with the description, documentation, and revitalization of two endangered languages, Rama and Francoprovençal, over a long period of time. Through ongoing discussions of our respective fieldwork situations over the last ten years we have become increasingly convinced of a great deal of common ground in our experiences, despite working in such different contexts as the Caribbean Coast of Nicaragua and the Rhône-Alpes region of France. One of the most striking parallels we have noted is our constant confrontation with ever-present and ever-changing ideological forces that are at work in our projects and are the theme of the present chapter.[1] As linguists originally trained to do fieldwork for linguistic description and dialectology, it is both the circumstances and the demands of the field that have made us turn our attention to issues that are specific to endangered languages. Therefore we do not claim to be experts in questions of ideology per se and will use the term 'ideology' as a 'catch-all' for mental representations, beliefs, myths, and attitudes.[2] We are interested in *how* ideologies are essentially built in opposition to others, how they are projected onto specific types of actions, and how they are explicitly articulated by some people and then adopted and absorbed, largely implicitly, by others. Taking a critical approach we will also ask ourselves *why* a certain ideology is evident at a certain time, and we will

* Since its first oral presentation in London, this chapter has evolved, fed by ongoing discussions of the LED TDR research group. We would like to thank James Costa, Jane Freeland, Alexandre Duchêne, and Julia Sallabank for discussions and comments that hopefully have improved this piece of writing. Any shortcomings that remain are our own.

[1] Another striking parallel between the two projects has been the theme of recognizable profiles of speakers of endangered languages (see proposals for a typology of speakers in Bert and Grinevald 2010).

[2] On the nature of language ideologies we refer readers to the Introduction of this book and other writings (such as Costa 2010; Duchêne 2008; Duchêne and Heller 2007) of fellow experts in sociolinguistics, sociology of language, political sciences, or anthropology.

try to trace *what* might be at stake *for whom*: community, government, and institutions, as well as academic linguists.

In section 17.2 we introduce the notion of an ideological 'road map' that delimits spatially conceived 'spheres' of ideologies, and discuss the '*who and where*' of what ideology, to construct a view of the ideological complexity of field situations of endangered languages. Next we add some dynamic dimensions to this road map, such as changing levels of intensity in the expressions of these ideologies, synergies, and conflicts induced by their constant ebb and flow, and effects produced by their interlocking. To illustrate this notion of a dynamic road map of ideologies, we then consider two case studies that are at the origin of our proposal. In section 17.3 Grinevald discusses the Rama Language Project of Nicaragua, many aspects of which have already been discussed elsewhere, and in section 17.4 Bert presents in more detail the little-known situation surrounding Francoprovençal in France and the latest developments there. For each case study we follow the evolution of the field situations over the last 20 or 30 years, from the start of our involvement to the present time. We also assess interesting new dynamics, taking note of illustrative situations of ideological convergence and conflict. We close this exercise of 'ideological clarification' (Fishman 1991) in section 17.5 by suggesting further directions this discussion of ideologies, in the context of endangered language projects can take, such as recasting the proposal of a road map of ideological spheres within wider dynamics, for example, a general global North–South axis of the world, and, within it, a Western academia/real-world contrast.

17.2 A Road Map for 'Ideological Clarification'

We consider the road map as our proposed contribution to an 'ideological clarification' for projects of endangered language revitalization. Although we address this primarily to fellow field linguists who are likely to find themselves as little prepared as we feel we were, we assume that our efforts at analysing the various kinds of sociopolitical and psychological realities of fieldwork on an endangered language ought to be of some help to all actors in revitalization projects, from academia and beyond.

17.2.1 An Overview of the 'Spheres' of Ideologies

The road map to be proposed identifies five spheres within which ideologies prosper, visualized in Figure 17.1.

As shown in Figure 17.1, four of the spheres are conceived as being stacked in a nesting arrangement, of international, national, regional, and local scope, from a world-encompassing domain to the local sphere within which fieldwork

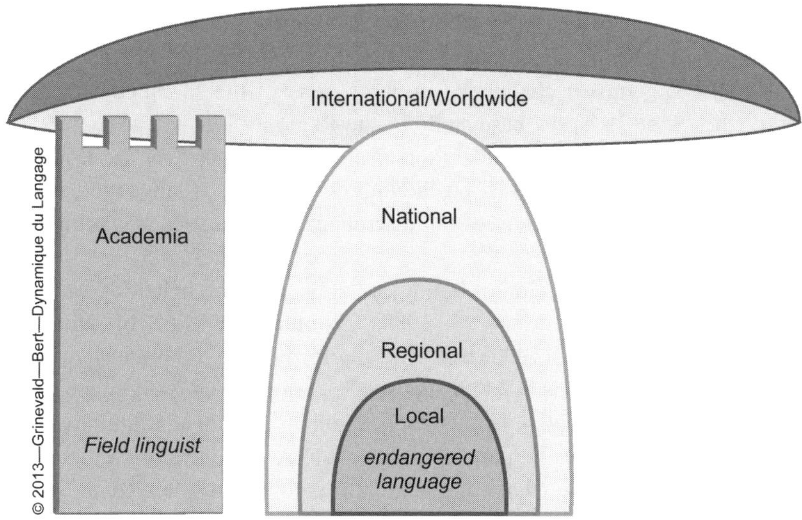

Figure 17.1 Spheres of ideologies.

takes place on the ground. Alongside these stacked spheres we have included a fifth—the academic sphere—which stands alone next to them. We have chosen to examine these spheres in 'reverse' order: first, from an inside view of academia and then on to the worlds of our respective field experiences, starting at the local sphere, noting the constant 'to and fro' between our 'isolated' base in academia and 'the field' with its varying links to the other spheres.

17.2.2 The Academic Sphere

This sphere is sketched as a stand-alone tower, specifically next to, but not touching, the other spheres, to help visualize how much it thinks of itself, and is perceived, as a world of its own. It definitely maintains an ambivalent relation to the 'outside' and/or 'real' world that it considers tainted by so-called 'politics' at all levels, although researchers have to deal with the 'real world' at the local level in any 'fieldwork'.[3]

Ideologies concerning the academic sphere abound, and include its own sense of its research (and teaching) mission, which is traditionally articulated around an ideological core of 'pure science', said to demand independence from what is perceived as the messiness of the 'real world'.[4] This ideological stance

[3] As in the warning frequently heard by Grinevald, when still Craig in the US, of 'not mixing academia and politics', in contrast to the pressure felt in Latin America to specifically make the link between academic linguistics and the politics of endangered languages in the field.

[4] The ideology of a pure science is said in some circles to be counterbalanced by a belief in the natural trickling down of the benefits of pure science to the people, given sufficient time.

can probably be situated in a North–South axis (see section 17.5) as it has emanated from older academic bases of the so-called 'first world' (the 'North'), while it is being further challenged in many parts of the so-called 'developing world' (the 'South'), as the case study of the Rama project will show.[5]

The academic world has undergone a radical evolution over the last two or three decades with respect to its positioning on the issue of language endangerment, at least in some quarters of the disciplines of linguistics, sociolinguistics, and anthropology.

In the US the mobilization of linguistic fieldworkers on behalf of indigenous languages towards the end of the 1980s first took the form of support for the Native Language Act (1990) that officially recognized the linguistic rights of Native American peoples.[6] Interestingly, the 'English Only' movement that fostered the defence of native languages was principally aimed at limiting the use of immigrant languages, in particular Spanish.[7] A mobilization for all native languages throughout the whole of the American continent followed, at the same time as a vast protest movement started in Latin America, led by numerous indigenous organizations, against the planned celebrations of the 500th anniversary of the supposed 'discovery of America' by Columbus. The first symposium on endangered languages that took place during the annual meeting of the Linguistic Society of America at the end of 1991 was intended to be a gesture from academia towards this movement.[8] In 1992 another symposium, on the same theme of endangered languages, took place at the International Congress of Linguists in Quebec (Craig 1993; Crochetière et al. 1993).

Within a decade, several foundations were established to foster work on endangered languages, first the Dokumentation Bedrohter Sprachen ('documentation of endangered languages') programme, known as DoBeS, of the Volkswagen Foundation in Germany.[9] After that came the Hans Rausing Endangered Languages Project (HRELP) in London, created in 2002, and later the Documentation of Endangered Languages (DEL) programme, through a consortium of

[5] See Grenoble and Whitecloud (this volume) for a discussion of conflicting postures between the standard academic research paradigm and community views of knowledge, in this case in the Arctic, so not literally in the 'south' but well within the paradigm of developed/underdeveloped worlds.

[6] Some of the dynamics to be mentioned derive from first-hand knowledge of one of the present co-authors, Colette Grinevald from the University of Lyon, having been, until her return to France in 1996, Colette G. Craig from the University of Oregon.

[7] An interesting European parallel will be mentioned later in section 17.4.2.1 in the discussion of the effects of the new Article 2 of the French Constitution, originally aimed at English but taken as a threat to regional languages.

[8] Its proceedings were soon after published in *Language*, to come out in 1992 (Hale et al. 1992). It was during these meetings that the Linguistic Society of America positioned itself with respect to the problem of endangered languages, with official statements and the creation of a committee on endangered languages and their preservation.

[9] See <http://www.mpi.nl/DOBES/volkswagen_foundation> (accessed 1 October 2013).

the US National Science Foundation and National Endowment for the Humanities. A new subfield of linguistics termed 'documentary linguistics' (Himmelmann 1998, 2006) took shape, led by the archive of the DoBeS programme in Nijmegen, the Netherlands. All in all, the momentum gathered around the turn of the twenty-first century has resulted in creating and establishing a new sub-discipline, centred on endangered languages, within the sphere of academic linguistics.

Over time, the various subfields of linguistics dealing with endangered languages—description, documentation, archiving, and revitalization—have developed with increasing overlap, as the result of an evolution of ideological positions within the academic sphere. Within linguistics, the activity of description has regained value (over 'theory'), both in its essential role of carrying out work on un(der)-described endangered languages and in its contribution to the development of the subfield of linguistic typology. A subfield of 'documentary linguistics' has been defined by specific norms, benefiting from the accelerated development of new technologies. These same new technologies have also allowed for the development of the subfield of archiving documentary material. At this point in time, discussions of work on endangered languages have been evolving to add revitalization as a new link in the chain. However, thus far it remains the least-acknowledged link in purely linguistic academic circles, while it is better established in sociolinguistics and anthropological linguistics.

Hence the formula that we propose in order to formalize the evolution of the new sub-discipline of endangered languages and its accompanying ideological evolution: 'D-D.A+R', as in Description, Documentation and Archiving, plus Revitalization.[10]

Needless to say, the mere schematization of work on endangered languages through this formula is in itself a manifestation of a certain ideological stance. For instance, it clearly maintains as the first link in the chain the description of these endangered languages, to the extent that linguists are trained to do this work, which we ultimately take to be their main responsibility. It also links documentation with archiving, both of which have their own norms, in the same way that the discipline of language description has its own standards.

More marked as ideologically divergent, to the extent that it runs counter to the 'pure science' independent stance of academia, is the addition of the revitalization link to the chain. Revitalization is an activity that needs to be 'owned' by endangered language communities, in a spirit of 'sustainable

[10] We are proposing this new formula of D-D.A+R (instead of DD-A+R) to better match well-established linguistic glossing conventions. The symbol '-' in 'D-D' is meant to resemble a morphemic segmentation, meaning 'description and documentation'; '.' in 'D.A' to show the unit formed by 'archiving of documentation'; and '+' in 'D.A+R' to mark the systematic addition over time of revitalization as an activity more and more systematically incorporated into the complex of work on endangered languages, as in 'D-D.A *plus* revitalization', although with another type of link, currently formulated more often as D-D.A '*for*' revitalization.

development' for which the participation of linguists can be essential, although it is still often discredited in academia as a kind of 'social work' (Newman 1999, 2003). Indeed, the issue of what linguists can do, ought to do, or are willing to do in revitalization is in itself ideologically charged. In particular, it remains to be seen how much of what seems to have become the politically correct discourse of supposedly necessary concern for endangered language communities is mere political lip service, and how much is real engagement.[11]

An even more ideological and more controversial issue in some quarters of the academic sphere is the general consideration of the relationship of linguists to the speakers of the endangered languages with whom they work, and to the communities to which those speakers belong. This topic usually falls into discussions often labelled as 'field ethics'.[12] Here again, a formula will be proposed to capture succinctly the evolution, over the second half of the twentieth century, of a line of thinking preoccupied with the issue of power relations between researchers (from the academic sphere in general) and those who are 'researched' in the field.[13] It indicates a progression from fieldwork *on* a language (the ideological schema of the 1950s, of field research with 'informants') to fieldwork *for* the linguistic community (the ideological schema of the period of civil rights, of the engaged linguist in defence of the linguistic rights of minorities for instance, but speaking for the speakers and the communities), to fieldwork *with* the speakers (an ideological schema that emerged in the 1990s, of empowerment and collaborative research, and of action research), to which was added, more recently, the final step: the ideal of fieldwork *by* the speakers (of speakers trained to be linguists of their own languages for their communities).[14]

In the end, the proposed formula can be reduced to the simple schema of 'fieldwork *on*, *for*, *with*, and *by*'.[15]

[11] See Grinevald (2006) for a case study of contradictions and tensions between stated concerns of a foundation supposedly on behalf of the community, and absence of commitment to support activities with the community.

[12] See Craig (1993) for an early discussion of this issue in terms of ethics. This topic still finds limited space in discussions of ethics in the field of endangered languages, which is more oriented to legal aspects such as property rights (and associated notion of informed consent) than to the nature of the human interactions involved in the process of collecting data, in the more legalistic approach of literate societies.

[13] The formula is an adaptation and extension of a proposition originally made by Cameron et al. (1992) in the field of sociolinguistics, imported into the field of endangered languages by Craig (1993), Grinevald (1997, 2000, 2007a.)

[14] For example see speakers of Mayan languages (England 1998, 2003; Grinevald 2005, 2007b). This addition was expressly requested at an international conference on Amazonian linguistics in Brazil attended by Amazonian indigenous leaders (Grinevald 2000).

[15] Literally as 'fieldwork *on* (a language), *for* (a community), *with*, and *by* (the speakers)'. This means, of course, a radical rethinking of the role of linguists in the field, and conflicting synergies in terms of expectations of the academic sphere and expectations of the communities concerned. As suggested by

This exploration of the first ideological sphere (i.e. the academic sphere) has attempted to retrace different lines of developments over the last two decades of a new field of 'endangered languages'.[16] It has been relatively more elaborate than the discussion of the following spheres will be, to the extent that the world of linguistics at large may not be much better informed of these developments than the general public. It is clear that much remains to be discussed concerning the ideological underpinnings of this relatively new academic discipline concerned with endangered languages, at least among linguists.[17]

17.2.3 The Local Sphere: Where Fieldwork Takes Place

The next sphere to be considered is the world that the researchers encounter on the ground, in the field, the sphere where linguists encounter the languages they intend to describe, document, and, in some circumstances, help revitalize. It is the sphere of contact with a community, and of face-to-face interactions with speakers and all the other actors involved with the fate of endangered languages. To start with, it might be worth noting that the notions of communities of endangered languages and speakers of endangered languages are still a matter of debate, as argued in Grinevald and Bert (2011); see also Chapter 1 of this volume. It is often not clear where an endangered language community is, what its delimiting boundaries are, or who its members and representatives are. This is particularly so the more endangered the language is.

To the extent that the major preoccupation of field linguists is ultimately that of finding speakers with whom to work on the language, a major issue for linguists is how to deal with the great variety of speakers that one encounters in endangered language situations. Speakers vary not only in their levels of pragmatic and grammatical competence and lexical knowledge, but also in their attitudes towards the language, as well as their interest in sharing their knowledge. These are some of the basic ingredients being considered for the elaboration of a typology of speakers of endangered languages, as proposed by Bert and Grinevald (2010).[18] In this sphere ideology resides in the different stances taken by the various actors involved (such as foreign or native linguists, speakers and non-speakers in the community, activists, or planners) towards

Costa (p.c.), this is rich material for an exploration of the links between linguistic rights, diversity, and neoliberalism.

[16] This discussion was admittedly based on the personal involvement of co-author Grinevald Craig in a number of these academic discussions, as shown by references of the time.

[17] Who may not be aware of Cameron (2007), Duchêne and Heller (2007), and Freeland and Patrick (2004), for example.

[18] Dorian (1977, 1981) was the pioneer in this field. Grinevald Craig (1997) offers a review of proposals as of that time; Bert (2001) includes a radical expansion of the proposal based on fieldwork on Francoprovençal in France.

language variation (inherent to all situations) and notions of purism (problematic in all activities on the language, from description to documentation and revitalization).[19]

Finally, whilst in the field, one major issue to be reckoned with is the level of consciousness and politicization of the community at large: whether there is an awareness of language endangerment and of the loss of vitality of the language, and, if there is awareness, whether there is any concern about it.[20]

17.2.4 The National and Regional Spheres

These are spheres delimited by constitutions, laws, and decrees, and the ideologies they convey. They include the domain of 'language planning', generally mandated to implement legislative decisions. The two case studies presented below will consider the importance of these spheres in shaping field projects. In Latin America and in the European Union, a particular characteristic is the essential role played by new autonomous regional governments in promoting the languages of their regions. In the French case this is in clear defiance of national legislation.

17.2.5 The International and Worldwide Sphere

The defence of the local is recognized today as a reaction to the phenomenon of globalization, and well-established organizations at the international level are now involved in the promotion of local endangered languages. This promotion is generally subsumed under larger concerns such as human rights, indigenous rights, or protection of the environment. Speaking in terms of the defence of endangered languages, declarations of institutions such as the United Nations (UN) and one of its branches, UNESCO, are the most visible in this sphere. However, it is important to bear in mind the composition of these international organizations, which are the sum of the nation states of the world. This translates into much necessary compromise in the statements that are agreed upon.[21] Meanwhile it is undeniable that these statements have a potentially deep local impact. What is striking, as seen from the field (at least in many places in Latin

[19] Purism is, of course, itself an ideology: see Dorian (1994, 1998).

[20] See the Ladefoged–Dorian exchanges in *Language* in 1992–3 about the role of linguists in raising communities' and/or speakers' consciousness of the situation of endangerment of their languages, and the question of supposedly free choice of speakers to maintain the transmission of their languages or not. This is certainly a debate loaded with ideology well beyond the realm of work on endangered languages, and one that tightly links the academic and the local spheres.

[21] See Minasyan (this volume) for an inside view of such entities in this respect. The detailed study by Duchêne (2008) of the process of creating legislation for the United Nations with regard to language rights, as part of indigenous rights among other things, is a case in point.

America) is the awareness on the ground, in the local sphere, of the declarations of such international entities. Intermediate level supra-national organizations, such as the Organization of American States (OAS) or the European Union (see section 17.4 on Francoprovençal) are also important.

Finally, part of the international network that may affect perceptions of, and attention to, endangered languages are the NGOs or other bodies with diverse philosophies that support or run development programmes (as will become obvious in the case of Nicaragua).

17.2.6 Evolution of Synergies and Conflicts

As mentioned above, the listing of spheres and loci of different ideologies regarding endangered languages makes for a rather flat, two-dimensional, schema. In all the spheres considered, issues of endangered languages can either become focal points of attention or not, which may account for variations in the ease or difficulty of carrying out a project in the field. Often, these changes of circumstances are very difficult to read and interpret on the spot, although they can generally be elucidated later, with hindsight.

This instability of the field probably constitutes one of the major elements of risk in such projects, for academics plan their field trips well in advance and generally from a distance, in order to satisfy the demands of funding agencies and to meet other work commitments (e.g. teaching). The discord between the requirements of foundations and the academic world for efficient planning, quantitative results, and scientific products, and the realities and demands of the field, often create a gulf of divergent interests and ideological views. This gap, which is a source of constant tension for any project of (sustainable) development, is another issue to be considered in the North–South perspective already mentioned. This is in itself ideological in nature and is clearly rooted in histories of colonialism (as will also be mentioned in the Conclusion).

The two case studies below will concentrate on the ebb and flow of such energies in the various spheres of ideologies as they were experienced by the authors in their respective projects, and will signal the various positions taken by the linguists at different times in response to changing circumstances.

17.3 Synergies and Conflicts in the Rama Language Project (1984–2010)

From its very beginning the 'Rama Language Project' (RLP) was cast into a web of political, sociological, and human rights ideologies emanating from all of the spheres at once. It started with a specific matching of a linguist with a heavily politicized field situation, and has provided plentiful food for thought about endangered languages and fieldwork approaches during the almost three decades of its evolution. It has also included all the links in the chain of possible projects on an endangered language: from description to documentation and archiving, with the driving force of its inception being a request made to the linguist for revitalization, which is locally still the justification for its existence today.[22]

17.3.1 Phase 1: Description and Demand for Revitalization

In the 1980s, the Rama people were the smallest and most minoritized ethnic group of the then Atlantic Coast of Nicaragua (now renamed the Caribbean Coast), and their language, Rama, was the most devalued and most vulnerable of the indigenous languages still spoken in that part of the country (see Figure 17.2).

17.3.2 The National and Regional Political Origins of the Project[23]

Soon after the 'triumph' of the Sandinista revolution in 1979, counter-revolutionary forces organized with strategic support from the US Government and enlisted a large number of indigenous people of the Coast (adding international and ethnic dimensions to the left/right political conflict). There followed the 'Contra War', in which the indigenous populations of the Atlantic Coast found themselves deeply involved and affected. This was also the case in the Rama community, with a large number of its members passing to the Contra side, and many crossing the border to neighbouring Costa Rica as Contra combatants or just as refugees.

Eventually a peace accord took the shape of a political gesture towards the whole Atlantic Coast region and its ethnic communities, in the form of granting it autonomy. This regional autonomy was sanctioned in 1987 in the national constitution, with a text that uniformly granted the same linguistic rights to all the different ethnic groups identified at the time: Creole, Miskitu, Sumu, Garifuna, and Rama. This happened in spite of the fact that the last two groups seemed to have all but lost their languages.

It was therefore in the specific context of the establishment of laws about linguistic rights, within a certain ideology of a one-to-one necessary relationship between ethnic group and language, that the Rama people found themselves at a loss for having abandoned their language. They had become speakers of a variety of the local English-based Creole known as Misquito Coast Creole (or MCC).

[22] The RLP has been amply documented, locally in Spanish in the Nicaraguan review WANI, in English more recently through overviews such as Grinevald (2006, 2007a), and most recently, more in depth and in French, in Grinevald (2010a, 2010b). Only the main themes pointing to specific interactions of ideologies will be sketched out here.

[23] For the political origins of the project, see Craig (1992), a contribution to the LSA panel on endangered languages of 1991; see note 12 above.

Figure 17.2 Location of Rama (1980), Nicaragua.

Under these circumstances the chief of the Rama at that time presented a request to the Sandinista Government asking for help in revitalizing the Rama language, their ethnic language. At that moment there seemed to be a strong ideological alignment between the regional, national, and local levels in the demand for the revitalization of Rama.

17.3.3 Bridging a Gap between the Academic Sphere and the Real World

A series of circumstances matched the request of the Rama community leader with a linguist, then known as Colette Craig, who was in the midst of an equally marked political and ideological situation. She happened to be travelling to Nicaragua as an interpreter for US human rights delegations organized by an NGO known as the Council for Human Rights in Latin America (CHRLA).[24] It was specifically because of pressure from some corners of her academic world (a disapproving department head at the University of Oregon) that she presented herself to the Nicaraguan Ministry of Culture as a linguist specializing in indigenous languages, and offered her services as a fieldworker.[25]

When the Sandinistas asked her in return to attend to the demand of the Rama for the revitalization of the Rama language, they had no information as to how to locate Rama speakers. It was said that Rama had only three speakers left, out of a population estimated at around 300.[26] The first step of the project started through academic networking in the US, from Lyle Campbell (a linguist specializing in Central American languages) to Barbara Assadi (who had been his assistant in a survey of endangered languages of the region in the 1970s), and from her to one speaker, an older woman, Eleonora Rigby, living on the island of Rama Cay, the largest and closest Rama community to the main town of Bluefields.

17.3.4 The Local Sphere: The Rama Language Project

The Rama Language Project started in 1985, with NSF support for a description of the language, on the basis of having located at least this one speaker who had expressed her eagerness to work on the language.[27]

[24] The story of her association with this NGO due to another warlike experience in Guatemala, her previous research field, is narrated in Grinevald (2010a).

[25] This is in the context of intense academic mobilization in the US against the involvement of the US Government in Central America (e.g. in El Salvador) after the movement against the Vietnam War. Although Craig's original engagement with the CHRLA was directly linked to the US involvement in the war in Guatemala, her services as an interpreter for Nicaragua had been solicited by this NGO.

[26] Interestingly, in spite of all the information provided through the activities of the RLP to counter this myth of three old men as the last speakers on the island of Rama Cay, not far from the major coast town of Bluefields, it is still believed, as a testimony to the tenacity of beliefs about endangered languages.

[27] The NSF is the US National Science Foundation: in itself an interesting political anomaly, considering the US Government source of NSF funding and the ongoing, US-financed Contra War in the same region. This was a silent gesture of academic solidarity, or an ideological stand, on the part of the then NSF director.

On the revitalization front, the project started with a search for more speakers (more than 50 were actually located, 30 of whom were native speakers, but all jungle dwellers). Two years into the project, Miss Nora (as she is remembered) threw herself into an inspired one-woman revitalization programme. Her first priority was the revalorization of the language she so profoundly loved, but which was thoroughly despised by the majority of the Rama, who called it a 'tiger language' (i.e. close to animal calls) that only 'tiger people' (savages from the jungle) spoke. She spent time and energy demonstrating at public assemblies on Rama Cay on Sundays how the language was indeed a 'real' language that could be written, studied, and taught, as she had learned from contact with the linguist.[28] Soon she started, of her own initiative and with the support of the linguist, to teach Rama in kindergarten on the island of Rama Cay (which she did for ten years).

17.3.5 Pressures and Challenges in and across Spheres

These were somewhat schizophrenic years between the stress of regular back and forth between linguistic circles within the academic sphere, where 'mixing politics and academia' was denounced, and the very politicized Nicaraguan national, regional, and local spheres, with their expectations of foreign academics.[29]

There was, in addition, the stress of the back and forth between the US and the Contra war zone it controlled, until the area became an autonomous region of Nicaragua, and the intense pressure of describing an almost extinct language with few speakers available,[30] in the midst of demands for its immediate revitalization.[31]

17.3.6 Phase 2: Documentation-Archiving + Revitalization (1994–2010)

Various circumstances of a personal and political nature ground the project to a halt in 1993 for several years, and by the time the linguist was brought back, the ideological configuration had largely changed.

[28] See Craig (1992) and Grinevald (2005) for a portrait of this language saviour and the attitude of Rama people towards the Rama language at that time.

[29] The project was one of several projects coordinated by volunteer linguists organized by an association called Linguists for Nicaragua (LFN), under the leadership of Ken Hale (colleague of Chomsky at MIT), who himself became the linguist for the Ulwa Sumu community, north of the Rama.

[30] The Rama grammar produced as the final report for the NSF grant in 1987 is one of the grammars used for the WALS project of the MPI of Leipzig.

[31] This was one of the field experiences discussed at the 1991 LSA meeting, part of the launching of the theme of endangered languages (Hale et al. 1992).

17.3.7 The International Sphere and the Defence of the Rama Territory

While much of the Rama territory was internationally recognized as the 'Biosphere Reserve of South East Nicaragua' in 1999, the same traditional territory has fallen prey to numerous serious threats: the construction of a 'dry canal'[32] with its coastal land speculations and the selling of Rama islands and beaches, and an invasion by mestizo settlers destroying the supposedly protected forest for agro-pastoral exploitation. Many denunciations have been made to the international court of law over the years, so far to no avail, and the situation on the ground is becoming more and more dangerous.

But in the midst of this accumulation of international protection and national and regional rights, matched by uncontrolled illegal speculations and invasion on the ground, the Rama have been reaffirming the priority of defending their language as a major element of their identity, and associating it with the defence of their territory.

17.3.8 Regional Sphere

In their regional sphere of Región Autónoma Atlántico Sur (RAAS—'autonomous region of the South Atlantic'), the principal activity of the newly created Rama autonomous government (GTR-K for Gobierno Territorial Rama-Kriol) has been the demarcation of the Rama territory, but the revitalization of the Rama ethnic language was listed as second to the defence of the territory in the regional government's 30-year development plan (PADA).[33]

17.3.9 The International Dimension of the Academic Sphere

An international academic project brought back the linguist Grinevald Craig at the request of the Rama in 2000.[34] A major grant was secured from the Endangered Languages Documentation Programme (ELDP) in London in 2004, bringing the RLP within the fold of a major foundation dedicated to endangered languages.[35]

[32] An alternative to the Panama Canal, a kilometre-wide highway through the forest for railway tracks transporting containers between two deep-sea ports, one right on the Rama coast, and impeding the passage of small embarkations.

[33] The GTR-K is the first such autonomous indigenous government in Nicaragua, and one of the first in Latin America.

[34] A cooperative project between the University of Tromsø, Norway, and the local URACCAN University (Universidad Regional Autónomas de la Costa Caribe de Nicaragua).

[35] To archive the materials of the first phase of the RLP and produce a dictionary with data gathered in the first phase, although notably with no support for revitalization activities per se, as discussed in Grinevald (2006). Financial support for them eventually came from unrestricted research funds from the Institut Universitaire de France.

17.3.10 Mobilization in the Local Sphere

The most striking feature of this new phase was the involvement of all sectors of the Rama community in various revitalization activities. At the workshops organized at the local university (Universidad Regional Autónomas de la Costa Caribe de Nicaragua, or URACCAN) and the GTR-K by the RLP team on several occasions, all sectors of the Rama community gathered, including many native and semi-speakers participating for the first time, new activists and neo-speakers, as well as non-speakers such as students, schoolteachers, and leaders and community members from newly recognized and isolated communities.[36] The RLP team shared its understanding and knowledge of the Rama language situation, and presented the website that contains the dictionary project, as well as the archives now available on the AILLA site (Archives of Indigenous Languages of America at Austin, Texas).[37]

This new phase of Rama revitalization had certainly been appropriated by the Rama community at large and seemed to provide a vehicle for identity building of apparently crucial importance to all generations.

17.3.11 Conclusion: 25-Year Perspective on the Rama Language Project

It has been a long and tortuous journey for the unprepared academic linguist dealing with such an endangered language, such a divided community, and such a complex and powerful political framing. But this experience has been the source of a growing awareness of the dimensions of fieldwork on endangered languages, particularly of the aspect of fieldwork in a fragile 'exhausted' community. Whatever has been achieved was absolutely unforeseeable at first, but the long-term perspective of over almost three decades has shown how the scene constantly changes, often in wholly unpredictable ways. It has provided fertile ground for reflecting on the role of linguists and the choice of fieldwork framework (practically imposed on all projects of that region by the political context but also willingly espoused by the linguists for Nicaragua).[38]

[36] Many of them ex-students of Miss Nora or witnesses to her teaching.

[37] Such as teaching that Rama is a Chibchan language, part of a large family of languages stretching from Honduras to Colombia, with a genetic tree and maps to support it; or the suggestion of thinking of the Rama language as a 'treasure language', not a mother tongue as the UNESCO and the bilingual education authorities would categorize it; to consider appropriate teaching methods in view of actual realistic use (Grinevald and Pivot, forthcoming).

[38] The Rama Language Project has provided a framework for a sustainable development project involving many of the same families, more precisely the next generation of Rama people. See <http://www.blueenergygroup.org/?lang=en>, (accessed 9 October 2012). This NGO is also participating in the new thinking of a social entrepreneurship framework, including a clearly new ideological approach to development.

One of the striking features of recent times is, on the one hand, the fading role of native speakers and the emergence of semi-speakers as some of today's 'best speakers' and, on the other hand, the takeover of most language activities by neo-speakers. These new dynamics provide a clear case study of how revitalization may not be a question of producing new generations of native speakers, but of adding a demonstrative value to a 'treasure language' for self-worth and defence of territory, as argued in Costa (2010) and specifically for the Rama in Pivot (2010, 2014); see also Austin (this volume) and King (this volume).

17.4 Synergies and Conflicts in the Francoprovençal Situation

The discussion that follows sketches the striking evolution of the situation of Francoprovençal in the Rhône-Alpes region of France over 20 years. This will be described in more detail than for the Rama language of Nicaragua, as until now little information has been published about Francoprovençal in English. As Francoprovençal is probably the least known of the regional languages of France, some general information about its status in France will be given first, before drawing a contrast between the situation in the 1990s and at the time of writing. Parallels and differences with the Rama context will be underlined throughout. Among the features they share are: a history of being extremely minoritized languages, relatively recent attention from regional governments within the larger context of dynamics within national and international spheres, and participation of academic linguists in some of the new dynamics set in motion at the regional level. On the other hand, we consider that the obvious differences between the two situations can be analysed principally along the North–South axis already mentioned, and will be further developed in section 17.5.

17.4.1 Francoprovençal as a Very Endangered Regional Language of France

Francoprovençal is a transnational language spoken not only in France but also in Switzerland and in Italy, in the Aoste Valley (see Figure 17.3). Only the French situation will be considered here.

In France, French is the sole official language and regional languages occupy only a marginal place. For instance, when they are taught in school (as is the case for Breton, Basque, Alsatian, and Corsican) it is only to a limited number of children. Francoprovençal is one of the 'poor relations' of these regional languages. Unlike its neighbour Occitan, it lacks a written tradition, prestigious literature, an established writing system, and an established and organized activist tradition. Furthermore, it is not included in the list of regional languages

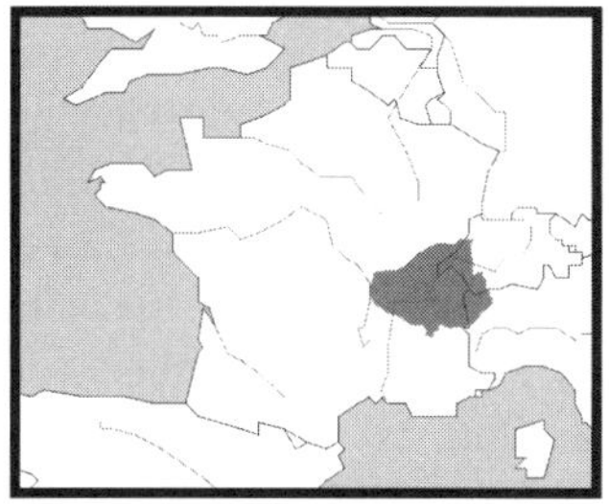

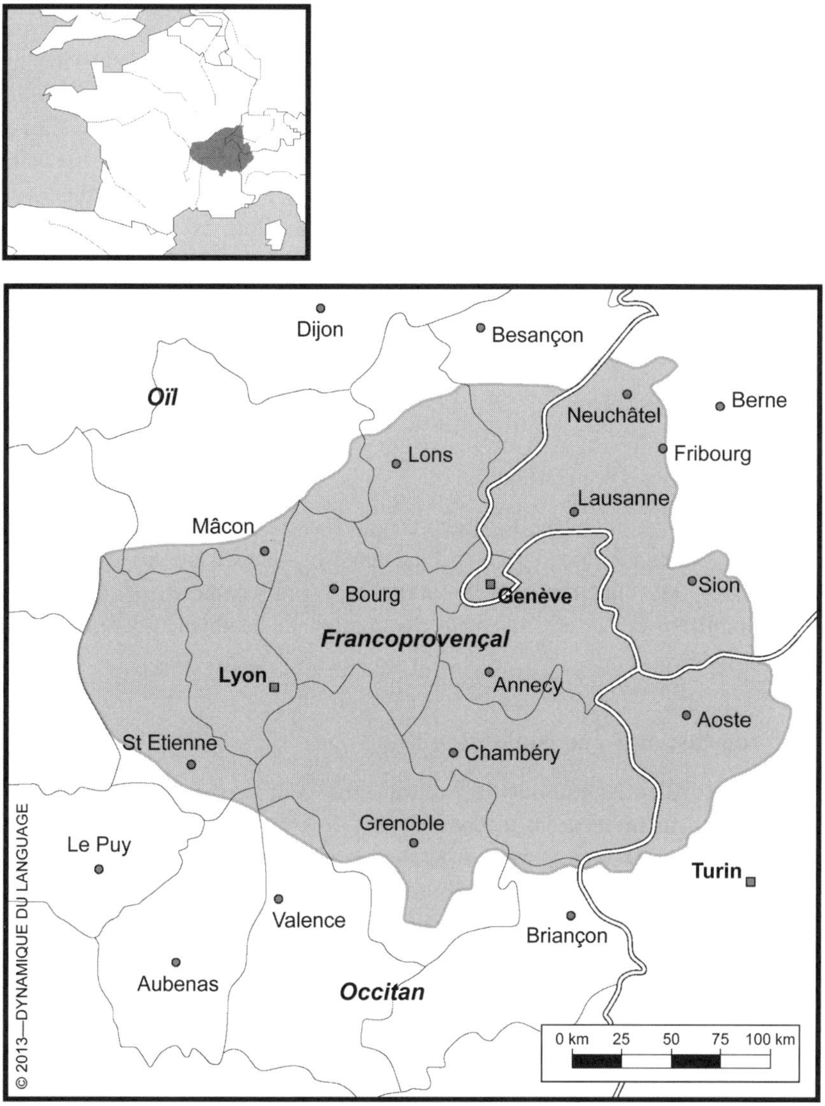

Figure 17.3 Map of Francoprovençal in the context of other regional languages of France.

that may be taught in schools.[39] Its level of vitality in France is very low, with around 50,000 speakers in a population of more than 5 million (i.e. 1 per cent) in the Rhône-Alpes region, with those speakers being over 60 years of age (Bert

[39] This means that it has no status of 'option' in any of the French public exams, either at high school nor at university levels.

et al. 2009). Those same speakers still have no name for the language; they use the generic term '*patois*' (a word for dialect in French), often identifying the language as only being the local form spoken in their own village. Meanwhile, a chain of dialects spoken over a vast territory has been recognized by linguists as constituting one larger language that they have called Francoprovençal, the name by which the language is known in the academic sphere. Unfortunately this name is a misnomer that causes ambiguity and confusion, as it evokes by its compounded form a mixture of French (Franco-) and Occitan (of the Provençal variant), which the language is definitely not. For these varied reasons, Francoprovençal finds itself at the bottom of the list of regional languages of France and is sometimes called an unknown language ('*méconnue*', Stich 1998), or a forgotten language ('*oubliée*', Tuaillon 1988).

17.4.2 The 1990s: Description

During the last decade of the twentieth century, which corresponds to the period of intensive doctoral research on the language by one of the co-authors (Bert 2001, 2010), the situation of Francoprovençal was characterized by relative general indifference, in contrast with the context of heightened activity in the international sphere.

17.4.3 International and National Spheres

The year 1992 was not only significant for endangered languages in the Americas (as mentioned in section 17.1.1), it was also a turning point for endangered languages in Europe, with the signing of the European Charter for Regional or Minority Languages proposed by the Council of Europe.[40] European states were invited first to adhere to this Charter by signing it, and then to ratify it by committing to adopt at least 35 of its 94 clauses.

France as a nation refused then and still refuses to adhere to the Charter, let alone to ratify it. In the same year, France actually added to Article 2 of its Constitution the statement that 'the language of the Republic is French'. By this, it meant to forcefully underline its nation state ideology of 'one nation–one language–one culture', an ideology strongly felt in France. This new statement drew a strong reaction from supporters of regional languages, so much so that the then minister of justice felt obliged to specify that the new statement in Article 2 was not meant to endanger regional languages.

[40] See European Charter for Regional or Minority Languages: <http://conventions.coe.int/Treaty/EN/Treaties/Html/148.htm>.

17.4.4 Regional Sphere

During that time the Rhône-Alpes region seemed indifferent to the defence of its regional languages. As the regions were still relatively new administrative entities in France (they date from the 1970s), the Rhône-Alpes region in particular was having a hard time defining itself, for a number of reasons. For one, it does not naturally constitute a historical entity nor a geographic one (extending from the glaciers of the Alps to the lavender fields in its southern part). In addition, it does not constitute a linguistic entity either since it includes two regional languages: Occitan, spoken in two of its departments, and Francoprovençal, spoken in the other six. In addition, the territory of Francoprovençal extends north into the region of Franche-Comté, where its vitality is even lower than in Rhône-Alpes and where there is even less interest in the language. All in all there is little overall sense of Francoprovençal unity and identity, and where there is some, it is at a more local level (as with the subregion of the two Savoys).

In sum, the region remained indifferent to the question of regional languages in the 1990s, in spite of some demands from movements on behalf of Occitan, inspired by activities in the regions to the south (Languedoc and Roussillon).

17.4.5 Local Sphere

On the ground there was no coordination at all in support of Francoprovençal. The great majority of native speakers, still quite numerous then, remained very marked by the stigmatization of the '*patois*'. They were convinced that Francoprovençal was not a real language, that it did not have a grammar or literature, and that it could not be reduced to writing. They suffered from the supremacy of French and the purist and normative language ideologies promulgated by the French nation state.

This does not mean that there was no interest in the language locally. Associations, often in total isolation or with little contact with each other (except maybe in Savoy), were active in local cultural conservation, mostly through the use of the local language but never with the goal of teaching it in order to create new speakers.

The actors in these associations were mostly semi-speakers, who were less sensitive to the stigmatization of the language than traditional speakers. They were attached to it for its cultural value, to provide an identity, although a very local identity at the village or regional level. There also existed a few activists, in very limited numbers, who individually presented demands to the Ministry of Education for the teaching of the language. Those demands were systematically rejected under one pretext or another: either that the language is a variety of Occitan and was already being taught, or that it is a variety of an Oïl language and thus too similar to French to require being taught.[41] The rejection was therefore based on the ideological bias that Francoprovençal simply cannot be a language of its own.

17.4.6 Academic Sphere

In the academic sphere, the research tradition of Francoprovençal specialists was one of language description within a well-established tradition of dialectological studies. This meant the production of atlases, monographs searching for local variants, and studies of linguistic geography, which systematically stressed the phenomenon of variation and differences across field sites (Bert 2011). In this tradition, studies are carried out exclusively with 'good' speakers, who tend to be older, rural, and sedentary males, while semi-speakers are systematically ignored. For those traditional dialectologists, the Francoprovençal language exists only in the range of its local variants, and there is no need to design a supra-dialectal writing system, for instance. These linguists consider themselves outside observers, never activists, and they limit their interventions to occasional acts of promotion. In this sense, their fieldwork framework could therefore be said to be limited to work *on* the language.[42]

In conclusion, the inaction of that period is clearly due to a predominance of negative factors, from widespread confusion about the nature of the language and negative attitudes towards '*patois*', to generalized resistance to the recognition of all regional languages at the national level. The turn of the century, however, is marked by the beginnings of a change in the dynamics of the region.

17.4.7 2000–10: Revitalization, Documentation

While an impasse continued at the national level, synergies were set in motion at the regional level, in which academic linguists began to play an active role, leading to much attention being focussed on the Francoprovençal language, as explicated below.

17.4.8 International and National Spheres

Following electoral promises, the French president at the time, Jacques Chirac, decided to push for the signing and ratification of the European Charter. Due to the addition to Article 2 in 1992, which specified that 'the language of the

[41] The Romance languages in France are generally divided into subgroups of Oïl (northern) and Oc (southern). Oïl languages are often seen as dialects of standard French.

[42] See section 17.2.1.1 above for the evolution of fieldwork frameworks, fieldwork *on* being the most traditional one.

Republic is French', a modification to the Constitution was required. To prepare for this, Bernard Cerquiglini, Head of the Direction Générale à la Langue Française (DGLF) within the Ministry of Culture, was charged with establishing a list of the languages concerned. The DGLF, which became the Direction Générale à la Langue Française et aux Langues de France (DGLF-LF), established a list of 75 languages of France which included regional languages, languages from French overseas territories, a new category of 'non-territorial'[43] languages, and French Sign Language (Cerquiglini 1999). By appearing in this list, Francoprovençal became recognized by the Ministry of Culture. Although France signed the Charter, at the last minute and because of electoral politics, it did not ratify it. A consequence of this is that Francoprovençal still receives no recognition from the Ministry of Education, meaning that it still cannot be taught in schools. This refusal by France to ratify the European Charter reflects the persistence of a nation state ideology that links a country to one language and one culture only.

17.4.9 Synergies between Regional, Local, and Academic Spheres: The FORA Study

At the regional level, under pressure from supporters of Oc and Francoprovençal languages, the Rhône-Alpes regional government decided in 2006 to sponsor a study of the situation of these two languages within its territory (conceived ideologically as part of its regional heritage). The study included both a sociolinguistic evaluation and propositions for language planning of the sort that already existed in other regions.

The fact that, contrary to expectations, a university research team won the bid to carry out this government-sponsored research is indicative of new dynamics within the academic sphere. For the first time, university specialists in regional languages became directly involved with the regional government, and established, on the academic front, a link between the French tradition of dialectal studies of regional languages and the newly developed international network of endangered language research (through the association of the co-authors, Bert and Grinevald, co-creators of the LED TDR research team at DDL).[44]

What has become known as the FORA (Francoprovençal–Occitan–Rhône-Alpes) project was carried out within the approach to fieldwork promoted by the LED TDR programme, with an emphasis on qualitative rather than quantitative

[43] This is a category for immigrant languages that have been spoken in France by a large number of speakers over a long period of time, and that have no official status anywhere else, in line with the ideology of France as the land of human rights.

[44] LED TDR = the 'Langues en Danger, Terrain, Documentation, Revitalisation' project at the Dynamique du Langage (DDL) laboratory, University of Lyon; see <http://www.ddl.ish-lyon.cnrs.fr/led-tdr/>, (accessed 10 October 2012).

research (as articulated in Bert et al. 2011) and paying special attention to the variety of profiles of speakers encountered in the field (as discussed in Bert and Grinevald 2010 and Grinevald and Bert 2011).[45]

It was also undertaken from a collaborative approach *with* the communities, through local associations that had multiplied all over the territory in the previous decade. On the ground, the process of fieldwork itself has contributed to the promotion of new contacts between the associations.

17.4.10 Recommendations of the FORA Study and of the Regional Government Vote

The FORA recommendations to the regional government of ways to promote the regional languages emphasized the planning of transversal actions in order to promote networking among Francoprovençal associations. The suggestions were to carry out two strands of documentation projects, to establish a corpus based on specific plans for collection, digitization, and dissemination as well as adequate conservation of the data gathered, and projects of collection and conservation of local toponymy, a threatened heritage possibly of interest for future sustainable development projects.

The FORA study and its recommendations were very well received and the Regional Assembly voted in July 2009 to 'recognize, valorize and promote Occitan and Franco-Provençal as regional languages of Rhône-Alpes'.[46] This vote is considered to be a symbolically important event by the actors who participated. Often an individual plays an essential role in facilitating synergies such as the one that made the realization of the FORA study and the implementations that followed the vote possible: in this case both owe much to A. Bengio, the General Director of the Services within the regional government, and his commitment to the issue of minority languages.[47]

Viewed within the schema of ideological spheres proposed here, the background to the discussion interestingly evokes the international sphere such as the European Charter at a regional European level, and the endangered language and intangible heritage discourses of UNESCO at the global level. At the level of the Rhône-Alpes region, the search for a regional identity tends to erase the differences between the two regional languages, Occitan and Francoprovençal, in a discourse where they are newly fused into a single and somewhat virtual 'vernacular language'. Therefore, the resulting discourse of 'one region, one

[45] The study was coordinated by Michel Bert (of DDL), Jean Baptiste Martin, scientific adviser, and James Costa, who was responsible for the language planning propositions (Bert et al. 2009).

[46] The text of the deliberation is available at <http://www.rhonealpes.fr/485-langues-regionales-rhone-alpes.htm> (accessed 10 October 2012).

[47] He also participated in the elaboration of the list of the Langues de France (see 17.4.3.1).

language' seems to replicate the ideological national model of 'one nation state, one language' (as discussed in Costa and Bert 2011).

17.4.11 Establishment of New Regional Language Policies

Currently, a team of linguists actively participates in the implementation of the new language policies of the region. Some are members of a special committee and are financed by the region for a project labelled 'Valorisation Langue Territoire: promotion du FP en Rhône-Alpes' (VLT). The project focuses on establishing a roster of associations through a database to be made available online, and on studying the modes of transmission of the language (see Pivot 2014). They are documenting a great variety of activities (theatre, *veillées* 'themed evenings', songs and local projects to create dictionaries, DVDs, etc.) that seem to result in some sort of language transmission, which is characteristically done mostly by immersion and away from school environments.

As of 2012, the approved Corpus project, which depends on the participation of the associations, had not yet started, partly due to the bias of the members of the various associations towards looking exclusively for the oldest speakers so that they may tell stories of earlier times and talk about forgotten practices, which correspond to what traditional dialectologists look for. They are not interested in language interactions and hold on to a purist vision of language, cast in a heritage ideology. Yet this type of corpus is of limited interest to linguists today, in part because it is of no direct use for teaching the language, being of limited use to would-be new speakers.

In contrast, the proposal for local toponymy has encountered much success. The associations have divided the territory to be covered and the linguists, in the role of scientific experts, are providing them with training in data collection, archiving, and digitization, in a real spirit of empowerment. At the same time it is worth noting how all these activities actually reinforce a certain ideology that equates a language with its local expression, and does not promote the sense of a Francoprovençal language at large.

17.4.12 Conclusion about the Francoprovençal Situation

Two main themes have dominated this account of the last 20 years in the situation of Francoprovençal: one focussing on changes that were unimaginable at an earlier period and which have been shaped by new dynamics in favour of the revalorization of the language, and the other highlighting the nature of the participation of academic linguists in those new dynamics.

The first period described was one of inactivity, due to a combination of low esteem or indifference towards the language, absence of interest at the administrative level of the newly established Rhône-Alpes region, and ambivalent attitudes and lack of ambition or vision at the local level, as well as among linguistic experts on the language. This situation of what could be labelled calm indifference towards Francoprovençal prevailed within the context of an openly hostile posture towards regional languages at the national level and other varying levels of activity on behalf of the other regional languages of France.

The favourable dynamics towards Francoprovençal that slowly emerged around the turn of the new century were marked by a relatively sudden acceleration due to a synergy resulting from chance encounters of a number of actors. The acceleration had much to do with the presence of a personality like Bengio in a key administrative position, and the meeting of field academics (Grinevald, Bert, and Costa) in a local university setting. Over the years they have made their experiences of fieldwork on endangered languages, and their shared interest in the fate of those languages, a subject of university research. So much so that the Francoprovençal situation has become a site of participant observation in the subfield of fieldwork on endangered languages, and has enabled reflection on their description, documentation, and revitalization.

17.5 Conclusions about Whose Ideologies, Where, and When

This chapter has drawn parallels between two field projects on endangered languages, one in Nicaragua and one in France, which could easily be taken to be more different than similar. However, as linguists involved both in linguistic work on those languages and in revitalization on their behalf, it is our conviction that strong parallels prevail. Both deal with languages at an advanced state of endangerment, and highly minoritized linguistic communities. Our focus here is on their equally complex webs of alternatively diverging and converging ideologies that we have situated in time and space.

17.5.1 Contrasts within the Frame of Analysis (Static Spheres and Dynamics)

It is obvious that the two situations are different on a number of parameters. One is in terms of the size of the respective local spheres and the nature of the linguistic communities. While the Rama situation is a case of a homogeneous and rather small population living in a well-defined territory, the Francoprovençal one is characterized by a heterogeneous population of several millions living across three countries.

Another very obvious difference is between opposite socio-economic contexts. At one end, the living conditions of the Rama speakers and community are marked by extreme poverty, discrimination, third-world conditions, and serious threats to their physical security. In clear contrast, the Francoprovençal situation is one of mostly older retired speakers in wealthy and safe countries, and a community that is diluted in the general population.

Another way of thinking of the differences is in terms of recasting the ideological dimensions of the two situations along a North–South world axis, in which the Rama situation is linked to discourse about post-colonial 'indigenous rights' and 'linguistic rights', against the backdrop of an intricate colonial history, and the Francoprovençal to a discourse of 'cultural rights'.

17.5.2 Shared Features

This co-authored chapter stemmed from the identification of overwhelming similarities between the two situations. It starts from similar experiences of academic actors that have followed parallel trajectories through long-term investment in their respective fields, and who share a willingness to become parties to linguistic revitalization projects, which after all is still not the case for many field linguists today. While involved in such projects, they have questioned the implications of such efforts from within, and have further espoused critical (academic) stances towards the nature of such projects and their evolution. In particular they have been interested in observing the roles of the multiple actors involved in each situation (local activists and speakers, higher-ranking planners and authorities at regional, national, and international levels, and academics from the ivory tower).

Several features stand out in the parallel evolutions of these projects situated as far apart as Central America and France. In both cases, the situations developed from strong stigmatization of the languages on the ground at the start of fieldwork, to a shift to differing degrees of pride. This pride emerged as part of a process of identity building in both places, but has moved more recently in both contexts into another phase of neoliberal commodification of language, in the shape of new pressure to instrumentalize the language, for example in the enterprise of eco-tourism. The discourses of identity that were initiated in regional and national contexts are therefore being reshaped by discourses coming from the international sphere (UNESCO for instance) about exhibiting and selling cultures. Thus, in both field situations, dynamics from the international sphere are being felt and adopted at regional level, and then pushed down into the local sphere.

Another aspect of the intricate relations in both contexts between the three upper spheres—international, national, and regional—is the interesting dynamics at the regional level. In both places this happened with strong ideological support from the international level in contrast to, at best, an inactive national level (Rama) or an openly negative one (Francoprovençal).

In addition, both cases share strong synergies between discourses of cultural, linguistic, and territorial identity. Although this synergy is much more marked in the Rama case, it is nevertheless part of the discourse of the Rhône-Alpes regional government. Finally, in both places the same variety of speakers of endangered languages with certain profiles can be clearly identified, leading to a joint proposal for a typology of speakers of endangered languages (Bert and Grinevald 2010; and Grinevald and Bert 2011). Here again, the perspective includes a dynamic dimension, because in both field situations the linguists also witnessed parallel evolutions in the attitudes of native speakers, from shame to pride, from hiding to coming forth and participating, as well as the fact that, by and large, most activists are generally semi-speakers or neo-speakers.

In order to analyse the complexity of ideologies that interact in situations of endangered languages in which discourses of revitalization emerge and develop, we have proposed a diagram of stacked and parallel identified spheres (see Figure 17.1) to talk about 'whose ideologies, where, and when'. This schema has enabled us to structure the analysis of very complex situations of endangered language ideologies through concrete examples from our respective field experiences. It also facilitates analysis of the impact in the field sites and communities of ideologies from this multiplicity of the spheres, as well as their impact on the field of documentary linguistics.

References

Bert, Michel. 2001. Rencontre de Langues et Francisation: l'exemple Du Pilat (Loire). PhD thesis, Université Lumière Lyon-2.

Bert, Michel. 2010. Qui parle une langue en danger? Locuteurs du francoprovençal et de l'occitan en Rhône-Alpes. In Colette Grinevald and Michel Bert (eds.), Linguistique du terrain sur langues en danger: locuteurs et linguistes. *Faits de Langues* 35/36: 79–115.

Bert, Michel. 2011. Documenter les langues régionales de Rhône-Alpes au début du XXe siècle: contexte et perspectives. In Christine Blauth-Henke and Matthias Heinz (eds.), *Où en Sont les Études sur des Langues Régionales en Domaine Roman?*. Tübingen: Stauffenburg Verlag.

Bert, Michel, James Costa, and Jean-Baptiste Martin. 2009. *Etude FORA: Francoprovençal et Occitan en Rhône-Alpes*. Institut Pierre Gardette, INRP, ICAR, and DDL, Lyon. <http://www.ddl.ish-lyon.cnrs.fr/led-tdr/> (accessed 1 October 2013).

Bert, Michel and Colette Grinevald. 2010. Proposition de typologie des locuteurs de LED. *Faits de Langues* 35–6, *Linguistique de Terrain sur Langues en Danger: Locuteurs et Linguistes*, 117–32. Paris: Ophrys.

Bert, Michel, Colette Grinevald, and Lucie Amaro. 2011. Évaluation de la vitalité des langues minoritaires: approches quantitatives vs qualitatives et implications pour la revitalisation. In Bruno Moretti, Elena Maria Pandolfi, and Matteo Casoni (eds.), *Vitalità di una lingua minoritaria: Aspetti e proposte metodologiche* [Vitality of a minority language: aspects and methodological issues]. Ticino: Osservatorio linguistico della Svizzera Italiana.

Cameron, Deborah. 2007. Language endangerment and verbal hygiene: history, morality and politics. In Alexandre Duchêne and Monica Heller (eds.), *Discourses of Endangerment: Interest and Ideology in the Defence of Languages*. London: Continuum.

Cameron, Deborah, Elizabeth Frazer, Penelope Harvey, Ben Rampton, and Kay Richardson. 1992. *Researching Language: Issues of Power and Method*. London: Routledge.

Cerquiglini, Bernard. 1999. *Les Langues de la France*. Rapport au Ministre de l'Education Nationale, de la Recherche et de la Technologie, et à la Ministre de la Culture et de la Communication. <http://www.culture.gouv.fr/culture/dglf/lang-reg/rapport_cerquiglini/langues-france.html#ancre79649#ancre79649> (accessed 1 October 2013).

Costa, James. 2010. Revitalisation Linguistique: Discours, Mythe et Idéologie. Approche Critique de Mouvements de Revitalisation en Provence et en Écosse. PhD thesis, Université de Grenoble.

Costa, James and Michel Bert. 2011. Rhône-Alpes en tension entre unité et diversité: francoprovençal, occitan et discours institutionnel. *Mots: Les langages du politique* 97: 4–57.

Craig, Colette. 1992. A constitutional response to language endangerment: the case of Nicaragua. *Language* 68(1): 11–16.

Craig, Colette. 1993. Linguistic fieldwork on endangered languages: issues of methodology and ethics. In André Crochetière, Jean-Claude Boulanger, and Conrad Ouellon (eds.), *Proceedings of the XVth International Congress of Linguists*, vol. 1. Sainte-Foy, QC: Les Presses de l'Université Laval.

Crochetière, André, Jean-Claude Boulanger, and Conrad Ouellon (eds.). 1993. *Proceedings of the XVth International Congress of Linguists*, vol. 1. Sainte-Foy, QC: Les Presses de l'Université Laval.

Dorian, Nancy. 1977. The problem of the semi-speaker in language death. *International Journal of the Sociology of Language* 12: 23–32.

Dorian, Nancy. 1981. *Language Death: The Life Cycle of a Scottish Gaelic Dialect*. Philadelphia: University of Pennsylvania Press.

Dorian, Nancy. 1993. A response to Ladefoged's other view of endangered languages. *Language* 69: 575–9.

Dorian, Nancy. 1994. Choices and values in language shift and its study. *International Journal of the Sociology of Language* 110: 113–24.

Dorian, Nancy. 1998. Western language ideologies and small-language prospects. In Lenore A. Grenoble and Lindsay J. Whaley (eds.), *Endangered Languages: Current Issues and Future Prospects*. Cambridge: Cambridge University Press.

Duchêne, Alexandre. 2008. *Ideologies across Nations: The Construction of Linguistic Minorities at the United Nations*. Berlin and New York: Mouton de Gruyter.

Duchêne, Alexandre and Monica Heller (eds.). 2007. *Discourses of Endangerment: Interest and Ideology in the Defence of Languages*. London: Continuum.

England, Nora. 1998. Mayan efforts towards language preservation. In Lenore A. Grenoble and Lindsay J. Whaley (eds.), *Endangered Languages: Current Issues and Future Prospects*. Cambridge: Cambridge University Press.

England, Nora. 2003. Mayan language revival and revitalization politics: linguists and linguistic ideologies. *American Anthropologist* 105: 733–43.

Fishman, Joshua A. 1991. *Reversing Language Shift: Theoretical and Empirical Foundations of Assistance to Threatened Languages*. Clevedon and Philadelphia: Multilingual Matters.

Freeland, Jane and Donna Patrick (eds.). 2004. *Language Rights and Language Survival.* Manchester: St Jerome Publishing.

Grinevald, Colette. 2000. Los lingüistas frente a las lenguas indígenas. In Francesc Queixalos and Odile Renault-Lescure (eds.), *As Línguas Amazônicas Hoje*. São Paulo: IRD MPEG Instituto Socioambiental.

Grinevald, Colette. 2005. Why the tiger language and not Rama Cay Creole? Language revitalization made harder. In Peter K. Austin (ed.), *Language Documentation and Description*, vol. 3. London: SOAS.

Grinevald, Colette. 2006. Worrying about ethics and wondering about informed consent: fieldwork from an Americanist perspective. In Anju Saxena and Lars Borin (eds.), *Lesser Known Languages of South Asia: Status and Policies, Case Studies and Applications of Information Technology.* Berlin and New York: Mouton de Gruyter.

Grinevald, Colette. 2007a. Linguistic fieldwork among speakers of endangered languages. In Osahito Miyaoka, Osamu Sakiyama, and Michael E. Krauss (eds.), *The Vanishing Languages of the Pacific Rim*. Oxford: Oxford University Press.

Grinevald, Colette. 2007b. Endangered languages of Mexico and Central America. In Matthias Brenzinger (ed.), *Language Diversity Endangered*. Berlin and New York: Mouton de Gruyter.

Grinevald, Colette. 2010a. Quarante ans de perspective sur deux langues en danger: le jakaltek popti' du Guatemala et le rama du Nicaragua. *Faits de Langues* 35/36: 39–78.

Grinevald, Colette. 2010b. Linguistique de terrain sur deux langues en danger: locuteurs et méthodes. *Faits de Langues* 35/36: 133–77.

Grinevald, Colette and Michel Bert (eds.). 2010. *Linguistique de terrain sur langues en danger: locuteurs et linguistes*. *Faits de Langues* 35/36.

Grinevald, Colette and Michel Bert. 2011. Speakers and community. In Peter K. Austin and Julia Sallabank (eds.), *The Cambridge Handbook of Endangered Languages*. Cambridge: Cambridge University Press.

Grinevald, Colette and Bénédicte Pivot. 2013.The revitalization of a 'treasure language': update on the Rama Language Project of Nicaragua. In Sarah Ogilvie and Mari Jones (eds.), *Language Endangerment: Documentation, Pedagogy and Revitalization*. Cambridge: Cambridge University Press.

Grinevald Craig, Colette. 1997. Language contact and language degeneration. In Florian Coulmas (ed.), *Handbook of Sociolinguistics*. Oxford: Blackwell.

Hale, Kenneth, Michael Krauss, Lucille J. Watahomigie, Akira Y. Yamamoto, Colette Craig, Jeanne M. LaVerne, and Nora C. England. 1992. Endangered languages. *Language* 68: 1–42.

Himmelmann, Nikolaus P. 1998. Documentary and descriptive linguistics. *Linguistics* 36: 161–95.

Himmelmann, Nikolaus P. 2006. Language documentation: what is it and what is it good for? In Jost Gippert, Nikolaus P. Himmelmann, and Ulrike Mosel (eds.), *Essentials of Language Documentation*. Berlin and New York: Mouton de Gruyter.

Ladefoged, Peter. 1992. Another view of endangered languages. *Language* 68: 809–11.

Newman, Paul. 1999. 'We have seen the enemy and it is us': the endangered languages issue as a hopeless cause. *Studies in the Linguistic Sciences* 28: 11–20.

Newman, Paul. 2003. The endangered language issue as a hopeless cause. In M. Janse and S. Tol (eds.), *Language Death and Language Maintenance: Theoretical, Practical and Descriptive Approaches*. Amsterdam: John Benjamins.

Pivot, Bénédicte. 2010. Évaluation d'une situation de revitalisation d'une langue en danger: le cas du rama, langue du Nicaragua. Masters thesis 2, Université Lumière-Lyon 2.

Pivot, Bénédicte. 2014. Revitalisation de langues postvernaculaires: le francoprovençal en Rhône-Alpes et le rama au Nicaragua. Doctoral thesis, Université Lumière-Lyon 2.

Stich, Dominique. 1998. *Parlons francoprovençal, une langue méconnue.* Paris: Éditions l'Harmattan.

Tuaillon, Gaston. 1988. Le franco-provençal, langue oubliée. In Geneviêve Vermes (ed.), *Vingt-cinq communautés linguistiques de la France*, vol. 1. Paris: l'Harmattan.

18

UN Discourse on Linguistic Diversity and Multilingualism in the 2000s: Actor Analysis, Ideological Foundations, and Instrumental Functions*

ANAHIT MINASYAN

18.1 Introduction

THERE ARE THREE possible attitudes towards the diversity of languages spoken by humanity: positive (what a blessing, this linguistic diversity!), negative (what a curse, this Tower of Babel!) and neutral (or in emotional terms, indifferent). While there are individuals and entities (including states) that steadily promote through discourse and/or through practice one of the first two views, many seem to have no strong opinion, or seem to oscillate between positive and negative, depending on the situation.

The task for the authors of this volume set by the editors, following Joshua Fishman's appeal (Fishman 2001), was to discuss beliefs and ideologies held by various actors involved in 'reversing language shift (RLS) movements' (Fishman 1991) (i.e. efforts to maintain or revitalize an endangered language). I will focus on the United Nations (UN) system and its constituent actors, exploring, through discourse analysis, the ideologies that bring about and shape these intergovernmental organizations' (IGOs) involvement in the cause.

18.2 Terms Requiring Preliminary Clarification

Certain terms used in this chapter call for a brief discussion to explain which of the many definitions are to be used and to focus the reader's attention on the relevant aspects of certain particularly multi-layered concepts.

Let us start with *culture*. Most of its definitions fall roughly into two categories: Culture with a capital 'C', defined from an aesthetic perspective, and

* The author is responsible for the choice and the presentation of the facts contained in this chapter and for the opinions expressed therein, which are not necessarily those of UNESCO.

culture with a small 'c', defined from the anthropological viewpoint. Within the UN discourse, it is the second perspective that has prevailed for several decades. The preamble to the UNESCO Universal Declaration on Cultural Diversity (2001) defines 'culture' as the 'set of distinctive spiritual, material, intellectual and emotional features of society or a social group, that encompasses, in addition to art and literature, lifestyles, ways of living together, value systems, traditions and beliefs' (UNESCO 2001).

As the concepts of *ideology* and *language ideologies* have already been discussed in Chapter 1 of this volume, I will instead highlight the relationship between ideologies, actors, and transnational policymaking (a more detailed discussion will follow). Recent sociological studies suggest that ideas, identities, norms, and beliefs affect policy-making more than has been presumed over the past decades. Campbell (2002: 24) argues that, under certain conditions, 'normative beliefs may be so strong that they override the self-interest of policy makers' who resultantly pass legislation that favours social groups other than their own (for instance, women or minorities), disregarding the majority's reluctance and 'risking their electoral fortunes in the process'.

These 'normative beliefs' shared by increasingly globalized elites are referred to, among others, as 'world culture,' 'global civic culture', or 'global ethics'.[1] These *global ethics* are based on the necessity for individuals to cooperate to ensure the survival of the group, a vital principle cultivated in all human societies and conceptualized in various spiritual traditions as the 'golden rule' of conduct (i.e. not doing to others what one would not wish to be done to oneself). They have been further shaped by the values enshrined in human rights and permeate current discourse produced by the international community and by most national and local policy-makers.

Girard (1982) defined *policy* as a system of aims and means, pursued by a group and applied by an authority. Miller and Yúdice (2002: 1) describe *cultural policy* in terms of 'the institutional supports that channel both aesthetic creativity and collective ways of life … [and are] embodied in systematic, regulatory guides to action that are adopted by organisations to achieve their goals'. These 'supports' and 'guides to action' take the form of funding, promoting, training, and distributing, including the definition of the very criteria of what is to be considered 'culture'. Cultural policies are sometimes explicit (or deliberate), and oftentimes ad hoc, designed 'on the run' (see Miller and Yúdice (2002) for a detailed discussion on this subject). The same observation can be made of language policies that are often established 'by practice and consensus rather

[1] For a discussion of 'global ethics', see World Commission on Culture and Development (1995: 33–51). The authors of this 'World Report' stress that 'The principles and basic ideas of a global ethics furnish the minimal standards any political community should observe' (World Commission on Culture and Development 1995: 47).

than by specific acts of language management' (Spolsky 2009: 167; Spolsky, this volume).

The first purpose of cultural policy, according to Girard (1982), is the 'right to culture' recognized in the Universal Declaration of Human Rights (1948) and the subsequent International Covenant on Economic, Social and Cultural Rights (ICESCR 1966), which asserts in its Article 15 that everyone has the right to 'take part in cultural life'.[2]

Finally, I wish to clarify the term 'discourse' and highlight aspects of 'globalization' that are relevant to this chapter. Fairclough (2003) defines texts as parts of social events and as tools for producing, diffusing, or changing ideologies; from this perspective, *discourse* can be described as 'a meaningful social action: a key instrument of individuals' and groups' participation in social roles, social contexts, social situations and social processes' (Fox and Fox 2004: 15). Discourse as action encompasses the processes of production of texts and of their interpretation (Fairclough 2001), and is a tool for mobilization and influence available to various types of social actors.

As regards the features of 'globalization' that are of interest to us, several observations come to mind. First, globalization enhances individual and social actors' capacity 'to act upon and shape the actions of others over considerable distances of space and time' (Fairclough 2003: 30). This increased capacity amplifies the process of policy diffusion or 'policy transfer': replication and adaptation of policies and institutions from one place to another (see Evans 2004). Some commentators describe this process as the 'internationalization of social policy', thereby highlighting the interplay between the national and international levels of policy-making that accompany globalization (see, for instance, Ervik et al. 2009).

With this in mind, it is not surprising that discourse has become a powerful tool of governance and policy-making throughout the world. In the following sections I will focus on how discourse was used (i.e. produced and interpreted) in the context of the UN and its agencies in order to support language maintenance and revitalization in the first decade of the twenty-first century.

18.3 The UN System in Relation to RLS: Agentive Actors and their Interactions

It has been observed that globalization 'emphasises both the international dimension of human welfare and focuses attention on international institutions as social policy actors in their own right' (Yeates 2001: 19). These institutions promote 'policy mobility', international cooperation, and invite comparisons and

[2] ICESCR (1966). To be discussed further in the section dealing with linguistic human rights.

learning (ibid.: 31). They derive their legitimacy from the assumption of their member states that they 'provide more efficient means of solving problems of common interest across nations than if each state tackled the problems on its own' (Ervik et al. 2009: 4).

The UN is an international (inter-governmental) organization founded in 1945 with the purpose of 'maintaining international peace and security, developing friendly relations among nations and promoting social progress, better living standards and human rights'.[3] In 2010, the UN had 192 member states, and the 'UN System' included 15 specialized agencies, the World Bank Group, as well as a number of programmes, funds, and other bodies.

The UN system can be analysed in terms of its constituent actors/stakeholders whose combined action has an impact on RLS. These can be considered to be agentic actors in the sense of Meyer and Jepperson (2000: 108), who define the main characteristic of modern agentic actors as their readiness and capacity to act as agents for other actors and to mobilize for 'potential actors' (e.g. foetuses, the unorganized poor), as well as for 'the imagined interests of non-actor entities', such as the ecosystem, animals, or endangered languages. In the UN system they are as follows:

18.3.1 Governmental Actors: Member States of the UN and its Agencies

As of 2010, UNESCO had 193 member states and seven associate members. These actors interact with the other constituent actors (e.g. the experts or the members of the UN staff) mainly through their National Commissions for UNESCO and Permanent Delegations to UNESCO and, on some occasions, through high-level officials such as heads of state or ministers, or through 'governmental experts'.[4] As regards the discourse of these actors, it is generally consistent at the national and international levels. However, given that decisions at the UN are taken collectively (through consensus or vote), their collective discourse does not always reflect the views of all member states. The main channels of this collective discourse are the decisions and resolutions of the Governing Bodies and Treaty Bodies (variously named the 'General Assembly', 'General Conference', 'Conference of Parties', etc.) and international normative texts (declarations, recommendations, and conventions). The governmental actors are directly involved in drafting, interpreting, and implementing these texts, and may spend hours negotiating a consensus over a single word.

As a case in point, I will cite here the 2007 UN Multilingualism Resolution, in which the member states *recognize* that 'genuine multilingualism promotes unity in diversity and international understanding'. Further, they *recognize* 'the

[3] See <http://www.un.org/en/aboutun/index.shtml> (accessed 1 October 2013).

[4] For more information, see <http://www.unesco.org> (accessed 1 October 2013).

importance of the capacity to communicate to the peoples of the world in their own languages', they *recall* 'that linguistic diversity is an important element of cultural diversity', and they *call upon* 'Member States and the Secretariat to promote the preservation and protection of all languages used by peoples of the world'.[5]

18.3.2 Epistemic Community: Experts in Linguistics and Anthropology and Other Relevant Fields, and NGOs

Meyer and Jepperson (2000: 103) claim that, due to globalization, high esteem for 'scientific authority' has now spread to nearly every corner of the planet, 'with scientists attaining substantial public (even philosophic) standing in world culture'. In order to account for their decisions before legislators and public, governmental actors claim to have been guided by 'scientific and professional advice'. To reinforce the legitimacy of their actions, organizations 'structure themselves to depend upon a host of professionalized consultants in every sector, and further, internalise the relevant professionals' (Meyer and Jepperson 2000: 114). Meyer and Jepperson (2000) argue that unlike power, which is perceived as infused with self-interest, authority seems to come in modern societies from the 'relative purity of otherhood' (i.e. the scientific discourse is generally believed to be neutral, objective, and unbiased). These actors have been referred to as 'epistemic communities' in sociological literature. Following Haas (1992), Campbell (2002: 30) defines such communities as 'networks of professionals and experts with an authoritative claim to policy-relevant knowledge, who share a set of normative beliefs, causal models, notions of empirical validity, and a common policy enterprise' and are instrumental in generating innovative policy ideas and disseminating them. Epistemic communities exert their influence through 'political insinuation of their members into the policymaking process and through their ability to acquire regulatory and policymaking responsibility and to persuade others of the correctness of their approach' (Adler and Haas 1992: 374).

In order to describe the 'activist' groups within these epistemic communities, the term 'transnational advocacy coalitions' has been proposed. Such coalitions are formed by people both from within and outwith the epistemic communities, based on shared beliefs and morals. They produce a shared discourse on a variety of issues (e.g. human trafficking, gender, the environment, endangerment of species, and endangerment of languages), and actively engage in 'seeking to shape the climate of public debate and influence global policy agendas' (Stone 2008: 31).

It has been suggested that, for the members of an epistemic community, the academic standing of the said members within their disciplines is most important

[5] General Assembly. 2007. Resolution 61/266. Multilingualism. A/RES/61/266, see <http://www.un.org/ga/search/view_doc.asp?symbol=a/res/61/266> (accessed 1 October 2013).

in terms of the potential impact that it can have on international policy-making and policy transfer. This takes precedence over the size of the community (Adler and Haas 1992: 380).

Governments tend to seek the best available expertise in times of uncertainty or crises, especially when officials realize the limitations of their own understanding of new developments and certain complex issues (Adler and Haas 1992; Ervik et al. 2009). They recognize the need for scientific explanations of the processes in question and their potential societal impacts, as well as suggestions for possible responses to these problems. Haas (1992: 4) qualifies this type of information delivered by epistemic communities to decision-makers as 'neither guesses nor "raw" data; it is the product of human interpretations of social and physical phenomena'.

The thematic debate on indigenous and endangered languages and Education for All (EFA) organized by UNESCO's Executive Board in 2008 at the initiative of its chairperson and as part of its 180th session, is an apt illustration of the above.[6] The state members of the Executive Board who convened for the debate invited the following scholars and public personalities to participate and share their views on the subject matter: Achi linguist Nikte' Maria Juliana Sis Iboy (Guatemala), writer and Yoruba literature professor Akinwumi Isola, Indian scholar and publisher Ganesh Devy, Venezuelan anthropologist Omar Enrique González Ñáñez, Finnish linguistic human rights activist Tove Skutnabb-Kangas, and the former Icelandic president and UNESCO Goodwill Ambassador for Languages, Vigdís Finnbogadóttir.

Their presentations were followed by an intense question-and-answer session, during which representatives of over 30 states took the floor to make statements on their country's position with regard to linguistic diversity, multilingualism, and education. A number of these representatives addressed very specific questions to the experts, soliciting their 'interpretations' and guidance. These questions included:

- Given the scarcity of resources, could rapid progress be made on EFA while at the same time investing in the preservation of mother tongues and indigenous languages? How could these two objectives be harmonized (Portugal and Thailand)?
- In countries with indigenous languages and a language of wider communication, would the most appropriate approach be to achieve literacy first in the mother tongue and only then in the language of wider communication (Cuba)? What factors need to be considered when designing an indigenous language programme to be introduced into the school system (Malaysia)?

[6] UNESCO Executive Board (2008).

- Could the existing international normative instruments guaranteeing linguistic human rights be used more effectively (Bulgaria)? If so, how could coherent efforts by various stakeholders be encouraged to that end (El Salvador)?
- Is there a limit to the number of languages that could be taught in a multilingual framework (Japan)?
- To what degree should governments promote language revitalization, and what were the procedures and conditions under which communities could reliably express their will as to whether they wished to keep their language alive or not (US)?

18.3.3 Speaker Communities, Activists, NGOs, and Indigenous Peoples' Groups

Spolsky (2009: 198) highlights an interesting discussion on grass-roots language activist groups, noting that while many of these groups have a wider socio-political agenda, language remains a central element and a lever for mobilization: 'While they lack the power to manage, they can be successful in supporting and spreading beliefs and ideologies which prepare the way for government management, and they can be successful in lobbying for legislation and other management decisions ... These language activists then are significant participants in national language management.'

The views and agendas of these types of actors often reach the UN through experts or governments, even though some channels of direct expression have emerged of late, the most notable of which is the UN Permanent Forum on Indigenous Issues (UNPFII). This is an advisory body to the Economic and Social Council with a mandate to discuss indigenous issues related to economic and social development, culture, the environment, education, health, and human rights. Indigenous peoples and others in the Working Group on Indigenous Populations felt that the structures of the UN were not well suited to considering issues of concern to indigenous peoples comprehensively. In addition, they felt that the participation of indigenous representatives in the UN was limited. In the light of these concerns, indigenous peoples and others proposed establishing a new body that would focus on global issues related to indigenous peoples and that would offer the opportunity for indigenous peoples to participate effectively.

In 2008, the UNPFII organized an Expert Group Meeting (EGM) on indigenous languages, during which representatives of various indigenous groups spoke about their language situations and discussed how they could benefit from a more pronounced UN involvement. The meeting produced a set of recommendations to the UN and its agencies, to national governments, and to the indigenous peoples on how to best promote and protect indigenous languages.[7]

[7] UN ECOSOC 2008.

Another important point to be made concerns the principle of 'free, prior and informed consent' (FPIC) which is built into a number of UN normative texts, such as the ILO 169 Convention concerning Indigenous and Tribal Peoples in Independent Countries, or the Convention on Biological Diversity (cf. Article VIII (j)).[8] The 2003 Convention for the Safeguarding of the Intangible Cultural Heritage supplies an example of a concrete mechanism to ensure such consent. It is articulated in Criterion 4 for inscription on the Representative List of the Intangible Cultural Heritage of Humanity, also in Criterion 4 for inscription on the List of Intangible Cultural Heritage in Need of Urgent Safeguarding, and in Criterion 5 for selection as a 'best practice'. These criteria require that the nominating state demonstrate 'the widest possible participation of the community, group or, if applicable, individuals concerned and with their free, prior and informed consent'.[9]

Another way to give voice to the speakers of endangered languages is to make use of the 'read/write' feature of the 'Web 2.0' (i.e. the Internet's interactive character). One of the first attempts by an IGO in this direction was the updating of the online version of UNESCO's *Atlas of the World's Languages in Danger* (Moseley 2009) as a result of users' feedback, many of whom were speakers of the languages listed in the atlas. Over 100 entries were revised within the first 18 months of its publication.

It should be noted for fairness' sake that segments of speaker communities who do not wish to maintain or revitalize their language are unlikely to organize into activist groups and lobby the international community not to support language shift.

18.3.4 The UN Staff or 'the Secretariat'

The extent of agency of these actors depends on their position in the organizational hierarchy, their experience, and their level of expertise. The duties of UN staff may include running peacekeeping operations, surveying and monitoring global trends, drafting human rights reports, liaising with the media, translating documents, and so on (see Alger 2005: 22–3). Stone (2008: 30, 33) highlights certain characteristics of UN staff, including their relative 'impartiality, objectivity and international loyalty rather than national particularism', their rather 'globalized' identity and outlook, but also the fact that they tend to travel too much, are geographically dispersed, and therefore meet irregularly and rely instead on information technology.

[8] For a discussion on FPIC in various UN texts, see Report of UNPFII Workshop at <http://www.un.org/esa/socdev/unpfii/en/workshopFPIC.html> (accessed 1 October 2013).

[9] See operational directives for the implementation of the Convention for the Safeguarding of the Intangible Heritage at <http://www.unesco.org/culture/ich/index.php?lg=enandpg=00026> (accessed 1 October 2013).

The Secretariat's functions include close cooperation on issues in their area of competencies with the three other types of actors. For instance, the Secretariat's interaction with epistemic communities involves:

- soliciting contributions to documents (reports, policy guidelines, position papers, etc.);
- soliciting participation in 'expert meetings' aiming to shed light on specific questions (for instance, language mapping or multilingual education); and
- involving committees, evaluation panels; or consultants in tackling a particular research task or managing a project.

It is noteworthy that UNESCO's Endangered Languages Programme was launched following the 1992 Congress of the Permanent International Committee of Linguists (CIPL), which focussed on language endangerment and loss, and specifically called for UNESCO to take action.[10]

All of the aforementioned actors agree in UN forums that language-related human rights (for a more detailed discussion see below) are to be 'respected', 'protected', and 'fulfilled'. They also agree that linguistic diversity is a cultural resource and a common heritage of humanity, and hence endangered languages should be 'safeguarded'. Note that 'safeguarding' is defined as 'measures aimed at ensuring the viability of the intangible cultural heritage, including the identification, documentation, research, preservation, protection, promotion, enhancement, transmission, particularly through formal and non-formal education, as well as the revitalization of the various aspects of such heritage' in Article 2 of 2003 UNESCO Convention. Thus defined, 'safeguarding' would cover both language maintenance and language revitalization.

Several UN bodies are involved in ensuring the 'linguistic human rights' of individuals, on the one hand, and in the elaboration and implementation of norms, guidelines, and projects designed to safeguard the linguistic heritage and promote the linguistic diversity of humanity on the other hand.

18.4 UN Discourse on Linguistic Diversity and Multilingualism: Cycle, Types, Functions, and Underlying Ideologies

A representation of the 'production-diffusion-interpretation' cycle of UN discourse on languages can be described as follows: the epistemic community produces and popularizes a particular idea or an argument, governmental actors interpret/develop it into resolutions and programmatic or normative texts; the Secretariat interprets/develops it into advocacy texts, reports, guidelines, and so

[10] See <http://www.ciplnet.com> (accessed 1 October 2013).

on, while also supporting the implementation of normative texts mentioned above; and the speaker communities appropriate and use the UN-generated normative instruments and other texts to substantiate their claims for language rights and status, and/or to secure funding for their safeguarding efforts.[11] There is a growing tendency for governments to cooperate with the speaker communities in these types of efforts, which is due, among other things, to governments' heightened awareness and familiarity with the discourse of linguistic diversity, as well as to the influence of social justice and equity-oriented normative beliefs mentioned in section 18.1.

For a concrete example of how this cycle works, let us look at the relatively new discourse on biolinguistic diversity. The concept of 'biocultural' and 'biolinguistic' diversity was developed during the 1990s by an epistemic community including Berkes, Harmon, Loh, Maffi, Mühlhäusler, Posey, Skutnabb-Kangas, and Zent, among others. Their argument that linguistic and biological diversity are interdependent has influenced such high-profile documents as the *UNESCO Universal Declaration on Cultural Diversity* (2001) and Decision VII/30 of the 7th Conference of Parties to the *Convention on Biological Diversity* (2004). This decision established a framework of indicators to be used globally and nationally in assessing biodiversity status and trends. One of the indicators is the 'Status and Trends of Linguistic Diversity and the Numbers of Speakers of Indigenous Languages'.[12] In addition to these documents, the UN has produced a number of guidelines, reports, and declarations in the subsequent years relying heavily on the work by the above-mentioned epistemic community. These include: *Sharing a World of Difference: The Earth's Linguistic, Cultural and Biological Diversity* (2003, co-published by UNESCO, WWF, and Terralingua), *Links between Biological and Cultural Diversity* (UNESCO 2008),[13] and a multi-agency *Declaration on Bio-cultural Diversity.*[14] Moreover, the Intergovernmental Committee of the UNESCO Convention 2003 inscribed a number of cultural expressions linking oral traditions, languages, traditional knowledge, and natural environment on to the Representative List of the Intangible Cultural Heritage of Humanity, while measures designed to safeguard such expressions have been funded and carried out by various state parties. Examples include: the oral heritage and cultural manifestations of the Zápara people, the whistled language of La Gomera (Canary Islands), the Silbo Gomero (language, dance, and music) of the Garifuna, and the Olonkho, a Yakut heroic epos.[15]

[11] The UN's normative texts and resolutions are available in, at least, the six official languages of the organization. The other texts are, as a rule, also available in a number of languages.

[12] See <http://www.cbd.int/decision/cop/?id=7767> (accessed 1 October 2013).

[13] See <http://unesdoc.unesco.org/images/0015/001592/159255e.pdf> (accessed 1 October 2013).

[14] See <http://www.unesco.org/mab/doc/iyb/Declaration.pdf> (accessed 1 October 2013).

[15] See brief descriptions of these practices and the safeguarding projects that were carried out at <http://www.unesco.org/culture/ich/index.php?lg=enandpg=00011> (accessed 1 October 2013).

As already mentioned, the UN discourse on linguistic diversity and multilingualism is generally produced, diffused, and interpreted either from the perspective of human rights or whilst invoking the idea of a common heritage and cultural wealth of humanity (i.e. emphasizing that languages are a vital component of 'global cultural goods').

In the 2000s, an array of interventions was used to diffuse these two types of discourse and their related policy recommendations: advocacy (through events, International Years, print materials, visual and electronic materials, etc.), operational projects, data compilation and clearing-house initiatives, the monitoring of trends (developing indicators, statistical analysis, reports), monitoring and supporting implementation of normative instruments (periodic reports of parties, their examination by treaty bodies and public comments on them, capacity-building activities, channelling international assistance), and so on. I will discuss both perspectives and the roles of different actors in their related discourse cycle below, noting however that this chapter focuses on the discourse in its various shapes and forms, and does not deal with the UN-funded field projects that have an RLS component. To inventory all the recent and ongoing projects and analyse their joint impact calls for a separate study.

18.4.1 Linguistic Human Rights

Spolsky (2009) observes that 'language rights' are typically interpreted in the following ways: rights assigned to individuals (i.e. part of universal human rights), rights assigned to groups (collective rights), and—more rarely—rights assigned to 'languages' (building on the analogy with biological diversity, it is assumed that linguistic diversity also needs protection from people's unwise choices and actions).

De Varennes (2007: 116–17) argues that it is 'unfortunate and erroneous' to interpret, as has often been the case in recent years, that language rights are essentially 'collective rights'. In his view, such an interpretation results in casting language rights 'as part of a new generation of rights' that are 'weaker' and less important than 'authentic', fundamental, individual human rights. He goes on to demonstrate that the vast majority of the existing language use related provisions in international law are 'examples of the direct application of general human rights provisions, mainly freedom of expression, non-discrimination, right to private life and the rights of members of a linguistic minority to use their own language with other members of their group'.

A number of UN bodies, programmes, and specialized agencies are involved in the advancement of human rights, which comprise civil, political, economic, social, and cultural rights. International law in general, and human rights law in particular, has been described as a 'broad social phenomenon deeply embedded in the practices, beliefs, and traditions of societies, and shaped by interaction among societies' (Glenn 2000 cited in Finnemore and Toope 2001: 743).

According to a recent UNESCO document (UNESCO Executive Board 2009a), the following language rights are provided, at the level of the individual, in other widely ratified international human rights legislation:

(i) the right to be educated in the mother tongue in state schools when the minority members so wish;
(ii) the right to establish and operate linguistic minority schools;
(iii) equitable access to state funding;
(iv) the use of minority languages in court and administrative proceedings (or access to interpretation where not available);
(v) the right to publish (in all media) in the language of choice, as long as minimum standards are met;
(vi) non-discrimination on the grounds of language in relation to the rights associated with work, social security, health, family life, education, participation in cultural life, a fair trial, freedom of speech, and taking part in public life;
(vii) the right to maintain their own language (as part of the right to participate in cultural life);
(viii) freedom of speech (to seek, receive, and impart information and ideas orally or in a form of art or media of one's choice);
(ix) the right to take part in public affairs and public service without discrimination on the grounds of language; and
(x) the obligation not to deny children the right to use their own language.[16]

The legal texts providing the above linguistic human rights are considered to be 'soft law', in which 'legal arrangements are weakened along one or more of the dimensions of obligation, precision, and delegation' (Abbott and Snidal 2000: 421). Critics have focused on the lack of enforcement and sanctions for non-compliance of this type of law, but a growing body of research has begun to look at the various strengths and advantages of the 'soft' law as compared to the highly precise, delegated, and enforceable 'hard law' which is typical in national contexts. Abbott and Snidal (2000) argue that the admitted weaknesses (i.e. the soft characteristics) with international law can also be interpreted as strengths. For instance, it is relatively easy to achieve an international consensus and high ratification rates in

[16] UNESCO Executive Board (2009a). See the same document for a full list and a discussion of the standard-setting documents in question. The legally binding documents are: Convention Against Discrimination in Education (1960); International Covenant on Civil and Political Rights (ICCPR) (1966); International Covenant on Economic, Social and Cultural Rights (ICESCR) (1966); International Convention on the Elimination of All Forms of Racial Discrimination (1966); Convention on the Rights of the Child (1989); and ILO Convention 169 concerning Indigenous and Tribal Peoples in Independent Countries (1989).

soft law as it allows states to retain a high degree of decision-making authority (weak delegation) and offers effective ways to deal with uncertainty and to learn by doing (imprecision and lack of sanctions). As a result, it facilitates compromise and cooperation between actors with different interests, values, and degrees of power. Finnemore and Toope (2001) observe that in a number of areas of international law, relative imprecision of norms goes hand in hand with high compliance. Parties to these normative instruments establish mechanisms to promote their implementation 'premised on the need for positive reinforcement of obligations rather than on adjudication and sanctions for noncompliance'.

Discussing these types of mechanisms with regard to cultural rights in the context of the International Covenant on Economic, Social and Cultural Rights (ICESCR), Donders (2007) finds it useful to distinguish between negative and positive obligations. Negative obligations essentially imply that the state should refrain from action, while positive ones entail state action (see also Kloss' (1968) distinction between 'tolerance-oriented' (authorities not interfering with what minorities do with their language in the private domain) and 'promotion-oriented' (authorities promoting minority language through institutional use in law, administration, and public education) language rights). In relation to linguistic rights, Donders (2007) evokes the shared understanding of the negative obligation not to interfere with individuals' language choices in private domains, but observes that there is no general agreement on providing language facilities for individuals to use their chosen language in their dealings with the administration.[17]

The implementation incentives in the case of ICESCR, ICCPR (International Covenant on Civil and Political Rights) and other relevant international norms are ensured by the monitoring mechanism, which involves a state-reporting procedure, examination of these periodic reports by a committee (e.g. the Committee on Economic, Social and Cultural Rights, the Human Rights Committee or another body, as the case may be), taking into account the comments and views provided by NGOs; the formulation of questions, comments, and observations by the said committee and the required response by the state; as well as special procedures such as the appointment of special rapporteurs.[18] All of the above takes place in public, rather than behind closed doors, and therefore tends to be rather persuasive, 'as governments are generally sensitive to public exposure of their human rights performance' (Levin 2004: 33).

In their periodic reports, states describe the legislative and other measures that they have adopted in the implementation of the normative instrument in

[17] In November 2010, the Human Rights Committee asserted that 'A State party may choose one or more national or official languages, but it may not exclude, outside the spheres of public life, the freedom to express oneself in a language of one's own choice' (CCPR 2010: 3).

[18] For a more detailed description, see, for instance, Levin (2004).

question. A 2008 compilation by the Office of the High Commissioner for Human Rights (OHCHR) of the work of ten treaty bodies with regard to the protection of indigenous languages in 1994–2006 supplies an interesting overview of these bodies' communications to the reporting states that expressly address linguistic rights.[19] I will cite below two examples to illustrate these interactions, whilst refraining from generalizations and analysis that would require more in-depth research than the scope of this chapter permits.[20]

In 1998, the Committee on the Elimination of Racial Discrimination encouraged the Russian Federation to take further measures to provide mother tongue based education (CERD/C/304/Add.43). In its reply submitted in 2008, the Russian Federation reported to the Committee, among other things, on the efforts made over the past decade to create or to support 'ethnocultural' public schools in which 18 per cent of all students were enrolled, as well as on the funding allocated to publish dictionaries of small indigenous languages of the north (Nenets and Selkup) and to support minority language media (CERD/C/RUS/Q/19/Add.1).

In 2001, the Committee on Economic, Social and Cultural Rights encouraged Algeria to 'preserve the language and culture of the Amazigh population and to take appropriate steps to implement the plans to accord constitutional status to the Amzigh language as a national language' and requested information on the access to print and broadcast media for the Amazigh culture (E/C.12/1/ADD.71). In its reply submitted in 2010, Algeria reported to CESCR that Amazigh was granted the status of a national language following the revision of their constitution in 2002, that a national teacher training centre attached to the Ministry of Education was established in 2003; that, at the time of the report, the 'Amazigh national language' was promoted and taught at all levels of education (at primary level in 768 schools, at middle school level in 282 schools, and at secondary level in 63 schools); and that in 2009 a new television channel was launched whose programmes were entirely broadcast in various forms of the Amazigh language (E/C.12/DZA/Q/4/Add.1).

18.4.2 Languages as a Global Cultural Resource

Almost every document dealing with languages or multilingualism produced by UNESCO in the first decade of the twenty-first century states that languages are more than communication tools, as they reflect our ways of being and conceptualizing the world. These statements can no doubt be traced to the famous 'linguistic relativity' or 'Sapir-Whorf hypothesis': the 'proposal that the

[19] OHCHR (2008).

[20] The replies of the states were retrieved from the OHCHR Treaty Bodies database <http://tb.ohchr.org/default.aspx> (accessed 1 October 2013).

particular language we speak influences the way we think about reality' (Lucy 1997: 291). The earliest powerful incursion of this idea into UN discourse is due to the late Professor Stephen Wurm who was the editor-in-chief of the first two editions of *UNESCO's Atlas of the World's Languages in Danger* (1996 and 2001). His assertion that 'each language reflects a unique world view and culture complex' (2001: 10), coupled with the statement of the *Language Vitality and Endangerment* paper (UNESCO 2003: 1)[21] that 'each and every language embodies the unique cultural wisdom of a people: the loss of any language is thus a loss for all humanity', have been taken up countless times in a variety of UN reports, policy documents, web materials, and press releases, which have, in turn, fed into printed and broadcast press, websites and blogs throughout the world.

Languages, thus depicted as an essential component of culture, depositories of knowledge, important identity markers, and essential vehicles of humanity's intangible cultural heritage, have been incorporated into the latest set of UNESCO's international normative documents that address the 'protection', 'promotion', and 'safeguarding' of cultural diversity and cultural heritage. They are:

- the UNESCO Universal Declaration on Cultural Diversity (2001);
- the Convention for the Safeguarding of the Intangible Cultural Heritage (2003); and
- the Convention on the Protection and Promotion of the Diversity of Cultural Expressions (2005).

The first of these three texts, adopted by the General Conference of UNESCO's Member States in 2001, sets out the framework in which the international community is to tackle the threat to linguistic diversity. Its Action Plan, inter alia, calls for member states to take appropriate measures towards the following:

- safeguarding the linguistic heritage of humanity and giving support to expression, creation, and dissemination in the greatest possible number of languages;
- encouraging linguistic diversity—while respecting the 'mother tongue'—at all levels of education, wherever possible, and fostering the learning of several languages from the earliest age;
- promoting linguistic diversity in new technologies and encouraging universal access to all information in the public domain. (UNESCO 2001).

[21] This paper was drafted collectively in 2002–3 by the UNESCO Ad Hoc Expert Group on Endangered Languages that included Matthias Brenzinger, Arienne M. Dwyer, Tjeerd de Graaf, Colette Grinevald, Michael Krauss, Osahito Miyaoka, Nicholas Ostler, Osamu Sakiyama, María E. Villalón, Akira Y. Yamamoto, and Ofelia Zepeda.

In 2003, with regards to education, UNESCO elaborated a policy guideline ('position paper') entitled *Education in a Multilingual World*. This document, based on a review of existing UN texts, puts forward three 'basic principles' summarizing its approach to language and education in the twenty-first century, which are:

1. UNESCO supports mother tongue instruction as a means of improving educational quality by building upon the knowledge and experience of the learners and teachers.
2. UNESCO supports bilingual and/or multilingual education at all levels of education as a means of promoting both social and gender equality and as a key element of linguistically diverse societies.
3. UNESCO supports language as an essential component of intercultural education in order to encourage understanding between different population groups and ensure respect for fundamental rights.

Another widely used guideline focussing on mother tongue based multilingual inclusive education is the 2007 *Advocacy Kit for Promoting Multilingual Education: Including the Excluded*. Produced by UNESCO Asia and the Pacific Regional Bureau for Education (Bangkok), this practical advocacy kit contains an overview of regional policy and practice, a 'Policy Makers Booklet', a 'Programme Implementers Booklet', and a 'Community Members Booklet'.

In a report submitted to UNESCO's Executive Board in 2008, the director general recapitulated the reasons why linguistic diversity should be protected, and outlined the organization's main policy recommendations as follows:

> Essentially, national policies should be aimed at (a) safeguarding linguistic diversity by protecting and revitalising languages and (b) promoting multilingualism as far as possible. These two objectives are intertwined since the promotion of multilingualism (including mother tongue education) also constitutes a means of safeguarding indigenous and endangered languages. On the international level, this is essentially a similar two-pronged approach (a) to preserve global linguistic diversity as a prerequisite for cultural diversity and (b) to promote multilingualism (including in administration, education, the media and cyberspace) in order to foster inter-cultural dialogue.

Finally, some texts—most notably, the UN Declaration on the Rights of Indigenous Peoples (UN 2007) adopted in 2007 by the UN General Assembly after many years of debate—deliver a hybrid rights–resources discourse, addressing indigenous languages both in terms of individual and collective linguistic human rights (see Article 14.3, Article 16) and as common cultural goods and resources (see Article 13, Article 14.1).

18.4.3 Main Functions of the UN Discourse on Languages

Both types of UN discourse on languages described above (i.e. linguistic human rights and common cultural resource) share the following functions:

(i) supplying 'rhetorical statements' (see Spolsky 2009 and as discussed below) for advocacy and policy formulation;
(ii) influencing policies and practices through the 'soft regulation' power of 'naming and shaming' (this mainly happens in the interactions between UN treaty bodies and states, but certain surveys and reports prepared in cooperation with renowned scholars also produce the same effect);
(iii) providing recognition through such highly charged performative acts as listing and making inventories (e.g. the 2003 Convention's Representative List of the Intangible Cultural Heritage of Humanity and the UNESCO *Atlas of the World's Languages in Danger*); and
(iv) furnishing methodological tools and data (e.g. *Language Vitality and Endangerment* paper with its set of nine criteria to assess the degree of language endangerment; UNESCO Framework for Cultural Statistics (UNESCO 2009b), World Culture Reports).[22]

With regard to the latter two functions, it is of note that Silverstein (1998: 414) identifies the field of 'institutionally focused sociology of language' (i.e. creating inventories of languages and surveying their status and trends) as 'policy science' or 'applied science'. He observes that 'people within local language communities actively position themselves with respect to the political orders of contemporary nation-states and more encompassing international political institutions ... For such interested parties, the data on linguistic "status" are fraught with implications, positive and negative.'

18.4.4 Underlying Beliefs and Ideologies

As demonstrated in the previous sections, the UN discourse of the 2000s on linguistic diversity (including 'safeguarding endangered languages', i.e. RLS) and multilingualism was informed by the normative beliefs of the epistemic community and, to a lesser but increasingly important degree, the views of the speaker communities (notably expressed though the documents of the UN Permanent Forum on Indigenous Issues).

The UN's beliefs and ideologies can be summarized as follows:

- Languages reflect worldviews, and are essential to identities, cultural heritage, and cultural diversity.

[22] These reports are produced by UNESCO every few years, the latest dating to 2011.

- They are also important to the fulfilment of human rights, to human well-being and development, and to the conservation of biodiversity.[23]

There is, of course, a much wider range of language beliefs and ideologies than these. At the level of individuals, Dorian (1998) describes three types of beliefs common among the speakers of dominant European languages:

- an 'ideology of contempt' for the languages of politically subordinate or economically less prosperous groups;
- the 'Social Darwinist' belief that some languages are 'naturally' well suited to modern life; and
- the belief that bilingualism and multilingualism are onerous, and that learning a new language diminishes the individual's ability in their first language.

At the level of states, Spolsky (2009) distinguishes essentially two types of official language ideologies:

- the highly centralized approach to language management inspired by the 'one nation, one language' motto; and
- a 'decentralized' approach that, free of the belief that national unity requires linguistic unity, allows for the official coexistence of more than one language corresponding to the territorial or regional divisions within the state ('territorial solution to multilingualism').

For want of an active and influential epistemic community that currently espouses these beliefs, they do not tend to enter into the body of international discourse (including individual statements made by member states in international forums).

18.5 Conclusion

Spolsky (2009: 258) summarizes a few other recent analyses (see, for instance, Grenoble and Whaley 2006) of the role of inter-governmental organizations in RLS:

> Because these supranational bodies lack authority over their members, their main participation in national language management has been in presenting rhetorical statements of international consensus, which are available to governments, and

[23] The idea of the link between language and human development comes from the highly influential 2004 UNDP Human Development Report: 'Cultural liberty in today's diverse world', whose main contributors included Amartya Sen and Will Kymlicka. See <http://hdr.undp.org/en/reports/global/hdr2004/> (accessed 1 October 2013).

> even more important to language activists, and helps account for the growing respect for linguistic diversity and the concerns of linguistic minorities.

Considering the examples discussed in this chapter, I conclude that the UN discourse of the 2000s on linguistic diversity, translated into international normative texts and implemented through national laws, policies, and measures, can claim to have had the following effects:

- the reshaping or adjustment of national discourses on cultural heritage and diversity;
- the legitimization of RLS efforts by speaker communities and activist groups; and
- the justification of 'affirmative action' by different tiers of government, including provision of funding, the changing of curricula, teacher training, the introduction of quotas for minority languages in public service broadcasting, and so on.

Thus, while it is true that the main leverage of inter-governmental organizations is discourse, and that they 'influence beliefs and ideologies more than practices' (Spolsky 2009: 258), I have argued in this chapter that the UN discourse, when analysed as social action and taking into consideration its cycle of production, diffusion, and interpretation, may lead to a pro-RLS impact at the national level.

References

Abbott, Kenneth K. W. and Duncan D. Snidal. 2000. Hard and soft law in international governance. *International Organization* 54: 421–56.

Adler, Emanuel and Peter M. Haas. 1992. Conclusion: epistemic communities, world order, and the creation of a reflective research program. *International Organization* 46: 367–90.

Alger, Chadwick F. 2005. *The United Nations System: A Reference Handbook*. Santa Barbara, CA: ABC-CLIO.

Campbell, John L. 2002. Ideas, politics and public policy. *Annual Review of Sociology* 28: 21–38.

CCPR. 2010. Draft General Comment N. 34 on Article 19. Document CCPR/C/GC/34/CRP.5. <http://www2.ohchr.org/english/bodies/hrc/comments.htm> (accessed 1 October 2013).

De Varennes, Fernand. 2007. Language rights as an integral part of human rights: a legal perspective. In Matthias Koenig and P. de Guchteneire (eds.), *Democracy and Human Rights in Multicultural Societies*. Paris: Ashgate and UNESCO.

Donders, Yvonne. 2007. The legal framework of the right to take part in cultural life. In Yvonne Donders and Vladimir Volodin (eds.), *Human Rights in Education, Science and Culture: Legal Developments and Challenges*. Paris: Ashgate and UNESCO.

Dorian, Nancy C. 1998. Western language ideologies and small-language prospects. In Lenore A. Grenoble and Lindsay J. Whaley (eds.), *Endangered Languages*. Cambridge: Cambridge University Press.

Ervik, Rune, Nanna Kildal, and Even Nilssen (eds.). 2009. *The Role of International Organizations in Social Policy: Ideas, Actions and Impact*. Cheltenham: Edward Elgar Publishing.

Evans, Mark (ed.). 2004. *Policy Transfer in Global Perspective*. Farnham: Ashgate.

Fairclough, Norman. 2001. *Language and Power* (2nd edn.). Essex: Pearson.

Fairclough, Norman. 2003. *Analysing Discourse*. London and New York: Routledge.

Finnemore, Martha and Stephen J. Toope. 2001. Alternatives to "legalization": richer views of law and politics. *International Organization* 55: 743–58.

Fox, Renata and John Fox. 2004. *Organizational Discourse: A Language-Ideology-Power Perspective.* Westport, CT: Praeger Publishers.

Girard, Augustin. 1982. *Développement Culturel: Expériences et Politiques*. Paris: UNESCO.

Grenoble, Lenore A. and Lindsay J. Whaley. 2006. *Saving Languages: An Introduction to Language Revitalization.* Cambridge: Cambridge University Press.

Haas, Peter M. 1992. Epistemic communities and international policy coordination. *International Organization* 46: 1–35.

ICCPR (International Covenant on Civil and Political Rights). 1966. <http://www2.ohchr.org/english/law/pdf/ccpr.pdf> (accessed 1 October 2013).

Kloss, Heinz. 1968. Notes concerning a language-nation typology. In Joshua Fishman, Charles Ferguson, and Jyotirindra Das Gupta (eds.), *Language Problems of Developing Nations*, 69–85. New York: John Wiley and Sons.

Levin, Leah. 2004. *Human Rights: Questions and Answers*. Paris: UNESCO.

Lucy, John A. 1997. Linguistic relativity. *Annual Review of Anthropology* 26: 291–312.

Meyer, John W. and Ronald L. Jepperson. 2000. The 'actors' of modern society: the cultural construction of social agency. *Sociological Theory* 18: 100–20.

Miller, Toby and George Yúdice. 2002. *Cultural Policy.* London: Sage.

Moseley, Christopher (ed.). 2009 (web version) and 2010 (print version). *Atlas of the World's Languages in Danger* (3rd edn.). Paris: UNESCO. <http://www.unesco.org/culture/languages-atlas> (accessed 1 October 2013).

OHCHR (Office of the United Nations High Commissioner for Human Rights). 2008. *The Protection of Indigenous Languages Compilation of the Work of Treaty Bodies (1994–2006) and Special Procedures (2006–)*. Document PFII/2008/EGM1/19. <http://www.un.org/esa/socdev/unpfii/documents/EGM_IL_OHCHR_2.doc> (accessed 1 October 2013).

Paten, Alan and Will Kymlicka. 2003. Introduction: language rights and political theory: context, issues, and approaches. In Alan Paten and Will Kymlicka (eds.), *Language Rights and Political Theory.* Oxford and New York: Oxford University Press.

Silverstein, Michael. 1998. Contemporary transformations of local linguistic communities. *Annual Review of Anthropology* 27: 401–26.

Spolsky, Bernard. 2009. *Language Management*. Cambridge: Cambridge University Press.

Stone, Diane. 2008. Global public policy, transnational policy communities, and their networks. *Policy Studies Journal* 36: 19–38.

UN (United Nations). 2007. UN Declaration on the Rights of Indigenous Peoples. <http://www.un.org/esa/socdev/unpfii/en/declaration.html> (accessed 1 October 2013).

UN ECOSOC (United Nations Economic and Social Council). 2005. *Report of the International Workshop on Methodologies regarding Free, Prior and Informed Consent and Indigenous Peoples*. Document E/C.19/2005/3. <http://www.un.org/esa/socdev/unpfii/en/workshopFPIC.html> (accessed 1 October 2013).

UN ECOSOC (United Nations Economic and Social Council). 2008. *Report of the International Expert Group Meeting on Indigenous Languages*. Document E/C.19/2008/3. <http://daccess-dds-ny.un.org/doc/UNDOC/GEN/N08/213/56/PDF/N0821356.pdf?OpenElement> (accessed 1 October 2013).

UNESCO (United Nations Educational, Scientific and Cultural Organization). 2001. *Declaration on Cultural Diversity*. <http://unesdoc.unesco.org/images/0012/001271/127160m.pdf>.

UNESCO (United Nations Educational, Scientific and Cultural Organization). 2003a. *Education in a Multilingual World*. <http://unesdoc.unesco.org/images/0012/001297/129728e.pdf>.

UNESCO (United Nations Educational, Scientific and Cultural Organization). 2003b. *Language Vitality and Endangerment*. <http://www.unesco.org/culture/ich/doc/src/00120-EN.pdf>.

UNESCO (United Nations Educational, Scientific and Cultural Organization). 2007. *Advocacy Kit for Promoting Multilingual Education: Including the Excluded*. <http://unesdoc.unesco.org/images/0015/001521/152198e.pdf> (accessed 1 October 2013).

UNESCO (United Nations Educational, Scientific and Cultural Organization). 2009. *World Report: Investing in Cultural Diversity and Intercultural Dialogue*. <http://unesdoc.unesco.org/images/0018/001852/185202e.pdf> (accessed 1 October 2013).

UNESCO (United Nations Educational, Scientific and Cultural Organization) Executive Board. 2008a. *Thematic Debate: Protecting Indigenous and Endangered Languages and the Role of Languages in Promoting EFA in the Context of Sustainable Development*. Consolidated record: document 180 EX/INF/Thematic Debate. <http://unesdoc.unesco.org/images/0017/001788/178893e.pdf>.

UNESCO (United Nations Educational, Scientific and Cultural Organization). Executive Board. 2008b. *Report by the Director-General on the Follow-up to Decisions and Resolutions Adopted by the Executive Board and the General Conference at their Previous Sessions*. Document 179 EX/INF.6. <http://unesdoc.unesco.org/images/0015/001585/158558e.pdf> (accessed 1 October 2013).

UNESCO (United Nations Educational, Scientific and Cultural Organization) Executive Board. 2009a. *Preliminary Study of the Technical and Legal Aspects of a Possible International Standard-Setting Instrument for the Protection of Indigenous and Endangered Languages*. Document 181 EX/14. <http://unesdoc.unesco.org/images/0018/001811/181141e.pdf#xml=http://www.unesco.org/ulis/cgi-bin/ulis.pl?database=andset=4D10A57C_3_367andhits_rec=9andhits_lng=eng> (accessed 1 October 2013).

UNESCO-UIS (United Nations Educational, Scientific and Cultural Organization-Institute for Statistics). 2009b. *2009 UNESCO Framework for Cultural Statistics*. <http://www.unesco.org/culture/ich/doc/src/00120-EN.pdf> (accessed 1 October 2013).

World Commission on Culture and Development. 1995. *Our Creative Diversity*. Paris: EGOPRIM.

Wurm, Stephen (ed.). 2001. *Atlas of the World's Languages in Danger of Disappearing* (2nd edn.). Paris: UNESCO.

Yeates, Nicola. 2001. *Globalization and Social Policy*. London: Sage.

19

Language Beliefs and the Management of Endangered Languages

BERNARD SPOLSKY

19.1 Introduction and Definitions

I USE THE COVER TERM 'language beliefs' to include all the individual and group reactions to language, languages, language varieties, language variants, and language users, whether attitudes, motivations, or values, or gathered into recognizable ideologies. Under language, I include not just named languages such as English and French and Swahili, but also their named varieties like British English, American English, New Zealand English, and Indian English, recognized dialects such as Estuary English, Appalachian English, and Afro-American Vernacular English, and distinct registers like formal academic English and Business English. By 'language practices', I refer to the complex socio-linguistic ecology of a speech community, with all the accepted rules for selecting varieties (whether named or not) and variants of one or more languages for appropriate niches, more or less what Hymes (1974) calls the ethnography of communication. 'Language management' then refers to efforts by individuals, groups, or institutions that have or claim authority over other members of the community to modify their language practices or beliefs, or the efforts of those without authority to influence those with it to modify the rules for practice (Spolsky 2009).

Efforts to rescue or preserve an endangered language are part of language management, involving an attempt to stabilize or even increase the number of speakers of a named variety and the range of functions for which it is used. My emphasis, it will become clear, is on speech communities and speakers rather on language and language varieties. I appreciate the aspirations and accomplishments of those of my colleagues who wish to salvage and preserve the grammar and lexicon of the language varieties themselves, with their record of the multiplicity of ways in which languages have evolved to capture and serve human perception and needs for communication, but my concern is not so much with varieties as with people.

Proceedings of The British Academy, **199**, 407–422. © The British Academy 2014.

19.2 Vitality

Looking at the linguistic ecology of a speech community, a language variety is considered to be endangered when there has been a steady loss in the number of speakers (resulting from death or shift to another variety) or a noticeable reduction in the domains and functions that it serves. Of these, perhaps the most critical is in the home domain and in what has been labelled 'intergenerational language maintenance', referred to by Stewart (1968) as 'vitality'. When parents or other caretakers no longer speak a language variety to their children, the age of the youngest native speaker rises, and soon the only speakers are beyond child-bearing age. Thus one comes to what Fishman (1991: 88) categorized as stage eight (the lowest) on the *Graded Intergenerational Disruption Scale*, when the variety is used only by 'socially isolated old folks'. Any attempt at rescue requires first salvaging language's vestiges.

Of course, it must be noted that the belief that the language is threatened is a matter of judgement, so that the French Government and its language institutions or the supporters of the English-Only movement in the United States see the need for active defence; but there are more objective criteria, such as evidence of loss over time, suggesting that in the foreseeable future there will no longer be active speakers. Such a state was reached, for example, with the Māori language in New Zealand in the 1950s, where in only a few neighbourhoods were children growing up speaking the language and when the age of the youngest native speaker was steadily increasing (see King, this volume).

Stewart considered vitality to be an actual practice, but Fishman wisely saw it, like many other factors affecting language shift and maintenance, as a belief, the belief that the variety should be spoken to children. In this chapter, I want to explore this and similar beliefs that help account for the decisions we make about the languages that we, our children, our employees, and our fellow citizens should know and use.

19.3 Complexity of Beliefs and Ideologies

Ager (2001) attempted to capture the complexity of what I call language beliefs as they appear in a theory of language policy. First, he makes clear that the actions produced by these beliefs can be either attempts to influence by 'individuals, groups, and governments' or actions of 'authorities' to 'control, favor or repress particular forms of language use' or 'encourage hatred, fear, or support for particular languages or language varieties'. The distinction is important, for at any level or in any domain of a speech community there will be individuals who have (or assume that they have) authority over others; those who lack authority may still try to influence, while those who have it may choose to 'control' or simply to 'encourage'. Domains are identifiable sectors of a speech community: they are made up of role-determined participants, social describable locations, and appropriate topics. The home is a domain: the participants are parents, children, significant others; the location is where the participants live; the appropriate topics are concerned with daily life. Other domains are school, church, workplace, neighbourhood, and government. Ager further distinguishes three components of motivation: motives, attitudes, and goals. He recognized three clusters of motive: political (identity, insecurity, ideology, and image), social (inequality and integration), and economic (instrumentality), any or all of which may be combined. Attitudes have to do with knowledge about language, feelings about it, and readiness to respond. From this emerge language goals, needs, and strategies.

Some scholars include these relevant beliefs in the concept of language ideology, a notion which Blommaert (2006) attributes to Sapirian and Whorfian linguistic anthropology (see especially Schieffelin, Woolard, and Kroskrity 1998). This ideology sets the values assigned to varieties, and since the seventeenth century, when John Locke argued for a pure elitist written standard, and the eighteenth-century addition by Johann Gottfried Herder of the folk or national tradition, the two have combined to produce the notion of standardized traditional languages, with names and norms, associated with defined national spaces and functioning as elements of national identity.

Speech communities may, as I argue generally, be multilingual, but the working of this ideology, Blommaert suggests, produces what Silverstein (1998: 130) calls a 'linguistic community' marked by 'an ideology of speaking the same language'. Silverstein (1996) characterizes this as a 'monoglot ideology', a belief that the community is in fact monolingual. It has, Blommaert (2006: 244–5) suggests, three significant outcomes. First, it leads to 'practical linguistic regimes' in public life and education. Second, it 'produces and regulates identities'. And thirdly, it leads to the common scholarly belief in a monoglot image of 'languages' as pure discrete and describable objects. It is, I believe, the widespread acceptance of this ideology and its usually unsuccessful adaptation by language revival movements that helps explain the difficulties they face. It is, however, important to realize that language ideologies are neither fixed nor undisputed within the group that holds them. Others (e.g. Bednar et al. 2010) are working on a model that shows how a culture can develop what they call an 'identity signature' while at the same time maintaining some internal heterogeneity, depending on the interaction of two forces, an individual pressure for consistency and a social pressure for conformity.

Beliefs about language are a fundamental factor in success in language rescue, for a shift of languages regularly depends on the values attributed to competing varieties. It has been suggested (Walker 1993) that Maslow's hierarchy of needs, seen as subjective perceptions, accounts for language choice.

Languages may be seen as enabling a speaker to stay alive, to be secure, to belong to a group, to be esteemed in one's society, or to achieve self-actualization (see its use by King, this volume). While language activists and managers commonly rank these values starting at the symbolic end, it is probable that speakers are more likely to start first with pragmatic and instrumental needs—getting food and shelter, obtaining and holding a job—and only when lower needs are met, to deal with the symbolic values.[1]

19.4 Whose Beliefs?

What I want to stress here is the difficulty of the task one undertakes when one tries to identify the beliefs that influence language policy. The problem is highlighted when one asks who is involved. In the simplest view, there are two groups of participants to consider, those with and those without authority. But if we look at the way in which speech communities are organized into separate levels or 'domains' (I take the term from Fishman 1972), things are quickly seen to be more complex.

Start with the home domain: the language policy of the home depends in part on the participants themselves, each with their own language proficiencies and preferences (just think of a normally multilingual cosmopolitan or immigrant family). These proficiencies depend on their previous language experience (those born in the old country and those born in the new), and their preferences are likely to come both from their level of proficiency (I know many language activists who do not speak the language to their children because of their own limited mastery) and from the values they assign to each variety. The values in turn come from the other domains in which family members function: their church, their school, their neighbourhood, their football club, or their wider family, for instance. They will also be influenced by management activities within the family (the father who insists on use of the heritage language when the grandparents are visiting, the mother who has been persuaded by a child-care centre to try to speak the new variety with preschool children, the older child who has seen the value of the new language with her peers or at school) as well as any efforts of authorities at other levels who try to impose their preferences on the homes. Needless to say, just as each member of a family is likely to have developed their own values, so each family within a community may well develop a different policy as a result of different pressures and values. I argue, then, that while we may look for the development of a consensus or even an ideology that

[1] However, Ginges, Atran, Medin, and Shikaki (2007) show how political ideologies that become sacred are difficult to modify.

makes generalization easier, most studies I have seen find differences within and between domains.

I want to start with a case of a common belief controlling the behaviour of one specific group: the linguists who work in this field.

19.5 Linguists as Lames

Labov (1973) raised the suspicion that linguists might be seriously different from the regular speakers of the languages and varieties they study. They all share what I call 'linguicentrism', the assumption that language is at the centre of human culture and existence.[2] The fact that so few people and governments, including so many of those most directly concerned, seem to care about the threat to the survival of the majority of existing varieties should warn us to think very carefully before we assume that the beliefs and ideologies of linguists are in harmony with the speakers of the language and varieties we try to save. This does not mean we are wrong when we argue for the importance or beauty or naturalness of all varieties of language, or even build elaborate rhetorical analogies of the linguistic diversity to biodiversity. But we should not be surprised to find these arguments echoing vainly in cabinet hearings or letters to the editor.

I do not want to overstate this. There are many speakers who see the spiritual value of their heritage language, as it provides a connection to their dead and living ancestors, and of a community language, as it provides a rallying point for claiming solidarity with an ethnic, religious, national, or gender community.[3] But these values, which come from the top of Maslow's suggested hierarchy, regularly conflict in the 'real world' with the more basic demands of acquiring and using languages and varieties that help meet the basic needs of physical survival, safety, and economic security.

But first, I must clarify the issue of the object of endangerment. We speak, misleadingly I believe, about 'endangered languages'. Blommaert (2001) has been among the strongest of those scholars who question the use of the term 'languages', criticizing the Asmara declaration on African languages, for example, for equating languages with language names, and arguing then for an impossible sociolinguistic equality.[4] In a number of papers, he makes clear that one must deal rather with the significant varieties (or even variants) that are

[2] I coined this word to distinguish it from 'linguacentrism', which on analogy with ethnocentrism would mean looking at things through a single language.

[3] I spent a stimulating week with such a group, the New Zealand Māori language revival-group, Te Ataarangi.

[4] He in turn is attacked by Skutnabb-Kangas, Phillipson, and Kontra (2001) in a strangely ill-tempered paper that seemed to hold that the only languages worth protecting are those whose names are recognized by the lawyers who fight human rights cases. They note that '"sociolects" and

marked attitudinally within the society (or domain) that one is studying. It is not enough to talk about English or Navajo or Māori without considering the sociolinguistically significant varieties that function within a particular sociolinguistic ecology. Thus, *r*-colouring may be stigmatized, as in Boston, or highly valued, as in New York; to simply ask about attitudes to English misses the point. Similarly, in studying language attitudes in Singapore, one needs to distinguish between attitudes to British, American, and Singaporean varieties (Xu and Wei 2002). It has recently been stressed that in the super-diversity of modern urbanism, where multilingualism is common, actual language practices involve mixed rather than pure language varieties. But it is probably the case that only a named variety will be thought of as endangered.

19.6 Endangered Speakers or Languages?

There is another important caveat that needs to be mentioned. In a recent paper, Labov (2008) expresses it in his title 'Unendangered dialects, endangered people'. He was dealing with Afro-American Vernacular English, and argued (in the days before the US elected a black president) that as long as social and economic discrimination against Afro-Americans continues to isolate them in ghettos and jails, their distinctive variety of English will continue to diverge from the standard dialects. From a human or civil rights position, our concern should be with the speakers rather than the variety.

It is here that the linguist (excluding the sociolinguist) is most likely to have beliefs and ideologies that are in conflict with the community. I noticed it most starkly a number of years ago when I had just started to work with Navajo language maintenance efforts and attended an international meeting in Mexico: the local linguists made it quite clear that once they had recorded the grammar and lexicon of a dying Indian language and placed the resulting book on the shelves of the museum, they had preserved the language. I am certainly not denying the basic value of salvage linguistics, but simply pointing out that it is more likely to be a value presented by linguists than recognized by speakers. This point is made clear by the chapter by Couzens and Eira in this volume dealing with Australian Aboriginal communities, and the chapter by Grenoble and Whitecloud on Greenland.

19.7 Language Diversity and Biodiversity

There is a related belief that probably distinguishes linguists (including some sociolinguists) from speakers of endangered varieties, and this is the belief that

"language varieties" are unknown concepts in international law' (Skutnabb-Kangas, Phillipson, and Kontra 2001: 147).

language diversity is analogous to biodiversity. The rhetoric of arguments for rescuing threatened languages regularly echoes the rhetoric of arguments for maintaining diversity in species of plants and animals. This argument is, I suspect, fallacious. Essentially, the biodiversity case assumes that natural ecology maintains a complex pattern with each species fitting into its appropriate niche. If one species become extinct, or if an alien introduced species invades a niche, the entire ecological balance will be thrown into chaos. Is this not true, they ask, of linguistic ecologies? Doesn't the loss of Eyak or the introduction of a world language destroy the natural environment?

To try to understand environmental changes, I spent a few rather depressing weeks reading the ambitious study by Diamond (2005) on the collapse of societies. He finds four sets of factors that enter into the picture in various degrees:

- environmental damage by humans such as the cutting down of forests or the failure to dispose of waste from mining;
- changes in climate;
- hostile neighbours, especially when overpopulation reduces available resources; and
- the absence of friendly trade partners.

These are all moderated by a fifth set of factors: the way the society responds to its environmental problems. In none of his analyses does language enter as a factor: Iceland has maintained its highly literate language in spite of the problems it produced by using up all its timber and more recently by venturing into international finance; Rapa Nui survived the statues that seem to have contributed to the collapse of civilization in Easter Island; the Australian Aboriginal languages were wiped out by the slaughter of their speakers just as the possibility of agriculture was destroyed by the introduction of rabbits and foxes; the Classic Maya collapse came in spite of the invention of writing.

The analogy between plant and animal diversity and language diversity does not hold. In the plant and animal world, we assume that ecological balance is upset when one species is destroyed or when its niche is taken over by another. The destruction of forested land has commonly led to erosion and not to the provision of good agricultural land. Overfishing of specific varieties has required the exploitation of wider and deeper areas of the ocean. A few years ago, those of us who like eating fish were excited to discover a new variety, 'Orange roughy', which we were told was being caught at the new depths. It turned out that the fish being brought increasingly to market in New Zealand and Australia and elsewhere were quite old—the fish takes 20 to 30 years to reach maturity—and signs were that by 2003 the quotas being imposed would not be able to assure sustainability.[5]

[5] The 2012 quotas were maintained even though there were signs of improvement in the restocking of the variety.

Examples of damage to the physical environment by the introduction of alien species—whether rabbits to Australia or sheep to Greenland—abound, and one can easily understand why people make or believe similar arguments about the effects of the introduction of languages. But languages are not biological species. Their life depends on use, and within the complex sociolinguistic ecology of a speech community each of the diverse varieties is in constant contact and change. Every new thought, every new concept, and every new item provides an opportunity for modification. Only when a language is no longer used can one map its limits. Speakers are constantly modifying their repertoires to meet new needs or serve new functions they have discovered in the increasing cosmopolitanism of all societies.[6] Similarly, as social patterns change, so do language varieties, so that the politeness formulas of more traditional societies disappear with increasing inequality and openness.

At the same time, the constant pressure for change in language means that new varieties are developing all the time. It is true that English is taking a greater part of the ecology of many speech communities, but it is an English that has been modified to fit new needs and functions, including the marking of identity that seems to be a special feature of language. The search for a pure, untouched language to be preserved ignores the reality of constant change, just as the decision to look only at grammar and lexicon loses the richness of variety that marks living sociolinguistic ecologies.

19.8 How Do Beliefs Fit the Model?

What leads to a change in language practices? In particular, what accounts for the fact that members of the speech community shift from one set of choices to another? The model suggests three answers to the question. If there is a change in the speech community as a result, for instance, of genocide or migration or other demographic changes, or a change in the sociolinguistic ecology as a result of technological or economic changes, or a change in communication channels, there will be a change in language practices to match the changing niches.

Let me put that more simply. Assume the immigration of a large group of people speaking a different language. Or assume the migration of members of the speech community to another country or to the city. In each case, the language practices of the community will be different and one obvious result will be changes in the value of the language varieties. The destruction by the Nazis of the Yiddish-speaking community of Eastern Europe changed the distribution of Yiddish irretrievably. The survivors in the Soviet Union lived in a community where Russian was the dominant language; the million who emigrated in the

[6] Obama (1995) describes the growing cosmopolitanism of his Luo grandfather's family.

1990s found themselves in speech communities where Hebrew was the dominant language. As roads and schools were built on the Navajo Reservation, and especially when repeater television stations were introduced, English moved into the community not just as a language spoken when you left the reservation for work or shopping, but as the language most Navajo children speak when they start school, so that bilingual programmes now teach Navajo rather than English. In Papua New Guinea, when young men returned from work in the plantations, they brought with them a new variety of language, Tok Pisin, associated with the treasures of the outside world (cargo)—see Dobrin (this volume). Similarly, the men in the small Jewish communities of the Rhineland in the ninth and tenth centuries picked up the variety of German spoken in the Gentile community, and probably showed their status by using it within their own community, just as the Israeli Palestinians employed outside the village were the main source of borrowings from Hebrew and the growing status of the variety.

Even without actual cases of language management, then, external or novel pressures lead to changes in the values assigned to language varieties, encouraging individuals to acquire proficiency in them, and to make crucial decisions about the language variety their children should learn. The most basic reason for acquiring a language is survival. This, of course, is most clearly shown in the case of children who go through the wonderful and complex task of acquiring language in order to take advantage of the adults around them. The combination of exposure and need would appear to be what sets off the process. Babies start recognizing voices and varieties early, perhaps even before they are born. As they develop, they quickly learn that mastery of a system of communication is a key element in satisfying physiological needs, whether for sustenance, warmth, or comfort.

But let us return to the question of whose values and beliefs are relevant. The model of language management that I have proposed offers a framework for answering this question. First, it assumes operation within a specified speech community, however small or large. It may therefore refer to an individual family or any other defined social group, up to and including a region or nation. Second, it assumes two main classes of participants within that community: the managers and the managed. Within the family, I would need to ask about the beliefs and values of the parents who are trying to manage the language of their children, or the beliefs of the children themselves who may accept or reject their parents' values and beliefs. Within the school domain, one must distinguish between teachers and pupils. Thirdly, my model distinguishes between internal and external management—between parents who try to manage family language policy, teachers or governments who try to persuade parents, and education departments that control schools and teachers.

19.9 Some Examples

The implications of this model will become clearer if we look at some examples. Te Puni Kōkiri (2002) aimed to learn about the values and beliefs that affected the Māori language regeneration programme in which they were engaged.[7] They were particularly concerned with understanding the loss of natural intergenerational transmission and the decline in the use of Māori within families. Their survey found that two thirds of the Māori sample studied believed that their language was not used enough. When asked why they thought it should be used  more, a quarter simply said because it is valuable or shouldn't be lost; under a fifth associated it with identity or culture. While most thought it had intrinsic value, few saw a functional value. The survey came up with eight statements of belief that it used to classify the respondents. I paraphrase them:

- Māori culture is part of the heritage of all New Zealanders.
- I can learn from all races in New Zealand.
- Māori should have special rights.
- If New Zealanders understood Māori culture there would be less racial tension.
- I want to be more involved in Māori culture.
- New Zealand would be better if there weren't so many races of people.
- Learning Māori is a very high priority.
- I think that Māori rights are important.

On the basis of the values assigned to the statements, the survey classified Māori respondents into three distinct groups: 'cultural developers' who made up two thirds of the population, a 'Māori only' or perhaps separatist group (27 per cent), and a small uninterested group (7 per cent).

Parkes (2008) conducted a study in New Mexico of the dual language programme in which English-speaking and Spanish-speaking children were learning both languages. This study concentrated on the reasons that parents sent their children to the school. The questionnaire offered the following choices of reasons for choosing the dual language programme:

'I chose dual language for my child because I want my child to be

- able to speak, read and write in two languages.'
- comfortable relating to different people and cultures.'
- better able to relate to his/her heritage.'
- with teachers that speak our language.'
- more successful in school.'
- successful in a global society.'

[7] Benton and Smith (1982: 3) had found in the 1970s more positive attitudes to Māori among Māori, especially the old groups.

The first (able to speak two languages) is simply restating the decision, although it does assume a belief in the possibility of bilingualism and perhaps in its value. The third and the fourth are associated with claiming membership ('his/her heritage', 'our language') in one's own parochial group. The last two place the emphasis on academic success and the economic value of bilingualism and a multilingual world. The second, on the other hand, rejects parochial solidarity and argues for tolerance in a pluralistic or cosmopolitan society.

If we translate these into beliefs, then we might guess that the respondents hold in various measures the following beliefs:

- Bilingualism is possible.
- Bilingualism is worthwhile.
- It is good to be able to communicate with the members of other groups.
- It is valuable to maintain connections with one's heritage.
- It is better to have a teacher from one's own community.
- It is valuable to have teachers who can communicate with students.
- Knowing two languages (or, alternatively, also knowing the other language in a bilingual community) is valuable for academic success.
- Knowing two languages (or alternatively knowing the other language that the dual-medium school teaches) is valuable economically.

These then are values that might account for parental decisions about choosing a school for their children. They also help account for decisions within the family about language policy.

When one looks at the attitudes and beliefs of other groups, one finds considerable differences. De Bres (2008b) was interested in the attitude to Māori among the general non-Māori population. Her sample consisted of mainly New Zealand-born adults with better than average education. Three quarters of them had had some experience learning Māori. On the basis of their responses to questions, she divided them into three clusters: more than half were classified as supporters of Māori, about 40 per cent as uninterested, and 5 per cent as 'English only'. This distribution was similar to that found in equivalent studies by Te Puni Kōkiri in 2000, 2003, and 2006. The three groups disagreed on specific attitudinal questions, but most respected people who could speak Māori fluently (93 per cent of the supporters but only 75 per cent of the English-only group). Most of the supporters (93 per cent) thought it good when Māori spoke their language in public, but only 42 per cent of the uninterested and 25 per cent of the English-only group thought so. Most agreed that it should be spoken on the marae (89 per cent of all), and disagreed that Māori should speak English at home. Similarly, almost all agreed that Māori children should learn some Māori at school and over 90 per cent agreed that all New Zealand children should learn some Māori. Most supporters agreed that Māori culture is part of New Zealand's heritage; so did half of the uninterested group, but none of the English-only group. Nearly 90 per cent of the supporters were interested in learning Māori, under half of the uninterested agreed, and a quarter of the English-only group. Half of the supporters thought Māori should speak their language, about 40 per cent agreed they should learn it, a fifth agreed they should pass it on to their children, but only 6 per cent thought they should send their children to immersion schools. Another study (de Bres 2008a) expands on this by investigating the concept of tolerability, which the author defines as the attitudes and behaviours of majority language speakers towards the minority languages in the community. Its absence obviously leads to overt repression, as in French policy towards its regional and immigrant languages, or Turkish policy banning Kurdish, or the English Only movement in the United States; even when this ceases, there can continue to be memories of past repression inhibiting minority parents from using their own language with their children or leading to their opposition to bilingual education or other language regeneration efforts. Studies in Wales and Catalonia similarly showed evidence of negative attitudes on the part of English and Castilian speakers respectively.

Although the National Policy on Education in Nigeria calls for a multilingual approach, Igboanusi (2008) claims that it has not been implemented. He carried out a study of attitudes among students, teachers, parents, and Ministry officials. There was evidence of an increase in the use of English in early primary school. Half of the respondents said they wanted their children to be taught in English, because it is the official language and an important international language. Half preferred English and the mother tongue together. Nearly two thirds thought English should be used beyond the third year. Primary school teachers tended to support English as the teaching medium, with the mother tongue as a subject; staff from universities, secondary schools, and the Ministry tended to support equal use.

A religious community working to isolate itself, as Fishman (1966) showed, will often manifest this in language attitudes. Tannenbaum and Ofner (2008) used questionnaires to study the attitudes of Israeli Haredi (ultra-Orthodox) Jews to three languages: Hebrew, Yiddish, and English. A number of striking differences emerged. Members of the non-Hasidic Litvak ultra-orthodox group had more positive attitudes to Hebrew than to Yiddish, and positive beliefs about English. Yiddish-speaking Hasidim (some sects more than others) valued Yiddish over Hebrew and English. Members of the Habad community in Israel had positive attitudes to Hebrew (which they mainly use) and also to Yiddish (the language of the Lubavitcher Rebbes). Sephardi Haredim are the most positive in their attitudes towards Hebrew. Haredi women generally had more favourable attitudes to both Hebrew and English than men. Both these studies are important because they show the complexity of attitudes: different classes of participants in the speech community or domain are likely to have different attitudes, as many of the studies in this volume show.

This has been shown even more clearly in the study of immigrant children in England (Blackledge and Creese 2009). First, their respondents, who were students in Bengali community-operated complementary evening and afternoon schools in Birmingham, did not see 'languages' as separate and discrete entities, disagreeing with each other as to what constituted a language. Secondly, the concept of 'heritage' turned out to be a more dynamic phenomenon, more a process of negotiation than a stable entity. The students were speakers of Sylheti, a vernacular regional variety the very existence of which tended to be denied by the Bengali administrators and teachers in the schools, who were concerned to teach the standard variety, leading to complex negotiations between students and teachers about language choice and identity. They conclude that 'the young people's attitudes to their languages, and their multilingual practices, constituted a sophisticated response to their place in the world ... [They] were flexible and adaptable in response to the environment, as they negotiated identities which were more complex and sophisticated than the "heritage" position ascribed to them institutionally' (Blackledge and Creese 2009: 552).

19.10 Conclusions

The chapters in this volume give us many more examples showing the complexity of attitudes towards endangered language varieties and the emergence of ideologies. They test my arguments:

1. Various stakeholders (e.g. government, experts, and speakers—and various age groups and social groups of speakers) regularly hold different beliefs. For instance, King in this volume compares institutional (government and tribe) ideologies for Māori to vernacular or popular ones. Costa shows the differences and complexity of children's beliefs about language when they are involved in Scottish and Provencal language revitalization activities. Marquis and Sallabank report a wide range of different ideologies among Guernesiais, ranging along a scale from static (French is the status language but current use of the indigenous language should be maintained) to dynamic (the indigenous language is a source of identity and new users should be found and encouraged).
2. Governments use evidence of language proficiency while communities are more concerned with language ownership. Boynton shows that an Australian Aboriginal group is more concerned about language ownership than language proficiency, but has been influenced by government policy to modify its ideology.
3. Linguists commonly have different goals from the members of the language communities with whom they are working. Grenoble and

Whitecloud, analysing cases in Greenland, show the wide differences between the approach of scientists and linguists and the community to the preservation of language and other heritage knowledge. Stebbins, using cases from Papua New Guinea, discusses how linguists create and interact with indigenous languages as objects of study. Minasyan analyses ideologies revealed by discourse in various UN bodies and argues that the UN's view of linguistic diversity and multilingualism is shaped by its experts, but is increasingly influenced by speaker communities. Couzens and Eira, looking at Australian Aboriginal communities, show the differences between the approaches of linguists and of the community to revitalization. Austin describes two Aboriginal communities who are satisfied with the use of their language in greetings and the opening of speeches, yet are not convinced of the need for full use. Räisänen has interviewed members of the Kven minority in Norway and finds that they see the language as associated with home as opposed to the wider significance of Norwegian.

4. Myths and mistaken beliefs can be as powerful as scientifically justified ones. Ó hIfearnáin suggests that Irish language policy is still largely driven by an ideology that Irish is everyone's language, ignoring how few speak it and the increase in immigrant languages.
5. Revitalization efforts can change, as well as follow, beliefs. Hadjidemetriou reports on a small community of Arabic speakers in Cyprus, and finds some evidence that revitalization efforts are leading to more favourable attitudes to the language. Rasom describes Ladin-speaking women in Italy, and conducts interviews and focus groups intended to raise their awareness of the value of heritage-language maintenance.
6. But ideology can be important in affecting change. Di Carlo and Good analyse a region in Northwest Cameroon and suggest that it is changing political affiliation and ideology rather than linguistic history that accounts for language shift.

There remains much to do in exploring the complexity of language beliefs, and significant questions have not been answered, but the studies in this collection provide a valuable beginning.

References

Ager, Dennis E. 2001. *Motivation in Language Planning and Language Policy.* Clevedon: Multilingual Matters.

Bednar, Jenna, Aaron Bramson, Andrea Jones-Rooy, and Scott Page. 2010. Emergent cultural signatures and persistent diversity: a model of conformity and consistency. *Rationality and Society* 22: 407–44.

Benton, Richard and Lee Smith. 1982. *Survey of Language Use in Maori Households and Communities: A Report to Participants in the Initial Investigation 1973–1978*. Wellington: New Zealand Council for Educational Research.

Blackledge, Adrian and Angela Creese. 2009. Contesting 'language' as 'heritage': negotiation of identities in late modernity. *Applied Linguistics* 29: 533–54.

Blommaert, Jan. 2001. The Asmara Declaration as a sociolinguistic problem: reflections on scholarship and linguistic rights. *Journal of Sociolinguistics* 5: 131–42.

Blommaert, Jan. 2006. Language policy and national identity. In Thomas Ricento (ed.), *An Introduction to Language Policy: Theory and Method*. Oxford: Blackwell Publishing.

De Bres, Julia. 2008a. Planning for tolerability in New Zealand, Wales and Catalonia. *Current Issues in Language Planning* 9: 464–82.

De Bres, Julia. 2008b. Planning for tolerability: promoting positive attitudes and behaviours towards the Maori language among non-Maori New Zealanders. Unpublished PhD thesis, Victoria University of Wellington.

Diamond, Jared. 2005. *Collapse: How Societies Choose to Fail or Survive*. London: Penguin Books.

Fishman, Joshua A. 1972. Domains and the relationship between micro- and macro-sociolinguistics. In John J. Gumperz and Dell Hymes (eds.), *Directions in Sociolinguistics*. New York: Holt, Rinehart and Winston.

Fishman, Joshua A. 1991. *Reversing Language Shift: Theoretical and Empirical Foundations of Assistance to Threatened Languages*. Clevedon: Multilingual Matters.

Fishman, Joshua A. (ed.). 1966. *Language Loyalty in the United States: The Maintenance and Perpetuation of Non-English Mother Tongues by American Ethnic and Religious Groups*. The Hague: Mouton.

Ginges, Jeremy, Scott Atran, Douglas Medin, and Khalil Shikaki. 2007. Sacred bounds on rational resolution of violent political conflict. *Proceedings of the National Academy of Sciences* 104(7): 357–60.

Hymes, Dell. 1974. *Foundations in Sociolinguistics: An Ethnographic Approach*. Philadelphia: University of Pennsylvania Press.

Igboanusi, Herbert. 2008. Mother tongue-based bilingual education in Nigeria: attitudes and practice. *International Journal of Bilingual Education and Bilingualism* 11: 721–34.

Labov, William. 1973. The linguistic consequence of being a lame. *Language in Society* 2: 81–115.

Labov, William. 2008. Unendangered dialects, endangered people. In Kendall A. King, Natalie Schilling-Estes, Lyn Fogle, Jackie Lou Lia, and Barbara Soukup (eds.), *Sustaining Linguistic Diversity: Endangered and Minority Languages and Language Varieties (Georgetown University Round Table on Languages and Linguistics)*. Washington, DC: Georgetown University Press.

Obama, Barack. 1995. *Dreams from My Father: A Story of Race and Inheritance*. New York: Times Books.

Parkes, Jay. 2008. Who chooses dual language education for their children and why. *International Journal of Bilingual Education and Bilingualism* 11: 635–60.

Schieffelin, Bambi B., Kathryn A. Woolard, and Paul V. Kroskrity (eds.). 1998. *Language Ideologies: Practice and Theory*. Oxford: Oxford University Press.

Silverstein, Michael. 1996. Monoglot 'standard' in America: standardization and metaphors of linguistic hegemony. In Donald Brenneis and Ronald K. S. Macaulay (eds.), *The*

Matrix of Language: Contemporary Linguistic Anthropology. Boulder, CO: Westview Press.

Silverstein, Michael. 1998. The uses and utility of ideology: a commentary. In Bambi B. Schieffelin, Kathryn A. Woolard, and Paul V. Kroskrity (eds.), *Language Ideologies: Practice and Theory.* Oxford: Oxford University Press.

Skutnabb-Kangas, Tove, Robert Phillipson, and Miklos Kontra. 2001. Reflections on scholarship and linguistic rights: a rejoinder to Jan Blommaert. *Journal of Sociolinguistics* 5: 143–55.

Spolsky, Bernard. 2009. *Language Management.* Cambridge: Cambridge University Press.

Stewart, William. 1968. A sociolinguistic typology for describing national multilingualism. In Joshua A. Fishman (ed.), *Readings in the Sociology of Language*, 531–45. The Hague: Mouton.

Tannenbaum, Michal and Hannah Esther Ofner. 2008. 'Tell me what you speak and I'll tell you . . .': exploring attitudes to languages in the ultra-orthodox community in Israel. *Journal of Multilingual and Multicultural Development* 29: 499–517.

Te Puni Kōkiri. 2002. *Survey of Attitudes, Values and Beliefs about the Maori Language.* Wellington: Ministry of Maori Development.

Walker, Roland. 1993. Language shift in Europe and Irian Jaya, Indonesia: toward the heart of the matter. *AILA Review* 10: 71–87.

Xu, Daming and Li Wei. 2002. Managing multilingualism in Singapore. In Li Wei, Jean-Marc Dewaele, and Alex Housen (eds.), *Opportunities and Challenges of Bilingualism.* Berlin: De Gruyter Mouton.

Languages Index

Subject Index